A VICTORIAN MARRIAGE

A Victorian Marriage

Mandell and Louise Creighton

James Covert

Hambledon and London

London and New York

Published by Hambledon and London Ltd, 2000

102 Gloucester Avenue, London NW1 8HX (UK)
838 Broadway, New York, NY 10003–4812

ISBN 1 85285 260 7

A description of this book is available from
the British Library and from the Library of Congress

Typeset by Carnegie Publishing, Lancaster
Printed on acid-free paper and bound in Great Britain
by Cambridge University Press

Contents

Illustrations   vii

Text Illustrations   xi

Preface   xiii

1   Who is That Girl?   1

2   The Nicest Man I Have Met   5

3   A Most Promising Scholar   23

4   Undoubtedly the Ablest Man   37

5   A Glorious Game   49

6   The Peak   67

7   A Charm about Oxford   83

8   Exile   105

9   The Happiest Years   127

10   A Great Work   155

11   A Breath of Fresh Air   175

12   Inspiring Influences   193

13   The Blow has Fallen   211

14   I Went to Visit the Queen   231

15   Fulham is a Nice Place   253

16   Tell Her That I Love Her   271

17   Dear Mrs Creighton   295

18   A Sincere Fine Old Thing   313

Notes   319

Bibliography   372

Index   393

Illustrations

(*between pp. 112 and 113*)

1 Carlisle's Castle Street in the 1880s with the cathedral at the end of the street. The Creightons' house was on the right side of the street near the church. (*Jim Templeton*)

2 The Creightons' former house on Castle Street (with shop on ground floor and living quarters above) as it looked in the 1880s a few years after the family moved to Kirkandrews. (*Jim Templeton*)

3 Durham cathedral from the railway station. (*James Covert*)

4 Durham Grammar School and playing fields. (*James Covert*)

5 Mandell's family, *c.* 1870. Left to right: James, Robert, Mary Ellen (Polly), Mandell. (*Joan Duncan*)

6 The Crystal Palace in Sydenham. *c.* 1900. (*Lewisham History Centre*)

7 Peak Hill Lodge, Sydenham, *c.* 1880, the house belonging to the von Glehns where Louise was raised. (*Lewisham History Centre*)

8 Sketch of Robert von Glehn, *c.* 1876. (*Christian Creighton*)

9 Louise von Glehn about the time she became engaged to Mandell Creighton in 1871. (*Christian Creighton*)

10 St Bartholomew's church, Sydenham, the parish church of the von Glehns where Louise and Mandell were married. (*Lewisham History Centre*)

11 Mandell Creighton,1862, during his first year at Merton College, Oxford. (*Christian Creighton*)

12 Mandell's college friends, the 'Quadrilateral', in 1864. From left to right: R. T. Raikes, Mandell Creighton, C. T. Boyd, and W. H. Foster. (*Christian Creighton*)

13 South bay of Merton College library. (*Merton College, Oxford*)

14 Mandell Creighton in 1864 at the age of twenty-one, just after taking his first degree at Merton. (*Christian Creighton*)

15 Mandell Creighton, an Oxford don at the age of twenty-seven in 1870, the year before he met Louise von Glehn. (*Christian Creighton*)

16 Merton College tower, watercolour painting by Louise Creighton, *c.* 1873. (*Mary Bailey*)

17 Beam Hall, where the Creightons lived for a time, directly across from Merton College gate. (*James Covert*)

18 Louise Creighton when she was nearly twenty-eight. Painting by her Oxford friend Bertha Johnson. (*Mary Bailey*)

19 Six of the Creighton children standing at the front entrance of Embleton vicarage with donkey ready for a picnic outing on the beach in 1884. Left to right: Lucia, Mary, Oswin, Walter, Beatrice and Cuthbert. (*Christian Creighton*)

20 Embleton vicarage, Northumberland, *c.* 1880, at the time the Creightons lived there. (*Christian Creighton*)

21 Mandell Creighton with three of his daughters, Lucia, Beatrice and Mary, 1888. (*Christian Creighton*)

22 Louise Creighton with her three sons, Walter, Cuthbert and Oswin, 1888. (*Christian Creighton*)

23 Mandell Creighton at the age of thirty-eight in 1881. (*Christian Creighton*)

24 Louise Creighton in the mid 1880s, shortly after leaving Embleton for Cambridge. (*Christian Creighton*)

25 The entrance to Emmanuel College, Cambridge. (*James Covert*)

26 Worcester Cathedral. (*British Travel Association*)

27 A family game of croquet in the palace garden at Peterborough, *c.* 1895. (*Christian Creighton*)

28 Bishop Mandell Creighton in the palace garden at Peterborough, 1893. (*Christian Creighton*)

29 Family and friends after a hockey game at Peterborough. Left to right: Basil, Walter, Winnie (kneeling), unknown, Lucia (seated on ground), Robert, Harold, Ella, Gemma, unknown, and Mary. (*Christian Creighton*)

30   Louise Creighton in the early 1890s. (*Christian Creighton*)

31   Mandell Creighton about the time he became Bishop of London.
     (*Christian Creighton*)

32   A family holiday in the Lake District in August 1897.
     Seated (left to right): Oswin, Ella (niece) Basil (nephew), Beatrice,
     Walter. Standing (left to right): Lucia, Cuthbert, Winifred (niece),
     Mandell, Marjorie (niece), Louise, Robert (nephew), Mary, Gemma,
     Harold (nephew), Aunt Polly (Mandell's sister). (*Joan Duncan*)

33   An outing on the banks of Ullswater near Glenridding in the Lake
     District, August 1897. Seated (left to right): Ella (niece), Louise.
     Standing on the shore (left to right): Beatrice, Robert (nephew),
     Aunt Polly (Mandell's sister), Mandell, Winifred and Oswin (far
     right). In the boat (left to right): Lucia, Basil (nephew), Walter,
     Mary, Cuthbert, Harold (nephew), Gemma, Marjorie (niece).
     (*Joan Duncan*)

34   Louise Creighton, painted by Glyn Philpot and unveiled at
     Lambeth Palace, c. 1920. (*Christian Creighton*)

35   The official photograph of Mandell Creighton as Bishop
     of London, 1897. (*Christian Creighton*)

36   Mandell and Louise Creighton are buried in the chapel of the
     Order of the British Empire in the eastern end of the crypt at
     St Paul's. The grave is located under the carpet near the entrance.
     (*St Paul's Cathedral*)

Text Illustrations

Mandell Creighton's report from Durham School, 1862   31

Von Glehn Family Tree   71

Creighton Family Tree   131

Cartoon in the April 1897 issue of *Vanity Fair* of Mandell Creighton soon after he became Bishop of London. (*British Library*)   252

To the Creighton Family

especially Mary, Rachel, Susan,
Kisty, Barbara,
and of course
Basil, Joan, Penelope, Hugh and Tom

Preface

Mandell Creighton (1843–1901), one of the leading British historians and churchmen of the nineteenth century, is now mostly remembered for his six-volume history of the Renaissance popes. Indeed, he introduced the subject to the English-speaking world. He was also one of the founders, and the first editor, of the *English Historical Review*; he wrote on various aspects of ecclesiastical and English national history, which elevated historical study in England; and he also contributed significantly to the debate over whether or not historians should make moral judgments about those who lived in the past.

Creighton became a bishop in the Church of England, first of Peterborough and then of London. Many of his contemporaries believed that he was destined to become Archbishop of Canterbury. He climbed the ecclesiastical ladder from country vicar to prelate and was a popular and effective leader of the Church of England during his later years, a man who seemed to possess a congenial temperament suited for compromise and common sense. He was one of the last scholar-churchmen in England.

Louise Creighton (1850–1936), née von Glehn, was a remarkable woman. Besides being the wife of a prominent Victorian, and the mother of seven children, she was a writer, biographer and social reformer. Not just content to sympathise with the early feminist movement, she offered a moderate, religious perspective to a wide range of women's issues. She wrote to educate a wide readership about national history, interesting people, and social and religious trends. She contributed to the dialogue over women's rights and church reform, bringing a reasoned voice to bear on a number of thorny issues.

Louise and Mandell Creighton are both worthy of biographical attention for what they accomplished. Besides their public roles, however, their shared private lives reveal a fascinating interplay of Victorian attitudes, values and tensions. Both, in a real sense, are just as interesting for who they were as for what they did.

Yet, with one minor exception, there has been very little written about Mandell since Louise wrote her two-volume biography, *Life and Letters of Mandell Creighton* (1904). The exception was a thin book, *Mandell Creighton and the English Church* (1964), by W. G. Fallows. With the exception of a published memoir and a volume of her letters to her mother, both edited recently by me, little has been written on Louise.

This book has been over thirty-five years in the making. I began researching the life of Mandell Creighton in the early 1960s. My plan in the beginning was to limit my research to Creighton himself. It seemed obvious to me that this colourful, sometimes controversial, scholar-bishop would repay scholarly investigation. Professorial obligations over three decades, however, interrupted my progress, but in the intervening years, while still collecting material for the biography, I happened to discover an autobiography written by Louise, along with a batch of letters she wrote to her mother and sisters over extended periods, both of which I edited and published. The years, therefore, have allowed me to turn the project into a dual biography of husband and wife.

So many individuals have helped me over the years of research and writing that I scarcely know where to begin in thanking them all. While it is impossible to mention everyone, I want to acknowledge as many as possible. To members of the Creighton family I offer my deepest gratitude for granting me permission to use materials deposited in various public and private libraries, and for allowing me free and complete access to all their papers, documents and photographs. Specifically, I wish to thank Mary and Susan Bailey and Rachel Moss (granddaughters of the Creightons), Christian (Kisty) Creighton and Barbara Creighton (wives of grandsons) and Barbara Adcock (grandniece of Mandell). I want to extend my special appreciation to Mary and Kisty for all of their help and advice. Without their interest and support this book would never have been completed. Five people gave enormous assistance but sadly died before they had the opportunity to see the fruits of their trust. They were Basil Creighton (nephew), and Hugh Creighton and Thomas Creighton (grandsons), and Joan Duncan and Penelope Fowler (grandnieces of Mandell).

I express my appreciation to the literary executors of manuscript collections who permitted me to microfilm or photocopy correspondence relating to the Creightons: Sir Peter Curtis (Sir Edward and Lady Dorothy Grey Papers), R. J. Stopford (J. R. Green and Alice Green Papers), and Sir Geoffrey Keynes (Samuel Butler Papers). I also offer my gratitude to countless librarians, archivists and staff members, many of whom have long retired, at the Bodleian Library, the British Library, Cambridge University Library, Carlisle Local History Centre, Emmanuel College Library, Fulham Palace, Harvard University Library, Lambeth Palace Archives and Library, Lewisham Local History Centre (London), Merton College Library, Peterborough Palace, the Public Record Office (London), the University of Oregon Library, and the University of Portland Library.

I would like to single out the following scholars, librarians and archivists who have helped me in more recent years: William Barnes (London), Sarah Bendall (Merton), Patrick Casey (University of Portland), John Coulter (Lewisham), Judith Curthoys (Christ Church), Susan Hinken (University of Portland), the Rev. Peter Karney (former vicar of Embleton), Valerie Langfield (Cheshire), Janet Morris (Emmanuel), Richard Palmer (Lambeth Palace), Keith Rooksby (Sydenham), Roberta Staples (Lady Margaret Hall), Marjory Szurko (Keble), James Templeton (Carlisle), Anne Thomson (Newnham), and Kay Seymour-Walker (Embleton). To each of them I offer my heartfelt thanks for their generous assistance.

I also owe considerable debt to Tony Morris, Eva Osborne and Martin Sheppard at Hambledon and London for their sustained enthusiasm and wise counsel in making this book a reality; and to a number of colleagues associated with the University of Portland, and others—friends and family—for individual encouragement and support, especially, James Connelly, Marc Covert, Jeanne Cummins, Madeleine O'Brien Faller, Valerie Langfield, Christine Covert Naylor and Elizabeth Covert Tobey. Finally, I must express my deepest and loving gratitude to my wife, Sally, who has been not only my chief constructive critic but also my firm advocate throughout, in sickness and in health, when it looked as if this book would never be completed; and to my children and grandchildren for their humour through it all.

University of Portland   James Covert

8 December 1999

1

Who is That Girl?

'Who is that girl who has the courage to wear yellow?'

Mandell Creighton to Humphry Ward [1]

For most of those who crowded into the Sheldonian Theatre that February afternoon in 1871 to hear John Ruskin, he was a familiar figure.[2] But for Louise von Glehn, having just arrived in Oxford a few days before, it was her first opportunity to see and hear the great art critic and social writer. Louise had a passion for art, and Ruskin, along with William Morris and Edward Burne-Jones, had shaped much of her thinking.[3] The year before she had travelled to Italy and discovered Italian art, notably Titian and Tintoretto. In England, the Pre-Raphaelites were also in the ascendancy. They became her focus. But if she were to choose one person to follow, it was Ruskin, her 'prophet'.[4] He stood above all others as a spokesman on art. For this impressionable twenty-year-old woman, the lecture was to be the high point of her brief visit to Oxford. It was, but she could hardly indeed have imagined to what degree it was to change her life.

Louise had come at the invitation of Lady Brodie, wife of Sir Benjamin Brodie, professor of chemistry. Lady Brodie had learned of the young woman through Louise's elder brother Ernest, who had studied at Oxford. The summer before Louise and Ernest had spent a week at the Brodies' summer house on Box Hill. This was not long after Louise had passed the first London University examination ever open to women, one of six women to do so. What Lady Brodie had heard of her and the London University examination 'disposed her favourably towards me', Louise recalled, so she was invited to stay for a few weeks with the Brodies when she came to Oxford in early February 1871. The Brodies lived at Cowley Lodge (which years later became St Hilda's College for women), a large house with a garden sloping down to the Cherwell and with a commanding view of Christ Church Meadow.[5]

A few years before, Louise had also come to know Humphry Ward, a fellow and tutor of Brasenose College. Ward was one of the few fellows in those days not to have taken religious orders; and, in his association with the von Glehns at Sydenham, he came to find Louise an attractive, clever and cultivated woman. His seeming fascination with this daughter of a rich London merchant caused many of his friends to speculate on his marital intentions.[6] A few weeks prior to Louise's arrival in Oxford, however, Ward had begun to adjust his sights towards Mary Arnold, granddaughter of Thomas Arnold of Rugby and niece of Matthew Arnold. Then, just before Louise actually stepped off the train at the Oxford station, Ward's feeling for Mary apparently cooled and he eagerly awaited Louise's arrival in Oxford.[7] For her part, Louise appeared circumspect about the relationship, regarding Ward as 'a great flirt, perhaps of a rather heavy kind, but he had a good heart and plenty of intelligence'.[8] She had become a friend of Ward's sister Agnes in 1869, but, as Louise came to know Humphry better, she could only regard him as a friend, 'a most unpleasing mixture of an evangelical parson and a fox hunting squire'. She admitted later that there had been moments when she could not help but find him 'a little dull and heavy' and 'doubted whether it would be wise to let our friendship go much farther'. Her mother heartily agreed.[9]

Louise arrived in Oxford on Wednesday 8 February. For the next couple of days, Ward—playing cat-and-mouse with Mary Arnold—energetically showed off Oxford to Louise, and Louise to Oxford. When Louise came to Ruskin's lecture on 'Light and Shade' on Thursday afternoon, Ward was there to welcome her.

Ruskin was not the only Oxford figure with strong views on the importance of art and on its social implications. To Mandell Creighton, a young fellow of Merton, his hero was his friend Walter Pater, the champion of the aesthetic movement sweeping Oxford at the time.[10]

Creighton, standing a few feet away, spied Ward chatting with an unfamiliar young woman. She was pleasantly attractive rather than striking, of medium height, about five feet five inches, and seemed to carry herself with confidence. Her hair was light brown, wavy, and pulled back loosely from her oval face and pinned in a bun. But it was her eyes that one noticed most, green and sharp, with a hint of a twinkle, in spite of the full eyebrows that dipped at the ends to suggest a slight sadness. What really caught Creighton's eye, however, was the bright yellow scarf she was wearing. Yellow was his favourite colour—a colour not customarily worn then. Immediately after the lecture, Creighton hurried up to Ward and inquired, 'Who is that girl who has the courage to wear yellow?' Ward promised an introduction, and a few days later Ward hosted a St Valentine's Day luncheon party at Brasenose, on Tuesday 14 February. Among the fifteen guests were six eligible young women, including Louise von Glehn and Mary

Arnold. On the table before each young woman was a St Valentine's card with a camellia.[11]

Louise recalled the event years later, writing that Ward

> gave me a large luncheon party in my honour when every lady found a card in her place on which were the verses written by him for her. I was rather disappointed to find that I was not to sit by him at lunch but had as my neighbour a stranger, Mr Creighton. I do not remember that we were particularly interested in one another during lunch.[12]

After lunch Ward gave his guests a tour of Brasenose. Creighton, however, witty and charming as was his way, seized the opportunity and snatched Louise away for a private tour of Merton and a walk along the river. Historic Merton, one of Oxford's oldest colleges, dated back to the middle of the thirteenth century. While the old buildings may have impressed Louise, her guide did not. 'I was interested but I do not think he made any real impression on me till the following Saturday when Mr Ward had a dinner party in my honour', she recalled. 'Then I sat between Mr Ward and Mr Creighton and there was a sort of struggle between the old friendship and the new. But Mr Ward had not much chance as a talker in comparison with Mr Creighton.'[13]

The Nicest Man I Have Met

'Mr Creighton is by far the nicest man I have met up here; he is so bright and intelligent and delightful to talk to.'

Louise von Glehn to her mother [1]

Over the next two weeks 'many arrangements were made to show me the sights', Louise said, and during that time both Mandell Creighton and Humphry Ward continued to express ardent interest in Louise von Glehn. At the Brodies' dance at Cowley Lodge on Thursday, 16 February 1871, for example, Ward thought Louise 'gayer than ever'.[2] Mandell also came to the dance, and though she could not remember dancing with him, Louise did recall that they 'sat out together and talked, and as we were talking, Humphry Ward passed by with Mary Arnold, and Mr Creighton said to me, "I wonder whether Ward is going to marry Miss Arnold". I fancied that I had good reason for assuring him that I thought not.'[3]

Ward, of course, sensed Creighton's interest in Louise as 'very ominous', and so 'contrived to lunch with her' over the next several days; but he soon realised he was 'all the time losing ground' to Creighton.[4] On Saturday, 18 February, Ward organised another Brasenose dinner, gallantly placing Louise between the two of them. This time Louise said she found Mandell 'delightful'.[5] On the other hand, Mandell proved not so gallant at a luncheon he hosted at Merton the following Monday when he put Humphry between Lady Brodie and Walter Pater's odd sister, Clara, causing Ward to note caustically in his diary that he was 'much edified' by the conversation. When they adjourned from their luncheon for a quiet walk along the Cherwell, Ward struggled to appear disinterested as he watched his rival courting the woman he wanted.[6] Louise said that strolling along the towpath with Mandell formed a good excuse for meeting; and that it was on such excursions over the next few weeks that she and Mandell grew to know one another better.[7]

Lady Brodie by this time was becoming concerned about her charge over Louise and about the 'rapid growth of intimacy' between her and Creighton. The question was should she write to Louise's mother, Agnes von Glehn.

Fortunately for Lady Brodie it was about that time that Louise's elder brother Ernest arrived in Oxford for an unexpected visit, presumably to reconnoitre the situation on behalf of a suspecting mother. Ernest knew the Brodies from his days as an undergraduate at Christ Church, where his tutor, Robert Brodie, was a cousin of Sir Benjamin.[8] With Ernest came George Grove, a close family friend from Sydenham, who was at that time secretary of the Crystal Palace Company. The visit had the effect of calming Lady Brodie.

On Tuesday Mandell took Louise for a boat trip on the river. It was now obvious to Humphry that, by not being invited to come along, he had irrevocably lost ground to his rival. Two weeks passed in Oxford; and after receiving a letter from her mother expressing concern about when she was coming home, Louise realised that a prompt explanation was required. On Thursday, 23 February 1871, she wrote her mother a long letter detailing why she planned to stay in Oxford a few extra days. 'Your note made me have a consultation with Lady Brodie,' she explained, 'the result thereof is that I do not return till Thursday or Friday in next week. I think it is not entirely inclination but also good sense that has led me to this conclusion. Lady Brodie is a very open person and I am convinced that she means what she says and would not press it if she didn't wish it.' Louise stressed the point that her Oxford friends had made plans for her in the coming week, adding: 'I hope you will think me right in staying. I am confident you would if you knew the circumstances and as I am once up here I fancy it is wisest to get all the good I can out of it. Don't think I delay coming home because you have nothing exciting to offer me. I am sure this time has been excitement enough to last me for a long while and there are things at home which make up plentifully for the absence of excitement.'[9] Then she described some of the highlights of her stay thus far:

On Saturday I dined at Brasenose; it was the most delightful little dinner. I went in the carriage from here to fetch Madeline at her lodging so that I might go into Brasenose properly chaperoned. We dined in such a lovely room, one of the public rooms of the college with dark oak panels and old Venetian looking glasses three hundred years old … I am continually astonished at the luxury of these entertainments. We were twelve people. Mr Creighton took me in and I sat between him and Mr Ward so I was well off. Mr Creighton is by far the nicest man I have met up here; he is so bright and intelligent and delightful to talk to. On Sunday, the Wards fetched me to go in the morning to hear [Henry Parry] Liddon preach,[10] then we went [for] a walk afterwards to lunch in Mr Ward's rooms, just we four – a quiet and cosy party; and he showed us lots of photographs afterwards. Then I went to meet Lady Brodie and we went and heard [Benjamin] Jowett preach,[11] such a splendid sermon.

The funny thing was that we went to church with [Thomas H.] Huxley and he walked part of the way home with us and said he thought it a noble sermon.[12] I should never have imagined that I should go to church with Huxley. On Monday, Lady Brodie and I lunched with Mr Creighton, it was a large assembly but very nice [and] my spirits rose when I found my place on Mr Creighton's left hand. Afterwards he made us stay a long while and showed me all his things and let me poke about and examine as much as I like. He has the most gorgeous rooms I have ever seen, splendid carved oak furniture, quantities of beautiful china and endless beautiful photographs and prints. It was such a treat looking over them all.

Afterwards we went for a walk all along by the river on the towing path which is most amusing as one sees all the boats practising. On Tuesday, Mr Creighton brought a boat to the garden steps and fetched Ethel and me for a row which was nice and I had my first lesson in rowing. It was a little cold and we had to take a good walk afterwards to get warm again. We are to meet Mr Creighton at Ruskin's lecture and shall make him take us afterwards. Yesterday I had a most scientific day, [with] Mr Clifton all the afternoon and in the morning Sir Benjamin made me walk down with him to the museum and showed me all over his laboratories. People up here do have a jolly life ... Sir Benjamin is always telling me that I must come and live up here for a year to study and suggesting how I am to do it.[13]

In delaying her return home by a few days, Louise gained added time to be with her enchanting don. By now, as far as she was concerned, Humphry Ward was nowhere in sight. Then two nights before she was to leave Oxford, Mandell decided to give a farewell dinner party for her in his rooms. Louise remembered the evening very well:

My visit was drawing to an end when on the last evening but one, I went with Sir Benjamin to a dinner party in Mr Creighton's rooms. It was a large party and he had arranged that I sat opposite him at a narrow table. He took in Mrs George and she ate her dinner in white kid gloves. After dinner I was standing by the table in his upstairs room looking at some photographs when the gentlemen came up. He at once came up to me and took my hand and then took me to a seat in the window where we could talk under the pretence of looking at photographs. I do not know whether he had meant to speak definitely then; he had already said that he would come to see me at home as soon as term was over, but somehow a very few words were said which we felt settled every thing.

Then wishing to bring things back to the ordinary plane he began to chaff Mrs George's gloves and her vague talk. I do not think I slept at all that night. It was all too wonderful.[14]

Though it was hoped that the engagement would remain private for a time, some in their circle soon learned of it. At Mandell's request the couple planned no meeting on Louise's last day in Oxford until the evening when, having secured tickets to a concert in the Town Hall, he invited her to attend as his guest.[15] 'I hoped that he might come to see me during the day,' she admitted, 'but he never came. We met at the concert and found plenty of time to talk.' [16] Mandell informed her that, because of his teaching duties, he could not get away to visit her home in Sydenham and to meet her family until the end of the term; and that until he had spoken with her father about permission to marry, he did not think they should consider themselves formally engaged, nor, indeed, should they write to one another. Louise, saddened by this, left Oxford for her home to wait for the Hilary term to pass. 'I told my parents and sisters who did not seem surprised, and during the fortnight was often teased with chaff about the unlikelihood of his ever appearing. All I could do was to send him my photograph in return for one he had given me of himself; but I was true to our compact and did not write a word ...' [17]

Louise did confide to her friend, the historian J. R. Green, about their engagement, writing to him soon after she returned to Sydenham. Green was in Cannes in the south of France, but responded immediately:

... I have been wondering at your long silence [occasioned by Louise's Oxford visit], dear Louise, and now I am only in wonder how you can have broken it. If I am ever engaged, my correspondents will have to give up all hopes of letters ... Still I am delighted that you have written and that the news of your engagement should have reached me from yourself, for happy as I am about it—and *indeed I am on all grounds most happy*—there is always a shadow of dread about a friend's marriage, and I have too few real friends to care to lose *one*. But such a frank, warm-hearted note as yours dispels all dread. I feel that our friendship will remain just as warm and true as ever, although you will have some one else now to treat you to 'wise conversation'. Indeed, indeed, Louise, I rejoice in this happiness of yours. As you say, I have just seen Mr Creighton, but he is a man one hears a good deal of and all one hears tends the same way. I have said hard things of 'Young Oxford', and perhaps there are hard things to say; but no one can deny that there is a great deal of real nobleness and refinement of life about it. I have always heard Mr Creighton spoken of as the representative of its best side. He must be a man of singular power—his influence over Merton and at Oxford generally shows that—and for all moral qualities I am content with your own assurance. I know you could not love a man who was not noble in heart and soul ... [18]

When the term ended, Creighton promptly caught a train to London where he made arrangements to stay with his close friend from undergraduate days, H. J. Hood, a Brasenose man, and his new wife of six months. From central London it was a short distance to Sydenham. Louise, of course, was both excited and fearful the day Mandell arrived at Peak Hill Lodge.

She felt confident, however, that her parents would approve of her Oxford don, and it pleased her that her father had thoughtfully asked her if she wanted him to remain home that day from his business in the City so as to greet her suitor. She quickly assured him it was quite needless, she recalled. And her mother being the gentle soul that she was, Louise felt confident she would welcome him with warmth and enthusiasm. It was her sisters that concerned her the most.

Being the tenth child of twelve children, sibling contests were the norm at Peak Hill Lodge. The usual 'critical atmosphere' in her family often resulted in cutting, hurtful remarks. As she described it, her family 'were not given to outward demonstrations of affection', and there was 'a good deal of rather rude plain speaking', and 'personal defects were far more likely to be criticised than personal merits to be admired'. She feared what Mandell would think of her family, while hoping they all would endorse her decision to marry him. The last thing she wanted was for one of them, particularly one of her 'critical elder sisters', to offer a biting comment in his presence. Being that Mandell was so academic, she was 'intensely conscious of how much there was in his nature' that could be misunderstood. She had hoped to prepare him as subtly as possible before meeting her family, 'what sort of things would hurt their susceptibilities, and to warn him of cherished views and opinions which must not be criticised'. But there had been no time, plus the fact that she realised, even having known him for just a short time, that he was a person who would be reluctant to accept such cautionary advice willingly. A blunt university man with a north country background visiting a pragmatic, business-minded, middle-class household in the metropolitan south could spell disaster. Mandell's tendency was to talk 'about things as they came into his head', playing with ideas as they amused or interested him, like a tutor with a group of students. She feared, therefore, that his 'ideas and ways' could be misunderstood by her family. His manner, Louise knew by then, seemed to go 'straight at things', treating topics of conversation rather impersonally, even flippantly.[19]

Fortunately only two of her older sisters, Olga and Mimi, were home that day. Mimi would probably be fine, but what of Olga? Louise felt apprehension all morning the day Mandell was to appear at their doorstep. Both sisters seemed to be hovering about the house like impatient vultures, eager to pounce and dine. Much discussion at lunch centred on the impending visit. As the early afternoon wore on, to Louise's relief, both Olga and Mimi found that they could not bear the suspense any longer and went out to run errands. 'Soon', Louise recalled, 'I heard the bell ring and was told he was in the drawing-room and went down alone to meet him. I remember pausing a second with my hand on the door to realise that he was really there.' [20] He rose from the chair when she entered and greeted her warmly, but somewhat awkwardly. Seeing him in her own drawing-room, miles away from the heady glow of Oxford, gave her an opportunity for the first time, it seemed, to really see the man she was intending to marry.

Mandell's demeanour was striking. He possessed what one might call 'presence'—distinguished and engaging, which in some odd way triumphed over his initial reserve and his slightly awkward physical mannerisms. Those who knew him were well aware that he could be disarmingly brusque or frivolously effervescent, depending on mood or circumstance. He stood erect, shoulders square, which had the net effect of making him appear taller than his five feet eleven inches; and his carefulness of dress, almost scrupulously so, and poised manner always produced a dignified air. His legs were thin and gangly, though his gait, she well remembered, was hurried and determined. His hands were soft and sensitive, with long artistic fingers extending well beyond his sleeves as if in search of something to touch.

It was Mandell's face that caught most people's immediate attention, like an imposing latch on a colourful door. His large aquiline nose hung down on a narrow face and acted as a bridge linking a high forehead to a bushy beard that dipped below his collar. His thinning, wavy hair was auburn; his eyes, framed by thin gold-rimmed spectacles, were greyish-blue—strong, steady and intense—and easily telegraphed his moods. They could dance humorously or become fixed with anger, producing a hawk-like stare. Creighton's voice was strong and rather high-pitched; and his words were precise, crisp, clipped, and seldom punctuated by gestures. He still carried traces of a broad Cumbrian accent. With a temperament that was highly strung and often impatient, Louise would later discover that his sometimes irritable manner tended to fall full force most often upon those nearest to him. All his close friends agreed that Mandell gave little attention to what people thought of him, and that he demanded high standards from himself as well as from others.[21]

After a brief embrace and some quiet words, they sat down opposite each other. Very soon Louise's mother entered the room. A thin woman, old and weary-looking, she seemed reserved, maybe nervous, and after introductions she and Mandell began talking, eventually getting around to a lively discussion about travelling in Switzerland. (Mandell had been there two years before and the von Glehns went there regularly.) Louise soon felt she had to rescue him and left momentarily to get a wrap so she could take him for a stroll in the garden. When she reappeared, her mother and Mandell were still going on about Switzerland, seemingly having never noticed that Louise had been gone. So Louise took possession of Mandell and the two of them went for a quiet walk in the garden where the sloping green fields and rolling Kentish uplands could be seen in the distance. 'As we walked round the field,' Louise recalled, 'I remember his asking me how many love affairs I had had, and I was able to tell him that though I have sometimes fancied that I cared for someone there had never been anything serious, and no one had proposed to anyone.' Then he surprised her by admitting that 'three girls had proposed to him, not very serious proposals perhaps', he added quickly.[22]

Olga and Mimi were there when they returned for tea, and happily the remainder of the afternoon was filled with light talk and laughter. Awkwardness slowly diminished and Louise was relieved that her gentleman friend was approved of by everyone. Then Robert von Glehn, Louise's father, arrived home from the City, and she felt apprehension again. After introductions and a few minutes of cordial talk, her father and Mandell disappeared into the study for a private talk. Nothing further was said about the engagement by anyone that evening. Louise must have felt the strain, though she never admitted it. Mandell took the train to London not long after dinner, promising to return early the following day. Before he arrived the next morning, Louise asked to speak to her father, and they talked in private for a few minutes. He warned her that she must be prepared to find herself 'in rather different social circumstances' to those in which she had been accustomed. He said he was concerned that Creighton's father, in his words, 'kept a furniture shop' in Carlisle, and that the family actually 'lived over the shop'. It was probably difficult for Louise's father fully to appreciate the status of Robert Creighton's business, which was in fact a successful furnishing and decorating firm of high reputation in the region. Robert Creighton was also a prominent figure in local government at the time, even serving once as mayor of Carlisle. He was certainly no mere carpenter.[23] Robert von Glehn, a successful City merchant, was just being chary of the rural shopkeeper or tradesman class of the north which he did not understand. For Louise, however, the issue scarcely troubled her.[24]

Mandell spent the better part of his Easter vacation with Louise, often visiting galleries and museums in London, sometimes spending hours studying Italian engravings in the print room of the British Museum. There were occasional teas and dinner parties in which Louise was able to show him off to family friends, but, as far as possible, they spent their time 'alone together, talking endlessly ... It was very hard when we had to separate and he had to go back to Oxford at the beginning of the term. I felt our parting terribly'.[25] It was during those early weeks of their engagement that Louise selected the nickname 'Max' for Mandell, something she regretted later in life because it just did not seem suitable given his success as a historian and clergyman. Nevertheless, for her, 'Max' his name became, and to many of Mandell's closer friends as well.

Their correspondence during the courtship was filled with questions about the future, not only about their lives together but also about his career. Colleges at Oxford and Cambridge in the early 1870s were still largely governed by ancient statutes, common for centuries, prohibiting married fellowships. At Merton, for example, the question of allowing married fellowships was raised in March of that year. Certainly the announcement of Creighton's engagement gave an urgency to the issue. The suggestion, however, met strong opposition from senior fellows at the March meeting of the college, with the result that action on a motion to permit a few married fellows was postponed. For Creighton it spelled a time of anxiety, and he began considering a possible career as a schoolmaster at a public school. He even contacted Harrow about a possible vacancy. In a letter to Louise on 19 April 1871, he stated:

> I am distracted by advice from every side what to do: several of the Fellows beseech me not to leave the College; they are good enough to say that my continuance here is important ... they beseech me at all events to do nothing hastily, to wait till June, when we have our next College meeting, when they will reopen the question of allowing marriage ... Others of my friends advise me at all events to keep my Tutorship, even if I vacate my Fellowship by marriage, and stay at Oxford taking pupils. I listen patiently and meditate.

He ended the letter with the comment: 'I should very much like to be a married Fellow here, but I see difficulties in the way ...' [26] The issue preyed on both their minds. A few days later, Creighton wrote to her: 'I am really touched by the anxiety of people here to do all they can for me ... My fellow tutors are prepared to do anything they can to help me, although by so doing they lose promotion and consequent income.' [27]

By early May, Louise was able to accept Mandell's urgings and make a visit to Oxford. It was arranged that she would be accompanied by H. J. Hood and his wife, but Mandell also thought one of Louise's sisters should come along too, so took it upon himself to ask Mimi. When she declined, Olga was asked. She accepted, much to Louise's sorrow, and Mandell soon discovered shortly why it was a 'great mistake', for Olga's 'jealousy prevented her from enjoying a time during which I was so much the most important person'. As a result Olga's letters home to Mrs von Glehn became a matter of some contention within the family.[28]

Louise, Olga and the Hoods stayed in lodgings in Merton Street near the college and took their meals in Mandell's rooms. 'We were much entertained by his old friends', Louise wrote later. 'In my mind it is all melted away into a sort of haze of May time in Oxford, of gardens and boating, of many delightful people, and of quiet times with Max in the Merton garden. Olga's disapproval and grimness was rather a blot, but she liked the Hoods and made friends with them.' During the visit Louise particularly enjoyed a river picnic arranged for all of them by Humphry Ward, and subsequently, a quiet conversation with Mary Arnold in the Merton gardens, during which Mary asked Louise if 'a certain young fellow of Brasenose had been much disappointed' over her engagement to Mandell. 'I did my best to reassure her', Louise said. Interestingly, Ward had written to Creighton on learning of the engagement: 'I, like a butterfly, flit from flower to flower, but oh to have found *the* flower.'[29] It was only a few weeks later that Humphry and Mary Arnold became engaged.[30]

After Louise and Olga returned home in mid May, Creighton finished Trinity term and made preparations for his summer. In early June, he visited Peak Hill where he and Louise attended picnics and made expeditions around Sydenham. As the haymaking season had arrived, they had 'delightful talks lying in the hay', discovering that their tastes on the whole 'were wonderfully alike'. When they did not agree, 'we would discuss the point again and again, often in letters when we were separated, till we found a basis of agreement or one converted the other'—Louise generally coming around to his point of view. Mandell claimed he never wished to overpower Louise with his opinions. This is no doubt true, for he sincerely believed that one had a right to form an own opinion on anything; but his persuasive skills were great and she found it difficult to resist both his reasoning and his manner, then and later. Nevertheless, their courtship, as most courtships do, brought special moments of discovery. 'I cannot imagine a more perfect companionship of mind than we enjoyed during those months of our engagement', she recalled fondly.[31]

The couple wrote long letters to each other, almost daily, when they were apart over the next seven months. Louise's letters have not survived. Some of Mandell's letters, however, were subsequently printed. Collectively, they reveal a good deal about Creighton's mentality as well as his moral approach to their developing relationship. They were his attempt to explain himself to her and also to prepare her to his way of looking at things. They were cerebral, moral and sermonic as the following excerpts reveal.[32]

[15 April] I am not blind to what the world might call your faults, but I feel and know they are a thousand times fewer than my own, and the question is, I trust, to us, and ought to be to every thinking person, not 'How much chaff' but 'Is there any wheat?' ... If we feel the other's heart is right, thoroughly right, the faults are of little consequence ...

[18 April] I don't want us to depend too much on one another. I want you to be you, and me to be me, and yet both of us absolutely one; and to do so we must each of us fuse together the ideal and the real, not rush too soon to grasp the real, and so sink the ideal ...

[28 April] I am not, as you know, and never was, conventional; my friends have always been the result of personal preference, and our friendship has mostly been of their choosing ... if anyone cares for me, I am glad ...

[19 May] I agree with you most entirely in reposing ourselves and all our hopes in God, and feeling confident that He who has already brought us to such wondrous great joys will never leave us or forsake us, and that if any evil befalls us we shall only have ourselves to blame ...

[25 May] I tried, if you remember, once before to put clearly the only way by which it seemed to me such a position (the discharging of domestic duties) in some degree was to be reconciled to real high culture on the woman's part—viz. to regard all duties and responsibilities, high and low alike, as to be jointly shared by both; by that means fewer difficulties are likely to arise. In my experience I have seen more disturbances caused in households by sheer carelessness and thoughtlessness on the part of the males than by anything else; while a woman, by being encouraged to brood over little cares, tends to forget the weightier matters of the law ...

[2 June] Your remarks about our manner to one another are quite true: I feel I cannot hope to conceal from myself that I am very much in love indeed; and that being the case, why should I try and conceal it from others as if I were ashamed of it? To say nothing of the fact that the process of concealment would be very painful ... Let us be happy as we can, however foolishly in the eyes of others; they will soon come round to our point of view ...

[23 September] You say you cannot see how one can reasonably believe in God's personal interference in the concerns of this life ... Your difficulties are merely those of reading flimsy articles or milk-and-water philosophy: the Divine government of the world no more requires 'personal interference' than it does perpetual miracles ... I am not in favour of milk-and-water heresies, let us have strong ones if any; I hate feebleness ...

[17 October] We must take ourselves as we are: such is my most decided view ... I quite see your impatient desire that everyone should think of me as you think; but then everyone is not like you. Human nature cannot be dealt with wholesale.

[11 December] You have a great capacity for losing your hold of moral principle at times: it is so hard a thing to hold it fast always, that no one could say he always had it; but it is a great help to firmness to hold to try and weave it into all one's actions, to make all one does seem great by keeping the great issues of every little act to one's moral self, clearly before one ...

One particular passage in the following letter, written less than a month before their wedding, must have caught her eye, perhaps causing her to ponder their future together. Years later she would lament the times he was away from her brought on by his professional responsibilities.

[12 December] I don't think you need fear we shall be too idle when we are married. I shall always have enough to do. That always strikes me as the nuisance of married life—strive as I may or as you may, still the practical side of life must be much more prominent to me than to you. I shall have a number of things to do, whereas your sphere will be all within my reach and knowledge, mine on the other hand will not be in your reach entirely. Will you mind? Will you make allowances for that? Will you not feel hurt when you think I am doing a number of things for other people that I had much better not do, but spend the time with you? I hope you will not do so, I hope you will trust me enough: it does not do to say that I might explain to you all that I am doing ... You must not ever think that I want to keep anything from you ... Please make up your mind to take on trust many things I do: if I am wrong, you can slowly convince me; but it will not be wise of you to lay orders on me to desist ...

These courtship letters, interesting examples of Victorian moods and manners, say much of course about Creighton's cerebral character.[33]

In June 1871, at the conclusion of Trinity term, Creighton went off for a couple weeks of examining at Marlborough. Returning in early July, he and Louise travelled to Carlisle to visit Creighton's family, where they spent several quiet weeks. It was her first time in the north of England. What followed were restful days when the newness of their relationship continued to fall away. They took long walks along the Roman wall and made expeditions deep in the Cumbrian hills and valleys, and down into the Lake District. Mandell surely must have waxed eloquent about the charms of his favourite landscape where placid, subtle green valleys spilled out into small lakes beneath sharp hills of stone and sod. He introduced her to the Italian languange, and she in turn promised to teach him German. He read Dante aloud, her venture into Italian literature, and they talked and talked. They discussed George Sand's novels and Goethe's poetry, and beautiful paintings.

What Louise found most intriguing and in some respects disquieting was Mandell's family and the culture of the north. The first night Louise met his family she found them 'so utterly unlike Max, in speech, in manner and appearance' that she felt 'he must have brought me to the wrong house, unless he were indeed a changeling himself'.[34] In her first letter home, she told her mother she 'felt a little strange here at first and still feel so a little at times. They are all quite kind to me and accept me as a matter of course ... It is hard to believe that these people are really [Mandell's] relatives. They are in every way so different from him'.[35] A product of the merchant class of metropolitan London, Louise was finding the Carlisle Creightons, and their circle of what she called 'well-to-do-tradesman class', very different. 'I was then very ignorant of ordinary middle class life', she said later, realising then that first impressions of other peoples and places can be deceiving. 'I knew nothing of the life of a provincial town, and really nothing of country life in England', she admitted. 'It was the defect of the life at The Peak, with all its intensity, that it really made us narrow and each of us only to like people or pay attention to people "of our own kind" as we called them.'[36]

Some members of the Creighton family in later years resented Louise for feeling the people of the north were somehow uncouth and humble.[37] Yet Mandell, though Cumbrian by birth and sentiment, had taken on cosmopolitan qualities at Oxford that transcended north country culture; and in some respects he *was* a changeling. It is probably true that he also never displayed close ties with his family in the way that Louise did with hers. But that was his manner. Louise said that this 'was one of the points on which we differed', claiming that Mandell in later times 'never understood family feeling or family life. It used often to strike me how absolutely alone he stood, and how detached he was from his family. Of course it would probably have been very different had he had a mother.'[38]

Louise had little opportunity to know Mandell's father well, for by the time she met him he was ill in mind and body. Robert Creighton had suffered a paralytic stroke the year before. Having turned over the family business to Mandell's younger brother, James, he now resided in the village of Kirkandrews four miles from Carlisle. Mandell's younger sister, Mary Ellen, known always as 'Polly', lived with her father, along with Aunt Jane, Robert's spinster sister who had been a part of the family since the death of Mandell's mother some years before. At times Mandell's father was perfectly alert and able to join in discussions, but at other times he would sit reading novels or musing in a kind of subterranean solitude. Mandell's brother, James, who had just become engaged to an attractive local girl, Caroline Hope, known as 'Carrie', lived in the city and managed the family business. As his father had done before him, James was emerging as a prominent citizen of Carlisle. To Louise's way of thinking, nonetheless, James 'had a rough north country manner' which she thought he rather liked to cultivate. He spoke with a strong Cumbrian accent. 'I felt him rather a difficult person to fit into my then rather limited conception of the universe,' she said, 'but as the years passed I grew to like him more and more, and I think he liked me, tho we had very few tastes and interests in common.' Like Mandell, James possessed a strong personality, though they 'had little in common except their liberal views'. Yet, she found that they shared a 'strong affection between them, based on the respect each felt for the others capacities, effective along such very diverse lines'.[39]

Louise found her relationship with Mandell's sister, Polly, somewhat strained, and it apparently remained so over the years. 'I expect this was a very trying time for Polly', she reasoned. 'She was a very plain girl, tall and thin with a Cumbrian accent and an incoherent way of talking. She had not at this time developed any special interests of her own, and owing to her father's illness had had a rather dreary girlhood, except for her times at a boarding school and the friends she made there.'[40] Louise to some extent failed to appreciate then, as she did years later, how much Mandell's impending marriage affected Polly. Louise was like a wedge being driven between Polly and her brother. Mandell occupied a special place in Polly's heart—more so than James, because he was her elder brother and because they shared similar interests in art and literature and music. Now Polly watched Mandell 'absolutely absorbed in a girl quite strange to her'. But like a true Cumbrian, Polly said nothing. 'I am afraid we were too absorbed in ourselves to guess her feelings', Louise believed. 'She was very kind and friendly to me, and I was only too glad to make friends with her.' Caught between two engaged couples—Mandell and Louise and James and Carrie—Polly found her existence awkward.[41]

In late August 1871 Creighton went off to the south coast and offered a series of lectures on Dante at Falmouth and Plymouth to groups of middle-class women. These lectures had been arranged by the newly formed Ladies' Association at Oxford that was intent on promoting university education for women who were still denied entry at both Oxford and Cambridge. After several weeks in Cumberland, Mandell and Louise both now knew they would not see each other for any extended period until the wedding; and that would be at Christmas. Life at The Peak in the following weeks was not easy for Louise. Only correspondence would keep them connected, and therefore she found Mandell's 'long daily letters' a 'great joy'.[42]

Taking up temporary lodgings in Falmouth, Creighton gave lectures several times a week, journeying to Plymouth on one day for a lecture there. Wherever he spoke, he inspired his students, who seemed to fall victim to his charm and wit, appreciating his command of language, his insights into Dante's relationship with Beatrice, and his ability to delve into the finer points of life in Renaissance Italy. His method was to inspire more than to instruct, most people felt, and in the words of one listener, he 'bore the burden of learning so lightly as to make us forget he had any. He would ask questions, suggest paradoxes, and listen most attentively to anything that was said in reply. He certainly succeeded in making us think', for 'his power to revel in pure nonsense was a striking characteristic'.[43] This was Creighton's style of teaching which he used the rest of his life, whether in classroom, chapel, church, or in the casual atmosphere of a drawing-room gathering or a stroll with a friend along a dusty path. Before he left Falmouth, he even introduced the locals to William Morris, wallpaper for which he then had a passion.

'My class at Plymouth is about fifty', he wrote to Louise. 'I was not quite content with my first lecture; I felt it was pitched rather too high for the intelligence of those I saw around me, and then don't you know how one becomes dogmatic, the less one sees criticism. I shall be better in my next [lecture, for] they must have more detail and fewer general principles.' A few days later he wrote about a Falmouth class: 'My lecture was a great success yesterday. I was in good form, and said everything in good taste. It is curious how one's audience affects one. I felt at once here that I was addressing a much more cultivated set of people than at Plymouth, and the difference on my mind was enormous. You see how wicked I am, what many people would call conceited; but if one is placed in a position of authority by people, I humbly submit the only thing to do is to use that authority.'[44] There were those who only knew him casually that thought him conceited. In reality he was confident and self-assured; and he could, in a curious way, be detached from those around him, sometimes seemingly from himself. He had an amazing ability to analyse people, himself included, and to render judgments that could either hurt or honour. It made little difference to him. He was honest to a fault.

An example of this honesty can be seen in the strange admission he wrote in the following letter to his impending bride. Describing one of his social outings in the south coast, he said: 'I was amused at the way in which I went. One of my class asked me to go—a very nice-looking girl to whom I had been introduced, I assented, expecting a great assemblage: she appeared, accompanied by two others of my class. There was no chaperone: the eldest of the ladies was, however, some thirty-five, and might claim the privilege. I thought, however, the arrangement was nice, human, and intelligible; I liked it.'[45]

And he always liked it. He was the consummate social creature who enjoyed the world of people and ideas. He was also, in Louise's mind, an 'ardent lover'. Her love for him never wavered. She found that Mandell exhibited an abiding interest in everything she did and thought; that he 'openly expressed admiration' for her, and delighted in all that she was. As a result his demonstrable affection had an overwhelming impact on her, seeing that she was, as she put it, 'accustomed to a very critical family atmosphere when admiration was certainly never expressed'. She felt that her 'love and admiration for him was so immense, that no harm came to me, only wonder, from his admiration. But critical elder sisters thought it must be bad for me; and I remember when I once ventured to confide in Mimi how wonderful I felt it to be so much loved, she told me that I ought not to think of that side of it, but rather of the love I gave ... Max just absorbed my life then and always.'[46]

> I remember later, when we were married in Oxford, Clara Pater once comparing Mary Ward and me, and she said that she always preferred Mary's company when Humphry was present, because if he was absent Mary was always wondering where he could be; but she preferred me without Max, for when he was there I was so occupied with him and with what he was saying that I was no use to anyone else ... I think this was true all my life; certainly during our engagement the outside world seemed hardly to exist[47]

Commenting on their courtship years later, Mandell reckoned that they had 'thought too little of others' during the engagement period, and that he had 'given way' to her 'against his better judgment' in spending so much time alone together. 'I could never bring myself to agree with him', Louise confessed. 'It was such a wonderful time for us, a time that could never be repeated; no one with any real understanding or sympathy could grudge it [of] us. I do not think my mother did.'[48] But it bothered her always that her family—with the possible exception of her mother and one brother, Willie—never fully appreciated Mandell 'or felt at ease with him. I believe that this arose really from a fundamental difference of nature, and also from an intensity and a certain narrowness in the family point of view which made them only like people of a certain type.' From Louise's point of view Mandell helped her to be herself, 'which I never could have been in the family atmosphere, but I do not think changed me fundamentally. Of course he influenced me profoundly ...'[49]

After Creighton returned to Oxford to commence the new term, anxiety over his fellowship bore on both of them. Even before leaving Falmouth he had written to her: 'A letter I got last night has proved to me, in a way which cannot fail to give you a most melancholy satisfaction, my justification in beseeching you not to count upon my position at Oxford as even approximately settled.' He went on to state that 'the demon of matrimony' had seized another don at Merton, which meant that four men wishing to marry were now applying to retain their fellowships. 'I don't feel particularly merry about the matter', he admitted. 'I must candidly own that ... the sooner I look about me for a schoolmastership the better. I still have a sentimental desire to stay at Oxford: I still feel that the work there would be most congenial to me.' Anticipating a December vote on the college celibacy statutes, he asked Louise: 'Tell me, do you think I ought to wait till Christmas, for the votes of the college, or ought I to turn away my mind at once elsewhere? I incline rather to wait and see, but our prospect of being married at Christmas becomes more and more shadowy.'[50]

The meeting of the college was scheduled for 23 December. While the proposal asking for a change in the statutes to permit four married fellowships had been given an affirmative assent by the Privy Council at the end of August, Merton still had to ratify the decision to grant four such married fellowships, and then to select those to be the recipients from the several men applying. Further, the vote would be secret, and there were many senior fellows still publicly adverse to this radical motion. Creighton was sufficiently realistic to know that he could not be certain of being one of the four accepted. It was all very trying. He wrote to Louise on 20 September: 'I had really, just as you had, quite counted on the consent of the College, and now everything is uncertain. The whole question has become now so complicated to the unhappy body of fellows, that my one source of content-ment is that I am not called upon to vote in the matter. It really is ludicrous ... Merton always has been regarded as the most advanced and maddest College in Oxford; but the spectacle of all its Fellows rushing headlong into matrimony at once will make everyone in Oxford die with laughter.' He concluded:

> If Providence decides that I leave Oxford, I have no doubt it is better for us. He may have greater work for us to do elsewhere: let us go and do it without repining. Look at it in that way: after the first disappointment is over, which one can't help feeling, a deep-seated belief in the goodness of the new course ought to take possession of us. Let us be prepared for all emergencies.[51]

Louise had begun to collect her trousseau that autumn. 'My parents gave me also all of my house linen and kitchen things, my bedroom furniture and my piano', she recalled. 'Choosing all these things was of course a great interest [to Mandell] and we corresponded too a great deal about the wallpapers and decoration of our house, though I did not go up to Oxford to see it.'[52] Creighton had begun searching for a suitable house in Oxford, which he found a painful distraction. Houses close in to the colleges were few and generally expensive to rent. He did locate a semi-detached villa just constructed off Banbury Road not far beyond St Giles's church.[53] With many misgivings, caused by the thought of leaving his Merton quarters, he rented it in mid November. 'Happy thought!' Mandell wrote to her. 'Our rooms shall be what we want, not what the faculty would prescribe for us. I would much rather have something that we agreed upon, though it might be all wrong, than be ever so right by taking other people's advice.'[54]

'My taste was not very formed yet,' Louise explained, 'but I knew pretty decidedly what I liked.' She claimed that Mandell 'had thought more on the subject; his taste was certainly more catholic than mine, and he was not so violent in his dislike. I still think he had some strange lapses into bad taste, tho' on the whole I have grown to appreciate much which he liked then both in great and small things.' Her tastes, of course, were heavily shaped by Ruskin. 'With us both, yellow was a favourite colour; my best evening dress was yellow silk, and our drawing-room wallpaper was yellow. Our future house was quite new, so we did not go to the expense of Morris wallpapers on walls which might prove damp, but got our papers from Woolam Co., who was reviving some of his old fashioned blocks, and we looked forward to Morris papers in the future.'[55]

As December approached, both Mandell and Louise waited with great anticipation, although support and consolation could only be shared in their letters. He had only managed two brief visits to Sydenham during Michaelmas term, and the stress of it all was taking its toll on both of them. 'Up till the last I was not allowed to speak of our marriage as certain, though our wedding day was fixed; it was only supposed to be fixed provisionally.' Reflecting on her feelings at that time, Louise wrote:

> I do not feel as if those months were very happy to me. I doubt whether such a transition time as an engagement is ever happy for a girl. Yet it has its great value as a correspondence, such as ours was, certainly brings out much that would not otherwise come out in ordinary [courtship] ... I expect that I was unduly sensitive and exacting, but I certainly found both Mimi and Olga very unsympathetic at this time, and when I once looked through the letters which I wrote to Ida [another sister] during these months I was surprised to find how full of complaints they were of the want of sympathy from those at home except my mother. Getting all my things was a great interest to her and she was unfailing in her love and kindness.[56]

Mandell, also experiencing moments of anxiety, wrote to Louise in November saying that he sometimes felt 'quite terrified to think what would occur if I did not get leave from the College. I should be fearfully disappointed.' Then a few days later: 'If you inquire about my general state of mind, it is that of a man who struggles to remain cheerful, and knows that unless he keeps his will a very solid one he will be absolutely lost. If ever I were to begin and speculate on the possibilities of not getting leave to stay here, and sometimes one feels tempted to do so, I should simply collapse altogether under my work.' A week later: 'I have been haunted to-day by a notion how horrid it would be if all our schemes came to nothing: there is yet a month to wait before we know, and here we go on arranging as if all were right: I shall never forgive myself if I cause you a disappointment.'[57]

Then, on the afternoon of Christmas Eve, the fateful word came. Louise was in the process of trying on her wedding dress when a telegram arrived from Mandell stating that Merton had elected him to one of the four married fellowships. The issue was settled. And as one of the senior fellows said, as he gleefully reported the decision to Creighton, 'My dear fellow, there were four seats in the matrimonial coach, and they were all immediately taken.' It was widely held at the time that Merton altered the celibacy rules in order to keep him. That may or may not be the case, though it is a story in itself how Mandell Creighton came to be one of the most celebrated dons in Oxford.

3

A Most Promising Scholar

'A most promising scholar and a thoroughly satisfactory pupil in every respect.'

Henry Holden, D.D., Headmaster, Durham Grammar School [1]

The city of Carlisle is an ancient border town situated on the River Eden in the rugged western border county of Cumberland. On bright days, particularly at sunset, many of its older buildings, because of being constructed of sandstone, gave off a warm pinkish glow. To the north are the purple hills of Scotland. Carlisle, located on the western end of Hadrian's Wall, began as a Roman encampment, one of those northern defensive outposts maintained by imperial legions for some three hundred years. Little of old Roman Carlisle, *Luguvallium* as it was called, can be seen except for occasional artefacts unearthed now and again. Considerable evidence exists of its medieval past, however, notably the city's castle, the abbey church-turned-cathedral and the remnants of old city walls. Near the guild hall is the old town hall, which dates from Elizabethan times. [2]

Over the centuries Carlisle's citizens lived amid romantic tales about their city: the stern Roman occupation, a succession of stormy struggles with invading Scots, Saxons, Danes, and Normans, and the constant bloody feuds of feudal nobles and dynastic families. It is tempting to consider that this ancient city, born in Celtic mists and fashioned by the muscles of Roman soldiers and medieval artisans, was in some way influential in forging Mandell Creighton's early intellectual and religious yearnings. [3] How could a boy not be influenced by a city that claimed such occasional residents as Agricola the Roman general, St Cuthbert, many kings of Scotland and England, Mary, Queen of Scots, Bonnie Prince Charlie, Sir Walter Scott, and—even in Creighton's youth—Dean Archibald Tait, later to be Archbishop of Canterbury?

Creighton believed Carlisle to be *the* city of the north of England. With the advent of the 'spirit of industry', as he put it, Carlisle and its environs became the cotton manufacturing and railway centre of Cumberland, yet even the economic boom of the nineteenth century failed to alter the county's pastoral setting. In fact, Cumberland seemed unique in preserving traces of old England, Creighton thought, and Cumbrians, he maintained, remained 'stalwart, sturdy and independent' and prided themselves on being 'kindly, homely and outspoken'. He was convinced that travellers passing through his county would easily sense they were 'amongst a folk who have their roots in an historic past', more so, perhaps than other regions.[4]

The most imposing structure in the city was—and still is—its castle, a low, squat-looking, square block medieval fortification constructed of red sandstone. The castle sits on a slightly elevated piece of ground at the end of Castle Street; its walls still bruised with the wounds of countless border skirmishes between Scots and English. The most memorable moment in the castle's long history was when it served as temporary place of confinement for Mary, Queen of Scots, after her surrender to the English. Walking down the hill from the castle through narrow streets, that Nathaniel Hawthorne once called 'mean and sordid', one comes to Carlisle's cathedral, which dominates the old centre of town.[5] A modest structure as English cathedrals go, the church's medieval remnants seem to fit nicely with modern additions. Across the way, on busy Castle Street and in the shadow of the cathedral spires, stood the Creightons' two-story home and business. It was here, on 5 July 1843, that Mandell Creighton was born. And it was in the cathedral precincts as a child growing up that he played and learned his school lessons.

Though he would ultimately leave Carlisle's cramped confines for good, Creighton genuinely prided himself on the fact that his roots ran deep in Cumberland soil.[6] His paternal grandfather, James Creighton, was a joiner by trade who had emigrated from the lowlands of Scotland to Carlisle early in the nineteenth century. It is known that the Creightons of Scotland (and possibly Ireland) sometimes spelled their name 'Crichton', and that some had settled in England before James arrived.[7] James, who became a partner and later owner of a successful furniture and decorating shop in the city, had several children, but only two of record, Robert and Jane.[8] Robert followed his father in the carpentry trade, slowly expanding the business, and eventually moving it to a prime location on Castle Street. There the business flourished, and by the 1860s Robert had built it into a successful cabinet-making and decorating establishment enjoying a wide reputation for manufacturing quality furnishings for gentry houses and mansions of the county. Robert Creighton also shrewdly tapped into the lucrative timber trade of the region.

In 1842 he married Sarah Mandell, tenth child of Thomas Mandell and Mary Rayson. Thomas Mandell was a yeoman farmer near Bolton in

Cumberland. Robert and Sarah's marriage commenced under a cloud, however. When Robert was refused permission to marry from Sarah's dominating brother, with whom she was living, Sarah agreed to elope to Gretna Green, Scotland, not an uncommon thing for impatient couples to do in those days. Gretna Green, once described as 'a spot which many people have visited to their woe', was just across the border from Carlisle. It was, until 1856, a place where couples—because of Scotland's liberal laws—could be married without a waiting period, a licence, a clergyman or parental consent. Although Robert and Sarah subsequently received a special licence, the union remained a source of tension among Sarah's family. Her brother never spoke to her again.[9]

The Mandells came from yeoman stock. The 'Mandell' name was recorded in the 1700s as 'Mandele', and the family possibly descended from the 'de Mandevilles', thus being related to the Earls of Sussex. A certain 'Walter de Mandeville' witnessed the Magna Carta being signed. An Edward and a Robert Mandeville were successive vicars of Holm Cultram Abbey around the turn of the sixteenth century. Sarah's uncle, William Mandell, was fellow and tutor at Queens' College, Cambridge, and one of her brothers, William Mandell, was a fellow at St John's, Cambridge. Her cousin, William Gunson, became fellow at Christ's College, Cambridge. He regularly visited the Creighton family in Carlisle while the children were growing up. Two of Sarah's brothers were also clergymen—John, curate of Milverton, and Rayson, rector of Ridgwell.[10]

Mandell's childhood was similar to other boys of his region, class and generation; it was merely that his particular energy and talents took him further.[11] He was the eldest of the four children of Robert and Sarah Creighton. His brother James was born the year after Mandell, and a sister, Mary, was born in 1846 but died the same year. Another sister, Mary Ellen, 'Polly', was born in 1849.[12] The following year Mandell's mother, Sarah, died unexpectedly from unknown causes.

Robert Creighton was now left with three children with only a slight memory of a mother's devotion and influence. He never remarried nor did he ever speak of his wife to his children again. His unmarried sister, always referred to as 'Aunt Jane', came to live with the family. With the assistance of a young Cumbrian girl named Ann, who cooked and did housekeeping, Aunt Jane tried to create some semblance of a family atmosphere for the children. Aunt Jane was described as a 'dear little person' who was 'very warm hearted and affectionate', although apparently accustomed to being teased and laughed at. She remained with the family for many years.[13]

The Creightons lived in quarters over the Castle Street shop. Though spacious enough, the rooms were furnished sparsely and virtually devoid of books or pictures. The impression is that the children were raised in a kind of cultural vacuum. One cannot but imagine home life being strict and dreary. Worse, Robert Creighton displayed a violent temper and an overbearing manner, more so after his wife died, and had little tenderness to offer his children. The children's relationship with their father was hardly a loving one, but then Victorian children often seemed unaccustomed to any real demonstrable love from fathers. Growing up with a dominating father, and a surrogate mother who was affectionate but rather ineffectual, had a telling impact on the Creighton children—at least Louise thought so, for she speculated that Mandell's loss of customary home life and 'family feeling' would not have been the case 'had he had a mother'.[14]

Although a regular attendant at church, Robert Creighton's heart and mind were elsewhere. He was a self-made businessman, instinctively anti-clerical, very secular-minded, and a firm Liberal in politics. His scant interest in religion seemed grounded on a strong contempt for the clergy because of what he considered their lack of practicality. The Creighton children were raised in a stern atmosphere spiced with Liberal principles of industry, thrift and duty. Robert Creighton, according to one of his favourite sayings, expected his children to have 'their heads screwed on the right way', a phrase that Mandell adopted as an adult.[15] Robert Creighton eschewed luxury and demanded an unfailing earnestness in all things. He despised weakness and shoddiness. He was easily given to improving or reproaching comments, and believed that insisting on respect for work and authority would surely forge character. These strong leanings, however, resulted in a concomitant virtue: a firm belief in individual liberty. As a result the Creighton children grew up with a sense of being independent, with a ready belief that they ought to follow their own inclinations. Polly Creighton recalled that her father was a 'great believer in allowing a boy to follow his own bent—only everyone must work and work hard', again a belief that young Mandell adopted readily in later life. Perhaps this explains why he was allowed, though hardly encouraged, to leave Carlisle and pursue an academic education. When he decided to take Anglican holy orders, his father—admittedly disappointed—remained true to his principles and made no objection, giving him help and encouragement to make his life his own way.[16]

Polly remembered that, as they all grew up, she was 'allowed to be with them when they and other boys played cricket in our garden and of watching Mandell while he played whist with his boy friends in the parlour'. Mandell had a tendency to be moralistic even then and took a rather serious interest in religion. Polly certainly felt his influence and claimed that it was 'his example which made me think seriously of religious things, and to go to Holy Communion'.[17] Both Mandell and James, she recalled, were strong-willed and 'hot tempered'; but though they had the customary quarrels of boyhood brothers, they were close companions. 'We grew up taking each other as we were without stopping to analyse each other's faults or good qualities', Polly said. Nevertheless, while studying at Oxford in 1865 and knowing that James was destined to take over the family business, Mandell wrote to a friend that his brother regarded him as 'an impracticable dreamer—good enough at grubbing in books, but with theories utterly useless on every material point', and that 'his only hope for me is that experience will put me right'.[18]

Young Mandell always seemed to go out of his way to look after his sister, then and later in life, as if, she used to say, their mother while dying had asked him to do so. Even after he had left Carlisle for school, he wrote home every week, mainly to her, until he married. He also took every occasion to introduce her to new books, supervising her reading habits vigorously. Once when she asked to read *Vanity Fair*, his response was emphatic: 'No need to meet knaves sooner than need be and fools you will meet plenty of.'[19] Despite her elder brother's concern for her, Polly regarded her childhood as 'horridly unhappy'. She recalled rather bitterly that Mandell warned her never to be 'a slave' to a husband, or a father or a brother; yet, as it turned out, she unselfishly considered it her 'duty in life' to take care of her father because she felt it her responsibility. It was 'what a girl was good for', she remarked with a shrug.[20]

Mandell was independent-minded and self-assured from the start, and Polly described him as 'a particularly active, restless child, never quiet' and 'generally in mischief'. He began attending a dame's school in Carlisle at around four or five, a school administered by a formidable matron, a Miss Ford, who once tied him to the leg of a table to keep him quiet—a punishment he himself employed on his children in later life.[21] Then in 1852 he went on to the local cathedral school across the street from their Castle Street home where he studied until 1857. Falling under the spell of an inspiring headmaster, the Rev. William Bell, Mandell discovered the joy of reading books. He soon acquired the nickname 'Homer' because of 'the rapidity and ease with which he could construe'.[22] Classmates, usually younger students, sought him out for help in translating and interpreting passages from their classical studies.

James never had the inclination, and Polly the opportunity, to pursue an academic education as did Mandell. James also attended the cathedral school for a time and then completed his formal education at St Bees boarding school, on the Cumberland coast near Whitehaven. But that was it. Robert Creighton expected James to join the family business which he subsequently inherited, becoming a successful businessman and civic leader in Carlisle. Like his father, James was active in local government, served as justice of the peace, and was twice mayor of the city. He was encouraged, but declined, to stand for Parliament for Carlisle. He became a director of North British Railways, and was the first person honoured in 1889 with the freedom of the city.[23] For Polly there was no choice apparently but to share in the caring of her father, which became particularly troublesome after his paralytic stroke in 1870 that left him an invalid. Sadly, her formal education—a brief few years at a girls' boarding school—was cut short, leaving her without the cultural refinement she always desired. She never married and spent her entire adult life in Carlisle engaged in civic and private philanthropy, most notably work in education—no doubt because it was one of the major omissions in her own life.[24]

Among family members, Mandell Creighton's scholastic success appeared to be only appreciated by an older cousin, William Gunson, a nephew of Mandell's mother, a Cambridge man who had received honour degrees in Classical and Mathematical triposes and stayed on as fellow at Christ's College. On regular visits north to his home at Baggrow, Gunson often stopped to visit the Creightons. He soon recognised Mandell's intellectual gifts and urged him to continue his academic interests. When Mandell went to Oxford and did not even try for Cambridge, Gunson became angry and wrote a sharp letter to his young cousin. After reading the letter, Mandell crumpled it up and flung it into the fire. Years passed before the two men mended their friendship.[25]

At the urging of his Carlisle teachers, Creighton sat for the King's Scholarship examination for Durham Grammar School in November 1857. For the first time Durham examiners had instituted Latin verse as one of the sections of the test, a subject for which Creighton's teachers at Carlisle had failed to prepare him. As a result, he left the Latin translation portion of the test blank and was convinced he had failed. The examiners, however, chose to make an exception in his case, reportedly because they were impressed with the overall examination. Young Creighton received special admission to the grammar school and entered the fourth form.[26] He was fifteen years old when he left Carlisle for Durham in February 1858, and he rarely looked back—indeed in a cognitive way he never quite returned to the city of his birth. Yet the border region remained forever dear to him; and he made no apologies for being a man of the rural north, a fact that usually carried some social liability in those days.[27] In a letter to his niece years later, he wrote of meeting a man 'who had been at the Carlisle

Grammar School soon after me ... I am always delighted when people from Carlisle come and talk to me'.[28]

The period 1858 to 1862 were the happiest of Mandell's boyhood years. Durham Grammar School offered a refreshing freedom to expand his intellectual vistas. The old grammar school forged formative impressions in his mind that shaped a good part of his adult outlook. And with regard to the venerable eleventh-century Norman cathedral with its massive presence and high church ceremony, it became the religious centrepiece in his mind. The school had been moved in 1840 from the cathedral precincts high above the River Wear to a facing hill across the river. The move was precipitated by the creation of Durham University a few years before. The new location gave grammar school students a spectacular view across the river of the cathedral's triple towers and the tops of city buildings off in the distance. Grammar school students were required to attend cathedral services on Sundays and holy days, and to get to the cathedral they had to make their way down a narrow, winding path to Prebends Bridge and up another path on the other side. The view from the old stone bridge over the meandering river was a treat and many consider it—even today— one of the loveliest spots in all of England. From the bridge the mighty towers of Durham's cathedral stretch high above the trees that cover the rugged cliff. Pausing on the bridge to view the massive edifice, the lines of Sir Walter Scott inscribed on a corner plaque conjure up all kinds of images of the past:

> Grey Towers of Durham,
> Yet well I love thy mixed and massive piles.
> Half Church of God, half Castle 'gainst the Scot,
> And long to roam these venerable aisles,
> With records stored of deeds long since forgot.

These words reveal more than the spirit of Durham's cathedral—they capture the essence of England's north country, something a young Creighton felt dearly.

The grammar school was then under the imposing headmastership of Dr Henry Holden, a Balliol man and a serious classical scholar. Holden, formerly headmaster at Uppingham before coming to Durham in 1853, was one of the 'new breed' of headmasters in that era of education reform. He realised, like Edward Thring (his replacement at Uppingham), the pedagogical benefits in treating young boys as individuals, something quite radical in those days. Creighton was fortunate in this and soon found Holden taking a keen interest in his studies.[29]

Flourishing under the rigorous academic programme, Mandell soon became a regular prize winner in Classics, Hellenistic Greek (New Testament), Latin, French, and English poetry and prose. Never becoming what might be called a 'scribbler of verse', he wrote occasional poetry then and at intervals in his later life. His strength, however, seemed more analytical than creative, and, as a result, he found mathematics easy. Not surprisingly, he enjoyed reading history.

It perhaps says something about Creighton's moralistic bent that in subsequent years he often regretted that he never sufficiently applied himself at Durham, but instead trusted too much to his natural cleverness and his ability to work slavishly at the very last moment. After a year he was admitted to the headmaster's class where his work was described as 'strong rather than neat'. When it came time for him to leave Durham for Oxford in 1862, Holden wrote in Mandell's final 'Report of Progress and Conduct' that the young student was a 'most promising scholar and a thoroughly satisfactory pupil in every respect', and that he was 'exemplary and highly useful in the management of the school'. Holden concluded: 'I greatly regret his approaching departure.' [30]

In that last year at Durham, Mandell was promoted to head boy, a notable recognition in that era when the monitorial system, the practice of using the brightest students to instruct and discipline the others, reigned supreme in schools across England. The role of monitor appealed to his instinctive drive to influence people, especially younger boys, and Mrs Holden, the headmaster's wife, had vivid memories of young Mandell in his final years at Durham, walking around the playground with each arm extended out over the shoulders of as many boys as could squeeze close to him, all wheeling playfully in a circle. The smaller boys, she said, always watched for him to appear and then would rush to him eager to hang on him and walk with him. It was at Durham that Creighton discovered his powers of hypnotism, a practice he experimented for a time on younger schoolmates until forbidden to do so. Though he discontinued the practice, never to take it up again, it reveals something about his magnetic personality and his ability to influence.[31]

An example of Creighton's moralistic precocity can certainly be found in the amazing letter he penned in August 1864 shortly after leaving the grammar school for Oxford. He wrote this 2200-word letter concerning the 'duties of the monitors' to a student friend at Durham who had succeeded him as head boy. He always called it his 'pastoral epistle', claiming that it took him 'three hours of hard work to think it out carefully and write it'. The letter not only offers a perceptive insight into his mind as a young man, it also reveals a great deal about English boarding school practices in that era:

DURHAM SCHOOL.

Report of *Creighton's* progress and conduct

from *Aug. 18th* to *Sept. 29th*, 186 2.

		Signed
CLASSICS.	*A most promising Scholar & a thoroughly satisfactory pupil in every respect — I had perfect confidence in entrusting him lately with the management of the IV form for a or so days during the absence of the master*	*H. H.*
MATHEMATICS.	} *Works diligently and has a firm hold on his subjects.*	*S. F. Creswell.*
ARITHMETIC.		
WRITING.		
FRENCH OR GERMAN.	*C*	
GENERAL CONDUCT.	*Exemplary & highly useful in the management of the School — I greatly regret his approaching departure. H. H.*	

HENRY HOLDEN, D.D.,
HEAD-MASTER.

Mandell Creighton's report from Durham School, 1862

1864: Carlisle: St Bartholomew's Day

My dear Sherlock,

I am going to take the liberty of writing a few observations on the duties of the monitors, and the best way of fulfilling them. They are such as my own experience as monitor taught me, and such as I have found out by thought since ... I know that I am laying myself open to the charge of presumption in thus volunteering my advice, but I am sure you will all of you forgive me, and take what I say in the spirit in which it is written. You will excuse me if I say that I think you need it: you are all of you still young to be monitors ...

I will, however, speak first about the duties of monitors in general; and then will give you in particular a few hints.

A monitor's duty, then, is, to try and benefit the school in every way he can, especially morally: a schoolboy can do nothing, of course, for the teaching of his fellows, but he can do everything for their moral good ... Boys are very easily turned and guided: a kind look, a kind word, a piece of advice from one of you may, humanly speaking, be the means of determining for good the course of many a boy's life: a few words of advice may often be the turning point to a boy hard pressed by temptations ... You will see then, at once, that the chief influence of a monitor lies in his example; but this is a point on which I have seen many people deceive themselves—they trust to what they call 'the force of silent example'. That is most pernicious: if you content yourselves with merely keeping school rules and doing what is right yourselves and keeping out of the way of any fellows who you know are doing wrong, or if you stand by and listen to them saying what they ought not, without reproof, you are doing wrong: fellows will only say, 'Oh! he's a monitor, and has to look rather solemn, but he doesn't mind': No, that won't do ... Never let a single thing go unreproved that your conscience disagrees with. Never be led away by pity of the offender, but regard rather the immense amount of harm he may do to others if you let him go on as he is.

... To be more particular: you will find it necessary to be very consistent: fellows won't stand being pulled up for breaking one school rule, when they know you break another. If you go out smoking, you cannot, without causing great ill feeling, pull a fellow up for going to publics [public houses], though the one thing is infinitely more important than the other ... The principal things you have to guard against are, first of all: talking filth, or any kind of indecency: that is the worst evil, by far the worst that can befall a school. I am glad to say I don't think that prevails, to any very great extent, at Durham; but if you find it, crush it with all your might ... Bullying, I think, you will not have much to do with, nor with dishonesty; but both of these your instincts, and popular feeling in general, would teach you how to deal with. The only other particular I need mention is: irreverence at prayers in the morning or in the Cathedral. It is a very bad sign if fellows talk ... during prayers. Be careful to attend to Holden's rules of being in school early in the mornings, and so on: reverence is a very useful habit for all to cultivate ...

And now I have told you all I think is particularly important as regards your duties. The next question is: how are you to fulfil them all, how [to] impress these lessons on others? Of course it is impossible to teach anybody unless you are first convinced of the truth of what you are trying to teach. Look at these things I have mentioned: consider them well ... Never think how little good all your endeavours are doing; how you are only getting hated, and not doing a bit of good; how things like this cannot be helped, and it is no good making a noise about them; how perhaps after all you are too strict, and things are not so bad as you think. Such are the thoughts, I well know, which will often occur to every one of you ... However as regards influencing boys, a kind word or a warning word, is the best way: be kind but firm: always be gentle as long as you can, and speak kindly to fellows, however much you may think or know they are trying to insult you. Do not be overbearing: ask them to do a thing rather than command them: do not stand too much on your dignity—a thing to which new monitors are rather prone. Do not be above talking to the little fellows and trying to help them: you may often be able to give them good advice by the way, and you will also accustom them—a great thing—to come to you for advice when they really want it. Be sociable with all ... As regards punishment, I strongly recommend giving a fellow a thrashing, the fellows like it best themselves—better than setting impositions or reporting. Setting impositions is essentially weak, and shams master too much: I should only recommend it in the case of fellows so little, or so weak, you did not like to thrash them, or as an addition to a thrashing when you felt the latter was not enough. For drunkenness and beastliness (also for bullying and stealing, of course) thrash a fellow once, as hard as ever you like—you cannot give him too much; but let me recommend that no fellow be thrashed by any of you hastily or in passion, but that before thrashing a fellow you consult some of your brother monitors. Remember, never thrash a fellow a little, always hard: and it is always well that he be thrashed by more than one of the monitors ... Try, all of you, to be cordial towards your brother monitors: often talk to each other and consult each other about things in general. As regards reporting to 'Bung' [Dr Holden], there are only two cases in which I should think it at all allowable: in cases of continued disobedience; e.g. if the monitors all together thrashed a fellow twice for disobedience, and he still was stubborn, then report him; or if you saw a fellow hopelessly bad, doing mischief which you had no power to stop, warn him that you will report him, and if you nail him again, do so. I should not recommend this, however, unless you had a strong enough case to get him sent away. And now if you ask me how you are to do all this, I am sure you will all feel where the best help is to be found; also you will find a frequent attendance at the Holy Communion a very great assistance to you indeed ... I have in this letter just jotted down such things as came into my head; they will, at any rate, supply you with food for thought and discussion; and if there is anything else on which I have not given you my opinion, and any of you would like to have it, I shall be most truly happy to give them it. You will pardon me, all of you, for having arrogated to myself the right of sermonising.[32]

Henry Scott Holland, reading this letter years later, wondered if 'there ever such a letter written at such an age? It has in it the earnest wisdom of a man who has thought everything out', he said.[33] Mandell had just turned twenty-one, and the letter does show a mature bent and smacks a great deal of Thomas Arnold's doctrine of 'godliness and good learning' where education was inexorably linked to personal morality.[34] The letter in retrospect is a fascinating example of Victorian pedagogical thought and practice, and in a way reflects Arnold's celebrated sermon a few decades before, where, in trying to elevate the moral tone of his school, he warned Rugby boys of the six evils of public school: sensual wickedness (sex, drunkenness, and the like); lying; bullying; disobedience; idleness; and choosing bad companions.[35] And it certainly explains a great deal about Creighton's mental and moral posture as a young man, and gives further evidence that his inclination at the time was both educational and religious. Finally, the letter contains numerous ideas later found in his adult notions on such things as balancing the role of the individual within the institution, individual rights versus responsibilities, cause and effect regarding private and public actions, how personal example can modify behaviour, proper and improper use of corporal punishment, and distinguishing delegated authority from residual power.

In a letter to another Durham school monitor written shortly after this 'pastoral', Creighton enunciated one of his cardinal principles: 'Remember', he stated bluntly, 'I am very far from presuming that my opinions are right: I simply wrote what seemed to me best', and that the purpose of the letter was that 'each of you consider ... and [then] come to what conclusion on the subjects ... you thought fit'. This became one of his chief educational traits, to offer reasoned advice, but then allow one to accept or reject it as one 'thought fit'.[36] Creighton often said he thought himself a 'terrible prig' during his school years, and perhaps he was, though there were some who considered him in later life 'too little of a prig'.[37] Most who knew him best, however, saw Creighton's early moral earnestness merely a portent of the caring pastor to come.[38]

This 'pastoral' letter proved not to be his final fling of advice to school chums at Durham. Creighton continued a personal interest in his old school after going up to Oxford. Once in 1866 he is said, obviously one of the perpetuated family myths, to have walked for three days from Oxford to Durham to hear school speeches.[39] On that occasion he stayed ten days saying that he enjoyed greatly, 'making new friends among the boys and prying curiously into the state of things in general in the school'. He regretted, nonetheless, that he did not find things as he would have wished, and thought the 'old monitors had not been firm enough'. So, he 'chummed violently with the fellows who will be monitors, and tried to impress upon them some notion of their duties ...'[40] He continued his close friendship with Dr Holden in later years, visiting him at the grammar school whenever possible.[41]

Creighton was never athletically inclined as a boy, although he did score for the school's cricket eleven at Durham and nearly won a steeplechase—if he had not fallen from exhaustion fifty yards short of the goal.[42] It was severe shortsightedness that really prevented him from serious participation in sports. Because of this he was forced to wear spectacles early, and had to read with one eye closed because of double vision.[43] Walking was his sport of choice. He enjoyed taking long walks over the countryside, 'rambles' as he called them, and this remained his favourite recreational activity which he continued throughout his life—although friends and family often considered it his wild obsession, particularly those reluctantly recruited on one of his forced marches. 'A walk in the blazing sun or pouring rain had never to be abandoned', a nephew recalled. 'All laziness and sloth were abhorred.' Creighton delighted in setting out with several friends on a walking tour of the Lake District or parts of Scotland, covering twenty miles or more a day.[44] Walking seemed to fit his natural sense of curiosity, especially for botany and buildings. He loved to roam the countryside examining wild flowers, for instance, once compiling a collection of dried flowers that won a school prize. He also delighted in exploring out-of-the-way villages, or strolling through towns and cities where he developed a keen eye for places and people, which is evidenced in his later writings on English shires and towns.[45]

Those who came to know Creighton in later life often speculated about when and where he acquired the religious feelings that led him into holy orders. Durham more than Carlisle seems to hold the answer. He was apparently deeply moved by the high church services at Durham Cathedral; because the school lacked a chapel at that time, students attended the cathedral services. The king's scholars—and Mandell was one—had the honour of wearing surplices as members of the foundation. Moreover, since the canons were often professors of the university, they took note of these young scholars, giving them special attention and responsibility. All this had a stimulating influence on Mandell and on his moral being.[46] In later years Creighton confided that it had 'always been his intention from boyhood' to become a priest. Further, 'his schoolfellows' confirmed this notion. Even the headmaster's wife said that he once told her in answer to a question, 'I intend to be a bishop, Mrs Holden'.[47]

Durham certainly left an indelible imprint on young Creighton. He once hinted years later that, because the school was situated on the opposite bank of the River Wear, the cathedral 'was always before our eyes, with its beautiful suggestiveness'.[48] The conventional view has often been that it was in the quadrangles of Oxford where Creighton first discovered his religious and academic vocations. Where Carlisle aroused his curiosity, it was Durham that charted his course, and Oxford became his path to the future.

4

Undoubtedly the Ablest Man

'He was undoubtedly the ablest man in the college at the time.'

Edward Caird, speaking of Mandell Creighton [1]

Oxford University was the ideal place for Mandell Creighton. Unlike Cambridge, which had always seemed rather too serious for him, Oxford was more spirited, more animated.[2] This liberal, self-satisfied ambience in the 1860s suited Creighton's temperament and character. Old Oxford of worn cloisters and weathered spires was undergoing a great transformation as the university began shedding much of its Elizabethan character, the result of a series of administrative and academic reforms that began in the 1850s. These reforms changed not only the university but also its colleges, long governed by obsolete or restrictive medieval statutes.[3]

The Oxford Movement that had set these staid quadrangles aflame a few decades before actually contributed little to the atmosphere of reform in the 1860s. The Tractarian cause largely remained a fragmented argument about religious rituals and was generally spent by the end of the 1850s.[4] In its wake, however, as if trying to clear away the wreckage, new, vital waves of change from other tidal forces lapped at the old college walls. These new intellectual and cultural forces created a weird cacophony of opinions and arguments. Leftover Tractarians argued vehemently against increased secularisation of the university, but the anti-clerical spirit of the younger liberals proved stronger. Then there were the arguments posed by men, such as the great classicist Benjamin Jowett, who urged that the curriculum should be more practical, preparing men for a world beyond Isis and Cherwell. This would be a significant departure from the mission of old Oxford as a place for training clerics; or as a place of learning for learning's sake, a belief championed by Mark Pattison, the respected rector of Lincoln College.

Other issues centred on the growing friction between natural science and theology. Testy geologists and biologists, advocating a rationalistic approach to their disciplines, advanced confrontational ideas about evolution that stimulated the rise of higher criticism which in turn produced the rising spectre of a destructive rationalism over religious belief.[5] In the early 1860s, for example, there was the stormy encounter between T. H. Huxley and Bishop Samuel Wilberforce on Darwin's theories, as well as rising questions over biblical interpretations and modernist doctrinal tendencies exemplified by the publication of *Essays and Reviews*. Also, the Colenso affair, which opened the flood gates on biblical criticism. John Colenso, the Anglican Bishop of Natal, began to question the literal interpretation of the Bible while translating parts of it into Zulu, with the result that his published *Pentateuch* and commentaries claimed portions of scripture untrue. What followed was a controversy leading to heresy charges and trials, clashes between religious liberals and conservatives, and protracted disputes over jurisdiction between the established church at home and its South African counterpart.[6]

In addition, philosophers and social scientists alike, with all their 'isms', had the effect of damaging if not discrediting the staunch defenders of the Christian faith and even traditional academic studies such as the classics. Running rampant were Herbert Spencer's positivism, John Stuart Mill's liberalism, Thomas Hill Green's neo-Hegelian idealism;[7] and aestheticism— the latter still in its embryonic stages and soon to be inexorably shaped by a young Brasenose tutor, Walter Pater. Each of these forces had its disciples and critics.[8]

It was in the midst of this hubbub of iconoclastic jousting that Mandell Creighton arrived at Merton College in October 1862 at the start of Michael-mas term. He had first applied for a classical scholarship to Balliol in the spring of 1862 at the urging of the school headmaster, Henry Holden. Failing to win it, he applied to Merton and was elected to a classical postmastership. Postmasters, dating back to the 1380s, were those scholarship students who formed the academic nucleus of Merton.[9]

Merton was founded in 1264 by Walter de Merton, Chancellor to Henry III, and later Bishop of Rochester. Merton's 'Mob Quad', one of the enclosed Oxford quadrangles, has been described as the cradle of college life in England.[10] Merton claimed many illustrious sons, including Roger Bacon, Duns Scotus and William of Ockham. The library, completed in 1379, had some of its early bound tomes chained to their shelves in 1862, and it remains one of Oxford's most evocative medieval relics.[11] The chapel, built decades earlier in the fourteenth century, had undergone numerous interior remodelling over the centuries, the most 'ruthless' alteration being earlier in the century when the college became caught up in the fervour of the Tractarians.[12] Noted for its ecclesiastical finery, the chapel's historic architec-ture appealed directly to Creighton's sensibilities. After being nourished by the elaborate ceremonies at the cathedral in Durham, he relished the chapel's music and high services.[13]

Merton in 1860 had the reputation of attracting the gentry and aristocratic 'men of the world', according to Mark Pattison.[14] The majority of the Merton men in Creighton's time came from the elite public schools and were a hunting set with large wealth and little intention of doing any solid academic work.[15] Yet if Creighton felt a tinge of social insecurity he never showed it. Edmund Knox, then a student at Corpus Christi and an undergraduate friend, recalled that Creighton avoided the 'expensive, non-industrial life' that he claimed was the norm at Merton, but yet seemed socially comfortable with the other students.[16]

Creighton's postmastership was £70 a year in 1862, enough to cover tuition but little else. For the remainder he had to ask his father, something not easy for him to do, he said, because his father's 'manner made it difficult to ask for anything'.[17] Unaccustomed to extravagant tastes in his youth, he found it easy to live frugally in his sparsely furnished attic rooms on the top floor of a Mob Quad staircase. It was only in his last year that he could afford to move from the college to share lodgings in the High Street with George Saintsbury.[18]

Merton was small in population at that time, numbering about forty undergraduates. After the opening of the New Building two years later, the undergraduate number increased to fifty-six. As all colleges, Merton demonstrated a strong sense of common life which Creighton found to his liking. Edmund Knox, a contemporary undergraduate at Corpus Christi, offered a picture of collegiate life not dissimilar to that of Merton:

> Called by our scouts [college servants] about 7.30 a.m., in time for a cold tub, a cold shave and hasty toilet, we rushed to Chapel at 8 a.m. where the porter ... marked out attendance. Prayers were still the full Morning Prayer with Litany on Litany days. They were read by the two Chaplains, the scholars [postmasters at Merton] reading the Lessons ... Then came breakfast. Economy dictated for the economical 'two eggs', cooked in our own saucepans ...
>
> After breakfast ... came lectures ... Lunch was followed by two hours on the river, or a walk or 'grind' [slang for 'a constitutional']. Boating, cricket, and, for those who could afford it, riding ...
>
> Dinner in the hall at 5.30 might be followed by a 'wine', till about 8 p.m. —and for those who affected it, a game of cards. The rest of the night was free for work, by candle-light or by a Colza oil lamp, a singularly mellow light when the lamp was in proper working order ... 'A dull life', do you say? Well, we did not find it so.[19]

Creighton was popular with his classmates and developed several lasting friendships. One was George Saintsbury who, after becoming a successful writer and critic (particularly on wine), went on to a distinguished academic career at the University of Edinburgh.[20] Arriving at Merton on a classical postmastership the same year as Creighton, Saintsbury recalled his friend's 'innocently Socratic habit of taking up ingenuous freshmen, whom, unlike most takers up, he never put down again'.[21] Reginald Copleston, later Bishop of Calcutta, was one of these younger students. He met Creighton in his first term and found him 'loved by many and liked by all ... He especially loved men who were boyish, frank, pure, and over-flowing with high spirits.'[22] When it came to high jinks, however, Creighton was more a spectator rather than a participant. Merton had its share of what Copleston called 'very foolish but not very harmful rowdyism'. A case in point was the notorious student bonfire that occurred in the Mob Quad on Guy Fawkes Day in 1865 and nearly burnt the college down. All undergraduates involved in the bonfire were 'gated' by college officials for the remainder of the term. Creighton, who was then living in rooms outside Merton, had no part in the bonfire incident, but when a crowd of students held a retaliatory demonstration one night in the Fellows' Quad to show their indignation at the punishment, Creighton supplied the penny-whistles and other noise-makers for the demonstrators' cause. It was a half-hearted effort to run with the crowd—one of the rare moments he ever succumbed to it. Throughout his life Creighton had that happy knack of standing aloof from the crowd and yet being the centre of its attention. Among Merton men his popularity was strong and steadfast

Because of his shortsightedness Creighton never played cricket or football at Merton, though he rowed in the college eight.[23] His passion for walking remained a constant. Walks around Oxford in the afternoon were routine for students in those days. According to one Oxford student, a 'great mass of men' would take daily walks for both exercise and discussion. 'At two o'clock, in pairs or threes, the whole University poured forth for an eight or ten miles toe and heel on the Iffley, Headington, Abingdon, Woodstock roads, returning to five o'clock dinner.'[24] Creighton's hikes were often more ambitious, for he had, in the words of his friend Saintsbury, that 'amiable knack of organising expeditions' that generally used up the entire day.[25] In one of their long walks together, his friend Copleston recalled passing a woman with a crying child. Creighton unexpectedly walked back 'and clapped his hands loudly to the face of the crying child, and rejoined me without a word. I was astonished both at the procedure and at its success; but he explained it as if he had done it before.' Creighton said simply: 'Anything that startles them will do. It changes the current of their thoughts.'[26]

Aside from rowing and rambles, Creighton's gregarious nature moved him in the direction of more cerebral, sedentary activities. He was one of the founders of the college's whist club and was said to be a 'keen player'.

The quintessential card game in nineteenth-century England, whist was the only card game he ever really cared for with, the exception of bridge.[27] Reading was his preferred pastime. As an undergraduate, he read books of various kinds besides those needed for his studies and virtually every book had to be discussed with a friend. His leisure reading consisted of the popular English prose and poetry writers; his favourites were Carlyle, Browning, Tennyson and Swinburne. Once Creighton was given a just-published book of poems and ballads by D. G. Rossetti which he proceeded to spend the day from lunch to chapel time reading aloud until a fellow student pulled it from his hand and took his turn at it. Regarding contemporary novels, he liked *Jane Eyre* and *The Mill on the Floss*. Later, he developed a strong taste for French novels, especially the works of George Sand and Balzac, and occasionally dipped into Italian fiction. He showed little interest in German literature, considering the language ugly, though he read Goethe's poetry once in a while.[28]

Being a voracious reader he often spent his vacations immersed in books, even to the point of logging his reading time. Friends were often perplexed by his ability to read as much as he did. His knack was to read quickly, absorb what he wished to retain, and leave the rest. Sometimes he remained at Oxford between terms so that he could read in peace. He liked to read in his friends' rooms, or on summer days he would carry his books out in a punt, reading for hours while moored under shady trees overhanging the Cherwell. A favourite saying of his was: 'A book is only useful in so far as it gives you ideas.'[29] Creighton often went on reading parties with friends during vacations, relaxing excursions generally under a tutor's direction. On one of these, he went to Lynton in Devonshire along the coast on a particularly memorable 'read' organised by Thomas Arnold, son of Thomas Arnold of Rugby and the brother of the poet Matthew Arnold. Another member of the party was Thomas Arnold's sixteen-year-old daughter Mary, the future Mrs Humphry Ward.[30]

In religion Creighton was now decidedly high church, and attended daily service in the chapel or the early morning communion service at St Mary's, the University Church, in the High Street. When he went home on vacations he claimed to be 'sickened' by the 'humdrum' services at Carlisle's cathedral. They 'never take the brown holland off the altar,' he complained, because the verger said 'it is too much trouble and gives the dust much more time to settle'.[31] Though evidencing a fascination with ritual, he was very much reserved about his deeper religious feelings. Some even wondered if he had any. A college friend wrote that he seemed to take religious principles for granted 'and did not talk much about them: if he did, it was to assert rather than to argue'.[32]

When it came to politics, Creighton was much more open. If pushed, he quickly acknowledged an unrelenting liberalism all of which was based on the principle of the sovereignty of the individual, who naturally possessed the freedom to choose right or wrong—a principle acquired from his father. Although a verbal person, Creighton generally avoided public speeches and public debates, not because of diffidence but because he hated talking for talking's sake, particularly about matters he regarded as trivial. Although he rarely spoke at the Oxford Union, he nevertheless became Union president, and also for a time its librarian.[33] More inclined toward informal discussions, he began to develop his early skill as a persuasive conversationalist. He thrived on that pedagogical custom so popular at Oxford of endless, informal conversations that had the effect of broadening undergraduate minds as well as forging lasting friendships. Students liked to wile away their evenings after dinner in each other's rooms over dessert and wine engaged in both frivolous talk or serious discourse about anything and everything—a custom Gladstone called the 'Oxford Agony'.[34] Reginald Copleston described how Creighton and Saintsbury, for example, would engage in discussions 'about the "immensities" and the "everlasting no", and divide all into those who were "in contact" and those who were not "in contact" with the great Heart of the Universe'.[35]

Possessing a natural tendency to instruct, Creighton went out of his way to influence classmates, particularly younger students who began calling him 'The Professor', or 'P' for short, a nickname he never lost among his Merton friends. Saintsbury, remembering the endless conversations with his friend Creighton, said that 'all things in heaven and earth, at all hours of the day and night' were discussed; and then added that 'nothing came up so often as a pet idea of Creighton's about influence. He thought that everybody ought to try to influence others as much as he could.'[36] In later years Creighton moderated this view somewhat, realising that a strong personal influence on another could have the negative effect of weakening character as well as independence of thought. 'Draw as largely as you like on my experience, but come to your own conclusions', he admonished Louise during their courtship. Despite such occasional outbursts of caution, his dominating personality generally held sway over those in his tow.[37]

For Copleston the most remarkable feature of Creighton's manner during the Merton years appeared to be his 'pleasure in discussing moral problems, or rather announcing his verdicts on questions of conduct', which could—and often did—offend others. 'His sharp repartee would often hurt a friend for a moment, but then he was quick and tender to make amends.'[38] Creighton, he said, was 'fond of analyzing the conduct' of others and 'estimating' their abilities. He was a 'shrewd observer of human nature at a stage in which it does not always command the sympathy of an under-graduate'. While he could be sarcastic, he could not be bitter, Copleston recalled. Creighton was 'profoundly convinced that unintelligent acquies-cence in opinions, though these might be true, was immoral and dangerous, that it was good for people to be shocked and to have their beliefs shaken up'.[39] Because of this, probably few at Merton really understood him. Those who thought they did found him intriguing, even captivating; for Creighton, friendship required unconditional trust, as one of his poems illustrates. The verse, penned in Creighton's hand, was composed for a friend, presumably on the spot because at the top of the poem is the inscription: 'Lines Composed and Written by Mandell Creighton, in the Album of Mrs Caroline Potter, at Stanley Mount, Oxton, Birkenhead: August 1865.'

Friendship

As each goes forth life's doubtful ways,
    How sweet it is some trusty friend to meet
Who now may guide him thro' th' uncertain maze,
    Now seek for aid for his own tottering feet—
Neither may be beneath the other's thrall;
    Still giving, still receiving each should be;
Each moulding each, each staying other's fall;—
    Equals themselves, tho' different their degree;
Each to the other's faults extending too
    The charity he shows unto his own;
Bareing [sic] his breasts unto the other's view,
    Knowing he'll find there sympathy alone.
Friends halve our sorrows, double all our joys,
    Aid us when dangers all around are rife,
Guard us when slander's biting tooth annoys,
    Equip us for the battle-field of life.
On the same path must friends still plant their feet,
    Towards their self-chosen goal together move,
But only then can friendship be complete
    When heavenwards is their path, their goal above.

                                                        M. C.[40]

Creighton's closest friends during his undergraduate years, other than George Saintsbury and Reginald Copleston, were H. J. Hood (of Brasenose), C. A. Potter, Robert T. Raikes and William H. Foster (of Merton), and C. T. Boyd (of University College). Hood became a barrister and eventually bankruptcy registrar of the Supreme Court; Potter became an Anglican priest; Raikes married and went into business in London; Foster died unexpectedly in Rome of cholera in 1867; and Boyd took holy orders and became Archdeacon of Ceylon.[41] In Creighton's second year he and the latter three—Raikes, Foster and Boyd—formed what came to be known as 'The Quadrilateral'. They became inseparable in term time and on vacations. They exchanged rings as marks of friendship, each pledging his loyal and lasting friendship to the others. In a letter dated January 1866, Creighton said that, however much he may like other people, 'my feelings towards them are entirely different to those I feel to the three within the mystic circle'.[42]

The 'mystic circle' was the nucleus of a small group of kindred spirits at Merton known as 'The Saints'. All being high church at the time, they fasted, often refraining from dinner in the hall on Fridays and on religious feast days, and enjoyed sipping tea in one another's rooms while reading aloud from St Augustine's *Confessions*.[43] While their clannish idiosyncrasies incurred ridicule from some students, it never lessened their individual popularity. A recent hint that the mystic circle or quadrilateral was possibly homosexual in nature lacks any evidence, anecdotal or otherwise, and is thus pure conjecture based on the assumption that such activity was common in boarding schools and college life at the time.[44] One of the abiding characterisitics of Creighton's life, from start to finish, was his high moral stance; and, whatever he was in other ways, a hypocrite he was not. In a letter written to Raikes during the 1865 Hilary term, Creighton explained two principal reasons for choosing a new friend at college: because 'he is a good fellow (I mean *morally* not *socially* good), and is very jolly'. One tutor described Creighton as 'a man of thoroughly healthy mind, who could be trusted to take a reasonable view of any question, and to help keep up the moral and intellectual tone of the College'.[45] As an undergraduate Creighton had, on his own, intellectually arrived at Thomas Arnold's widely-accepted point that the primary goal of instruction was moral perfection, and that education and religion were inexorably intertwined—a Victorian principle known as 'Godliness and Good Learning'.[46]

From all evidence Creighton never succumbed to any serious romantic interlude until he met Louise von Glehn. He had female friends in Carlisle whom he visited off and on when he was home on vacation; and there were several young women in Oxford with whom he and his friends associated, but these relationships were platonic and never amounted to much. Rather, his habit was to follow the love affairs of his friends with only a modicum of interest—more a detached curiosity than a desire to be involved in a similar experience. Surveying the situation of one classmate who had loved but lost, Creighton mused that his friend was 'very sad this term: he is still in love, I am afraid, and thinks about it more than the ideal wise man ought to ...' He also wrote to a college friend in 1866, just before his final term, that he found that 'ladies in general are very unsatisfactory mental food: they seem to have no particular thoughts or ideas ...' Then he added: 'Of course at a certain age, when you have a house and so on, you get a wife as part of its furniture, and find her a very comfortable institution.' 47 Louise cannot have appreciated this comparison.

Creighton could convey a sense of genuine sympathy and tenderness to others, yet he jealously guarded his own inner feelings. Louise always attributed this, in part, to his north country background. 'Few,' she explained, 'recognised that, a true Cumbrian at bottom, he was fundamentally then, and always, a man of profound and proud reserve.' 48 This reserve, however, was probably rooted more in his acquired belief that rational relationships should transcend physical or emotional ties than in his north country origins. When it came to exhibiting demonstrative affection, even later toward members of his own family, he found it awkward—almost impossible—not unlike many Victorians if we are to believe historians.

In 1864, after two years of study, Creighton received a first in 'Moderations'. This intermediate honours examination in classical studies prepared him for a final two years in the honour school of *literae humaniores* which generally attracted Oxford's most gifted students and included intense studies combining history and philosophy. For Creighton it was the natural course of subjects because ancient history and philosophy appealed to him. In this curriculum there was a number of scholars who guided him in his study and ultimately shaped his undergraduate perspective, men such as T. H. Green and Benjamin Jowett (of Balliol), Edward Caird and William Sidgwick (of Merton), Mark Pattison (rector of Lincoln), James Bryce (then fellow at Oriel), Walter Shirley (professor of church history), and William Stubbs (appointed Regius Professor of Modern History in 1866).

Edward Caird, the Scottish philosopher, his favourite, he later credited as being his most influential mentor because of Caird's approach to philosophy, which he regarded as the most valuable knowledge he learned in his university career.49 Caird was equally impressed with Creighton, referring to him once as 'undoubtedly the ablest man' at Merton and as possessing 'common sense in a degree which amounts to genius'. According to Caird, Creighton's philosophical work 'was always done carefully and thoroughly, and in it he gave proof of a well balanced judgment and considerable critical power', adding that, though he was not 'specially attracted towards philosophical studies', he 'already gave evidence of practical sagacity'.50

Creighton took a first class in 'Greats' and immediately began reading in the School of Law and Modern History, which was not divided at that time. While one might assume that the decision to pursue history was natural

for Creighton, the choice was more accidental than planned. He had toyed
with the idea of reading philosophy, presumably because of T. H. Green;
and he may also have pondered classics because he often took essays to
Jowett. But serendipity intervened. By chance he sat through a series of
lectures given by W. W. Shirley on the life and works of St Anselm. 'I went
with absolute ignorance of medieval history', he admitted.[51] This, coupled
with his fascination about the 'conduct' of people of the past, left church
history as the only form of literature acceptable to him.[52] In a note scribbled
off to James Bryce in 1864, after reading Bryce's recently published work
on the Holy Roman Empire, one can see how ecclesiastical history had
entrapped him. The note also illustrates his maturity and candour as a
young undergraduate.

> Dear Sir,
> Might I point out to you a slight omission in the Chronological Table at the
> beginning of your 'Holy Roman Empire'? On page xxv the name of Pope Nicholas
> V has been omitted: and also the name 'Eugene V' occurs while the form Eugenius
> has been used of all his three predecessors of the same name. Very probably you
> have discovered these before; but, in case you had not done so, I thought it
> worthwhile to mention them with a view to the next edition.
>
> > I am yours truly,
> > M. Creighton [53]

As he approached his B.A. degree, Creighton pondered the possibility of
an academic career at Oxford. In 1866 he confided to a friend that he was
'determined, in case I get a fellowship, to give myself up to study and
literary labour in general, and seek to do nothing else'. History offered him
a real possibility of a scholar's life, he wrote, claiming that as his 'duty' in
life 'only slowly dawned on me', he reckoned that he could 'do much more
positive good at present as a don at Oxford than in any other capacity ...
and could besides have plenty of time for study and no social duties or
troubles'.[54] It was not long until he felt that his destiny was to spend his
life at Oxford.[55]

He began to read for the School of Law and Modern History during
the summer of 1866. On his route home to Carlisle for the summer, he
stopped off at Durham to visit Dr Holden. While there he wrote to a
friend stating that he had to 'go home soon and commence the Great Law
and History trick, though I feel very disinclined to begin, and regard the
amount of work I have to do as to some extent hopeless'.[56] A month later
he wrote from Carlisle: 'I want to do my best for Law and History, and I
foresee that I need more reading than I can by any means get.'[57] The
examination was scheduled for the autumn and the required number of

books to read seemed insurmountable. As the day of reckoning grew nearer, he declared: 'I like the history business much; it is amusing and at the same time instructive', but added regretfully that he was unable 'to get up my work sufficiently well; but hang the expense! what's the odds of a [first] class?' 58

After less than six months reading Creighton took the Law and Modern History examination. William Stubbs and James Bryce were two of the examiners. Although impressed with his basic intellect, the examiners believed Creighton failed to demonstrate sufficient knowledge of detail to take a first class. Creighton wrote to Bryce soon afterwards: 'I am very glad that I only got a second class for I should have thought very poorly if I had got a first'.59

A second class did little to weaken Creighton's academic reputation. Just as in the case of T. H. Green, who had received a third in the School of Law and Modern History a few years before, the scholastic honour of the older, more respected classical curriculum of the *literae humaniores* was sufficient to prove potential.60 In fact, Jowett personally asked Creighton to stand for a fellowship at Balliol. Creighton, however, decided to wait, hoping that his own college would offer him something—as Merton did. On 22 December 1866 Creighton was elected to a clerical fellowship with tutorial duties, which he happily accepted since he had previously decided to take holy orders. He immediately dashed off a note to a college friend: 'I just scribble you a line because I think it may interest you generally to know that I have got a Fellowship ... Do you know already I feel an old, old man?' 61

He spent that Christmas vacation in Carlisle with his family, where it must have been an especially satisfying several weeks, preparing as he was for his new role as fellow and tutor. For the first time in his life Creighton would be relatively independent, where he could take pleasure in the fact that he had chosen his own course. In replying to Bryce's note of congratulations on winning the fellowship, Creighton wrote that being a tutor in the 'same College in which I was an undergraduate is a great help to me', and that it was his intention to continue his studies towards a graduate degree.62 He formally received his B.A. degree in 1867 and his M.A. two years later.63

Thus, with the beginning of the Hilary term in 1867, Creighton settled into the comfortable life of a don, teaching students little younger than himself.

5

A Glorious Game

'Fascinating as he was in his talk, he always ... treated conversation as a glorious game, an intellectual frolic ...'

Henry Scott Holland about Creighton as a don.[1]

When Creighton became fellow and tutor, Oxford's reform movement was well under way.[2] A new Oxford was emerging, and old ways were melting away.[3] Reform actually began with the passage of the Oxford University Act of 1854, itself the result of a parliamentary commission report two years before. This Act ended many of the university's quaint medieval statues and obsolete regulations, thereby encouraging modern administrative procedures. Representation on the Hebdomadal Board, Oxford's governing body, was expanded to allow broader diversity of opinion, and its meetings were now conducted in English rather than Latin.[4] Eventually these university reforms seeped down into the colleges. Mark Pattison, one of the leaders of reform, wrote happily of the new 'keen airs of intellectual activity' that were blowing across the university; and he believed that a 'restless fever of change had spread through the colleges—the wonder-working phrase "University Reform" had been uttered'.[5]

From the 1860s through the remainder of the century, innovation reigned over tradition. University professors, those scholars with specialised research interests and generous stipends, were given increased responsibilities when it came to lecture and publication requirements. Professors were also attached to specific colleges as active fellows, thus strengthening the linkage between the university system and the teaching colleges. Moreover, newly endowed chairs emerged in various disciplines across the university.[6]

Colleges systematically increased the role and presence of their fellows, men who were usually distinguished graduates, held stipendiary positions and constituted their governing boards. Before the reform era, fellows often enjoyed privileges without precise duties. Many were either non-resident or unconnected to the daily life of their colleges. By the 1860s, however, colleges began abolishing life fellowships, exerting more control over their fellows and establishing specific prize fellowships for research. Fellowships

were either clerical or lay, and by the 1870s colleges were easing the traditional celibacy restrictions. By permitting a certain number of married
fellows, not only did the 'common life' of the colleges change but also the
city itself. There began a sizeable expansion of houses on the outskirts of
the city as married dons moved to the new suburbs. J. R. Green spoke rather
cynically of the 'hundreds of medieval little villas' beyond the fields of St
Giles where 'learned young ladies invite young Oxford to early tea'.[7] In
short, merit emerged as the principal basis for granting both fellowships
and scholarships.[8]

There also occurred what might be termed a tutors' revolution beginning
in the 1860s that shifted instructional accountability for preparing undergraduates to take university examinations from the professorate to the
colleges. Tutors were awarded greater latitude in teaching undergraduates.
Besides Oxford's customary tutorial method of coaching students in their
rooms, tutors began to give lectures in college halls. These lectures at specific
colleges were eventually opened to undergraduates from all colleges.

Oxford's traditional life of learned leisure was to some extent passing.
Although teaching duties increased, the number of tutorial fellows rose
more slowly—from eighty-one in 1858 to ninety-eight in 1874.[9] At the
university level the tutors lacked voting power, but at the college level they
gained much. This brought about a certain backlash from both the professorate and the students—as the following verse from an undergraduate
magazine of 1874 suggests:

> And surely to the world it needs must seem,
> A little strange in this our Academe,
> How easy to the heights of College sway
> The Don all youthful wends his gladsome way ...
> Securely great, examinations o'er,
> At twenty-three they tread the path of power.[10]

Colleges also expanded traditional disciplines, offering wider studies in
literature, languages, history, geography, mathematics and science, providing
an emphasis that seemed to fit better the needs of a modern, urban, industrial
society largely directed by the middle class. Also, through cooperative efforts,
professors and tutors began to launch new 'Schools' in natural sciences and
modern history which cut across traditional lines of collegiate control.[11]
There were other reforms. When Gladstone's government abolished religious
tests for matriculation and degrees in 1871, the established church found its
monopoly eroded at both Oxford and Cambridge. With the creation of local
examinations in the 1850s, the germ for the university extension movement
was born, and various towns joined in forming the association for promoting

higher education. By the 1870s, tutors were offering courses across England. And higher education for women was now in its embryonic stage with the decision to permit women to attend heretofore male-only college lectures.[12]

By the end of the century medieval Oxford had been transformed into a modern university. This rejuvenation of Oxford (and Cambridge too), however, was not substantial enough to break the 'Oxbridge' hegemony over the newer civic (redbrick) universities of the nineteenth century, such as Durham and London, but the weakening had begun.[13] And there were those who charged, as G. M. Young did, that Oxbridge had 'surrendered the freedom it was meant to guard'.[14] Nevertheless, tutors, fellows and professors were demonstrating a new and impressive commitment to teaching and scholarship; and this renewed vitality and cooperation could be seen best at the colleges. There was a feeling of youthfulness and energy. 'Oxford is young, and oddly enough it is this peculiar characteristic of the place which has been intensified by modern reforms', wrote J. R. Green. 'The old Don of port and prejudice has disappeared. The new teachers are hardly older than the boys they teach.'[15] Perhaps the most significant feature of the reform was the severe weakening of the vested interests of both church and aristocracy which together had controlled Oxford for centuries. 'The Oxford of the clergy and squires passed during those years', lamented one former don.[16] Oxford became less theological, more secular, less aristocratic, more middle-class.

For Mandell Creighton as he approached his final undergraduate studies, a clerical fellowship at Merton became his likely goal. Where he stumbled into the discipline of history, he grew into religion. As a matter of fact, he was moving in the opposite direction to many of his intellectual contemporaries, for many of the mid century Victorians, while starting their lives in solid Christian homes, ended their years in religious doubt or disavowal. A whole score of social and intellectual forces of that century produced an unforeseen backlash that caused denominational dilemmas for both the middle and lower classes. Immediate worldly conditions became more important than the promised rewards of an afterlife.[17] Nevertheless, the assertion has been made that evangelical morality was 'the single most widespread influence in Victorian England'.[18] If true, these spiritual obstacles scarcely challenged Creighton's course. He never experienced anything like a crisis of faith, or a Damascus event. He came by his faith slowly, but once it became fixed, he never questioned it again. He, like his friend George Saintsbury, found religious conflicts, dramatic conversions and personal confessions 'repugnant'. Their 'fires burned deep with smokeless flame'.[19]

By the time he became a don, Creighton had moderated his high church views slightly, more inwardly than outwardly, all of which confused a few of his friends who worried that he was drifting into scepticism or worse. Others were surprised that he even considered the prospect of taking religious orders.[20] Henry Scott Holland, while at Balliol, watched Creighton with interest and said that he 'took his stand for God ... at the extreme hour of intellectual tension', and that at 'the close of the [1860s] it seemed to us at Oxford almost incredible that a young don of any intellectual reputation for modernity should be on the Christian side'.[21] The controversies between religion and the utilitarian spirit, so prevalent at the time, barely caught his attention. He remained undaunted and never gave the natural or social sciences a fleeting glance; his feeling about the burning questions that confronted science vis-à-vis religion was simple: both were legitimate as long as they stayed within their own appropriate boundaries. The Darwin controversy, for example, amused him more than bothered him, and he wrote to Louise in 1871: 'You have the advantage of me in reading Darwin: I am afraid I don't take sufficient interest in the subject of his speculations.'[22] As far as Mill's secular liberalism was concerned, it provoked only a minimal shrug from Creighton; and T. H. Green's idealism, while perhaps somewhat more palatable because of its Platonic connection, never really occupied his thought. Herbert Spencer's positivism was much too speculative for him.

Interestingly, when Creighton accepted the clerical fellowship, Merton College was becoming more secular in character, this in part due to the 'afterglow of Ritualism' when the few remaining Tractarians were being replaced by younger dons, laymen who shared non-theological perspectives.[23] Moreover, the reform winds blowing across Oxford were only then piercing the thick walls of Merton. The aged and nearly blind Robert Bullock Marsham was the only lay warden at an Oxford college at that time. He had been the head of Merton for fifty years but, while venerated for his kindliness and longevity, was regarded by younger fellows as an ineffectual leader who should resign. Heresy or leprosy, however, were the only grounds for removing a warden according to the ancient statues of the college; regrettably, for those who desired a change in administration, he showed the signs of neither.[24] Most of the senior fellows were laymen and many of the junior ones also, which had the effect of discouraging clergy from holding on to their fellowships. This probably worked in Creighton's favour because, when a clerical fellowship became available, he became the obvious candidate.[25]

Appointed fellow in November 1866, he was given full tutorial assignments one month later commencing with the new Hilary term. He spent his entire Christmas vacation cramming, preparing his history lectures. As an Oxford don, Creighton had to put aside his undergraduate mind and adjust anew to his role as a teacher. He was not much older than the men he was to teach. Another challenge he soon found was the prevailing 'spirit of insubordination', as it was called, among the undergraduates of Merton. This resulted in part because of a general laxity of leadership from the older resident fellows along with the normal kinds of student rowdyism. It was hoped that Creighton would be a calming influence. His student friends, however, found it difficult to accept this young don as a disciplinarian. They could not comprehend the notion that he could walk or talk with them in the afternoon, sometimes with his arm on their shoulders as was his custom, and then reprimand or punish them for some misdemeanor at night.[26] The simple fact was, however, that whether or not the students understood him, he understood them.[27] But as he now emerged from his narrow undergraduate-mindedness into a larger arena of responsibility, he tried to some extent to restrain his tendency towards sarcastic criticism or intellectual contempt.[28] Creighton painfully shared his challenge with a friend in October 1867. After almost a year of teaching he felt he had become

in many respects a wiser man; but I am at present much perplexed and troubled in my mind. It has just begun to dawn upon me now that my actions and sayings are of any consequence: before, I used to think they mattered to no one outside the walls of Merton and to few inside, but now I see that I cannot hold that theory anymore—that I am seriously responsible for all I do, and so I feel a need of broader sympathies. You know that up to this time I have been careless on this point—that I have liked a few, have looked on the majority of men with indifference and on some with contempt. Is this right? [29]

Apparently, Creighton was able to quell some of the undergraduate unrest. As one former student remarked, his 'influence in the College was great. He never forgot that he was a don, and yet he always treated us as his personal friends', adding that even the 'wildest' students would 'bow to him, when if any other don had interfered it would certainly have increased the trouble'. His approach to discipline was to reason with students, to argue for 'gentlemanly behaviour' and 'common sense', which reportedly brought success along with 'the sincere affection and admiration we all had for him'.[30] He found it impossible, however, to rein in his penchant for puzzling paradoxes and cutting repartee.

What proved a liability with students, served him well in the verbal combat of the common room. Inclined to favour overstatement and even inconsistency, Creighton both shocked and amused his colleagues. Edmund Knox, elected fellow in 1868, remembered with fondness Merton's picturesque common room which was 'panelled with oak, lit by candles in silver candlesticks, [and] heated by a noble fire'. But the heat that stimulated most of them came from those common room 'debates' where Creighton held forth against his fellows; and Knox recalled them as being 'of supreme educational value' to him.[31] Henry Scott Holland said of those years how Creighton—ever the welcome guest of any college common room—was always fascinating in his talk, claiming that he 'treated conversation as a glorious game, an intellectual frolic … playing the game with gusto, for the joy of liberating his faculties in the keen amusement of a gymnastic exercise'. Holland concluded: 'As a game it was delightful. It allowed him to throw off the burden of responsibility. But it was only a game that he was playing, like a conjuror tossing magic balls.'[32] As a conversationalist Creighton was supremely gifted, according to Edmund Gosse, recalling that those who might have 'doubted his gravity, never doubted his sincerity; nor would there be many ready to denounce their own appreciation of good company by declaring his conversation anything but most attractive'.[33]

Creighton's friend Reginald Copleston, a tutor at St John's College, who watched him in action, believed that he 'allowed himself at that time to be seriously misunderstood'.[34] Another friend, J. R. Thursfield, tutor at Jesus College, reckoned that 'dull and solemn people thought him flippant: shallow people thought him insincere'. Thursfield claimed that no Oxford man in those years 'was so constantly, so freely, and so variously canvassed, not only favourably but invariably as a rare and strange portent, not to be readily classified in any familiar category of human nature'.[35] Creighton's future wife gave perhaps the best explanation of this enigma. She maintained that he was often misunderstood throughout his life because 'he never troubled about what people thought of him'. She believed that he was

absolutely unself-conscious, and had that kind of simplicity, produced by a want of self-consciousness, with which no one ever credits a clever man, and which sometimes leads to his being called egotistical. He was too much interested or amused by the subject he was discussing, by the ideas he was playing with, to consider whether he was shocking his hearers or not. If anything humourous occurred to him, it had to come out; he did not stop to ask himself whether it might be misunderstood. But it certainly puzzled people.[36]

When it came to university politics, Creighton showed no interest whatsoever. His view of such busy work resembled that of his friend Mark Pattison, who hailed his own failure to be elected to the Hebdomadal Council because it would surely have 'wasted years in idle and thankless pursuit which they call doing university business'.[37] A contemporary noted that Creighton displayed 'rather a contempt for the business side of Oxford life', meetings and committees; and he cared little for the 'man that was wrapped up in them'.[38] College meetings were a drudgery for him and it was during those occasions that he developed his art of writing letters while listening to someone drone on and on about something or other. The only college committees he found useful were those that had some direct relationship to the question of student life, notably instruction.

Teaching rather than research was Creighton's interest in the early years of his fellowship; and, because of this, much was expected of him as there was a shortage of effective teachers. Three leading tutors left Merton during his first two years: in 1867 Edward Caird accepted a professorship at Glasgow University, William Sidgwick retired because of poor health, then T. L. Papillon—a Balliol man who had come to Merton in 1866—left in 1868 for a Rugby mastership. The greatest leadership problem, however, occurred because non-resident fellows showed little or no interest in daily college life while resident fellows were either too reclusive or too scholarly to care about students altogether. As a result, Creighton tried to fill the vacuum, and thus his overall duties increased significantly, bringing inevitable promotions, such as junior dean, principal of the postmasters (which as main disciplinary officer corresponded to senior fellow in other colleges), and Knightley lecturer for a year. After his ordination to the priesthood in 1873, he served as the principal preacher of the college from 1873 to 1874.[39] 'I remember the rapidity with which he rose to be the dominant spirit in his own College', recalled a fellow at Oriel. 'Merton was already a brilliant, active, lively, sociable College: but when he came to join the Common Room, he seemed to step easily into first place.'[40]

Creighton's income as a junior fellow with tutorial stipends was a little over £300 per year in 1867. By 1871, his annual salary amounted to £719, which broke down as follows: £300 fixed payment as fellow, £332 additional payment for being senior fellow, £50 for holding the office of principal of the postmasters, £37 as senior dean.[41] This was a comfortable income for a young man who a few years before had been one of the more impoverished undergraduates, dependent largely on a frugal father to pay the bills. Aside from his tutorial duties, the clerical fellowship allowed him to serve on the governing board of the college, subject to two conditions: he must take deacon's orders within a few years; and he must not marry.[42]

Concerned about residential conditions and the quality of instruction, Creighton joined forces shortly after becoming a fellow with another young tutor, Robert Wilson. Wilson proved to be a man of like mind and sympathies.[43] Wilson, elected fellow the same year as Creighton, was promoted to junior bursar soon after. Together they did much to urge improved living conditions for the students; for example, in 1869 through their initiative the college passed a series of regulations decreasing student meal expenses and improving the dining facilities, notably the hall, kitchen and wine cellar. Creighton, always interested in the college's common life, promoted the idea of all the tutors attending breakfasts and lunches on a regular basis. He sponsored weekly tutors' meetings to discuss curriculum ideas, going so far as to suggest greater interdisciplinary cooperation among the tutors. He also led the way by assuming responsibility for some of the general passmen along side of his work with the ancient history honour students studying *literae humaniores*.[44]

Early on Creighton recognised the potential benefits of working with other colleges. An experiment by Merton tutor William Esson to initiate an intercollegiate study in mathematics failed miserably in 1867 because he could not gain support from his own college. University and college regulations at that time only permitted students to study under their own college tutors, or at best to attend those occasional lectures given by university professors. If an undergraduate needed the instruction in a particular area of study not available in his own college, he was forced to hire a private coach. Creighton, however, liked Esson's concept and decided to join forces with him in February 1868 to gain college authorisation for what some called the 'combination system' of lectures.[45] Eventually becoming the acknowledged leader of the cause, Creighton went outside Merton to win the assistance of several other history tutors, notably Robert Laing of Corpus Christi, C. L. Shadwell of Oriel and Edward Talbot of Christ Church. Together, they launched a series of intercollegiate lectures described as 'an almost unconscious manifestation of the new spirit' of Oxford reform.[46] Merton, Corpus and Oriel opened their tutors' history lectures to all undergraduates; and before long other colleges joined the system, thus creating in 1869 the Association of Tutors.[47]

The Association of Tutors ultimately included all history tutors in the university. The organisation met, usually once a term, to organise the lectures for the following term, trying as best as possible to cover the required material in the history schools. This organisation, along with the creation in 1866 of the Regius Professorship in Modern History at Oxford, did much to enhance the study of what was then called 'scientific history' and promote the Oxford history school.[48] William Stubbs, who was elected the first Regius Professor of Modern History—'modern' being anything beyond the classical era—brought special distinction to the effort.[49] As Creighton said:

> With Stubbs began the scientific pursuit of modern history, as he impressed his views upon us younger men. We worked out among us a scheme of lectures covering the whole field, and were the pioneers of the 'Intercollegiate Lectures' which now prevail at both Universities. The needs of this scheme threw upon me the ecclesiastical, and especially the papal history, which no one else took.[50]

The impact was even greater than suggested above. The object of college instruction was to prepare their students for the university examinations. Lectures by the various university professors often had little connection with the examinations. Although Creighton did not intend that inter-collegiate lectures be construed as an attack on the professorial system, it spotlighted the growing division between tutors and professors and 'tended unconsciously to oust the Professors even more than before'.[51] What the intercollegiate lecture system did was to point the way toward the modern concept of higher education by increasing the role of tutors on the instruct-ional side of the university while allowing the professors to concentrate on more specialised scholarship. Edmund Knox, a Merton fellow without tutorial duties at that time, was sufficiently impressed with the intercollegiate lecture system to write later that while 'professors like Stubbs and Burrows still drew round their chairs only small companies of the select, these young tutors had sprung into the position of deputy professors, and filled college halls with crowds of hearers from all the associated Colleges'.[52]

Acutely concerned about this dichotomy of instruction and the mounting criticism of the professoriate, Creighton explained it in an article he wrote in 1876 entitled 'The Endowment of Research' for *Macmillan's Magazine*.[53] Unusually blunt, even for him, the article goes far to explain his view on education at Oxford. 'On all sides complaints are heard that the professors' lectures are unattended', he wrote. 'This has become more and more the case ... partly to the fact of greater energy among tutors, and partly to the greater organisation of college lectures.'[54] He indicated, after delineating the course of the reform movement at Oxford since the 1850s, that it was difficult to know under the existing system precisely what 'a professor ought to do'. He noted that the chief object of college tutors was to prepare students for university examinations, and that tutors were more likely to be adept at what he termed 'the tricks and knacks' necessary to achieve that end than 'the professor of maturer years and larger knowledge'. He added that because examinations had increased in intensity, the 'art' of preparing men for them had become more and more of a 'trade'. The tutors, he stated,

> have youth on their side. They have themselves come more recently from the Schools. They have a direct interest in the success of their pupils, because it redounds to their own credits. They have a greater familiarity with the under-graduates in other ways, and can adapt their teaching to their shifting needs. It is, in fact, their business to do for their pupils what it would be degrading for a professor of any eminence to do in public lectures delivered in an academic capacity.[55]

Creighton admitted that by not lecturing on material related to the examinations, professors were destined to face small audiences; but such was 'the tyranny of the system of examinations'. The primary function of a professor was research, he felt. 'The increase of the professoriate is to be looked upon as a desirable step, only because it is another name for the endowment of research', he said, urging that greater care be taken in the selection of professors to end the competition between tutors and professors.[56] He declared that if the duties of professors were properly recognised as being essentially related to research, they would 'embody the idea of the value of knowledge for its own sake'.[57] Ultimately, Creighton believed that by clearly acknowledging the professorial duty to be primarily involved in research, professors would in effect counter-balance what he called 'the feverish sophistry' which the system of examinations inevitably generated.

As always, his basic concern was for the student, and the examination system was a persistent source of irritation to him. 'The examination system', he stated, 'may be an admirable means of stimulating young men to acquire a great mass of varied information and to develop readiness of thought and expression; but', he concluded, 'it does not kindle in them a thirst for knowledge', which, of course, was Creighton's principle aim in education.[58] In some respects this article resembled the 'pastoral epistle' he had written to his friends at his old grammar school a little over ten years before, for it reflects the manner and the mind of a young don fresh from the struggles of an archaic structure in the process of being remodelled. Throughout the essay one can sense the gentle rebelliousness, rather common in his manner, where a mixture of ethical realism and educational idealism often reside in a somewhat uneasy alliance.[59] By the end of the century, most of Creighton's ideas had become the educational doctrine at both Oxford and Cambridge.

Creighton welcomed the expanding role of the tutor. Previously, tutors taught pupils in their private rooms by means of informal discussions on readings or assigned essays. Now they were giving lectures to larger groups of students.[60] As the popularity of the intercollegiate system grew, attendance at these lectures increased sizably. When Creighton first became a tutor, he only worked with a handful of students it seemed. By 1871, however, he could write to his fiancée that one of his lectures 'surpassed my wildest expectations', adding: 'To-day I began my lectures, and was at first frightened, though afterwards gratified, to find my class for Italian history numbered the huge amount of sixty-three.'[61]

Creighton's lecture method was to prepare his ideas carefully, setting them down on paper, and then to present them extemporaneously. His aim was to be lucid and incisive, to create excitement and interest He preferred his students not to be dependent upon him for specific information. He wanted to enlighten rather than to be eloquent, and always tried to avoid flowery imagery in his lectures and writings. Most students seemed to find him a compelling if not a dynamic lecturer.[62] One wrote that instead 'of the usual dry lectures of the other tutors, his were always bright, and we looked forward to them as a pleasure instead of trying to cut them'.[63] 'How fascinating it all was', wrote Edmund Knox of Creighton's lectures; 'how vivid and sparkling!' He recalled how the lecture hall would be 'full of men from all colleges, listening with real attention to lectures which were quite unlike the typical Oxford lecture of the day'. According to Knox, his lectures 'made the old days live again: we saw and knew the actors in the scenes; we understood the connexion of events. Yet always done with such ease and simplicity that it seemed as though any one might have delivered the lectures.'[64]

Tutors, nonetheless, continued to invite students to their rooms for personalised instruction. It was Oxford's tradition. One of his pupils claimed how he always remembered taking his first essay to him in his rooms. After reading it, Creighton said to the young man: 'This essay might easily have been worse. There are some good things in it, but good things in an essay don't make an essay good.' Then, in his matter-of-fact manner, which mixed blunt honesty with a glimmer of gentleness, he added: 'A good essay ought to have a beginning and a middle and an end. You must do better next time. You must learn to put a middle in and you'll do all right.'[65] Another student recalled an incident that was typically Creightonian:

I have never forgotten how when I was in for Mods, and he saw I was treating it very casually, and was more interested in athletics, he asked me to his room one night, put me in an arm chair with a pipe, and began to talk about athletics; and then I suddenly found that I was having a most interesting talk on the athletic pursuits of the old Greek heroes, and so we passed to my Greek books, and I saw for the first time their great interest, and from that day I always loved my Homer. He often repeated his invitation ... He generally had a kitten on his lap, and if I ever got sleepy or inattentive he used to throw it on to my knees.[66]

Two of Creighton's more famous pupils were Prince Leopold, Duke of Albany, the sickly son of Queen Victoria, and Lord Randolph Churchill. To the former, he gave private lessons in history and literature, and encouraged the prince to attend his lectures on the history of the Renaissance in Italy.[67] Lord Randolph Churchill arrived at Merton the year Creighton became a don. Several tutors saw little hope in the young Etonian who once remarked innocently after reading some Aristotle that he 'had no idea these old Greeks knew such a lot'.[68] Apparently Creighton discerned some redeeming scholastic capabilities in the young aristocrat and bore down hard on Churchill's studies. The story was told that, while walking with a friend one day in Oxford, they spied Randolph swaggering and strutting along with 'a big nosegay at his buttonhole and a moustache curled skyward'. Creighton's companion could not resist making a 'gesture of disdain'. Creighton looked at his friend in a matter-of-fact manner: 'You are like everybody else. You think he is an awful ass! You are wrong. He isn't. You will see that he will have a brilliant future, and what's more definite, a brilliant political future. See whether my prophecy doesn't turn out true.' [69]

Creighton wrote two letters to Lord Randolph's mother, the Duchess of Marlborough, at the time of Churchill's final examination. The following excerpts go far to illustrate Creighton's candid approach in dealing with people—no matter who they were. In the first, he shared his views about preparing Lord Randolph for the examination.

14 November 1870

... As regards Lord Randolph, I still think that he is wise in going in for examination now rather than in the summer. It is, of course, always difficult to predict the result of an examination; but I think that it would be very improbable, so far as my experience goes, that he should get any lower class than a second: some of his subjects he knows remarkably well—quite up to the standard of a first class—others he is not so much interested in. At present he is quite in earnest with his work, and has vigour and freshness in his treatment of it. He might no doubt, and probably would, be better prepared in six weeks' time; but the interval of six months would be too long, and would give him temptation to listlessness and idleness which might leave him in worse position at the end of that time than he is now.

I shall, however, require from him a rigorous account of what he does in examination; and if I think he has not done himself justice, I shall advise him to remove his name before the end, and so put off his examination to the summer. Do not, however, suggest this to him as a possibility. It is bad for anyone to have an alternative before him, and it were better that I judged after the event than that he thought of it during the process. At present I certainly think he will get a second class at least ...

In the second letter he offered an opinion about the results of the examination in which Lord Randolph received a second class.

15 December [1870]

... I must own I was sorry when I heard how narrowly Lord Randolph missed the first class: a few more questions answered, and a few omissions in some of his papers and he would have secured it. He was, I am told by the examiners, the best man who was put in the second class; and the great hardship is, as your

Grace observes, that he should be in the same class with so many who are very greatly his inferior in knowledge and ability.

It is rather tantalizing to think he came so near; if he had been further off I should have been more content. Still I am glad he went in for examination this time. I think he would only have idled the six months before the next examination.

On the whole I think he has learned a good deal during his time at Oxford ... I am sorry to lose him ...[70]

Lord Randolph did not forget Creighton, and some years later wrote to his indulgent tutor: 'It has always been pleasant to me to think that the historical studies which I too lightly carried on under your guidance have been of increasing value to me in calculating and carrying out actions which to many appear erratic, and if they ever lead to any substantial result it will be owing to those years at Merton when you alone so kindly and continually endeavoured to keep me up to the mark.'[71]

It was a major characteristic of Creighton's life that he placed a large emphasis on teaching values. To him the moral character was as important as scholarship. To be an influence for good as well as a promoter of knowledge was his sublime balance, he thought; and that teachers should be enormously important in building the character of their students. 'When old schoolfellows meet in after life,' he used to say, 'what they discuss is not their old lessons, but their old teachers.'[72] Or as Creighton told an audience years later: 'It is not the skilful educator, versed in new methods, urging men on to run with skill and dexterity the race of competition, who leaves a permanent mark on the mind ... What men look back upon is not the advice how to get on, but the lofty ideal of life and character which was implied rather than impressed.'[73]

It has been sometimes suggested, in part by Creighton's own admission, that he fell under the spell of the aesthetic movement during these Oxford years. Walter Pater, the champion of aestheticism, greatly influenced an entire generation, especially those young Oxonians like Creighton who implemented their 'taste for beautiful things'.[74] Aestheticism certainly smacked of a cult. Though not 'an aesthete', he skirted the edges of the movement as evidenced by the way he furnished his rooms in the Fellows' Quad. His quarters, overlooking Christ Church Meadow, consisted chiefly of a large ground floor room which he used as a combination library, teaching room and dining-room; off this room was a small private stairway leading to a sitting room and bedroom above. Overall, Creighton's decorative interests were more eclectic than harmonious. He purchased musical scores by Wagner—then virtually unknown in Britain—for his friends to play for him; he wore stylish clothes, neckties of Helbronner's silk, and he collected *objets d'art*, often frequenting curiosity shops; and he furnished his lodgings with William Morris wallpapers, scenic photographs, Italian prints, and random selections of blue china and old oak furniture. Though many young Oxford bachelors followed the trend to various degrees, Creighton's tastes was regarded by many as exemplary. In fact his rooms were considered 'show rooms', with his friends bringing visitors to see them. 'He was always delighted to show hospitality, and many were the entertainments he gave.'[75]

Creighton found in Pater a kindred spirit, and could delight audiences with stories of Pater's popular drolleries and epigrams, like Pater's comment about Oxford society: 'I wish they wouldn't call me "a hedonist"; it produces such a bad effect on the minds of the people who don't know Greek.'[76] Creighton admired others in the movement, including Ruskin, Morris and Burne-Jones; and though he admired the Pre-Raphaelites, he was never seduced by them. Still his early enthusiasm for aestheticism proved to be a young man's fancy, and it waned decidedly as he reached the third decade of his life and disappeared for all intents and purposes in later years when he came to call it 'artistic paganism'. After having lunch once with William Morris, he wrote to a friend:

> Surely the Greeks loved beauty in their persons, their dress, their manner, every-thing about them. Why cannot the modern pagan try to reproduce what was valuable in the Greeks, that would make any man a social missionary at all events? Why cannot they construct a gospel of taste and show some slight self-sacrifice in carrying it out? To convert mankind to clean linen, to rebuke vice by a graceful wave of the hand, and rise to power over men's hearts by the exquisite refinement of a smile—these are the fruits one expects from them and never gathers.[77]

Walter Pater was the only exception. Creighton's view was that 'Pater is the only man who carries out his view in the least. In him you feel the idea of beauty absolutely dominates, and all that does not come under its influence is to him external.'[78] He came to make the strong distinction between Pater and his followers, knowing full well that the leaders of most movements are often judged by the extravagances of their followers. The extravagances of the followers in this instance also bothered Creighton. Pater has often been charged with the actions of his followers, who often slipped from the higher aesthetic principles he asserted in his 'doctrine of beauty', and indulged in overly ripe and reckless practices.[79] It was this question of 'recklessness' that disturbed Creighton. Years later he expressed this reservation to a niece, stating that he believed Ruskin's main theme was not entirely true, to wit that 'beauty is goodness and art is morality'; and that people will be made good through the process of teaching them 'to admire beauty'. Creighton was too rational to go that far and warned his niece that 'there is even a moral danger in the love of beauty for itself alone. The feeling may uplift, or it may debase, according to previous habit of mind.'[80]

When it came to recreational reading Creighton possessed a passion for English, French and, later, Russian novels in French translation. He relished Balzac and George Sand, the latter to the point of once inquiring of a publisher about his desire to write an article on her because she was 'an author whose writings I have long been greatly interested in—more than those of any other writer of literature in this generation'.[81] He even read some of Renan, though not *La vie de Jésus*, a book Stubbs could state with dogged jocularity that he had destroyed without ever reading it.[82] Creighton could never have brought himself to destroy a book. He could fling it aside and refuse to read it, but never to destroy it. It would not have squared with his unwavering liberal views. About Renan's controversial book Creighton told his future wife: 'I never read it myself, so I don't know anything about it. I am opposed to protection, as you know; but, on the other hand, I am opposed to reading a book because it is naughty or unorthodox. Read it if you have any reason to believe it contains anything you want to know, but don't ever read a book because it made a sensation and obtained a notoriety by being naughty or unorthodox.'[83] He felt similarly about Darwin's works. 'I have not time for it, and would rather read some Italian history.'[84]

A descriptive portrait of Creighton is drawn by Mary Ward, who wrote that her first recollection of him was 'when I was fifteen, and he was reading history with my father on a Devonshire reading-party. The tall, slight figure in blue serge, the red-gold hair, the spectacles, the keen features and quiet, commanding eye ...' Then a few years later she came to know him better and recalled visiting his 'beautiful Merton rooms, with the vine tendrils curling round the windows, the Morris paper, the blue willow-pattern plates upon it, that he was surely the first to collect in Oxford'. And she recalled the luncheon party at Brasenose 'where the brilliant Merton Fellow and tutor, already a power in Oxford, first met his future wife'.[85]

Mary Ward, before her marriage, also happened to be with Creighton one day when a party of them went to view the boat races from Christ Church Meadow. On the barge with them was George Eliot (Mary Ann Evans) and G. H. Lewes. This was at a time when their lives were still subject to open scandal. Mary recalled that, on the way home, Creighton escorted them through the gardens of Merton, and how the carnival of colours engulfed them all. 'The chestnuts were all out,' Mary remembered, 'one splendour from top to toe; the laburnums; the lilacs; the hawthorns, red and white; the new-mown grass spreading its smooth and silky carpet round the college walls; a May sky overhead, and through the trees glimpses of towers and spires, silver gray, in the sparkling summer air—the picture was one of those that Oxford throws before the spectator at every turn, like the careless beauty that knows she has only to show herself, to move, to breathe, to give delight'. And continuing in her colourful prose, one novelist studying another, Mary remembered George Eliot standing 'on the grass, in the bright sun, looking at the flower-laden chestnuts, at the distant glimpses on all sides, of the surrounding city, saying little ... but drinking it in, storing it in that rich, absorbent mind of hers'.[86] Creighton, as he walked his guests back to Lincoln College, felt in his element.

In the course of those years he discovered the Continent, and most importantly Italy. He spent four holidays travelling in Europe during those years. In 1867 Creighton began, as most Englishmen did of that generation, with a trip to Switzerland. One of his companions was his former tutor William Sidgwick, who was a member of the Alpine Club. Climbing, he soon found out, had its exhilarating moments, but it never caught hold of his imagination. 'Switzerland is very stupendous, but I own that a week of mountains at a time is enough for me', he wrote home, adding: 'To descend into Italy was lovely ... from the barren fir trees of the Alp to the lovely chestnuts, vines, olives, and acacias of an Italian valley; from the chilling tints of the snow to the brilliant colours of an Italian climate: also from the ugly stupid faces of the Swiss to the finely moulded faces and quiet expressions of the Italians.'[87]

Creighton fell in love with Italy and Italy never disappointed him. On this first trip he also travelled through Germany. It was at Dresden that he first heard some of Wagner's operas. In the following year he went to Belgium with a friend, rambled through old towns and then travelled up the Rhine to Heidelberg. 'I smoke a good many pipes, and consume a good deal of wine which this country produces, and which seems to me to be the most perfect wine made anywhere. In such occupations who would not be more than content.'[88] During his 1869 vacation he travelled with another friend to Holland and then northern Germany, returning again to Dresden. 'We saw many pictures, heard much music, talked a certain amount of bad German to the natives, and of profound rubbish to one another. It was amusing: I should like to do it again.'[89]

Creighton's hope was to study art and collect photographs and engravings. In the following year, 1870, the Franco-Prussian War curtailed much of his journey to the Continent. He had probably planned to return to Germany but, due to hostilities, headed south from southern France to Italy. About this fourth trip to the Continent, Louise later wrote:

This journey did much to fix the direction of his future studies. Books about art and the Italian Renaissance were then far from being so common as they have now become. Photographs were comparatively dear, and not as yet very good. Italy, except for the larger towns, was but little visited. Only a few in England read Dante. To Creighton a boundless field of study was opened out, which exactly suited his natural tastes and inclinations. He had found his subject, though it was some time before he defined it.[90]

In 1870 Creighton was ordained deacon by the Bishop of Oxford following months of speculation to whether or not he would actually go ahead and make the commitment. The ordination prompted much open discussion. It was the habit in Oxford, he later said, to assume that a man who took holy orders was either a fool or a knave, and since he doubted that anyone would think him a fool, he reasoned that he must have been judged a knave.[91] Nonetheless, he never attempted to explain or justify his decision. Again, his closest friends were not surprised. Perhaps Mary Arnold explained it best when she wrote that the 'intellectual doubts and misgivings on the subject of taking orders, so common in the Oxford of his day, Creighton had never felt. His life had ripened to a rich maturity without, apparently, any of those fundamental conflicts which had scarred the lives of other men', such as J. R. Green, who actually abandoned an ecclesiastical career.[92] Creighton preached his first sermon in April 1871.

By the start of 1871 Mandell Creighton had basically mapped out his career. He had chosen his scholarly interest—Renaissance Italy. He had chosen his vocation—priesthood in the Church of England. Fully embarked on his academic and religious journey, he now pondered the prospect of marriage. Like other young dons the anxiety of the decision to marry, once accepted, resulted in the stress of finding a wife. For Creighton, unaccustomed to romance, the prospects of finding a wife would not be easy. He may have even considered Mary Arnold. One suspects she thought of it. Then on an afternoon in February, at a Ruskin lecture, he happened to notice Louise von Glehn, an attractive girl who had the courage to wear yellow.

The Peak

'Peak Hill Lodge, known to us and our friends as "The Peak", has many happy memories for me.'

Ernest von Glehn, brother of Louise [1]

Peak Hill Lodge, the von Glehn family home, was hardly the 'small gabled house' that Louise told people years later, but rather a large, rambling structure with sufficient room for all the children, guests and a bevy of live-in servants; the house stood on seven acres of rolling hills, meadows and woods in Upper Sydenham and commanded a scenic view of the Kentish uplands. 'The Peak', as the von Glehns customarily called their house, was built around 1835 in the Jacobean style—then the fashion of Sydenham architecture—for the Rev. Thomas Bowdler (nephew of the noted expurgator of Shakespeare who gave his name to the verb 'bowdlerise'). Robert von Glehn purchased it on a sixty-year lease in 1845, and over the years added on to it twice to meet the needs of his growing family. The von Glehns alternated their living between The Peak in the summers and their London residence in the winters, 34 Upper Harley Street, not far from Marylebone church, in what was still a district of fine homes and rich homeowners. The house originally belonged to Louise's grandmother. After her death in December 1849, Robert von Glehn moved his family completely to Sydenham in 1850, the year Louise was born.

Prior to the 1840s Sydenham was a sleepy village a few miles south east of London, well beyond the metropolitan sprawl. When the railway stations at Sydenham and Forest Hill opened in 1839, the commuter service became as good as today, with regular trains to London Bridge taking only fifteen or twenty minutes. This produced the first building boom as business and professional men like Robert von Glehn or Scott Russell, the noted architect, began moving to Sydenham. The London Brighton and South Coast Railway line ran directly along the edge of the Peak Hill hay field, often sending its bubbling black, sooty smoke drifting up toward the house on the hill when the wind was from the south east. 'Trains were constantly passing', Louise remembered, and were a 'never ending source of amusement for us children'.

One of her earliest recollections was of watching trains bringing back troops at the end of the Crimean War in 1856. 'Great was the excitement,' she recalled, 'when a camel's head was seen looking out of a horse box. We had taken down the dinner gong and flags and made great demonstrations as the trains passed, and were puffed up with pride when this was mentioned in some newspaper which described the return of the troops.' [2]

Life in Sydenham changed dramatically in 1854, the year the new Crystal Palace opened there on 10 June. The original structure of glass and steel at Hyde Park, designed by Sir Joseph Paxton for the Great Exhibition of 1851, was moved to Sydenham after the Great Exhibition closed. The new and larger structure was even more magnificent than the original, and the palace became a popular tourist attraction, especially for concerts and special exhibitions. It was the announcement in 1852 that the Palace was coming to Sydenham that launched the second great building boom there, in Norwood and Forest Hill, and in other neighbouring suburban villages.[3] Population increased considerably, Sydenham lost its picture postcard character, and this quaint little English village grew so rapidly into a suburban town that, in Louise's words, it 'had no real character, no history. We looked down upon the newcomers as vulgar and common.'[4] Of course the really old Sydenham families must have felt the same about the von Glehns, the Scott Russells and the other newcomers who had moved into the area the decade before.[5]

Louise Hume von Glehn was born on 7 July 1850, at Peak Hill Lodge, the tenth child of twelve. The middle name 'Hume' was given to her in remembrance of her godmother, Elisa Hume, daughter of the radical MP Joseph Hume. Robert von Glehn, Louise's father, was a shrewd businessman who owned a successful import-export firm in the City, first in Martins Lane and then subsequently in Mincing Lane, Fenchurch Street and, finally, in Idol Lane. He was a distinguished member of the Baltic Exchange and possessed numerous contacts across Germany and the Baltic region which helped his commercial business. Few other things are known now about it, however, though the firm was certainly prosperous enough during his lifetime. By the 1870s Robert von Glehn had added 'Sons' to the company name and created a joint-partnership with Alexander (Alick) and William (Willie). His son Ernest, temporarily affiliated with the business, left to make his career as managing director of the Ragosine Oil Company. By the end of the century, however, a decade and a half after the death of Robert von Glehn, the business went into sharp decline and was sold.

Louise remembered that her father's business employed 'many clerks', and that it was 'very prosperous'. She always regarded her father as 'a very good business man', but doubted whether his business acumen was ever inherited by her brothers.[6] The precise income of her father or his overall wealth was a guarded secret in the family. All Louise knew was that they were 'not rich', though they lived well. 'With such a large family, careful management was necessary and we were always brought up to be economical and careful about all, even the smallest expenditure.'[7] During the years Louise lived at Peak Hill Lodge, the von Glehn family's life style was comfortably upper middle-class. Louise's father's diary, for example, showed the family's annual expenditure for 1857 at £2700, a substantial sum in those days.[8]

Robert William von Glehn was born on Christmas Day, 1800 (Old Style), or 6 January 1801 (New Style), in Reval (Tallinn), capital of Estonia and a major Baltic port on the southern coast of the Gulf of Finland. He was often referred to as a 'Russian merchant', but he was actually half-German and half-Scottish. The von Glehn side of the family had originated in the Rhineland and moved to the Baltic provinces during the Thirty Years War. The von Glehns were of the merchant class. A descendant, Peter von Glehn, was born in Reval in 1751. He married a daughter of a Scots merchant who had emigrated from Dundee with his wife in 1798. Peter and his wife had several children, of whom Robert, Louise's father, was the second son.

After some semblance of a formal education, first at a dame school in Reval and then a year at a gymnasium in St Petersburg, young Robert joined the family import-export business, first in St Petersburg and later in Berlin. He then spent a few years travelling throughout Europe, mostly in France and Spain. In September 1828, Robert von Glehn sailed to England and remained there sightseeing for several months. He returned to the Continent, but after a period in St Petersburg and Hamburg, he again visited England in March 1831. Then, after several more years of wandering on the Continent in an apparent search for a permanent home and career, he travelled back to London in 1832 and again in 1833, whereupon he established a small commercial business in the City. Eventually becoming a naturalised British citizen, Robert von Glehn formed a close personal friendship and business relationship with a Mr Reierson; Mrs Reierson had a daughter by a previous marriage. Her name was Agnes Duncan. 'Miss Agnes is a most perfect young girl', Robert wrote in his diary.[9]

Agnes Duncan was born about 1813 near Dundee. Her father and mother were both Scottish. After her father died while working in India—when she was still a small child—her mother married Mr Reierson, a prosperous merchant of Danish origin. He and Agnes's mother eventually settled in London, and raised Agnes as an only child in luxury and comfort. Agnes first met Robert von Glehn when he visited her mother and stepfather in 1832. Mr Reierson began to advise Robert in business matters during his visits to England, and probably encouraged him eventually to settle in

London. Louise credits Mrs Reierson, her grandmother, with shaping Robert's religious conversion and encouraging him to join the Church of England.

Both Mr and Mrs Reierson apparently found the young foreigner acceptable as a son-in-law, and Robert and Agnes married in June 1835. 'There must have been something specially attractive about him,' Louise felt, 'considering that he was only an obscure foreigner without position or wealth', and considering Louise's mother 'had been most carefully educated and watched over; it was a great testimony to my father's character and religious views that the marriage was allowed'.[10] Mr Reierson, who died in 1839, greatly assisted Robert in business after the marriage. When Mrs Reierson died ten years later, Agnes received a substantial inheritance which included two pieces of valuable property—the London house in Harley Street and a country home in Surrey known as 'Woodhill'.[11]

Louise, along with her six living brothers—Alick, Willie, Ernest, Alfred, Harry and Oswald (one brother, Edward, died at the age of nine, and another child died at birth), and her four sisters—Sophie, Olga, Mary Emilia (always known as Mimi) and Ida—thrived on the continental connections her father brought to the family. They all were 'proud of being von Glehns', Louise stated, especially knowing there was no other family in England with their name.[12] Also the fact that her father was 'a foreigner' produced a noticeable lack of British customs in their home, Louise thought, because Robert von Glehn was 'not in touch with real conventional English life, above all he had never lived in the real country, in country circles. His connexions and interests were cosmopolitan.' Further, she said, 'he took no part in English politics or public life. His views were liberal and I believe he always voted liberal, and he was an idealist, having grown up in days when Byron was the inspirer of young men ...'[13]

Robert von Glehn was a tall slender man, handsome and, to friends and acquaintances, 'a great favourite, very sociable, a good dancer, musical and lively, with a good deal of German sentiment. He was a good linguist, speaking English, French and German absolutely well and Russian also. I don't think he knew any classics but he was always a great reader, though in no sense a student.' As a father, he was kind but remote, seemingly the classic 'Papa' one reads of in Victorian literature. Louise never felt him as a friend or 'play fellow'. In part, it was the culture of the times, but also, she reckoned, his German nature made it difficult for him to unbend. 'I never saw him play the fool, and I think he was always puzzled at English jokes, particularly when older people talked nonsense. I do not think we were ever quite at our ease with him and when we wanted anything it was always to our mother that we went ...'[14]

The von Glehn Family

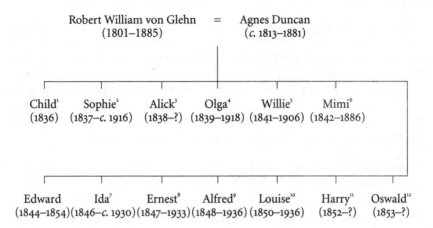

Robert William von Glehn = Agnes Duncan
(1801–1885)   (c. 1813–1881)

Child[1]	Sophie[2]	Alick[3]	Olga[4]	Willie[5]	Mimi[6]
(1836)	(1837–c. 1916)	(1838–?)	(1839–1918)	(1841–1906)	(1842–1886)

Edward	Ida[7]	Ernest[8]	Alfred[9]	Louise[10]	Harry[11]	Oswald[12]
(1844–1854)	(1846–c. 1930)	(1847–1933)	(1848–1936)	(1850–1936)	(1852–?)	(1853–?)

[1] Died at birth.
[2] Sophie married Paul Hasse.
[3] Alexander. Married Fanny Monod.
[4] Never married.
[5] William Robert. Married Sophie Löwe.
[6] Mary Emilie. Never married.
[7] Ida married her cousin, Nicolai (or Nicholai) Koch.
[8] Ernest married Marian Bradley.
[9] Alfred married Lucile Gros.
[10] Louise marreid Mandell Creighton. See Creighton family tree.
[11] Never married; ordained an Anglican preist.
[12] Oswald married. Agnes was her first name.

Louise regarded her mother as clever and cultivated, possessing a 'superior intelligence' in comparison to her father Robert, and certainly more demonstrative when it came to expressing love toward the children. While strong in character, her health was generally weak, presumably in large measure from having a large family. She had had thirteen children overall, the eldest being stillborn. 'I remember she was often tired', Louise remarked, and 'had many small illnesses'.[15] Robert von Glehn started early for the City each morning during the week after prayers at 8 o'clock, a brief glance at the newspaper, and breakfast. The children apparently breakfasted with the parents from an early age, not an English custom at the time. Louise claimed that she had no recollection of a nursery breakfast. 'Whatever it was, the breakfast was very simple, I know that there was no marmalade or jam till after I was married.' [16] Her father arrived back at Peak Hill for dinner around half past six,

> often bringing with him a bag with a bit of fish from town. My mother always grew expectant some time before his train arrived and was very fidgety and anxious if anything detained him. I remember her eager face and smile of greetings and the kiss at partings and meetings. He always said good evening to each of us with a kiss when he got back, and there were times for games too sometimes, when he would jump us high in the air or make us lie stiff like pokers on the floor and he lifted us straight by our heads. But I do not remember his telling us stories or even really romping or playing games with us.[17]

Growing up in a large family, Louise was influenced in her childhood years as much by her brothers and sisters and her nurses as she was by her parents. All her memories of her parents were 'as of decidedly old people', which made them seem more like grandparents than parents, even though her mother was only about thirty-seven and her father was fifty-one when Louise was born. Of course the size of the family kept her and her younger siblings from any real closeness with them. 'I was in many ways the special care of my eldest sister, Sophie', Louise recalled. Sophie was about twelve years older than Louise. 'I had an immense devotion to her and always called her Puss, whilst she called me Brown Mouse.' [18] The six younger children—Ida, Ernest, Alfred, Harry, Oswald and Louise—played together. Her elder brothers and sisters were less influential companions. The tragedy of her brother Edward's death from scarlet fever in 1854 at the age of nine affected the family deeply. As a result, Edward's name was never spoken in the family afterwards.

The 'schoolroom hours' were rigidly kept in the von Glehn household, though Louise remembered that during non-school hours of the day there was 'no objection' to her making her way 'to any part of the house when I was free from lessons'. Her ambition was to be old enough to go downstairs after dinner and mix with the adults, as was generally the custom for older children in that era. 'I do not think we especially dressed on these occasions beyond having pinafores removed and hair brushed; neither did the grownups then dress for dinner on ordinary occasions.' Schoolroom tea was in the late afternoon, and it was considered 'very terrible to have lessons to do after tea and only necessary on some rare emergency or as a punishment'.[19]

Punishments were not severe, though discipline was strict. 'I remember no case of corporal punishment, certainly I never suffered it myself. There were dark suspicions as to what might have happened when, for some exceptional crime, one of the boys was summoned to my father's dressing-room, particularly when Ernest broke the looking-glass above an oak cabinet in the dining-room by throwing a book against it.' The 'ordinary punishment' was to be placed into a dark closet near the schoolroom. 'It was roomy, and had no unpleasant smell so it only induced a feeling of boredom and slight disgrace', she said.[20]

Louise's earliest nursery memories included 'playing with toys and talking out loud in a room where other people were reading and working'. The smaller children played with bricks and tin figures, and on rainy afternoons they were allowed to have 'feasts of biscuits, apples and figs'. This was the era when children were raised virtually by nurses and governesses. The nurse who reigned over Louise's early life was a strict woman named Burnham, who was 'not particularly kind', and could exhibit a temper. According to Louise, Burnham personified grouchy Mrs Crabtree in Catherine Sinclair's 1844 novel *Holiday House*.[21] Louise's later governess was Miss Brunn, a strict German woman who controlled much of her life until well into her teenage years. Miss Brunn was an institution at The Peak. 'I could not imagine life without her', Louise confessed.

She was engaged primarily as a nursery governess to keep order, superintend dressing and walking and giving elementary teaching, for higher subjects there were masters and classes. She was excessively tidy and punctual, and neat and orderly in every particular and insisted upon us being the same. She had coarse black hair twisted in a very tight coil behind and so tidy that we thought each hair must be separately arranged. All her ways were methodical, a clear place on which to wipe her face every morning was kept in her towel; needles that had lost their eyes had a ceiling wax head given them and were used as pins. Of course she had headaches, and these were dire events, for we had to try to keep quiet, and we somehow felt that her suffering was tremendous and awe inspiring.

I don't think she ever played with us, and she had not much sympathy with our foolish ways. It was a terrible thing to get a giggling fit at schoolroom tea. The first offender was ruthlessly ordered out of the room to be followed generally by a second and a third till there were several helpless giggling children in the passage outside the schoolroom door. Miss Brunn was strict; she was sometimes decidedly cross. I do not think that we either liked her or disliked her as children; we accepted her, she was perfectly just and straight and aroused no resentment. As we grew older we appreciated more her absolute loyalty, her genuine sympathy in everything that concerned us. She gave the best years of her life to us and we learnt from her, method, neatness, punctuality and many good habits, though it was not in her power to give us any intellectual stimulus. Her special gifts were invaluable in the discipline of a large family of boys and girls, all with strong characters, vigorous health and decided tempers ...[22]

In general, despite some Teutonic features, Louise's childhood life at The Peak was filled with conventional Victorian experiences—nursery and schoolroom study and teas, playing Indian chiefs in the garden, charades and storytelling in the parlour on rainy days, Christmas parties with ventriloquists and conjurors, skating on icy ponds in winter, picnics and hay parties in summer, and playing hoops along the dusty roads. One of the great events each summer occurred at hay cutting time, Louise remembered. 'Every moment of the time was a delight from the waking on the first morning to hear the mowers sharpening their scythes to the carrying of the last cart-load. Little wooden forks were cut for us to help in tossing the hay'. she said. 'We had many and varied games which we played in the hay, making nests, burying one another, playing hide and seek behind the cocks. The crowning joy was when the carting began. We followed the full carts to watch them unload and then were allowed to ride back in the empty cart.' [23]

Then there were the annual summer picnics on Hayes Common, not far from their home, 'a beautiful wild spot' where the heather and tall bracken grew 'in which a small child was quite lost, and here and there a fine tree, and a steep slope covered with aged oaks of great girth. In one of these, which was quite hollow, my father used to like to collect the whole family, helping us to climb onto the outstretched branches of the old giant.' [24] For summer holidays a trip to the south coast was always a popular family outing. 'Life was very simple at our home in the days of my childhood', Louise explained. It was not thought necessary for the children to go away for change of air, 'unless we had been ill, and that seldom occurred, or on one occasion when the house was painted. Hastings was the place to which we then went and we loved it passionately. We stayed as near as possible to the old fishing town, and loved to watch the boats go out, and enjoyed the walks on the cliffs ... then unspoiled by tourists.' [25]

Ice-skating on cold winter days was the chief form of recreation for the von Glehn children. Not yet customary in England for girls to skate, Louise claimed she and her sisters were among the first in Sydenham to do so. 'I learnt on our pond. The brothers put on our skates, took me to the middle of the pond and left me there and I spent a whole day tumbling about alone without help, with the result that the next day I was able to join the party which went to skate on the large fountain basins in the Crystal Palace grounds.' Louise regarded herself as 'a good skater and loved it more than any other amusement. We used to start at 10 o'clock taking our lunch with us and skate all day till it was dark; sometimes going again in the evening and skate in the moonlight ... What glorious fun it was and then the deliciously tired feeling in the evening when we all sat on the floor round the fire at the end of the drawing-room too sleepy to do anything but laugh and talk nonsense ...' [26] The Crystal Palace, of course, added a great deal to the cultural life of the family on Sunday afternoons. Robert von Glehn was a shareholder, which allowed his family to gain special admission.[27] Another winter activity was the annual dance at Peak Hill Lodge. As Louise described the event,

> The long narrow drawing-room was cleared out and a white Holland tacked down over the carpet. My elder sisters used to make red paper roses and stuck them among wreathes of evergreen to decorate the house; my mother super-intended the preparation of a wonderful Russian salad which was always a much appreciated feature of the ball supper. The young ones were allowed to stay up for the first part of the party, and sometimes some kind man would dance with us. On one occasion when I may have been ten to eleven one young man petted me a great deal and I enjoyed sitting on his knee and being made much of. The next year, forgetting the difference made by a year in a girl's life, he wished to treat me as before. I was miserable and shy and escaped early to bed, and fearing a repetition of this distasteful intimacy, preferred to stay away altogether from the dance in the following year.[28]

While there was no lack of family social 'life and stir' at Peak Hill, Louise felt her childhood was marked by 'its real simplicity, the absence of any unnecessary expense of display, the strict economy that was always practised'. It was 'so bred in us that we became naturally economical without being stingy,' she said, 'for from our earliest days expense had always had to be considered. Food and dress were both simple. Schoolroom tea consisted of plain bread and butter, the butter very thin and sometimes bread and treacle. If we spoke of other children who had cake and jam we were told, as no doubt many others were in those days, of the children in the royal nursery who were said to have nothing but plain bread and butter.' [29]

To manage such a large house in mid Victorian times, a small army of servants was required. According to the 1871 census, the von Glehns regularly employed five female servants, as well as a gardener and his niece who lived in a small cottage near the main house.[30] According to Louise, the relations between 'master and mistress and servants were always most pleasant'.

> Many trusted servants stayed with us for long years. My parents treated them with the utmost consideration and we were always made to do the same. My father was invariably courteous, with a graceful old-fashioned courtesy to every-one, and he showed his servants this same courtesy. He always spoke with admiration of their willingness to oblige and help, and used to say, 'I often wonder why when I ring the bell and ask a servant to do something, she should at once agree. Why does she never refuse to do as she is asked?' [31]

The von Glehns were broad church Anglicans and attended St Bartholomew's Church in Sydenham, although the family 'held rather aloof from
the regular church families', considering themselves 'in some vague way
superior to them', Louise said.[32] Her father's favourite religious readings
were those of Thomas Arnold, the famed headmaster of Rugby, whose
homilies are still regarded as some of the finer sermons of the Victorian
period.[33] Their broad church tendency was perhaps encouraged by their
acquaintance with Sir George Grove, then secretary of the Crystal Palace
Company, who was a close friend of Arthur Penrhyn Stanley, Dean of
Westminster. Through Grove, Louise claimed, Thomas Arnold 'became the
object of much admiration in our family circle and his books, and
F. D. Maurice's and Fred Robertson's sermons were much read'.[34] Although
Bible reading and theological study were required of the von Glehn children,
one senses that religion was not a dominant force in their early lives. 'I
had no religious crisis', Louise said, 'and never went through any period
of doubt.'[35] Later in her life, however, religion did become her principal
focal point, particularly the church's social and missionary work.

Louise's early cultural outlook was also fashioned by the dynamics of
Sydenham society. Sydenham had emerged as a lively cultural centre with
the arrival of the Crystal Palace, attracting prominent figures in the arts
and professions. Many of the 'new' Sydenham society came to know the
von Glehns well,[36] and Peak Hill Lodge served as a favoured gathering spot
for lively entertainment and serious discourse by a coterie of musicians,
artists and writers. As one of Louise's brothers recalled, his parents made
it a habit of keeping 'open house' for 'men and women well known in the
world of music, art and literature'.[37] There was Sir George Grove, who, as
a frequent visitor, later became smitten with Louise's older sister, Mimi;
though they never married, he carried his profound fondness for her for
the rest of his life. Louise remembered him stopping by the house every
morning on his way from his late seventeenth-century weather-boarded
house on Sydenham Road to the Crystal Palace. Often on his return in the
evenings, he would drop in again, staying for long talks.[38] Sir Arthur Sullivan,
of Gilbert and Sullivan fame, came often and entertained. It was at The
Peak that one of the first performances of Sullivan's Cox and Box was
given, with Sullivan himself playing the role of 'Box'.[39] And then there
was John Richard Green, one of the leading historians of the century, a
writer who perhaps more than any other of his era could relate complex
social and political history in a way that both educated and entertained
a wide reading public.[40] Green visited The Peak often and delighted in
conversing with the von Glehn girls, particularly Louise.

There were never any 'feelings of fuss or difficulty about entertaining guests,' Louise recalled, 'and there was no idea of the need of making any show or display in the method of entertaining them. They were simply admitted to the ordinary life of the family. In consequence, people always felt free to drop in without any formality; there was never any stiffness in the social atmosphere of the house ...' This hospitality combined with an absence of formal entertaining gave a character of its own to the society at Peak Hill, Louise admitted, 'and made us all grow up with the feelings that it was the obvious thing to be hospitable'.[41] Louise, as one would expect, profited from all of this. The von Glehn home, despite its cultural environment, was noticeably an un-English enclave, and it seems to have at times taken on a kind of Gothic Puritanism, what came to be known in the family as 'The Gloom is on the Glehn'. 'The critical atmosphere of the family and the personal remarks', Louise explained, made her 'very self-conscious and in consequence rather shy'.[42]

Like her mother and her sisters, Louise never attended school in the formal sense—not unusual for girls of that era. The von Glehn sons, however, all went in succession to the Blackheath Proprietary School located near Greenwich, which, as most proprietary schools of that era, gave middle-classes families a less expensive schooling than public schools and yet a more practical curriculum. 'My father', Louise explained, 'had no traditional feeling about English public schools, and my parents did not wish to separate their sons too much from home life. They came home every Saturday at midday and stayed till early Monday morning so that they never lost touch with home life.'[43]

After Blackheath, Robert von Glehn sent two of his older sons abroad for business experience, Alick to Petersburg and later to Mauritius, the British colony in the Indian Ocean, for three years. One of Alick's sons was Wilfrid de Glehn, the noted British impressionist painter and a close friend of John Singer Sargent.[44] Willie went to Le Havre, France. Ernest, academically the brightest of the boys, went to Christ Church, Oxford, before going into the business. Alfred, deciding to be an engineer, studied at King's College, London, and later in Zurich. Harry, displaying little aptitude for business, grew restless, and journeyed to the United States, first joining Thomas Hughes's settlement of farmers known as New Rugby, then enrolling at the theological college at Harvard. He was ordained in the American Episcopal Church and ultimately returned to England. Oswald, the youngest, went to New College, Oxford; later, he studied at the Slade School of Art in London and had two of his paintings exhibited at Royal Academy in 1879 and 1880.[45]

Louise's early education took place at home, a strict regime of daily supervised study conducted by her mother, her elder sisters and her governesses. Classes commenced early every morning in the schoolroom with a writing lesson of twenty minutes. She learned French and German, along with English literature and music. She soon began 'to read everything on which I could lay my hands', she said.⁴⁶ As it turned out, her home schooling was first rate; nevertheless, she always regretted not having an opportunity to receive formal education, and in later life she became an ardent advocate for women's education at all levels. A fortuitous opportunity did provide Louise with a semblance of 'formal' schooling in her teens when Crystal Palace officials inaugurated enrichment classes for young women, using a suite of rooms formerly reserved for the royal family when they visited the exhibition hall while it was at Hyde Park. There for two or three years Louise took courses in such subjects as German literature and composition, French, physical geography and arithmetic, as well as dancing and drawing.⁴⁷ To her credit she mastered an array of academic subjects that enabled her to sit for the first London University examination for women. Hearing that London University planned to offer a higher examination for women, Louise decided to take it. 'I crammed it all up. The examination ... lasted several days. Eight young women went in for it and of these six, of whom I was one, passed with honours. This was the only examination for which I ever went in, and I have always been rather pleased that I passed the first higher examination for women that was held.'⁴⁸

Louise found early on that she possessed some talent for sketching and watercolour painting, and art became one of her life-long activities. Music, however, was never one of her recreational skills, though it was an important part of von Glehn family life. Both her father and mother were musical, and her sister Mimi became an accomplished pianist. Louise said that growing up in such a musical atmosphere, she 'loved music and understood at least something about it. Every evening after dinner my father called for music and there was playing and singing for an hour or two; he still sang himself when I was a child.' The weekly concerts at the Crystal Palace were then under the direction of the conductor August Manns. 'I can remember beginning to go to them when I must have been very young, for I know that I had no idea what a symphony was, and always wondered why the music seemed to come to an end and then to begin again ...'⁴⁹

Of course, with the von Glehns' continental connections, Louise travelled abroad with her parents occasionally, which not only broadened her social horizons as a young girl but also afforded her a European outlook that many young women of her day could never hope to acquire. When Louise was thirteen she made her first trip to visit her married sister Sophie, who lived in the Black Forest of south-west Germany, and then on to Paris. It was while in Paris that Louise's mother caught a chill and became acutely ill. For the first time, Louise faced heavy responsibility. 'Much of the care of her fell on me', she remembered. 'When my father was out I was alone in charge, and my mother was mostly dozing and sometimes rather wandering in her mind. It was a dreary time for a girl of thirteen on the fifth floor of an enormous French hotel. I had no books to read but some volumes of German stories ... It was an immense relief when my mother was well enough to travel slowly home ...'[50]

A couple of years later Louise made her second journey abroad with her parents, first to Paris and then on to Switzerland. 'When I travelled with my parents', she said, 'my father and I always walked a great deal together. We used to go out for a first walk of exploration before breakfast in a new place and for several other walks during the day, but we never left my mother for long', she being unable to take lengthy walks.[51] From that time forward, Louise became a frequent companion on their journeys. She took her third trip three years later. 'Few things affected my intellectual development more than a journey I took with my parents in 1869', she said. 'My mother was to drink the water [at a spa] in the Black Forest for her rheumatism ... We were then to make our way into Italy and spend the autumn there so as to give her a complete change from English damp ...' The journey included a swing south to Italy, her first trip there and an experience, she confessed, for which she was 'utterly unprepared'.

> The only advice I had received was given to me by a delightful old English gentleman I had met [in Germany] who told me to read [Edward] Gibbon before going to Rome.[52] When I did get Gibbon out of a library in Rome, though I read him with interest, I was too ignorant to understand how he was to help me to see Rome. My father and mother knew little more than I did about Italy. In those days the craze for Italy had not begun; the thousands of little handbooks which explain the different cities and the works of the different artists did not exist ...
>
> My mother could only do a limited amount of sightseeing, but my father was ready to do anything I wished. I studied the guidebook and dragged him about to picture galleries and churches without end; one day in Rome he said wearily as we entered a church, 'I wonder how many hundreds of churches we have seen since we came to Italy and what you remember of them?' What he liked was to walk about the streets and look at the people. Rome was very picturesque in those days. The Pope was still supreme and drove about in a great coach.[53] If we met him, our driver compelled us to get out of our carriage and at least stand as he passed, the devout Romans knelt. I saw him carried to mass with great white peacock feather fans before him. The Cardinals drove ... in their great coaches, getting out to take walking exercise in their purple robes whilst lacqueys and coach followed slowly behind.

The villas had not yet been sold to the speculating builders and the city was full of gardens, roses and creepers tumbling in profusion over the high walls. I was keenly interested in everything and admired all the wrong things. Guido Reni was my favourite painter,[54] being aesthetically absolutely under the spell of Ruskin I had no interest in anything but gothic architecture and the monuments of the Renaissance said nothing to me. Fortunately Ruskin helped me to love San Marco at Venice and to find my way a little amongst the Venetian painters. But ignorant and blundering tho I was, this journey was a great awakening for me and sent me home keen to study and understand art.[55]

This was Louise's introduction to the seductive charms of the Italian Renaissance—something she came to appreciate more after she met Mandell. Before her trip to Italy she had never visited the National Gallery in London. Now she became a regular visitor. 'I was keen about ... making a definite study of art, reading a great many histories of art and inclined to make Ruskin my prophet', she admitted.[56] The trip had broadened her perspective on art. And about this same time she developed 'a new friend' in Agnes Ward, sister of Humphry Ward, who had come to know the von Glehns through his friends, J. R. Green and Stopford Brooke. Louise had initiated an essay society consisting of several young women friends in Sydenham, shortly after returning from Italy. The purpose of the society was to study and write about art. J. R. Green, a friend of the von Glehn family, apparently had a romantic interest in Louise at the time. He agreed to read and advise the women about their essays at Louise's suggestion, and in one of his letters to her he stated that his suggestions were 'simply hints' for writing good English. 'Simplicity is half of it, I think', he stated. 'But the true way to write well is to write constantly—ease of style can only come by habit; and grace of style can only come with ease ... Above all, don't let any idle fun of mine make you think me careless about your work.'[57] According to Louise, Green had the 'strongest intellectual influence' on her during her girlhood years.

> He was first introduced to us when I was thirteen and after that was a constant visitor at The Peak as our home came to be called. He had great sympathy with young girls and soon won my unbounded devotion. He talked to me about my reading and my studies, told me books to read and gave me much wise advice and showed me much affection.[58]

Louise's friendship with Green never became romantically serious, for she began to feel he was becoming too intimate. 'Mr Green liked tender relations with young women and during the long years of his friendship with our family, his friendship for Olga, Mimi and me passed through many phases. I remember at one time being afraid that it was going further than I desired and drawing back a little, but on the whole I gained nothing but good from him and am most grateful for the intellectual stimulus he gave me.' [59] Green later asked Stopford Brooke, then still a clergyman at the Bloomsbury Chapel, to take over and suggest subjects and criticise the essays. 'There were only very few members, at most six ... in this essay society. As our essays were all founded on our own personal study of the things we wrote about, it was of real educational use, and the help Mr Stopford Brooke gave us at the beginning was most valuable. But other work interferred and he became unable to give any more time to us.' It was then that Humphry Ward agreed to take over the reviewing of the essays.[60]

Ward and Louise were 'growing to be great friends', she confessed, and one day he wrote to tell her that his sister, who had been ill, was being sent with a maid to lodgings in the village of Anerley, just a few miles south west of Sydenham, in order to get her out of London. Ward asked Louise to visit his sister. Almost from the first moment of meeting, Louise and Agnes Ward became friends, and for some weeks she visited Agnes almost daily. Over the next couple of years the two young women continued their close friendship. Agnes Ward's health being uncertain, it was decided that her father should take her to Capri for the winter in 1870, and Humphry appealed to Louise to go along as Agnes's companion at his expense. 'It was a great disappointment to me that my mother would not allow this, I think because she felt very far from being attracted by Mr Ward', Louise remarked later. 'I am sure my mother's decision was wise.' [61]

It was certainly a 'momentous decision', Louise recalled, as she would have been out of England that winter of 1870–71. Her friendship with Humphry Ward's sister brought her in close contact with him, and while she never fell completely under his spell, romance was beginning to bloom. When it was arranged that Louise should visit Oxford in February 1871, Ward was delighted. He may well have assisted in the arrangement. So, Louise went to Oxford to visit Humphry Ward and discovered Mandell Creighton.

7

A Charm about Oxford

'With all its faults of idleness and littleness, there is a charm about Oxford which tells on one ...'

J. R. Green to Louise von Glehn [1]

Mandell Creighton and Louise von Glehn were married on 8 January 1872, at St Bartholomew's Church in Sydenham. It was a quiet, modest ceremony with only a few friends present beyond the immediate family. Mandell's sister Polly was the only one of his family to attend. The Rev. Robert Wilson, Mandell's friend and a fellow of Merton, officiated at the ceremony. Louise wore a plain white poplin dress with a net veil. There were no bridesmaids. To the strains of 'Through All the Changing Scenes of Life', Louise and Mandell walked out of the church and into their newly-shared life.[2]

After a lunch at The Peak, Louise changed into a fine wool dress and sealskin jacket; and as she walked into the drawing-room, Mandell smiled and said for all to hear: 'What a swell you are.' The couple drove to Herne Hill that afternoon, caught the train to Dover, and stayed that night at the Lord Warden Hotel. The following day they crossed the Channel to France and caught the train to Paris. There they spent their honeymoon sightseeing, visiting galleries and going to the theatre. 'I don't think we either of us ... felt any real love for Paris', Louise said. 'We never did more in later years than spend a couple of days there on our way elsewhere.'[3] In a letter to her mother on 10 January, she happily noted:

> We two people are in a generally flourishing and satisfactory condition; things altogether having gone very well with us, even the weather has smiled upon us so that we had a calm crossing and bright sunshine to welcome us in France ...
>
> My cold unfortunately went on increasing and I was rather tired on the journey yesterday ...
>
> Max [Mandell] takes the most wonderful care of me so don't you think old mother mine that I shall do too much. The worst of it is that we neither of us know our way about. I find I know even less than I expected of the directions and of the streets which is a severe blow to my pride. I suppose it comes from my having always been led about by Papa and not having to find the way for

myself. However we don't mind wandering about; the only thing we object to is losing our way, and so we wander till we find it for ourselves.

I don't know how long we [took] getting back here from the Louvre. We got there quite successfully but getting back we wanted to come a different way and in consequence walked many miles. Max is enchanted with the pictures which infinitely surpass his expectations and mine too; also we find many old curiosities shops, and he has already bought one old mirror and very nearly another ...

I daresay also we shall wander endlessly through the streets and poke into many shops. We feel generally very contented and also very idle and mean to have a regular holiday. I need not tell you how good Max is to me and how happy he makes me—you will know that without my telling it ...[4]

Their honeymoon was short, only a week, because Mandell needed to be back at Oxford for the beginning of the new term. The house they rented was off the Banbury Road, a little over a mile from Merton. Because it was located in a new residential area of Oxford and not yet numbered, the couple named their home 'Middlemarch' after George Eliot's novel. When they arrived in Oxford they discovered that Creighton's college servants had moved all his things from his Merton rooms to their new home. Mandell prided himself on managing his male servants, claiming the best approach was to be 'fearfully strict with them, though never losing your temper or being put out'.[5] Presumably he was pleased with how his former servants prepared the house before their arrival, doing virtually everything except hanging his pictures. Louise said they found their house warm and cosy with a new blue carpet—a wedding gift from her father—on the drawing-room floor, a kettle boiling on the fire, and Mandell's white Persian cat peacefully preening herself on the hearthrug. The cat was prolific and wound up being the mother of many kittens subsequently given to friends, such as the T. H. Greens and the Paters.[6]

Louise recalled that they 'worked hard' over the next few months to get their house furnished, visiting 'every old furniture and curiosity shop in Oxford' in the afternoons until she 'ached with fatigue standing about whilst [Mandell] explored their innermost recesses, and discussed their contents with their owners'.[7] The Creightons originally employed one maid and a cook. Writing to her mother shortly after getting settled, Louise said she was 'in every way pleased with our cook as far as she has gone. She could not have done better. The other girl also is more decent than I had ventured to expect. We have been doing more unpacking since lunch ... I am very busy and don't see much prospect as yet of being able to write many letters.'[8] She later employed a second maid and a house parlourmaid.[9]

Married life brought adjustments for both. Louise soon learned that her husband was 'very particular about all the arrangements of his domestic life', and wanted what was done in their home to be done well. He 'accepted no excuses and over-looked no shortcomings', she observed. 'From everybody he asked the best they could give.' [10] Having been an unmarried fellow ruling supreme over male college servants with fairness but firmness, he now had to modify—to some extent at least—his household management. Louise had been raised in a large household where servants and governesses were ubiquitous and dutiful, virtually underfoot, handling all the daily domestic chores. Louise, therefore, had to learn how to supervise her small staff, sometimes unable to avoid the wrath of her new husband which could fall swiftly and directly on her. She wrote to her sister Mimi a little over three months after her wedding that Mandell was 'not the sort of husband who overlooks one's faults, so I have a help always at hand and a severe critic also', adding that 'nothing could be better for me'.[11] Years later, she attempted to explain away his sometimes volcanic temperament, saying: 'Like all men of highly strung natures, he had a somewhat impatient and irritable temper. This was, as a rule, absolutely under control.' [12] Mandell always displayed a kinder, gentler side to his friends, colleagues and students, but in the privacy of his home, he could 'express displeasure or vexation in sharp and cutting words', Louise admitted, and 'those nearest and dearest to him alone seemed to arouse his irritation, partly, I think, because his very love for them made him expect so much from them, partly because he so absolutely identified himself with them that he felt their shortcomings as his own. But once the sharp word [was] spoken, the temper was gone.' [13]

Louise was a perfectionist too. As a child she had struggled to overcome self-doubts; but in later life she gained more than a measure of self-confidence to the point that she was sometimes characterised as formidable and domineering—suggesting that her assertiveness was a veneer covering basic feelings of insecurity.[14] Only Mandell seemed able to handle her, and her submission to his will was striking to those who observed them together. He literally became the centre of her life, and from her point of view he could do nothing wrong, say nothing unwise.

Louise found a great source of comfort and support in her mother. They corresponded with each other weekly. Louise usually wrote her letters on Sunday evenings. 'Have you any other cookery books with simple receipts which you could send me to keep for a little while and which might contain some information about soups more especially?', she asked in one dated 25 January 1872. 'Mine is of very little use; all the receipts are fearfully extravagant. However, my cook is good in many things and especially roasts meat very well which is a good quality; and meat we get here is very good.' Then she added proudly, 'I went round the other day to all my tradesmen to pay their books and felt very important; they are all so very humble and desirous to please, as Max—on account of his position in Merton—is a person of importance in their eyes.' [15] In another letter that spring she asked her mother, 'Tell me, ought I have any of the chimneys swept this spring? The kitchen chimney has been swept but none of the others'; concluding at the end of her letter that she was 'in dispair [sic] because things cost so much and I shall have to end by going without flowers in the house half the summer. Fancy 4d. for each pansy root?' [16]

Louise recalled their early married days at Oxford with special fondness. 'There was a wonderful glamour over them for me. The place enchanted me; the life was just the kind that I delighted in.' [17] Her life with Creighton was certainly enhanced by the fact that his popularity brought numerous social activities. She met new friends and, as their circle expanded, she found their public life congenially busy. Oxford was 'very sociable', she recalled. 'We dined out a great deal and gave many little dinners ourselves. These were always very simple ... and we used to have little dinners of six or eight without extra help. Only when we went to ten did we get in a very beautiful man [servant] ...' Mandell was accustomed to entertaining and Louise obviously enjoyed the opportunity to play the role of hostess. 'I was glad to fall in with his ways and try to make our little parties as nice as possible. It took up a great deal of time, getting and arranging flowers and dessert, and I sometimes found that most of the day before a party went in preparation. Max [Mandell] was always interested in the clothes I wore; he even chose which necklace I should put on ... When we went out to dinner we always walked; even on wet nights we seldom indulged in a cab. We often went out as many as four times in a week.' [18] There were times, of course, when social commitments became burdensome for the newly-weds. In a letter Louise wrote to her mother in April 1872 she complained: 'To-morrow we dine at the Max Müllers and next week we have two invitations, one a fearfully dull one to an old clergyman and his wife. I wish there would not be so many.' [19]

Most of the fellows gave dinners in college, and the Creightons willingly accepted a majority of the invitations. Andrew Lang at Merton was a regular. A man with enormous and versatile talent, and a disciple of the poet Matthew Arnold, Lang subsequent career as a poet, historian, folklorist, editor, journalist, humourist and translator was just beginning.[20] 'We did not know many of the great and seldom dined with heads of Colleges. It was an event when Jowett first invited us', and they had some 'very pleasant dinners with him and met interesting people. It was there we met the George Howards,[21] and made great friends at once.' [22] Their older friends with whom they often dined included Professor Bonamy Price and his wife and Professor Max Müller and his wife.[23] Their chief friends, however, came to be Thomas and Charlotte Green, Humphry Ward and Mary Arnold, Walter Pater and his sisters, and a little later Arthur and Bertha Johnson. Humphry and Mary were married in April 1872, just four months after the Creightons' wedding. 'He had finally made up his mind and proposed some months after we were engaged', Louise said. Ward was, she reckoned later,

> certainly fortunate above his desserts I think. She [Mary] thought him a very great man. We used to wonder, as did many of his friends, whether she would ever find out that he was not as great as she thought, but she never did; and in many ways he was much better than people thought. He was a most true and faithful friend, and one who would take any amount of trouble for his friends.[24]

According to Louise, they lived by Oxford standards a modest existence, leisurely frugal. One of the social events coming into vogue at that time was afternoon tea. 'We only had it if anyone came to see us,' Louise said, 'but I found that I acquired a habit of going out to see a friend about tea time and having tea with them, or else asking someone to tea with me; and in time afternoon tea became the regular thing.'[25]

Creighton's daily routine during term was simple. He left for Merton early. Louise's routine was to make him a cup of cocoa on the 'gas ring' in their dressing room and then stand at the window, watching 'his black gowned figure disappear' down the narrow road. He always turned back to wave at her before reaching the corner, she said. Arriving at Merton, he attended morning chapel service and took his breakfast in hall. Early morning would be taken up with lecturing and teaching. Louise generally walked to Merton in the late morning to 'fetch him back to lunch'. In the afternoons, unless there were meetings to attend, they took walks together around Oxford, often strolling along the river where they had first got to know each other the year before. Sometimes they took in a lecture by one of the professors, which were usually given at the convenient hour of 2 o'clock in the afternoon.

On certain afternoons, Mandell would join a group of older tutors, known as the Ancient Mariners, and they rowed on the river. Louise would usually walk along the tow path and watch. 'He was proud of his skill in punting, and we had happy afternoons on the Cherwell, which was then not really so crowded with boats as it became later. He tried to teach me to row, but I never did much in that way, and used to be a good deal bothered in steering on the lower river, finding it difficult to remember the right sides in order to keep out of the practising eights.'[26] They particularly enjoyed exploring the upper river with its row of aspen poplars on the side opposite to Port Meadow; and in the beginning of the summer vacation the

Creightons, like other young Oxford residents, 'rowed up to Godstowe, walked to Witham, and ate bowls of strawberries and cream in the cottage gardens there'.[27] In a letter to her mother, Louise described an afternoon expedition in July 1872.

We went [on] a long rowing expedition with [Mrs Thursfield] and her son [Richard] and two other men the other day which was very nice. We explored quite new regions to me going up higher than Oxford and getting into narrow branches of the Thames which were almost entirely choked with reeds and where it was a matter of great difficulty to advance at all, then pulling the boat over a bit of land and by degrees getting out again into beautiful wide open river flowing through lovely meadows. It was a beautiful evening and altogether most jolly.[28]

At 5 o'clock there were pupils to meet followed by dinner at 7, after which Mandell would work the remainder of the evening writing lectures or reading. 'He used to prowl amongst his books, and then dictate his notes to me. Most of my letters home [to her mother and sisters] were written in the intervals between these dictated notes', Louise declared.[29] The Creightons, when not going out in the evenings for dinner, enjoyed their quiet suppers together. Louise always took an interest in the preparation of meals, making sure to find the newest recipes for her cook. The cookery book she favoured, she told her mother, was Mary Jewry's *Warne's Every-Day Cookery*, though she probably consulted Isabella Beeton's *Mrs Beeton's Every-Day Cookery and Housekeeping Book*, the most popular of the day.[30]

The Creightons were often invited to luncheon parties at Merton or other colleges which Louise claimed were sometimes 'of formidable length and great magnificence'. They both felt obliged to attend most of these luncheons, 'always rather groaning' about having to go, Louise confessed. 'In those days too one sometimes went out to breakfast parties in College, particularly when any of the fellows had friends up. Altogether there was a great deal of entertaining in College as there were then very few of the fellows who were married. Even some of the married people gave their dinners in College. On the whole I enjoyed the social side of our life immensely', Louise said. And at those college affairs she was often the only woman, as women were still rare in Oxford.[31]

On Sunday morning they usually attended service at Merton chapel at 8 o'clock, and if there happened to be an interesting preacher scheduled, the University sermon later in the morning. Sunday afternoon was for visiting friends. On Sunday evening there was evensong at Merton 'where a choir of undergraduates sang drearily'. Then Mandell would usually dine in college leaving Louise to spend 'a solitary evening' writing letters at home.

During the remainder of the term 'there were many calls to be returned', to all those who had visited them in their first few weeks at Oxford. 'It was then etiquette for the husband to call also,' Louise observed, 'a proceeding which bored Max much, and made us always choose an exceptionally fine afternoon for our calls. He considered it a good afternoon's work if we could achieve eight [calls].'[32] Their principal friends in the early days, besides the Greens, the Wards and the Paters, were J. R. Thursfield and his mother, and Arthur and Bertha Johnson, along with several bachelor fellows, including J. F. Bright, Reginald Copleston, Andrew Lang, Robert Wilson, and H. G. Woods. Others in their circle at that time were the Frederic Harrisons, George Saintsbury, Edward Caird, the Henry Cromptons, C. P. Scott, Robert Bridges and J. R. Green.[33]

Creighton, possessing a strong feeling for the common life of his college, always insisted it was 'the duty' of every college man 'to contribute what he could to raise it morally and intellectually'. In the wake of the Young Oxford reforms, there was a dramatic lessening of fellows' commitment to the college life alone. In the words of Edmund Knox, a fellow of Merton, the 'Oxford of the clergy and squires passed during those years', in part because of what he called the 'pursuit of academic reputation' that was replacing 'loyalty to the College', where there began the desire of fellows to be 'free from the burdens of scholastic discipline' that was being replaced by a 'desire to shake off responsibility for the conduct of undergraduates and to let them learn by experience and self-expression how to govern their own lives'. Added to this was the increase of married fellowships. Tutors no longer lived within the college walls and their homes 'were more than a mile from the College, and that in days when bicycles and trams were still unknown'.[34] Men like the historian Edward Freeman lambasted the trend to allow married fellowships, and declared that it was destroying college life.[35] And he was not alone in this notion.[36]

Creighton, caught between being one of the earliest married fellows and his desire to promote active common life of the college, went out of his way to preach the need for preserving the tutor-student relationship. He no doubt spent more time at Merton during term time than Louise wanted him to, and certainly the greater part of his chapel sermons at Merton dealt with the need to promote common life experiences, as his *The Claims of the Common Life*, a book of his collected sermons as a don, eloquently reveals.[37] Reflecting on one of his sermons on the subject, he said: 'I rather liked my sermon ... It was a very rational sermon ... Its point was that men here ought to remember that their common life was the great means of the education of one another, and ought consequently to regulate most rigidly their life, so as to not only work out their own culture, but also contribute to the general culture of the whole society, and help everyone else in so doing.'[38] His sermons, then and later, tended to be more social than spiritual. It was his way, his rational approach to living. While devotion was important, it was to be kept personal. He was more a teacher than a preacher.

In 1871 the Law and Modern History School was divided, and Creighton was appointed one of its examiners for the new school of History. This increased his work but also his income and reputation.[39] Creighton's involvement with the women's higher education at Oxford was minimal at that time, largely a part of his participation in the broader university extension movement. Tutors and professors were being invited to give lectures in various towns and cities to women who were still barred from the universities.[40] Throughout England, 'Ladies' Associations' were being formed. Prior to his marriage Mandell had given lectures at Falmouth and Plymouth. Now, in the Hilary term of 1872, he began delivering a series of lectures on Dante and the Italian Renaissance at Clifton and Falmouth, and later at Birmingham.

Both Oxford and Cambridge were being pushed to adopt a more inclusive policy toward giving women higher educational opportunities, and Louise became keenly interested in this; more so than Mandell, who accepted women at lectures but never supported awarding them degrees. Louise, on the other hand, wanted full educational opportunities. She expressed initial criticism in the way the ladies' committees arranged women's courses taught by visiting tutors in the various towns, reckoning that the courses were too uncoordinated, too abbreviated, 'jumping from one subject to another'. To her mind the system was 'most uneducational', and it was not long until she decided that in order to 'do better in Oxford', there needed to be better organisation.[41]

Louise joined with several similarly-minded women, including Mary Ward, Charlotte Green, Georgiana Müller and Lavinia Talbot (wife of the Edward Talbot, first warden of Keble College), to produce a scheme for offering lectures in specific periods of English history with each historical course followed by a course on the literature of the times.[42] Up until then, women could not enrol in courses or officially attend tutors' lectures at Oxford. Arthur Johnson, a fellow of All Souls, agreed to begin the new plan and other tutors soon followed. In 1873 Louise and her friends reformed the ladies' association, which in 1877 became the Association for the Education of Women, thus moving Oxford closer to a complete course for women. Two women's colleges were established by the end of the decade at Oxford: Somerville and Lady Margaret Hall, the latter being of special interest to Louise over the years. Later in 1886 came St Hugh's, and then

St Hilda's in 1893. At Cambridge, also in the throes of a similar change but ahead of Oxford, two womens' colleges were already in hand: Girton which opened in 1873 and Newnham in 1875.[43] Both Cambridge and Oxford in the 1880s came to permit women to sit for university examinations, but balked at allowing women to receive anything but diplomas. It was not until well into the next century that women were granted the right to earn degrees, first at Oxford and then at Cambridge.[44]

Bertha Johnson and her sister Charlotte Green were collaborators in Louise's educational efforts. Bertha described years later how she got involved with the 'committee of ladies'. She recalled that Louise, 'then a remarkably handsome young woman in the aesthetic costume of the period', came up to her one day and asked that she 'join a Committee of ladies for providing a system of lectures and classes for women in Oxford ... I joyfully assented and found myself with an interesting little company of organisers ...'[45] Recalling a visit one day to Middlemarch in 1873 (after the birth of the Creightons' first baby), Bertha Johnson, Mary Ward and Clara Pater were gathered around a drawing-room table with Louise pre-paring a newsletter for distribution and were, as she said, 'introduced at once to the theory of "equal rights" of husband and wife'. While the women worked and took turns caring for the one-year-old baby, Mandell secluded himself away in his study—indicating he wanted nothing to do with helping out.[46]

Louise also became a district visitor in Oxford, a new venture by the Church of England to visit the poor in an effort to raise the religious standards of the urban working classes. Clergymen divided their parishes into districts and assigned women to them so they could visit homes and assist families in special need. District visitors were then to report back on the physical and spiritual conditions of the families. Along with Clara Pater, Louise signed up and was given one of the poorer sections of the city to visit periodically. 'It was a great effort to me to visit my street, and I do not remember anything interesting about the people', she admitted. Louise and Clara Pater also established a small lending library in their parish district where they were volunteers, encouraging families to take out books.[47] All this provided Louise with her early experience in social work, broadening her perspective on working-class conditions.

Mandell, interested in introducing Louise to the study of history, began to advise her on her reading, giving it direction and focus. Because of her knowledge of German, he asked her to translate one of the volumes of Leopold von Ranke's *Englische Geschichte*. The project, having been initiated by several Oxford tutors, was then well underway. They wanted to make this important historical study widely available in English in the history schools, and early on Creighton had agreed to translate one volume of this monumental work on his own.[48] Mindful of her linguistic ability, he thought the project was ready-made for Louise. She agreed to do a volume and completed it by the end of 1873. 'We revised it together', she said later:

> It was an unsatisfactory piece of work from the literary point of view as old Ranke wished it to be very literal and that we should as far as possible keep to the order of sentences and words ... In the preface to the translation it appears as done by Max, who had really undertaken it. I took a great deal of trouble to verify the notes, and enjoyed hunting up the references at the Bodleian. My delight in that part of work makes me believe that had circumstances permitted it, I might have become a real grubbing student. Wealth did not come to the translators of Ranke. It was a labour of love for the benefit of the History School [at Oxford], and it was a pleasant surprise when some time after the appearance of the book I received £5 for the work. I bought with it our silver tea pot.[49]

The Ranke project introduced her to the charms of the Bodleian Library. She began spending her mornings there reading under her husband's direction and found the atmosphere enchanting. The 'prince of librarians' Henry O. Coxe—or 'Bodley Coxe' as he was sometimes known—'pervaded the library with his gracious personality, and his easy manners and delightful humour brightened its whole atmosphere', Louise claimed.

> I was allowed to use one of the large desks in the wide space at the end of the reader's corridor. The other half of the desk belonged to Professor [William] Stubbs,[50] and he would often look round the back of the desk that divided us, with one of his ridiculous jokes, or sometimes to ask me the meaning of a German word. Sometimes Mr Cox [sic] would come wandering along and sit on the top of the desk and talk to us. I was finding out how to study; wasting a good deal of time I have no doubt, but enjoying it all immensely.[51]

Mandell encouraged Louise not only to read history but also to write. He saw this as her means of pulling ideas together; and he frequently suggested topics to write about. Creighton was a great believer in the notion that it was better to learn everything about something rather than something about everything.[52] Her first project was to study medieval guilds. 'I hunted up all I could find on the subject', Louise tells us, 'and became deeply interested in the Staple', that late medieval guild of English wool merchants engaged in export under royal authority.[53] Shilling primers were those thinly bound and relatively inexpensive survey studies designed for young students. They were just beginning to appear in Britain at that time, and since one of the first history primer series was edited by Louise's friend J. R. Green, she began to consider doing a book herself. Creighton had already agreed to do a volume for the Green series. Since he was teaching Roman history at the time, he found it relatively easy to whip out a thin book, some 127 pages, on the subject. It was eventually published in 1875 and became highly successful, selling several thousand copies annually well into the next century.[54] Interestingly, Creighton maintained that one reason for the huge success of these primers was that 'they were just a convenient size and shape to be used by schoolboys as missiles to hurl at one another, and their consequent speedy destruction served to promote a rapid sale'.[55]

Louise eventually also turned her research into a small primer also, a book dealing with England's foreign policy in the middle ages published under the title *England: A Continental Power. From the Conquest to Magna Carta, 1066–1216*.[56] Mandell further encouraged Louise to review books, a form of academic writing in itself. Knowing C. P. Scott, editor of the *Manchester Guardian*, from undergraduate days, Creighton arranged for Louise to submit reviews. 'My first appearance in print was in the pages of *The Manchester Guardian*', she said; and, after having several reviews published, she was paid a total of six guineas. 'But I did not take to reviewing', she confessed, and 'was glad to give it up for historical work.'[57]

Louise discovered in the spring of 1872 that she was expecting a child. 'We both would have liked to wait a little before having children', she admitted. 'It did not interfere much with my life, only my walks had to grow shorter. My mother undertook to provide all the baby clothes. She was an exquisite needle-woman, and and made them all herself, very simple but beautiful workmanship.'[58] Louise's letters during the pregnancy certainly underscore the delicate language Victorians used in discussing such things. The following letter shows how Louise first broached the subject to her mother:

18 April 1872

Dearest Mother,

I am much amused at the way in which you and Mrs Muriel put your two old heads together and consult about me and then prescribe for me without knowing that anything is the matter with me. I will [have] none of your prescriptions. I am perfectly well—never was better in my life, as may be testified by the fact that I have this afternoon walked over seven miles with Max and am none the worse for it. Also Max says I look more flourishing than he ever saw any human being look, so you see I am not in a very bad way.

As for the matter which I mentioned, it is nothing serious; my habits are perfectly regular, daily I may remark and the only thing that struck me was to put it medically—that occasionally my, shall we call them bowels, were not quite active enough. Now as I was taking magnesia which is said to have an aperient effect, this think me as absurd. I now take no more magnesia and am just as well if not better without it. I may also remark that I rarely if ever feel sick now and am in fact quite flourishing. I think that by eating as much fruit and vegetables as possible I shall keep all right. Rhubarb I have stewed long and with much sugar when it becomes nice and is altogether superior to rhubarb in tarts. We both eat it in quantities thinking it to be most wholesome.

I want none of your medicines or machines you see, and and write at once to save you trouble in uselessly getting or sending such. Send me diapers when you have an opportunity with directions as to how the articles must be made. Also will you be kind enough to think of any other simple articles such as perhaps shifts or flannels which I might make if you showed me how.

Is there not a sort of soup to be made of spinach and lettuce things which is thick and green and nice? I wonder, if there is, you would send me the receipt ...

> Goodbye. Much love to Papa from your loving child,
> Louise [59]

The Creightons began the custom of spending a few weeks each summer, from late July to the middle of August, visiting Mandell's family in Cumberland. For Louise at least these visits were 'certainly more a duty than a pleasure for us in many ways as life there is not exciting, still one does not like to think of that; they, poor people, have so little pleasure of any kind that of course they count greatly upon our visit'. Elsewhere she wrote that Kirkandrews 'was not a very amusing place to stay, and the immediate country was not interesting, but we made some nice expeditions always and otherwise used the time for a lot of quiet work'.[60] From the Creighton's family home in Kirkandrews, Louise wrote to her mother on 27 July 1872 saying she was feeling well toward the end of her sixth month, and that she found her medical doctor at Oxford

> quite unobjectionable tho' not [a] mildly exciting old man. He delivered a short address to me which I suppose he keeps ready for such occasions, the upshot of which seemed to me to be that I was not to fuss and do whatever I liked and felt able for, which seemed to me excellent advice. He seems to be much occupied in attending upon such cases and is apparently a good old soul ... [61]

In September, Mandell and Louise spent a few weeks in Falmouth where Mandell lectured again to the ladies' club, and where they both combined his lecturing responsibility with a relaxing holiday for the two of them on the south coast.[62] Then they returned to Oxford in early October, just three weeks before the expected birth of her child. Louise had written to her mother about this time to assure her that she need not come to be with her, that a Mrs Giles, a midwife, 'will do all things needful; and you see I am so ridiculously well and strong that I am sure everything will pass by most quietly. Mrs Fox and Mrs Genn neither of them could ever get over their surprise at my state of health. They always wished to treat me as an invalid and then soon perceived how utterly unnecessary it was.' But Mrs von Glehn apparently insisted on being there at the birth. Louise told her mother that when they had gone to Falmouth a few weeks before, she had learned to her 'disgust,' that a childhood friend, a Mary Schwabe, 'had published abroad in Falmouth everything about my state of health, when I expected my confinement and so on ... Of course [everyone in Falmouth] would have found it out soon enough but I don't see the fun of publishing those things to the four corners of the world.'[63] Concluding her letter, Louise wrote:

> May I trust in you blindly to supply me with all things needful? Perhaps you won't have time when you come home [from Europe]? Is there anything I ought to get? For instance how about a bassinet? Then again will the little creature require any sort of bath beyond an ordinary foot bath at first? Perhaps that, however, will do when Mrs Giles comes but just tell me if there is anything I ought to do or get. I can assure you that if moving is a sign of health, mine will be a most healthy child; its nature is decidedly very rampageous.[64]

On 31 October 1872 a baby girl was born at their home with only the assistance of a midwife. The daughter was named Beatrice after Dante's great love. The baby arrived earlier than expected. Her mother, who had planned to be there at the birth, was 'to have brought all the clothes and other necessaries with her; there was no nurse in the house and we two young and inexperienced people were alone. However, Max soon fetched Dr Freeborn; he produced a nurse, borrowed clothes [and other necessities] from a neighbour and all went well. My mother came in the afternoon to find Beatrice safely there. I knew nothing about children.'[65] Louise had to admit that she found motherhood more challenging than she had previously thought, and expressed serious doubt about

> the value of what is called the maternal instinct in rational human beings, who love and care for their children for other reasons than instinct. We both felt much interest in our neatly shaped little brown baby; Beatrice was not red, or fat, or in any way unsightly, but what my family would have called a very neat baby. I, of course, nursed her myself, as I did all my other children, for nine months. Without being as particular as the young mothers of the next generation in all sanitary and health matters, I studied them as far as I could, and tried to make the nursery life in every way healthy and simple. The baby clothes were simple and practical. I learned how to wash and dress her and do everything for her myself; but as I had a capable and experienced nurse, she did not interfere very much with my life; only the fact that I nursed her kept me from going about much, and this as it went on with the other children did prevent me sharing many of Max's expeditions and walks which was a very real deprivation.[66]

Louise's nurse, whom she described as 'fat and ugly, and essentially vulgar tho' very kind', was an experienced woman named Eliza, and she remained with the family for seven years.[67]

Being a parent took some getting used to for Mandell also. Before they were married he had candidly expressed the view to Louise that for him to show affection to children would hardly be easy. 'It would be a ghastly piece of hypocrisy on my part to do so', he confessed, 'Let us tell the truth and shame the devil; I will learn all those things in good time.' Now that a child was born to them, Louise also found him slow to express any real affection for the little one.[68] Like most parents, Louise and Mandell had 'great talks' about the education and the future of their children as they came to be born; and they decided that they were 'the kind of people who might be expected to have distinguished children', though in later years Louise admitted

> we never had any illusions as to the nature and extent of their gifts. I expect that we were really too critical of them. We were never a family given to mutual admiration. I believe Max and I were really over-critical because we wanted so much from our children. But in spite of being so critical I fancy that I really thought there were no children that could be compared with ours. I expect we both praised too little. I have often wondered whether it was a real loss to the children that we never had an entirely satisfactory nurse, never one who played a great part in their lives.[69]

In the middle of August 1873, the Creightons took their first journey together to Italy, leaving nine-month-old Beatrice at Sydenham. They reached Milan on 20 August and then travelled on to Piacenza, Modena, Pistoia, Lucca, Pisa, then to Siena, and from there to Florence. They avoided the 'smart big hotels full of tourists', and wandered through the towns and villages soaking up the culture. At that time of year the 'heat was excessive. We used to get up between five and six, and after breakfast outside our café, wander about seeing churches till lunch at ten o'clock, after which we took refuge from the heat in picture galleries or museums. The afternoon had to be spent resting with closed shutters till, after dinner at five o'clock, the cool of the evening tempted us out again.'[70] They rounded off the day sitting outside a café, Mandell smoking his cigarettes with Louise beside him, reflecting on the day as both watched people pass by. After spending two weeks in Florence, they journeyed on to Cortona, Arezzo, Perugia, Assisi, Ancona, Loreto, Rimini, Ravenna and Bologna. Creighton was particularly impressed with the town of Assisi; as a result, he developed a special fondness for St Francis, whom he called the 'poet among the saints' because he considered that his life had been lived like a poem. Louise remembered later that while in Italy, they were very diligent sightseers; not from a sense of duty, but because we loved it; we went to very poky little inns, and travelled as simply as possible. One of the little troubles which I remember was that Max never seemed to get hungry, and after a breakfast of only a cup of coffee and a roll in some small café I used to become very starving long before he wanted lunch or had found a place where he wished to lunch. We did not this time discover the joy of country rambles and walks which played so great a part in our later journeys. We confined ourselves entirely to the little towns.[71]

Of the several letters Louise wrote to her mother during their journey, the one from Turin on 25 September 1873 is an interesting example:

Dearest Mother,

I write to warn you that you may see us a little sooner than I first thought. We have as usual changed our plans and are going back by the Mont Cenis, instead of the Brenner. We suddenly remembered that the cholera was particularly bad at Munich and that it was perhaps hardly wise to stop there. The Brenner trains are anyhow very inconvenient and quite impracticable unless one stops at Munich, so we had to give up that scheme and come home this way.

I was sorry because I had much wished to stop at Verona again and also see Munich, but this way is really much more convenient, the trains are much quicker, and leaving Italy just at the same time as we otherwise should have done, we shall have a couple of days in Paris instead of at Munich and yet get to you two days sooner, namely on Tuesday instead of on Thursday next. This will not I hope be inconvenient to you; if you haven't got room for us, we can sleep at the Greyhound [inn] you know, and if you have a large dinner party on Tuesday evening, you know it won't disturb us and we will eat a crust of bread in our bedroom.

Max is glad to get to England in good time and it is much better for him than to come racing home only just in time to his work. We have been travelling about a great deal lately and I think he is beginning to feel that he has had enough of railways. Since Perugia we have been at many jolly places. Assisi we enjoyed greatly, and Loretto was very interesting and curious. Then we had a day at Rimini where there is a wonderful church and where Max had a letter. Unfortunately I got no letter there as we were much too soon, and not going to Innsbruck. I shall get no letters now any more, which is very sad, and I am so sorry to have given you the trouble of writing uselessly, but it is not worth while to write for them, as they would never succeed in catching us till we got to Sydenham. I feel a little sad at hearing nothing for so long, but it can't be helped, and I must trust that all is right.

From Rimini we went to Ravenna, where I was delighted to see the mosaics and we also had a drive to the famous pine forest where one sees acres of stone pines, which are too lovely. Then we went to Bologna where we staid [sic] two days, as we had neither of us seen it very properly, and also we wanted to get some clothes washed. Then yesterday we came here; to-morrow we start on the long journey to Paris, which however we mean to break at Mâcon, getting to Paris on Saturday night. We shall stay there Sunday and Monday as we want to see the pictures a little, and also repose ourselves after such a long railway journey. We are thinking of going to the Hotel du Louvre so as to be near the pictures.

As far as we know at present we shall come on Tuesday by Calais and Dover, so you may expect us to dinner. We have had some more very hot weather at Ancona, Ravenna and Bologna, but here it is cooler, and we feel that to-morrow we shall be plunged into winter at once. It is very sad to think that to-day is actually our last day in Italy; but we have enjoyed ourselves thoroughly and are quite satisfied with what we have had, as indeed we ought to be. Turin seems to me like a small Paris and there is apparently nothing to be seen but the pictures; they, however, are very interesting.

I shall see you so soon now that I may as well keep my news till we meet. I am rejoicing much at the prospect. I wonder whether Beatrice will have quite forgotten us. Much love to you all.

Your loving child,
Louise [72]

Creighton's interest in Italy was significantly enhanced by this 1873 trip. His studies over the last several years had been moving toward Italian topics. Now his first-hand impressions of contemporary Italy, its simple, unpretentious people living amid great legacies of fine art and sumptuous architecture—relics of a glorious medieval past—only convinced him the more to delve further into the Italian Renaissance. The trip proved to be a turning point in his academic outlook and career, for when he returned to commence the new term, he began to lay plans for a research project on the popes in the Renaissance, which would fulfil his scholarly dream and bring him national acclaim. In his lectures the next year, Italy and the Renaissance began to shine forth.

By the beginning of 1874, the Creightons had decided to look for a house nearer Merton College. The distance of their house from the college 'added much to the fatigue of Creighton's work', Louise claimed, and upon learning that Beam Hall, a house directly across the cobblestone street from the college entrance, was about to become vacant, they jumped at the chance to rent it. 'We had always wished to live in the town of Oxford and nearer to College, and to get away from the atmosphere of villadom.' [73] Beam Hall, formerly known as Biham Hall after Geoffrey Biham, was owned by Corpus Christi College; it still stands virtually as it did in August 1874 when the Creightons moved in. The house was in 'a rather dirty and dilapidated condition' but, after some preparation, it was made ready for occupancy. 'It had a beautiful panelled room which was painted white and arranged as Max's study; all the rooms were exceptionally charming. There was one room with a high oak beamed-pointed ceiling, like a small college hall which—as it was difficult of approach, only to be reached either through the kitchen premises or the drawing-room—we made into our bedroom, and a very uncommon bedroom it was.'[74]

That summer Louise was expecting their second child. A baby girl, born on 26 July 1874, was named Lucia after the lady who comforted Dante in his Earthly Paradise. Since Louise was unable to travel that year, Creighton took a ten day trip shortly after Lucia was born, visiting Normandy by himself, seeing such places as Caen, Bayeux and Mont-St-Michel. Polly, Mandell's sister, had come down from Carlisle to help Louise in the early days of her confinement. It was after Creighton returned from Normandy in early August that they moved to Beam Hall, with Louise directing things from her bed. They were still getting things organised in Beam Hall when the Creightons were suddenly confronted with one of the biggest decisions of their married lives. As Louise recalled it, 'I used to sit in one room after another during the days that followed and direct the willing Polly where to hang pictures, arrange books and etc. It was whilst we were so engaged that Max came in one day and said that the vicar of Embleton, one of the two best livings of the College, had died, and that the living would certainly be offered to him as the fellows senior to him were sure to refuse it.'[75] As it turned out, two senior fellows turned the offer down and Mandell was now certain to be presented with the opportunity of becoming the next vicar of Embleton, a large rural parish located some forty miles north of Newcastle on the North Sea coast.[76]

Creighton, both as deacon and priest, had preached regularly in the college chapel; and his sermons, many having been reprinted, reveal an ethical practicality—more so than spiritual insight—which targeted the lives of undergraduate students. A predominate theme was to attack that 'languid indolence which only feebly hopes to fill up somehow the hours spent out of bed'.[77] His preaching, admittedly dry by modern homiletic standards, was generally well enough received by the collegiate congregations, though he was probably more effective from the lectern than the pulpit in his earlier years.

By the summer of 1874, he felt his life was becoming too confined. Marriage and children no doubt coloured his outlook. When he had accepted a clerical fellowship a few years before, the prospect of the peaceful bachelor life of a tutorial fellow had appeared sufficiently satisfying. Now, with a family and a desire to write serious history, and possibly even to gain a coveted professorship, Mandell came to realise that his undergraduate conception of a tutorial fellow's life was ostensibly at a dead-end.[78] He must have been toying with these ideas when he announced to Louise his interest in considering accepting a rural living if it were offered to him. Of course this option was fuelled greatly by his decision to do a thorough study of the Renaissance papacy. Pastoral work and financial advantage were not serious factors in his decision to leave Oxford. He had sufficient opportunity in Oxford to preach and carry out clerical duties; and the salary gain would not be great. As a don his annual income as fellow and senior tutor was about £720, not counting examining fees from the modern history school and vacation lecture stipends. The annual income as vicar of Embleton was only marginally better, £840.[79] What really tipped the scales in favour of the move north was simply the fact that he desired a less demanding environment where he could enjoy more leisure time reading and writing. What he may have really had in the back of his mind was, ultimately, a professorship; and a professorship would only come with the leisure to research and publish.[80] For him at that time, the church may have seemed a better path, oddly enough, than the university.

Creighton, who once described Oxford life as trying to live 'in a house which always has the workmen about it', wanted to inspect Embleton. While visiting his family in Cumberland in mid September he made a short trip to Northumberland and liked what he saw. While he found the old medieval church to his liking, he particularly relished the large vicarage that would surely afford him the ample peace and quiet he desired. After his return to Oxford, Louise said there followed a period of agonising indecision. The decision, however, was more agonising for Louise than for Mandell. For all intents and purposes Creighton's mind was made up. He wanted to accept the living if it was offered to him by the time he returned to Oxford.

From Kirkandrews, Mandell wrote to Louise about the pros and cons of the matter, pointing out to her that the advantages of staying at Oxford were the 'stimulus of intellectual society' and the 'facilities of consulting libraries', while, on the other hand, the advantages of going to Embleton were 'quiet and energy undisturbed by struggles concerning [my] work' and an 'opportunity of uninterrupted work all the year round, and concentration of intellectual energy on one subject'.[81] Louise did not favour the move, having just settled into their new home adjacent to Merton College with all its conveniences—including the use of college servants—and having given birth to her second child. The prospects of being uprooted were not appealing and to move to a remote corner of Northumberland must have seemed like social exile. In her letters to her husband while he was at Kirkandrews she showed no real endorsement of the move, which brought a response from Mandell, dated 23 September 1874:

Your remarks about Embleton and the necessity for meditation are just: we cannot exaggerate the importance of the determination taken in the matter; it will decide our future. Your immediate remarks do not seem to me, however, to be of any great value. You give me two reasons against Embleton, which, you will permit me to say, are futile. When you ask who will take my place in Oxford, I am inclined to smile: never was a place where men are so easily replaced and so soon forgotten ...

You next ask, what is the best thing for me to do? Where would I be most useful? I answer, a man is equally useful everywhere if he is doing his best. In talking about what is best for me there is a certain ambiguity. Do you mean best for my fame or for my happiness? About it being best for my fame, so far as that is concerned with being talked about by the set of people who do the most talking, that is best consulted by staying at Oxford; as to my abiding fame, if I ever had ever so little, I am not sure; as to my happiness, again, I am not sure. If you helped me on these points with your views, you would be doing more that was definitely useful.

Your considerations, however, omit the most essential point. By going to Embleton I get quietness and security ... What is it that makes an Oxford life seem agreeable? You will answer, quiet, pleasant occupation, congenial society. I answer, at present I have no quiet ... A Cabinet minister has not to be more careful of his proceedings, or feel that he holds office on a less secure tenure ... I am, though nominally a Fellow of the College, really a subordinate official in the employment of the unmarried Fellows, of whom certainly a strong minority have expressed their opinion that they may treat a tutor as a governing body does a head master ... A change of Warden might render the College intolerable to me at any moment ... If I were unmarried I could hold my Fellowship and do work for other colleges, which would be pleasant enough; it is impossible to do enough teaching in Oxford without a Fellowship. I have no chance of any University office at present, or I would not dream of going. An Oxford life is delightful, if one has it properly; but in seven years more I have to sue for re-election ... Really, the state of things is this: I want to lead a literary, not an active life. Which helps me most, Embleton or Oxford? [82]

The answer to that question was clear enough to Louise. Then on the following day he wrote to her that his letter yesterday 'consisted of matter for your reflection. Don't suppose that the arguments there put forward are considered by me as conclusive of the matter. I only feel them to be very strong.' He stated that they could not 'look to Oxford as our abiding resting place. Shall we let ourselves grow old in its allurements before we quit it? We cannot secure a College living just when necessary ... That is the worst of it; literary application and tutoring don't run side by side. They may at a swell college ... The tendency of Oxford is to make me a teaching drudge, and prevent me from being a literary student.' [83]

Then two days later Creighton wrote of the matter again from Kirkandrews:

> You say you like Oxford society more than I do: I grant it: you are younger, and have not had so much of it. I have long felt how trumpery it is ... an interchange of things meant to be clever, but not containing much that is real or true. It is more pleasant to talk over schemes of education in a drawing-room than to work them out in a poor parish; and 'society' gives you all the advantage of looking very wise and very good without much cost of actual effort. I only make these remarks to clear up another point. I think on this matter our being separated for a week has done us much good. We have had to think and write away from one another, and, perhaps have thereby, learned to see the question more clearly.
>
> I submitted the question to Mr [William] Gunson [Creighton's cousin] yesterday, as an impartial person, knowing me and knowing colleges, and being worldly wise. I feel much strengthened by the fact that he, after carefully inquiring into the facts of the case, concluded that I would not be justified in letting Embleton pass. He concluded by saying, 'You will miss books, but you must just economise and buy them ... My general view is certainly to take it if it comes, unless ocular inspection discloses some horrors.' [84]

Louise claimed that her 'one desire' was to do what would be best for her husband, admitting that she 'hated the thought of leaving my delightful life at Oxford'.[85] From her point of view the issue remained in doubt, for she wrote to her mother on 22 October that they were 'still more undecided than ever about Embleton, and what will happen I know not in the least'. She felt they would make up their minds by early November, but added that she would 'be at a loss' to say what decision they would make. 'There is so much to be said on both sides', she explained. 'People here mostly object greatly and say that Max ought not to leave the work which he is doing here ... As far as I can discover my own sentiments, I think that I personally wish for it a good deal, but I do not want to influence Max one way or another in his decision ...' [86]

In another letter to her mother a couple of weeks later, she said she felt that the situation had not changed and that advice on what they should do was coming from all quarters of Oxford. 'It is endlessly discussed', she wrote, 'so that, were the subject not so important for us, I should quite weary of it. People give very different advice and we get torn different ways in turn. There is so very much to be said on both sides, and it is very hard to get at a quite satisfactory conclusion.' As a rule, she said, 'married people advise us to go and single men advise us to stay', Louise told her mother. 'Shall we not judge therefrom that to go is the wisest course for the married man with a large family?' She concluded by saying that things generally pointed to their going to Embleton.[87]

Students drafted a petition imploring Creighton to remain at Merton, while some of his colleagues also urged him to stay with promises of his being nominated for the position of warden of Merton when the post became vacant. The petition and the faculty support pleased Creighton to be sure, but the prospects of being made warden or given some other promotion was of little consequence. Years later he wrote to a friend: 'When I left Oxford for parochial work, I received a petition signed by all the undergraduates of Merton asking me to stay. It was a sore thing to turn away from such an expression of goodwill, but I have not regretted that more and more arduous work has followed on my decision.' [88] Elsewhere, Creighton explained more succinctly his reasons why he chose to leave Oxford:

> I had felt that the manifold activities required of me—I was the Senior Tutor, and taught both ancient and modern history for honours men, besides taking a share of pass work—were an obstacle to gaining any thorough knowledge. I thought that the period of papal history between the Great Schism and the Reformation had never been adequately considered. In England, Gibbon skipped it, and Milman was tired out before he reached it. In German there was no connected book. So a desire for less mental dissipation led me into the country.[89]

By 12 November 1874, when Merton College formally offered him the Embleton living, Creighton was ready and eager to accept it. When hearing of the appointment, a fellow tutor unwittingly predicted: 'Then you will end by being Archbishop of Canterbury!' [90]

8

Exile

'In a sense I felt it as an exile; my friends and the social intercourse of
Oxford had meant much to me. It used to come home to me, especially
during the dark winter days, that there I was, far away, and there were
all those delightful people quite out of my reach.'

Louise Creighton [1]

Embleton is located along the barren North Sea coast about midway between
Newcastle and Edinburgh. At the time the Creightons came to Embleton,
the village was a mixture of random grey stone cottages, several modest
shops and five public houses, all clustered along the one road that ran
through the village. The villagers, some 600 of them, were mostly people
who worked in the nearby whinstone quarry. Probably Embleton's most
famous son was William T. Stead, the noted Victorian journalist and author
who went down on the *Titanic* in 1912.[2]

The parish, roughly seven miles long and five miles wide, had a population
of about 1700. Within the parish there were several other villages, including
Newton-by-the-Sea, two miles north of Embleton, which was really two
fishing hamlets—Upper Newton and Newton Sea Houses—and Craster
three miles south of Embleton. Men of these villages, for the most part,
fished for herring and haddock in the winter while the women spent their
days in the curing yards cleaning, salting and packing fish for export. To
any suggestion that the work was dirty, the reply was: 'Aye, but the money's
clean.' [3] The remainder of the parish population consisted of farm families
and agricultural labourers living in the isolated houses and cottages that
dotted the countryside. There were only two links to the outside world
from Embleton. One was the dirt road, always muddy in the winter and
spring, that connected Embleton to the market town of Alnwick seven miles
south; the other was the North Eastern Railway that ran from London to
Edinburgh, with trains occasionally stopping at Christon Bank station two
miles west of Embleton. The small village of Christon Bank near the station
was largely given over to railwaymen and their families. Nearby was Fallodon
Hall, one of the houses of the powerful Grey family.[4]

'Travellers who rush swiftly through Northumberland by the North Eastern Railway on their way to Edinburgh', Louise observed,

> can think of it only as a rather dreary, featureless country, and if they knew where and when to look, they might catch glimpses of blue sea, of a stream at the bottom of a deep wooded glen, or of a grey tower rising above some trees; but they will have no idea of the treasures of interest and beauty which they are passing by. Many may even visit a Northumbrian village and come away with no impression except that it is grim and grey and quite without any beauty. One must know Northumberland and its people to feel their special charm, and then there will be no other county that can compare with it.[5]

Much of the 'special charm' of the region is associated with the scenic Embleton coastline that stretches from the rocky headland ten miles to the north, where Bamburgh Castle sits securely on the black basalt cliff, to the brooding remains of John of Gaunt's Dunstanburgh Castle two miles to the south, ruins that rise like broken fingers of some primeval giant. On one summer's day in the 1870s the colours of the beach and sea, thought one visitor, rivalled the French Riviera in beauty.[6] The long, wide beach along the Northumbrian coast, a curious mixture of sand and crushed yellow shells, when caught under a sky of sun and wind-bundled clouds gives off a blazing golden hue. Moving inward, the beach gives way to low ochre-coloured sandhills and then green undulating slopes lined with irregular rows of scattered stone houses. Looking inland to the west are broad fields of green grass and bracken, low hedges with random clusters of wood that shelter old pele towers and grey farmhouses; from there the land rises towards the sweeping moors of Charlton and Chillingham, and on to the violet hills of Cheviot in the distance. The bracing air of Embleton, someone once said, is cool, keen and invigorating, like champagne—even in summer.[7] Winters, of course, were harsh, often violent, with biting gusts and flying snow, but the summers, as if in nature's great apology, brought extended sunny days and persistent winds that scoured the landscape of winter's harsh residue.

> As one approaches Embleton along the Alnwick road from the south—in 1875 or even today—the grey stone tower of the medieval church peeks above the tops of old oaks, willows and sycamores. Then where the road dips and rises again, the fortified vicarage house comes into view, then the old walled garden beyond the line of red-tiled stables tucked within a cluster of trees; and further on stretches a field with an old stone dovecote.[8] The church shows traces of twelfth-century stonework; its nave and tower, with some Norman features, were constructed of grey sandstone between 1330 and 1340. The remaining parts of the church, such as the chancel, porches, windows, pulpit, tablets and brasses, are more modern. In the churchyard, no longer used for burials, are the graves of

former vicars and many prominent locals including some members of the Grey families, notably Sir George Grey, former cabinet secretary and son of Prime Minister Earl Grey of Reform Bill fame.[9]

The vicarage, privately owned after Merton College sold it in the early 1980s, has been restored to much of its nineteenth-century elegance. A 'large and convenient house', in Louise's words, the vicarage stood on about eight acres of land adjacent to the church.[10] The original structure was the fourteenth-century 'pele' (or 'peel') tower, a massive fortified structure of thick sandstone built for protection during all-too-frequent border raids. The term 'pele' or 'peel' probably comes from the Celtic word for 'hill-fort', although there is no universal agreement on this.[11] After the parish was laid waste by marauding bands of Scots in the 1380s, the vicar was granted permission in the reign of Edward IV to build the tower. Narrow openings in the corners of the walls were placed so that an archer could shoot in two directions. The vaulted chamber on the ground floor was used for sheltering livestock, with upper rooms protecting as many parishioners as managed to squeeze in. The tower, not strong enough to stand a lengthy siege, however, only afforded limited security during a raid.[12]

The modern additions to the vicarage, now the main living quarters, were built of black basalt and attached to the tower. The first addition was constructed in the 1780s; the remaining parts, designed by the famed Northumbrian architect John Dobson, were added in the early 1830s. The conservatory was built a couple of decades later. The vicarage, when combining the tower and the additions, is approximately 8000 square feet with seventeen fireplaces, a number of large and small ground floor rooms, and a vaulted foyer with its own fireplace to warm frozen visitors who came to see the vicar. At the far end of the foyer is an elegant spiral staircase that leads to the upper level bedrooms, dressing-rooms, nursery and servant quarters. Just off the foyer, on the right, is a small waiting room for guests. Across the way, opposite, is the library study. On the garden side of the house, running parallel to the pleasant terrace and large sloping tree-studded lawns, are the drawing-room, dining-room, pantry and kitchen. The drawing-room opens onto the conservatory with its Georgian roof composed of small pieces of glass arranged as a dome. The kitchen and utility rooms in the rear lead to a large kitchen garden bounded by a lovely long wall of old Dutch bricks, brought by some ship as ballast during the early part of the nineteenth century when Alnmouth exported grain to Holland. The vicarage was certainly large enough for live-in servants and the expanding Creighton family, with sufficient rooms for guests sleeping over.[13]

In the Creightons' time, there was a narrow lane running along side the property and behind the stables, barn, and other outbuildings that connected to the old station road beyond the hill in the rear. For visitors coming to the vicarage, however, the approach was through the gate along the Alnwick road, just south of the village, and down the tree-lined gravel driveway to the circular turn-about in front of the old tower and adjoining house with its parapets, protruding upper bay window and small Tudor-Gothic porch. This must all have caught the eye of Louise when she first saw the vicarage in March of 1875 as the carriage drove up the Alnwick road and turned into the shaded lane.

Over the Christmas vacation of 1874 Creighton had travelled north from Oxford to Auckland where he was installed as vicar by C. T. Barring, Bishop of Durham; he then proceeded to Embleton to look over the vicarage, the church and the parish. Having arrived earlier than expected, Creighton found no one to greet him and wandered off on his own in the direction of the vicarage, soon becoming lost in a sudden snow storm—a characteristic winter welcome of Northumberland. He eventually found refuge in the farmhouse of one of the churchwardens. Mandell wrote to Louise of his experience the following day from the safe confines of the vicarage:

Romantic adventures befell me on entering my parish which at the time I reached it was something like the North Pole. When my train had got a little way from Newcastle, a great wind began to arise from the sea. When I landed at Christon Bank Station the snow was drifting fast before the wind, and the sky was black with clouds.

No one was there to meet me, as I had said that I did not expect to be there before eight, whereas I got there at four. I started, however, to walk, as I thought the way was straight, and I could not miss it. But the sky grew blacker and the wind fiercer and the drifting snow dimmed my spectacles so that I saw not, and I often sank up to my middle in a great bank of snow blown across the road. After an hour of simply struggling blindly onwards I saw a house, to which I made my way. I found I had come a wrong road, and on being directed rightly retraced my steps, though with some doubts, since the wind was rising more and more, whether I should ever find my way after all, since it was now five o'clock and getting dark. However, the lady of the house had seen me and dispatched her household to bring me back, which with great difficulty they did.

As luck would have it, this was the house of one of my churchwardens: his wife had guessed who I was when she heard a stranger had been inquiring the way, and her heart had warmed towards me. I asked for a man-servant to show me the way.

Meanwhile we had some tea. The wind waxed higher; at six o'clock, when I rose to go, the drift against the front gate prevented it from being opened. I had to stay all night, the roads being impassable. It was a fearful night; the house shook before the blast, and the fine snow was blown in at every window ... This morning is a fine bright sunny morning, and the snow-drifts being somewhat hardened on the top, I made a kind of Alpine expedition hither: my great doubt now is whether it will be possible by any means the art of man can devise to get my luggage hither.[14]

The next day he wrote that the thaw was beginning to set in and, with all the snowdrifts, the roads were reduced to 'a state of slush perfectly awful to behold, and almost impossible to walk in'. Mandell said he did his 'first Sunday school this morning, and found it not so bad; but all the arrangements of every sort have fallen into waste during this interim, and I shall have to devote some energy to working them up', adding:

I like the house at Embleton more and more; it has great capabilities, but will want heaps of money to furnish: I quite shudder at the thought ... At present I go on slowly trying to find out things gradually, as there is so much quite new to me, and I have not yet got my views together. The village and the people are very much as I expected, and will require much labour to make an impression on. They will find our quiet ways a great change from the Rookes [the outgoing vicar and family] with their large family.[15]

A couple of days later, he wrote that the 'thaw goes on, but only makes the roads more impassable. I am regularly weather-bound, and see no chance of getting to see my parish in its length and breadth. The thaw turns the roads into deep mud, alternating with partially thawed snow-drifts, on which when you tread you stick up to your middle in slush.' Creighton, in his words, 'staggered over' to see the Greys at Fallodon Hall, a two-mile walk. Fallodon Hall was one of the two houses of the Grey family, the other being Howick Hall, a few miles to the south. Originally a part of the barony of Alnwick in the twelfth century, Fallodon belonged to a number of owners before the Greys of Howick acquired it in 1755. The second Earl Grey, famous for his connection with Catholic Emancipation and the Reform Bill of 1832, was born at Fallodon.[16] The Greys were one of the old local aristocratic families of the region. One branch of the family occupied Howick Hall, the other resided at Fallodon.[17]

In his last letter before returning to Oxford, Mandell wrote about his visit to Alnwick, stretching out along the River Alne within the shadows of the Duke of Northumberland's castle. He thought the town 'a nice old place, not much of a town, but the castle is splendid, and the church very fine'. He continued:

The people are very friendly, and generally well disposed. I find the villagers very kindly, and a general desire to be hospitable: they are quite prepared to take me on trial, but they will not accept one without fair criticism, and their approval will never be without reserve. Blind enthusiasm is not to be expected; but they are not the least cantankerous, and will give everyone a fair chance. Drunkenness is their great weakness; otherwise they are just the good sturdy people I expected ... Embleton as a village is not much; it is scattered about and huddled together along the ridge of rock between us and the sea. I have been down to the sea, which has the loveliest coloured sand I ever saw. I never saw sand so yellow ...[18]

Before he left Embleton, Creighton made necessary arrangements for moving into the vicarage later that spring. Recalling their move north in Easter week, March 1875, Louise wrote that there was

a tremendous time of hard work getting settled in. We had to arrange the house so as to be ready to receive the Arthur Aclands as well as ourselves. It had been decided that he should come and be Max's curate for the first six months, and as there was no possible accommodation for them in the village and the vicarage was large, we arranged that they should live with us. They had one boy, Francis, and another was to be born that summer. We shared household expenses, and settled our life so that we could be as independent as possible of one another, each having a sitting-room into which the other did not enter, but sharing the drawing-room and dining-room. I think the arrangement worked well. We had no disagreeables.[19]

Creighton wanted to make the move to Embleton before the spring, but he had been asked to teach through the Hilary term. The Rev. George Rooke had been vicar at Embleton since 1830 and had lived in the vicarage for forty-four years with his large family. The house needed a thorough cleaning and refurbishing. As it turned out, Louise set about redecorating large portions of the vicarage, including mounting the latest Morris wall-papers, expensive ones. In the dining-room, for example, she put up the popular dark blue-on-white swirling leafy pattern known as the 'Indian design'. She also re-landscaped the gardens, even adding a lawn tennis court off the terrace. What the parishioners thought of all this new elegance after the spartan years of the Rookes is not known. One of the Creightons' neighbours recalled all the change and said that they 'warned us that we were to be roused from our old habits and thoughts, and made to see things with new eyes'.[20]

Creighton's annual income as vicar was £840 in 1875, a fair sum; but for a man with an expanding family and a large house to maintain, he needed more and decided to enhance his salary by taking in resident pupils during the summers and agreed to be an examiner for the history school at Oxford. With fees for tutoring, stipends for examining and some royalties for published writings, Creighton enjoyed a comfortable income.[21] In order to share the work of a large parish and still have leisure time to read and write, Creighton decided to employ a curate to assist him, paying him from his own funds. He first selected Arthur Acland, a young tutor from Keble College. Unfortunately for Creighton, Acland did not remain long as curate at Embleton. At first he seemed interested in parochial work but after several months he left, eventually laying aside his religious orders and turning to politics.[22] Creighton then acquired C. E. Green who came and stayed. He was a man who proved 'excellent as a loyal fellow worker in every way', remarked Louise, though she thought his sermons 'were decidedly dull'. Nevertheless, he became a true friend to the family and Creighton regarded him as 'a jewel of a curate'.[23]

Embleton demanded a great adjustment from the Creightons, more so by Louise. She felt it as 'an exile' and missed Oxford society desperately. 'It used to come home to me,' she confessed, 'especially during the dark winter days, that there I was, far away, and there were all those delightful people quite out of my reach. But really there were hardly any regrets. We never felt that we had made a mistake in leaving Oxford and as I look back on our life I realise more and more how immense was the gain of those years.' [24] Creighton's challenge, of course, was learning to be a pastor, having come from a purely academic life with no pastoral experience and no first-hand knowledge of working people. Presumably his Cumbrian roots helped to some degree in his understanding of the northern character of his parishioners. At first, the Creightons thought the people cold and unfriendly. When meeting someone on the road, for example, the person would pass them by without a word. When told that a Northumbrian expected the vicar or his wife to speak first, the Creightons were then met with a cheerful response that usually began with a comment about the weather. The regional dialect was soft with a sort of plaintive cadence and characterised by a burr, a roll of the r, which was pronounced in the back of the throat.[25] While the character of the people was sturdy and stubborn, their morals left a good deal to be desired, the Creightons thought. Drunkenness barely surpassed graver vices of fornication and adultery. The lack of moral standards in the region convinced Louise that the slums in urban cities were not the only place that turned 'men and women into beasts'. Because Embleton had no resident squire to set standards and demand conformity of behaviour—unlike Craster and Christon Bank—the Creightons came to think they must do more to set the moral standard for their village people who 'were not tolerated in the villages around, and it had a bad reputation in the neighbourhood'. Yet they found some residents of Embleton 'as saintly as could have been found under the most favoured circumstances' anywhere.[26]

After a month and a half in Embleton, Mandell wrote that his life was 'tolerably busy'. He planned his daily routine to fulfil both his ambitions—to be an active pastor and to write history. He spent about four hours each weekday morning closeted in his library reading. Then, after lunch, he made his parish rounds from two to about seven in the evening, 'rambling', as he said, 'among my parishioners'. Evenings were usually spent with his family. After the children were sent to bed, Mandell and Louise would sit in the study until around 11 o'clock, he smoking an occasional cigarette while reading and she writing letters or working on one of her historical projects. 'I like my life here very much,' he wrote to a friend, 'and am far from regretting that I left Oxford.'[27]

Sundays were the busy days. Besides the regular morning service at Embleton, afternoon and evening services were conducted at the villages of Craster and Newton. Both Mandell and his curate, and even Louise, taught at Sunday school. Baptism often followed Embleton morning service; then, after a hasty lunch, either Creighton or Green would walk to Craster and the other set off for Newton. Louise would often walk along with her husband. Then all were back at Embleton for evensong. Creighton generally preached extemporaneously, which is why there are no recorded examples of his homilies. His method of preparing a sermon was to settle on a topic every Monday and then let ideas roam around in his mind for the remainder of the week so that when it came out in the pulpit he had thought it all out logically. If he had any particular problems in preaching it was in communicating his ideas to country folk, to speak plainly and make his points as simply as possible. Eloquence was never his goal according to Louise. As his curate generously remarked: 'Occasionally he might be a little over their heads, but ... in every sermon he preached, there was something which the people might, and I know did, carry away with them.' Creighton believed his sermons should be about one subject, and not leave the impression that it was merely better to be good than to be bad.[28]

Perhaps the most satisfying part of his parochial life was those informal visits in the villages and to farm families in the isolated cottages of his parish. It became an important activity and in a sense fitted his natural gregarious nature, though as his neighbour Albert Grey (later fourth Earl Grey) observed, it was 'a most amusing thing in the world' to watch the learned historian from Oxford 'endeavouring to be at ease with the sunburnt field-labours of Northumbria'.[29] Nevertheless, Creighton seemed to find refreshment in these chats, sometimes giving legal advise on how to make wills or settle disputes within families and among neighbours. He would pray or read with those that were old and ill, and was 'a sympathetic listener to their long yarns about their ailments', Louise said. As one old woman told her: 'Mr Creighton he says it's my digester that is out of order, but I say it's my whole cistern.'[30] He even handed out home-made elixirs on

1. Carlisle's Castle Street in the 1880s with the cathedral at the end of the street. The Creightons' house was on the right side of the street near the church. (*Jim Templeton*)

2. The Creightons' former house on Castle Street (with shop on ground floor and living quarters above) as it looked in the 1880s a few years after the family moved to Kirkandrews. (*Jim Templeton*)

3. Durham cathedral from the railway station. (*James Covert*)

4. Durham Grammar School and playing fields. (*James Covert*)

5. Mandell's family, *c.* 1870. Left to right: James, Robert, Mary Ellen (Polly), Mandell. (*Joan Duncan*)

6. The Crystal Palace in Sydenham. *c.* 1900. (*Lewisham History Centre*)

7. Peak Hill Lodge, Sydenham, *c.* 1880, the house belonging to the von Glehns where Louise was raised. (*Lewisham History Centre*)

8. Sketch of Robert von Glehn, *c.* 1876. (*Christian Creighton*)

9. Louise von Glehn about the time she became engaged to Mandell Creighton in 1871. (*Christian Creighton*)

10. St Bartholomew's church, Sydenham, the parish church of the von Glehns where Louise and Mandell were married. (*Lewisham History Centre*)

11. Mandell Creighton, 1862, during his first year at Merton College, Oxford. (*Christian Creighton*)

12. Mandell's college friends, the 'Quadrilateral', in 1864. From left to right: R. T. Raikes, Mandell Creighton, C. T. Boyd and W. H. Foster. (*Christian Creighton*)

13. South bay of Merton College library. (*Merton College, Oxford*)

14. Mandell Creighton in 1864 at the age of twenty-one, just after taking his first degree at Merton. (*Christian Creighton*)

15. Mandell Creighton, an Oxford don at the age of twenty-seven in 1870, the year before he met Louise von Glehn. (*Christian Creighton*)

16. Merton College tower, watercolour painting by Louise Creighton, *c.* 1873. (*Mary Bailey*)

17. Beam Hall, where the Creightons lived for a time, directly across from Merton College gate. (*James Covert*)

18. Louise Creighton when she was nearly twenty-eight. Painting by her Oxford friend Bertha Johnson. (*Mary Bailey*)

19. Six of the Creighton children standing at the front entrance of Embleton vicarage with donkey ready for a picnic outing on the beach in 1884. Left to right: Lucia, Mary, Oswin, Walter, Beatrice and Cuthbert. (*Christian Creighton*)

20. Embleton vicarage, Northumberland, *c.* 1880, at the time the Creightons lived there. (*Christian Creighton*)

21. Mandell Creighton with three of his daughters, Lucia, Beatrice and Mary, 1888. (*Christian Creighton*)

22. Louise Creighton with her three sons, Walter, Cuthbert and Oswin, 1888. (*Christian Creighton*)

23. Mandell Creighton at the age of thirty-eight in 1881. (*Christian Creighton*)

24. Louise Creighton in the mid 1880s, shortly after leaving Embleton for Cambridge. (*Christian Creighton*)

25. The entrance to Emmanuel College, Cambridge. (*James Covert*)

26. Worcester Cathedral. (*British Travel Association*)

27. A family game of croquet in the palace garden at Peterborough, *c.* 1895. (*Christian Creighton*)

28. Bishop Mandell Creighton in the palace garden at Peterborough, 1893. (*Christian Creighton*)

29. Family and friends after a hockey game at Peterborough. Left to right: Basil, Walter, Winnie (kneeling), unknown, Lucia (seated on ground), Robert, Harold, Ella, Gemma, unknown, and Mary. (*Christian Creighton*)

30. Louise Creighton in the early 1890s. (*Christian Creighton*)

31. Mandell Creighton about the time he became Bishop of London. (*Christian Creighton*)

32. A family holiday in the Lake District in August 1897. Seated (left to right): Oswin, Ella (niece) Basil (nephew), Beatrice, Walter. Standing (left to right): Lucia, Cuthbert, Winifred (niece), Mandell, Marjorie (niece), Louise, Robert (nephew), Mary, Gemma, Harold (nephew), Aunt Polly (Mandell's sister). (*Joan Duncan*)

33. An outing on the banks of Ullswater near Glenridding in the Lake District, August 1897. Seated (left to right): Ella (niece), Louise. Standing on the shore (left to right): Beatrice, Robert (nephew), Aunt Polly (Mandell's sister), Mandell, Winifred and Oswin (far right). In the boat (left to right): Lucia, Basil (nephew), Walter, Mary, Cuthbert, Harold (nephew), Gemma, Marjorie (niece). (*Joan Duncan*)

34. Louise Creighton, painted by Glyn Philpot and unveiled at Lambeth Palace, *c.* 1920. (*Christian Creighton*)

35. The official photograph of Mandell Creighton as Bishop of London, 1897. (*Christian Creighton*)

36. Mandell and Louise Creighton are buried in the chapel of the Order of the British Empire in the eastern end of the crypt at St Paul's. The grave is located under the carpet near the entrance. (*St Paul's Cathedral*)

occasion, the larger the bottle and the nastier the taste, the better the medicine was thought to be.[31]

Even Louise found herself dispensing medical aid, and wrote that after a while:

> there fell into my hands a little book giving directions how to treat ulcered legs, with an account of what a lady had done in this way in some south country parish. I knew one woman who complained of a very bad leg so I got her permission to let me do what I could for it. I made ointments and prepared bandages according to the directions in the book, and having consulted the village doctor started to do what I could. It was a terrible leg with ulcers eating almost down to the bone. She was a big, heavy woman and cure would have been impossible unless she had been willing to go to a hospital for a considerable time which she refused to contemplate; but by keeping the wound clean and bandaging the leg I gave her much relief. I used to try to dress it once a week. I treated some other milder cases, which it was possible to cure.[32]

The Creightons discovered that, in coming to know the Northumbrians, they learned more about themselves. 'It was a splendid thing to be able to share all these new experiences together. I had done a little visiting in a poor street in Oxford, but it did not come to much. Max had never done any. We had neither of us ever taught in a Sunday school. We had no knowledge of the mechanism of parochial life, and we found a large, scattered parish without any organisation.'[33] According to Louise, it was helpful being young and active in carrying out their visitations:

> We did not visit together tho' we used to walk together to a particular village and then separate to visit different families and meet again to walk home together and talk over what we had discovered. I, of course, could not visit nearly as much as he did, and got to know Embleton itself much better than other places. There were some of the scattered farms, practically little villages, to which I seldom if ever went. All this visiting had to be done walking, and in winter the roads were intolerably muddy which greatly increased the fatigue of walking. The roads have been much improved since then by the use of steam rollers.[34]

Both claimed to enjoy visiting and were 'always received with great friendliness whether the people were church people or not', Louise said, 'but Northumbrians are reserved and pride themselves on their so-called independence. They do not give themselves away and it was not easy to get at their hearts.' She went on to suggest that:

> On the whole the less respectable they were the more amusing they were to visit. There was a woman hawker whom I used to visit when I was feeling very dull and whose talk was so amusing that her whole family would gather around to listen whilst she held forth to me. The visits to the farmers' wives were generally

a little stiff and solemn. We were received in their best parlour and sometimes kept waiting whilst they changed their clothes; but with some of them I made real friends. Very few of the houses were unpleasantly dirty or smelly, and it was wonderful how smart even some of the one-roomed cottages were. I don't suppose my visiting was of much, if any, spiritual use to the people, but it promoted friendly relations and I was sometimes able to help them about their children.[35]

A friend visiting Embleton remarked about Creighton's congeniality while out on a walk across his parish: 'Never a walk hardly without turning into some cottage—"Well, Mary, how are you to-day? And how's the old man?"—and all with such charming freshness and naturalness; not a touch of condescension ...'[36] In another instance, when the death of the parents in one family left several children orphaned, Creighton made sure they were taken care of properly. The youngest, a ten-year-old-girl named Eleanor McDonald, lived until she was eighty-nine and remembered the vicar's kindness, saying that he 'always seemed to take such an interest in what we were doing. It didn't matter what it was, cleaning up, sewing, or baking. He used to ask all sorts of questions; really I have never seen a clergyman since who took half the interest that he did. I could tell him all my troubles.'[37] The girl went on to marry, and moved to Yorkshire, eventually returning to Embleton. Creighton stayed in touch with her over the years and went out of his way to visit her on a couple of occasions.

'We were generally given tea when we visited at a farmer's house and sometimes in the cottages', Louise said. 'Visiting taught much about the lives of the people and certainly enlarged my experience and I hope my sympathies.'[38] What she disliked most about parochial life was Sunday school teaching and directing the choir. Even Mandell the teacher did not relish Sunday school teaching: 'We used to wake on Sunday morning with the sense of a weight hanging over us', Louise explained. 'We had to teach several classes in one room, where each class was distracted by the next; such other teachers as we could get to help were very inefficient, and very rare.'[39] When they came to Embleton the practice was to have both a morning and afternoon Sunday school, but they soon dropped the afternoon session. The vicar's wife was generally responsible for the choir. Louise found that, though she admitted she had 'very little ear' for handling the choir, the experience proved successful enough. She had about twenty-five women from the village, or nearby farms, and conducted choir practices every Friday evening.

Creighton instituted an annual Christmas ball at the vicarage for the choir members when they rolled up the rugs in the drawing-room and, with local musicians, stepped lively to old country dances the evening long.

Mandell enjoyed dancing with each woman and was adamant about not allowing a person, tired and gasping, to stop in the middle of a dance in hopes of securing a retreat to the dining-room for refreshments or rest.[40] There were dances in the vicarage on other occasions too. Louise wrote of one in January 1877:

> Our dance came off on Wednesday with great success ... Tuesday the drawing-room was all turned out and prepared for the dancing; Wednesday there was enough to do getting the supper table etc. ready. Our guests arrived at 7; we were forty-four altogether; our music was the only thing which was not quite successful. The fiddler whom we had engaged had felt so bashful in coming to what he considered such a grand house that he had cheered his spirits by a little whisky first, and the whisky seemed to have gone to his fingers and made his playing muddled. We varied his playing with quadrilles on the piano from me and polkas on the concertina from some of the young men.
>
> You would have been surprised to see the number of dances they performed. They did everything that is danced in the ordinary ballroom, though their valsing did not come to much, besides they danced four or five different kinds of country dances, schottishe, reels and polkas. Some of them danced extremely well, and it was amusing to watch the difference in their dancing to that of people of our position. They put their whole energy into the dancing and thought of nothing else, conversation played no part in the proceeding, but the dancing was everything and had to be done as well as possible. In fact the faces of most of them were solemn all the time as if they were accomplishing an important task ... I did my duty, polkaed with our gardener, danced country dances with others, but was not so vigorous as the gentlemen ... We fed them on claret cup and biscuits between dances, and then had sit-down supper in two divisions, when enormous quantities of cold beef and pie were devoured. At 1.30 they all went home and left us very tired.[41]

The Creightons found some local customs quaint and others disturbing. Usual village entertainments were concerts, dances, lectures or penny readings, the latter when people paid a penny each for admission to a programme of reading from books with the proceeds going to the church or charity. Most of these events took place in the village school directly across the road from the vicarage and church. Creighton himself favoured the penny readings and sometimes agreed to read Shakespeare or Dante or some other literary work which presumably flew high over the heads of his villagers. One woman after hearing him speak on Shakespeare and recite from *Macbeth* commented several days later: 'Oh, it was too terrible. Generally when I go home, I try to remember the vicar's sermons, but this time I tried to forget as quick as possible.'[42] Years later, shortly after the turn of the century, a village hall was constructed and named 'Creighton Hall'.[43]

When it came to village dances, local weddings and the annual village fete celebrated on Holy Trinity Sunday ('Holy Trinity' being the dedication of the village church), Creighton found that drunkenness was a major problem. He immediately tried to curtail the excessive use of alcohol at social functions, which irritated some locals. When a party of fisherman visiting the vicarage one afternoon failed to receive the customary drink following their meeting with their vicar, one rose and uttered mournfully, 'A dry visit, this', which prompted Creighton to reply, 'Yes, very dry'.[44] In a letter to her mother Louise described one village dance:

> We had a village ball last week; it was given in the school with Max's permission on condition that no spirituous liquor was provided, and went off in a most orderly manner. Max and I went up for half an hour and were much amused by the perfect solemnity of the entertainment. As we drew near we could hear no sound issuing from the school; it happened to be a pause between two dances, and when we entered, we found the girls ranged on one side of the room and the men on the other and not a word being spoken. Then after a moment or two, the school master who directed the proceedings said 'Take your partners for a polka'. Whereupon the young men marched across the room and with a solemn bow offered their arm to a girl and proceeded to march round the room in perfect silence till the music struck up. They then set to work and danced without once stopping till the music stopped, when the girls went back to their seats and the men to theirs, and so on. There was occasionally a song between the dances, but they went on from 8 o'clock till 6 in the morning.[45]

Creighton was no teetotaler and enjoyed a drink now and again, usually wine, but he did see the need for controlling the abuse of alcohol that he deemed a problem in the parish. With Louise's help Mandell started a branch of the Church of England Temperance Society and, later, a Band of Hope which sought to discourage alcohol consumption among children and young adults.[46] In a letter to her mother in May 1875, Louise wrote:

> To-day and to-morrow are what is called the Embleton feast. Each village about here has a feast, which always covers a Sunday and Monday. The people all have their friends to come and see them, and on the Sunday they walk about in new clothes. On the Monday there are sports, races etc. for prizes, and a ball in the evening. Booths are set up in the village, and I am afraid a good deal of drinking and disorder accompanies the feast ... On Monday we went to see a cottage tea drinking of temperance people there. They first drank tea and then listened to discourses about total abstinence. We too sat down and listened and were a good deal amused.[47]

Louise developed an interest in the Mothers' Union. This was a movement, beginning about that time in rural England, that encouraged mothers to take greater responsibility in the religious upbringing of their children.

Louise formed a committee in 1879. 'I started my mothers' meeting to-day', she told her mother, 'and ten women came, which Max thinks very good to begin with. If they only go on. I want the young mothers most and I had four of them, and shall hope for more another time. I read and discoursed to them, [and] I spent most of my afternoons last week going round to hunt them up, and did a deal of visiting. I am so glad to find that I grow to like the people more and more ...' [48] Louise was learning to be an organiser, a strength at which she later excelled. 'I wanted to give [the mothers] some religious help', she said, and tried having them read books, 'but it was difficult to find what just suited them. I knew the kind of lives they led and knew what sort of teaching they needed, or thought I knew. So I made up my mind that I must discourse to them myself. I had never done such a thing and the prospect was terrifying.' She described how she adapted herself to managing the mothers' meetings that met every Monday.

> For a long while I used to prepare very full notes, and so I learned to speak and found it really came very easily to me. But it was impossible to know what the women thought about it. It certainly was a grim experience. We met in a gloomy little room which had been arranged as a men's reading room. About sixteen women used to come and there were generally several babies or older children who ran about. Sitting on a level with them, I had to hold forth. Of course they never spoke. I doubt whether anyone could have them to ask or answer questions; certainly I could not. I suppose they liked it ... but the prospect of the afternoon cast a black cloud over my awakening on Monday morning. For me this was the school in which I learned how to speak, and certainly speaking in that little room to that group of women was more trying than I found speaking in the Albert Hall or Queen's Hall in later years. [49]

The Girls' Friendly Society (GFS) was another one of those socio-religious organisations like the Mothers' Union that was ideally suited for wives of country parsons. The GFS was founded in the early 1840s in the hope of encouraging parents to be more responsible in promoting the moral and educational well-being of their daughters, such as keeping them in school until the age of fourteen. Louise eventually formed a chapter in Embleton and conducted a class twice monthly. [50] Lady Frederick Grey, widow of one of old Lord Grey's brothers, happened to be the national president of the GFS, and Louise found herself summoned to a meeting at Howick Rectory to 'hear her discourse about it'. As a result, Louise 'had to start a branch', but

> it was not easy work. I had a class of girls at Embleton, but they were very ... unresponsive, and I could not get into real touch with them. On one occasion

we had a great GFS gathering at Howick. I had to address them out of doors, the first time. I had to speak to so large a gathering. I had decided to speak about their relations with men, and in the middle was a little dismayed to see standing on the outskirts of the crowd and listening eagerly the coachmen and grooms who had accompanied the different vehicles which brought the people. However, I was told afterwards that one of the coachmen had told his mistress that I had spoken words of gold.

To my surprise I was, after some time, elected first diocesan president of GFS and had to attend meetings in Newcastle and organise a conference there. This brought me into connexion with many local people and I was pleased to be told when we left the north that I had made the committee meetings amusing. But GFS never provoked much enthusiasm in my mind, either then or later, though it no doubt helped me to know something about the girls and perhaps more about the associates.[51]

Louise also taught occasionally in the day school, instructing girls on 'domestic economy', a new subject at that time. Her students, she thought, seemed interested, 'but I could not coach them up in the way necessary to make them satisfy the Inspector, and as payment by results was then the rule, the schoolmaster was inclined to consider the time given to Domestic Economy wasted. So after a while my lessons were discontinued.'[52] This was the period shortly following the national government's educational revised code of 1862 (the so-called 'payment by results' plan), when that ubiquitous army of freshly-formed government inspectors were spreading across the landscape like a wave of locusts, making annual visits to voluntary (private or church-related) schools to test children and study facilities in order to determine what grant-aid schools could receive. At the time the Creightons arrived at Embleton there were four voluntary schools in the parish, all under the authority of the Church of England: at Embleton, Dunstan, Newton-on-the-Moor and Rennington. There was also a private squire's school sponsored by the Greys at Fallodon, and by 1883 another voluntary school at Newton-by-the-Sea had been established.[53] As vicar, Creighton played a supervisory role over the schools in his parish and was their legal overseer.[54]

As would be expected, Creighton showed a deep interest in his parish schools. Embleton village school of course was small, with fifty-three pupils if they all showed up. Most of the other schools in the district, all voluntary, had a similar enrolment.[55] Creighton served as chairman of the local school attendance committee which had been formed, as had other districts across the land, under the Compulsory Attendance Act of 1876.[56] Creighton regularly visited the schools in his parish and on occasion agreed to teach the children. He found the experience far more challenging than he expected.

'I can only tell you', he remarked years later, 'that my own attempts at
teaching the young when I had a country parish were disastrous.' He went
on to explain that Louise and his curate experienced similar results, saying
that all three of them:

> regarded ourselves as intelligent persons, and we took great pains in teaching the
> children. But when it came to the inspector, they failed in the subjects that we
> had taught. That raises the question, who was to blame for such a result? Was
> it the teachers, the children, or the inspector? I was so conceited that I thought
> the fault was the inspector's. It was quite natural. It was his business to examine
> in a kind of knowledge which I was not trying to give.[57]

Creighton lamented the fact that when it came time for him to depart
Embleton, 'no pang was so great' as his leaving the children in the village
schools.[58]

Never subscribing to the government policy of 'payment by results' and
the use of inspectors, Creighton often spoke of the day he visited one of
his schools and found the teacher forcing the children to memorise the
names of the capes of China in preparation of the inspector's visit, a favourite
question of that particular inspector.[59] He decided thereafter that it was
better for him just to loan books to the teachers whenever possible. But
his pastoral experience convinced him that the success of teaching children
anywhere, in village or town, depended entirely on the teacher; 'an intelligent
teacher will teach intelligently, and you can't invent a system which will
make an unintelligent teacher intelligent'. From that period on, he believed
that the aim of a teacher was to inculcate both a sense of curiosity and a
power of observation, and that this would be achieved best by designing
a course of study that followed the order of the child's mind.[60]

After several years at Embleton, Creighton began to serve as an examiner
of schools outside his district, regularly visiting such schools as the new
secondary school for girls at Middlesbrough and various schools in Leeds,
Shields and elsewhere. He lectured in Newcastle at the Literary Philosophical
Institute on occasion and gave talks on educational topics at the Young
Men's Improvement Association in Alnwick and at various poor law conferences in the northern district. Creighton was also elected chairman of
the Alnwick board of guardians and the local sanitary authority, important
local governmental bodies for rural England in those days. The new poor
law of 1834 established a commission to create rules of administration, but
the actual implementation of the poor law regulations was handled by local
elective bodies called boards of guardians. With the passage of further
health and educational reforms, the boards of guardians had by the 1870s
assumed increased responsibilities in parishes and towns. When Creighton

joined the guardians, there was an important proposal being hammered out to supply the district with pure, plentiful water 'which would be an immense advantage', Louise explained. 'It seems that in a dry summer all the wells about have got dried up and one is left without water, which is not cheerful. So I hope something may come of this new scheme.'[61] Two years later, Louise wrote of Mandell's work on the guardians' board:

> We have been leading a very peaceable life this week mostly buried with parishional visiting. On Friday we went to Alnwick, as Max had a meeting of the new Educational Committee of which he has been made Chairman and I went in to do some shopping. One never realises till one lives in the country the enormous amount there is to be done by different local boards, in sanitary, poor law and educational matters. I never thought before that Guardians were such important people, and would do so much either for good or evil. We hope to get compulsory school attendance in this district, which will be a great boon ...

In 1877 and again in 1878 Creighton presented two papers on 'Duties of Guardians with Regard to Education'.[62] In both papers he argued for the increased responsibility of parents in following the requirements set forth in the recent Education Act of 1876 that established compulsory education in its initial forms. He also gave a paper in 1881 on workhouse management, pleading for sanitary and infirmary reforms. Along with the vicar at Alnwick, Creighton started what was called a 'provident dispensary' in the town.[63] These were still the days when parish clergy served a supervisory civic role in their parishes, something that was lost for the most part by the end of the century when the duties of rural clergymen had become strictly ecclesiastical.[64]

Creighton never left academia entirely. He occasionally went south to preach at Oxford in his role as a select preacher, once preaching on 'The Sense of Freedom' at Oxford, where he contrasted the mental freedom given by popular culture and the spiritual freedom given by religion, stating that the purpose of the university was to bring the two into closer union.[65] He gave other sermons at Oxford on such topics as 'Public Worship' and 'The Christian Aim'.[66] Creighton began examining for both the Law and the Modern History schools at Oxford also, which permitted him to visit former colleagues, something he very much savoured. In 1879 he was also appointed examiner for the Lightfoot Scholarship at Cambridge, his first official connection with that university.[67] Louise wrote to her mother:

> You may be entertained to know that Max has been asked to examine for the Lightfoot scholarship at Cambridge. It is a great honour as of course he is an Oxford man. One of the examiners for this scholarship has to be an Oxford man in accordance with the conditions in which it was founded and the men who

have preceded Max have been very distinguished historians; he is very pleased
of course; it is nice to be honoured and besides he will enjoy going to Cambridge
and seeing the people he knows there and making new friends ... [68]

That same year, after Joseph Lightfoot succeeded to the diocese of Durham,
Creighton was named rural dean of Alnwick, requiring him to attend periodic
meetings over the next several years in Alnwick and Embleton. As rural
dean, he helped to solidify the local clergy and give them a renewed regional
focus since the ruridecanal chapters had been inactive for several years. He
wrote to a clerical friend about his meetings saying that: 'At present I am
trying to make my position as Rural Dean a means of promoting clerical
co-operation and free discussion on all points. So far I have succeeded
beyond my expectations. But I made a rule for myself at the beginning that
I would not declare myself needlessly on any point, but would aim at a
position as moderator. Situated as I am, I can do more good that way than
as an agitator.' [69] This appointment offered Creighton his first position of
leadership in the church and proved to be an opportunity for him to hone
skills in working with the rank and file clergy, though he complained to his
friend Reginald Copleston a year later that:

> As Rural Dean I have much to do and find the older clergy very difficult to stir
> up. Under Bishop Baring we never had any common life: he distrusted his
> clergy and thought that when two or three were gathered together they were
> sure to make fools of themselves. Probably he was right, but he did not draw
> the obvious moral that they must go on doing it till they learned not to do
> it. Under him we had no rural dean at all; he thought us [clergymen] too abom-
> inable. Consequently the old folks have all learned to look upon themselves
> as such.[70]

At the 1880 diocesan conference in Durham, Bishop Lightfoot spoke of
dividing the diocese and establishing a see of Newcastle. This came to pass
two years later, and it appears Creighton played an important role in getting
it underway.[71] When E. R. Wilberforce was consecrated Bishop of Newcastle
in the summer of 1882, Creighton was named one of his examining chaplains
and appointed to an honorary canonry. In the year previous Creighton
worked on organising a church congress in Newcastle, and in 1883 he was
appointed secretary of the first diocesan conference in Newcastle.[72] These
appointments placed an increasing burden on him. Because he was efficient,
effective and available, the new bishop turned to him often, describing
Creighton as being 'always there when wanted for anything'.[73]

It was also about this time that Creighton delivered a paper 'Clerical
Inaccuracies in Conducting Church Services' at a clerical meeting, later
published in the *Clergyman's Magazine*.[74] In it he urged clergy to regard

liturgy as a work of art in which no detail, however small, should be allowed to mar the harmony of the service as a whole. 'The more intent a worshipper is upon his devotions, the more fatal is a trifling diversion', he stated, chastising priests for not conducting church services with proper preparation and solemnity. 'It is worth while to stand up for a brief space before beginning,' he advised, 'to have one's throat cleared, to fill one's lungs, to make the very first word penetrate through the church, to read the sentence in such a way as to rivet attention, and then to settle down more quietly to the sober and practical tone of the Exhortation.' He called for the choir not to be a distraction. He also thought that, in the readings, the priest should put the correct emphasis on specific words. 'Never emphasize a personal pronoun', he asserted, maintaining that it was better to read, as an example 'Come unto me', rather than 'Come unto Me'. 'None of the hearers wish to seek any other saviour', he insisted. In short, he said that 'everything connected with the service should be carefully settled before-hand', concluding that ministers 'cannot consider too carefully any suggestions which may enable us to perform more adequately the services of the Church. Their meaning, their capabilities, their expressiveness, deserve our fullest consideration.'[75] This is Creighton's first public expression of liturgical thought and illustrated his leanings with regard to ritual, something that would be more evident in later years.[76]

The Creightons discovered Northumberland social life as compared to Oxford was minimal, to say the least, but they managed to make the best of it. 'We knew, of course, all the gentry that were to be known within reach, that is a few county families, and the neighbouring clergy. There was hardly anyone whom I would under other conditions have been liable to make a friend of,' she said, 'but it was very good for me to be obliged to make friends with people whom in Oxford I should have dismissed as hopelessly uncongenial.'[77] They were on friendly terms with the two Grey families, particularly Sir George Grey of Fallodon, nephew of the Reform Bill Prime Minister, and his wife, Lady Anna Sophia Grey. Sir George was a kindly old man and greatly took to the new vicar. 'He was so young in mind that he was readily interested in the books and subjects for which we cared', Louise claimed. 'Lady Grey feared sometimes that we were corrupting him. She was always very kind and warmhearted, and we never minded her sharp sayings, tho' we had been told that we should find her very alarming. I expect we shocked her sometimes.' Lady Grey reportedly said to Mrs Acland, the curate's wife, shortly after she met Louise, 'Mrs Creighton seems very nice but why does she not wear gloves?'[78]

The Creightons often dined at Fallodon Hall, meeting what Louise called 'interesting people' there. And when out on their parish visiting expeditions the Creightons regularly dropped in at Fallodon for afternoon tea. Mrs Harriet Jane Pearson Grey, wife of Lieutenant Colonel George Grey (the son of Sir George Grey) was living at Fallodon with her children, the eldest being Edward, the future Sir Edward Grey and Viscount Grey of Fallodon.[79] In spite of the fact that Louise found her a 'rather dull and commonplace woman', the Creightons became 'great friends' with her seven children, particularly Edward who, when they arrived at Embleton, was away at school at Winchester. Constance Grey, the youngest girl, was about Beatrice's age and they became good friends. Indeed, all the Grey children became play-mates of the Creighton children, and over the years there were an abundance of joint games and picnics. As the children grew older, they were often invited to tea at Fallodon.[80]

When Sir George's health began to fail in the summer of 1882, Creighton visited him often, reading to or praying over the old man who was confined to bed and unable to speak. After he died, Creighton wrote to his sister Polly he was 'very grieved at the death of Sir George Grey, more than I can say. He is an immense loss to us in every way. But it was most painful to me to see him day by day for the last month, suffering greatly as he did, and being fully conscious till the last two days. However, he is gone; may we all go like him. His funeral is today, I shall be relieved when it is over.'[81] The funeral brought many dignitaries from across England to the village of Embleton to pay honour to the old statesman. Sir George was buried in the little churchyard under a simple Celtic stone marker. Later, five stained glass windows were commissioned and added to Embleton church as a memorial to Sir George. A few months later Lady Grey asked Creighton to write a memoir of him, which he did, a tender tribute to the man. The family insisted the book be privately printed and only given to family members and close friends, though Sir Edward Grey later gave permission for the book to be published in 1901.[82]

At Howick Hall, the old Lord Grey, son of the Reform Bill Earl, reigned with his elderly wife. The Creightons dined with them occasionally where they found it 'interesting to meet these old people belonging to a past age', Louise said. It was at a dinner at Howick that the Creightons met Lord Halifax, the Anglo-Catholic leader.[83] Then into 'the midst of the aged society at Howick', she reported, came Albert Grey, Lord Grey's heir, 'like a radiant meteor, bringing life and joy wherever he went'. Albert Henry George Grey had been educated at Cambridge and was planning to enter politics. In 1880 he won a seat in the House of Commons for a Northumberland constituency. Albert became good friends with the Creightons and, when at Howick, would often walk over on Sunday evenings to hear Mandell preach and stay for supper afterwards.[84]

The other nobleman of their neighbourhood was the Duke of Northumberland at Alnwick Castle. The earldom of Northumberland had been created in the fourteenth century, and the first Duke of Northumberland was created later in the eighteenth century. In the 1870s the title was held by Algernon George, sixth Duke of Northumberland. His wife, the Duchess, was Louisa Drummond (daughter of Henry Drummond of Albury Park, Surrey, the banker). During their first winter at Embleton, the duke and duchess invited the Creightons to come and spend a few days at Alnwick Castle, once the residence of Hotspur and certainly one of the more picturesque and inhabitable medieval fortifications in the north country. Though Louise may have found the ancient ambience enticing, the current tenants she did not. 'It was a strange and dreary experience', Louise remembered.

> I was not used to country house visiting, and as we had merely driven over from home I had taken no occupation with me, and when after a very stiff tea I was shown into my room at 5:30 and told that dinner was at 8, I simply did not know what to do till then. There was not a book that could be read in the room, and I felt at first that the only thing to do was to go to bed, but as there was some writing paper, I ended by writing letters instead. Never after that did I stay away anywhere without taking a book.
>
> That evening when we came to dinner the great and titled took one another in and marched off; the men, who were in the minority had been told who to take in, but about five of us women were left helpless in the drawing-room, till the elder of us said 'Well, I suppose we had better follow', and we went in and found seats as best we could, no hostess paying any heed to us. The next day having been shown the Castle, and found my way to the library, I fared rather better; and in the evening even played whist with Lord Percy, who went to sleep during the game. It was a most dreary visit. Later on I think the Duke discovered Max's [Liberal] politics [and] we were never invited again to the Castle except for the two general annual functions, the Christmas Tree and the Flower show, both desperately stiff and formal affairs which we did not often frequent.[85]

Among the clergy of the region, their chief friend was C. W. Streatfeild, rector of Howick. Of the gentry in the area, their closest friends were George Robertson and his wife of Embleton Mill. Robertson was in Louise's words 'a really interesting and intelligent man, a thorough Northumbrian. He never gave himself away, but he had a great admiration and a very real liking for Max, and was his churchwarden. They often drove into Alnwick together on Saturdays when he was going to his market and Max to the Board of Guardians.'[86] One of the more memorable events in the history of the parish was the tragedy that occurred on the Robertsons' farm one day in November 1879. As Louise explained it to her mother in her weekly letter:

We have had a most terrible tragedy in our neighbourhood which had made us very sad. Mrs Robertson the farmer's wife was found yesterday morning in a well in their cellar, the well so narrow that she had not fallen to the bottom but had her feet sticking out, and her little baby four months old at the bottom of the well. No reason can be assigned at all, she was the most unlikely woman to commit suicide, had gone to bed in a usual manner the night before, talking to her husband quite cheerfully before they went to sleep, and had got up and dressed herself and the child as usual and seen after the preparations of the breakfast and then was missed, till her poor man after hunting for her everywhere found her like this. The well is in the corner of a cellar where nothing is kept and where there can have been no reason for her to go.

It seems the most terrible mystery, and the inquest which sat to-day returned an open verdict. Max was with Mr Robertson almost immediately afterwards and has of course tried to be of much help to him as anyone can be, but it is terrible to think of what the poor man's distress must be, for besides the horror of the death they were so happy together, and she was such a sweet, gentle woman. There are four little children left.

It is a sad story to tell you but knowing them as we did it so fills our thoughts that I could not write without telling it; it is not often that one is brought near such a terrible tragedy.[87]

Of the Robertson children, the eldest was Katie, a girl not much older than Beatrice Creighton. As Katie and Beatrice were playmates, and having been good friends with Mrs Robertson, Louise offered to educate Katie with Beatrice; however, according to Louise, 'after a while Mr Robertson in true Northumbrian way refused, saying it might lead her to think herself above her station'.[88]

Two other families the Creightons came to know well were the Peases, John William Pease of Newcastle and Alnmouth, and Sir Joseph Whitwell Pease of Hutton Hall in Yorkshire. Both families were members of the Society of Friends (Quakers); Joseph and John Pease were cousins and had married sisters, Helen Fox and Mary Fox of Falmouth. The Fox family, coincidentally, had come to know Creighton when he gave his series of lectures in Falmouth in 1871. The Peases were a prominent business family and had investments in a number of ventures in the north east, including coal, textiles, railways and locomotive construction, iron ore mining, limestone quarrying and banking (Hodgkin, Barnett, Pease, Spence and Co. of Newcastle).

It was at a dinner at Pendower in Newcastle, the home of John W. Pease, that Creighton met Thomas Hodgkin, also a Quaker and related to the Peases by marriage; as a result a long and strong friendship was fashioned between the two. Though a banker in partnership with the Pease family, Hodgkin wrote several significant history books, and at the time Creighton met him he was working on his multi–volume account of the Germanic migrations into the late Roman Empire, *Italy and Her Invaders.* Hodgkin recalled that dinner saying that they 'talked history hard all evening, and I felt at once that I was in contact with one of the ablest and best stored minds that I had ever known. [Creighton] gave me all sorts of tips, but more than all he raised my standard of the way in which history ought to be written.' Hodgkin said that it was during their conversation that Creighton 'said—and the saying has been a watchword to me ever since—"I always stay close to my authorities".'

On one particular day in late August of 1879, Hodgkin led Creighton on a walk where he introduced him to the Northumbrian part of the Roman Wall. Coming from Cumbria, Creighton was familiar with the west end of it, but now saw its opposite side. 'My dear Hodgkin,' he wrote later, 'I don't think that I properly conveyed to you my thanks for the delightful, and to me, most interesting expedition which we made last week ... I think more and more of the enormous importance of the Roman wall as an historical monument. I feel as if I shall often go there again, and I feel that having been there once under your able guidance I shall be better able to appreciate it on future visits.' [89]

Hodgkin urged Creighton to keep his eyes on his planned history of the popes. The life of a country clergyman had given him an opportunity to read around the topic, but he had yet to produce a publishable manuscript. Creighton knew first hand about dilly-dallying on such a project. He recalled the sad story of an old Merton fellow who had amassed an enormous amount of notes for a book and then died before he actually began to write. Creighton had been asked to sort through the fellow's lifework in hopes of salvaging something from all the notes. Unfortunately, it turned out to be only one article. He then resolved not to wait any longer before commencing with his writing. 'I was full of horror', he declared, 'at the possibility of ending in the same way, so I began to write at once ...' [90] He concluded that reading and writing should go side by side. Two years later, in September 1881, Creighton wrote to his publisher: 'The first two volumes of my book, *The Papacy of the Reformation Epoch,* are almost ready.' [91]

9

The Happiest Years

'At Embleton I spent ten years, and I have not hesitation in saying that they were the ten happiest years of my life.'

Mandell Creighton in 1899 [1]

By all accounts the years the Creightons spent in Embleton *were* the happiest in their married lives. There, Mandell said he 'got to know people, and to know English people: two things which one does not learn at a University'.[2] Louise felt similarly. She came to Embleton with a sense of dread as if it were exile, but came to realise what an immense gain it was for them both. 'We were thrown back on ourselves; we were in close touch with the elemental facts of life; we were saved from the pursuit of vain shadows, and from the narrowing effect of university life which is almost inevitable for those who do not spend some time in the wilderness.'[3] For Louise it afforded her an opportunity to discover 'for the first time the beauty of the country in winter, at night and in all its varying moods'.[4]

Even so, the Creightons missed their Oxford friends. Winter days, though short in light, were often long and lonely. But summers proved ideal for friends to visit their comfortable vicarage which offered plenty of room for stay-overs. Indeed, in those days with transport being what it was, the term used for such visits was 'dine and sleep'. Louise explained how it worked:

In the summer we had successions of our old friends from the south and elsewhere to visit us. We were on the high road to Scotland which made it easy for people to stop with us; the Andrew Langs came every year on their way. We would take in two married couples and a single person at once, or more if the couples would do without a dressing-room, and very delightful were the parties of friends we gathered together. There was bathing before breakfast in the first days when we were all young. Even Mr Hood bathed and gathered mushrooms before breakfast; there were walks and expeditions, and in the evening often whist, but always plenty of good talks, discussion about everything under the sun.[5]

In one year the Creightons' visitor's book recorded sixty-nine separate house guests, and these visitors did not just drop in for an afternoon or an evening; they stayed for days or even a week or more. Their guests over the years included Thomas and Charlotte Green, Humphry and Mary Ward, and Humphry's sister Agnes. Humphry Ward, having been forced to resign from Brasenose because the college had yet to allow married fellows, was searching for a new career. He eventually settled upon being a journalist for the *The Times*. Mary Ward, who seemed to bask in what she called 'the humanizing, educative life at Embleton', was beginning her climb to fame as a successful novelist.[6] Arthur Johnson, a fellow of All Souls, and his wife Bertha were occasional guests, and it was probably during one of their visits that the decision was made that Bertha should paint a portrait of Louise, which she did in 1877.[7] Creighton's undergraduate friends came too, such as Reginald Copleston, C. T. Boyd, the poet Robert Bridges, H. J. Hood, R. T. Raikes, George Saintsbury, and James Richard Thursfield, who usually brought his mother along. There were Andrew Lang and his new wife, Leonora Blanche Alleyne (Lang, a writer-poet and Merton don, had decided in 1875 to leave the safe Oxford cloisters for Fleet Street), and Creighton's new friend Edmund Gosse and his wife.

Others visitors were Hugh Bell, later provost of Oriel College, Oxford, and his wife; several of Louise's childhood friends, such as Mary Schwabe (née James), and her husband Colonel G. S. Schwabe, and Edith and Bunnie Wetton; H. G. Woods and his future wife Daisy Bradley of Oxford, who met at the Creightons' home; Edward Talbot, later Bishop of Winchester, and his wife; Robert Wilson, a former Merton colleague, then warden of Keble College, Oxford; C. T. Cruttwell and N. Freeling, both fellows of Merton; Dr J. F. Bright, later master of University College; C. P. Scott, editor of the *Manchester Guardian*, and his wife; Dr Charles Edward Appleton, editor of *Academy*; Clara Pater; Archibald Henry Sayce, fellow of the Queens College, Oxford, and classical lecturer at the time; John Morley, writer and later politician, who at that time was editor of the *Fortnightly Review*; George Howard, afterward Earl of Carlisle; Signor Costa, an Italian painter and friend of George Howard; Sir George Grove, then editor of *Macmillan's Magazine* (Louise's family friend); and the historian J. R. Green, Louise's long-time friend, and his new wife, Alice Stopford Green.

Alice Stopford met J. R. Green in the mid 1870s shortly after she arrived in London from Ireland, where she was born. Green was then engaged in writing his classic *Short History of the English People*. The couple married in June of 1877, but J. R. Green's health soon declined. He died of consumption in 1883. Mrs Green, herself a writer of history, developed quite a cerebral affinity with Mandell as is strikingly revealed in their correspondence.[8] Her letters are examples of high repartee. 'I was naturally much interested in your essays,' she once wrote to Creighton, 'the more so perhaps because I felt there was reason enough for a tremendous argument.' In another letter she states: 'You are so stimulating and so helpful that you come a very long way in front of the people whose sympathy and counsel matter.'[9]

There were also other guests who visited, such as Louise's parents, several of her brothers and sisters, Mandell's sister, Polly, and his brother James and his wife; and there were also local or regional friends who came to 'dine and sleep', particularly clerical associates, as well as the Peases, the Widdringtons of Newton-on-the Moor, the Trevelyans of Wallington (George Otto Trevelyan was a prominent historian of the era),[10] and the Bosanquets of Rock Hall.[11] Distances between houses being relatively far for those days and travel being problematic because of weather and road conditions, to 'dine and sleep' over was customary, and in the spring, summer and autumn, when weather was likely moderate and predictable, Embleton vicarage seemed more like a hotel than a secluded, scholarly hermitage. Guests enjoyed the run of the large house, drifting from room to room—men pausing in Creighton's study which was the smoking room, women chatting in the drawing-room, absorbing whatever weather there was that came through the large bay windows. After lunch, Creighton's habit was to make his rounds of parish visits, and any visitor who seemed aimless was taken by the arm along with him. Evenings were given over to talk, reading aloud from favourite works, such as one of Browning's books of poetry or Mark Twain's *American Drolleries*, or playing whist.[12]

When alone in the evening, Mandell would be hunched over documents in his study while Louise wrote her letters. 'I often wonder how I ran this large household, with a very small staff of servants', she once confessed. Her staff, however, was hardly small, even by late Victorian standards: a cook, a parlourmaid, a nurse and a nursemaid, a gardener, a groom, sometimes a second housemaid, and usually a kitchenmaid.[13] 'I think we lived comfortably', Louise asserted, and

> had quite good and well cooked food, tho' of course it was not up to country house standard. Meat could only be got twice a week, fish was uncertain, and I found the wisest plan was to say that whenever fish was brought to the door it was to be taken. Groceries I got in large supplies from London; and Alnwick supplemented. I went in some times on Saturday with Max, and the pony carriage used to be laden with the most varied goods and parcels so that we could hardly get in ourselves. One thing living in the country taught me, that one could get on very well without shopping. I ordered most things by post. Our own garden supplied fruit and vegetables. We had masses of peaches and even figs on one wall.[14]

The following letter written on 12 September 1875 to her mother illustrates one of Louise's all-too-typical weeks at the vicarage:

We have had a busy week with visitors. The Hoods came back on Monday and stayed two nights. Then on Tuesday Mr Raikes and his boy left and we had Mr Walker, the head master of the Manchester grammar school, with his boy for two nights.

It was strange to have successive visits from two widowers each with an only son. Mr Walker's boy could not compare advantageously with Mr Raikes'; he was a most spoilt youth of seven, to my mind exceedingly disagreeable. It seems strange that a man who can manage an enormous school like Manchester as successfully as Mr Walker does should not be able to bring up his son to be anything but a little prig ... Mr [Andrew] Lang and his wife, Nora Alleyne that was, came on Wednesday and are here now. The two Wards left us yesterday. I think they enjoyed their visit and the country very much; it is the only outing they have from London this year.

We are getting near to the end of our list of visitors now and shall not have many more now. They are making me sadly neglect my duty to the farmers and people about here; however I shall have plenty of time for them in the winter. On Wednesday we go to the George Howards at Naworth, which is a very pleasing prospect particularly if this weather continues.[15]

Like most middle- and upper-class Victorian women—especially wives of successful professional men residing in the country—Louise found it a full-time job managing a large home on acres of property with a galaxy of servants and over-night house guests, along with several children. Four more children were born during the Embleton years. Their first son was born in July 1876 and named Cuthbert after the patron saint of Northumberland and Durham; Thomas and Charlotte Green became his godparents. Two years later a child was born prematurely and named Walter after Walter de Merton, the founder of Merton College. In 1880 Louise gave birth to a third daughter, Mary, named after one of the women who aided Dante on his pilgrimage; and in 1883 Oswin was born, their sixth child and third son. He was named after the popular Northumberland saint and martyred king of Deira, who was betrayed and murdered in 651 by a rival group on the orders of Oswy, king of Bernicia.

Louise felt her 'chief concern' in those years was civilising her children, and even with a staff of servants her time was understandably, as she said, 'pretty well occupied'.[16] 'We were always well and strong', she remembered, claiming that never once during their years in Northumberland was she called up at night to a sick child. Something about the climate, she reckoned, made it a splendid place to raise a family.

We had a donkey with panniers which used to take them all down to the sea, the little ones in the panniers and perhaps an older one sitting on the donkey's back. In the summer they all went down to bathe. We undressed on the shore

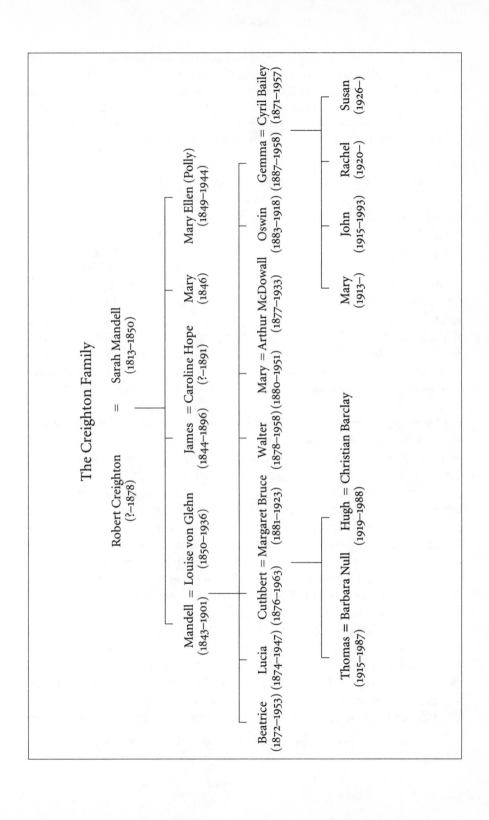

The Creighton Family

which was quite private in those days; the sea was always bitterly cold and small children could not do much more than dip and they much preferred paddling. I invented flannel dresses and knickers for them which could be easily slipt off or in which they could paddle without fear of wetting their clothes. It was a jolly sight to see them starting off for the sea with pails and spades, generally bare foot, with their blue flannel frocks and red felt hats.[17]

As parents, the Creightons were probably more giving than many Victorian couples of their class and circumstances. Louise chose not to employ a governess because she wanted to supervise the children's education herself. 'The children', she maintained, 'lived with us as much as possible. They came to breakfast and lunch with us at a very early age. I, from the first, undertook their teaching. How far this was the best thing for them I do not know. I had had no training as a teacher, but I read all the educational books I could discover and tried to get hold of wise and modern methods.' She confessed not being 'always very patient, but I don't think that I was either very irritable. We always began with a Bible lesson. I wanted to make them love Bible study. We did not have regular holidays. I thought that for little children occasional holidays were much better; and when there was a very fine hot day in summer, or an expedition was proposed, holiday was given on the spur of the moment, and of course there was always a holiday on birthdays.'[18]

Mandell, once the children arrived, became more relaxed and comfortable with them, ready to show his affection towards them, though he could express his temper instantly when things did not go as he wished. Where Louise was more reserved, he was more open. He delighted in rolling and romping with them on the hearthrug before the fire or strolling with them across a meadow hand-in-hand, telling impromptu and contrived nonsense stories about the antics of fictitious characters he made up on the spot, like Tuttery Buttery, Timothy Toozelwits and Kezia Hubbock.[19] Years later, Mandell reminisced in a letter to a young nephew: 'I remember when I was a big boy at [Durham] school I used to go at night and tell stories to the small boys. It developed a power, which I afterwards carried on, of inventing rubbishing tales on a moment's notice.'[20]

Beatrice recalled later how her father used to play with all the children. She remembered how she climbed up on his 'shoulders, and there stand proudly, with one foot on each, while he ran about the room skilfully dodging a hanging candelabrum. Many were the acrobatic feats we performed together, to the imminent peril of life and limb, onlookers used to think, but I didn't know what fear meant when I was with him', she said, adding:

No children ever had a more delightful playmate than we had, and all our best games and romps are bound up in our minds with him. No paraphernalia were ever needed; we cast aside toys and bricks when he was there, he himself was all we wanted. One moment he would be an awful giant, who with mighty roaring would seize us by the legs or pinafores or anything else he could lay hands on. This was a thrilling but a noisy game.

Then—this was what we loved—he would be a rocking-horse. This meant lying upon the floor with several of us seated upon him, and rocking violently up and down. It was exceedingly exhausting for the horse, I expect, but for the riders most exhilarating. Outsiders looking on at our games used to wonder sometimes why no one was killed, so wild and violent were the romps, so daring the gymnastic feats when we scrambled and clambered all over father, and fell in a heap of indistinguishable arms and legs and tangled heads, only to extricate ourselves again and start afresh. I cannot remember any sort of accident ever happening, beyond the occasional damaging of his spectacles in the fray. Sunday evenings in the drawing-room were always a great time for romps, and the wildest and most furious took place then. Perhaps he found them a rest and relaxation after his Sunday duties.[21]

Beatrice remembered those rainy days when all the children were restricted to the nursery and could not go out and play in the garden. Towards the end of the afternoon on those days, when Mandell had returned from his parish rounds and about the time when the children were getting bored with their games, the nursery door would 'open gently and a face peep round the corner, and in he would come to be seized upon by us with screams of joy'. Mandell had a habit of reading to them while lying on the floor, a favourite position for him with all of the children huddled around him as close as they could get. 'How real those stories became to us when he read them', Beatrice said. 'One day, I remember, he had picked up a book and was reading to us a sweet, sad little tale. We were all so quiet that mother looked into the nursery, wondering what had happened, and she found us on the floor as usual, but father and all of us in tears over the touching story he had just finished.'[22]

On hair-cutting afternoons, Mandell would turn the enterprise into a game. Beatrice said they all 'thought it great fun to be perched on a high chair with a towel round us, and have our untidy mops snipt by him. Never failing was the joke, when we had each had our turn and the nursery floor was strewn with curls, that we must be sure and gather them all up carefully and take them to cook.' The joke was that, after cutting the hair, he always demanded to have 'hair soup' for dinner. 'He did not need a book to amuse us,' Beatrice claimed, 'for what book ever written had in it such wonderful and delightful stories as he wove for our amusement? They would perhaps hardly be called stories. It was amazing nonsense, often in verse, in which strange weird creatures with still stranger names played a part ... These stories he would tell us generally out of doors, on walks or picnics, or seated among the sandhills by the sea.'[23] Beatrice recalled they all regarded him

> as the most delightful of playfellows, some one who, in spite of being the wisest and best of all grown-up persons, could yet understand and care for the things of children, and without whom no games and fun would be quite perfect. He could be very stern and angry sometimes, though, when we were naughty. Then it was very terrifying, but it never lasted long.
>
> We knew that there were some things we must never do, or he would be angry, things fairly harmless in themselves we sometimes thought, but which he considered criminal, such as talking and making a noise on the stairs or in the passages, banging doors, aimlessly coming in and out of the room where he was sitting, being, as he called it, 'disorderly and futile'.[24]

When it came to the intellectual development of his children, however, Mandell's instruction met with limited success. His mercurial moods often took their toll. When he started teaching Greek to Beatrice at the age of six, for example, sessions often ended in frustration for him and tears for her. 'I liked going into the smoky study,' she recalled, 'sitting on his knee or on a stool by his side, while between puffs of his cigarette he would hear me [recite] my verbs and correct my feeble exercises. It was delightful when all went well.' But many times, she admitted, her lesson would 'end in tears, when in my carelessness I forgot a word he had told me over and over again, above all when I made excuses. Then with a bang the book would be thrown across the room, and I would be told to go.'[25] Louise said her husband 'was always a very severe critic of his own children, and cherished no delusions as to their capabilities'. Years later after the children were raised and on their own, Louise wrote that although Mandell

> was morally convinced of the supreme importance of character, and the comparative unimportance of intellectual gifts, it was, I believe a real disappointment to him that none of his children showed anything exceptional in the way of intellectual powers, and did not have very distinguished school or college careers. He would always tell strangers that his children were quite stupid ... At all times the standard which he applied to his own family was absolutely different from that which he applied to others ...[26]

Louise generally handled the schoolroom chores which lasted from early morning to about 1 o'clock. 'I have barely time to get the most needful letters and business notes written before lunch at all', Louise said, and 'then we go out directly afterwards and visit hard in the parish trudging about in wind and mud till 5 o'clock and directly after tea down come the children and I have to occupy myself with them till time to dress for dinner. So after dinner is the only time I get for my own work and I generally work hard till 11 and seldom get a minute for any miscellaneous reading.'[27] Teaching the children reading and writing in English, French and German came most naturally for her, she remembered, but musical instruction proved to be her 'great difficulty'. She even drove into Alnwick for a few lessons in harmony from a teacher in the hope that it would help in her instructions. She required the children to sing a great deal, and when they came downstairs after morning tea they usually spent some time 'singing nursery songs of all kinds or in playing singing games'. What Louise enjoyed most, however, was reading stories to them. There was the regular half-hour of reading aloud after lunch while both boys and girls alike did some sort of needlework. 'I read them Walter Scott novels when they were quite young, missing out of course a great many long descriptions.'[28]

The following are random selections from Louse's letters to her mother about her children:

[8 October 1876] Cuthbert is getting on nicely and grows big and fat, and will be pretty I think. He is such a very white baby. Lucia is troubled with her last tooth and has a sore ear, but is very good and cheery over it. She is such a little chatterbox, her tongue never ceases when she is awake. Bice [Beatrice] again insisted upon going to Sunday School to-day. I think she would put up with any thing for the sake of being thought a big girl.[29]

[12 February 1877] [Once when the nurse was away] seeing the children so constantly for a week made me meditate much on their wickednesses, and tempers, and I came to many conclusions which I hope are valuable. But I don't think I am [a] good person to be constantly with children. When I am going on amusing them, telling them stories etc., I do so with a constant sense of labour, and the strain becomes so great towards the end of the day that I find it hard to go on answering their questions etc.

Children never let one have any rest; they are so terribly remorseless. Of course Bice is just at an age when she needs much attention. She is tired of playing on peaceably in a babyish manner, and wants to be taught to do things which will interest her more. Lucia amuses herself alone much better, and will play away peaceably for any length of time, if not disturbed by Bice.[30]

[2 April 1878] Cuthbert has been very cross with his cold, and his conversation has consisted chiefly of violent 'Non', 'Non', with intermittent shrieks. I find that during his visitings he has been so spoilt with jam and cake, that he now refuses to eat plain bread and butter, and crumbles it on his plate instead. I never saw a creature of such determined temper ...

Lucy is amusingly affectionate with me. She comes into my room when I am dressing and says, 'I can't leave my old mother alone', and is always demanding good hugs. Beatrice amused me the other day [with] her sharpness. She has a puzzle given her by a certain lady with whom we have a sort of business acquaintance, and she asked me what her name was so I responded Miss Stables. To which she at once replied, 'What a funny name, does she have horses inside her?'

I can't exactly make out the effect which *Alice in Wonderland* produces upon her. She listens to it with wrapt attention and is very fond of the book, but she hardly ever laughs at it, and when she does laugh, it is never at the absurd portions. I think that all its incongruities seem quite natural to her, and hardly more strange than the ordinary course of things ...

We have begun a habit which much interests the children of throwing crumbs out of the dining-room window every morning and watching what birds will come and it is just as amusing to us as to the children. We have already got quite a little family, tomtits, blackbirds, robins, chaffinches, and of course the inevitable sparrows. I want the children to get to take an interest in natural history, but we ought to have a really good book about birds with coloured pictures; uncoloured ones are no good. We must hope to pick up one at some sale someday.[31]

[22 April 1878] It is curious how readily children learn from one another to be naughty. It seems to me that where there are three children each child individually is at least three times naughtier than it would be were it alone. Even Beatrice initiates the naughty ways of the other two. Cuthbert amazed everybody by his voracious appetite; he will eat anything and everything. The ordinary rule that a child will stop when it is satisfied does not seem to answer with him.[32]

[13 May 1878] Beatrice was most excellent last week in helping me dust the books and was really of great use. It is sad that children should grow naughtier as they grow older.

Beatrice is certainly naughtier now than she used to be, and she is so cute that she can plan naughty things to do. However it is easy as a rule to make her sorry, and I think that what she needs is plenty to occupy and interest her. She clearly enjoys her lessons and will go on reading as long as I will let her.

Cuthbert has got much better behaved. He amuses himself splendidly alone. He has a good many bursts of passion if anything goes contrary to his views, but otherwise gets thru' life most contentedly, and is very cheerful unless he has made himself stolid by eating too much.[33]

[21 May 1878] You speak about B. [Beatrice] learning wool work; she has done so long ago. Both she and Lucy are immensely fond of sowing [sic], and are always delighted to get a needle and a piece of rag, and stitch away contentedly for a long while together. Beatrice can hem fairly and also does her wool work quite neatly now. She is very fond of singing now and can sing several hymns very nicely indeed.

I have also begun teaching her the piano. Miss Herbert who is very musical and has had plenty of experience in teaching recommended me to begin at once, when she was with us ... She enjoys it immensely, even the wearisome process of learning the notes which is of course all we have got to at present, and also wants to go on endlessly. In fact I am pleased to say that that is what she generally wishes with each of her lessons; she never cares to stop.

I do not teach Lucy anything yet but hymn singing, and it is difficult enough to get her to attend to that. She will be over at the other side of the room in a minute to see what Cuthbert is doing. I summon her back and another line is sung, then something else attracts her attention or she wishes to make a remark to me. But she can sing very nicely when she tries, and I think making her do so is an easy way of training her to habits of attention.

Baby [Walter] has been better altogether this week, and seems to be growing much plumper now, and cries less. He sleeps very well at nights and has done so for some weeks now.[34]

[4 June 1878] The children are all most blooming. Lucy is developing an amusing talent for telling stories, if Beatrice can't get any one else she calls upon Lucy to come and tell her a story and then Lucy sits at her feet and with extended eyes gazing into space, and many contortions of her mouth and much gesticulations proceeds to tell a tale about some very naughty little girl, which generally ends with 'and then she was *dead*', with a tremendous emphasis. Some times they are more imaginative and all kinds of invented words are introduced.[35]

[10 June 1878] Baby [Walter] is growing tremendously now, and has taken to sleeping all night without even waking, so I am sure Eliza [the nurse] has not cause to complain of him. He laughs and is most merry now, and seems very knowing and wide awake. Beatrice's greatest delight is to be allowed to hold him in her arms for a few minutes.

Cuthbert makes great progress with talking, and it is very amusing to hear the way in which he mixes up French and English words, He copies all Lucy's passionate tricks, and it is most comic to see the way in which he will stamp his feet and give short sharp shrieks, more because he thinks it the proper thing to do than because it comes naturally. They two are always quarrelling and teasing one another, and yet one cannot keep them apart; they always want to get together.[36]

[24 June 1878] On Saturday afternoon they went with me into a field where I was sketching and played most happily. I was amused at a game they invented because they found a little break in the ground where there were bits of loose rock; they called the rock chocolate and proposed to keep a shop, having daisies and buttercups to represent other articles. Lucy kept exclaiming, 'Oh B., what fun we are having', or 'Oh B., ain't we having a jolly time?'[37]

[1 March 1880] I am beginning to plan spring clothes. It takes such a long time to get everything necessary, that one must begin in good time; and it is a puzzling problem to arrange for the needs of five children ... There was a meet [fox hunt] near here this morning and Bice and Lucy went off with the nursemaid to try and see the hounds but do not seem to have succeeded in finding them. I daresay very few hunters were tempted out in this storm.

Cuthbert is developing a great capacity for singing, he has such a clear little voice and a very good ear and sings so neatly all by himself. We have some German songs now which they learn, and learning the words by heart is of course a help to their German. That book of [Nathaniel] Hawthorne's which you sent Lucy has been a great delight. They have enjoyed it more than any book I have read to them for some time, and were quite grieved when it was finished.[38]

[30 March 1880] On Saturday morning [before Easter] we went out with the children and clambered about on the sand hills to get the moss which grows among the tall grass [for church decorations]. We filled the donkey's panniers with moss, and then rested from our labours perched on the highest sand hill with a lovely view over the sea. The children by degrees rolled down onto the shore and then I had to get the donkey down which was a more difficult under-taking but she struggled down safely. In the afternoon we decorated the church with our flowers and moss. I had so many helpers that I got quite done by four o'clock and the church looked very nice.[39]

[12 July 1880] The children have just been having a little feast of strawberries and cream in Lucie's toy tea things and the girls have been washing up the things at enormous length and with much slopping. They managed to get a bath this morning between the showers, and we are hoping for a fine day to-morrow for Mrs Widdrington has promised to bring her children here to bathe and picnic on the shore with ours ...[40]

Louise wrote often about the 'good deal of quarrelling and temper' dis-played by her children, and she claimed that she 'tried to make punishments fit the offence as Herbert Spencer enjoined'. Spencer, an early social scientist, was thought by many Victorians as a sensible exponent of behaviour modi-fication because of his linking of biology to psychology. Louise said she 'always objected to anything of the nature of a judicial punishment' but admitted in later years that some of their punishments 'may be considered brutal by some people'. Those were different times, of course, and today one should be wary of passing judgments even though the punishments do seem severe by modern standards. 'Cuthbert', she wrote once, 'was a very mischievous boy, and used to play with fire and cut things with knives, so when he played with fire I held his finger on the bar of the grate for a minute that he might feel how fire burnt, and when he cut woodwork with his knife I gave his fingers a little cut.' Yet Louise stated that she 'never whipt any child'.[41] As another example of trying to employ various kinds of instructive punishments for the children, on one afternoon Lucia 'began to pull the china about, so [Mandell] put her under a chair and tied her leg to the chair. After a moment's struggle, she submitted calmly to her fate and remained passively lying on the floor for nearly ten minutes till she chose to say she was good. Then the moment she was released she was as cheery and friendly as ever and seemed utterly to forget what had occurred.'[42]

Much of Louise's letters to her mother centred on children—discipline, health, clothing, etc; another major theme was house management. Louise valued her mother's advice. In the summer of 1876 Louise wrote of doing her weekly shopping at Alnwick The journey there by dogcart or carriage, over roads either muddy and slippery or dusty and bumpy, was never pleasant. On one particular occasion, Louise told her mother that she purchased 'a cask of some eighty lbs of butter from Cork which promises to be a successful experiment. It cost 1s. 4d. a pound, and the carriage will I suppose make it come to 1s. 5d. but it is very good butter and as we already pay 1s. 8d. here and shall pay more, it is a decided economy.'[43] Elsewhere in the same letter, she wrote:

> My cows are not doing very well, and the butter we get from them now is very nasty tasting from the turnips which they get. We have just taken up twenty sacks of potatoes from our field, all very fairly good, so we shall be well stocked for the winter which is a comfort. My fowls are doing nothing just now. I am going to get Indian corn to feed them on instead of barley; farmers tell me it is both cheaper and better. Of course their main food is scraps from the house, but they have to have a little corn.[44]

A year later in the middle of summer she wrote of 'making rhubarb jam and green gooseberry jelly, and I shall advance to strawberry jam in a fortnight or so. The haymaking has not got on very well, we have had such showery weather. It has been just like April, most violent showers followed by brilliant sunshine. It is just what the farmers want for their dearly loved turnips but is not so useful for our hay.'

Then that autumn she wrote of having just imported 'a keg of Irish butter, seventy-three lbs at £1 4s. 4d., and it is lovely butter, quite nice to eat, in fact we like it better than any other in the winter'. One of their chief problems, naturally, was the difficulty of getting food provisions for the winter. Louise told her mother that she was 'glad to lay in stores of anything. How are you off for apples? Ours are so small that they seem hardly worth cooking, and none can be found really big enough to satisfy my love for baked apples. Pears we have none and our poor figs tho' they have grown to a good size have never ripened.'[45] Louise was highly conscious about the cost of food and livestock, something that did not concern her as much before moving to the remote north. 'We have got another cow, a young one who has just had her first calf, and who at present is troublesome to milk and makes my kitchenmaid groan, and we have two small pigs. Pigs are a ruinous price; these were 35s. each. One of the cows cost £18 and the other £20. Is my five and a half pounds of butter too much or too little that you express amazement at it? We only made three and a half pounds since the Aclands came, but now of course shall make more with the two cows.'[46] In another letter, she states:

> I have discovered what perhaps you know, that lard makes the most lovely crust for meat pies, better than butter crust. We indulge in rabbit pies or fish pies on Sundays which are very good and economical; a chicken pie with a little beef steak is also very good. I am sure a second Sunday dish is a great economy; nothing is such expensive food as blocks of roast beef.
>
> We are in a melancholy predicament for want of milk. Any kind of pudding or sauce made with milk is an impossibility. So is coffee in the morning. The children's puddings have to be made with condensed milk, and are not very nice. My cook is getting on very well on the whole; she is not a genius but is teachable. We have a baking once a week, and get some very nice bread tho' of course not enough for everything.[47]

The major cross Louise had to bear at Embleton, however, seems to have been managing her servants. Louise often spiced her letters to her family with countless references to her 'domestic troubles', ordeals with servants that caused her anguish, as can be seen from the following random selections:

> [25 April 1875] My idiotic housemaid has departed to be under housemaid to Mrs Craster for £12 instead of the £17 she demanded from me. I have another coming to-morrow, who I hope may prove more successful. Our gardener has also come. He is a wonderful man for he brought some plants with him, and has already got the greenhouse to look a little decent.[48]

> [8 October 1876] I shall have to change my nursemaid, this one will never answer. She is a sulky sort of girl, very thoughtless and seems to have no interest in children. She has lovely eyebrows but I am afraid they are not enough to constitute a good nursemaid. I think I shall have no difficulty in hearing of one here now, as at the November time all the girls look out for places; and I can keep this one till I hear of another satisfactory one.[49]

> [22 April 1878] You ask about Marie [Louise's Swiss nursemaid]. I think she does very well, and I like her on the whole extremely. She seems to me to have very good principles, and be thoroughly conscientious. Eliza [head nurse] is a little fond of fault-finding, and comes to me with stories of Marie's having disobeyed her orders and so on; but I can generally trace them to some misunderstanding resulting from the difference of language. Upper servants seem to me far more exacting in their demands on underservants than mistresses are. Marie has nice ways with the children and tries to be firm with them, tho' of course the language difficulty is not easy for her always to make them obey.[50]

> [13 April 1880] I have my needlewoman back making many frocks and hope to get all my work for the summer done this time. Five children seem to need so very many frocks, it is quite awful to contemplate.[51]

On one occasion she hired a cook and considered it fortunate that the woman's husband could be the groom and take care of the animals. The cook's name was Mrs Holmes and she worked out well enough, but her husband proved a disaster. Louise complained to her mother that 'domestic troubles will never cease', telling her sadly that she saw

> no hope of lasting peace for us at present for that wretch Holmes is as unsatis-factory as possible. I have always tried to speak up for him, and hope he was not so bad as he seemed; but now Mrs Holmes spoke to Max and asked him to try what he could do by speaking to Holmes to make him go less to the public house. He spends most of the day there so no wonder all his work is left undone. Mrs Holmes says that nothing she can say or do makes him any better and she wished Max to try.
>
> So Max has done his utmost to instill virtue into Holmes but is afraid it won't be much good. Moreover we hear from the policeman who is a most respectable trustworthy man, that Holmes uses the most fearful language all about the village, worse than any of the quarrymen and they are renowned for their swearing.
>
> You will see the prospect is not very hopeful. I am so sorry for Mrs Holmes; she naturally enough says that it makes her very miserable; she is such a good creature, and takes such a wise view of things and quite sees it will never do for us to keep him unless he improves. Of course we can do nothing but try and look after him and keep him in order if possible. At present he is a clear loss to us; he neglects everything—cows, pigs, poney [sic], carriage.
>
> The pigs won't be ready to kill for Christmas, the poney [sic] and the carriage are in a disgraceful state. I wish he would die and we could keep her forever; I shall never wish to have a better or more faithful servant. But I am afraid that with a drunk and swearing groom, our reputation in the village will be no better than ever.[52]

The problem soon reached the crisis stage. Louise decided she had to dismiss the groom and therefore lose a worthy cook. But employing a new cook was never easy, she knew, and a couple months later she told her mother she was still 'struggling' to find a suitable cook. 'Mrs Holmes would gladly stay on a little after he [the groom] goes and join him when he has got work, but at present he says he won't let her. It seems that when she has paid one or two bills which they owe up here they will have hardly any money left.' Then Louise became 'perfectly disgusted' at the condition in which she found the pony one day which was used to pull their dogcart. The animal was in a sorry state,

> so thin and wretched; and has to be urged along when one drives her. From all sides we hear tales of the furious and cruel manner in which he [Holmes] drives her, and of course that especially with these winter roads in destruction, besides he does not feed her regularly so that she does not get half enough. One of our

cows is nearly going dry with no prospect of calving because he neglected to take her to the farm when he was told; so she is simply ruined. With all this I am impatient to get him out of the place as soon as possible and yet should like to get another cook before parting with her; perhaps we may manage somehow to get him to go off.[53]

A few days later, Louise wrote to her mother with better news. 'You will be glad to hear that I have at last, I think so, got a cook', she said. 'I hardly like to count upon her till she is actually in the house, but I hope there will be no slip. She comes from Edinburgh, is thirty and very ugly which is a recommendation to my mind. I have also got another nursemaid.'[54] Then a month later, she wrote:

My dearest Mother,
    You will soon begin to laugh at me and my domestic worries. They are really too absurd. This wretched old cook of ours arrived on Wednesday, and has spent the time since then mostly in tears, and saying she never was in such an awful spot in her life. Now she ends by saying she must go away to-morrow or she will die, and her state of mind is so imbecile that the only thing to be done is to let her go, or she will either fret herself into an illness, or make the other servants so wretched that they will all want to go too. The reasons of her conduct I cannot discover. She says she never in all her life saw such a frightful hole as our kitchen, that no human being ever could do the work here, that she has felt ill since the moment she entered the house etc.
    The truth I think is that she caught a slight cold coming down and that she naturally feels a little strange here at first, and does not easily understand the Northumbrian housemaid, and has not enough pluck to try and get over it. I have given her hardly anything to do, and gave her a woman all Saturday to do her cleaning, and promised her further help of the same kind as long as we have these two pupils, but all to no purpose; there is no response but tears. Max is furious and gives me one indignant message after another to give her, which naturally I don't give, in fact I don't go near her. It is only disgusting that I have to pay her fare from London, 26s. for the pleasure of these three days.
    Our new boy [groom] is the great joke; he is aged but fourteen but is at present a model of virtue, and immensely delighted with being here. He says to the cook 'You don't know what's the matter with you, wait three weeks and then see how you'll like it'. Eliza [the head nurse] is indignant with her, and my housemaid says, 'She seems quite broken hearted. I don't know what to make of her'. However here we are left cookless once more. I don't know whether I shan't try and get Mrs Holmes back. She said the last thing, she would come if this cook didn't stay and leave Holmes in London. But till she writes I don't know her address.
    I have managed to get an old woman about seventy to come in and do for us to-morrow; she was once a cook so perhaps we may manage to get on with her. The bother is not knowing Mrs Holmes' address, so we can do nothing but wait,

and see if we hear anything. She promised to write shortly, but did not know where she was going to, and so could not give us her address before going ...

Goodbye dearest mother. This is a stupid letter I fear, the absence of a cook does not tend to make one more capable of writing amusing letters.

Your loving child,
Louise [55]

In a month's time, however, Louise had secured a new cook and wrote happily that her spirits 'have just been cheered by hearing of a cook who will come on Saturday. It is to be hoped she may be a success; but she is rather an experiment; as she has been at home for a year, but her character as head kitchenmaid from her last place is a very good one.' [56]

Louise, as many Victorians did, took special interest in her gardens and shrubs and flowers, all of which were important ingredients to their everyday life because they added colour to an otherwise—at least to the modern mind— cosmetically drab and dreary existence. An enjoyment of flower-cultivation began in the late medieval period and continued to grow in popularity. By the middle of the nineteenth century no country could equal England in the flower-gardening craze, a socially wide appeal that cut across both the island and the various classes.[57] To the Victorians, their garden was more than just a physical place of wild, irregular profusion of kaleidoscope colours, it held a deeper meaning that bordered on mystery or mysticism. Louise, though never spending time working in the soil, took serious note of every bloom and sprig in her garden, and must have been like a bee buzzing around the head of her gardener. 'The garden was a great joy to me. Everything flourished there, as it was very sheltered and the soil was very good. We improved it a great deal', she said. 'We planted many roses taking in a bit of rough vegetable ground to make rose beds. We had a most worthy and industrious gardener, Egdell, and I enjoyed superintending him, but did not garden myself.' [58] In one letter to her mother, Louise wrote of being 'busy with great improvements on our garden, which will I hope be as successful as we imagine', adding:

I am quite alarmed at our gardener; he has such a tremendous love for destruction, which could be all very well if one could hope that new things would grow up as high as the old in no time. Every time I go out into the garden he meets me with some new demand for cutting down a tree, pulling up a shrub or pulling down creepers. He has made me consent to the destruction of all the old creepers on the house and to plant new ones. I believe he is right tho' of course we are condemned to a temporary period of bareness, but the creepers were in a wretched condition; mouldy old roses which never flowered and were only a home for slugs. We have got a lot of new roses; they do so wonderfully here that I am tempted to go on and get more and more.[59]

Whenever the weather was decent, both Mandell and Louise loved to be outdoors; when at home, much time was spent walking in the gardens and fields of the vicarage. For Louise, who preferred landscape sketching and painting, Embleton provided her an opportunity to take up her pencils and brushes again. At Oxford she had done some watercolour paintings before Beatrice was born. Now at Embleton she managed to resume her sketching and painting, often while on outings with the children and their nurse. She claimed that in painting she discovered 'the special charm' of the region's winding shoreline and broad skies. 'Perhaps it is making too much of my small efforts to say this,' she later said, 'but I think that it was through my sketching that the country got hold of me and became part of me. What I learnt by sketching at Embleton was a help when later I managed to sketch during our journeys abroad. At first I never could find the oppor-tunity; later I tried always to do something when we rested in the middle of the day.'[60] Louise's sketches and paintings were mostly of landscapes and seascapes; and, though they reveal some basic talent, her style tended to be taut and unimaginative.

The Creightons made four journeys to Italy while at Embleton. The first was in January 1878. Louise was expecting her fourth child. The Creightons planned on leaving in late December 1877. Their party consisted of Mandell's sister, Polly, along with Emma ('Effie') Pease and her younger brother Joseph ('Jack', later Lord Gainford of Headlam); both were children of Sir Joseph Pease. Also joining the ranks was Vincent Hamlyn, one of Creighton's former pupils. It was not long afterward that Effie and Vincent became engaged and were married.[61] Louise said 'it seemed very difficult and unpleasant to put off our proposed journey' because she was expecting in the spring, so she consulted her physician who assured her that 'he thought I could quite safely go as I was so strong and my confinements had all gone so well'.[62]

In October, while still debating whether or not she should make the trip, Louise wrote to her mother:

> Your remarks about the Italian journey go far to convince me, if I needed convincing, that there is nothing risky in it. I am not in the least afraid of doing too much in Rome; there is not nearly so much risk of that as there often is of my doing too much at home. Here often I feel tempted to go on slaving rather than leave things half done or undone, or leave them to other people. There I should only have to amuse myself; and Max is not one of those dependent husbands who can enjoy nothing without his wife; he would never want to drag me about more than I was able.[63]

As Christmas approached Louise was confident that she could make the trip without difficulty. Leaving Beatrice, Lucia and Cuthbert at Peak Hill

Lodge with Louise's family, the Creightons and their party left England two days after Christmas, travelling at a leisurely pace through southern France and over the mountain passes into Italy. At Turin, Louise wrote home that 'the weather was lovely and the sea fairly calm, and we should have had a splendid and quick crossing only that when we reached Calais the tide was so low that we were kept waiting quite an hour tossing about in rather a horrid manner in a very cold wind. Polly succumbed utterly and I only saved myself by a retreat to the cabin, whilst the others managed to bare [sic] up on deck.' She also assured her mother that she was 'very flourishing except for a horrid cold in my head which I think I must have caught from the children and which makes life rather a burden ... We mean to be at Pisa from Monday till Wednesday and I shall hope to find a letter there. We shall stop afterwards a day at Siena and Orvieto each and get to Rome Friday I expect; and you will let me have a letter there.'64 From Rome, Louise wrote: 'We are a most jolly party, and all seem to possess endless capacities of enjoying ourselves.'65

While in Rome, Victor Emmanuel II, King of Italy, died and, as they discovered, many public buildings such as museums and galleries were closed in consequence of the mourning. This was Creightons' first time together in Rome, though Louise had been there once before with her parents. The party travelled on to Naples for a few days before returning to Rome where misfortune struck. Polly and Effie came down with what was diagnosed as a form of malaria; and then Mandell received word that his father had unexpectedly died. Polly returned to England immediately, accompanied by Effie Pease, though Mandell decided to remain on, it being too late to get back in time for the funeral.66 They made their way from Rome to Florence and then on to Venice. 'It is most delightful to be in Venice again', Louise wrote home, 'and I think we shall enjoy our four days here thoroughly. Then we go to Verona and so home. We mean at present to get to London on Thursday week.'67

It was while they were at Venice that Louise was taken ill with a fever, and what followed was 'a nightmare journey home'. They decided to curtail their trip and return to England. Louise 'had the most violent headache and at night I think I must have been in high fever for I never slept at all and could hardly eat anything all the way. Tho' Max did all that was necessary to take care of me, I felt him rather unsympathetic and imagined that he could not realise how ill I felt.' She said that he later told her that 'his one idea was to give me courage to get back to England by making as if he did not think me very bad, and hiding his anxiety'.68 When they reached Sydenham in early February, Louise was immediately put to bed with 'a raging delirium'. She explained what happened next:

It is useless to describe the miseries of the illness for me or the horrible terrors and delusions I suffered from. For Max it must have been awful, as not only to watch me, but to be told by the doctors that probably my mind might not recover for a year. He was a wonderful nurse. He could always soothe me, and I am afraid I constantly screamed for his help even when he was away at his meals. At last they decided that the labour must be brought on by forced means. They were very doubtful whether the child could be born alive. But all went wonderfully well. Walter was safely brought into the world, of course a very small, but a perfectly healthy baby. As soon as he was born I was quite myself again, able to nurse him from the first and my recovery was uninterrupted. For many days afterwards Max still twitched all over with nervousness and could not keep himself quiet. But all went well and he was able to leave me and go back to Embleton.[69]

This serious illness, Louise confessed, caused her to reflect in later years about 'what illness does, or should do, for one. Perhaps this illness made me realise more than ever the reality and greatness of my happiness. Certainly my convalescense was a happy time, and it was a joy to get back to the children and to our full home life with all its interests, and its work.'[70]

In the month of May the following year, 1879, the Creightons returned to Italy, again asking Polly to accompany them. 'It was not a very successful journey', Louise remembered, as 'it rained a great deal, and Polly was not a very tactful travelling companion. She never realised that we might like to be alone sometimes, but came every where and did every thing with us so that we were always à trois.'[71] They went through southern France stopping at Avignon to see the old palace of the popes, and on to northern Italy to Mantua, Pavia and Trent, the scene of the great church council in the sixteenth century, and finally on to Venice—having missed many of these sights the year before because of Louise's illness. Leaving Italy, they then crossed over the Brenner Pass en route to Munich, stopping at Constance, the site of the momentous council in the fifteenth century that not only condemned John Hus to death but struggled to end the Great Schism. While on their way home Mandell received a telegram announcing the death of his Aunt Jane.

In January 1881, another death rocked the family: Louise's mother died. 'I had been to see her only a little while before,' Louise said, 'a strange visit—she lying in bed mostly half asleep, the poor father wandering about distraught, and many of the usual family friends gathered downstairs.'[72]

My last, happiest memory of her is sleeping like a quiet child when I went up to say goodnight. She died on January 14. On the 16th there was the most terrible blizzard I have ever known. We were all imprisoned in the house, and many were the adventures of the brothers who had to go up to London. The funeral had to be put off till the roads were opened up, and then it was with difficulty that we got through the snow to the cemetery. They were strange sad days of waiting at The Peak. We spent them largely in reading aloud old letters from our grandmother about her journey to India which we had discovered by chance. My father was wonderfully patient and good all the time, but a little puzzled and bewildered. This grew worse as the years passed. I think I had two more visits from him at Embleton and I went to Sydenham as often as I could. My mother's not being there made a great emptiness.[73]

In her memoir, Louise described their special relationship and wrote that she doubted 'if one ever fully realises the place one's mother fills in one's life till she is gone. There is no one who like her feels an interest in every little thing that concerns one, whose sympathy can always be counted upon. In my case too I felt a rather special responsibility for my mother, as I had so often travelled with her, so often taken care of her in illness, and I knew that she leant upon me, and that my happy life was a great joy and interest to her.'[74] Louise shared a closer bond with her mother than with her father.

In the spring of 1881 the Creightons went off to Italy again, this time just the two of them; and—understandably after the melancholy events of the last two trips—they left England with some 'forebodings' which they never mentioned to one another until they returned, having had 'one of the most delightful journeys we ever had'.[75]

We were mostly in the little towns of Umbria and did a great deal of driving from one place to another, a method of travelling in which we grew more and more to delight, and which seemed to bring us into touch with the country and the life of the people. We were very rapid travellers in those days. We seldom stayed more than one night at a little town. We wanted to see as many places as we could and we saw them pretty thoroughly. But we did not explore the country outside, or take long walks as we did in later years, when we more fully discovered the charm of Italian country and were less exclusively occupied with art and history. On this particular journey we visited twenty-six different towns between April 26 and May 29, some of them only for the day. We made acquaintance for the first time with Assisi, [and] went as far south as Spezia [and also visited] Terni, Vallombrosa, Rimini, Gubbio, Urbino, etc.[76]

Creighton discovered Pienza, a village favoured by of one of the more interesting Renaissance popes, Pius II (Aeneas Sylvius Piccolomini), who adorned it with new buildings and art works. By 1881, however, much of the village stood depressingly desolate and nearly in ruins. Mandell and Louise often abandoned the railway to rent a light one-horse carriage so they could explore the countryside. They never took a guide, always trusting to their sense of direction and good fortune to come upon interesting places and common people far from the tourist's haunts. In the late afternoons they would stop at country inns, both of them spending the evening between dinner and bed sitting in front of some café, chatting with locals while Mandell smoked his last cigarettes of the day. 'A journey of this sort was a most complete refreshment', Louise said. 'Eye and mind alike were fed almost without effort.' This trip they both thought later was one of the most pleasing holidays they ever shared, and for him it was an opportunity to experience rural Italy. 'Is not Italy delightful?', he wrote to a friend later, claiming that 'one takes in new ideas through one's pores, it seems to me, without any conscious effort'.[77]

In the spring of the next year, 1882, they went to Italy again, travelling straight to Rome where they spent ten days studying the sites related to Renaissance papal history. Leaving the Eternal City, they journeyed into the neighbouring countryside, eventually going north to Florence and Milan before returning to England.

> During these journeys [Louise said] Max would gladly have done without any letters at all, but I insisted on having news of the children and so we had to have addresses. We did not mind roughing it and put up in many very primitive places, and did for days with very little luggage, only hand bags. We enjoyed it all immensely. I am afraid that we neither of us had perfect tempers. I was exacting and he was irritable, and I used to be foolishly hurt by sharp words which meant nothing. I don't wish to imply that any of this was very serious, but it would be false to suppose that we were one of those angelic couples who never spoke a sharp word to one another or had any disagreement.
>
> Travelling always brings out these small difficulties; fortunately it brings also opportunities for very great happiness ... We liked the same things and wanted to do the same things. We did not want to make acquaintances by the way, except with people of the country, on whom Max practised his Italian. We disliked the life in smart hotels, but could thoroughly enjoy a brief plunge into a really comfortable hotel. My view was that I did not mind how rough a place was in a little out of the way town, but that in a big town I liked to go to a good hotel. I took very few clothes with me, just one change in case of accidents. The chief difficulty was to have enough books for the evenings. I used at times to feel a little homesick for the children and the prospect of getting back to them made the journey home very delightful.[78]

On each of the trips to Italy during those years, Louise managed to sketch and paint landscapes and buildings of interest whenever she had the time to sit an hour or two. 'I accomplished it by making up my mind always to sketch whatever was possible when we stopt for lunch on a ramble.'[79] Because cameras had not yet become the normal appendage on tourists' bodies, Mandell purchased photographs and drawings for those sites that caught his interest.

It was in the winter of their first year at Embleton that Creighton was asked by a fellow academic, Dr Percival of Clifton College, to tutor a young man who had failed the Indian Civil Service examination. Louise said she hated the idea of a resident pupil living at the vicarage, but Creighton felt it financially necessary. He had previously agreed to be an examiner at Oxford and the University of Durham. So to Louise's 'great disgust' the first student, Trevor Berrington, arrived in January 1876. 'I minded very much the interruption of my quiet life with Max', Louise said.

> It had always been my habit to sit in his study and do my writing and reading there, now I had to sit in the dining-room that he might have his pupil in the study. However, in the end Trevor became so dear to both of us that I felt the gain more than the loss. He was the first and the dearest of a long series of pupils. Only a few came for a long period and the more usual plan was to have several together, men already at the university, for a few weeks in the summer.[80]

In a letter to her mother she wrote that the 'pupils are a little provoking. We had quite made up our minds to having four together for a month and devoting ourselves to them, but now they will go draggling on all through the summer.'[81] Louise, however, soon came to think it was a 'very good plan' for her husband to take in pupils, thus adding to their income. 'It was all most informal', she said. The pupils 'quite belonged to the family and I liked most of them very much. I was interested to discover how fond most young men were of children, and our children thoroughly enjoyed the pupils, and on the whole so did I.'[82]

Creighton was particular about the young men he took in as resident pupils, and after a year or two, wrote that he was 'deluged with applications'. He believed that reading assignments 'must be hard work, and the subject must be stiff', yet his study routine for pupils, Louise thought, was 'most unconventional', very relaxed and conversational. Students would sit working in his study while Creighton read or wrote.

> At times he would break off in his writing, and spend an hour, not so much in definite teaching, as in discussing the point which the pupil had been reading. His object was to make those whom he taught think for themselves, to guide them and arouse their curiosity, to fertilise what was in their mind rather than to find out how much they knew. Sometimes the historical discussion would take place pacing up and down the terrace in the garden, and he would talk about the period of history the pupil was reading just as he might have talked about it to a friend in society.[83]

Among his pupils at Embleton were Trevor Berrington, Paul Bevan, young Stopford Brooke (son of Stopford A. Brooke, an Anglo-Irish clergyman, literary writer and art critic), Sir George Sitwell, Lord Lymington (later Earl of Portsmouth), T. G. Carmichael (later Sir Thomas Gibson Carmichael), Lord Porchester, Hugo Charteris (later Lord Elcho), Alfred Pease (later Sir Alfred Pease), and Edward Grey (later Sir Edward Grey, afterwards Viscount Grey of Fallodon). Louise could never disguise her feelings easily, and regarding resident pupils she was less than subtle about those she liked or disliked. She considered George Sitwell, for example, 'conceited and rude', and wrote to her mother that he was 'a conceited prig, but he will not trouble me long for he does not seem to mean to read more than about three weeks and he cannot be said to read much as it is. He thinks it is bad for his digestion to read for more than an hour without taking a walk in the garden or playing a game of tennis.' And she regarded Lord Lymington as 'very greedy'.[84]

About others she noted that young Stopford Brooke and Lord Porchester 'irritated me by their untidy, slovenly ways'. Next to Trevor Berrington, who was Creighton's first resident pupil and Louise's favourite, she liked Alfred Pease, T. G. Carmichael, Hugo Charteris and Edward Grey, though she never quite thought of Grey as a resident pupil since he lived at Fallodon Hall two miles away, and only once during a summer did he actually live at the vicarage.[85] After a mediocre performance at Winchester, Edward Grey went up to Oxford where his academic performance was less than stunning. Sir George Grey asked Creighton to take charge of his grandson's reading in the summer of 1881, to which Creighton replied:

> My dear Sir George,
>   I have been thinking over the plan that Edward should read with me. I cannot help thinking that if he does so, it would be a help to him if he stayed here. Besides the supervision of work, there is need for a general atmosphere of work, and that I think I can provide. I find that the best thing I can do for anyone is to show him how to work, and I have been pleased with the testimony of pupils, not only that they did work here, but that they actually began to enjoy the process.[86]

In this note to Sir George are two of Creighton's cardinal principles of sound scholarship, that the enemy of study is distraction and that true teaching is to show a student how to learn, not what to learn. Young Grey's passion was not in books but in fly-fishing streams, a passion that he never lost. Yet Creighton saw promise in him, much as he had with Lord Randolph Churchill. Grey came to Embleton and benefited greatly, coming to regard Creighton, along with Jowett at Balliol, as one of the two great men in his educational upbringing. In his autobiography, Grey wrote of Creighton as 'a very remarkable man' who took

> certain specially recommended pupils in history. He had a great admiration for my Grandfather, and my Grandfather found the greatest delight in his society. There

sprang up between them a peculiarly close friendship and my Grandfather asked Creighton in my first long vacation if he would take me as a pupil in Classical Moderations. Creighton replied that I needed no coaching for Classical Moderations, but he could provide the atmosphere of work only if I would come and live in his house. This was arranged, and I spent a month or two at the vicarage.

Creighton had wonderful power of concentration. He was at the time writing his history of the Papacy. In his study there were two pupils reading history, and Creighton would break off his writing in order to take them out one by one, in summer weather, to walk up and down the garden path and talk to them about the period of history of which they were reading, and then return to his writing again. I meanwhile was left alone in the drawing-room, to read books which were required for Moderations In this way I did read a certain amount during the hours which were set apart in the vicarage for work, and to this no doubt it was due that eventually, in the autumn of 1881, about one year after I went up to Oxford, l got a second in 'Mods'. More than this I certainly did not deserve by the amount of reading I had done.[87]

In many ways, Edward Grey became like an older son to Creighton, and his friendship with both the Creightons became lifelong. Grey loved to visit the vicarage as a student, and the old weeping ash tree in the garden just beyond the conservatory, blown down by hurricane force winds in the 1950s, was remembered as the tree that Sir Edward Grey and Creighton would sit under on a summer's day while discussing some historical point. Grey loved the Embleton garden and sometimes wished, while imprisoned with his books in the drawing-room at Embleton, that he could trade places with the gardener who happened to walk by the windows pushing a wheelbarrow along the terrace.[88] When in 1885 the young baronet married Dorothy Widdrington from Newton-on-the-Moor, he found a companion whose mind had also been greatly broadened by Creighton. A handsome, proud and silent young woman who was much too critical of herself and others, Dorothy had found in Creighton a sympathetic mentor. 'It was extraordinarily comforting that he understood how much I wanted to be good', she admitted. 'I had been in a perpetual state of self defence, and was hostile and superior because I was in such a fright of people. Then I was filled with gratitude to him and began to understand that I had better be kind too to other people.'[89]

Alfred Pease, after leaving Grove House School and taking his entrance examination to Trinity College, Cambridge, was sent by his father in 1876 to Creighton for a summer of reading . Like Grey, Pease found Creighton stimulating and helpful, and subsequently a good friend, though he had some private reservations about his tutor's character. Alfred wrote in his diary that he thought Creighton a short tempered man with a great confidence in himself, a great delight in outrageous propositions and great powers of a certain sort in conversation and argument. He appeared to despise everyone around him save the visitors he hospitably entertained which hailed from Oxford. He had all sorts of people there from time to time who appeared to me to be most weird and dull ... I never regarded him in any way a religious man but rather as a good actor in the different parts he played. I was always fond of him. He had a warm heart and was faithful to his friends. The things which shocked me were his violent quarrels with his wife alternating with such demonstrations before Berrington and me of affection for Mrs Creighton as I had never seen before. He would have her on his knee in our study or library and they would fondle and kiss each other. No doubt it was a bore to them to have two boys with them in their first years of married life.[90]

Like many brilliant men of talent, charm and energy, Creighton tended to be self-centred and confident. Wherever he was, he managed to be the centre of attention, particularly among his family and friends. He could be explosive and, like many perfectionists, easily vented his annoyances on those nearest and dearest too him. Young Pease, coming to know Creighton, became puzzled about the vicar's personal religious beliefs. Most of Creighton's friends were also puzzled because his spirituality seemed like a mixture of childlike faith and sophisticated moral reasoning. Actually, Creighton's métier was more ethical than religious, and even though he often wrote or spoke on religious themes, his deeper, personal spirituality remained mysterious. In his letters to Alfred Pease during these years, however, one finds something about Creighton's views on specific religious questions, such as the thorny issue over the nature of the eucharist. Perhaps the specific problem for Pease in this matter rested on the fact that his Quakerism never quite squared with Creighton's views of history and orthodoxy. Whatever the case, Alfred Pease later joined the established church.[91] Another interesting theme in Creighton's letters to Pease concerned their mutual interest in politics. 'Knowledge about the history of this century is quite necessary for anyone who looks to politics', he once wrote to Alfred. 'Foreign politics must for some time be prominent, and the woeful ignorance of the facts which prevails among public men is really distressing.'[92]

Creighton's political beliefs were less obscure than his religious beliefs. He came from a Liberal family in Carlisle, and for the most part remained so the rest of his life, though he favoured the Unionist-Conservative coalition during the Irish Home Rule crisis in the mid 1880s—which forced him quickly to assure Sir Edward Grey, then in politics: 'Please do not imagine that I have turned Conservative.'[93] When Albert Grey decided to enter politics, running for a south Northumberland seat in Parliament during the general election of 1880 on the Liberal ticket, Creighton gave him his support. Though reluctant to express his political ideas publicly because of his position as a clergyman, he became known as a 'blue priest', blue then being the Northumberland Liberal Party colour.[94] Creighton accompanied Albert Grey to several political rallies and even spoke for him in the mining districts of the southern Northumberland constituency, justifying it on grounds that it was not in his parish. Just before the election in February, Creighton agreed to attend a political dinner and speak at a Liberal demonstration in Alnwick, a Tory stronghold. The only active part he took in Embleton itself during the election was to lend his pony carriage to carry voters to the polls, and to cast his own ballot—the only time in his life, according to Louise, that he voted in a parliamentary election.[95]

Creighton also spoke for his friend George Howard at a Liberal meeting in Carlisle. 'His speech received immense applause', Louise tells us, 'and created real excitement.' The citizens seemed particularly pleased, not only with his ideas, but with the fact that he was a fellow Cumbrian.[96] After the election, Louise wrote to her mother: 'Well I suppose the political excitement is over for the present. Mr Albert Grey's election was the last we personally cared about and that was got over satisfactorily last week. It is amusing to hear the political talk of the villagers now as one visits. The contest has certainly woke them up to take more interest in affairs. One old fisherman took Max most severely to task for being a Liberal.'[97]

Creighton was again tempted into a making a minor political gesture in 1884, with the result that, his actions being misconstrued and criticised, he abandoned forever his public role in secular politics. The issue arose over Edward Grey's role on the franchise question at a political meeting in Alnwick. The House of Lords had refused to pass the government's Bill to enfranchise the working classes in county constituencies, as had been granted to the towns in the 1867 Act. Agitation against the Lords erupted across England. The few Liberal squires in the north saw this as the moment to lead, and Sir Edward was asked to chair the meeting. The young baronet had just left Oxford; he was twenty-two and had never made a public speech, not even at the Oxford Union.[98] He sought Creighton's advice on his speech. In a letter agreeing to help young Grey, Mandell wrote on 29 July 1884:

Dear Edward,

I am very glad that you are coming on Saturday. It is quite the right thing to do. Use every opportunity that may offer itself of making yourself a political personage, with a distinct line. Though I did not want to do anything myself, when I was shown your letter I said that I would go to the meeting. Frankly, it is rather hard work to keep Liberalism respectable in these parts, and I have been more political than I could have wished, from a feeling that it was my duty to do what I could to keep Liberal politics respectable and serious.

I should say that a speech of a quarter of an hour was about the right thing. If you aim at a quarter of an hour you will perhaps hit twenty minutes, which will do very well. It does not much matter what you say; you are sure to say what is all right and proper ... Have before yourself some point which you are going to lead up to and with which you are going to finish, and have the strength of mind to sit down when you have reached it, and have fired the shot which you meant to be your last.

There is a great temptation not to have an ending definitely prepared. This leads a speaker to wander about aimlessly at last, and repeat himself and flounder about and do away with the effect of the first part of his speech. He is like a bore who has come to see you, and does not know how or when to say 'good-bye' ...

Remember that it is better people should say 'I am sorry it is over', than 'I am glad that it is over'. Therefore, I say, prepare a definite statement carefully which you are going to lead up to. You may trust your inspiration of the moment how you get there. But when you have gotten there, say it clearly and sit down. I shall hope to see you on Friday.[99]

Grey prepared his speech, and rehearsed it for Creighton in the library at Fallodon Hall on the day of the meeting. 'He said it was exactly the right thing for me to say', remarked Grey. Then, hopping in a dogcart, the two men drove the six miles from Fallodon to Alnwick. At the meeting Creighton said a few words of introduction that, according to Grey, 'pleased the people very much'.[100] Sir Edward's speech was a roaring success, so much so that he was urged to run for the House of Commons as a Liberal candidate for the constituency of Berwick in the 1885 election. He did and won the seat from Lord Henry Percy in the November election, a seat he held onto for the remainder of his long political career.

During the election, rumours were circulated by Grey's political opponents that Creighton had written the young man's speech at Alnwick and was indeed writing all of Sir Edward's speeches throughout the campaign. This annoyed both of them. Creighton, of course, had not written the speeches, and, the fact of the matter was, he disapproved of some of Grey's political sentiments on the grounds that they were too radical.[101] From that point on Creighton eschewed public politics and came to hold the view that clergy should refrain from secular politics. In subsequent years, therefore, he became less and less a party man, caused also in part by his growing disenchantment with Gladstone's policies on widening the franchise, on the disestablishment of the Anglican Church and over the Irish question.

10

A Great Work

'I can assure you from experience that life is not complete unless one has a 'great work' on the stocks; I think one's happiness is increased if the work is so great that one has no hopes of ever finishing it.'

Mandell Creighton to Oscar Browning [1]

Mandell Creighton's reason for going to Embleton in the first place was so he could study and write about history in a quiet atmosphere of peace. And though his life as a rural vicar was hardly quiet and peaceful, he and his wife, collectively, managed to publish a total of fifteen books and a number of articles while there. In Mandell's case, his writings brought him national acclaim as a scholar. For Louise, her several primers established her as a respected writer of children's history. When placed within the context of everything else they did in the course of those busy years, their literary achievements are even more remarkable. And for Louise, it is especially impressive when realising that during the greater bulk of those years at Embleton she was only in her twenties.

Creighton's primer on Roman history, which was published in 1875 after they arrived at Embleton, had, of course, been written at Oxford. Likewise with most of Louise's first book, *England: A Continental Power. From the Conquest to Magna Carta*, which appeared the following year.[2] The publisher, Longmans, had asked Creighton, while still at Oxford, to edit a series of primers on 'Epochs of English History', which he agreed to do, arranging to have Louise write the volume on English foreign policy for the series. The result was her primer *England: A Continental Power*, a slim volume of some sixty-six pages that outlined the impact of the Norman invasion and its influence on Anglo-Saxon England. As this was her first real literary effort, her writing style was slightly awkward compared with her later writings. Mandell's school books at that time were *The Tudors and the Reformation* and *The Age of Elizabeth*, the latter being a volume in Longmans' new 'Epochs of European History' series. Both were published in 1876. As it turned out, the book on Elizabeth proved to be one of the more popular primers of that era. He accepted £100 for the copyright, thus giving up future royalties, an arrangement that he subsequently regretted. Thereafter, both for them always retained the copyrights in their books.

Creighton had definite feelings about books directed towards young people. He wrote to his publisher that the 'great danger' was that such educational books 'turn out to be extremely useful and very interesting to *grown-up people.* He told C. J. Longman, that everything he had seen 'intended for beginners has slipped away from its purpose'. He felt it his duty as editor to keep school books focused on what young readers needed.[3] In another letter to Longman, he explained his philosophy about school books, stating that they should run to about eighty pages, and that each ought to be written 'in the simplest possible way for the use of beginners, and should avoid all unnecessary names and details which did not bear on the subject'.[4] In a follow-up reply, Creighton said he hoped he was 'not too sanguine in anticipating that the "Epochs of English History" will be used in all kinds of schools', such as in the lower forms of the public schools, in the grammar schools, and in the broad spectrum of board schools. 'Also I think they would be of great service in Girls' Schools, which seem to me to be just now an element in the demand for school books, which is daily becoming more important, and I have kept my eye on them in this series.'[5] It should be remembered that while popular education was a new phenomen sweeping the country—what some have termed a 'silent social revolution'—school books specifically geared to the young middle- and lower-class students crowding into these new classrooms across the landscape were an innovative curricular feature in Britain.[6]

Creighton also agreed to edit a series called 'Historical Biographies' for another publisher, Rivingtons, and in this series he wrote the *Life of Simon de Montfort, Earl of Leicester,* published in 1877. Louise had written the *Life of Edward the Black Prince,* which came out the year before, for the same publisher. Louise also added to this particular series by writing the *Life of Sir Walter Raleigh* (1877), and the *Life of John Churchill, Duke of Marlborough* (1879).[7] Both Mandell and Louise possessed the knack for writing books for young people because both were good story-tellers possessing easy, unencumbered writing styles with a flair for the picturesque word and the dramatic phrase that could catch a child's imagination. Being excellent writers, their narratives were readable and uncomplicated. As far as Louise is concerned, she claimed no difficulty in writing, saying that it always came easily for her: 'I do not suppose that my style has any distinction, but I think that it is easy and direct. I know what I want to say, and can say it ...'[8] The following passage from her little biography of the Black Prince, describing a medieval tournament, is a typical example of her prose:

Though the tournaments were only looked upon as sport, they were often attended with great danger, and the knights engaged in the combat were not seldom severely wounded, and even killed. But no thought of this danger, incurred for no good reason, diminished in the least the enthusiasm for them. They were attended with every possible kind of magnificence. The lists within which the combatants were to fight were superbly decorated, and were surrounded by pavilions belonging to the champions, and ornamented with their arms and banners. Scaffolds were erected for the noble spectators, both lords and ladies; those upon which the royal family sat were hung with tapestry and embroideries of gold and silver. Every spectator was decked in the most sumptuous manner. Not only the knights themselves, but their horses, their pages, and the heralds, were clothed in costly and glittering apparel. The clanging of trumpets, the shouts of the beholders, the cries of the heralds increased the excitement of the fray.[9]

In her letters of that time Louise mentions interesting details about her writings. In March of 1876 she wrote, 'I am very busy with proofs again for my little Epoch [*England: A Continental Power*]; fortunately it is all printed now, so no mad printer will be able to destroy any more of it.'[10] A few months later she wrote:

We have been living on very quietly. I think I am busier than I ever was in my life, and only by making use of every minute in the day can I get done at all and then I have to leave many things undone. I have come to the melancholy conclusion that I shall not be able to finish my biography of Raleigh before we go away, which is saddening, as I hate not having a thing done when I promised it. But I hardly get any time except the evenings to write, and tho' a long evening is something to be thankful for even that comes to an end.[11]

In November 1876 Louise told her mother that she and her husband were getting 'generally puffed' about the response to their biographies, adding 'we have now been favourably reviewed in the *Saturday Examiner* and *Academy*, and everyone seems to think the series a very good idea, so I hope it may be good for our pockets'.[12] A year later, while planning for Christmas and a trip to Italy, Louise wrote about attempting to coordinate all her activities while writing her biography of John Churchill, the Duke of Marlborough: 'I shall be very busy till then trying to get on with my life of Marlborough and also trying to prepare a little for Rome, and getting everyone in the parish well visited.'[13] Then six months later she said: 'I have got back again to writing a little of my life of Marlborough, and shall be very pleased when I can get it finished but it will take some time yet.'[14] The Creightons salvaged every moment they could from their busy lives to pursue their literary efforts. In one of her letters Louise described a hectic scene in the library: 'I write with the children playing around me in the library, where Max in spite of their noise, is busy with his Popes over his big folios.' [15]

In January 1879 Creighton completed *The Shilling History of England*, part of Longmans' 'Epochs of English History' series. The reviews were again favourable and Louise told her mother that a 'Mr Rowley' (the reviewer who had picked holes in J. R. Green's *Short History of the English People*) thought Creighton's book 'admirable'. Louise hoped 'the British public may think so too'. About her current writing project, she complained of the lack of progress she was making on *A First History of England*, concluding: 'I don't get on with my babies' history as fast as I should like. Live babies take up too much time, but I suppose I shall get it done some day.' [16] By the autumn of the following year, 1880, Creighton was in the final stages of wrapping up the first two volumes of his history of the Renaissance popes and Louise had finished the *First History of England*. She happily wrote that her husband was staying

> peaceably at home to write, as for a wonder we are alone to-night, which is very pleasant ... Beatrice reads aloud the proofs of my little history [*A First History of England*] and I explain and tell them more about it. Lucie listens without moving in an attitude of the deepest attention. She was much puzzled as to which to sympathise with, Harold or William the Conqueror and kept saying 'I can't quite make it out, it was that bad wind I think which drove Harold over to Normandy'. Then I read them the account of the battle of Hastings in Freeman's *Norman Conquest* and about the death of Harold and Lucie said when I finished 'I don't like that, that's sad'. I wish she was as attentive to her reading and writing lessons as she is to the history. [17]

Rivingtons had been urging Louise to write more children's history, and the lasting popularity of her books over the years proved them right. All her works of this genre enjoyed several reprints. Louise was at her best with biography because she was effective in portraying people in their natural surroundings—kings in castles, knights in combat, and all the other medieval characters who stalked forests trails or bartered their goods in the mean streets of the towns. She was descriptive but not tedious in capturing people and events with a minimum of flowery prose. Theories, trends and the larger lessons of history, however, were less engaging to her. The basic story was a sufficient lesson. Louise accepted Rivingtons' request to do a book on interesting tales in history which appeared in 1883 as *Stories from English History*. She then wrote a textbook on the evolution of Parliament from its origins down to the Reform Bill of 1867 entitled *The Government of England* (1883). This volume became a part of a 'Highways of History' series, a project Louise now agreed to edit. It was 'a great mistake to get to feel too hurried', she said later. 'It is flattering that I should have received by two successive posts two reports to write two different books about English History. I am probably going to do one of them.' [18]

Louise claimed she had 'always been ambitious to write a novel', and around 1880 she set about working on a Jane Austen-style story. Once completed, it was published in two volumes by Rivingtons in 1882 and entitled *The Bloom off the Peach*. 'I don't think it was either very bad or very good', she declared. 'It was fairly well reviewed.' [19] She chose not to publish it under her own name, but took as a *nom de plume* Lois Hume ('Lois', being a childhood friend's name and 'Hume' because of her godmother, Eliza Hume).

The story centred on a beautiful and highly-educated young woman, Mary Auckland, the daughter of a country clergyman. She is so attractive that all the men she comes across fall in love with her and all the women become admirers. Rejecting the marriage proposal from her father's curate, Louise's heroine seeks greener pastures in London. There Mary becomes the fascination of society, deeply admired for her beauty and her talents. After the strain of pleasing everyone, her health breaks and Mary returns to country life to become a resident governess where she soon meets a man with whom she becomes deeply in love. Her life as a governess is scarcely dull. After an unsatisfying relationship with her lover, who departs for foreign lands, Mary falls in love with her lover's friend, a country gentleman. A struggle follows—a mixture of honour and passion—and then marriage and title. As fate would have it, Mary's husband turns out to be less than perfect. Fortunately he dies and Mary now must seek a new life. At this point in the story we know three things: she is now a lady with a stately home, her former lover will surely return from foreign shores, and the bloom is truly off the peach.

Sadly for Louise, reviews of her novel were not enthusiastic. The following is an excerpt from a review in the *Spectator*:

As a novel, *The Bloom off the Peach* has many merits. It is carefully put together, it is entirely free from all mannerisms, its characters are sufficiently life-like, and in all respects it bears the mark of being the work of an educated and careful writer. But something more than negative qualities is needed to make a first-rate novel ... Want of imagination, and an entire absence of humour are the chief faults of the book. The story has been well thought out, but there is such a sense of deliberation over the whole work as to suggest a determination on the part of its author to write a novel at any cost, while at the same time, we doubt if the writer has sufficient sympathy with suffering and broken lives to be able to accomplish the highest kind of imaginative work. The book, however, is good in its way. If novels are to be written by people who have no special gift for writing them, *The Bloom off the Peach* is a fair specimen ...[20]

Louise seemed to shrug off this failure. 'I was therefore never known as the writer of a novel and few of my friends have read the book', she said. Later on she wrote a second novel, but it was not accepted by a publisher.[21]

While he laboured over his history of the popes, Mandell was also busy writing articles and book reviews. He published in the course of three years—April 1875 to June 1878—a total of twenty book reviews in the weekly *Academy*, for example. One was on a new biography of Simon de Montfort by the historian George W. Prothero, which he gently criticised, concluding with the comment: 'We can only regret that ... so much valuable labour should have led to so little that is new.' About a book on Dante, he wrote that the author 'has written over-hastily about a writer who requires careful and reverential treatment more than anyone else in the roll of modern literature'.[22] Creighton's articles covered a wide range of subjects. Before coming to Embleton he penned four articles for *Macmillan's Magazine*, two on Aeneas Sylvius, Pope Pius II, and two on Dante.[23] Through Louise he had met Sir George Grove, then editor of *Macmillan's*. Creighton, therefore, had a natural entrée to the magazine, and as a result he published four more articles in *Macmillan's* while at Embleton. Two were on Renaissance characters he had encountered in his readings on the popes, Vittorino da Feltre, the humanist schoolmaster whom Creighton called 'a true Saint of the Renaissance', and Olympia Fulvia Morata, a sixteenth-century woman from Ferrara who had been caught up in Reformation politics and religion.[24] The third article was his forceful call for professorial reform at Oxford discussed earlier.[25]

The last article appeared in an 1884 issue of *Macmillan's* and dealt with the history of the Northumberland border. It evidenced Creighton's growing interest in a region he had discovered at first hand while on his many rambles across the countryside.[26] When a book by the historian Frederic Seebohm was published on English village communities in 1882, Creighton was sufficiently confident to write to Thomas Hodgkin to say that, while the author had made many points clear, 'I cannot agree with his conclusions. He has considered the economic as apart from the historical facts.'[27]

Creighton's consummate love of England's rural history and architecture can also be seen in a two-part article he wrote for the *Magazine of Art* (1881–82) on historical and architectural aspects of Alnwick Castle. 'It is but natural that we should find in the Land of the Border the most imposing survivals of the Middle Ages,' Creighton stated, 'and that historic associations should have so far prevailed as to preserve in a modern palace the outward semblance of a feudal castle.' His sensitive description of the castle's many charms—exterior and interior—reveal the cogent eye of both artist and historian. 'Many as are the beauties of Alnwick Castle,' he wrote, 'its medieval character robs it of one charm. The courtyard of a feudal fortress has no place for flowers, and the descent of the hill down to the river leaves no scope for a garden outside.' [28] This was the castle's only flaw, he thought. Because of his growing interest in the north country he contemplated initiating a project on border history and seriously began to collect materials. But it was not to be. His eyes never swerved from his history of the popes, so the closest he came to fulfilling this border studies project was his membership years later of a committee sponsoring a multi–volume work on the history of Northumberland.[29] He once assured the vice-chancellor of Cambridge that there were 'abundant remains of medieval art' in rural parish churches, and encouraged him to promote this 'ample field of research' which was close at hand, and which 'an intelligent young man can do much in his own neighbourhood'.[30]

A few years after leaving Embleton, Creighton wrote an article for the *Magazine of Art*, in a similar vein to the Alnwick Castle piece, about Hoghton Tower, a stunning artefact of late medieval architecture located between Preston and Blackburn in Lancashire.[31] He appreciated the notion of a combined study of history and architecture to capture the English past. Like a tourist guide, he sought to walk his readers through the past in hopes of interpreting these weary, weathered structures as meaningful symbols of English civilisation. One cannot help but wonder which came first, his fixation with the English landscape and all its historical accoutrements, or his acquired love of the Italian Renaissance. Whichever way, each enhanced the other.

Creighton exhibited a sophisticated but tender touch when it came to writing about English regional history. His narratives were readable and direct, and display a certain elegance of style that lifted them above ordinary prose.

Sentences often sang with poetic cadence: '. . . Alnwick Castle, as it rises proudly on a height above the little river of the Alne, with the town clustering round it for protection, tells at once the tale of the beginnings of civilisation in that rude district where life was for so many centuries precarious, and order and security were only won by the sword'.[32] Even in his more technical writings, his comfortable prose was always more literary than scientific.

In 1880 Creighton published an article in the *Magazine of Art* on the Renaissance rascal Gismondo Malatesta of Rimini, a man who sternly ruled his city from 1432 to 1468 and made it a lively centre of art. The visit to

Rimini the year before had aroused his interest in Malatesta, and the article illustrated Creighton's way when dealing with controversial historical figures, that is, even when describing a man like Malatesta, whom he described as 'a brutal ruffian', he would balance out his narratives with redeeming qualities. In Malatesta's case, he clearly admired his courtesy and culture, often excusing private excesses when some notable public good was achieved—a tendency that characterised his later writings on Renaissance popes.[33] Creighton also wrote an essay on the influence of John Wyclif's ideas on the Reformation in England for the *Church Congress Reports*,[34] and 'John Wiclif at Oxford', for the *Church Quarterly*.[35]

In February 1877 Creighton broached the subject of his proposed history of the popes to the publisher Charles J. Longman: 'You are very good in expressing your hope that our connexion may not cease. I am at present busy on what I intend to make my life's work—a History of the Papacy during the fourteenth, fifteenth, and sixteenth centuries.' Then a year later, still juggling his pastoral commitments in order to find time to work on the popes, he wrote to Longman again in frustration: 'I really must make a stand against my habit of being worried and fussed', he said. 'It is quite absurd; when I am quite alone I feel just as much driven as if I had any quantity of pupils and children and wives.'[36] The problem, however, lay not in the pastoral life but the pastor, for he seemed to be unable to refuse anyone anything.

Two years later, having made progress on his 'great work' as he called it, he wrote to Longman again: 'I have already mentioned to you that I am busy upon a book, *The Popes of the Reformation*', adding that he felt he should like to have 'an understanding, at all events a general one, about it'. Then he explained his project in more detail in hopes of interesting Longman in publishing the work:

> The object of my book is the History of the Papacy and of the Reformation in Europe from the year 1378 to the end of the Council of Trent. My book would be in no sense polemical nor ecclesiastical—it aims at dealing with the large political aspect of the time, and would embrace the history of Italy, its art and literature, at the time when these flourished most, as well as a survey of the whole of European history ... At present I have nearly finished one volume ... The book, as I at present contemplate it, would extend to about five such volumes.[37]

A month later Creighton commented to the Cambridge historian Oscar Browning: 'I can assure you from experience that life is not complete unless one has a "great work" in the stocks; I think one's happiness is increased if the work is so great that one has no hopes of ever finishing it. I have been for some time engaged on such a one: it is to be called, *The Popes of the Reformation*, and I have advanced in three years from the outburst of the schism to the Council of Constance, in which I am now plunged.'[38] As it turned out, Longmans did indeed become the publisher of his great work, but, as Creighton predicted, he was never able to finish it.[39] Finally, towards the end of 1880, Louise could joyfully announce that the first two volumes of her husband's 'great work' were being printed, saying how 'very jolly' it all was, and that 'it is immensely interesting correcting the proofs'.[40]

Thomas Hodgkin recalled those Embleton years when Creighton was submerged in his research. 'I always like to think of him standing at his desk in the library at Embleton', he remarked, 'with a volume of his green parchment-bound Muratori before him, writing his *History of the Popes*; or else rolling and smoking one of his multitudinous cigarettes by the library fire when the household had gone to bed, and talking the while.'[41] What Hodgkin refers to by 'his green parchment-bound Muratori' was Creighton's copy of *Antiquitates italicae medii aevii* by Ludovico Antonio Muratori (1672–1750), the Italian Roman Catholic priest-historian who was a major source relating to papal history. This was one collection essential for his project and served as a foundation source for the multi–volume series; and it explained the major research problem confronting Creighton at Embleton—finding primary source materials. These were years prior to the opening of the Vatican archives.[42] Thus Creighton had no opportunity, unlike later papal scholars, to explore the critical documents that had languished for centuries within the Vatican walls.[43] He had to search else-where. Besides major depositories in England, such as the British Museum and the Bodleian, which he frequented while on his trips away from Embleton, he was forced to purchase personal copies of printed documents and collections, such as Muratori. Creighton, needless to say, was abundantly aware that there would be charges levelled against him for only using printed sources and for not having explored what one historian euphemistically called 'the twilight world of the archives'.[44] In a letter to Lord Acton, shortly after the first two volumes appeared, he explained his problem:

> I have written my book so far practically without consulting any one, because I know no one who is at all interested in my subject. I live away from any literary friends, and I very seldom am able to consult libraries. I do not think that the entire time I spent in London and Oxford for the purposes of study for my two volumes reached the period of a month. I frequently have had to leave points unsolved till I could go, or get some friend to verify points for me—I am obliged to buy most of the books I want when they are possible to be bought, and I lose the opportunity of seeing stray articles that might help me, though I find the excellent abstracts of periodicals in the *Revue Historique* very useful.[45]

This was a time when British scholars were discovering the Renaissance era, prompted in large measure by the work of continental scholars such as von Ranke and the Swiss historian Jacob Burckhardt. Burckhardt was the father of modern Renaissance studies, and his seminal work *The Civilisation of the Renaissance in Italy*, published on the Continent in 1860, had just appeared in English translation in 1878. And certainly John Ruskin's five-volume work on *Modern Painters* (1843–60) also fuelled the fire of enthusiasm in Britain for the Renaissance. Two other works were Pater's *Studies in the History of the Renaissance* (1873) and John Addington Symonds's three-volume *The Renaissance in Italy* (1875–77). Having fallen under the influence of James Bryce, Walter Shirley and William Stubbs—all Oxford scholars then probing the margins of late medieval history—as well as Pater and Ruskin who satisfied his aesthetic nature, Creighton was thrilled at the notion of expounding Renaissance ecclesiastical history. The Reformation, he believed, was a direct result of continental forces embedded in the Renaissance and he considered the English population largely unknowledgeable of historical events beyond their shore: 'The ignorance of the British public about any other history than its own is so great that no one ever writes in English about anything except England', he told a student.[46] He once wrote to his friend Reginald Copleston: 'I have been busy ever since I came here on a general history of the Papacy and the Reformation, considering that the British public are profoundly uninformed on that point and have no real notion what the Reformation was. Perhaps they don't want to know: however, it amuses me, and that is the main point.'[47]

From Mandell Creighton's perspective, the Reformation had been a tragic necessity. Intuitively, he would have preferred that a theologically unified civilisation had continued, but unfortunate political circumstances prevented this, he thought. Some of his learned friends reckoned, like Hodgkin, that Creighton was too Roman Catholic after the first two volumes appeared, which caused him to respond promptly by saying that his 'Protestantism will be more obvious in succeeding volumes. My arraignment against the Papacy is that it rendered a violent reformation necessary, because it refused to make a mild and wise one.' He went on to explain that his

first two volumes go to show that a reformation was universally demanded, that its necessity was allowed, that defective organisation rendered it impossible by any ecclesiastical parliament, that men stayed their hands from revolution to give the Papacy a chance. My third volume will show the Papacy plunging into a career of secularity in Italian politics, and increasing instead of amending its aggressions; my fourth volume will show the inevitable revolution; my fifth the reaction of that revolution on the papal system, and the internal reform which converted the Medieval Church into the Ultramontane system which we now are familiar with. This is my entire scheme.[48]

In the preface of his first two volumes, Creighton defined his aim as being 'to bring together materials for a judgment of the change which came over Europe in the sixteenth century, to which the name of "The Reformation" is loosely given'. He added that he wanted 'to do this from a strictly historical point of view—by which I mean that I have contented myself with watching events and noting the gradual development of affairs. I have taken the history of the Papacy as the central point for my investigation, because it gives the largest opportunity for a survey of European affairs as a whole. I have not begun with the actual crisis itself, but have gone back to trace the gradual crisis formation of opinions which were long simmering below the surface before they found actual expression.' Then, with characteristic honesty, he admitted that his work 'has been written under the difficulties which necessarily attend one who lives far from great libraries, and to whom study is the occupation of leisure hours, not the main object of life'.[49]

To study the causes and not the conflict known as the Reformation of the sixteenth century was Creighton's aim. Both intellectually and intuitively, he felt more at ease in the glitter of the Renaissance than the glare of the religious explosion triggered by Luther, Zwingli and Calvin.[50] The initial two volumes, as they were presented in the final reconstructed edition in 1897, dealt with the conciliar movement, beginning—after a lengthy prelude of growing papal power and politicisation—with the disputed election of Pope Urban VI in 1378 following the humiliating Avignon era and the subsequent Great Schism, through the councils of Pisa (1409), Constance (1414–18), Pavia-Siena (1423–24), to the council of Basel (1431–37).[51] Creighton's view was that the noble effort for reform, that is, to create a parliamentary-governed church, failed utterly in the nationalistic rivalries and political machinations of its conciliar supporters, thus leading the way to the revival of an unfettered papal monarchy. 'The Council of Constance failed because it represented Christendom too faithfully, even to its national dissensions', he maintained. 'The Council of Basel failed because, in its endeavour to avoid that danger, it represented nothing save the pretensions of a self-elected, self-seeking body of ecclesiastics.' His conclusion was simple: 'The failure of the Council of Basel showed the impossibility of reforming the Church from within.'[52]

Scholars welcomed Creighton's contribution to serious historical literature, and many, like Lord Acton, marvelled at the fact that a remote Northumbrian vicarage—which he called 'a rare and enviable spot'—could contain a library capable of supporting such scholarship.[53] The reviews were generally good. One stated: 'Cold and dry as much of the *History of the Papacy* is, it is never dull; for the working of a keen intellect on a problem of great intricacy makes itself apparent on every page.'[54] Creighton never wished to take sides or prove anything, and all reviewers admitted that his approach was balanced and straightforward—to a fault. He was criticised for being too even-handed when it came to the popes. Acton, himself a Roman Catholic and generally recognised as the icon of erudition in England at the time, took Creighton to task, stating that the first two volumes leaned towards a 'Scotch verdict' (referring to the Scottish criminal law verdict of 'not proven'). The fact that Creighton was hesitant to make a moral judgment bothered Acton, as in the case when Creighton showed sympathy for both John Hus and for those at the council of Constance who sent him to the stake.[55] In a letter to Alice Green a few years later, Creighton explained his dilemma while writing about the controversial Dominican friar Savonarola: 'I have to take his halo off', he said, 'and look at him as an ally of France and a disturber of Italian politics. A few good souls put the halo on; but the mass of his contemporaries did not see it.'[56]

Creighton regarded Acton as the only person in England who possessed the learning to judge fairly the merits of his study and asked the editor of *Academy* to have him review his work. It was sometimes said of Acton that, however much one knew about anything, he was certain to know more.[57] Acton did write a review and, while differing with Creighton's views on many points, gave a frail nod of approval. Acton wrote that the 'history of increasing depravity and declining faith, of reforms earnestly demanded, feebly attempted, and deferred too long, is told by Mr Creighton with a fullness and accuracy unusual in works which are the occupation of a lifetime', adding that the author 'speaks with regret of his imperfect command of books, but it is right to expose the guile that lurks in this apology'. Acton added that Creighton's 'use of right materials is as thorough as it can well be where completeness is unattainable'.[58] The *Academy* review appeared 9 December 1882, and on that same day, after reading it with some measure of satisfaction, Creighton penned a gracious letter to Acton whom he had never met: 'My Lord, Will you permit me, though personally a stranger to you, to express my gratitude for your review to my book in the *Academy*? I specifically asked the editor to get you to review it, as I wanted to be told my shortcomings by the one Englishman whom I considered capable of doing so. I am only afraid that you have estimated my knowledge too highly, and have credited me with a motive where I erred through mere ignorance.' He continued saying that he thought it 'very hard for a Protestant writer, with the best intentions, to be accurate in his reading and interpretation of medieval theology ... I am only glad that you have not discovered more serious misconceptions in my work'.[59] A few days later, from Cannes in the south of France, Acton replied:

My dear Sir,

I did not write to thank you for the gift of your two volumes, supposing them to come from the *Academy*. When I knew my mistake I was already deep in the review, and uncertain whether the expression of difference of opinion might not appear presumptuous. For I think we are at variance on one fundamental point—the principle on which you judge and acquit the Conciliar party, and I could not help regretting that the Introduction had run to a length detrimental to the essential topic. So that I am much more grateful to you for the gift and for your letter than you could be for the critique. As you consider it my proper function to pick holes, I wish I could justify the imputation. Your book has passed into the hands of a literary friend; but I remember one or two things, which will show you how little the most captious of cavillers could find to say ...

As I know well that you did not mean to write a history of dogmas, I have not perhaps made out clearly my meaning about ideas. Looked at from outside, as Ranke or Macaulay look at things, I am not sure that the Papacy was weaker in 1514, after the stultification of Councils and the new combinations connected with the Medici and with the foreigners, after the establishment of the State and the development of absolutism based on Pelagianism, than in 1378. The change for the worse was very great if one looks to the progress of certain ideas, to what was going on underground.

To justify so long an Introduction, the outer change is not enough, and one wants to hear you about the other. You will not escape theological exposition when you come to the explosion at Wittenberg, the negotiations of Augsburg, the debates of Trent, about which there may not be much to say that is new. But there are two questions: What made Luther? and What made him so strong? which occur in the introductory period, and have never been properly answered. Here I think you could give much light which, from your sovereign impartiality, would be particularly valuable.

There are not many families, with education going on in them, to whom you are a stranger ...

I remain very sincerely yours,
Acton [60]

'Sovereign impartiality.' Those words of Acton have become Creighton's scholarly epithet.

After receiving Acton's letter, Creighton wrote to Hodgkin: 'Lord Acton has done me a real service, but he has estimated far too highly my learning, which is as nought compared to his. His minute criticism in details rejoices me to find that I have omitted nothing important, and have made no positive errors. The things which he points out are trivial, and arise from a necessary difference of point of view.' Later on, 'Lord Acton in his letter is good enough to speak of my "sovereign impartiality" as likely to throw a light on the causes of Luther'.[61]

Over the next weeks congratulatory letters of praise and appreciation streamed into the vicarage. Upon reading Creighton's work, J. R. Green wrote to Humphry Ward, in what was one of his last lettes before his death, describing it as 'remarkable ... both in its learning and its vigour of execution; but it would have been better had he written in his own person and not in the person of old Ranke ... Still the book shows great power, and sets Creighton among real historians'.[62]

As would be expected, many scholars did compare Creighton's work with the English translation in 1840 of von Ranke's *Ecclesiastical and Political History of the Popes during the Sixteenth and Seventeenth Centuries.* The comparison, however, never mattered much to Creighton. Ranke, who Acton regarded as the 'Columbus of modern history', was an exponent of the new scientific method of objective historical investigation.[63] Creighton appreciated Ranke's style and method but could never quite emulate it, in spite of J. R. Green's assertion. Creighton liked to think that he was writing *scientific* history, but his style was too literary and undocumented to be regarded as such beyond the shores of Britain, and certainly not in Germany, the homeland of the new historiography. 'It is an old controversy whether history is a branch of literature or a branch of science', Creighton maintained, 'but there is no reason why the controversy should ever be decided. A book is written; it must take its chance.'[64] Nevertheless, in his heart of hearts, he viewed serious historical research and writing in its most elemental form as 'a branch of science, not of novel writing'.[65]

Ranke's three-volume work on the popes was considerably different to Creighton's. Ranke's papacy was like a deep, still pool with layers of shadows and currents. Creighton's study, on the other hand, flowed like a waterfall, spreading out across the political landscape of Europe. Creighton was never really interested in the church as an institution but in its overall impact on society, or as he explained to Alice Green: 'I don't want to show how the Popes lived in Rome, but how they affected Europe.'[66] Ranke and Creighton, however, were similar in the sense that both tried to raise the subject of papal history from the polemical to the objective, and for this, especially, Creighton should be saluted.

Early in 1884, the Oxford historian William Stubbs was appointed to the bishopric of Chester, and the regius professorship of modern history fell vacant. Creighton had for some time felt that 'he would have to choose between the life of an historical student and teacher, and the life of ecclesiastical and administrative activity into which he was being drawn almost against his will'.[67] Since the regius professorship was a crown appointment, he decided to contact several influential friends expressing a desire to be considered for the post; among them was Prince Leopold, his former pupil at Oxford. The prince wrote a letter of support to the selection committee stating that 'Mr Creighton I know very well indeed; he is a most clear, unprejudiced, and enlightened man. I studied *much* with him at Oxford, and had a great respect for him. There *could not* be a better appointment.'[68] Creighton claimed it was the only time in his life that he ever asked for anything.

Mindful that there were other candidates seeking the post, he never really got his hopes up. And when Edward Freeman was appointed to the professorship, he accepted the decision with characteristic resignation. Ironically enough, however, just as he heard the news, he received word from Cambridge asking whether or not he would be interested in applying for the newly-created professorship of ecclesiastical history. Oscar Browning, fellow at King's and also an editor of historical primers, suggested Creighton apply having known that he had tried for the regius professorship. The new Cambridge professorship was being established as a result of an offer by Emmanuel College to provide income for the study of ecclesiastical history, partly out of funds from the bequest of Sir Thomas Dixie to the college in 1594, and partly from the stipend of a fellowship which the new professor would automatically hold. Creighton realised, of course, that if he applied and won the post he would have to take a cut in annual income. As vicar of Embleton, he was earning over £840 per year; while his projected first year's annual salary at Cambridge would be £700, £500 from the Dixie fund and approximately £200 as senior fellow at Emmanuel College.[69] But that did not seem to dissuade him. Still, he could not believe that the ten electors (one of whom was Oxford's James Bryce) would select an Oxonian for this new Cambridge position officially known as the Dixie Professor of Ecclesiastical History.

Creighton went ahead and applied for the professorship, and in May of 1884 he received word he had been elected, beating the popular Cambridge candidate Henry M. Gwatkin. In one of the most gracious letters ever written to a victor by one having been just vanquished, Gwatkin wrote to Creighton as soon as the announcement was made:

My dear Professor Creighton,
   Will you allow your rival of yesterday the consolation of giving you to-day an individual and hearty welcome to Cambridge? I envy you the splendid work before you: but it is your work, not mine.
   For twelve years I have taught Ecclesiastical History, I may say almost alone in Cambridge. I have worked faithfully and to the utmost of my power

hitherto, and I trust not without success; and now that my work is taken up by stronger hands than mine, I pray the Lord of all History, before whom we both are standing, to give you health and strength and abundant blessing to carry on far better than myself the high and arduous work entrusted to your charge.

For myself, I am ready to work under you, and to support you loyally in all that falls to me to do. So far as I know my own heart, no jealousy of yesterday shall ever rise on my side to mar the harmony and friendship in which I ask and hope to live with the first Professor of Ecclesiastical History in Cambridge.

I am yours faithfully,
H. M. Gwatkin [70]

Creighton later told a friend after meeting Gwatkin that the 'most touching thing that has ever befallen me is the conduct of the Cambridge man who hoped to have been made Professor, when I was taken', he said. 'He had for five years been preparing himself for it, and had written a book for the purpose. He is a simple student whose one aim in life it was, and who had no other prospect. All this I did not know at the time; but he wrote to me immediately on my appointment, and I asked him to come and see me. He took to me and has now formed a strong friendship for me.' [71] Happily for Gwatkin and Cambridge, he was be elected to the Dixie professorship at the conclusion of Creighton's tenure, no doubt in part due to Creighton's insistence. [72]

Merton, sorry to lose Creighton, offered the living to a fellow of the college Edmund Knox, who made a quick trip to Embleton to see what was there, quickly found little there that interested him and declined. 'Though far off in the North,' he said, 'it was not out of the world ... Still, it was two hours' railway journey beyond Newcastle, and seemed to me a very Ultima Thule, to which I was not prepared to be banished.' [73] Another Merton man, Montagu Francis Finch Osborn, then rector of Kibworth Beauchamp in Leicestershire, expressed interest in Embleton if he were offered it, so Knox agreed to exchange Embleton for Kibworth. Thus, Osborn replaced Creighton. [74]

After the appointment became public, Creighton wrote to Oscar Browning saying: 'It was you who suggested to me some time ago to become a candidate, or I would never have thought of it. I feel that is very good of Cambridge to find a home for an alien, but I am quite willing to lend myself to the process of adoption.' [75] When Mary Ward learned of Creighton's appointment to Cambridge she wrote:

> It will be a great change from Embleton to Cambridge, and from the Oxford to the Cambridge associations; but I am sure it will be a change worth making,

though for the last ten years you have had a humanising, educating life at Embleton, in the broadest sense, that anyone might envy. How few of us can ever come as close to the soil from which we all sprang as you have done in the North. You have seen the elemental human things nearer [by] far than most men of letters have a chance of seeing them, and now you will carry with you all this fruitful experience to enrich the scholar's life that is to be.[76]

Creighton probably thought that by making his decision to return to academia he may have ended further ecclesiastical preferment for the time being. He was still battling in his own mind the career question that had long dogged him—church or university. In a letter to Alice Green he asked, more hypothetically than not: 'Is my line practical or speculative, or both? How far can I combine the two? How far am I justified in abandoning one for the other?' But having decided to return to academic life he concluded: 'I have devised a fresh departure by way of trying a better solution.'[77] Then he told her what his old friend at Oxford, J. F. Bright, had warned him about choosing academic life over the church, that it was 'a better thing to manage men than to write books. It is more amusing and more satisfying. You should have gone on and become a Bishop, and made yourself a practical power.'[78]

In an another letter to Alice Green, Mandell spoke of the 'ominous absence of congratulations from Oxford' after his appointment, which he took to suggest that his 'friends there are all disgusted with me' for going to Cambridge.[79] He decided not to settle in Cambridge until November of 1884, thus giving him the summer and early autumn to prepare for the departure from Embleton. At the end of May, the Creightons made a quick trip to France—merely to get away for a couple of weeks—and spent their time exploring the countryside along the River Loire. Upon their return the couple visited Cambridge, where Mandell formally received his fellowship to Emmanuel College.

In the autumn, he attended the church congress at Carlisle where he read a paper on the influences of the Reformation on England. It was the first of a number of papers he delivered at successive church congresses. As a result of the first paper, he began to think more and more about the Church of England's relationship to national life. Louise wrote years later how his thoughts began to come together:

More and more as years went on did the thought take shape in his mind, that his message to the world was to try and get people to understand the meaning of the Church of England. At that time this thought had not been formulated; indeed, I do not think he spoke to me on the subject till some fifteen years later in the garden at Fulham. But looking back, reading the utterances of those early days, it is easy to see how his studies and experiences alike combined to form the views to which later on he was able in part at least to give expression.[80]

It should be remembered that the established church was being sorely tested throughout the nineteenth century, besieged not only by conservative and evangelical religious forces, and secular and scientific movements, but also by the steady rise of an urban, working-class population that felt itself alienated from denominational religion. The Church of England was losing ground. It was moving from a national entity to a mere denomination.[81] The Victorians had fervently built new churches and chapels, and restored old ones, especially in the earlier part of the century, which by the 1890s were relatively empty.[82] Yet whether or not people went to church every Sunday, the Victorians, according to one scholar, 'preserved a country which was powerfully influenced by Christian ideas and continued to accept the Christian ethic as the highest known to men'.[83] As for Creighton, whose vision was always keener in looking backward than forward, he failed to see the enormity of this challenge that was confronting the Church of England. Still, he can hardly be faulted for acquiescing in the common sentiment of the day, supported by many notables such as Thomas Arnold who thought the church and the nation were identical.[84] It is interesting, however, that by the end of the century, when this once popular assumption of a national church had plummeted nearly out of sight, Creighton was one of the few who still found it comfortable to hold this opinion, and he said so in February 1900 in a major address entitled 'The Church and the Nation'.[85]

Creighton spent the rest of the autumn bidding farewell to his flock. He, with Louise often going along, visited every house in his parish, giving them a personal goodbye and a small photograph of himself. Everyone regretted his leaving but, in characteristic Northumbrian manner, most found it difficult to express their inner feelings. 'Well,' declared one woman, 'if you ain't done no good, you've done no harm', which was probably about as close to glowing praise as one could expect.[86] Louise, though excited about the move to Cambridge, still felt a twinge of regret in leaving the north country—once hated and now fondly appreciated. 'There were moments when I realised sharply what going meant,' she said. 'One stands out clearly in my mind. I was coming up from the sea with the children, and their donkey, the little ones in the panniers, the three eldest walking and it came over me with bitter regret to think what they were losing in giving up this free country life.'[87]

For Creighton the move was bittersweet. He preached his farewell sermon in Embleton church on 9 November 1884, on the position and duties of a parish priest in the Church of England—a rather lengthy homily that evidenced his sadness as much as his practical, commonsense approach to life. It captured his particular blend of ethical sense and subtle spirituality. He concluded with the words: 'If I have taught you anything, you have taught me much in return. I go away ... a wiser and, I trust, a better man.'[88] And of course, he did. And Louise had to admit she gained much too, as a vicar's wife. Embleton had crystallised both their characters. It had taught them as much about others as it taught them about themselves; and in large measure, while the nine years in the north became important years in *their* lives, the years that followed Embleton became more important for what they did for the lives of others.[89]

A Breath of Fresh Air

'Mandell Creighton ... whose vigorous intellect, wide literary sympathies, and absolute disdain of the common-place, seemed to bring a breath of fresh air into the College.'

E. S. Shuckburgh of Emmanuel College [1]

The Creightons arrived in Cambridge at the end of November 1884, finally securing a house for their large family of six children and several live-in servants. Louise, unfortunately, was not happy with their rented house—Langdale Lodge on Brooklands Avenue—and thought it 'ugly' and too small, though she found its setting pleasant amid old trees in about three-quarters of an acre of garden.[2] Having lived in a spacious vicarage for nearly a decade, the Creightons found themselves cramped and confined. Louise, however, decided to make the best of it and, as with the old vicarage in Embleton, she immediately set about having the interior of their house 'completely done up'.[3] Louise managed the house with a staff of three maids, a nursemaid and her nurse, Janie Thompson, whom she brought from Embleton.[4] She also assumed that responsibility for the schooling of her children, not employing a governess, though one of Louise's nurses, a Miss Allnut, eventually assumed that role.

Of course the Creightons immediately found themselves caught up in Cambridge society with its frequent rounds of dinner parties and social gatherings. It reminded them of the delights of Oxford, fond memories they both treasured. During the first term at Cambridge, Louise recalled that 'an immense number of people called upon us, and I was kept pretty busy returning calls; we were asked out to many dinner parties. They struck me as being on rather a larger scale than our dinner parties in our old Oxford days, but we were of course older and belonged to a rather different strata [sic] in university life.'[5] Louise remembered that Mandell was most often the centre of attention at all of their social events. 'It was always the same in every new circle into which he entered', she maintained, 'one could see the growing interest he awakened and how by degrees everyone who was not frightened off, was drawn to listen to him. It was not that he held forth, or tried to domineer, but he was so amazingly fresh and full of life.' She claimed that his 'point of view' was so different from others in their society, that he was 'arresting, challenging, inspiring, always a surprise to people who had not met him before'.[6] He was never ignored and always attracted attention.

> I think [Louise felt] he puzzled Cambridge people a good deal. They were inclined to be serious, and even more inclined than some Oxford people had been in [the] old days to judge him to be frivolous; but I think most of them, and perhaps specially his pupils, delighted in him; and I think that he enjoyed his new life, getting back ... to teaching and lecturing. To me it was almost bewildering to be plunged again into the society of so many people of my own kind, and to meet so many people who interested and attracted me.[7]

While at Embleton, women friends were few and far between for Louise, but now she was 'confused' by the number of possible friends she soon met. 'I felt that I should never have the time and opportunity to make real friends unless I gave my mind to it.' So Louise 'quite deliberately' selected several women 'to try to see a great deal so that we might really make friends'.[8] One was Kathleen Lyttelton, wife of Arthur Lyttelton, formerly tutor at Keble College, Oxford, then master of Selwyn College, Cambridge, and later suffragan Bishop of Southampton. Kathleen became her closest friend at Cambridge. As with her Oxford friend Mary Ward, Louise and Kathleen shared many interests, especially in literary matters and religious questions.[9] Then there was Ida (Emma Cecilia) Darwin, wife of Horace Darwin, a prominent civil engineer and fifth son of Charles Darwin. She was the daughter of Sir Thomas Farrer, later Lord Farrer. Another was Mary Frances Prothero, wife of the historian George Walter Prothero, tutor at King's College and, after 1884, university lecturer. He was later, in 1894, appointed professor of modern history at the University of Edinburgh.[10]

Another woman Louise came to know during those years was Beatrice Potter, later Beatrice Webb. The Creightons met her in August 1887, and as Beatrice Webb wrote later in her diary, 'from that time onward I enjoyed [the Creightons'] friendship, a privilege extended to The Other One [Sidney Webb] when, four years later, he appeared as my betrothed'.[11] Indeed, it was while at the Creightons for dinner that Beatrice had her noted 'interesting talk' with Professor Alfred Marshall, the economist, about whether women were subordinate to men. 'If you compete with us we shan't marry you', Marshall quipped, upon which Webb rose eloquently in defence of female species.[12] Years later Webb wrote about meeting the Creightons, stating how much she admired Mandell whom she described as that 'versatile and pleasant ecclesiastic and don', and her 'attraction to the handsome and direct-minded Louise'. Both, she thought, were 'so different from each other, and yet so completely complementary. From that time forward I remained a friend, and ... used constantly to visit them ... And from the first they liked and trusted me—liked me for my best side. When I engaged myself to Sidney, they accepted him as their friend without hesitation.'[13]

Louise was three years older than Beatrice Webb, but both women were similar in that they readily exhibited a determined rationality that came across as very self-confident, even brash. Yet their demeanours really camouflaged a vulnerability, a fundamental shyness. Both women appreciated each other's cerebral gifts and on the surface at least seemed friendly, though one senses that there was a distinct competitiveness between them. Louise said that Beatrice once told her she possessed 'a masculine intelligence'. Interestingly, there is a hint in later years, as Beatrice drifted closer to Mandell in friendship, that their relationship cooled.[14]

All in all, Louise thought it a delight to be among so many intellectual and literary people again, hosting dinner parties and soirées. 'We had many people to stay with us, though the house was too small for the large parties of visitors we had had at Embleton', she said. 'We had only one double and one single spare room. Our dining-room was small and ten was the outside number we could dine. I had dinner invitation cards printed to save trouble, and felt inclined to have printed on them: "This is not swagger but only to save time". It was a very full and busy life.'[15] Francis Jenkinson, a Trinity fellow, was a regular at the Creightons' home, often coming for an afternoon tea or evening dinner and then writing cheerful entries in his diary that these visits were 'very lively and cosy'.[16]

It was at Cambridge that Louise came to grips with the notion that many people perceived her to be formidable and domineering. 'It has always been a trouble to me that so many persist in considering me alarming', she complained more than once. 'I think ... that it is because I am really shy myself, and have a shy manner. That makes me stiff and self-conscious, and being told that I am alarming does not help matters.'[17] Louise, as the years passed, grew more serious, perhaps more moral and humourless, finding social situations increasingly awkward. Creighton on the other hand was the quintessence of congeniality, and his beguiling personality grew more whimsical. He had no problem mingling in Cambridge society, and was in the words of one Emmanuel fellow 'a perpetual fountain of light and talk'. One of his students proclaimed him as a 'master of fun', and when the fellows gathered in the combination room at college for tea in the mornings, and drinks, or smoking after dinner, Creighton took delight in holding forth as he had done in the common rooms of Oxford.[18]

According to William Chawner, a college fellow and friend, Creighton seemed

> to be made up of two entirely different persons who had no connexion with one another. There was the real Creighton, the incarnation of common sense who discussed some question of general interest at a College meeting or on a board or Syndicate, or in a private talk with acuteness and sagacity. There was a quite different person who you often met at dinner parties or College high tables who blurted out the most outrageous paradoxes and supported them with fantastic arguments in defiance of all conventional views which no serious man would have adopted. No wonder that a sober head of the college complained, 'Professor Creighton is so frivolous ... Nowhere did he talk such nonsense as in our Combination Room on Sundays'.[19]

Creighton's tendency to delight in blunt, almost irreverent conversation was not new, of course. He thrilled at every opportunity to engage in such, at Oxford and at Embleton, whenever there were others around him capable of matching his mental gifts. He took great pleasure in blurting out an idea that struck his fancy even when he knew it was questionable, such as the time he declared in donnish fashion that the difference between a Russian peasant and English peasant was that the former swears, gets drunk and goes to church while the latter swears, gets drunk and never goes to church.[20] Hodgkin said he remembered one of Creighton's evening discourses at Embleton where he strongly predicted—in total opposition to his guests— that socialism would be the wave of the future, even advancing the thought that government policies would 'more and more assume a socialistic bias, and rightly so, and that the rights of the individual will be less and less regarded when they evidently clash with the welfare of the people as a whole'.[21] Creighton at times possessed a prescient quality that fell part way between the absurd and the shrewd.

But it was not long before Creighton discovered the social atmosphere at Cambridge too stiff compared to Oxford, that people often misunderstood his humour, and seemed perplexed by his 'outrageous paradoxes'. He wrote to a friend that people in Cambridge were rather too serious for him, that 'they don't often make jokes, they think it right to be wise, and I never was wise, and I don't see any chance of becoming so in my old age'. He once declared that the difference between an Oxford man and a Cambridge man was that an Oxford man 'looks as if the world belongs to him. A Cambridge man looks as if he did not care to whom the world belongs.'[22] Elsewhere he remarked that 'people look at me as a sort of strange beast'.[23] The esteemed F. J. A. Hort, senior fellow of Emmanuel and professor of theology—whose cautious, wrinkle-browed temperament was a far cry from Creighton's more light-hearted manner—eventually did come around to find his younger colleague beguilingly entertaining. The two fashioned an odd but sincere friendship, and Creighton readily admitted after Hort's death in 1892 that at Cambridge there was 'no one to whom I personally owed a greater debt of gratitude than to him. He will live with me always as being one of the highest types' the academic world could produce.[24]

Creighton greatly respected Lord Acton because of his scholarly reputation and looked forward to meeting him when he came to Cambridge. In a letter to a friend back in Northumberland he remarked: 'To-morrow I am going to London to meet at dinner Lord Acton, whom I have long been pining to see. He is a Roman Catholic, and is the most learned Englishman now alive, but he never writes anything .'[25] Creighton's observation was on target. The general consensus held him to be the 'most learned' man of his generation in England, though for some mysterious reason he acquired this reputation without having written much up to that point. Sadly, his only tangible scholarly legacy, other than conceiving the idea for the Cambridge Modern History series, came after his death in 1902 in a collection of published lectures, essays and edited letters.[26] James Bryce organised the dinner in early December 1884 for Creighton to meet Acton and Robertson Smith, the eminent Hebrew and Arabic scholar. There is no evidence of what Creighton thought about his meeting with Acton, but perhaps he might have echoed what Mary Ward once asked: 'Was there ever a more interesting or a more enigmatic personality than Lord Acton?'[27] Creighton surely must have found the conversation engaging. Acton did. In a letter to Mary Gladstone, daughter of the Prime Minister, Acton wrote afterwards: 'Did I tell you of my pleasant dinner with them on Wednesday, and meeting Creighton? He is an agreeable and superior man, whom you would like; and he is full of general knowledge. But I am afraid you will find his book [on the popes] a severe study.'[28] Bryce, recalling the dinner conversation, said it 'turned first upon the times of Pope Leo the Tenth, and then upon recent controversies regarding the dates of the books of the Old Testament, and it soon appeared that Lord Acton knew as much about the former as Dr Creighton, and as much about the latter as Robertson Smith'.[29]

Just as Creighton assumed his professorial duties at Cambridge, a simmering dissatisfaction over the historical tripos reached boiling point. The history and theology tripos, those dreaded B.A. honours examinations once termed 'cruel monsters' by Edmund Gosse, had been modelled on the venerable science, mathematics, and classics examinations created earlier in the century.[30] As it was, the majority of undergraduates at Cambridge had the option after three years of study to read for either a pass degree or an honours degree. Most took the pass degree. Those who sought an honours degree took the tripos in a selected field. The term 'tripos' was derived from the word 'tripod', the three-legged stool occupied by a student being examined.[31] John Seeley, who succeeded Charles Kingsley as Regius Professor of History in 1873, had been the driving force behind the creation of the history tripos. Seeley, known widely for being the anonymous author of the controversial book *Ecce Homo*, held the view that the subject of history should be studied within a political context. In his inaugural lecture of 1869, for example, Seeley insisted that history was indispensable in the preparation of young men for public service, particularly politics. He stated bluntly that 'history is the school of statesmanship'.[32] No historian of the time took a more limited view of the discipline of history; thus, the historical tripos was in reality a *political* tripos.[33]

By the time Creighton arrived, a serious movement was afoot to reform the historical tripos, and two of the leading reformers were Gwatkin and Prothero, the latter having just been appointed university lecturer. Both men hoped Creighton might counter-balance Seeley's influence and liberate the history school from its narrow course. This thrust against the politicisation of history at Cambridge, however, was part of a larger movement in the historical profession of the day. At that time revival of interest in the study of history was in part due to the growing German influence. Prior to this time, historical study was largely the work of amateurs who wrote history as literature. Beginning with Oxford men such as Stubbs and Bryce, however, history in Britain became an integral part of the university curriculum.[34] Stubbs and Bryce were noted for gathering young men around them to form a new 'scientific' history school; but Seeley and Kingsley showed little inclination to do the same. And Seeley remained defiant in the notion that historical knowledge was to fit men for a practical profession in politics or economics or even law. The Cambridge theologian J. B. Lightfoot, on the other hand, was more like Stubbs and Bryce in arousing great interest in history among a broad range of students. As professor of divinity, Lightfoot encouraged historical method in religious studies, and when he left in 1879 to become Bishop of Durham, his protégé, Henry Gwatkin, carried on his work. The only problem was that church history at Cambridge at the time meant what Lightfoot and Gwatkin had made it, namely the history of the early church.[35]

In writing to Gwatkin before he left Embleton, Creighton had warned his new colleague that he was *not* intending to shape his lectures to fit the history tripos. 'My desire', he said, was always 'to lecture in such a way that anybody may come if he likes … You see my notion is that I want to teach Ecclesiastical History to anybody who wants to learn.' Then he added emphatically, 'I don't want to commit myself simply to teach for that Tripos by taking a period as prescribed for examination'.[36] It is obvious from his appointment to this *new* professorship that Creighton was expected to broaden the perspective of church history because his scholarly interest was more medieval than classical and more historical than theological. The stage, therefore, was set for the creation of a curricular bridge linking theology and history at Cambridge. Seeley and Creighton were always on personal good terms and respected each other, though their academic views were somewhat at odds.

In the spring of 1885, the board of historical studies at Cambridge, of which Creighton had become a member, conducted a series of meetings on the question of reforming the history tripos. Creighton played little role in the debates, though he sided with Prothero and the other reformers. A compromise was reached later in the spring and modifications to the tripos were adopted by the Senate in the autumn that declared that in future preparations for the tests there would be a reduction in the number of required subjects the students would need to study; but there would be a greater emphasis on the knowledge of primary sources within those subjects. The scandal was that a student could receive a first class in the tripos without ever having consulted a primary source.[37] The compromise sufficiently satisfied all parties so that when the history tripos were revisited, twelve years later, no principal changes were made. As far as Creighton was concerned, he cared little about the pedagogical value of examinations and held the view that, if they had to be, it was best to make them as little harmful as possible.[38] Besides the historical studies board, he served on the university press and the library committees, which in general he found wearisome and unsatisfying.[39] He was, however, keenly interested in promoting new dissertation requirements that afforded students opportunities to select their own research subjects rather than relying on topics set by the board.[40]

In January 1885, Creighton gave his inaugural lecture in the hall at Emmanuel.[41] In many ways his lecture, 'The Teaching of Ecclesiastical History', was novel for the day, more so than one would think today. He turned to the theologians rather than the historians for examples of the way history should be studied; he also argued that history ought not be politicised; and he asserted that church history was no mere auxiliary branch of history but a legitimate speciality which needed to be recognised and studied independently of any other branch.[42] It was one of Creighton's more innovative lectures and possibly the most influential defence of ecclesiastical history as a precise discipline in the nineteenth century. Being the first occupant of this church history chair, he laid out his thoughts on the special responsibilities of the post. He recognised the strong existing traditions of theological learning at Cambridge, saying that while theology had become historical, it was not necessary that history should become theological. He assured his audience that ecclesiastical history must be pursued in precisely the same way, methodologically, and in the same spirit as any other branch of history. The 'aim of the investigators', he stated, was simply to discover truth, no matter what branch was being studied. Science, Creighton reckoned, 'knows no difference of methods'.[43]

As the issue surrounding the history tripos was in full swing, he made it clear that he favoured what he termed the 'historical conception', that is, the study of pure history for itself and not the 'political conception' which asserted that the past is to be understood through the politics of human affairs. History 'knows no special sympathies', he said, 'for it sees everywhere the working of great elemental forces which are common to human society at all times'. He explained his notion of history, saying he turned 'to the past to learn its story without any preconceived opinion about what that story may be. I do not assume that one period or one line of study is more instructive than another, but I am ready to recognise the real identity of man's aspirations at all times.'[44]

In asserting that the aim of historical study is the 'formation of a right judgment on the great issues of human affairs', Creighton went on to discuss the 'special advantages' of studying ecclesiastical history, concluding that while his lectures would no doubt be helpful to students reading for examinations, he hoped to attract more of those interested in a general understanding of the sweep of church history. 'The highest result of a professor's labours', he maintained, 'would be the formation of a small class of those who were willing to prolong their university course, that they might study methods of research, that they might begin some work which would be capable of expansion into a worthy contribution to historical literature.'[45]

Following up on another theme in his inaugural lecture, he pointed out some of the advantages of studying ecclesiastical history, particularly for a man preparing for clerical life. A deeper knowledge, he reckoned, would encourage clergymen to take a greater interest in the history of their own districts and parishes, thus affording them excellent means for giving instruction. 'Great truths are to be taught in many forms,' he observed, 'and many valuable lessons are to be learned from the history of places. Simple folk can learn much from things before their eyes', an obvious lesson learned from pastoral work in Northumberland.[46] Moreover, he underscored the fact that pastors, as guardians of the churches and parish records, 'had not always shown themselves to be intelligent guardians in the past'.[47] Better training in church history would remedy this, he thought. Finally, 'for the sake of their own mind', Creighton held that every clergyman ought to have an intellectual interest beyond his professional calling. Drawing on his own experience again, he said that anyone 'who has felt the burden of parish work will at once admit the necessity of some intellectual pursuit to restore his mental balance when overborne by details. A taste for ecclesiastical history gives an object for reading which is at once large and ennobling and not alien to his immediate duties.'[48]

Creighton lectured twice a week as a rule, and his lectures were 'fairly well attended as lectures go at Cambridge', filled with students studying for the tripos as well as members of the general public.[49] Apparently they were popular enough that, if someone happened to be showing a visitor around Cambridge, one option was to attend one of them.[50] He never limited his lectures to the number required by statute—as most professors were wont to do—and in fact even undertook a fair share of the teaching duties for the history school. His lectures covered a variety of aspects of medieval church history, such as the crusades or the rise of the mendicant orders, because he hoped to kindle popular interest in the church as a factor in European civilisation.[51] It was his view that, to understand European history up to the seventeenth century, one had to know the church. Church history, he maintained, 'is concerned with the ideas round which medieval civilisation centred, and from which modern ideas took their rise'. To his mind this was 'the surest guide to the comprehension of European history as a whole'.[52]

His lecture style was much the same as at Oxford. He spoke extemporaneously from extensive notes, trying to curb his tendency to drift into humour or flippancy. Occasionally, however, he would let slip a remark that could offend a listener, such as the time while lecturing on the policies of Mary Tudor, he suggested her defects were caused by her 'feminine mind'. In this instance it brought an immediate rebuke from a woman lecturer who happened to be in the hall. Louise, when telling of this incident later, showed once again her willingness to excuse her husband by suggesting: 'I think he must have intended to show that in his search for truth, he did not consider himself bound to respect the special susceptibilities of any part of his audience, when in his next lecture he insisted emphatically that the mistakes of Cardinal Pole were due to his having an essentially clerical mind.'[53] One pupil remembered his lectures, saying that a 'curious quality of all his teaching was its vividness at the time, and the sharpness of the impression it made'. He went on to say that, in Creighton's lectures, historical characters 'never seemed to be in the grip of relentless circumstances, determining them to a course of action perfectly inevitable. He made you see them as men and women swayed not only by considerations of high policy, but by those commoner feelings and passions which influence the action of all human beings. He made you feel that you knew them.'[54] The historian John Figgis, then a student at St Catharine's, often attended Creighton's lectures; he maintained that, unlike other professors— notably Acton or Frederic Maitland—Creighton never delivered 'finished compositions' that could be published as they stood, but rather his lectures were 'interesting monologues, in which new ideas ... were constantly being brought to mind'.[55] Figgis concluded:

> As a lecturer, and still more as a private tutor, the main cachet of Creighton's teaching was the constant stimulus he gave to thought and activity. What struck us most was the wide range of his interests, his sense of the absolute importance of knowledge, and, as I once heard him say, 'the appalling levity' with which the members of the so-called educated classes deliver opinions on every conceivable topic. It would be truer to say that he tried to make men discipline themselves than that he endeavoured himself to discipline them.[56]

Pleased that the Dixie professorship carried with it a fellowship at Emmanuel, Creighton delighted in college life as he had at Merton; and it was probably at Emmanuel that he did his best teaching. In these informal sessions with undergraduates, he allowed 'any species of historical conundrum to be put to him', according to Edmund Gosse.[57] The best example of this was the conversation classes he conducted in his college rooms after dinner on Wednesday evenings. While such classes were not new at Cambridge, it was novel to invite women students to them. Creighton supported both Newnham and Girton women's colleges; he often preached at the Sunday evening service at Girton and taught a series of weekly conversation classes for Newnham students. One female student in his first conversation class reported that he soon acquired the nickname 'the Admirable' by the women, and said that he made them feel 'that historical problems were after all problems of life, and that by learning how to deal with them ... we should learn also how to deal with the problems of life'.[58] It was while giving classes at Newnham that Creighton took notice of Alice Gardner, a history lecturer at Newnham, and Mary Bateson, a talented student. Both represented the first generation of women scholars at Cambridge, and both in some measure owed their inspiration to pursue historical research to his mentorship, especially Mary Bateson.[59] As was his custom, Creighton sought to inspire all his students, but often singled out those whom he regarded as the most promising, and then would encourage them to narrow their research focus, to write articles, even books. This was the case of Mary Bateson who, having come under his scholarly spell, became almost a part of the family during these years. She went on to become an accomplished historian, teaching most of her life at Newnham and publishing several significant works on British medieval history.[60]

Although Creighton thoroughly identified himself with Emmanuel, college politics bored him to the core; about the only thing he did was to attend the college meetings each term, though he rarely spoke and seldom argued a point. He did preach in the college chapel, which he regarded as just another venue for teaching. As at Merton, his preaching was more practical than spiritual. On one occasion he caused some indignation when he castigated young men for playing too much football at the expense of leisurely afternoon walks and talks with fellow students, a time he felt when questions of philosophy, art, religion, and other like minded subjects could be discussed. A colleague described his homilies as 'seldom doctrinal', adding that they were 'the sermons of a scholar and of a student of human nature, rather than of a profound theologian. The subjects he most affected had usually an educational aspect ... His sermons always arrested attention and made men talk about them; no one could call them dull.'[61] William Chawner, a fellow of Emmanuel, agreed, saying that they were 'short and mostly plain and practical, but not dogmatic ... They were never works of art. They always showed the speaker to be a man of masculine strength and intelligence, but they were not—and were not meant to be—eloquent.'[62] His preaching was best summed up by a fellow historian, Charles Bigg, who said that Creighton was

> amazingly ready; all his knowledge, all his powers were instantaneously at command. He did not care for eloquence, indeed he despised it; what he aimed at was instruction, and for this he always looked more to principles than to facts. He was not moving or pathetic, but stimulating and persuasive. His voice filled the largest building without effort and yet did not raise an echo ... He was never rhetorical or sensational, but you carried away the impression of a man who had given not his heart only, but a fine intelligence, to the cause which he preached.[63]

The key point here is that he aimed at *instruction*. This was Creighton's *raison d'être*. He was—by temperament—a teacher. He often said, 'I am nothing if I am not educational'.[64]

In the first year of his professorship, he and Louise enjoyed the most relaxing months of their married lives. For the first time since Oxford days he had the time to read, write and lecture at his own pace. 'I go to the library: I get out books and read and write', he wrote to a friend. 'My time passes quietly, and it is a great relief to me to feel that I can go on with my books and not feel that perhaps I ought to be doing something else, which always troubled me at Embleton.'[65] His schedule was simple: mornings were for work, afternoons were for leisure, which generally meant taking walks or visiting friends. Recalling those placid days, Louise said: 'In the afternoons we used to go out for walks, very often with all the children, and I was told that it was considered a novel and amusing sight to see us going out with a troop of children.' [66] It had been decided shortly after arriving in Cambridge that Beatrice and Lucia should attend the Perse School for Girls, a private day school in Cambridge.[67] The Creightons may have considered sending Cuthbert, Walter, and Oswin to the Perse School for Boys, but opted to have them schooled at home under Louise's super-vision until each reached twelve years of age. At that point, each was sent off to Marlborough, the public school founded in 1843 for the sons of clergymen.

At the end of the Easter term of 1885, however, the family's peaceful life was sorely challenged. Creighton was examining for the history schools in Oxford that June, something he had agreed to do in order to preserve his connection with his university, when out of the blue came a letter from the Prime Minister, W. E. Gladstone, offering him the appointment to a residential canonry at Worcester.[68] The offer recognised his responsibilities at Cambridge by only requiring a three-month residency, which could be easily fulfilled during vacation times. Ironically, Creighton had become disenchanted with the Liberal Party and regarded Gladstone's politics that winter as either weak or misdirected on three particular issues: the failure to relieve the siege at Khartoum; the push for Irish home rule; and the proposed working class franchise bills. He had told the Liberal Sir Edward Grey in February that, in his view, Gladstone's policies were in a 'perfectly deplorable condition'. He called them 'the policy of dawdle, the policy of sentiment, the policy of good intentions without definite purpose ... I doubt that Gladstone has the wisdom and the courage to come to a clear decision on our national business as a whole'.[69] Nevertheless, the Worcester appoint-ment was a distinguished one, if not a plum one, and certainly suggests Creighton's rising prominence in both ecclesiastical and political circles—an omen of things to come.

After a speedy trip to Worcester, Creighton decided he liked what he saw and accepted the appointment—after being assured by an old and venerable canon that harmony prevailed among the canons. It is said that he 'quite horrified' the elderly man when he innocently asked if members of the chapter quarrelled. 'Quarrel! What put such an idea into your head?' [70] The last thing Creighton wanted of course was to join a group of clergymen who bickered or fought. The decision to accept the Worcester post was sure to upset the family's tranquil existence, since it required three months of residency every year. Each vacation period, including Christmas, there-fore, the family would have to pack up and move to Worcester, returning again at the start of each term time. That meant six moves a year. Louise at first was a little annoyed at the prospect of having to share their life between Cambridge and Worcester. 'This came to us at first as a disturbance', she declared. 'We were just settling in to our new life at Cambridge, and it seemed almost too much to face another new life.' [71] Creighton's canonical duties of preaching, serving as examining chaplain to the bishop, and participating in chapter activities squared with his interests—seemingly filling a needed pastoral gap in his life; and he felt confident that the time spent in Worcester would still afford him opportunity for his research and writing. Yet, as he readily experienced when a rural vicar, a canon's life can also be subject to 'constant interruptions'. [72]

While in Worcester they lived in a comfortable and spacious red brick Queen Anne house with a small walled garden at the entrance of the cathedral precincts. They began their double life in September 1885. 'It was indeed a double life and both halves were very crowded', Louise explained. 'I arranged that the move from house to house which had to take place six times in the year should be accomplished as swiftly and easily as possible. We were always tidy and settled down in the new place on the evening of our arrival.' Their introduction to Worcester, however, occurred during a painful time for Louise. Her father passed away a few weeks earlier and now her favourite sister, Mimi, was in the late stages of consumption. 'I was there at his death; and for some sad and difficult days afterwards, Mimi was at home.' It had been Mimi's habit those last few years to spend her winters in a drier clime, such as the Riviera, but this had not checked the disease. 'She was often weak and exhausted, much troubled with cough', Louise explained. 'I used to go and visit her as often as possible.' [73] Unfortunately, Louise was not with Mimi when she died at Peak Hill on 8 January 1886, the anniversary of their wedding.

Both Mandell and Louise came to enjoy their periodic respites at Worcester, with its charming cathedral and congenial community life. 'The Cathedral captured us at once', Louise said, 'I could hardly realise as I came out one morning after an early service that I was really going to have the privilege of being a regular worshipper in such a place. Then came the business of settling down in the delightful roomy house that was to be ours.' [74] Both Mandell and Louise had found they missed the active life of the church, and now became 'caught up into what was a strong, real living centre of church life. We loved the services. There were a specially good set of preachers amongst the canons, and the great nave services in the evenings on Sundays were wonderful and very stirring with their large congregations.' For Louise, it was 'the first time I learned what church life at its best meant', and it became a 'time of real religious development' for her. 'For both of us the organised life of the Church came to mean more. We both loved Worcester, and I think Worcester liked us and our family.' [75]

It was customary for these canons to preach on Sundays, and Creighton delivered his first sermon in the cathedral on 6 September 1885. As was his manner, his homilies were more ethical than devotional. 'The essential feature of his sermons was lucidity', claimed a member of the Worcester congregation. 'He was not a preacher to please those who go to have their ears tickled.' [76] As was his custom, he generally spoke extemporaneously but from notes, and while no record of them exist, these Worcester sermons were considered by Louise as 'probably the best he ever preached', with the exception of the carefully written ones he preached at university chapels. [77]

In October 1885, Creighton read a paper at a church congress in Portsmouth on the topic of the teaching work of the church which, among other things, pointed out the need for clergy to continue to educate themselves, to read and study so that they would become more knowledgeable in subjects such as church history. Presumably he recognised the revolutionary trend of his age, namely, that laymen were being better educated and trained than before. His obvious worry, therefore, was that the clergy, once the best and the brightest of their community, would fall intellectually behind. 'The dangers of the present day do not so much spring from ignorance as from half knowledge.' [78] In the summer of the following year, he established an evening course at Worcester, a series of weekly lectures on church history in the hopes of attracting clergy and lay people alike. These lectures were sufficiently popular that he decided to continue them in successive years. His topics were varied, usually drawn from something that happened to be on the tip of his mind at the time, subjects like the architecture of cathedrals and activities of kings, to more controversial issues, such as Thomas à Becket or Wyclif. [79]

He naturally took a keen interest in the historic King's School, one of those English medieval grammar schools built from the ruins of an ancient abbey. The school fell more firmly under his sympathetic gaze because its headmaster had been his pupil at Merton. In one of Creighton's talks at a Christmas prize-giving assembly at King's that first year, he declared that it was fortunate for Worcester to have a school such as King's 'to which its children can go without interrupting home influences. Nothing would induce me to send a child to a boarding school if I could get a good education elsewhere', he exclaimed. 'My ideal of a complete educational organisation would be, that within a radius of ten miles there would be a first-class school, to which people could send their children, so that they might return home every day.' [80] Creighton favoured day schools over boarding schools for social rather than educational reasons, and that is why he never sent his own sons off to a boarding school until they were entering their teens, after what are considered the formative years for family bonding.

The Worcester experience shaped Creighton's outlook in two particular ways. First, he formed new thoughts about cathedral life and its cooperative role with the parish churches of the diocese which he later expressed in a paper he delivered at the Exeter church congress in 1894. Stating that the cathedral and the parish church should not be in competition, he admitted that there was sometimes 'a kind of jealousy of the cathedral in the mind of the parish priest, who complains that popular services in the afternoon or evening have the effect of detaching congregations from their own parish'. Rather than remove this competition, he reminded his listeners that many in society did not even attend church. 'Granted that some prefer to go to the cathedral,' he said, 'there are others who go nowhere.' And then telling the parish priest looking at a dwindling congregation: 'What he loses at the top he can replace at the bottom.' The problem was, of course, that denominations could not replace their diminishing flocks as church attendance, particularly in London and the manufacturing cities in the midlands, was plummeting.[81] He concluded that the 'cathedral ought not, even in its popular services, to be merely a glorified parish church'. Each had its own mission, so to speak. The cathedral 'should seek to discover how it can best supplement parochial activity. In many cases the cathedral and the parochial clergy might cooperate for special services.'[82] Creighton could well recall his school years at Durham where the beautiful services at that ancient cathedral had so impressed his head and heart; and now at Worcester he realised again how comfortable it was to be in a cathedral setting where stirring music and preaching could be the norm.

Secondly, Worcester introduced both Mandell and Louise to the realities of urban life in the late nineteenth century. Both had lived in the country, the suburbs or university cities all their lives until now, where the harshness of the industrial conditions was largely non-existent or greatly sanitised. They really had no realistic experience of the grim life of the working classes. Worcester, on the other hand, was a manufacturing city with many industries, notably some of England's best china and glove factories. For both, therefore, it was their first encounter with the breath of urban society.

Creighton soon found himself involved with the Worcester Diocesan Penitentiary Association, which led him to consider the plight of inmates and to say on one occasion that society could not have its 'moral sense stirred to pity, and then simply rest content with that pity, without evil results. Acts of Parliament cannot work a radical reformation; all they can do is register a higher moral standard, but the mere registration effects no practical purpose.'[83] He later argued that the mission of the penitentiary association ought to extend to more preventative work, and moved to establish a chapter of the National Vigilance Association which, having been founded by social reformer Ellice Hopkins in 1885, sought to raise the level of morality among women and children with an emphasis on preventative tactics rather than providing them with remedial work.[84] He also helped to establish a chapter of the Charity Organisation Society (COS), another one of those middle-class organisations of that era designed to help the poor. The society, founded in the late 1860s, sought to systematise philanthropic assistance and promote 'friendship' between the middle-class givers and the working-class receivers.[85] In some ways it was a radical venture in the history of professional social work and might be described as the beginning of the whole settlement movement.[86]

Perhaps Creighton's earliest public utterance indicating a genuine concern for the plight of the urban poor was the sermon he preached before the members of the Sanitary Congress of Worcester in 1889. Here was the civic leadership of Worcester, and his message was powerful in its simplicity. He began with a general recognition of the qualities and virtues of English life and then moved to the point that they all had 'to admit that the rapid development of modern days, all that we proudly speak of as progress, as civilisation and the advance of industry, has done much to deprive the great mass of Englishmen of many blessings which they enjoyed in simpler times'. He spoke of God giving the world 'free pure air' for everyone to enjoy. 'Aye, but modern industry, remember, has poisoned that clear air of God ...' He spoke of God providing pure water, but now it was polluted, and he went on to outline other contradictions in modern society, finally stating poignantly:

> The conditions under which life is lived, the unwholesome air of the factory, the crowded workshop, the ill-ventilated room, all those things rob the body of its vigour, how they must react also upon the soul! You heard in the Epistle this morning of the works of the flesh—uncleanliness, hatred, variance, drunkenness, revelling. Do not these things, think you, come very largely from, and are they not greatly affected by, the physical conditions under which life is lived?[87]

In the course of those years, Mandell began to shape his brand of social consciousness, which, interestingly, fell under the shrewd gaze of Beatrice Webb about that time. She eventually managed to comprehend her friend's point of view, once writing in her memoir:

> For outside the spiritual side of life, Creighton believed implicitly in the scientific method of observation and verification. And he believed in organisation and machinery, in the regulation of conduct by law or public opinion, according to some deliberately conceived idea of social expediency. He had no faith in

democracy; though he accepted it as necessary: his contempt for the politician amounted almost to intolerance. Lack of brains was to him the greatest social danger: with brains and goodwill no change was impracticable. Without intellectual leadership, the average man, however good his conduct, would remain in a state of squalor and mediocrity.[88]

Both Creighton and Webb, in the 1880s, were still developing their social philosophies. She went further than he, of course, for he never succumbed to Fabian social engineering; but in the course of those years one sees him slowly abandoning major parts of his Liberal viewpoint for a slightly more socialist perspective, perhaps a Christian Socialist position. While Webb may have exaggerated Creighton's social views to some degree, her assessment has more than a ring of truth in understanding his mind as it had evolved in the 1890s.

Louise's brand of social action, however, was in some respects more creditable than Mandell's in that she actually turned her thoughts into action. She began, however, taking little steps. As at Oxford, she became a district visitor again, going from house-to-house in a particular poor parish neighbourhood, visiting families, encouraging religious activities, and bringing back reports regarding educational needs, poverty and sickness. Her district was in the Barnwell section of Cambridge, a grim area along 'a long unlovely street', where she said she 'did not feel it easy to make friends with people with whom I had no defined relationship. I hated standing knocking at a door, waiting till someone opened, uncertain of the reception I might get; but I made friends with some of the families and hope that I may have been able to be of some little use to them.'[89] As in Embleton, she became involved with chapters of the Mothers' Union and Girls' Friendly Society, one year giving a course of lectures to middle-class mothers in the town hall. 'This speaking to mothers and the consequent preoccupation with educational questions', she said, 'fitted in naturally with all that I was trying to do with my own children. Their care was naturally my chief concern.' She went on to say:

> Talking to working class mothers made me feel how much something of the same kind was needed by more educated mothers; so with some friends I started a mothers' discussion society ... We began with a short paper on some subject connected with the education or training of children and went on to a discussion. In these ways I continued to develop my capacity for speaking. I had great natural fluency and a strong voice, and was seldom in the least nervous ... Not nervous before speaking, I often felt depressed afterwards. I realised that I had not said the things I wanted to say, and was bored by the kind of things people said to me, and the futile remarks made by those who proposed votes of thanks.[90]

Louise was emerging as a more public person, and now both she and Mandell stood on the threshold of a time when their public images would soon be fixed in the minds of their generation.

Inspiring Influences

'I often wonder how many of the young intellectuals of the 'eighties and 'nineties have, in later life, looked back on the days in this delightful family circle at Worcester or Cambridge ... as one of the inspiring influences of their lives.'

Beatrice Webb about the Creightons [1]

It was after coming to Cambridge that Louise began her long association with the National Union of Women Workers (NUWW), a non-political organisation comprised of middle-class women who wished to help working women in their domestic lives. The organisation was founded in Birmingham by the social reformer Ellice Hopkins.[2] Louise, along with Kathleen Lyttelton, attended the Birmingham meeting. 'I knew none of the women who were concerned in it, and I was much interested by those I met', Louise recalled later, and said she thought it

> a great joy and surprise to find amongst this collection of rather ordinary looking middle-aged women so much intelligence, capacity and zeal. My eyes were opened to discovering all the work that was going on. By degrees I got more and more drawn into it; and I discovered a latent power for organisation which I did not know that I possessed. We worked away at schemes for bringing the women who were doing social work more together than by merely an annual conference. So we thrashed out a constitution ... When the constitution was finally drawn up I was surprised to be told by Mrs Pearsal Smith, that it was obvious that I must be the first President. So I became President of the National Union of Women Workers as we called it and presided at the Conference.[3]

Mary Ward and Beatrice Webb also became early members, though both later grew disillusioned with the policies of the organisation—Webb because it was not political enough and Ward because, in at least one instance, it was too political. In the case of Webb, she resigned in the late 1890s, ostensibly over the executive committee's insistence on holding prayers before the business meetings, but really because she never felt comfortable with the NUWW's agenda. Webb wished it to be a stronger, more socialist-minded force for change. By the 1890s she had moved far to the left of the

NUWW's mission and thus found it a dull group of bourgeois women. After one of last meetings she attended, at the Manchester conference in October 1897, she penned in her diary: 'Louise Creighton has distinctly a statesmanlike mind—and the group of women who now control the policy are a good sort: large-minded and pleasant-mannered. The "screeching sisterhood" are trying to invade them, but Louise's battalions of hard-working religious and somewhat stupid women will, I think, resist the attack.'[4] Webb was joining the 'screeching sisterhood' camp.

For Mary Ward, the NUWW became too political when the controversy over suffrage rippled through the organisation, causing waves of argument and creating strained friendships. Ward was vehemently against the vote for women and became instrumental in organising the draft petition against suffrage at a dinner with J. T. Knowles, editor of the *Nineteenth Century*, in January 1889. She brought Louise into the picture and they drew up a petition against women suffrage; and then, with the help of others, they gathered signatures of 104 prominent women willing to support the document.[5] 'The worst of it', Louise said,

> was that a very large proportion of the signatories were not in any way distin-guished themselves, though they were the wives of distinguished men. Mary Ward and I did not oppose female suffrage for exactly the same reasons. She held that in certain directions, especially in matters of foreign policy, women were not capable of forming a wise judgment. My opposition was based on the belief that it was a great advantage to the country to have a large body of intelligent and influential opinion which was outside party politics.[6]

Besides Louise, signatories included Charlotte Green, Alice Green, Mrs T. H. Huxley, Mrs Max Müller, Mrs Arnold Toynbee and Beatrice Webb. For Louise, the question of women voting in parliamentary elections, as opposed to local government balloting, was presumably based on her distrust of political parties and the national government—something she acquired from both her father and her husband. 'I have always hated everything that was concerned with [political] parties', she declared.[7] Louise reckoned that moral persuasion could still affect positive change, and wondered whether, by obtaining the vote, women would lose their 'potent moral influence if once they plunge into the political arena'. She recalled that her 'opinions on this question were a source of many discussions with Kathleen Lyttelton who was a strong suffrage enthusiast'.[8]

The petition appeared in the June 1889 edition of *Nineteenth Century* and was instantly attacked from several quarters. In the July issue two staunch suffragists, Millicent Garrett Fawcett and Mrs Ashton Dilke, penned acid 'Replies'. Louise then wrote a response for the August issue entitled 'The

Appeal Against Female Suffrage: A Rejoinder'.⁹ It has been suggested that Mary Ward really wrote the 'Rejoinder'. While it may have reflected her thoughts, Louise clearly wrote it and signed it.¹⁰ In the words of Louise, 'Mrs Fawcett naturally attacked us and I wrote an answer to her in the *Nineteenth Century*'. Mary Ward's daughter, Janet Trevelyan, makes no assertion that the 'Rejoinder' was anything but Louise's, concluding that 'Mrs Creighton's "Rejoinder" was regarded on the anti-suffrage side as a dignified and worthy close to the discussion'.¹¹

The 'Rejoinder' was a six-page explanation of the anti-suffragists, signed simply at the end: 'Louise Creighton'. For Louise, this became her first real moment of national fame. In the 'Rejoinder', Louise stated that the manifesto signatories 'expected that it would be the beginning of a new discussion', adding that everyone 'has known for a long while that Mrs Fawcett, and Mrs Ashton Dilke, and a large number of other women eminent in various ways, were in favour of female suffrage. We thought that the time had come when it was well that it should be understood that there were still some women who were not convinced that such a measure was desirable.' ¹² Louise stated that it was 'surely hard that we should be twitted with our insignificance', deploring Fawcett's comparison of the 104 women with the doomed 'five hundred' (sic) of the Light Brigade at Balaclava.¹³ In response to Fawcett's assertion that all but a few of the women who had signed the manifesto could hardly be considered in any way leaders of the women's movement of that time, Louise pointed out that 'it would be charitable to suppose that many who are not known to fame have yet worked in some quiet and obscure manner for the advancement of female education and the good of women'.¹⁴ The advocates of women's suffrage, Louise declared, 'seem to labour under two delusions: first, that the vote is a good in itself; and, secondly, that change is necessarily progress, and must be welcomed, at any price, by all who do not wish to remain hopelessly behind'.¹⁵ Louise was convinced that extending the vote to women might endanger the traditional character of the family unit, suggesting for example that if married women could vote, it might make marriage a contract rather than a union.¹⁶ There is 'no magic about the vote', Louise wrote, stating that

> it is merely a necessary part of the machinery of government. The act of voting is not, as some would wish to make it, the chief way in which the individual can share in the work of the State for the good of all. The question is not whether women are not as qualified to vote as men. We are very tired of the rich and cultivated lady who may not vote whilst her coachman may. If the vote was the privilege of the wise and the educated, many women might justly claim it. But it is the propelling power of a part of the machinery of government which has always belonged to one sex.¹⁷

Louise was arguing that to be anti-suffrage did not imply anti-feminism—a term yet to be coined.[18] Louise's arguments, however weak they may appear today, centred chiefly on the notion that the 'existing social fabric rests upon the assumption that the family is the unit, and not the individual. It is impossible to deny that an attack upon the existing social fabric must imply an attack upon the family.' For Louise, a wife was 'purer, nobler, more unselfish' than her husband, and a woman 'must be a power for good or evil over man. In her hands rest the keeping of a pure tone in society, of a high standard in morality, of a lofty devotion to duty in political life. She is often not alive to her power, and if her power became conscious, it would lose much of its potency.' To give the vote to women, she thought, would 'debase her sex and lower the ideal of womanhood amongst men'. The moral power of women, she warned, 'will be lost if women are to go with men into the strife and bustle of political life'. She concluded by asserting that 'those women who, not content with what they have, still demand the franchise, are like those who, deaf through misfortune or their own fault, stand within the concert hall but cannot hear the music'.[19]

Years later Louise changed her mind on women's suffrage and spoke forcefully for it.[20] Indeed, many of those who signed the 1889 anti-suffrage appeal later regretted it, and, as the issue progressed, most came to support the vote for women.[21] At the time, however, the prevailing argument of the anti-suffragists was that women should confine themselves to the family while men should act as mediating agents between family and the wider society. This controversy by the way occurred well before the creation of the Anti-Suffrage League in 1908.

Louise's participation with the work of the NUWW brought her 'many new friends', and, as she said, 'opened my eyes to many different kinds of work that were going on, and in general proved a most instructive and enlightening experience'. She thought it added greatly to 'my opportunities for public speaking of all kinds, and developed my capacity for business and organisation. I discovered that I could be a very good chairman.'

I could keep order, and get things to go briskly, with plenty of life and go, and could keep people contented and amused. It was a pretty exacting task to chair one of the long executive committees, with a vast number of subjects coming up and many eager, clever women all anxious to speak. To preside at the big conferences was in its way even more exacting, but also more exciting. I enjoyed it and enjoyed the credit I won, and the praises and compliments showered upon me. I am afraid I had plenty of vanity and loved praise and being made much of; but my pride helped me to hide my vanity, and I was never gushing, and hated anything like flattery. But it has taken long to grow indifferent to what others think of me, and to lose consideration of myself and of the effect I am producing in the work I am doing. The victory is by no means won yet, and I do not suppose it ever will be, and yet as the years pass I grow more and more convinced that to achieve anything like the character of a follower of Christ one must lose oneself.[22]

Louise over the years served three times as president of the NUWW, besides holding a number of other executive posts. All of this forced her to travel more throughout England where she spoke at various chapter meetings. 'In consequence,' she said, 'my acquaintance with England was largely extended, even if only superficially, as often my visits were only for one day. Still I gained some idea of the character of very many towns and of the nature of the people living in them and the kind of lives they led.'[23] In the course of all this she acquired more knowledge of various kinds of social work. 'The circumstances of my life', she admitted, 'have always tended to make it difficult for me to specialise in any direction, and about social and religious work it has been my fate to know a little of many things, rather than to have become anything like an authority in one. I have often called myself simply a maid-of-all-work.'[24]

In June of 1886 Mandell and Louise took a short trip to Flanders, visiting Antwerp, Bruges and Ghent; then in August Creighton was asked to represent Emmanuel at the commemoration of Harvard University's two hundred and fiftieth anniversary of its foundation in America. John Harvard, after whom Harvard College was named, had been a student at Emmanuel, and Harvard University was anxious to have a representative from Emmanuel attend the celebration.[25] Dr Samuel Phear, the master of Emmanuel, invited Creighton to go to America in the autumn of 1886. At first Creighton declined saying that he felt it impossible to leave his work at that time. He had his classes, his lectures, and was then reading proofs of the third and fourth volumes of his history of the popes. He told Phear that he 'would be doing wrong in absenting myself from term'. Phear remained adamant, however, and so Creighton consented, writing to Phear: 'I will go, and Mrs Creighton will go with me. I will do my best as the representative of the College, and I feel very highly the honour which it has conferred upon me.'[26]

The Creightons set sail from Liverpool in early October 1886. The weather across the Atlantic was stormy and they both found, as Louise said, that they 'were not good sailors'.[27] On board the liner they met Charles Loring Brace, the noted philanthropist, who was returning from Europe with his wife and daughters. Creighton struck up a conversation with him, and was delighted to learn that Brace knew his friend James Bryce, who by that time had left Oxford and was under-secretary at the Foreign Office, later, in 1907, to be appointed British Ambassador to the United States. This all led to a warm onboard friendship between Creighton and Brace. When they landed in New York, the Creightons were received 'everywhere as most honoured guests', Louise remembered. 'We were passed on from one place to another with many introductions, always really in the same sort of set of university people, and we made many friends.' [28] As favoured tourists, they were escorted around to many sites in New York City. Brace made a special effort to show the couple some of his special charity enterprises in the city, such as the Children's Aid Society, of which he was one of the founders, the language school for Italian immigrant children, and a lodging house for newsboys. 'We walked around New York a great deal', Louise said, and 'delighted in the brilliancy of the atmosphere and the beautiful views of the harbour.' [29]

They then travelled up the Hudson River, spending a night at Brace's imposing house. The next day they visited West Point, proceeded on to the Catskill Mountains, and then on to Niagara Falls. Making their way south to Philadelphia, the Creightons visited Haverford College and Bryn Mawr. It was while in Philadelphia that Creighton met the historian Henry Charles Lea, who was then immersed in the concluding chapters of his first book on the history of the medieval inquisition. Creighton had corresponded with Lea earlier but had never met him. Before going on to Harvard, the Creightons squeezed in a short trip to Cincinnati to visit Louise's younger brother, Harry, who—having left the failing Tom Hughes cooperative farming settlement in Tennessee known as 'Rugby'—was teaching languages in the city. In a letter to Bryce, Creighton remarked that while in Cincinnati he was 'much amused by a glimpse of western life'.[30] They finally reached Harvard University in early November.

The four days of celebration at Harvard were crowded with festive activities and the Creightons found themselves in the spotlight.[31] 'Everybody wants to show me something or explain something, till my brain reels and I can scarce contain my knowledge', Mandell said in a letter to Dr Phear. 'The president has asked me to lecture on Wednesday to the students, and I felt bound to obey.' [32] Creighton was thrilled to meet many of the prominent academics and intellectuals of America who had gathered to honour the United States's oldest and most distinguished university. They included men like Francis Parkman, the professor of American western history; Charles Eliot Norton, the professor of the history of art; Charles W. Eliot (the cousin of Norton), the president of Harvard University and probably the most influential and innovative educational leader in America at that time; Daniel C. Gilman, a noted author and president of Johns Hopkins University; Joseph H. Choate, eminent lawyer and later ambassador to England; Oliver Wendell Holmes, then associate justice of the Massachusetts supreme court; James Russell Lowell, a professor at Harvard and foremost man of letters of America, and scores more.

The highlight of the celebration for Creighton came at the Alumni Day event in the Sanders Theatre on Monday, 8 November. There he received, along with other dignitaries, an honorary degree conferred by President Eliot of Harvard. Prior to the awarding of the degrees, however, came a commemoration address by James Russell Lowell and the reading of a poem by Oliver Wendell Holmes. But it was the Lowell address that Creighton would long remember. After offering his general welcome to the distinguished audience, Lowell singled out Creighton by acknowledging him as the representative of Emmanuel. 'Brethren of the alumni,' he told them, 'it now becomes my duty to welcome in your name the guests who have come, some of them so far, to share your congratulations and hopes today. I cannot name them all ... I should single out none by name, but I should not represent you fitly if I gave no special greeting to the gentleman who brings the message of John Harvard's college, Emmanuel', Lowell declared. 'The welcome we give him could not be warmer than that which we offer his colleagues, but we cannot help feeling that in pressing his hand our own instinctively closes a little more tightly, as with a sense of nearer kindred.' Creighton stood up briefly amid enthusiastic applause.[33]

The Creightons remained at Harvard for several days following the anniversary celebration, and on Wednesday evening Mandell delivered a guest lecture. With customary wit and wisdom he spoke on the rise of European universities. The next day his remarks were fully reported in the *Boston Herald* with the comment that 'a larger and more cultured audience has seldom been seen in Sanders Theatre than that which gathered to hear Dr Mandell Creighton ...'[34] Leaving Harvard, the Creightons visited President Gilman at John Hopkins University in Baltimore, where again Mandell was asked to deliver a lecture to students; then the final few days in the United States were spent at the house of Joseph Choate in New York. The return voyage at the end of November proved uneventful, and upon arriving in England Creighton went directly to Cambridge to report to Dr Phear and his colleagues about the trip, while Louise caught a train to Worcester.

Years later, well after the First World War, Louise penned the following observation about their trip to the United States. 'My impressions of America and the Americans were very happy', she said. 'I felt that similar ideals were cherished by us and them, and that if in the future England should go to pieces, the best ideals she stood for would be pursued by the Americans.' Then she added: 'I am sure one cannot really know Americans till one has seen them in their own country. Certainly one should not judge them by the tourists one meets in Europe.'[35] And in a Kiplingesque way, Creighton felt that the future of the 'Anglo-Saxon Race' was assured with America, and that the United States would likely carry on many of the British traditions and ideals.[36] He readily admitted, however, that in his view nations become strong as they produce national character, which led him to tell a friend one that while England was at the top of the list, America was 'yet an experiment'.[37]

Louise's principal occupation during the Cambridge and Worcester years was managing her household. Her literary efforts were limited and her major social work was still yet to come. The time spent looking after her houses and children prevented her from being 'in any real sense a student', she said. 'I believe I had it in me had there been any opportunity, for I always enjoyed hunting up special subjects in connexion with my various little historical books, and reading history has never ceased to be a delight.'[38] She did manage to write the Social History of England (1887), another school book in the 'Highways of History' series for Rivingtons. This book, she said,

> involved a great deal of research and every morning as soon as the children's lessons were over I used to race down to the University Library, a twenty minute walk at least, walking so quick that my legs ached. I loved those hours in the library enjoying the delicious freedom allowed at Cambridge of getting one's own books from the shelves, a freedom which led to some waste of time, because of the temptation to look at other books by the way. I never had time to go to Max's lectures which I have often since regretted as I have realised how interesting they must have been; indeed my days were so close packed that I hardly had time to think and felt that I did nothing really well.[39]

In the summer of 1890, Longmans asked Louise to write an introductory history of France as a companion volume to her A First History of England; she agreed and set about to read French history in preparation for it. The book came out in 1893.

It was during this period that Louise experienced the first serious illnesses of her children. Beatrice was the first. She reportedly came down with typhoid fever and diphtheria combined, not uncommon in those days. Louise said that it was 'discovered that the ventilating shaft of the drains was so placed that the fumes were often blown into her window. [Beatrice] was very ill and had to have all her hair cut off, but she made a good recovery. My natural instinct for nursing which had shown itself when I cared for my mother in my young days, proved most useful here.'[40]

Next came Walter. He had an attack of 'congestion of the lungs'. Louise always believed that this could have been avoided

> had I then known the use of the clinical thermometer, which was not yet considered even a desirable instrument for ... any mother to use. Walter had looked

pale and weary but complained of no pain, so there seemed no need for a doctor; but when I did send for one, his temperature was found to be 104. He too made a quick and rapid recovery, but sometime afterwards at Worcester he was taken ill again and this time more severely with pericarditis [inflammation of the double-membrane sac that encloses the heart]. This was a severe illness and he was prayed for in the cathedral. When he was getting better Max asked him one day whether they might not now stop praying for him, but he said that he would like them to go on a little longer. I had always dreaded to have to nurse sick children, but I now found how much easier they are to nurse than grown-up people. They are so absolutely submissive and have no anxieties or apprehensions, and do not worry about the things that have to be left undone because they are ill.[41]

In the summer of 1887, now in her thirty-eighth year, Louise gave birth to their last child, Gemma, named after Dante's wife. Because of her pregnancy, she was unable to accompany Mandell on the annual holiday—which turned out to be a 'short ramble' in the north of France. Creighton invited a colleague from Emmanuel to go along and the two men inspected cathedral architecture in Ypres, Tournai, Noyon and Laon. Louise also regretted missing all of the Golden Jubilee celebrations in London honouring the Queen. After Gemma's birth, however, Louise and Mandell took a trip the following September in the Adriatic travelling down the Dalmatian coast on a comfortable Austrian Lloyd steamer, staying a day or so at various places.[42] They returned through Italy and spent several relaxing days in Venice. 'It was a very interesting trip, but rather spoilt by the heat; a dry hot wind prevailed during most of the time and made life rather difficult', Louise recalled. Mandell, writing to Sir Edward Grey, mentioned that they had 'kicked up their heels' through Dalmatia, Montenegro and the Venetian region. 'I quite lost my heart to the Slavic peoples with their magnificent costumes, their primitive habits, and their simple ways. I went with an open mind into their complicated politics; but Montenegro did not convince me that small independent states were desirable.' He was, however, 'favourably impressed by Austria as a civilising and governing power' in those Balkan territories ruled by the Habsburgs, for Austria seemed to him to be 'doing a very difficult work with great skill and no unnecessary fuss. They are much better rulers than the North Germans.'[43]

On their holiday to Normandy and Brittany in the summer of 1889, they took the two older children, Beatrice and Lucia, with them. 'I think they enjoyed it very much, but I do not think it is good to take children travelling too young', Louise felt, adding:

There is a general idea that people, old and young, are interested in seeing anything new, but I believe that knowledge and experience are needed in order to appreciate new sights and new ideas. Children easily get bored by the incidents of travel after the first novelty is over. On one other occasion [in 1895] we took the two boys, Cuthbert and Walter, with us for a little trip in Normandy and Brittany, but on nearly all our journeys we were alone, and found this the best rest of all. I often longed for the children and sometimes even for the regular home life. I don't think I was by nature a vagabond, but it was an immense gain to get away from everything, to be alone together, to have time to think.[44]

Years later Louise offered some revealing insights about her trips abroad with Mandell. In her memoirs she stated that he 'did not talk much on these journeys except about the things we saw. He was content as a rule with French novels for his reading, and we also read any Italian novels we could find. I wanted something a little more serious and liked to take some biography with me and always some poetry. I could not go on reading novels endlessly.' She continued:

> We did not talk much to fellow travellers and never sought introductions or wished to go and see people. I remember that we almost felt ashamed of our want of sociability on our steamer trip down the Dalmatian coast when we always sat on our two chairs together in a quiet corner of the deck. These journeys meant a great deal in our life together.
>
> I am sure it would have been very bitter to me if he had been one of those husbands who liked to take their holidays alone or with new friends. Indeed any separation from him I always found very hard to bear ... His interest in architecture was constantly growing and I learned much from him. It was always intensely interesting to go over a building with him. Under his guidance my taste grew much more catholic and I escaped from the influence of Ruskin which had entirely dominated me in my youth. It is strange to me now to think that never before my marriage had I even been inside St Paul's nor dreamt that there could be anything to be said for the city churches. A Gothic cathedral was the one thing that I admired. It was only slowly under Max's influence that I grew to appreciate Renaissance buildings.[45]

In the spring of 1890, between the Cambridge term and the start of their Worcester residence, the Creightons took a five-week holiday to Spain, their first visit to the peninsula. 'We both set to work to learn Spanish in preparation and read a good many Spanish novels. I got on quite well, though it was large part guess work and I used to feel as if I were reading in a fog sometimes; and I never managed much in the speaking line.' Mandell, however, survived better, boldly but successfully communicating with ordinary folk.

> We were surprised to find how few of them spoke any English or French. I was immensely interested in this journey, though Spain did not get hold of my heart. With all its wonderful interests I did not feel that it had the charm of Italy; it

struck me as stern and cold; there was even a surprising want of colour in the clothes of the people. The women dressed mostly in black and we saw no costume except the great cloaks of the men. We were both absolutely captured by the beauty of Granada. Utterly different in every way. I felt that it caught hold of one and overwhelmed one with its beauty in the same way that Venice does. There seemed to be no need to do anything but enjoy, and just let the beauty sink in. Then the pictures in the Prado at Madrid were a revelation. For the first time in all our travels we visited the same gallery morning and afternoon; we could not have enough of the pictures. We could only see the chief towns in Spain on this journey, and we had very few rambles in the country ...[46]

It was while they were on their Dalmatian excursion in 1888 that their son Cuthbert went off to Marlborough. 'It seemed horrid that his first plunge into school life should be made in our absence', Louise admitted later, 'but it was impossible for Max to get any other time in which he could go abroad. So before starting I got all Cuthbert's school outfits ready, and we asked Mr Woodward the Worcester Precentor and head of the Choir School to take Cuthbert to Marlborough.'[47] As soon as they returned from their trip, Louise went to visit Cuthbert. 'It was a disappointing visit in some ways, for on the very morning of the day of my arrival he had had a fall in the gymnasium, exploring it at an unauthorised time, and had broken his nose and had a slight concussion; so I found him in bed in the sick house.' As the eldest boy, Cuthbert in many ways suffered the brunt of both Mandell and Louise's high expectations for their children. Louise regarded Cuthbert, even at the age of twelve, to be

very careless about his correspondence and at first often forgot his weekly letter and made many futile and often false excuses for so doing. This worried me a great deal, and Max was determined to cure him of this carelessness. During one holiday he was ordered to write and post a letter to me every day, and if this letter did not arrive by the morning post, he was not allowed to come to breakfast. I followed his school career with great interest and considerable anxiety. He was often idle and irresponsible, and I do not think that he made the most out of his school life in any way. He did not get into any very serious scrapes, but there were some very disturbing episodes after he got into the sixth [form], and in 1895 we were alarmed lest he should have to leave ... In this case, as always, Max's great desire was to get people to face reality and see the thing as it really was ... Cuthbert pulled himself together and left school with a quite satisfactory character.[48]

Cuthbert's departure diminished Louise's educational responsibilities somewhat, though she still had plenty of other children to occupy her schoolroom every morning. 'I have always been grateful that we kept the boys at home till they were twelve', she claimed.

I believe that it enlarged their interests and made them much more companionable all through life. No special fuss was made over them in holidays; they ... dropt back into the ordinary family life, and they joined the other children in my daily Bible classes. I expect they sometimes were bored at this, and envied other children over whom more fuss was made, and who had more treats. The fact that I did not allow them to take back boxes of cakes etc. to school was rather resented, but I believe that, though in after life they have never failed to criticise their upbringing, they were very content and happy ...[49]

Yet Louise believed that there were 'inevitable losses', as she put it, from the fact that neither Cuthbert, Walter nor Oswin had formal schooling prior to their leaving for Marlborough at the age of twelve. 'Had they done so I think they would have done better intellectually, and become more proficient in games, and had a stronger sense of *esprit de corps*, about their school; but I believe the gains of our system were greater than the losses ...'[50]

One of the interesting ideas being floated around by a group of historians when Creighton arrived at Cambridge was the thought of establishing an English scholarly journal—in the order of the French *Revue historique* or the German *Historische Zeitschrift*—a professional quarterly where articles by leading scholars on historical topics could be published along with critical reviews of current English or foreign books. J. R. Green, James Bryce and Edward Freeman had argued for such a periodical as early as 1867. It was even thought at the time that either Green or Stubbs would be a suitable editor for such a journal. Early in 1885 Creighton was invited to a dinner at Bryce's house to discuss such a possibility, along with Acton, R. W. Church, Dean of St Paul's, Adolphus Ward, professor at Owens College, Manchester, and Frederick York Powell, lecturer and tutor in law at Christ Church, Oxford. Before they reached the dessert, Creighton had been invited to be the first editor if such an enterprise could be initiated.

As in all cases, Creighton could not refuse such offers and let it be known that he would accept this unpaid position because he wanted to advance the role of historical inquiry in Britain, as well as to promote scholarly dialogue among scholars in other countries. 'I will edit for nothing, to start the concern, for a year', he wrote to York Powell later that spring after getting assurances that C. J. Longman would publish the journal, which became known as the *English Historical Review*.[51] The Oxford historian R. L. Poole agreed to be assistant editor. By the summer of 1885 they were well underway into launching the first issue, and managed to secure a number of leading historians to write for the first number, which appeared in the following January. Bryce, although not credited, wrote the introductory remarks, and there was an impressive array of scholarly articles and reviews by noted historians who included Acton, Freeman, Seeley, James

Gairdner and J. B. Bury.[52] Acton's lengthy but powerful thirty-five-page essay on 'German Schools of History' was the lead article. 'I congratulate you very sincerely', wrote Acton to Creighton after the first issue came out. 'The review is solid, various, comprehensive, very instructive, and sufficiently entertaining. It is not insular; there is no preference for certain topics, and no secret leaning towards any opinions.'[53] Interestingly, a book review of the Charles Greville memoirs was signed simply and mysteriously with the Greek letter for 'D' (Δ); it had been written by W. E. Gladstone—a month before he became Prime Minister for the third time—after some negotiation by Creighton.[54]

Being editor added substantially to Creighton's work; yet he seemed to enjoy the extra burden, writing to his sister that it was 'rather amusing ... but one has to offend a good many people'. While working on the second issue in early 1886, however, he spoke of being 'in the midst of more toil and labour than I have ever had'.[55] Despite initial problems of attracting suitable articles and critical reviews as well as establishing a sound financial footing, the *English Historical Review* evolved into a leading academic periodical, becoming the oldest journal of historical scholarship in the English-speaking world. Much of the credit for this success and longevity can be attributed to Creighton's early direction. When he resigned the editorship in 1891, because of pressing commitments, S. R. Gardiner replaced him as editor; Poole, who remained as assistant editor, continued his association with the journal until he resigned the editorship in 1920.

Before Creighton left Embleton, he had put together much of the material for volumes three and four of his history of the popes. The decision to become editor of the *Review* slowed his progress, however, as did his decision in 1885 to edit a series of 'Epochs of Church History' for Longmans. Creighton originally agreed to write the volume on the Reformation in Germany, but had to forego it because of other writing projects. In 1888 his biography *Cardinal Wolsey* appeared. It was a sympathetic treatment of a man who had received little sympathy from English historians.[56] Creighton wrote it swiftly, but it became one of his most engaging books, possibly the best of his monographs. He treated Wolsey kindly, stating that he was 'probably the greatest political genius' England had ever produced.[57] In his mind, Wolsey's spirit and diplomacy paved the way for the great Elizabethan epoch—a period Creighton believed typified England's great moment before the Victorian era. He described Wolsey, the son of an Ipswich butcher, as 'a very wise man, more wise than good, and he was a learned man as well ... He was fond of learned men and liked to gather them round him. He wished to make men more learned in England, for in those days Englishmen were not so learned as were men of Italy, Germany, Spain, or France.'[58]

The Wolsey biography, curiously, says almost as much about Creighton's instinctual belief in the English church's natural connection with the English state as it did about the controversial cardinal's political grand scheme for England and Europe.

In the following year Creighton wrote a volume on his home town of Carlisle for Edward Freeman's 'Historic Towns' series.[59] Concise and perceptive, he briefly captured Carlisle's Roman and medieval roots and then traced its flowering as an agricultural and manufacturing centre during England's national development. He also in the course of those years managed to write or lecture on a variety of other topics. He published an article on the Italian Bishops of Worcester, examples of non-residency in the Renaissance, which appeared in a Worcester diocesan publication.[60] He delivered at least two papers at church congresses, both of which were printed in their *Reports*—one on the teaching work of the church and the other covering some of his thoughts on the church in history.[61] He also wrote an article for *The Times* on the Harvard anniversary and several articles for Emmanuel's *College Magazine*, one comparing American and British educational systems in which he suggested that one of the major differences between the two was that American youth have their 'character' largely shaped by home life rather than by the 'discipline of school', since they do not leave home until enrolling in college.[62] His sermon on Sir Walter Mildmay, founder of Emmanuel, was also printed in the college magazine.[63] Finally, he wrote several biographical sketches for the new *Dictionary of National Biography* during those years, notably one on J. R. Green. This prompted the following comment from Green's widow, Alice: 'I cannot feel that this is a sort of account that ought to go in the Dictionary, and remain as a permanent record', she chastised him. 'It is rather the character of a passing notion in some newspaper.'[64] It is never easy to write about people when their close relatives are still living, Creighton knew, finding his article on Philip II for the *Encyclopedia Britannica* less controversial.[65]

In February 1887, the second two volumes of his papal history were published, and like the first two, they expressed Creighton's 'sovereign impartially', to use Acton's term. Even the acerbic Lytton Strachey later paid Creighton a faint compliment saying that a 'perfectly grey light ... the biscuit is certainly exceedingly dry; but at any rate there are no weevils in it'. Creighton considered the part dealing with the Borgias as 'high comedy'.[66] Volumes three and four dealt principally with specific popes—especially Sixtus IV, Alexander VI and Julius II—and it is clear that, while he did not whitewash them, Creighton could not bring himself to make them scapegoats for all the vices of that era either.[67] As he said, he thought it unfair 'to isolate the Popes from their surroundings and hold them up to exceptional ignominy'.[68] For example, he thought that Alexander VI fairly represented the tendencies of his era and that the 'exceptional infamy' associated with him was 'largely due to the fact that he did not add hypocrisy to his other vices'.[69] In the preface to volume three Creighton enunciated his point simply, stating that he tried 'to deal fairly with the moral delinquencies of the Popes, without, I trust, running the risk of lowering the standard of moral judgment: but it seems to me neither necessary to moralise at every turn in historical writing ... All I can claim is, that I have not allowed my judgment to be warped by a desire to be picturesque ...'[70]

Creighton asked Lord Acton to review these new volumes for the *English Historical Review* and Acton agreed, though when Acton sent in his review in early March 1887, he warned Creighton that it was 'the work of an enemy', adding that there was a 'yawning difference between your view of history and mine'.[71] At first surprised and hurt, Creighton eventually found humour in his predicament—for not only was the reviewer making an onslaught on the writings of the editor, but also the review itself was, in Creighton's words, 'terribly obscure' with many passages 'quite unintelligible'. As Creighton confided to a fellow historian, 'I asked Lord Acton to review my Popes, and he graciously consented. Now he sends me a review which reads to me like the utterances of a man who is in a furious passion, but is incapable of clear expression.'[72]

Creighton wrote to Acton advising him to re-examine his review for style. Acton did so, making some corrections and slightly toning down his rhetoric; nevertheless, when Acton returned the revised review, it remained long, harsh, convoluted and still obscure. And not to let it rest there, Acton blasted Creighton with another salvo—a lengthy, contentious letter on 5 April 1887 detailing more criticisms based on the charge that the author failed to make sufficient moral judgments.[73] Acton, playing the role of 'a hanging judge', demanded that historians judge past rulers and leaders according to a universal yardstick of justice.[74] It was in this letter that Acton wrote his famous dictum: 'Historical responsibility has to make up for the want of legal responsibility. Power tends to corrupt, and absolute power corrupts absolutely. Great men are almost always bad men, even when they exercise influence and not authority.'[75] Of course most people conveniently forget the concluding sentence when quoting Acton.

Creighton, showing a surprising measure of charity, immediately replied with a letter that began: 'My dear Lord Acton, Your letter is an act of true friendliness, and I am grateful to you for it—more grateful than I can say. It is a rare encouragement to me to have such a standard set up as you have put before me.'[76] He followed that with a lengthy explanation of his views on historical analysis which, in part, is revealed by this one sentence: 'Selfishness, even wrong-doing, for an idea, an institution ... an accepted view of the basis of society, does not cease to be wrong-doing; but it is not quite the same as personal wrong-doing.'[77] In trying to explain his treatment of papal policy on the Inquisition, for example, Creighton made a distinction between public actions—culturally driven—and private actions—personally motivated. He believed a public person should be judged more by his public actions than his private life.[78] 'You judge the whole question of persecution more rigorously than I do', Creighton wrote to Acton, 'Society is an organism, and its laws are expression of the conditions which it considers necessary for its own preservation. When men were hanged in England for sheep stealing,' he said, 'it was because people thought that sheep stealing was a crime, and ought to be severely put down. We still think it a crime, but we think it can be checked more effectively by less stringent punishments.' He concluded that men who regarded heresy as a crime in those days 'may be accused of an intellectual mistake, not necessarily of a moral crime'.[79]

Creighton ended his letter with a gracious remark: 'Your letter will give me much food for meditation, and may in time lead to an amendment of my ways.' He subsequently urged Acton to write an article for the *Review* on the ethics of history, promising that as editor he would have 'no objections to find my place among the shocking examples'.[80] Acton never wrote the article.

A few days later Creighton decided to challenge Acton again. 'I have no love for heroes', he said, but admitted that he hesitated 'to find men so villainous as in your scales of moral judgment they would be. I like to stand aside as much as possible, and content myself with the humble part of a chorus in a Greek play'; he stated that he felt compelled to 'find out men's good qualities before their bad ones, their good intentions before their evil means'. Creighton explained that—as a person—he tended to judge individuals more harshly for their personal immorality than the wrongdoing they did following public policy.[81] All this correspondence occurred before the actual ten-page review appeared in the July issue of the *Review*.[82] Other book reviews were much less harsh, indeed generally praising the work for its 'calm judicial discernment'.[83]

Historians still argue on whether it is better to follow Acton or Creighton with regard to making moral judgments. Acton's view of course may seem easier: one universal, moral truth applied to all people at all times. In his inaugural lecture at Cambridge in June 1895, Acton the idealist stated that 'Opinions alter, manners change, creeds rise and fall, but the moral law is written on the tablets of eternity'.[84]

It seems a case of the Ideal being the enemy of the Real. Creighton was a realist, a gentler man who understood the frailty of the human condition. As a person and a scholar, he was chiefly interested in what people did, where Acton's focus was on ideas—what people thought. That was the way each approached the past; and, as a result, each possessed a different recipe for evaluating the past. Thus, for example, it bothered Acton that Creighton seemed too tolerant of the Borgias. Creighton the realist, however, was not hoodwinked by the Borgia family by any means. In a letter to his friend Hodgkin, while deep in volume three, Creighton said that working on the Borgias was like 'spending one's day in a low police court'.[85] Yet he cautioned Alice Green that while Pope Alexander VI was 'an unscrupulous politician', he was 'not a villain; and Cesare Borgia was neither better nor worse than most other folk'.[86]

What bothered Creighton was that he thought Acton 'would reduce history to a dreary record of crimes'. Writing to Henry Charles Lea, the historian of the Inquisition and one who could not be accused of being overly gentle with the Renaissance popes, Creighton summed up his view about historians making moral judgments: 'I cannot criticise the Papacy of the fifteenth century from the point of view of the nineteenth century.'[87] Avoiding the thorny question of moral equivalency (of comparing one era with another, one regime with another, or one person with another), Creighton offered wise counsel, this notion of only judging pope, king, president, or whoever, within the context of the culturally accepted values of the times. Nevertheless, Acton's attack did give him pause; and he did move a little closer to Acton's judgmental approach later on, as can be seen in the series of lectures he presented at Cambridge in 1893–94 under the general title 'Persecution and Tolerance'.[88] Also in a paper he delivered in 1895, Creighton went even further to meet Acton's criticism, saying that the papacy which 'had been established for the promotion of morality' actually 'provided means for the utmost immorality'.[89]

Although Acton never wrote an article on historical ethics, Creighton did. An essay entitled 'Historical Ethics' was discovered among his papers after his death, but for some inexplicable reason the essay was not published during his lifetime. Louise reckoned her husband must have written it in about 1887, the time of Acton's attack, and after discovering it she sent the essay to the *Quarterly Review*; it was published in 1905 and then reprinted in America.[90] In the essay Creighton set out his reasoning about the question of historical moral judgments, and argued that the historian 'cannot make history a moral matter', stating that he did not 'feel comfortable in an attitude of lofty superiority over the men who, well or ill, have somehow done the work of the world'. He pointed out that 'public morality is not quite identical with private morality', and went on to state that 'rulers are to be judged by their public, not by their private life. The question of their personal virtues or vices is entirely subsidiary to their discharge of their public duties. Of course a king's private life possesses some historical significance for a full knowledge of his times; but his private character ought to be proved by overt acts, not by gossip.'[91] Creighton concluded that he 'liked to stand upon clear grounds which can be proved and estimated. I do not like to wrap myself in the garb of outraged dignity because men in the past did things contrary to the principles which I think soundest in the present'. About the only exception Creighton allowed on the question of making moral judgments was when the actions of a ruler or pope or statesman could be judged as 'treacherous or deceitful'. He thought that this 'simple issue' should be the 'sole standard of our moral judgment in historical matters'.[92]

Creighton's cautious historical approach never satisfied Acton, nor has it satisfied all the moral-minded historians of the twentieth century.[93] A century later it can be said that Creighton was perhaps too lenient with some of the rogues of the Renaissance and some of their policies; on the other hand, Acton's abundant and tiresome moral indignation was strong medicine indeed. History, following Acton's direction, would surely become a dismal science, a dreary exercise of moral finger pointing. Creighton's more judicious path was better.

13

The Blow has Fallen

'As soon as the children had gone to bed he said to me, "Well, the blow has fallen." I asked whether he felt clear that he was bound to accept. He answered that he was afraid so …'

Louise, recalling Mandell's appointment as Bishop of Peterborough.[1]

It was in the early months of 1886, just as Creighton was preparing the second number of the *Review*, that Bishop Henry Philpott of Worcester invited him to become his examining chaplain. Although sure to be an added burden, he found it impossible not to accept, especially because Dr Philpott was losing the one chaplain he had after twenty-five years of service to him. Already examining chaplain for Bishop E. R. Wilberforce of Newcastle, he felt he could resign from that post, however, as he was just one of several chaplains assisting Wilberforce. It was one of the rare times that he ever resigned from anything. Before leaving Embleton a pupil asked him if he would ever like to be a bishop. In one of those prophetic remarks that came to haunt Creighton later, he replied: 'No, I should not; but if I were offered a Bishopric, I have no doubt I should take it, as I always do what I am asked.'[2]

In early December 1890 Creighton received a letter from Lord Salisbury, then Prime Minister, asking if he would be willing to exchange the canonry of Worcester for a similar post at Windsor. 'To the Queen the matter, of course, is of considerable interest', Salisbury wrote, 'and the Canonries of Windsor are always filled up in deference to the Sovereign's personal wishes. She would be glad to be able to nominate you to this vacancy.'[3] Salisbury indicated that the annual stipend would be £1000, £225 more than he was receiving for the Worcester canonry.[4] One can easily speculate that both Lord Salisbury and Queen Victoria, sensing that Creighton was destined for higher preferment, felt it would be helpful to learn more about him first. There was no better place for this than Windsor.

Creighton must have seen the writing on the wall; but if he did not favour the change, he probably felt he could not decline and so with little hesitation accepted. He broke the news to a friend, claiming that 'life at

Worcester was much to my liking. I do not know that Windsor will be so much so'.[5] Upon learning of the Windsor appointment, Alice Green wrote immediately to congratulate him saying she 'felt a little surprised' when she saw the announcement in the newspapers; 'Windsor does sound a little courtly, and it has never done anything in the way of scholarship so that you will do a splendid service by bringing there the scholar's ideal.'[6]

Louise, however, regretted abandoning Worcester. 'I did not feel at all attracted by the prospect of life at Windsor and the connexion with the court', she recalled later. 'Had I known more about it then I expect I should have liked the prospect even less.'[7] She always dreaded the prospect of court life, and presumably recalled her previous experiences at Alnwick Castle with the Duke and Duchess of Northumberland, whom she regarded as intellectually dull. Mandell and Louise visited Windsor for one day before Christmas to look things over, and had lunch with Randall Davidson and his wife. Davidson was then Dean of Windsor. 'We went over what was to be our house on the Castle wall,' Louise recalled, 'and the one thing that attracted me was the wide view from its windows. It has never been my lot to live looking out on a wide view, and I have always wished for it and felt that it would be most inspiring to one's imagination. A day was fixed when I should go to Windsor to measure the rooms in our otherwise not very attractive house for carpets and curtains. But it was not to be.'[8]

As so often happened to the Creightons, unexpected events conspired to alter circumstances in their lives. On 12 February, just as the Lent term began, another letter arrived from Lord Salisbury. Louise was away from their Cambridge home, having taken some of the children up to London to the National Gallery to see an exhibition of Italian paintings. Mandell read the letter, but said nothing to Louise when she and the children returned home. That evening he seemed rather quiet and preoccupied, restlessly meandering around the house. After supper, when the children had retired and they were alone, Mandell turned to her: 'Well, the blow has fallen', he said. Then he told her the Prime Minister had written that the Queen wished to nominate him Bishop of Peterborough following the translation of William Magee to York. Louise asked if he felt obliged to accept. 'I'm afraid so', he sighed. That night neither of them slept much.[9] Mandell had had a premonition about this happening, Louise claimed, and once told her that he 'should like to put a special petition in the Litany that I might be saved from becoming a bishop', but adding, 'and the worst of it is, that I believe I should make quite a good bishop'.[10]

Mandell Creighton, of course, was an ideal candidate for a bishopric. To the leading politicians, men like Gladstone and Salisbury, he was intellectual, but level-headed, and not seemingly ambitious.[11] To Queen Victoria, who held firm views on ecclesiastical patronage, he was so moderate and sensible.[12] When his name surfaced as a potential candidate, Salisbury told the Queen that Creighton would be 'the best nomination for the vacant diocese of Peterborough'. Of those available, he conjectured, 'he is certainly the most distinguished in a literary sense. He is a popular man, and he has had some pastoral work which he has done well. He is a High Churchman, but his history of the Papacy shows that he is a man of philosophical mind with no tendency to extravagance.'[13] Creighton was more broad church in doctrine, though he favoured high church ritual. The fact that he liked wearing a cope and mitre, and relished the pomp of ritualism for example, stemmed more from his rich sense of pageantry and history than from any spiritual belief. This distinction was picked up by Randall Davidson, who corrected Salisbury, telling the Prime Minister he was in error calling Creighton a high churchman. Davidson assured him that Creighton was 'rather broad than otherwise; an able man'.[14] Salisbury hoped that since he thought the clergy in the diocese of Peterborough were mainly high church, Creighton being 'a Bishop of that colour would have the best chance with them ...'[15]

As it turned out, Creighton was destined to become one of Queen Victoria's favourite bishops, precisely because of his broad, moderate sympathies that matched her own. Louise, however, may not have fared so well in the Queen's royal esteem, for her growing reputation as a person of exceedingly strong opinions and a no-nonsense air for the commonplace—not unlike Her Majesty's manner—may have come to Victoria's attention. At least that was suggested by Laurence Housman who years later, after Victoria's death, wrote a short play 'Promotion Cometh' with the principal character being a formidable bluestocking named 'Mrs Clayton'—a thinly disguised and exceedingly uncomplimentary portrayal of Louise.[16]

Creighton went to Bishop Philpott for advice on whether or not to accept the offer. 'You know what kind of person I am, and how little fitted I am for the office, so I want you to advise me not to be bishop', he said. Philpott stared back at him and exclaimed: 'No, you must go, you must do what you are told'; then said, 'but let me tell you that a bishop's life is a happy one. It is full of troubles, full of hard work, but it has got this advantage—it gives you endless opportunities of doing little acts of kindness ...'[17] Few who knew him fully appreciated where his heart was and that it was a supreme sacrifice for him to leave his books and scholarly friends. 'My life has been that of a man who tries to write a book, and is the object of a conspiracy to prevent him from doing so', he confessed. Then he bemoaned that his 'wandering career seems to have come to an end. My peace of mind gone: my books will be shut up: I shall offer nothing but platitudes for the rest of my life, and everybody will write letters in the newspapers about my iniquities.' [18] To Reginald Copleston, then Bishop of Colombo, he lamented: 'No man could have less desire than I have for the office of bishop. Nothing save the cowardliness of shrinking from responsibility and the dread of selfishness led me to submit ... I am struggling to be submissive and pull myself together.' [19] To another friend he wrote what perhaps was one of the more revealing insights into his character and personality: 'I feel my function in life is changed. It is no longer to teach, but to edify. I have no longer to startle people out of self-complacency, but to be kindly, sympathetic, humble, and helpful.' [20]

Edmund Gosse recalled Creighton once confiding to him after he had become bishop that sometimes he asked himself

> whether it would not have been wiser to stay where I was; but I think, on the whole, it was right to come here [to Peterborough]. One is swept on by one's fate, in a way; but one thing I do clearly see—that [it] is an end of me as a human being. I have cut myself off. My friends must go on writing to me, but I shan't answer their letters. I shall get their books, but I shan't read 'em. I shall talk about writing books myself, but I shan't write 'em. It is my friends I miss; in the future my whole life will be spent on railway platforms, and the only chance I shall have of talking to you will be between the arrival of a train and its departure.[21]

Creighton continued his professorship and teaching throughout the Lent term. Of course the Cambridge community regretted his departure, for he had brought a decided vitality to his college and indeed the university. 'We knew only too well that we should not be permitted to keep him with us long', wrote a commentator in an 1891 issue of the *Cambridge Review*, 'that sooner or later we should have to part with him. But we had hoped with a selfishness which we trust is pardonable, that it would be later, and that Professor Creighton would have had time here to finish the *History of the Papacy*, to complete the reform of the History Tripos ... to impress the spirit of his teaching on the Cambridge school of history, both elders and juniors, while he represented it, as he alone could represent it, to the outside world.' [22]

The family went to Worcester at the end of the term for the last time where Creighton took over Good Friday services and gave a farewell sermon that evening, although he also preached on Easter Sunday. 'I am conscious of a personal tie which binds me to you all', he announced from the pulpit in his closing remarks, 'a tie which is sad to me to sever. The memories of Worcester and its great Church have become a part of my being ...' [23] And thus it was again, as it had been at Oxford and at Embleton; and when it came right down to it, to leave the comfortable known for the unknown was never easy, yet Creighton seemed to rejoice in the prospect of a new adventure. He was not a sentimental man, and was always ready to substitute the old for the new—more so than Louise.

Having resigned from the editorship of the *English Historical Review*, Creighton's connection with the *Review* was now limited to occasional pieces submitted to the journal, usually book reviews.[24] His replacement as Dixie Professor of Ecclesiastical History was also of some concern to him. He felt that his colleague Henry Gwatkin should receive the honour and strongly urged his selection to the electors. He wrote a forceful letter, marked 'Private' at the top, to his friend James Bryce, still one of the electors. Creighton implored him to support Gwatkin's cause, and described him as 'a born teacher' who had 'done more for the teaching of history than anyone in Cambridge'.[25] According to the historian George Coulton, who came to know Gwatkin well, the Creighton-Gwatkin friendship was strong and sincere, and the 'stimulus of Creighton's example raised Gwatkin from a wonderful tutor into a great lecturer'.[26] It was also obvious that future volumes of his history of the popes were in jeopardy. To Bryce, he wrote: 'Thanks for your congratulations ... but I suppose one must take one's chances ... I don't mean to drop my history.'[27] Creighton realised soon enough, however, that being a bishop drastically interfered with his scholarly life, as William Stubbs had acutely discovered when becoming bishop left him little time for serious research and writing.

The move to Peterborough proved especially difficult for Louise, as she did not relish leaving the collegiate environment and felt—as she had when she went from Oxford to Embleton—uprooted again and sent into social exile. There is even some hint that she may have experienced a form of depression. In all of the years together, this period may have tested their marriage. Soon after he became bishop, Mandell announced to Louise that they 'must never have any more quarrels', that he wished to leave all their disagreements behind. To dwell upon past or present disagreements now, he said, was 'to live in a sewer'. Louise admitted that they 'did not quite live up to this ideal'. When they did argue', she added, it was 'such bitter pain'; for Mandell, the incidents were 'sharp and short', but with Louise they were 'long and deep'.[28] It was, of course, difficult for two people with such intense temperaments not to quarrel. On one occasion Louise's teenage niece, Rachel von Glehn, came to spend a few days with them just before their move to Peterborough. In a letter Rachel wrote to her mother, she said that the 'first night I felt so sad and after half a day of noise quareling [sic] and angry words between the Creightons I longed so for my quiet home'.[29] The Creightons on the whole, however, had a happy marriage and balanced out their home life with affection for each other, as evidenced when Mandell's young nephew happened to walk into the bishop's study one morning and was both surprised and embarrassed to find his aunt and uncle in a romantic embrace.[30]

Nevertheless, leaving her Cambridge friends was a 'very real grief', Louise admitted later, and in a letter to her friend Kathleen Lyttelton she explained her feelings about going to Peterborough:

No, I have not the least fear that separation will make any difference in our friendship. Some friends are friends of circumstance, companions and associates in one's daily walk, and to such a friendship distance does make a great difference. But if ours has been that too, it has been a great deal more, and I still see in it great elements of growth and so I am quite happy about it. I suppose my ten years at Embleton without a kindred woman's spirit at hand has made me more stoical about separation than you are. I can only feel thankful for the gift of the last few years, a gift that is sure to be an abiding one. Don't think I am cold and don't feel. I simply can't sit down and feel about leaving Cambridge, and Worcester too ... I need all my strength for what has to be done and I am consoled as to my queries whether I have learnt to feel less by learning to discipline my thoughts more, since reflection makes it clear that I love ever so many more people now than I did in more sentimental days. I hope you are happy you have done very much to make my life at Cambridge happy, and I bless you for it. Don't give up making me happy; we owe a duty to our friendship, and life, which is too busy for friendship, is neither good nor wholesome; so we will see a great deal of one another.[31]

Preparations were made for Creighton's consecration as bishop on St Mark's Day, 25 April 1891, at Westminster. At the same time as Creighton, Randall Davidson was consecrated Bishop of Rochester. Just prior to this auspicious event, the Creightons decided to take a short holiday in Devon before wrapping up their affairs in Cambridge and Worcester. After arriving, they took an invigorating walk by the sea, and that night Creighton fell ill—one of those rare times when his body gave way, presumably from the stress of recent events. The diagnosis was muscular rheumatism and they were forced to return to Worcester. During his recuperation Mandell was invited to stay at Borough, Humphry and Mary Ward's rented farmhouse near Hindhead in Surrey,[32] while Louise remained at Worcester and at Cambridge, making final preparations for moving the family to Peterborough. There, in the Surrey hills, Mandell delighted in long walks and long conversations with the Wards as he regained his health.

By this time, Humphry was a struggling art critic for *The Times*, but Mary Ward had become a noted romance novelist, as Mrs Humphry Ward. Over the years Mandell had remained her ardent but friendly critic, someone she could depend on to offer frank suggestions. After reading her early novel *Miss Bretherton*, for instance, he advised her that she was writing more as a critic than a creator, and it proved to be sound advice.[33] Once, after writing a letter which harshly assessed one of her novels, Mandell concluded: 'There, I have told you what I think just as I think it. I would not have done so to anyone else save you, to whom I am always, Your most affectionate, M. Creighton.'[34] On another occasion, following one of his letters that was chock full of frank advice about her *Robert Elsmere*, which reportedly became the best selling novel of the century, Mary Ward shot back: 'I have been deeply interested by your letter, and am very grateful to you for the fairness and candour of it. Perhaps it is an affection to say always that one likes candour!—but I certainly like it from you, and should be aggrieved if you did not give it [to] me.'[35] Mary Ward never forgot her old friendly critic as she went on to write more than two dozen novels and became, in the words of one recent biographer, 'the most famous living novelist in the world' by the early part of the twentieth century.[36]

In mid May 1891, Creighton was enthroned at Peterborough Cathedral. Among the clergy assembled was his former headmaster from Durham Grammar School. The family was in the process of getting settled into the palace quarters the week after the enthronement when Mandell fell ill again, this time with acute influenza, which was especially serious in those days. It struck just at the time he was to begin interviewing ordination candidates; because he was so weak, most of the interviews had to be done from his bedside. During all of this, Louise struggled with the final modifications of their new quarters of the palace which she described as a 'rambling and somewhat inconvenient house'.[37]

The palace, situated literally within the shadow of the cathedral, was indeed a rambling structure that had evolved out of the abbot's hall of an ancient monastery founded in the seventh century. Parts of the outer wall of the hall's front entrance dated back to the ninth century. The two-story residence was set within the old monastery precincts, and had a large, walled garden—an ideal playground for the Creighton children as it turned out. In fact, the extensive lawn became the battleground for many a rough-and-tumble game of hockey with the bishop joining in after watching it from his ground floor office window. Louise did much to improve the gardens, adding many flower borders, although she complained that 'the poor soil and the smoke from the brickfields and the railways made gardening a constant disappointment'.[38]

In those early days at Peterborough, while trying to ready the house for comfortable occupancy, Louise confided to her friend Kathleen Lyttelton about her depression at leaving Cambridge and Worcester. 'Perhaps you may like to know that I am still alive after a hard struggle', she said. 'The desolation at the Palace is complete. My present feeling is that I hate the house, but perhaps that is natural considering its condition. There are workmen in every corner and I have done nothing but turn more on, order extensive sanitary works and pave the way to ruin. It is awful doing all this on my sole responsibility. Everyone has been very kind to me.' She concluded her letter by stating: 'My gardener and my butler are quite angelic. I am trying to be good but all the depression comes on at times, and I feel horribly stranded and cut off from all my old moorings; and very much separated from my family, and very ashamed for feeling these things difficult.' [39] Even by July her depression had not yet lifted. She wrote to Kathleen:

> I have written you many letters in my head but they did not come off; if they had they would have been grumbles or bits of foolish introspection and there would have been no use in that. I shall get used to it in time and find out what all this means. In the meanwhile, on the one hand, I am more than ever possessed with a sense of the difficulties of leading a spiritual life, difficulties which seem to me being a bishop's wife increases a thousandfold; and on the other hand, I am very rebellious at losing most of the things which made at least the external part of my life pleasant before.
>
> Grumbling isn't very much fun because it makes one so ashamed of oneself, so I am not going to indulge in it; but I have come to the conclusion that I have been very much spoilt during the last few years; people have been much too nice to me, and the evil result is seen now when I realise how much I miss it all ... It is the tiresome separation of the wife from the husband's work which bothers me. He may have ordinations and quiet days in which he cares for the souls of others; all that the wife has to do is to feed their bodies. He goes about giving new energy to the spiritual life of the diocese and the wife stops at home to look after the tidying etc. of a stupid big Palace and garden and to pay tiresome calls. Well, I suppose I shall find out what it all means some day if I try to see light somewhere.[40]

Formerly a Benedictine abbey, the cathedral became a diocesan church and the seat of one of the six new dioceses in 1541 after the dissolution of the monasteries by Henry VIII. It was constructed in the twelfth and thirteenth centuries in Norman style bearing flashes of continental Gothic in its later arches and facades; and, as at Durham and Worcester, Creighton was immediately taken with the cathedral's history and its architectural development, wasting little time before studing every nook and cranny, and taking his friends on guided tours through its decorative inner recesses. Interestingly, the cathedral was the burial site of two queens, the unhappy Katherine of Aragon, Henry VIII's first wife, and the tragic Mary Stuart, Queen of Scots, who, forsaking being a queen to be a woman, became a victim at the hands of Elizabeth I. Mary's body for a few years rested at Peterborough until her son James I moved it to Westminster Abbey to lie only a few feet from her cousin and executioner.

The city of Peterborough, growing up around this monastic foundation, is situated on the edge of the fens—that vast swamp of sluggish waters which washed up against the great limestone shelf stretching from the Dorset coast through the Cotswolds into Lincolnshire. Since the middle ages the fens have been reclaimed, and its flat, spongy lands have become arable and productive; but in prehistoric times it was wild and wet—a refuge for untamed men and game. Then, with the coming of the railway and industry, the city of Peterborough, perhaps unfairly, gained the reputation of being a colourless, nondescript town lacking scenic topography or cultural charm. By the 1890s, it was said that Peterborough had the dubious reputation of being the ideal place from which to catch a train.[41] Nevertheless, Creighton could never fail to see the unique beauty in the varied landscapes of England, and once wrote of the region as possessing 'smiling meadows with their flocks and herds, the ancient villages which nestle round their beautiful churches ...'[42]

The diocese of Peterborough at that time was large, consisting of 676 parishes with major centres at Leicester and Northampton. Creighton, nonetheless, was undaunted by the size and responded to the challenge by becoming familiar with his ecclesiastical territory, applying the same policy he did as vicar of Embleton—of visiting every corner of his ecclesiastical realm as soon as possible. During the first year as bishop, Louise sadly recalled, his 'days at home were few; the greater part of his life was spent in travelling about his diocese'. Many days and nights at a time were spent away from home, visiting churches and staying with clergy, though as a rule he tried to be at Peterborough on Sundays.[43] On some occasions, Louise would go along on his trips, especially those times when he went to Leicester for his annual three-week visit in the autumn. Then the Creightons would settle in some comfortable inn. Still, she regretted that his schedule left him little time for her. She wrote to her daughter Beatrice about one of their Sundays in Leicester:

> We had a tremendous day yesterday. First we went to an eight o'clock celebration in Mr Robinson's church, where father celebrated, and then we went to breakfast with him ... After breakfast father and I drove off to another church in the outskirts of Leicester, where he preached, and after service we lunched with the vicar, quite a young man, living in lodgings, and a curate. After lunch we drove to another church in Leicester, the great Evangelical church, where father instituted a new vicar and gave a little address ... After that we drove back here to tea and then soon we went off again to a great ritualistic church where father was to preach. I got there about a quarter of an hour before service, but it was crammed, and I got about the last seat. There were chairs all up and down the aisles and people stood all through the service, and some hundreds were turned away. After that the day's work was over, and we came back to a quiet and frugal meal.[44]

One observer in the diocese suggested that Bishop Creighton was 'utterly ignorant of the Midlands' when he became bishop, but that after a year 'he seemed to know the history and the geography and the distinguishing characteristics of his diocese better than any of his predecessors after many years'.[45] Not surprising, for Creighton was a swift learner. It is true that he was in the beginning of his episcopate a stranger to the larger world of church politics and hierarchical affairs, and felt more inclined to labour among the pastors and curates where he could promote cooperation and clerical unity.[46] He was ever ready to speak or preach when needed and felt it important that he try to meet every clergyman in his diocese. As he settled into his new life, the weeks were crammed full of routine work: preaching, ordaining clergy, inspecting old churches and dedicating new ones, conducting meetings with clergy and laity, confirming young people, giving away prizes at schools, cutting ribbons at civic events, attending social functions in cities and villages, hosting garden parties at the palace and, in general, being everywhere and being all things to everyone. In the first eight months his engagement book recorded 115 sermons and speeches—a pace exhausting even for a man who possessed boundless energy and could never conceive the possibility that his body would weaken under such strain. Of course some of the real joys in all of this were the times he met and talked to young people. People revitalised his energy and always lifted his spirits. He wrote once: 'I have been away from home confirming. I always like that part of my work; it is very nice going from one village church to another ... seeing all the young people, and trying to say something which they may remember.'[47]

According to Louise, her husband seemed always on a train, criss-crossing the diocese. She said that the only concession he made to his new status as a bishop was to travel first class so as to spare himself from fatigue and to gain some semblance of solitude in order to work on sermons and other projects.[48] Of course his life-long habit of taking long walks came in handy too, for he often used the excuse of taking a ramble to visit rural parishes, demanding his clerical associates walk miles with him to inspect a neighbourhood church. In one instance he wanted to inspect Newtown Linford church which at that time was in the gift of the Earl of Stamford and therefore 'a sealed book to a bishop'.[49] After walking miles over meadows and through woods, the bishop and the priest he was with reached a ten-foot stone wall with a locked gate. 'I discovered that my private key would not fit the lock', the hapless cleric said later. While he thought he might be able to scramble over the wall, he was sure that Creighton wearing his 'episcopal tights and orthodox gaiters' would never make it over. 'The Bishop, however, declared he would go wherever I could', and so they both scaled the wall. 'It was a scene I shall never forget', said the clergyman.[50]

It is probably true that, in his dealing with his clergy, Bishop Creighton enjoyed working with the younger men the most, always striving to prepare and guide them in their apostolate. When he arrived at Peterborough, it is said, he found the clergy had been living for years in terror of Bishop Magee, the previous prelate, who was described as 'remote and awful'.[51] Creighton's methods and manner, of course, changed that atmosphere, for he could put even the humblest curate at ease with his sparkling humour and down-to-earth practicality.

Certainly his letters to them show a sensitivity and understanding that must have given them encouragement. On one occasion, when one clergyman was in financial difficulties, Creighton arranged a bank loan for the man, giving his name as security. On other occasions, he offered pastoral assistance and career advice, and his teaching background seemed to give him an edge in reasoning with the younger, sometimes restless men. One of his rural deans claimed that Creighton's popularity among the clergy was because he 'took the keenest interest' in all of them, 'and was always prompt and thorough in dealing with any question great or small which they put before him'.[52] It was dealing with those cases of scandal and immorality among his clergy that was most vexing to him.[53] At Peterborough he experienced only slight problems over ritual. Those difficulties were yet to come.

Regarding dissenters and Roman Catholics, he was conciliatory up to a point. His personal liberality caused him to take people as he found them, and to accept them on those points with which he could understand or sympathise. He held fast to the notion, however, that to be English one ought to be Anglican. He reckoned that dissenters were simply non-conforming and therefore misguided Englishmen, but that Roman Catholics were essentially disloyal since they belonged not to just a separate denomination but—in his view—to a separate state as well.[54] For him, nationality meant culture and race as well as politics. This explains one of the paradoxical remarks Creighton made before a large group of clergymen: 'I am not ashamed to own that I am an Englishman first and a Churchman afterwards.'[55] Of course he did not say he was English first and a Christian second as some may have thought he meant. Yet it does underscore his persistent sense of national feeling (culture, race and government) and how it superseded nearly all other commitments.

One of the more telling aspects of Creighton's tenure as Bishop of Peterborough was his resolve to understand the working classes of his diocese. Leicester and Northampton had seen the rise of radical politics over the years, not unlike other manufacturing towns in the midlands. These commercial communities had large and of course influential non-conformist elements. Creighton's increased, albeit limited, contact with the working classes at Worcester had also sharpened his social sensibilities and alerted his concern for class harmony. Hard-headed businessmen and uneducated workers he knew were a recipe for urban strife and discontent, but his wide sympathies and quick intelligence, combined with his broad-mindedness, helped him considerably in dealing with his various constituencies. To whichever group he spoke, at Leicester or Northampton or elsewhere, his message was a call for genuine understanding and Christian compassion.[56]

It is safe to say that in the beginning of his urban ministry, Creighton got on best with the business classes because of his appreciation of their capacities and contributions.[57] When he spoke to worker organisations like the Literary and Philosophical Institute or the Co-operative Society, topics such as the defeat of the Spanish Armada or the role of Benedictine monasteries in the middle ages were probably too esoteric; he may have struck more of a resonant chord in a series of sermons he gave, the first being at St Martin's church in Leicester. The general theme of his homilies was 'The Church and Economics'.[58] In the first one he spoke of the spirit of Christianity and how it always led to the 'fullest recognition of the equal duties and of the equal rights of all men', although he made sure his listeners understood that he thought equal duties preceded equal rights. His words apparently met with some opposition, but the fact that their bishop was willing to raise the issue of worker rights was regarded by some as a positive step. One worker who heard him wrote that he 'had been a doubter in religious matters', but listening to the bishop's talks on industrial relations was a 'turning-point for me'. The man then admitted that he made sure to hear Creighton whenever he preached at Leicester thereafter.[59]

Often Creighton's personality and common sense examples were the stuff that charmed his listeners the most, as in the case when he exhorted some working men that it was their duty as 'members of Christ's Church' to take their children to church every Sunday and to sit beside them. 'You know', he said—no doubt with a hint of a smile poised on his lips—'that we have a crook in our arm. Why was that given to us? It was given to us that we might put it through the arm of another fellow and guide him on the straight way.'[60] Bishop Creighton's approach was to get people to see the connection between religion and the everyday life.

Creighton was still learning and growing. Much of organised Christianity in that era tended to be a religion of the more comfortable and successful, where material rewards were the expected result of sound Christian living.

As a result, a substantial separation of working-class people from active church membership became a reality.[61] But not long into his episcopate Creighton became known as 'a friend of organised labour', which propelled him ahead of most of the Anglican hierarchy at the time.[62] The event that helped him to understand organised labour was a boot and shoe industry strike that occurred in 1895, principally in Leicester and Northampton. It started as an employer lockout in March by the manufacturers' federation in which 120,000 workers were thrown instantly out of work. In a letter to a Leicester clergyman, Creighton decried the strike as 'very grievous', asserting that he thought the 'gravity of the crisis' was sure to have a devastating effect on the communities involved. 'If I can be of any use, I need not say that nothing would stand in my way.' But at that point he felt it a matter of principle to rule out overt 'episcopal interference with economic questions', adding quickly, 'but I am ready to sink anything for the purpose of helping'.[63]

Creighton's strategy was to write an open letter to the clergy in Leicester on 18 March. It clearly expressed his concern about the 'industrial dispute now so seriously affecting the welfare of the community'.[64] In urging his clergy to work with all sides on the outstanding issues, Creighton went on to state:

> The complexity of industrial life raises from time to time questions of great difficulty to decide fairly. The boot and shoe industry has passed through several stages, with exceptional rapidity, during the last few years. It is, I am willing to believe, hard for the most fair-minded and best-informed man to decide with any certainty how it can best be organised. Industrial disputes always involve matters about which certain knowledge is almost impossible ... But we are equally bound to impress upon both parties that suspension from work is to be regarded as affording time for a careful examination of the points of dispute, and a search for a basis of agreement ... The dispute must be settled, not by an appeal to the brute force of endurance, but by wisdom and conscience, quickened by a heightened sense of responsibility. The whole community has a right to demand that no time be wasted by pride or obstinacy ... I think that it is the great duty of the clergy to urge these great moral considerations, without any spirit of partisanship ... to uphold the standard of justice, to sympathise with every effort for peace.[65]

As the strike progressed, organised talks began in London among all representatives, including the permanent secretary of the Board of Trade. The bishop continued to work behind the scenes, mostly writing letters, eschewing public attention about his efforts. Creighton's tactic was to serve as a conduit for all bargaining parties, sharing information and feelings derived from his local clergy, who, being on the spot, possessed insights and sympathies that needed to be known and expressed. All sides, no doubt wary at first, soon came to sense his rational even-handedness over the broad issues and then welcomed his support. The secretary of the North-ampton Trades Council, representing some 9000 workers, wrote to Creighton to say that he offered his 'hearty approval' of the bishop's support, while the secretary of the Board of Trade praised Creighton for sending a letter of suggestions, stating that 'A navigator in a strange sea highly values a chart'.[66]

By the end of April the basic issues were resolved and the strike ended. The secretary of the Board of Trade then wrote to Creighton, saying that his efforts 'were largely helped by your information and counsel, which enabled me to see where danger lay and where safety was to be sought'. One of his clergy, who had strong views on the strike, told him that they were 'rejoicing beyond words to describe the prospect of social peace. Rightly or wrongly, I cannot help tracing your Lordship's good hand in the matter, and as a Leicester man to the core, I most heartily thank you in the name of Leicester.' [67] Another Leicester clergyman later said of Creighton:

> He helped the leaders on both sides to settle the dispute, not only by being a good listener to the statements of their different points of view and the arguments in support of them, but by suggesting at the right moment the method of intervention and the choice of a reference. But the action taken at the critical moment, with such good result, would have been impossible if he had not previously in many ways won at least a certain amount of confidence in many quarters.[68]

The strike was an educative experience for Creighton and it certainly indicated to others his growing statesmanship qualities. Another indication was his primary charge to his clergy in 1894 which one might consider a revealing expression of his views on the role of the church in society. [69] He delivered the first instalment on 29 May from the pulpit at Peterborough Cathedral; the remaining portions were given at six separate churches across the diocese. The entire text covered some of the principal questions of the era: the disestablishment of the Anglican Church, local government reform, biblical criticism, and various education and social problems. Certainly the document illustrated his evolving thoughts on the role of the church in dealing with socio-economic issues. An underlying principle was that the 'Christian Church is the necessary link which binds men together'. He admitted that part of the problem facing the church was that the clergy as a rule was 'little suited as a body to decide economic questions'. The great need of the day he believed was that 'all human relationships should be moralised and then spiritualised', and that in bringing this about, the clergy needs 'not only good intentions, but knowledge and wisdom'. Therefore, if the function of the church was 'to turn men's hearts toward one another', then, he reasoned, 'men of all kinds of opinion' had to seek 'benevolent neutrality in trade disputes'; and to be not only an outspoken critic of 'all unfairness', but to be committed to an 'unswerving maintenance of the great principle of justice'.[70] In the words of his wife, this primary charge 'makes clear what manner of man he was, more perhaps than anything else he ever wrote. It is equally full of humour, of learning, of common sense, of practical wisdom, of deep spiritual insight.'[71]

Some of Bishop Creighton's more spiritual sermons of this time, preached in various churches, were published in 1896 in a book entitled *The Heritage of the Spirit*.[72] Other presentations revealing much about his religious temper can be seen in the following: his address on 'Christian Ethics', delivered at the Folkestone church congress in 1892; his address on 'Science and Faith', given in the autumn of 1893 at the Birmingham church congress; his address 'The National Church: Its Continuity in Order, Doctrine and Autonomy' at the Norwich church congress in 1895; and his keynote address, 'The Idea of a National Church', at the 1896 Shrewsbury church congress, considered by some the most 'successful' of his church congress papers because, by building on previous papers, he went far to explain his thoughts on the nature and need of an established church that accommodated the twin forces of modernity—nationality and liberty.[73]

One of the most striking lectures he gave during these years, because it revealed a good deal about Creighton's confusing high church inclinations, was his sympathetic presentation of Archbishop William Laud's role in the Church of England at All Hallows church in Barking on 10 January 1895, the two hundred and fifthieth anniversary of Laud's execution. He saw in Laud a tragic figure misunderstood by history because history 'can make no allowance for good intentions'.[74] As one who believed that Cardinal Wolsey was not fully appreciated, Creighton believed Laud too was trying to preserve the universal faith in its English cloak, that is, to protect the national church from the pressures of both Rome and Geneva. To Laud— and one would say, to Creighton—the historical English church was inextricably identified with the historical English nation, and Puritanism was a threat to sound patriotism. 'Now, herein lies Laud's claim to greatness, that he recognised the possibilities of the English Church, not merely for England itself, but as the guardian of all that was best and most fruitful for the future of religious progress.'[75]

Creighton argued that Laud made a distinction between 'an English Church and an Anglican Church'. The former was clearly tied to the people of the nation. Laud's so-called 'ecclesiastical revival' promoted 'outward things' (high church ritual) because he believed that 'worship of the Church was the best form of teaching. Argument and controversy had done little; let the voice of devotion be heard, and it would prevail.'[76] Where Laud went wrong, Creighton thought, was in his secular policies, not his religious policies. Laud reflected one of the 'great evils' of the medieval church, of clergy holding political power at the expense of their religious authority. 'Laud shut his eyes to its obvious dangers, and believed that civil power was best in the hands of Churchmen.'[77] By being a state official, Archbishop Laud identified the English church with a policy that ran counter to the wishes of the people, but that should not lesson the fact that, in Creighton's mind at least, 'Laud's conception of the Church was sounder, larger, and more practical than that of his opponents. Events justified his wisdom.'[78] Years later, when Creighton was caught in a ritualist crisis of similar, albeit minor, proportions, when shrill ultra-Protestant cries rang out against high church practices creeping into Anglican services, he must have often recalled the tragic fate of the seventeenth-century archbishop.

Other addresses with a historical bent were his Rede Lecture on the early Renaissance in England delivered in the Senate House at Cambridge in June 1895, the Romanes Lecture on 'The English National Character' delivered at the Sheldonian Theatre in Oxford in June 1896, his address on 'Saint Edward the Confessor' at Westminster Abbey in October 1896, and his course of lectures presented between 1893 and 1895 on 'The Coming of the Friars' and 'Robert Grosseteste and his Times' in St Paul's in London.[79] The common theme running throughout all of these lectures is that England's religious heritage gave direction and flavour to its evolving national character. In 1894 a group of Anglican churchman formed the Church Historical Society. As would be expected, they asked Creighton to serve as the first president. He consented and remained president for the next six years.[80] To that organisation he delivered a paper, 'The Abolition of the Roman Jurisdiction', in 1895.[81] In June 1894 Creighton was given an honorary doctorate by Oxford University in recognition of his ecclesiastical scholarship, one of several honorary doctorates he received over the years.[82]

As Creighton had predicted, his life as a bishop left slight room for serious historical research, and therefore his *magnum opus* fell measurably short of its intended mark. The original scheme was to have his history of the papacy end with the final session of the council of Trent in 1563, but as it turned out the fifth volume that appeared in 1894 proved to be the final one and only dealt with the beginnings of Luther's career up to the sack of Rome in 1527. Because the initial edition had the title *History of the Papacy during the Period of the Reformation*, the publisher released in 1897 a second edition that came out in six reconstructed volumes with a new title, *A History of the Papacy from the Great Schism to the Sack of Rome, 1378–1527*, which is how the work is usually known today.[83]

James Bass Mullinger, a history lecturer and the librarian at St John's College, Cambridge, reviewed the fifth volume for the *English Historical Review*. It is not certain whether the editor S. R. Gardiner seriously considered asking Lord Acton to take on this assignment again or if Acton turned it down. Mullinger's review, however, resembled Acton's critical approach, though more clearly put. In a twelve page review, Mullinger frequently chastised Creighton for lack of evidence and perspective, declaring: 'The culture of the Renaissance, the sentiment of nationality, political divergences, the abuses connected with the temporal power, the growth of scholarship and enlightenment in Germany, all alike, in Dr Creighton's narrative, are scarcely perceptible as currents in the mighty tide which bore the Reformation into actuality.' Although Mullinger's criticism was more about professional judgments than moral judgments, his parting assessment was no less harsh than Acton's. 'This volume, especially when viewed in connexion with those 1600 pages by which it has been ushered in, is disappointing both as regards new material and originality of view.'[84]

Modern historians seem less ready to pounce on Creighton's history of the Renaissance popes, considering the fact that he was ploughing new ground for the English-speaking reader and that he lacked the primary sources which became available to those historians of the twentieth century. Creighton, aware that some would criticise his study for these very reasons, wrote to the American historian Henry Charles Lea that he considered his task to pull details together, that he never regarded his study as being the definitive interpretation. 'The study of institutions in detail must be done before general results can be summarised', he said. 'The history of the future will be less concerned with facts and more with internal development. We are only preparing the way.'[85] Nonetheless, it is generally agreed that his final volume was the weakest one. To be sure, Creighton's life had become fragmented and over-burdened, but just as important, his scholarly sensibilities lay south of the Alps. As a result he never really appreciated Luther or his cause. For Creighton, Erasmus always seemed much more sympathetic than Luther.[86] Still, one cannot help but wonder how the planned volumes covering the Reformation and including the council of Trent would have turned out.

One of the residual effects of writing his history of the popes was the series of lectures he delivered at the University of Cambridge in the winter of 1893–94. Known as the Hulsean Lectures, he chose the theme of persecution and toleration. Delivered in sermonesque form, they were apparently well received by the Cambridge community. Dr John Peile, then master of Christ's College, announced afterwards that he 'had not heard a sermon like that for twenty-five years', which brought responses from three other listeners: 'I have never heard a sermon like that in England'; another, 'I don't call that a sermon, but an essay'; and another, 'It was too deep for me; I went to sleep'.[87]

Subsequently published in 1895 under the title *Persecution and Tolerance*, Louise regarded these essays as revealing a great deal about the slant of Creighton's mind, more so perhaps than anything he ever wrote.[88] She thought that collectively they explained his life-long judgments on church, state and individual liberty.[89] Also, as has been pointed out, these essays show that Creighton had come to modify, albeit only slightly, his views on the question whether or not historians should make moral judgments, the result of Lord Acton's severe criticism a few years before.[90]

Although Creighton regarded the book as a trivial effort on an important subject, he recognised early on that it was difficult indeed for him even to approach the subject of persecution 'in an impartial spirit' because one either tends 'to represent persecution as especially inherent in all religious systems' or there is a tendency 'to plead the generally beneficent action of a particular form of religious organisation in relation to the world's progress as an extenuation of its particular misdoings'.[91] The conclusions he reached in this series of essays were several: that persecution of those holding 'erroneous opinions was contrary to the teachings of Christ, and was alien to the spirit of Christianity'; that persecution was adopted by the church 'from the system of the world, when the Church accepted the responsibility of maintaining order in the community'; that persecution was 'really exercised for political rather than religious ends'; that persecution was 'always condemned by the Christian conscience'; that persecution was 'felt by those who used it to land them in contradictions'; that persecution 'neither originated in any misunderstandings of the Scriptures nor was removed by the progress of intellectual enlightenment'; but that persecution 'disappeared because the State became conscious that there was an adequate basis for the maintenance of political society in those principles of right and wrong which were universally recognised by its citizens, apart from their position or belief as members of any religious organisation'.[92]

In a letter to Lea in June 1894, Creighton suggested that his lectures were a plea for 'a reconsideration of current judgment on the whole issue' of toleration. Creighton knew he was in the minority view when he argued that when power became absolute and corrupt, particularly over issues of liberty, persecution was more than likely to reside in or at least resemble the secular state rather than the spiritual church. 'I am just about to publish some lectures which I gave at Cambridge lately, on "Persecution". My position is that persecution is not necessarily inherent in the conception of a Church, but is inherent in the possession of power' he said, adding: 'I therefore traverse some of your conclusions in your *Inquisition* and regard the Church when vested with coercive power, not as a religious body, but as a branch of secular institutions. I will send you the book when it appears. It is a very slight and superficial, but is meant to plead for reconciliation of current judgment on the whole question.'[93]

In short, Creighton found it necessary to separate the medieval church's mission from its inquisitory machinations. For him the worst features of the church's practices in forcefully implementing orthodoxy resulted from the secularisation or politicisation of church policy. As he explained to Alice Green: 'My only point is that persecution is not inherent in religious opinions more than in any other set of opinions which are taken as the basis of common life. All I urge is that these things be considered separately. Christianity in itself as a system of thought and practice is one thing. Christianity as a necessary basis for common life is another ... If tolerance is a virtue, it is only because Christianity has learned to regard it so—if indeed it has so learned.'[94] It has been rightly pointed out that Creighton's description of a tolerant person is virtually a self-portrait:[95]

> The tolerant man has decided opinions, but recognises the process by which he reaches them, and keeps before himself the truth that they can only be profitably spread by repeating in the case of others a similar process to that through which he passed himself. He always keeps in view the hope of spreading his own opinions, but he endeavours to do so by producing conviction. He is virtuous, not because he puts his own opinions out of sight, nor because he thinks that other opinions are as good as his own, but because his opinions are so real to him that he would not have anyone else hold them with less reality ... Tolerance is needful to the individual; for it is the expression of that reverence for others which forms a great part of the lesson which Christ came to teach him. It is the means whereby he learns to curb self-conceit, and submit to the penetrating discipline imposed by Christian love.[96]

Creighton, ever the realist, knew that he would have to abandon his 'great work', the history of the popes, when he became bishop; and he wrote dejectedly to historian Richard Garnet in November 1894 that there was 'very little hope of any more continuous work. I may be able to do something, but I think it will have to be on a smaller scale, and of slighter character.'[97] That 'something' proved to be his biography of Elizabeth I, published in 1896.[98] This volume was a part of an illustrated biographical series and has worn well over the years; it and his biography of Cardinal Wolsey are Creighton's two best minor works. In fact the Elizabeth biography has remained one of the better interpretations of the queen throughout the twentieth century.[99] Although he cared little for Elizabeth the person, because of her personal flaws, or even the sixteenth century, because of its radical theology, he felt that she gave England direction and purpose.[100] Because he was so familiar with the Elizabethan era and had been lecturing on it for years, writing the book was relatively easy and required little research. It was a project he could do in bits and pieces, filling those gaps of time during the day and evening when he was able to turn his attention away from episcopal matters. 'I wrote it for my own amusement', he admitted later; because it was written with such a relaxed style and fulness of historical knowledge, his portrayal captures the personal character of Queen Elizabeth better perhaps than any book written since. It is more literary biography than 'scientific' history, but what it lacks in specifics it makes up for in insight.

In August 1892 Creighton delivered the opening address of the historical section at the Cambridge gathering of the Archaeological Institute. The topic was on the fenlands and his remarks carried forcefully the flavour of his enthusiasm for historical England, and how the forces of nature often conspire to make great things happen, as in the instance of how Cambridge University blossomed along the edge of the great marshland. English history, he felt, was in essence provincial history, which he noted had been long appreciated only by novelists and poets. Perhaps nowhere does one find this so well expressed as in Creighton's book *The Story of Some English Shires*, which appeared in 1897. A beautiful example of a nineteenth-century folio-size volume—or what would come to be known in the twentieth century as a coffee-table book— this compilation of essays on seventeen of Creighton's favourite shires and counties had been previously printed in a popular magazine of the time, *Leisure Hour*.[101] Finely balanced with picturesque prose and scenic line engravings, it was the fruit of many walks across England's rural landscape, from border counties in the north to Hereford and Gloucester in the west. His tender treatment of rural England, particularly areas in Cumberland, Northumberland and Durham, seems most compelling and rings with sensitivity and familiarity. Places have characteristics of their own just as much as persons, he thought, because 'they owe their distinctive features to the same causes as do men—to their ancestry in the past'.[102]

The concluding sentence in the preface of Creighton's book, however, rang loudly and sadly, tolling a prophetic dénouement that he might not even be able to finish that collection of essays: 'Increasing occupation has prevented me from finishing the series; but I still sometimes hope that I may succeed in doing so.' [103] As it turned out, this was the last history book he wrote.

14

I Went to Visit the Queen

'I went to visit the Queen and preach to her on Sunday. That was exciting, was it not?'

Mandell Creighton to his niece Winifred [1]

Bishop Creighton's new life forced him to be away from the palace often, travelling throughout his diocese visiting clergy and performing routine episcopal duties. This greatly agitated Louise. 'We had been very little separated in our lives,' she said, 'and now I suppose he was away at least half the week and sometimes more. There were no motors then, and he had always to sleep away if he had work to do in the evening. I sometimes went with him, but of course it was not always convenient for the clergy to put us both up, and besides I could not leave the children too much.' It disappointed Louise that, for the first time in their married lives, she could not really share in his work. 'There were more things with which he was concerned about which he could not talk to me freely', she said regretfully. 'There were more things which I had to do, about which I could not consult him.' [2]

Louise had always been dependent upon his companionship, to a fault. Prior to coming to Peterborough his work had allowed him to be frequently at home and to be about the house for the great part of the day. 'We talked over everything together', Louise remembered. 'I knew all about [his work], and could help him in some things.' [3] Now, the situation was different. Looking back on those years, she admitted that they were not the happiest of times for her:

I do not mean that they were unhappy, but they had not many compensations to offer for all the interruptions and upsets they caused in our usual way of life. In Peterborough, as a place, there was nothing attractive nor in the country round. It did not win my love in any way; only the Cathedral was a constant delight ... I was probably more lonely than I had been since I married. [4]

Although being the wife of a bishop had its 'special opportunities and special duties', she had to admit it was not easy. A bishop's wife 'must always think of how what she does may affect her husband's position and reputation'. In her particular case, she thought it 'fortunate that in all important matters our agreement was so complete that I really never had a desire to do things he would not approve of', and that she 'never wanted to do otherwise than fit my life to his; what I minded was that circumstances inevitably made our companionship less complete ... I generally had to go about alone, endless train journeys for meetings. Of course there was in one sense no loneliness in my life as I always had the children, and the house was never dull or empty.'[5]

It was 'ridiculous', she knew, how much she minded being away from her husband, but as she explained: 'I have always been most foolishly prone to fears and anxieties as to what might happen to members of my family when out of my sight.' She admitted having 'a horrible capacity for imagining vividly misfortunes of every kind. Though I have tried hard I cannot conquer this foolish habit, which caused me much misery, and which I think is really sinful. All I can hope to do, and in that I am far from successful, is to hide my fears and not let them interfere too much with other people's doings.'[6] Her loneliness seemed to goad the insecurity that had possessed her since childhood.

From an intellectual point of view, Louise felt starved. She had agreed to write a primer on the history of France for Longmans before leaving Cambridge, and spent the first year at Peterborough trying to complete it. It appeared in 1893.[7] She claimed the book 'kept my mind alive', but it was the last book she would write for some years. Like Creighton, her new life left little room for literary projects. And what made matters even worse, she discovered at Peterborough that she could no longer sit in her husband's study with him every day, each working separately on their articles and books. Now Mandell had to make room for his secretary in his office, and for others who might come to call. For the first time in their married life, she had a separate sitting-room.[8]

The hustle and bustle of the episcopal life, nonetheless, had a positive impact on Louise. It plunged her into 'the great ecclesiastical world outside', where she came to know various church leaders, lesser clergy with their wives, many county families, and the families of manufacturers and tradesmen, many of whom Louise described as 'able and cultivated, narrow-minded and limited in outlook'. All of this certainly also enlarged her own outlook.[9] Yet she found these social obligations often tedious or even boring. It was while visiting the Duke of Rutland at Belvoir Castle that she said she 'first realised the social position of a Bishop's wife' was considerably less than that of a bishop. It was a very large party, she recalled, and Creighton had the honour of taking the duchess in to dinner. He 'sat amongst the great;

I was far off at the other end amongst curates and other humble gentry. It amused me to find that I minded even a little, but only because it made me feel separated from [him] and in another world to his'.[10]

Louise found her visits to rural vicarages and churches of comparative interest, having spent nine years as a vicar's wife herself. 'I was genuinely interested in their parishes and their work and so there was always plenty to talk about. I wanted to help them and be of use to them as far as possible. I often wished that I could have urged them to be less conventional in their standards of living, to take their restricted means more simply.'[11] She said she came to feel the need 'to learn how to make poverty beautiful. But naturally I was the last person who could have attempted to speak to them on such a subject. There were very few of whom I saw enough really to make friends.'[12] While it can be argued that there is a valid connection between poverty—economic or otherwise—and spirituality, the comment about wishing to make 'poverty beautiful' tends to smack of an all too popular confusion of social attitudes with theology which was sometimes conveniently espoused by those who were materially better off.

During these years Louise attended many of the church congresses with Creighton in such towns and cities as at Birmingham, Folkestone, Exeter, Norwich and Shrewsbury. She enjoyed the congresses because, as she said, 'they helped me to know more about church people generally, and to understand more about church affairs'. Listening to her husband speaking at meetings of churchwomen she saw 'how much greater effect was produced by a man saying certain things to women than by a woman saying almost the same things ... This led me to see how desirable it was that women should speak to some of the men's meetings and for the same reason.'[13] Soon Louise managed to get herself invited to address specific men's sessions at congresses where she spoke on the life of the clergyman's wife in the country.[14]

The Mothers' Union became one of Louise's principal activities while at Peterborough. She wrote to her friend Kathleen Lyttelton in the June 1891: 'I begin my MU campaign ... in a fortnight, but I am going to take it gently at first and feel my way. I have not yet found a country parson's wife who wanted to do anything about anything, so I must not frighten them.'[15] A chapter of the Mothers' Union had not yet been established in the Peterborough diocese when Louise arrived, and therefore she launched one, though she let it be known that some of her organisational plans would be different from its founder Mary Sumner. She did not see the need for a central organisation, for example, and suggested a more local approach by promoting guilds of mothers in each parish. 'I wanted it to consist solely of mothers, or women who stood in the place of mothers ... I wished all to join on an equal footing and that we should think of ourselves as a community of mothers who were joined together to help one another in bringing up our children.' [16] Louise spent much of the first two years starting up branches which meant travelling across the diocese, going over and over the same planning which she frankly admitted was 'wearisome'.

Being interested in the relationship between children and parents, her work with social outreach programmes like the Mothers' Union caused her to become more interested in the problems of working-class families. 'It was a disadvantage knowing so few of the working women, really none, in their homes', she admitted, 'but I had memories to draw upon, and I took every opportunity to learn about them from the clergy and others.' [17] On one occasion a woman questioned Louise, in effect saying she found it hard to believe how a bishop's wife could understand her problems of raising children, to which Louise replied crisply, 'You see I have children of my own'. Louise said she possessed a 'constant desire to feel one with them, one mother amongst others. This was what I tried to feel too with the clergy wives.' [18] Although she still had a way to go, she was beginning to understand better the real life conditions of the urban working classes.

Louise also did volunteer work with the Girls' Friendly Society as she had in earlier years, but much of her 'outside work' at Peterborough came to centre on the rescue movement—further evidence of her growing social conscience. Late Victorian England witnessed a good number of new religious and social organisations bent on salvaging and reforming the lives of urban workers and their families, particularly with a thrust to promote moral values. The most notable example was William Booth's Salvation Army. The Church of England established its version with its Church Army. Throughout the 1880s and 1890s there were other variations concerned with revival and rescue work, notably the Church Salvation Army, the Church Gospel Army, the Church Mission Army, the Church Militant Mission, the Christian Social Union and the settlement house project.[19]

All this rescue work along with the creation of 'rescue homes' in larger cities emerged as a major social force for moral and physical intervention and the rehabilitation of wayward individuals, especially women. Louise admitted that the whole 'rescue' notion was new to her. 'I had never had anything to do with it before', she said, and 'it was with much shrinking that I realised that it was my duty to take it up and organise it in Peterborough'. She, along with some other interested women, were able to enlist the aid of a Church Army worker, and one morning every week they 'discussed all the cases and we considered what was best to do with them. I did not have much to do personally with the girls; my share was organising and directing. In this way I learned to know a great deal about all the problems of this most difficult matter.' [20]

Louise believed that their work in Peterborough led to the Church Army seriously taking up rescue work of young women as a regular activity, training workers specifically for this effort. 'At first we had only one of their ordinary mission workers, nurses as they called them then,' she said, 'and their rule was that these should only stay two years in one place; but I got them to relax this rule in our case. I also interested myself in the Refuge that already existed in Leicester, and in the Diocesan Home that we had started at Ketton under the Wantage Sisters.' [21] Louise spoke at various civic and church meetings promoting rescue and found that a committee of similar purpose in the National Union of Women Workers proved to be a helpful resource for her efforts. All of this prompted her to focus more diligently on what she called the 'purity question'. Years later she reflected on this:

> I think in all this purity question, women suffer from looking at it too much from the woman's point of view and not considering the man's side; and I believe that as a whole the subject suffers from being left so much to spinsters. Since those days there have been great changes, and men and women have learned to work together much more. I have myself come to feel more and more that this subject must not be segregated, but must be treated in connexion with all other efforts to raise the moral standard of the people; that as hospitals are needed for the study of physical diseases and their causes so that the health of the people as a whole may be improved, so rescue homes are needed for the study of this social disease and for the causes that lead to it in order that we may more wisely deal with the training of the young and the eradication of those social habits which lead to impurity. [22]

Taking up the cause with her usual enthusiasm, Louise began to speak out on the 'purity' issue challenging middle-class society to 'recognise that chastity must be demanded of men as well as of women and that it is not impossible for men; neither have women sufficiently recognised the special difficulties of men. I learned a great deal and thought a great deal about these subjects during the years in which I was so much occupied with organising rescue work.' [23]

Another activity that caught Louise's eye was the free library movement that began about this time in an effort to encourage book reading within working-class districts of the city. She joined a committee sponsoring the project and found that it brought her into close touch with workers and tradesmen. There were 'no gentlefolk' on the committee, she remembered, but the women who were involved proved interesting to her. She got to know 'their point of view', and though they were not in the least literary-minded, 'they were always ready to listen to me as regards the choice of books. I was proud of being able to persuade them to buy the *Encyclopedia*

Britannica, the price of which at first staggered them.'[24] Louise also joined the Women's Cooperative Guild in Peterborough, and spoke once or twice at their meetings; and when the group decided to start a women's Odd-fellows lodge, Louise was elected to be its first president, and eventually the lodge was even named after her. She also became a member of the Women's Friendly Society lodge in Northampton, another one of those non-denominational, non-political organisations that had as its underlying mission the social advancement of women.[25]

The NUWW continued to be one of her favourite activities outside the diocese. She served as president in 1895–96 for the second time, and nearly always attended their annual conferences. 'At these conferences I had some of my greatest successes as a speaker and also as a chairman', she said.

> It was not always easy to keep all these eager women in order and above all to make them speak to the point. I enjoyed my work ... with them all very much and made many faithful friends among them besides numberless acquaintances. I gained a wide knowledge of all kinds of women's questions; of course the suffrage question came up constantly, and the number of advocates of women's suffrage probably increased, though we were not at all as a body active in the matter, and my opinion did not change, that women would be more useful if they kept outside actual political life and free from party politics. It was a matter on which I had constant discussions with Kathleen Lyttelton, a keen suffrage advocate.[26]

Women in those years were beginning to make great progress in the public realm of that male-dominated society, organising meetings, speaking out on social and political issues; and this was certainly true in her case with regard to the NUWW. She gave talks and read papers whenever possible on topics she called 'women's work and women's questions'. Her experience helped her, as she put it, 'to get into a wider world'.[27] Certainly her involvement in this wider world counter-balanced the fact that she could not share as much as she would have wished in her husband's professional life and travels; for example, it particularly bothered her that he did not take her along the day he took his seat in the House of Lords.

As bishop, Creighton was not immediately eligible to sit in the Lords, not until a vacancy opened with the death of one of the sitting senior bishops. Spiritual peers were limited to twenty-six, consisting of the two Archbishops, Canterbury and York, the Bishops of London, Durham and Winchester, and twenty-one senior bishops. Creighton, therefore, was not eligible until a seat became available at the opening session in February 1896.[28] The following day he wrote to Louise from London that he had 'been busy all day: went to service at ten, opened the Church House, then lunched with Gore [canon of Westminster], went to the House of Lords, took my seat, which is a ludicrous process, but not so ludicrous as for lay-lords, of whom I saw six introduced. It was like a circus. Then I heard some debate, to the end of [Lord] Rosebery's speech, when I retired with a headache.'[29]

Louise felt she could well relate to the 'circus' metaphor. Life at Peterborough palace was often like a three-ring circus. On the whole, she said, she managed her 'big household and all the varied entertaining without much difficulty'. They had no desire to 'be smart', she said, stating that they felt a bishop should not 'live on a grand scale, but we wished to show hospitality to everybody'.[30] Indeed, both Louise and Mandell felt it essential that their children should grow up with 'habits to be as simple as possible', and not be allowed to assume a sense of unearned superiority or privilege because they were living in a grander style than before. Mandell once told the headmaster of Marlborough that the 'thing that weighs upon me' was the 'difficulty, and the absolute necessity' of making his children understand 'that they have to make their own way in the world'.[31]

There were constant visitors and entertainment 'of every sort, and for people of many different kinds', at the palace, Louise said.[32] She had to organise 'endless gatherings', dinner parties, garden parties, regular diocesan conferences, rural deans, ordination retreats, over night and week-end visits of both friends and others stopping by to meet the bishop. Visitors of all kinds often stayed for lunch after a meeting or just turned up unexpectedly. There were times Louise said that her children had 'to fly from the table to make room for the guests brought in by their father'.[33] And there were some 'amusing big suppers for people of very different kinds', she recalled, no doubt remembering the day they served a Christmas supper to the fifty workmen who had completed the alterations to the palace which Louise had demanded when they moved in.[34] Louise did have a gift for organising. 'I always liked everything to go easily and without fuss', she said, 'and I liked things to be well and comfortably done, but more or less to get on with all kinds of people; and I hope I grew less alarming, but I don't think I was ever much good at small talk and I never encouraged gossip.'[35] Mandell always tried to be at home on Sundays, so they often hosted weekend parties. 'We did not make these Sunday parties at all smart', Louise said, and 'kept up our habit of having a more or less cold supper instead of late dinner on Sunday evenings. Our excellent butler, Wilkin, helped to make all the entertaining go easily, and I was troubled by no domestic crises. The large house enabled us to have big Christmas parties.'[36]

The older boys, Cuthbert and Walter, were of course both away at Marlborough during these years; Beatrice was nineteen and now at home, often engaged with her singing lessons, and Lucia, seventeen, was attending Newnham College in Cambridge. Of the younger children, Mary, age eleven, Oswin, eight, and Gemma, four years old, were all at home. Louise found that she had to abandon for the most part her daily lessons with them, though she tried to keep up her Bible-reading every morning and her daily reading aloud after lunch when she was at home. Her succession of nurses in those days also served as governesses-of-sorts when she was away from the palace. Both Beatrice and Lucia helped out in the schoolroom as best they could. 'It was a great help to have the girls growing up and able to take some part in entertaining the many people who came to the house. Beatrice especially was of much use with her music. Her singing was then very delightful and natural and a great joy to us.' 37

Family life, when all the children were home, usually bordered on the hectic. Louise, of course, protected Mandell as much as possible from the 'perplexities and problems' of home life, as she had throughout their marriage, handling all the financial affairs of the family, keeping the accounts and paying the bills.38 When possible the family would take afternoon walks, which had been their habit since Oxford days. Sometimes Louise and Mandell would bring many of the children along, and possibly one or two servants, which brought some amusement to the faces of passers-by in the city as they watched the bishop's brood trooping off to Milton Park or strolling along the north bank through the fens.39 Occasionally, Creighton took some of the older children on his long walks about the diocese, stopping at churches and vicarages along the way. He still could not resist his habit of telling whimsical stories to the younger children, or rolling with them on the hearthrug. Louise confessed that she 'never had any chance with children', when Mandell was around. 'He was naturally more fond of them than I, and could invent enchanting games and romps, and tell fascinating stories.' 40

The summers were filled with picnics and parties, and daylong excursions into the countryside. Creighton relished challenging those who dared going along on one of his rambles. Describing to his niece a particular hike years later, he said 'the day was lovely and we went for a walk on the hill, and did not get back till 7. I positively dragged Aunt Louise up 2500 feet, but it was hard work for her and she remains very stiff.' 41 In the winters the chief outdoor activity was the family hockey matches in the fields in which guests, or even young people in the precincts or community, were invited to participate. Any visitors staying at the palace were forced to join in, Louise said. 'We had games when three and even four bishops [were] playing. We did not play according to strict rule or with regulation sticks; it was a game in which children, girls and boys and elderly women and men could all join. I enjoyed it much myself, tho' I could not really play, but it was a splendid way of getting exercise in the winter.'[42] One year, when there was a great frost and the fields were flooded, everyone found the ice-skating 'magnificent'.[43] The great entry hall at the palace, with its tiled floor, proved ideal for dances in the winter evenings. Creighton had danced occasionally at their annual Embleton Christmas party for the choir, but his taste for dancing at Peterborough came as a bit of a surprise to Louise, who said his 'love of dancing, dormant since our marriage, revived. I never knew till then how fond he was by nature of dancing, and there were of course often dancers staying in the house. I never cared for dancing and was only an on-looker. We had also an occasional big dance for the neighbourhood, and then danced in the dining-room.'[44]

In the summer of 1896, when his brother James fell grievously ill, Creighton travelled north to Carlisle twice to visit him, soon realising that the end was just a matter of time. In September James died, leaving six children. This was not the first sorrow to befall the Carlisle Creightons. Five years earlier, in 1891, James's wife Carrie had died unexpectedly, and then in the following year his thirteen-year-old son Gilbert died of appendicitis. Both Mandell and Louise were with James when he died and were able to console Polly and the children.[45]

Louise said that Mandell 'felt very strongly the call to do all in his power for Jim's children now left without father and mother. After this they always spent Christmas with us and joined us in the summer holiday, and the girls paid frequent visits in between, and Max wrote to them regularly.'[46] The following letter to his seventeen-year-old niece Winifred, about his first meeting of Queen Victoria, is a good example of his attempt to entertain and amuse:

7 December 1894

My dearest Winnie,

I have been so very busy lately that I have had no time to write to anybody. Now I have a morning which is comparatively free, though I have two Confirmations to-day. I have been for the last three weeks established in lodgings at Leicester. But last Saturday I went to visit the Queen and preach to her on Sunday. That was exciting was it not?

I arrived at Windsor Castle about seven on Saturday and was shown to my room. Then a series of officials came to tell me what I was to do. At nine I went to dinner with the royal household, the lords and ladies in waiting. It was the Princess of Wales' birthday, and all the royal family almost was at Windsor. After dinner we went into the Queen's drawing-room, when she presently came in followed by the royal family. She is a little old woman, very much crippled in the legs by rheumatism, walking with a stick, leaning on her Indian attendant, who was clad in a turban and a magnificent Oriental dress. There were the Duchess of York, the Princesses Victoria and Maud of Wales, Princess Louise, Duke of Connaught, Princess Beatrice and Prince Henry of Battenberg, besides some Prince and Princess of Schleswig-Holstein. They sat in a circle and we sat behind them. Then we had a concert; a violin and a tenor singer who sang and played vigorously. Then the Queen departed about 11.30 and we presently retired.

On Sunday morning I breakfasted with the household and, at eleven had to preach in the Queen's private chapel. It was rather awful having a congregation of about fifty, with the Queen and the royalties in a box up above, just opposite the top of the pulpit. In the evening I dined with the Queen. It was not so awful as I had expected. I sat next to Princess Beatrice, who was very nice. After dinner the Queen sent for me and we had a little talk in the drawing-room. She has a beautiful voice, and was very nice and friendly.

Then on Monday morning I departed. I have scarcely been at home since the beginning of October. Next week I am going to settle down till after Xmas. Much love to you. God bless you,

Your loving uncle,
M. Petriburg.[47]

After this initial visit to Windsor Castle, Creighton was frequently invited back, or to Sandringham in Norfolk, thus bringing him closer and closer to royal attention and approval. He in turn enjoyed these visits, met many persons in high places, and became popular with the children at court, such as little Prince Edward—the future Duke of Windsor—who was then four or five years of age. Creighton on one occasion was found having a 'tremendous romp' with him when he perched the prince 'standing with one of his legs on each of his shoulders, from which perilous height the descent was made by a somersault, a performance which the bishop had often practised with his own children. The little prince was delighted, and came up again and again to have the exciting experience repeated, whilst the bystanders were a little alarmed lest these wild romps might lead to some accident ...'[48] Later, however, the boy reportedly muttered: 'I don't like riding on giraffes!'[49] It is fairly safe to say that, if the Queen had witnessed such antics, she would not have been amused.

Creighton was an inveterate letter writer, often writing two or three dozen a day. As his letters in general are first-rate samples of the fine art of Victorian letter-writing, so his kindly letters to his orphaned nieces and nephews are some of the finest examples of his narrative skill to entertain and influence. Indeed, they have been described as the 'most touching evidence of his absorbing interest in conduct and character'.[50] Overall, his letters to them reveal clear evidence of his love of children and the gentle method he employed to give them personal guidance, as well as to entertain.

Creighton once declared to Ella Pease of Northumberland, another one of his regular correspondents:

> To be a good letter writer one must of course be egotistical. Letters are not history, nor are they essays, but they are jottings of small things as they strike *oneself*: records of one's own impressions: and they owe all their interest to the belief that the person to whom they are addressed is interested, not in things in general, but in *oneself* ... In talking or letter writing all depends on giving oneself rein: if one stops to be judicious or wise or discreet, one simply becomes dull. If I can't trust the person I am writing to with all I think, I am simply bored by the conversation, and would much rather read a book.[51]

Of all the Carlisle Creightons, Ella and Winifred took the most advantage of visiting Peterborough in the course of those years, and young Basil, who was 'rather forlorn at home', came to live at the palace for two years, from 1894 to 1896, before he went off to Uppingham. Louise thought 'it would be a help for him to join our schoolroom party'. It was not long before Louise began to feel that Mandell was being an overly indulgent uncle to his nephews and nieces, and it troubled her that he seem more interested in them than his own children. But Mandell justified his attention to his brother's children by telling Louise that their children had her to look after them.[52]

Three-quarters of a century later, Basil Creighton recalled those days with fondness, remembering his uncle's visits to their family in Carlisle, especially after his mother died. '[Mandell] almost adopted us', he said, and recalled how he was struck by the kind and affectionate interest he took in him:

> I was then eight and soon afterwards my father asked me whether I would like to go and live with my uncle and cousins ... I therefore saw a good deal of him. He was friendly to children ... He liked company, games, romps and family occasions. He took us for afternoon walks and told us stories which he made up as he went along. When he came out of his study at the end of the morning it was like the sun emerging from the clouds of business and care. He walked with a sprightly elegance and would look about for someone to engage in conversation ... He was altogether genial, stimulating ... never sentimental, knowingly earnest or edifying, or given to making 'improving' remarks ... He was quick-tempered, however, as I knew when I put a ball through a glazed door.[53]

Louise and Mandell made nine trips together to the Continent during the Peterborough years. After nearly five months of being a bishop, he was ready for a holiday to sunny Sicily; they left Peterborough on 22 September 1891 and returned on 23 October. For both it proved to be an intriguing journey as they encountered much that was quite new to them. 'It began with the worst sea passage I have ever experienced,' Louise recalled, 'from

Naples to Palermo, seven hours of violent sea sickness in an exceptionally swift boat which indulged in every sort of exaggerated motion ... It was really too hot for perfect enjoyment and rest, tho' no blazing sun could destroy the intense beauty and interest of Syracuse.'[54] They spent a couple of weeks visiting such places as Palermo, Syracuse and Messina, all the while marvelling at some of the remaining vestiges of Greco-Roman theatres, temples and fortresses in Sicily. Returning north, they spent some leisurely days in Naples, Rome and Verona.[55]

The following year, 1892, they managed three trips out of England. In the spring they travelled to the Rhineland for a couple of weeks, taking Beatrice and Lucia with them. One day, while all of them were walking around a large lake, they discovered a young man trapped in a cave after his girl companion had notified them of his predicament. After some difficulty and with Louise's assistance—while Beatrice and Lucia ran three miles for help—Mandell managed to drag the body from the cave heavy with volcanic fumes, but unfortunately the man was dead from asphyxiation. Creighton became a hero in the village, however, by risking his life in trying to save the man.[56] In July Mandell and Louise went to Dublin for the tercentenary of Trinity College, where he received an honorary LL.D. Creighton, with memories of the Harvard celebration vividly in his mind, enjoyed these festivities. Both enjoyed the city of Dublin, but saw nothing beyond the Pale. He did preach at an Anglican church in Parsonstown, however. It was their only visit to Ireland. Then, in the autumn of 1892, they both spent roughly five weeks in Italy again. The weather was beautiful and Mandell wrote to a friend that they were 'perfectly revelling in Italy; it is too nice for words'. Louise years later claimed it was the holiday she 'enjoyed the most. We wandered amongst Etruscan cities studying the different kinds of Etruscan tombs and ... visited many beautiful places ...'[57]

In June of 1893 they made a journey to the southern slopes of the Alps and the Italian lakes. Prior to the trip they both read the account *Alps and Sanctuaries of the Piedmont and the Canton Ticino* (1881) by the writer Samuel Butler. For Louise the book was 'enchanting' and led to the beginning of a casual friendship of sorts with Butler.[58] Creighton, who often displayed an affinity for unconventional characters, wrote to Butler in July 1893: 'I find myself on many points relating to art and literature, and to Italy in agreement with you: and it would be a great pleasure to me to compare notes.'[59] Butler possessed little sympathy for clergymen and balked at this invitation to visit Peterborough. It was said that he received the bishop's letter with 'some trepidation', and that he would have rejected the offer to visit out of hand except that a crumb of tobacco was discovered in the letter. Creighton was an inveterate cigarette smoker and Butler must have reasoned that the bishop was not so hidebound and haughty as he might have expected; so he borrowed a prayer book, making sure the pages were cut open—as was necessary in those days—and made his curious pilgrimage to Peterborough for dinner and discussion with Creighton.[60] Years later Louise said that their friendship was 'spoilt' when details of Butler's iconoclastic life became public after his death. 'It has given me probably an exaggerated feeling of distaste so that I feel unable to enjoy his books any more.'[61]

In the spring of 1894 the Creightons went to Algeria, where Mandell found the cultural differences engaging at exotic places like the ruins of Carthage, the bazaars of Tunis and Constantine, and the old Roman fortress at Announa. Louise said she 'enjoyed Algeria', but 'was not captivated by the Arabs and felt the want of seeing women about in the towns, or any evidence of family life. I was never tempted to sketch there.'[62] As it so happened, Creighton's former Embleton pupil Alfred Pease and his wife Nellie were staying at Biskra, and the Creightons arranged to meet them. In his journal, Pease wrote tersely: 'Mandell Creighton (now Bishop of Peterborough) and Mrs Creighton arrived—and left again after one day, disgusted with Biskra.'[63]

Later that same year the Creightons went to Bayreuth in Bavaria, home of the Wagner festival, taking along Beatrice, Polly, and Dorothy Ward, daughter of Mary and Humphry. 'I was immensely interested by the Wagner operas', Louise remarked, 'and felt that it was the right way in which to enjoy them, when there is nothing else to be done or to be thought about and one could give oneself entirely to them. When some years later I heard *Siegfried* and the whole Ring Cycle in London I did not get nearly so much out of it; the operas did not fit in with the London life outside, and did not get hold of me as they did at Bayreuth.'[64]

The next spring they went to central Italy, taking Beatrice along, but the weather turned cold and uncomfortable. Then at the end of August they spent a couple of weeks travelling though Normandy with Cuthbert and Walter. Of course Louise, having relatives and friends of the family in Germany, made an occasional trip to the Continent; for example, she and Beatrice visited her sister Sophie Hasse in Königslutter, although as a rule she hated to travel without Mandell.[65]

And of course she hated to have Mandell travel without her, as in the instance of Creighton's trip to Moscow in 1896 for the coronation of Tsar Nicholas II. Negotiations between the Archbishop of Canterbury, E. W. Benson, and Lord Salisbury had been going on for several months about selecting someone to represent the Church of England at the coronation; it was decided finally to send Creighton. Archbishop Benson wrote in his letter to Creighton in April 1896 that 'Lord Salisbury thinks such a mission may do a great deal of good spiritually and politically. Spiritually I believe, politically I hope, it will.' For various reasons, ill health mostly, the archbishop thought he should not make the long journey himself, and in his letter gave the same excuse for Randall Davidson, Bishop of Winchester, who 'as Prelate of the Garter, would be our ordinary official in such a case; but I have ascertained privately that it would be very undesirable on account of his health. This being the case,' he added, 'I have no doubt whatever that you are the right person to go.'[66] This was not universally felt by the hierarchy and politicians, however, which sparked a keen but quiet controversy over why Creighton was raised to third in line to be chosen.[67] Louise did not go, as Russian bishops were not married and she would, in her words, 'have been quite out of place'. Nevertheless, she was annoyed over this 'because of the separation it entailed and his going so far away. I felt the parting very keenly. I knelt down in his study asking him to bless me before he went; and had many foolish fears and anxieties during his absence.'[68]

Being advised by Archbishop Benson that he 'ought to go in the smartest clothes the law allows', Creighton borrowed one of the coronation copes of crimson velvet and gold used in Westminster ceremonies, but took his own mitre and pastoral staff.[69] After being briefed, even by the Prince of Wales, Bishop Creighton left on his journey in early May, arriving in Moscow on 18 May 1896. 'This place is so turned upside down, and everybody is so busy, and I can speak no Russian—so that, on the whole, I can only obey', he wrote home.

Creighton's letters are punctuated with picturesque descriptions of the coronation events over that two-week period. On the day the Tsar entered the city of Moscow, for example, he said the 'great bell of Moscow, the largest in the world, boomed out over one's head. Then suddenly it burst out into a rapid clang, and all the bells in Moscow [began ringing] at the same time. There are more than 2000 of them; you can imagine the din ... To add to the noise ... guns were fired.'[70] Later Creighton was escorted to the palace to meet the Tsar and Tsarina. Everything in the palace was 'very magnificent', he wrote, and M. Pobiedonostzeff, chief procurator of the Russian Holy Synod, 'took charge of me and walked me through the rooms, then introduced me to Briennios, the Patriarch of Constantinople ...' Then after meeting a number of dignitaries, Creighton was:

quite suddenly ... seized and told to go through a door, where in a little room stood the Emperor and Empress. I really felt quite casual, and had a little conversation with them in English. I made great mistakes in my court manners, but I dare say they forgave me. The Emperor is a very attractive man, with blue eyes, and a great charm about his face, which lights up and is very kindly. We talked and laughed, I am sorry to say. The Emperor said that I would find the coronation fatiguing: I said, what must it be for him? ... The Empress looked very nice dressed in white silk, and occasionally smiled. Then I went and lunched at a restaurant.[71]

On the day of the coronation Creighton was up early and in the cathedral shortly after seven in the morning, and was pleased to learn that he 'had about the best place possible' to view the ceremony. 'It was far beyond anything I could have imagined', he said, 'and the service was, from a religious point of view, wonderfully impressive.' On leaving the cathedral later Creighton was mobbed, along with all the other guests, by the crowds of people that thronged the cathedral area. 'Poor dears,' he said, 'they are just like children, but such nice children.' As he rode in his carriage, he recalled with some fondness giving his blessing as he went through the streets of Moscow.[72] Reportedly at one of the state banquets following the coronation, Creighton was the only non-Russian invited to attend.[73] Everything in Russia seemed to be on a grand scale. At a state ball in the palace there were 8000 people in attendance and 2800 came to a theatre performance. 'I was in the front row of the stalls, and had a splendid view. All the stalls were filled by officers in magnificent uniforms and the boxes gleamed with ladies.' [74] And on one occasion when gifts were distributed to a crowd of citizens—some 400,000 in the square—fully 1700 were killed in the crush at the beginning, thrown down and trampled. Mandell wrote to Louise that it was 'the sad fact that more people were slain in a holiday than would have perished in a battle'.[75]

Creighton found those days of high ceremony a dazzling spectacle of autocracy, and he thoroughly enjoyed it . When he arrived back in England in early June, he went straight to Lambeth Palace to report to the archbishop about his mission before returning to Peterborough. And while those operatic events of the coronation were still fresh in his mind, he wrote an interesting article for the *Cornhill Magazine* describing it all with rhetorical flourish.[76] Creighton was summoned to Windsor in the autumn to give the Queen a verbal account of the coronation, and she was thrilled with his article, later requesting in a letter written in her own hand that he send her several copies for her children and other relatives. She concluded by lamenting: 'How the Queen wishes she could have seen it.' [77]

It has been suggested that Creighton should have seen the writing on the wall concerning the future demise of imperial Russia some twenty years hence, which of course is unfair criticism.[78] In Creighton's case, however, when he looked beyond the present, it was more often than not to the past. It is probably true that he failed to see the real Pobiedonostzeff, a sinister figure who had been Alexander III's tutor and was one of the most powerful men at the Russian court. Creighton considered him 'one of the most able and interesting men' he had ever met, a person he regarded as 'clever, spare, and sharp—a man who could be disagreeable', but one who possessed sincerity and had the best interests of his country in mind.[79]

Creighton wrote to him after returning to England, thanking him for his courtesy, and included in the letter was a photograph of himself and a copy of his paper 'The English National Character'. Pobiedonostzeff responded in a letter written in French: 'I thank you from the bottom of my heart for your good and friendly letter accompanied with your photo which remind me of the agreeable hours spent in your company ... There are so many themes to consider in our conversations, topics of common interest', he stated. Expressing a wish that Creighton had gained new and worthwhile impressions of Russia, the procurator said: 'I hope nonetheless that these impressions revealed to you a few aspects of the spiritual life of our people in the very sanctuary of their history: "National character is the abiding product of a nation's past", as you said so well, explaining it in your discourse that I have just finished reading with great interest'. He concluded by asking Creighton to send him a copy of his history of the papacy.[80]

In that highly charged pragmatic diplomacy of the 1890s, Bishop Creighton's geopolitical assessment of Europe was of course coloured by both his innocence and his insularity. Nevertheless, he was mindful that Russia—one of the traditional adversaries of Britain in that century, along with France—would play an important role in future European affairs; and he sensed that a potential danger to Europe might well be a struggle involving three of the four great empires: some sort of contest between Russia and Germany with Austria in the middle.[81]

While in Russia, Creighton had an interesting interview with Patriarch Gennadius, the Archbishop of St Petersburg. Creighton delivered a letter to the patriarch from Archbishop Benson. The patriarch was a venerable figure, magnificently attired in purple velvet when he met Creighton. He only spoke Russian so that all communication had to pass through an interpreter. The interview lasted about an hour, and at the end the patriarch presented Creighton with an icon in great solemnity. 'He kissed me on both cheeks', Creighton said, 'and we kissed one another's hands. The interview was quite successful, I think. I was dressed in my Convocation robes and tried to look magnificent.'[82]

Both Bishop Creighton and Patriarch Gennadius expressed the hope that the interview would lead to better understanding of both churches. Gennadius stated that the Church of England was not well understood in Russia. During the course of the meeting, the patriarch claimed that there was 'great interest in Russia about your Apostolical Succession'. Gennadius then raised the question about the validity of Anglican orders. He was referring to the Roman Catholic Church's official position that the church in England adopted new ordination procedures in the mid sixteenth century substantively altering, in 'form and intention', the authoritative canonical rite for ordaining priests, thus breaking apostolic succession. Countless theologians in both camps—Roman and Anglican—had argued this validity question over the years since, as one would expect, but the official voice of Rome held fast to its strict interpretation. Creighton listened politely to the patriarch's question, but his reply was straightforward: 'The change in the ritual observed', Creighton said confidently, 'did not touch the essence of the rite. It was merely translation into English and simplification. All else remained the same.' It was the question of simplification of procedures, however, that upset Rome. The patriarch, taking note of Creighton's point, remarked that he approved of the expression '*tyrannus papalis*'.[83] Mandell must have nodded.

The reason the patriarch raised the issue in the first place, Creighton knew, was because of a question then being raised in England. With the growth of the Anglo-Catholic party in the Church of England in the wake of the Oxford Movement, the question of the validity of the Anglican orders had become an issue in some quarters again. A chief promoter for reconciling this long-standing disagreement between Rome and England was Lord Halifax—sometimes called the 'Holy Fox' by his detractors—who was president of the English Church Union, an Anglican society espousing Tractarian principles. As one of the Anglo-Catholic leaders, Halifax wanted to explore the question of reunion with Rome. In March of 1894 Halifax sent Bishop Creighton an article written by a French priest, Abbé E. F. Portal. The article raised the possibility that the time was ripe for seriously exploring ways to reconcile the issues over Anglican orders. Halifax knew Creighton from Embleton days, and recognised him as one of the more scholarly prelates who would likely to be valuable in the cause.[84]

Referring to Portal's article, Creighton replied to Halifax that the essay was 'very fair, and practically admits all that we [the Church of England] want. But it is very difficult to take him seriously at the end', he said, since Portal expressed the erstwhile view that only through the approbation of a general council could the issue be adjudicated. Then Creighton in characteristic fashion unravelled the knot with simple reasoning: 'Now a general council means to them [Rome] a council summoned by the Pope, and passing decrees which the Pope sanctioned. As the Church of England owed its rise to the necessity for abolishing the papal jurisdiction, it manifestly could not claim the papal consent to that step.' Creighton's point was clear: according to Rome, the Church of England's ordinations have been invalid since Henry VIII's reign, and for a pope to validate Anglican orders now, whether by general council or by his own pronouncement, he would have to destroy his own historical claims to ecclesiastical jurisdiction.[85] The real desire with Rome, however, was to overturn the Reformation rather than to give consideration to Anglican orders.

Halifax, however, continued to pursue the matter, and in the summer when Abbé Portal was visiting England, he and the French priest visited Creighton at Peterborough. Creighton later expressed genuine pleasure at their meeting, saying that Portal was 'quite charming, and I sincerely hope that his visit to England may be productive of fruit. Good understanding can only come from knowledge and sympathy.' While admitting that arguments about Anglican orders may 'go on for ever', Creighton pointed out that a 'great step to agreement' was the discovery that 'except in opinion we do not greatly differ', adding: 'Then opinion is reduced to its due proportion.'[86] Creighton gave Halifax little encouragement, however, but the Anglo-Catholic peer continued to pursue the matter. While in Rome in the spring of the following year, 1895, Halifax had meetings with a number of leading Roman ecclesiastics and wrote to Creighton that he felt encouraged by what he heard.

Creighton wrote back setting out the issue squarely and calling it 'much food for meditation'. But he explained that, as far as the Church of England was concerned, there was 'no doubt amongst us of the validity of our Orders; we are quite satisfied'. Then he pointed out the broader question of unification, saying bluntly that the 'restoration of the unity of Christendom will be—not by affirming any one of the existing systems as universal, but by a federation. What we have to do is to sweep away foolish and one-sided controversy, and see the unity of the spirit in the bond of peace.' He suggested that national differences along with cultural habits and questions of individual liberty were too entrenched and strong now 'to be set aside'. Comparing current Christianity with the medieval church, Creighton noted that the church in the middle ages 'was very liberal to those who were only positive, and not negative. Men might be as simple as they chose in their beliefs and in their practices', referring to the Franciscans, 'but it was not for them to object to what the Church had once allowed. Now some such conception as this must be at the bottom of reunion. We do not differ—any Christians—about the contents of the Christian faith, but about the proportion of them, and the means of their application to the individual soul.' Summing up, Creighton asserted that 'if any recognition of our [Church of England] were given by the Pope, it would be of enormous use: but we cannot ask for it without putting ourselves in the wrong. We have done nothing to invalidate our Orders: Rome has wantonly denied them in the past. We at our worst have never unchurched Rome: latterly we have been almost too kind to her.'[87]

Believing the time was right, Lord Halifax submitted the question of Anglican orders directly to Pope Leo XIII. In April 1895, the pope issued a letter, *Ad Anglos*, to the 'English People'.[88] The letter, patronising in both tone and message, offended many in Britain. Creighton in his response took the high ground and announced publicly to his clergy that the fact that Leo XIII issued a letter to the English people is 'at least a manifestation of good will. I do not like to criticise that letter in detail ... Controversy is unfruitful when it is blinded by prejudice; it is only useful when it is directed towards the discovery of truth. It is premature to discuss at present the methods of reunion, they must be left in the hands of God.'[89] Leo XIII, probably under some pressure, decided to appoint a papal commission to consider the question of Anglican orders but, after study and by a very close vote, the commission recommended not to accept validity. On 13 September 1896, the pope issued his apostolic letter *Apostolicae curae* that forcefully concluded: 'We pronounce and declare that ordinations performed according to the Anglican rite have been and are *irritas ... omninoque nullas*', that is, absolutely null and utterly void![90] Regrettably, as time would show, this papal bull raised more difficulties than it solved; and it was a smashing defeat for Halifax and his supporters. Further, the decision would be considered over the next hundred years by more than a few Roman Catholic theologians an embarrassment in an era of increasing denominational sensitivity and the beginnings of an ecumenical dialogue.[91]

Creighton's immediate reaction to the papal bull was that the 'Pope in Rome has been at his old games; and doubtless [Cardinal] Vaughn and Co. are chuckling. I think their victory will not profit them even in the next world.'[92] Cardinal Herbert Vaughan, the Roman Catholic Archbishop of Westminster and the leader of English Catholics, was consistently cool to any notion of accepting Anglican orders. Now the Anglican hierarchy were forced to consider an authoritative response to *Apostolicae curae*. Creighton was called upon to be one of three bishops to draft of a letter of reply to Rome. The sudden death of Archbishop Benson in October 1896 intervened, however, causing a delay in the final draft. Frederick Temple, formerly Bishop of Exeter and later of London, became the new primate. Archbishop Temple moved swiftly and, after some minor amendments, the letter was issued in February 1897 entitled *Response of the Archbishops of England to the Apostolic Letter of Pope Leo XIII*. The heart of the reply centred primarily on the weathered issue of the rightful use of papal power and the notion of proper jurisdiction.[93] Creighton's main role in drafting the letter was to give the Anglican response a solid historical footing.[94]

After Archbishop Benson's death in the autumn of 1896, Creighton's name was mentioned, both privately and in the press, as a possible successor. Then a few days after the announcement of Temple's appointment to the see of Canterbury, Creighton received another letter from Lord Salisbury, who was Prime Minister again as the Conservatives returned the previous year. The letter, dated 28 October, was brief and to the point: 'My dear Lord,' it began, 'I have the Queen's authority for asking you whether you will be willing to accept translation to the See of London, which as you are aware is vacant by the recent appointment [of Bishop Frederick Temple] to the archbishopric of Canterbury.' Salisbury was being as persuasive as possible, and concluded that there was 'probably no one in Christendom whose mind is better equipped for appreciating the importance of the work to which you are invited, or the injury which an ill-considered refusal might inflict upon the Church'.[95]

Queen Victoria had been pleased with Creighton's performance at Peterborough, describing him as 'very clever and agreeable, and so sensible and large-minded'.[96] Negotiations between Salisbury and Queen Victoria over who should be the next Archbishop of Canterbury, however, were interesting. Salisbury favoured either Creighton or Randall Davidson, then Bishop of Winchester, believing at first that Temple did not wish to leave London. The Queen told the Prime Minister that, in the case of Creighton, he was 'very able, very agreeable, with a good presence, and is an excellent preacher. But ... it would hardly do to place him above all the other Bishops.'[97] She wrote to Bishop Davidson expressing her view that Bishop Temple was 'eminently *unsuited*' for Canterbury and related that she understood the Archbishop of York, W. D. Maclagan, and the Prince of Wales, tended to favour Creighton as primate. Lord Salisbury, however, finally secured agreement from Temple to undertake Canterbury, and then suggested to the Queen that Davidson be translated from Winchester to London. The Queen thought differently, and told her minister rather forcefully that London should not be offered to the Bishop Davidson 'as his health would not allow his doing so ... The Bishop of Peterborough would do admirably for it'. Lord Salisbury then agreed and informed Creighton of his appointment by letter.[98] Two days later one of the Queen's maids-of-honour wrote to her mother from Balmoral, 'The Queen told me yesterday that Creighton is to be promoted to London and I am delighted London should have such a vigorous Bishop to stir it up. I wish I knew him, I feel sure I would like him.'[99]

Creighton 'had no desire nor expectation' that he would be selected as Bishop of London, Louise maintained later. 'I don't remember that I had either, and fortunately the days of uncertainty as to our future were very few.' But with the announcement of Temple's translation to Canterbury, both Mandell and Louise thought the possibility of his appointment to London was very likely. When Creighton showed Louise the letter from Lord Salisbury, she must have had an immediate flashback to that winter day in Cambridge when a similar letter had come offering him the bishopric of Peterborough. 'I cannot remember anything particular as to our feelings at the time', she recalled. 'It was of course nothing like so overwhelming a change and upset of our life as the appointment to Peterborough had been. Together we sought rest and quiet to fit us for the time that lay before us.' [100] It has been suggested that Creighton's nomination to London would never have been offered if such decisions were only left to the church, but that the government establishment found Creighton a politically attractive candidate because he was sufficiently worldly. The higher clergy, on the other hand, often misunderstood Creighton, thinking him too frivolous and professorial, and felt that he had never worked his way up the ladder, as was expected, by serving on the church's central committees, or even sitting on Convocation.[101] There is even some hint that the translation to London might have come with a promise of an eventual move to Lambeth (the palace of the Archbishop of Canterbury) after Fulham.[102]

Both Mandell and Louise felt it necessary to get away for a few days and took a short trip to the south of France, at Hyères, in early December where they walked the hills overlooking the sea or along the shore basking in the warm weather. Then came the busy Christmas season with family gatherings and seasonal responsibilities; on 8 January, their silver anniversary, the Creightons enjoyed a farewell party hosted by Peterborough friends, and then came preparations for departure to London.[103]

One of the very last things Creighton did before leaving Peterborough was to create, on 9 January, what he called 'Memorials of the Bishops of Peterborough', a scrapbook of collected hand-written jottings and memoranda by previous bishops over the past century. To this memorial, Creighton—ever the historian—wrote this entry: 'Handwriting has a special power of recalling a person; and I trust that those who come after me will leave something written in these pages which may serve to recall them.' [104] His hope was that his successors would also contribute a few lines and keep the tradition going. They have.

Creighton was formerly translated to the see of London in January 1897. Henry Scott Holland, canon of St Paul's, welcomed Creighton to London, writing: 'All our arms are open to receive you, as you know well. The old Dome [of St Paul's] is alive with delight', and as if with the gift of prescience, he warned: 'It is a frightful burden to lay on you: I hope you will use up everybody except yourself.' [105]

Cartoon in the April 1897 issue of *Vanity Fair* of Mandell Creighton soon after he became Bishop of London. (*British Library*)

15

Fulham is a Nice Place

'. . . we are not our own masters, nor are we, any of us, allowed to dispose of our own lives. I must go and do my best ... Fulham is a nice place.'

Mandell Creighton to Count Balzani [1]

Being Bishop of Peterborough had offered Creighton new and enticing vistas, and one senses he was beginning to savour episcopal life and seemed to look forward to moving to London, despite his comments to the contrary. 'My dear Brother', he penned to his longtime friend Bishop Reginald Copleston, 'We little thought in old days what was in store for us. Certainly I never wished for the office of bishop, or thought myself qualified for it ... But we can only go where we are sent, and do what we are bidden.' [2]

It is true that Creighton was not ecclesiastically ambitious, but his boundless self-confidence and a willingness to confront challenges of any sort allowed him to feel comfortable on any stage. In looking back over his life, one may conclude that he never went anywhere or accepted any postion he really did not want. Now in his fifty-third year, he seemed to resign himself fully to the idea that he should now go as far as he could in the church, always imagining there would be ample time in the future to reclaim scholarly joys. Still he knew the move to London would by necessity bring to an end his study of the popes. Louise wrote to James Bryce shortly after they learnt of the London appointment sadly observing that the 'bishop has become convinced during the last year or so that it would be quite impossible for him to continue a book [on the papacy] needing so much research in libraries; but I trust he may perhaps still find time for some historical work, it is such a refreshment to him.' [3]

As for then and there, however, the opportunity of becoming a major figure in the church appealed to Creighton. Was he thinking of becoming the next Archbishop of Canterbury? Perhaps, because underlying all of his instincts was an inherent sense of fatalism, that life was like a journey and he was not the ultimate navigator. He wrote to Count Balzani, an Italian friend the Creightons had met on one of their many trips to Italy, that he agreed with the view that, next to being Bishop of Rome, being Bishop of London 'was the most important position in Christendom'; and that while he had no personal wish for increased responsibility, 'we are not our own masters, nor are we, any of us, allowed to dispose of our own lives. I must go and do my best. The family were all plunged in woe at first, but we are growing more reconciled. Fulham is a nice place.'[4]

Yet there was a thread running through his letters during the first few months after his translation that indicated his deep frustration at losing touch with the *human* side of life. To Dorothy Grey, Sir Edward's wife, he wrote in June 1897: 'I never see anyone as a human being, it is all business. I never see any children, which is a great pang to me. I never see young people. I have no joys left.' To a clerical friend in Australia he wrote of the 'mass of business' that falls on the shoulders of the Bishop of London, 'immensely more than Peterborough'. Then he lamented that it was 'a very inhuman life'. And to a friend from Embleton days: 'I do not find so many human beings in London as there were in Peterborough.'[5]

The Creightons moved into Fulham Palace, the official residence of the Bishops of London, in late January 1897, two days before Creighton was to be enthroned at St Paul's. The palace, on the River Thames near Putney Bridge in the borough of Fulham in south-west London, was an irregular cluster of connected two-story brick buildings that had been constructed and remodelled several times over the centuries, with the result that the interior was a confusing maze of rooms, small and large, linked by ribbons of winding corridors and flights of stairs. When the Creightons moved in, Louise often said that they surely needed a map to find their way. The children, however, especially the younger ones, must have found its labyrinthine ways exciting.

The spacious palace grounds were idyllic. There were picturesque courtyards, sheltered flower beds, and broad lawns dotted with walnut, maple, oak and tulip trees, all enclosed by a mile long medieval moat. Because the palace grounds were so scenic Creighton continued the policy of his two predecessors of allowing public use of twelve acres, thus creating the riverside area along the Thames known as Bishop's Park.[6] Fulham, indeed, was a serene place to conduct the official affairs of the London diocese, but by Creighton's time—when daily administration was more demanding and automobiles were still in the future—Fulham proved too distant from central London, being several miles away by road, to handle normal business effectively. To get around, the bishop had at his disposal three horses for carriage use: a standard four-wheeled landau to be driven by a pair, a regular two-wheel brougham for a single horse, and a victoria, one of the newfangled four-wheel carriages.[7] A carriage ride into the city, especially on warm

summer days, would have been relaxing for an eighteenth- or early nine-
teeth-century bishop certainly. Fulham Palace Road boasted one of the finest
wood pavements in London. But Creighton found a horse-drawn carriage
much too slow and inconvenient for his animated style, and so to economise
on time he most often caught the District railway at Putney station for
central London or destinations beyond.

Fortunately the bishop had the use of London House at 32 St James's
Square, across from the beautiful Wren church in the West End near
Piccadilly Circus. Since 1771 that town house had been the auxiliary residence
of Bishops of London, though Creighton's predecessor, Bishop Temple,
rarely used it except as an urban office.[8] Creighton's plan, however, was to
spend most of the winter season at London House and reside at Fulham
from spring through the autumn. Louise preferred Fulham with its semi-rural
setting to the hustle and bustle of the city house and nearly threw up her
hands when she first saw London House, calling it a 'great barrack of a house,
dirty, unattractive and inconvenient'.[9] As a result most of the first year was
devoted to renovating the place from top to bottom, even to the point of
installing electric light; at Fulham there were only gas lamps and candlesticks.

Moving into Fulham Palace, however, proved no easy task. Louise supervised the transfer of furniture, and every day for about a week a carriage
took her to Fulham from their temporary quarters at St Paul's to receive
her arriving furniture, one day being forced to huddle by the front door
in the middle of a snowstorm directing where the different things were to
go. 'On one or two days we lunched in the servants' hall, a very merry
party', she recalled. 'The house was so rambling with endless little flights
of stairs that we were always getting lost.'[10]

With the move to the London diocese the family's domestic staff necessarily increased. The Creightons brought along their faithful butler, Wilkin,
from Peterborough along with Mrs Allnutt, the nurse-governess. Under
Wilkin were two footmen and a boy. Louise secured a gardener, Turner,
as well as an 'admirable cook-housekeeper', a Mrs Hardman. Then there
was the necessary supply of housemaids and kitchenmaids who, as Louise
put it, 'sat down thirteen every day in the servants' hall. I had no ladies
maid, but there was a sewing maid who looked after our clothes and after
Gemma.'[11] At Fulham the 'girls had bedrooms to themselves in the wing
called the rookeries, and the boys below them', Louise said. 'Each of the
girls had a fire in her bedroom once a week. My sitting-room opened out
of the drawing-room and into the garden. It was a very charming
room.'[12] In a prophetic letter to Mary Ward on her silver wedding anniversary in the spring of 1897, Louise wrote about the new stage in their lives,
saying that it was 'a wonderful thing for us to look back upon these

twenty-five years is it not and feel how they have been blessed, and how we begin the next stage of our life each with the home circle unbroken, and still full of possibilities for a full and useful life; may we use them to the full, and face whatever sadness and pain the future may have in store with hope and courage.'[13]

As far as income was concerned, Creighton received well over £10,000 a year while at London, mostly ecclesiastical income supplemented by book royalties and the legacy from his father's estate. As Bishop of Peterborough his yearly income was £5000; as Bishop of London his income precisely doubled, equal to that of the Archbishop of York and only surpassed by that of the Archbishop of Canterbury.[14] Louise regarded it as one of the blessings of her life that she 'never really had to trouble about money or known money anxieties. Perhaps this is one of the reasons why I have cared so little about money', adding that she 'never desired to be rich, and when we had the large income provided in Peterborough and London, we both quite naturally felt it to be simply a trust given us for the good of the diocese. I never travelled otherwise than third class except when I was with Max, nor had, nor wished to have, a maid, nor fine clothes.' For them, she said, their 'chief luxury was travelling'.[15]

Besides his normal responsibilities as bishop, Creighton served as a member of the Privy Council and as *ex officio* member of numerous boards and committees which required his periodic attendance. For example, Arthur Balfour, the Conservative leader in the House of Commons, invited Creighton, 'notwithstanding that you are one of the hardest-worked men in the Kingdom', to become a trustee of the National Portrait Gallery.[16] He was also appointed trustee of the British Museum and of the Natural History Museum. One day he wrote to a friend: 'I am writing this at a meeting. I am Trustee of the British Museum ... It is interesting work: one sees all the new things that come in.'[17] Indeed, many of his extant letters from this era, especially those to his young nephews and nieces, were written while sitting in some meeting with opening sentences such as: 'I am writing at a meeting. I see that we are to have a row amongst our officials. It is odd how people like to quarrel about nothing ...'; or 'I sit here as usual at a meeting talking about concrete and galvanized iron ...'; or 'I am sitting at a stupid meeting and going to fill up the time by writing to you ...'; or 'I am writing at a meeting: if I wander, forgive me ...'; or 'I am sitting at a meeting which does not seem to require much attention ...'[18]

One of Creighton's first decisions upon becoming Bishop of London was to manage the return to the United States of the famous log of the *Mayflower*. For Creighton, the historical scholar, it was simply historical justice. Even before being installed he found a letter waiting for him from the American

Ambassador requesting that the *Mayflower* log be given back to the American people. The log contained important accounts about the fortunes of the pilgrims in their travel across the Atlantic, notably the diary of William Bradford, afterward the governor of New Plymouth, along with a register of births, deaths and marriages of the New England colonists in their early decades in the new world. The document had apparently languished in the library at Fulham since the American Revolution, having been brought there at the time of the outbreak of hostilities in Boston because the Bishop of London was the religious authority for foreign and colonial clergy. Creighton immediately wrote to the Prime Minister, Lord Salisbury, saying that he supported the return of the manuscript 'to the country whence it came'. Both Salisbury and the Archbishop of Canterbury concurred, giving Creighton permission to undertake a convoluted process which ultimately allowed the legal transfer of the log to the governor of Massachusetts in April 1897. To commemorate Creighton's efforts, he—along with Archbishop Temple—were given honorary membership of the American Antiquarian Society.[19]

It was in the midst of the *Mayflower* log issue that Creighton became enbroiled in the passage of the Voluntary School Bill of 1897 that was winding its way through Parliament. The issue over public funding of private (voluntary) schools, particularly denominational schools, had been simmering since the passage of the 1870 Education Act which created elementary schools managed by local school boards and supported by local rates. While various schools fell under the broad umbrella of 'voluntary schools', such as Roman Catholic, Wesleyan, Jewish and British schools[20] and National schools,[21] the preponderant number were Church of England schools. The crux of the controversy centred on the complicated question of whether of not religious schools should be directly subsidised by the taxpayer. Advocates of Anglican schools had long argued for increased public financial assistance, beyond the customary annual grants given to certain schools meeting local education authority standards, on the grounds that if church schools were abandoned, an enormous burden of work would necessarily be thrust upon board schools. Yet critics of public support of voluntary schools felt that rate-aid should support only board schools, thus assuring the continuation of a dual system of elementary education on England.

Bishop Creighton favoured preserving the principle of the dual system in English education, but thought that, with the growth of secular board schools, there was a growing economic disadvantage affecting church schools, which at that time comprised the bulk of the voluntary system. And as bishop, he could point to the near equal distribution of educational chores in his London school district, for the number of board and voluntary schools were just about even—though the student population was slightly larger in the board schools.[22]

Over the years Creighton had made known his espousal of improved elementary education across the country—voluntary and board schools. This issue fitted comfortably with his staunch belief in the liberty of the individual, in this case parents with the right to choose the desired education for their children. Since Embleton days he had advocated the real need to keep the focus of education centred more on students than systems, and he often said that the main educational question was what the child should be taught and how best to teach him or her.[23] As Bishop of Peterborough he defended the right of the church to insist upon the full measure of religious education for society, and he spoke frequently and firmly on this, as in the case of his address to the Northampton Educational Society on 'The Value of Religious Education' in June 1891, and likewise his speech on 'Religious Education and Voluntary Schools' at the opening of one voluntary school in his diocese, and his 1892 sermon at Leicester's St Peter's Church entitled 'The Place of Religion in Education', and, of course, his primary charge to the clergy at Peterborough in 1894 of which a significant portion was directed to school matters.[24] In this charge, for example, he was especially blunt in asserting that the principle of religious teaching being provided at the public expense did indeed square with 'our English conception of liberty'.[25] For Creighton it was a matter of common sense and of history. As he explained to the headmaster of Marlborough a couple of years before: 'I am a student of the Renaissance. Then they understood education to be the development of the whole man', meaning religion as well as secular subjects.[26]

On 30 March 1897, Bishop Creighton rose in the House of Lords during the debate on its second reading, to speak in favour of the Voluntary School Bill that by all intents and purposes was a modest effort to correct the economic disparity. As was his nature, he called for a cessation of controversy that he said obscured the real issue of educational progress, and he urged the Lords to consider what he called the 'contents of education' rather than administrative machinery.[27] He challenged critics of religious education, especially nonconformists who feared that the government might weaken the 1870 conscience-clause that permitted Bible instruction in board schools but not any form of denominational religion.[28] Creighton told the Lords that while much had been said of the 'nonconformist conscience', they should remember 'that the Church of England had also a right to possess a conscience'. He went on to say:

> The advocates of the voluntary system are convinced that in maintaining that system they are maintaining principles which are essential for the maintenance

of education itself ... If religious education is to be genuine it must be denomi-national, and have a definite point of attachment to the life and character of the child who is being taught ... The suppression of voluntary schools by the brute force of financial pressure would leave behind it an inextinguishable sense of wrong, and would produce results most dangerous to the well being of society.[29]

He concluded that those who supported the Bill were 'animated by a nobler conception of the nature of education, and a higher ideal of civil and religious liberty, than their opponents of to-day. (Cheers)'.[30] His speech was received well, and described as 'graceful, full of culture ... perhaps the best and freshest second reading speech on the bill in either House'.[31] Two days later Creighton wrote of the event to his niece Ella observing that making such a speech was 'about the most awful thing' one can do. 'As a rule nobody listens, but they all talk to one another. There is no applause except that when you sit down one or two people say "Hear Hear". I believe my speech was thought a success; but is very nervous work making a maiden speech, as you are not sure of the sort of tone to adopt, and do not wish to seem cheeky.'[32]

The Voluntary School Bill eventually passed; and in its wake Bishop Creighton gave the presidential address at the London diocese conference in May, at which time he stated that the new Act proved two things: first, that the public truly desired an alternative system of elementary education; and, secondly, that the public recognised that voluntary schools provided the 'sole guarantee' for religious education.[33] Finally, in a letter jointly drafted by Creighton and the Bishop of Rochester, which was circulated within the school board district of London the following year, the two bishops adamantly condemned undenominational instruction as something 'which cannot be ultimately satisfactory' for society, stating that so-called undenominational instruction of any school subject cannot be what it professes to be, that is value neutral, because a teacher will inevitably reflect his or her own particular bias to children in a class. They further stipulated that: 'We only ask that the wishes of parents be consulted about the [religious] education of their children, and that every child in England should receive instruction in the religious beliefs of the denomination to which its parents belong.'[34]

Fortunately for Creighton, he never heard the remark by his good friend, fellow historian and Quaker nonconformist Thomas Hodgkin, who uttered cynically that the 'clergy of the Church of England can no more run the Elementary Schools of the nation than they can manage its railways'.[35] Regrettably the critical problem of the late Victorian society, missed by most at the time, was the growing number of parents who were professing no religious beliefs at all.

The amount of daily work increased measurably for Creighton compared with Peterborough. For some inexplicable reason, he chose not to employ a full-time secretary even though he admitted that he was 'perpetually over-whelmed with work'. He felt confident that he could handle the bulk of the paperwork and correspondence himself utilising only a domestic chaplain whose secretarial duties accounted for only a part of his responsibility.[36] As fortune would have it, however, Creighton found an admirably suited person, Lancelot Percival, son of his old Oxford friend, John Percival, who had recently become Bishop of Hereford. On the day Lance Percival came to be interviewed for the position of chaplain, Creighton—true to form—not only put the young man completely at ease with his comfortable conversation that blanketed pointed questions, but finagled Percival into a rousing family game of hockey out on the Fulham lawn. Percival liked the bishop's family and the job, and accepted the post eagerly; and a strong bond of friendship developed between the two men over the years.[37] Of course any unsuspecting person who came to visit Creighton at Fulham might very well be dragged off for a game of hockey. The bishop told a niece once about a fellow bishop who 'had a fall and hurt his leg' after being coaxed into a game of hockey. 'I do not know how much [he was hurt] as I have not heard from him since. This is a sad result of hockey. It must not produce dilapidated bishops.'[38]

Bishop Creighton's first year in London, according to his notes, saw him delivering 294 formal sermons and addresses of various kinds and on various topics.[39] And besides the usual ecclesiastical venues, he was often found at other places in the city speaking casually about history at some function associated, for instance, with the London School of Economics or the London Church Reading Union or discussing educational questions at a working-men's club meeting at Toynbee Hall, or giving witty, scintilla-ting after-dinner remarks at the Architectural Association or the Artists' Benevolent Society, or promoting some charity cause like the Prince of Wales' Hospital Fund. An example of one of his typical days is be found in the following letter to his niece Winifred:

> On Friday I had a good sample day. I left home at 10.30, had a Confirmation at 11. Then I went to Paddington, caught a special train, and at 1.10 went to Windsor with the Duke of Devonshire, Lord James of Hereford, and Lord Balfour of Burleigh; had lunch, and then took oaths as a member of the Privy Council; got back to Paddington at 4.30, went to Liverpool Street, and took train to Lower Edmonton; had a little dinner, and then a service at 7.30; got home at 11. This is the sort of way in which my days are spent. Do you think it interesting? In many ways it is. One sees a good deal going on and the business is much more important than it was at Peterborough.[40]

On one occasion an article appeared in the *Westminster Gazette* that said of Creighton: 'In the last eight days he has been at four public dinners, attended eight public meetings, consecrated a church, laid the stone for another, besides preaching, confirming, giving personal interviews to clergy, and writing endless letters. Well may Lord Salisbury say that he is the hardest-worked man in the country.'[41]

As the Creightons entered what they termed 'the great current of the world's life', the bishop soon became one of the bright stars of London society.[42] 'Fulham tea cups tinkled as they never tinkled before', joked Lytton Strachey some years later.[43] London at the close of the century was, in the words of Margot Asquith, 'the centre of the most interesting society in the world'.[44] It was a society of overlapping cliques that stretched from the reactionary, class-conscious 'Incorruptibles' to the free-minded 'Souls'. At the centre was the 'sporting set' with its base at Marlborough House and its acknowledged doyen, Edward, Prince of Wales. It was the London of the outrageous *Yellow Book*, the plays of Oscar Wilde and the suggestive drawings of Aubrey Beardsley; of weathered imperialists home for the season and weary liberals looking for an agenda; of Fabian socalists arguing with practical-minded socialists; and anarchists throwing bombs; of the hotly-debated Tower Bridge and the steaming motor car.[45] But Creighton was no puritan or world-rejecter and found all segments of London society amusing, from Buckingham Palace to the Webbs' house, the 'New Machiavellian' on Grosvenor Road in Westminster, where he was a frequent raconteur at their intellectual *salon*. Interestingly, although a political Liberal, Creighton often felt more at ease with Tories and socialists.

He had been a charter member of the Savile Club before arriving in London and for ten years a member of the Athenaeum. Now he was welcomed into some of other city's fashionable dining institutions—The Club, Grillions and Nobody's Friends. Here he mingled and mixed with the rich and famous, and because of his ubiquitous presence he no doubt expanded his reputation, gaining higher profile across the popular press. In the April 1897 issue of *Vanity Fair*, for example, there appeared a full-page caricature of him in a jaunty stance, wearing his black clerical coat and tights, casually fingering his top hat, with piercing eyes peering out from behind wire spectacles and wearing an impish grin that creased his bushy grey beard—as if he were preparing to cast one of his enticing epigrams to a receptive listener.[46] Following suit came articles on him in the *World*, the *London Illustrated News*, the *Review of Reviews* and the *Strand Magazine*, sometimes with photographs or pictorial likenesses. One of the more amusing was a cartoon sketch drawn by Max Beerbohm in the Christmas number of *The World* in 1900; it showed a spindly Creighton with a long, over-large head under a wide-brimmed hat and wearing his black clerical cloak, standing pensively as if he were some modern Socrates on a street corner.[47] Of course Creighton loved it all.

The 'rush of life was tremendous', Louise claimed, and the Creightons found themselves booked for endless social gatherings—parties, concerts, teas, receptions, soirees and charity benefits—all competing with more serious work.[48] During the day the bishop was either away from Fulham or London House, or closeted in his study with some clergyman or writing a batch of letters or preparing a sermon. Louise, while not seeing him much during the day, had the advantage at least of being able to join him in many of the social functions in the evenings; unlike Peterborough where he was often gone from the city administering his large diocese, now nearly everything Creighton did was within the radius of the metropolitan area. It was, of course, expected that the Bishop of London should entertain often, and Louise found herself hosting functions both at London House and Fulham. 'We are giving a series of dinner parties,' Mandell wrote to his young nephew Basil, 'so as to do our duty to mankind.'[49] It was a busy life, Louise admitted, claiming that she was becoming a 'maid-of-all-work', forced to 'provide the food and stand and shake hands'.[50] It was not her métier, to be sure, but she rose to the occasion and became, in her mind, 'quite a good hostess'; and she had to admit she was finally outgrowing her basic shyness, something that had haunted her since childhood.[51] Of these many 'endless entertainments in the garden', she recalled that they had to have a

> great marquee put up for the garden parties and for all the smaller meetings and meetings of mothers from the East End that we arranged. Mrs Hardman made the cakes for everything. She took pride in making all the cakes for the great garden parties, which on one occasion at least reached the number of about 4000 ... The sending out of the invitations was an immense business. Lucia helped me in this in the years after she had finished Newnham. I had no secretary. Max had no shorthand secretary and no typist. I often wonder whether the work is done more efficiently now than it was then.[52]

Louise said she especially looked forward to the Foreign Office parties which she considered the 'most brilliant society functions', along with those elegant dinners at Mansion House with the Lord Mayor of London where she often sat between Creighton and Archbishop Frederick Temple.[53] And she recalled two other events, the 'great dinner' given by Joseph Chamberlain, then Colonial Secretary, for the Prime Ministers of the Dominions visiting London, and the opening of the Wallace Collection at Hertford House in 1900, a collection of continental art, notably eighteenth-century French art given by Lady Wallace to the government. Attending that gala event, Louise remembered, was 'all the beauty and fashion of London'. And, though never invited to Windsor or Sandringham, she did attend a number of functions at Buckingham Palace and once went to the House of Lords.[54]

A major event for Bishop Creighton that first year was the Diamond Jubilee in June 1897, commemorating the sixtieth anniversary of Queen Victoria's accession. It was an attempt at high extravaganza, but it failed to recapture the beguilement of the Golden Jubilee ten years before—'a good thing repeated is seldom quite so good the second time', as one historian wisely observed.[55] Victoria was quite satisfied with Creighton's role in the affair, however, especially the thanksgiving service he masterminded at St Paul's on Jubilee Day, 20 June 1897. Creighton preached one of his better sermons to a packed congregation of national and international notables. He explained that they were honouring Queen Victoria 'as the unchanging and unswerving representative' of Britain's great desire 'to moralise all human relationships which is the flower of our civilisation'; and he confidently declared that it was not the material prosperity or the comfort and cultivation of their society that would 'make the Victorian age conspicuous in the future', but rather the deeper 'motive' that lay beneath the surface. 'Nations', he said, 'are strong in proportion as they have a clear conception of a national destiny—a destiny not limited to the convenience of the passing moment—but animated by a noble conception of truths to be taught and lessons to be learned, for the good of all mankind.' Then he said: 'No nation has continued great that has not had a growing consciousness of a universal mission, founded on a genuine belief in justice and righteousness, a burning passion to apply these first within her own limits, and then to carry them wherever her influence could reach.' Creighton spoke proudly that the Queen's reign had raised the level of national consciousness throughout the empire, adding that the 'great characteristic of the Victorian era' was this 'awakened conscience about our duties to our fellows'.[56]

For Mandell Creighton the Victorian age possessed shades of the Elizabethan era, and the Queen must have been duly impressed because a few days later she wrote to her bishop ostensibly to express her concern that Creighton might have suffered from the heat while standing on the steps of St Paul's in the hot sun without a hat waiting to greet her carriage. Then in her letter she asked him if he would write for her a 'short description of the memorial service', adding that 'no one could do this for her so well as you, who sent her that beautiful description of the Coronation at Moscow'.[57] Creighton, of course, willingly wrote an account of his impressions on the Jubilee and sent it to her.[58] The Prince of Wales's private secretary had also written to him praising the service and saying that the prince 'never saw anything better managed, or any service better done or more impressive'.[59]

The following month, July, Creighton had to turn his attention to a Lambeth conference, better known as the Pan-Anglican Conference, a meeting fashioned because of the opportunity that had presented itself when so many church dignitaries throughout the world were in London for the Jubilee. Fulham Palace was nearly overrun with a succession of American and colonial bishops who brought their wives and children along, many families even staying at the palace for a couple of days. By the end of July 1897, in the wake of the Lambeth conference, Mandell wrote to a niece about taking a holiday: 'I never looked forward to anything so much.'[60] Then in early August, all the family—including several nieces and nephews and Mandell's sister, Polly—adjourned to a large rented house along the banks of Ullswater near Glenridding in the Lake District. Louise always planned their holiday locations in advance, sometimes travelling to the area the month before to select the particular house to rent.[61] From the Lake District, Creighton wrote to Dorothy Grey and told her that he had 'the melancholy feeling' that he was 'now quite played out. I must go on as I am till I fizzle away'.[62] On the heels of this family outing, Mandell and Louise departed for a few weeks in the north of Italy, where they explored new places in Lombardy along the south slopes of the Alps and then went on to visit their friends Count Balzani and his two daughters. This became the basic format for the Creightons' annual two-part holiday. In the first part, Louise explained, the bishop

> devoted himself very much to the children, and I did not feel that I got so much of him, but in the latter when we were abroad I had him for the most part entirely to myself and we had many long walks together. He used to walk a great deal in silence, and we did not talk very much, but we loved the beauty and the peace of it ... Perhaps sometimes I would wish that he would talk more, but I believe that in his busy life with the constant strain there was upon him, these long quiet walks were a great rest and refreshment. We seldom made any acquaintances or even talked with fellow travellers, but we always spent some time with the Balzanis ... I did a good deal of sketching there and we all made excursions into the mountains.[63]

Both Louise and Mandell agreed that it was 'a great delight' to have so large a house as Fulham Palace so that it was 'always possible to take in anybody we wanted'.[64] It no doubt reminded them of the pleasant years spent in their spacious Embleton vicarage. Family gatherings at Fulham, particularly at Christmas time, were especially convivial. Mandell always invited his sister, Polly, along with his nieces and nephews to come south for the holidays, just as Louise would invite her sisters and brothers to join them. Punctuating those short winter days in December, the Creightons enjoyed rough-and-tumble hockey games on a nearby field or carefree ice-skating on one of the frozen ponds; sometimes they would arrange a sightseeing trip to London or Hampton Court. And in the evenings there would be dancing in the great hall with servants being 'fetched in to dance with us', Louise recalled, where she chuckled over the vision of Oswald, her youngest brother, 'dancing with our very comely kitchenmaid'.[65]

During these London years, Cuthbert took his B.A. degree from Cambridge in 1898 (a second class in the classical tripos) and went off to study in France after deciding to become a schoolmaster. Both Mandell and Louise felt that he had not quite lived up to their intellectual expectations, but as far as Cuthbert was concerned he seemed satisfied with the way things were. Being the eldest son, perhaps more was expected of him. Cuthbert once said that the chief characteristic of his father's relationship with the children was 'a combination of sympathy and sternness which made us regard him both as our delightful playfellow and companion, and also as our most exacting judge'.[66] Cuthbert had an active extracurricular life at Cambridge; he played forward for two years in the Emmanuel rugby team, and was first in his second year of competition in hammer throwing (with a distance of 73 feet 6 inches). He also participated both in the college debate team and the essay club.[67]

Walter, on the other hand, was even less enterprising in the eyes of his parents. Having gone up to Emmanuel with the thought of becoming a doctor, he left after two years at the end of the Lent term in 1898 when he decided to pursue what his father called a 'wild career' as a singer—much to the chagrin of both his parents.[68] His academic achievements lacked real lustre, but his winning personality made him popular; and he demonstrated some serious musical talent by playing the violin in the college string quartet and singing in concerts.[69] Louise, who is thought to have favoured Walter above the other boys, may have been more inclined to defend his decision to leave Cambridge without a degree. She said he had only considered a career in medicine because it pleased his father. Mandell argued against Walter leaving Cambridge, but in the end 'made no objection when he realised that he was really bent on it'.[70] True to his principle of individual liberty, he reluctantly gave in to Walter's request. The following letter—which any modern parent can relate to—was written to bring a closure to the father and son discussion over Walter's decision to abandon his academic studies. It certainly reveals much about Mandell's manner when fundamentally disagreeing with someone for whom he had great love or friendship:

Dearest Walter,

My only wish can be for your happiness. Your life is your own life, and you must decide about it. You may rest assured that I shall not be distressed by your decision ... I can only accept your decision and help you to do what you want to do. But I want you to understand that when I have accepted your decision, I do so entirely, and will never go back on the subject. Whatever you do, do it hard and well, and I shall be satisfied ... Don't think any more of my objections ... I suppose you had better pass as many examinations as you can. You might want to take your degree some day. Get on as far as you can. I suppose you had better get to singing as soon as possible. We will make all plans in the vacation. God bless you, my dear boy.[71]

It was then arranged for Walter to study singing in Paris. But this was short-lived when he became seriously ill with tonsillitis and had to return. He subsequently took up formal lessons again, studying for a year or two in Paris and Frankfurt. Oswin was finishing up at Marlborough during these years. As far as the girls were concerned, Beatrice and Lucia worked at day jobs in London and lived at home. Lucia, who began at Newnham in 1894, took a second in the history tripos in the spring after they arrived in London and then began training as a secretary. Mary showed real artistic talent and enrolled at the Slade School of Art in London, while Gemma, only ten when the family moved to London, continued her schooling at home.[72]

Basil Creighton, the bishop's young nephew, often stayed with the Creightons in London in the course of these years, and he recalled that his uncle was 'very much more critical and impatient with his own children' than he was of his nephews and nieces. Basil thought as a small lad that his uncle's children 'were rather afraid of him and uneasy in his company. None of them came up to his standards. He liked successful, brilliant, sociable people.' Basil remembered his uncle as 'an affectionate and anxiously considerate father' to his own children, 'but also an impatient and critical one. My own impression of him is that he inclined to vanity as opposed to conceit. He liked to be a success and always asked his children when they returned from a party: "Were you a success?" He himself was always a success!'[73] Mandell Creighton, however, was probably no more difficult or critical than most other fathers of that time who were well-educated and enjoying successful careers. To be sure, he could be rigid, demanding, and even self-indulgent when it came to his own family—Louise included—but Mandell's one overarching and redeeming quality was his staunch belief in individuality and personal responsibility. His usual retorts when there was a serious difference of opinion with one of his children were: 'It's a free country.' 'Do as you please.' 'Don't if you would rather not.' 'That's a point which you must decide for yourself.'[74]

Louise possessed many of these same traits when it came to her children, but unlike her husband evidenced them more openly beyond the home. Where Creighton, outside the family, radiated charm and conviviality, Louise found it difficult to sugarcoat what she thought needed to be said at any given time, often appearing critical and alarming. Lady Asquith reportedly once said of her: 'Uncomfortable woman—always expecting people to be what they are not.'[75] To be fair, however, both Louise and Mandell, while having high expectations for others, always applied their same high and demanding standards to themselves.

Continuing to run her schoolroom with an iron hand, Louise, with the help of Miss Allnutt, managed Gemma's early education in a variety of subjects including Latin, French and music. But Louise dearly missed her literary life, and deeply regretted that she was unable to do any serious writing during the London years. 'There was very little time for anything like intellectual work or serious study', she said. 'Any spare was given over to her women's work.'[76] She remained closely connected with the National Union of Women Workers, the Mothers' Union, and the Girls' Friendly Society, as she had been in past years, and helped get the Rescue Work Association in the London diocese better organised. As at Peterborough she saw the need for shelter houses, and it was at a Church Organisation Society meeting at Fulham one day that she recognised the specific need for a settlement house in the borough of Fulham which resulted later in the founding of the Bishop Creighton House.[77] She admitted that the circumstances of being a bishop's wife made it impossible for her 'to take up any one thing and go into it thoroughly. I had to be ready to be interested in anything and everything. Sometimes I felt it very unsatisfactory, and longed to have the opportunity to get to understand any one thing thoroughly.'[78]

Louise became active in the London Council for the Promotion of Morality, something Bishop Creighton helped to get started. She also developed a new interest in the foreign mission movement as a result of her connection with the Society for the Propagation of the Gospel in Foreign Parts (SPG), an off-shoot of the Society for Promoting Christian Knowledge (SPCK). Further, as the Bishop of London's wife she was entrusted with the Women's Diocesan Association (WDA), an informal organisation that was started in the 1860s as a means of getting women in London for the Season to do some useful charity work. Over the years the organisation had expanded its activities, but under Mrs Frederick Temple, Louise's immediate predecessor, the WDA had not prospered, and was when Louise found it, 'a rather dwindling, lifeless body'. Nothing excited her more than to breathe life into something she regarded as moribund, so she began to develop it into an agency of active women church workers across the diocese, organising it according to the structure of rural deaneries with regular meetings to stimulate work and to consider the needs of the diocese.[79] Out of the WDA grew the more successful Girls' Diocesan Association movement with Louise's daughter, Beatrice, becoming its first president. The GDA was a case, as Louise put it, of the child surviving while the parent perished.[80]

It was in 1898 that Creighton was asked to serve on the London University commission, the result of being hand-picked by the Webbs, Beatrice and Sidney. Beatrice Webb wrote in her diary about his selection to the seven-man committee, referring to it as a 'successful packing' of the commission, and stating that 'we have had two very good friends helping us—[Richard, later Lord] Haldane and the Bishop of London, both trusting us completely'.[81] Haldane was a member of the House of Commons and instrumental in getting the London University Reorganisation Bill through Parliament.[82]

Born in controversy, the University of London developed in the nineteenth century under persistent attack from various quarters, the principal criticism being that it was only an examining and degree-granting institution with little administrative control over the loosely affiliated schools comprising the teaching side of the university.[83] As one observer remarked, it was 'a university without students, a university without professors—a university, in fact, which is very willing to test your abilities, but does not attempt to fulfill its essential duty—to instruct'.[84] After two recent royal commissions of inquiry, educational reformers—particularly Liberals and Fabian socialists, such as Haldane and the Webbs—were determined to reconstruct London University, hence the creation of the statutory committee to force a new, government-inspired constitution.

According to Lord Davey, who was chairman of the committee, Creighton brought a sense of compromise to the highly charged issue and demonstrated his penchant for reconciling divergent opinions; Davey claimed that the bishop was 'most valuable in solving a difficulty or subject of difference amongst our colleagues by some middle course'.[85] For a man who had been caught up in the contentious boot and shoe trade strike a few years before, this must have been like holding forth in a college common room. But beyond his unifying ability, what Creighton brought to the bargaining table was his vast knowledge of university education and a wealth of experience as a teacher. What surprised most, however, and what was just as important as anything else he did, was Creighton's ubiquitous fairness. Indeed, he never showed a hint of Oxbridge superiority or denominational prejudice against this urban, non-denominational institution during the proceedings.[86] The commission reported its decisions in January 1900 and the new governing statutes for the University of London, which established a more efficiently organised teaching university, were immediately approved by Parliament and sealed the following month.[87]

It was during this time that Creighton lent his support to the fledgling London School of Economics (and Political Science) that had become affiliated with the reorganised London University. Again with Beatrice Webb pulling the strings, Creighton was manoeuvred into the post of president of this newly incorporated institution, though it was largely an honorary position with little or no specific duties. He also was appointed trustee of a building fund for the school, and in July 1900 laid the foundation stone in a ceremony opening the school's new building, Passmore Edwards Hall.[88]

In the spring of 1898 W. E. Gladstone, the Grand Old Man of British politics, died. It seemed like the passing of a political era, for Gladstone's life nearly spanned the entire century. Now the Liberal Party that he virtually founded was in tatters, and though England and its Empire seemed invincible to most, some—like Creighton—saw threatening storm clouds on the horizon, domestically and abroad. The funeral ceremony took place in Westminster Abbey; Bishop Creighton, who walked immediately behind the flag-draped casket, gave the final prayer which he composed for the fallen statesman.[89]

Holy Week services were especially grinding for the bishop that year, and the remainder of the spring and summer was crammed with a full schedule of confirmations, ordinations, sermons, an occasional lecture or address, and work on a time-consuming committee of the convocation dealing with the question of divorce. In June he wrote to his niece Winifred about their summer holiday, stating that he was 'looking forward to August. I count the weeks with impatience. I always think each week as it comes is going to be easier; but it never is.'[90] In early August, the bishop, eager as a schoolboy anticipating a vacation, took his family—including the Carlisle Creightons—off to Wales for three weeks, to a house in the woods near Betws-y-Coed. Then Mandell and Louise journeyed to Italy, France and Switzerland for five weeks, exploring the countryside, walking around lakes and on glaciers, enjoying both rural scenes and country people. It was one of their happiest holidays, and Mandell shared with Louise one evening after returning from a long walk: 'Well, whatever happens nothing can ever rob us of this day.'[91]

Upon returning to London, Creighton travelled north to Carlisle so he could be present at the unveiling of a stone memorial to his brother James, an event planned by the citizens of the city. The memorial stands in the town square opposite the city government building, near the south end of Eden Bridge. It was, and is still today, an impressive stone pillar—thirty-one feet tall with a figure of St George smiting the dragon and placed on a large stone eight-step pedestal; it features the following inscription to James Robert Creighton, twice mayor and freeman of the city:

> On his death bed he sent a message to his fellow citizens expressing his profound conviction that the greatness of England depended upon its capacity for local self-government. He trusted that Carlisle would never be without a due supply of men who regarded it as both their duty and their pleasure to devote their zeal and energy to the promotion of the welfare of the city.[92]

There were many dignitaries and speeches, including one by the Speaker of the House of Commons who had travelled north. Then, at the end of the ceremony, it was Creighton's turn to speak. Standing near his sister Polly, he thanked everyone on behalf of his family. 'Those who have spoken have only spoken of what [my brother] did', he said. 'I will only say for my own part, if I may, happy is the city that can inspire strong sentiments of local patriotism in its inhabitants; happy is the city which by its recognition of their labours can make that sentiment an imperishable possession. May Carlisle always have those of its citizens who are ready to give their lives and energies to serve its best interests ...'[93]

After the ceremony there was a reception, hosted by Polly in the County Hotel, where many citizens gathered. Who would have thought that the stately, energetic, fifty-five-year-old bishop, who with friendly animation mingled among the guests exuding his usual charm and wit, swapping old Cumbrian tales in thick, rich idiom, had little more than two years to live.

16

Tell Her that I Love Her

'I want to think what message I shall send to the Queen. Tell her that I love her and obey her, and will always obey her in all things—Now go.

Mandell Creighton's last words.[1]

The South African War, or what came to be known as the Boer War, began in early October 1899. Reports of the war rang out across Britain, eventually echoing over the Empire like a soulful bell tolling some frightening omen and breaking the long silence of peace. The Creightons at the time were visiting Mary and Humphry Ward at Stocks, their country house in Hertfordshire, once the summer home of Sir Edward Grey's family.[2] Friendship between the Creightons and the Wards had seasoned well over the years, and Mandell always enjoyed his discussion with Mary about religious questions and her books. But the cloud of war in South Africa hung like a pall over their visit. In a letter to a young friend whose husband had just been ordered to South Africa, Creighton wrote from Stocks about the young men being called to military service. 'Everybody I know is going. Of course they like it in a way: but there is always another way in all things.'[3] A few weeks later, back in London, he wrote to Winifred as the conflict deepened.

> The war is horrible in some ways. But we will never get rid of war, and we have to learn its lessons. A nation's life, after all, depends on its belief in itself: and we have to settle whether South Africa is to be brought under our ideas or those of the Boers. I do not know whether or no it was necessary to raise the question now. Mr [Joseph] Chamberlain [Colonial Secretary] thought so decidedly. But if the question is raised, it must be settled. We are having some of our conceit and self-confidence abated—that is good for us. We have much to learn after a long period of having our way.[4]

By the autumn of 1899, however, Creighton's gnawing pessimism over the way things were in Britain had been heightened by problems caused by his own little 'war'—what he came to call his 'ritual difficulties'.[5] These so-called 'difficulties' involved a growing, protracted debate over a couple of decades concerning ritual forms being used in some Anglican churches.

In Creighton's case, however, these forms seemed to erupt anew when he arrived in London and discovered that low church advocates were being provoked into direct and disruptive action by high church proponents using various rituals that suggested a Roman Catholic bent. The opening shot was fired at a special service in late January 1897 at St Mary-le-Bow church confirming him as new bishop. John Kensit, secretary of the Protestant Truth Society, provoked a disturbance at the service by trying to read aloud a protest objecting to the fact that Bishop Creighton had chosen to wear a mitre, and had—in Kensit's mind, at least—promoted clergy at Peterborough who appeared to be too high church. Upon leaving the church after the ceremony, Creighton noticed Kensit standing at the door. He greeted him kindly with a handshake, invited him to tea at Fulham, and assured him that they would surely come to understand each other once they got to know one other.[6] There is no record of what Kensit said in reply, but Creighton, who had spent his life mixing with intelligent, reasonable people, must have seen something different in the man's eyes.

The ritual turmoil Creighton encountered began as an outgrowth of the Tractarian legacy. By the 1890s there was a Catholic revival going on within the Anglican Church. This could be seen with the growing popularity of Lord Halifax's Anglican group, the English Church Union, along with the publication of the controversial *Lux Mundi* book, a collection of essays that appeared in November 1889 edited by Charles Gore, fellow of Trinity College, Oxford. Gore was one of a group of high church intellectuals—among them Creighton's friend, Henry Scott Holland—all of whom enthusiastically espoused Anglo-Catholic ideas.[7] This so-called 'dangerous book', along with other high church tendencies of that time, led to a deeply religious 'Catholic Way' in the 1890s. And this 'Catholic Way' inexorably seeped down amongst the laity, thus creating an indelible imprint upon the public religiosity and acting as fulfilment of what has been described as an 'Anglican spiritual tradition'.[8]

What exacerbated the anti-ritualist cause at this time, of course, was the issue raised over the validity of Anglican orders and Leo XIII's uncompromising and undiplomatic 'null and void' response. To further irritate a vocal segment of society coming to believe some popish conspiracy was afoot, there was in 1897 the publication of a book entitled *The Secret History of the Oxford Movement*, written by a Walter Walsh, assistant editor of the evangelical newspaper the *English Churchman*.[9] This had the effect of unleashing more attacks by evangelical and nonconformist groups, such as the Church Association, and several ultra-Protestant Erastian societies, like the Protestant Alliance, the National Protestant Church Union and the Protestant Reformation Society.[10]

About the time Kensit was making his presence known in London, five evangelical clergy signed a petition imploring Creighton not to introduce the use of the mitre in the London diocese. Creighton, from the start of his episcopal life, had chosen to wear a cope and mitre on great occasions in his cathedral, but was careful not to do so at other churches in fear that it might offend that particular congregation. He was not the first bishop in the Anglican Church to wear a cope and mitre since the Reformation, but was the first Bishop of London to do so in recent times. When the specific question about wearing a cope was posed to him directly by another priest, for example, Creighton replied that the position of the Church of England was that 'the Rubric of the First Prayer Book of Edward VI. prescribed a cope for holy communion and for a bishop at all times. The advertisements of Queen Elizabeth and the canon of 1603 prescribed it for cathedral and collegiate churches. The question is, did they exclude it from other places? ... I prefer to deal with such matters on the ground of common sense.' [11]

Although Creighton's doctrinal beliefs were largely broad church, his liturgical taste favoured the high church; and it had ever since his Durham and Merton years, when he had become comfortable with Pusey-style ritual. As Louise put it, Mandell liked a 'dignified service', but not 'anything fussy or elaborate'.[12] One can see, therefore, why those who knew him only a little thought his fundamental sympathies were avowedly Anglo-Catholic. This was not the case, however. His notion was that since the Reformation the real Catholic Church consisted of a collections of 'national churches', with their own special cultural characteristics, and that these external differences should not necessarily threaten doctrinal unity.[13] The purpose of the Church of England, he felt, was to teach the people in England about the Catholic faith.[14] The ultramontanism of Rome, he asserted, was excessively narrow and legalistic; and concurrently, he believed that the extreme wings of the Church of England—the reactionary high church party and the radical low church party—were both too divisive and dangerous. 'Dissension and disunion are in themselves disastrous', he said. 'Where misunderstandings arise there is a period of mutual recriminations, which do not help forward a solution. Peace is only possible when the real points at issue are fairly stated, and are admitted.' [15]

Of course the 'ritual difficulties' involved more than copes and mitres. There was an array of liturgical practices being widely conducted throughout the churches in London and elsewhere that either were not prescribed in the Book of Common Prayer or were bending certain permissible practices out of shape. Creighton, for instance, claimed that he soon discovered after coming to London, that 'there were certainly one or two features in the conduct of services in some churches which awakened natural anxiety'. He was concerned about 'the introduction of unauthorised services and ceremonies in addition to those contained in the Book of Common Prayer [and] the addition to, or omissions from, the Communion Office contained in the Book of Common Prayer which seem to me to be made with a view of reading that service into the terms of the services of the Church of Rome'.[16] First, there were the 'unauthorised services and ceremonies' not contained in the Common Prayer Book, such as confession, reservation of the host, benediction, the rosary, litanies, crossing oneself, the use of incense, vestments, statues, holy water, and services for the dead which incorporated the Roman view of purgatory, and the wearing of a continental- style biretta. Secondly, there was a variety of Roman terminology that had crept into many high church services, particularly the use of the word 'mass'.

It had been suggested that when Creighton came to London he found the diocese 'in chaos', and though his predecessor Bishop Temple had 'worked like a horse himself', he had 'let everyone else work in the way they liked. Every church had its own type of service'.[17] Creighton, however, rapidly came to the conclusion that a stricter ceremonial conformity was necessary, lest the clergy begin to think the Church of England 'an imperfect system, to be supplemented at each man's option from any source he thinks fit'.[18] Speaking at his first diocesan conference in 1897, he said he conceived his duty as bishop was to show 'sympathy with all forms of service and all forms of religious zeal, which are loyally in accordance with the principles of the Church of England'.[19] Elsewhere he pointed out that it was his duty as bishop 'to see that permissible liberty be not unduly extended, so as to impair the distinctive characteristics of the services of our Church'.[20] 'Permissible liberty be not unduly extended'—these words may seem problematic for a man who always argued strongly for personal responsibility. In a general way, Creighton's basic assumption was that the individual was wiser than a group of individuals, but only of course within the context of the rule of law. Here was a case, he thought, where the need for collective responsibility overshadowed individual rights. Thus reasonable conformity to the law—which in this case meant adhering to the Book of Common Prayer with all of its designed latitudes and toleration—was not only prudent but also necessary. Creighton, however, never desired a narrow Church of England and sought reasonable comprehensiveness of religious expression, always hoping to avoid insularity and trying to belay any suspicion of the Church of England's great medieval heritage. Therefore, he was desperately committed to finding moderate solutions somewhere between the two polar points—the extreme evangelicals and the conservative Anglo-Catholics.[21] As a result he was destined to be accused by the unreasonable in both camps of being too reasonable, too patient, too temperate, too willing to rely on private persuasion over public prescription.[22]

It was not long until the controversy spilled over into politics. Sir William Harcourt, former Home Secretary, Chancellor of the Exchequer and Liberal leader, emerged as a strident voice for the ultra-Protestant cause. He personally raised the level of noise and agitation by bringing in the press, taking it upon himself to send letters to *The Times* and other newspapers during the winter of 1899 calling on the bishops to force the high church party into obedience.[23] Being a Member of Parliament, Harcourt and others like Samuel Smith sought to make ritualism an issue in the House of Commons by interjecting it into debates on Bills that had little or nothing to do with ritual, such as the Benefices Bill or the Church Discipline Bill.[24] At Windsor, Queen Victoria wrote solemnly in her journal: 'Had some conversation with the Bishop of London on the most unfortunate squabbles in the Church. The low church, who started the whole thing, was quite as violent and more so than the extreme ritualistic party, and very unreasonable. The bishop said he was shocked to see that there was still as great a feeling for persecution in this nineteenth century as hundreds of years ago, which is very dreadful.'[25]

All the while John Kensit and his fellow extremists continued their anti-ritualist onslaught by direct, frontal assault, using irreverent language and mischievous actions to disrupt services in churches where ceremonies were regarded as too high. Kensit, who wanted publicity, found Creighton an adversary unwilling to do public battle. Creighton preferred to wage his war by seeking accommodation in private, always hoping to persuade both sides through reason and good will. Imbedded in his psyche was a profound horror of persecution that stemmed both from his appreciation of history and his inherent belief in individual liberty.

Creighton had no wish to impose strict and severe ceremonial uniformity on what he reckoned were 'non-essentials' or 'trifling matters' being urged by those whom his wife's described as 'the foolish and the fanatics' in describing Kensit's party; nevertheless, Creighton feared in his heart of hearts that it might come to that.[26] What he discovered in the course of his early dialogues with both the Anglo-Catholics and the evangelicals was that persuasion seemed to work better with the high church clergy than the low church party, perhaps due to the fact that the former, with their medieval mindset, tended to be more attuned to the argument from authority. Appealing to authority and medieval tradition did not set well with the evangelical party who considered themselves not only purifiers of the past but harbingers of the future. Creighton could understand the former but never quite the latter. When, for example, the question of the 'real presence' was raised concerning the sacrament of the eucharist, he said that the theology was quite simple and best expressed by Queen Elizabeth:

> Christ was the Word, and spake it:
> He took the bread and brake it,
> And what His Word did make it
> That I believe and take it.[27]

A more complete explanation of Creighton's broad church views on holy communion was expressed to a low church writer who had criticised him on that very question. The bishop replied:

The Church of England repudiates two views of the sacrament of the Lord's Supper, first, that it is merely commemorative; secondly, that there is the change in the elements known as Transubstantiation. Between these opinions any other has to be judged by its argument with the language of the Communion Service. You say 'this is *the* crucial question'. Pardon me if I say that I wonder why people are so heated about this particular matter. The faith of Christendom is contained in the Creeds: none of them mention the sacrament. All branches of the Catholic Church are agreed in their practice, in the nature of the rite, in the value which they assign to the sacrament. Differences of opinion are not about the virtue received, but about the mode of the reception: there is no real difference about the receptivity of cooperation on the part of the recipient, i.e. the *faithful* reception. The difference is solely about mode and nature of the process which precedes reception. Now is this a *crucial* matter? It is not a matter of revelation: it is not a question asked in the early Church. It is simply the desire of man to satisfy his curiosity ... The Church of England is Primitive, in the sense in which early Christianity did not ask questions impossible to answer with certainty.[28]

In April 1898, Creighton addressed a diocesan conference, eager to assure his clergy that he desired to foster consensus and cooperation in resolving the ritual issue. He told them that his duty was to deal 'straightforwardly and frankly' with them in the 'spirit of kindliness and in the spirit of Christian love' by means of offering reasoned arguments, 'not by attempting to coerce ... or to bring pressure upon [the clergy] to go in directions which are contrary to their own consciences'. He said he hoped to 'bring them all together equally into agreement upon the great fundamental points of our Christian practice, because in matters of Christian faith, of course, we are not divided'; and assured them all that he favoured 'personal persuasion and personal influence, by talking and conference with those who seem to be divided, to bring all together into an understanding at least of one another's position, that we may discover exactly what are the points upon which we differ; for until we have discovered those, any attempt at agreement is obviously quite impossible'.[29]

A few weeks later Creighton wrote a circular letter to the London clergy pointing out that in a diocese such as his

> where there is so much work to be done of a missionary character, and where the circumstances of parishes vary so greatly, it is natural that there should be a tendency to make new experiments in various ways. The natural tendency has affected the conduct of public worship, and must, in some degree, always do so. But it is a tendency which must be subject to certain obvious limitations, to which I would call your attention. It is absolutely necessary that nothing should be done which affects the due performance of the services of the Church as laid down in the Book of Common Prayer, and that any additional services which are used should conform entirely to the spirit and intention of the Prayer Book. There must be no confusion in the minds of the people as to the standard of worship in the Church of England, and there must be no opportunity for personal eccentricities to invade the system of the Church.[30]

Creighton made every effort humanly possible to communicate with men of differing opinions on this controversy, desperately trying to understand their point of view, always trying to explain his. Even many of those who differed most with him, especially those of the ritual party, had to agree that their bishop was acting out of fairness and goodwill.[31] He must have thought often about the Northampton and Leicester strike in the boot and shoe industry he had laboured behind the scenes to resolve, coming to the conclusion that the difference between trade unionists and ritualists was that the former seemed to be more willing to negotiate.

Over the months, as the issue continued to boil over, he received numerous visits and frequent letters from his clergy of all persuasions on the issue, suggesting some semblance of support, even obedience, albeit begrudgingly. 'I shall carry out your wishes in every particular', read one letter. 'If there is anything in my service not approved of, I will alter it', read another. A letter signed by eighty-nine of his clergy read in part: 'We desire to assure your Lordship of our dutiful and loyal compliance ...'[32] And the more he explored specific cases, the more he found that it was not just high church clergy who were guilty of unauthorised Roman practices, but a number of low church clergy were accustomed to omitting authorised Anglican practices which, needless to say, caused him further irritation and led him to chastise them as well.[33]

All of the bishop's efforts to deal with Kensit in a reasonable way were rebuffed. In a personal letter to Kensit in January 1898, Creighton suggested that he 'attend a church with which the services suit you rather than a church in which they do not suit you'. Kensit immediately forwarded it on to the newspapers.[34] When one of the bishop's supporters urged him to take public steps to vindicate himself, however, Creighton's courageous response was: 'I never wish to defend myself—and I prefer not to be defended ... I am the father to all my clergy. It is my duty to bear the burden of their mistakes. I never make public what passed between them and me.'[35]

Then Kensit wrote to Creighton in October 1898 threatening that if the bishop did not intervene more directly in certain churches, hundreds of his followers were ready to take matters into their own hands. He asked that the bishop make a public statement that could be shared with the Protestant Truth Society and its supporters at a great demonstration that was planned. Creighton replied with a letter specifically to Kensit: 'Sir, It is my duty to see that the principles of the Church of England are duly maintained and expressed in the services held in her churches. This duty I steadily perform.' He went on to say that when differences of opinion 'disturb the peace of the Church, it is the duty of those in authority to behave with strict regard to justice, and to remember that they are dealing with matters which are connected with the deepest sentiments of the human heart and the most profound convictions of the human mind. Human wisdom as well as Christian charity prescribes tenderness and patience in dealing with conscientious convictions.' Then he added: 'I regret that the tone of your letter implies that neither wisdom nor charity has any place in your consideration.'[36]

At the protest rally in Exeter Hall, Kensit read the letter from Creighton; but before much else could transpire at the gathering, opponents of the low church party who had crowded into the hall staged a vociferous disruption so that the platform speakers could no longer not be heard.[37] The controversy dragged on. On one occasion Creighton was mobbed when coming out of a church in Bethnal Green by some protesters shouting 'No Popery!' In a letter to a niece, he reacted philosophically: 'I have to go my way and be abused by people who want to stamp on someone else, or rather want me to stamp on them.'[38]

It was about this time that Creighton unveiled a window at Gray's Inn chapel in memory of Archbishop Laud. Deep in the morass of religious ritual controversy, caught in the middle of a modern Cavalier-Roundhead civil war, Creighton must have felt a kinship to that tragic seventeenth-century archbishop whom he described as 'a martyr for intellectual freedom'.[39] In his homily, he praised Laud and called him 'a man of great ideas, and a man who was unflinching and unwavering in his pursuit of truth', adding that Laud's 'idea of the Church of England was probably higher and truer than of any other man, certainly of his time ... Personally, he was large-minded and tolerant, but he was prepared to use intolerance as a means of establishing a system of tolerance.' Laud, caught between two

subversive groups—ultra-Protestants and Roman Catholics—had the misfortune of being trapped in the first modern revolution in history; and
while his religious beliefs may have been judged sound currency by some,
his methods were decidedly bankrupt. Laud, Creighton contended, 'upheld
great principles of spiritual freedom, which were as yet imperfectly understood; but he upheld them by methods which threatened the very
foundations of English liberty.'[40]

Creighton's attempt to regulate services and control ritualist actions was
meeting with some success by the end of 1898, though prospects of a full
and sustaining peace with the more entrenched clergy seemed remote. 'Our
lot has fallen on evil times', he wrote to a fellow bishop, 'but we must hope
to get some good out of it ... May God give us wisdom and patience.'[41]
For some time the high church party members had felt they never had a
real opportunity to explain their case to the archbishop in a formal hearing,
a standard process for resolving church issues that was suggested in the
preface of the Book of Common Prayer. Archbishop Temple, after deliberation with the Archbishop of York and a few other prelates, publicly
announced at the beginning of the new year that they would hold a hearing
that spring at Lambeth Palace for the purpose of considering specific
practices which the high church party claimed were rightful, within the
Anglican liturgical guidelines. It was decided that the hearing would deal
first with the ceremonial use of candles and incense. Other matters would
be discussed at subsequent hearings.

In April 1899, at the diocesan conference, Creighton gave the presidential
address and spoke sadly of the quarrelling over 'holy things' and the 'suspen-
sion of good works for barren disputation'. He said that 'diversity must
have its limits', and added that ceremonies are 'nothing in themselves, and
differences of opinion cannot be composed by attacking ceremonies. It is
useless to deal with them as subjects for legal decision.' And he ended by
driving home a fundamental point:

> I do not wish to command so much as to persuade. I wish to induce people to
> see themselves as others see them, to regard what they are doing in reference to
> its far-off effects on the consciences of others, to cultivate a truer sense of
> proportion of things, to deal more with ideas than with the clothing of ideas; to
> pay more attention to the reason of a thing than to its antiquity; to remember
> that the chief danger which besets those who are pursuing a high object is to
> confuse means with ends; to examine themselves very fully, lest they confuse
> Christian zeal with the desire to have their own way ...[42]

The Lambeth hearing was held in May 1899, and after listening to the
pros and cons on the use candles and incense, the decision of the two

archbishops—formally issued in August—went against the high church party. The ruling was of course celebrated by the evangelical side. Creighton found that within his own diocese the great majority of clergy who were in the habit of using candles in processions and at the gospel as well as burning incense were willing to give them up, though a few sent him resolutions of protest. On one occasion a priest defending incense told the bishop: 'But my Lord, you must remember that we have a cure of souls.' Creighton shot back: 'And you think that souls, like herrings, cannot be cured without smoke?' The remark apparently caused some offence; and Louise, upon hearing of it, reportedly chastised her husband: 'You ought not to have said that.' He replied: 'Yes, I know I ought not, but it was irresistible.'[43] The remark evidently continued on as an irresistible topic for light conversation in academic and religious circles for years.[44]

After a couple of conferences, Creighton was able to persuade all but three of his priests to obey the Lambeth injunction, yet he did not discipline them, deciding to leave them be and hope that time would eventually dissolve their stubbornness.[45] The ritualist controversy dragged beyond Creighton's episcopate, and though he and his suffragan bishops in the metropolitan area did much to restore some semblance of conformity among the ranks of the clergy, harmony and peace in London and across England on this issue remained elusive—waiting for a later era when more ecumenical minds might prevail. One of his historian friends later remarked that Creighton's 'respect for liberty preserved him from making mistakes', and that being convinced

of the truth of his main principles, imbued as he was perhaps more strongly than any other thinker since Hooker with the genius of the Church of England, despising the frivolity and ignorance with which the Latinisation of the Church was being pushed forward, and deeply opposed to the legalist conception of religion in general, and to 'canonist' Christianity in particular, Creighton's strong hand alone prevented an outburst of the persecuting spirit which would have entirely defeated its own object, and would have left the Church shorn of some of its best elements. He felt that the dangers of competing creeds and the emergence of every form of unbelief into articulate prominence, would also justify the attempt to leave dangerous tendencies to work themselves out rather than by repression to leave the evil smouldering. Episcopal authority stood very high to his mind, but he was not prepared to support it by coercion, if men (committing as he deemed a sin) refused to bow to that authority.[46]

Bishop Randall Davidson later said that he found in Creighton 'a frequent touch of something appealing to the deeper spiritual side of things, and it always seemed to me that he had a sound appreciation of the true proportion of great things to small in the Ritual Controversy'.[47] Davidson, however, tended to find Creighton too conservative and unprogressive, for when he proposed a resolution that the Church of England extend official approval for public libraries, galleries and museums to remain open on Sundays, Creighton was one of the bishops who objected. 'They all', wrote Davidson in disgust, 'spoke as men belonging to another generation than ours.'[48] Creighton to the end believed in limiting such activities on Sundays, and even claimed he tried to dissuade a London newspaper, the *Daily Telegraph*, from printing its Sunday issue; he himself said that it was his rule to avoid writing letters on Sunday, although he admitted not being able to hold to it.[49]

For the Church of England overall, this ritual issue in general at first seems to represent the wider social confusion that affected, among other things, the religious expression and practices of the *fin de siècle*. Yet of course it was only one of the several concerns confronting the established church, the principal one being not quarrels among the faithful over matters like ritual, but rather that the faithful were either switching to nonconformist chapels or abandoning denominational religion altogether. Statistics show that only about two out of eleven people were attending services in London at the turn of the century. Compared with a few decades earlier, this was a major falling away; indeed, there was a widening gap emerging between the theology of the theologians and the social beliefs of the people.[50] For Creighton personally, the ritual experience seemed to him to be one thing that he reckoned he had failed to reconcile through his usual combination of reason, charm and wit. History, nonetheless, suggests that Creighton's tactics were the wiser path. Sadly, however, the ritual battle wore him out and shortened his life by placing too much stress and strain on his constitution.[51]

'I think that the recalcitrant clergy are falling in', he wrote to Ella, his niece, in October 1899, 'but this is merely a trifle and does not touch the real position. There is no hope of people agreeing: they must learn to argue, to differ and live in peace. But the public mind is now taken up with the [Boer] war. Luckily it can not keep two things before it at once. This is a mercy.' Then he added: 'It will pitch into the Boers instead of the Bishops. All the same I would much rather bear the fruit of all things than have this horrid war going on. We are suffering great losses for nothing. All that is now happening is doing nothing for an ultimate settlement.'[52] Six weeks later he wrote to his niece Winifred: 'The war is terrible. Never have I been so low. No one can foresee the future. We have been for a long time much too arrogant and insolent, and we must repent and learn humility. It is too dreadful ... We must think and pray and humble ourselves. Life is becoming a very serious matter to us all, and we must learn to face its seriousness.

But the joys of quiet affection still remain, and nothing can affect love which abides when all else goes.'[53]

Like so many other British in those last days of their long and relatively peaceful epoch, Creighton was also beginning to sense the dénouement of that great era of optimism—for the public conviction that 'God's in His Heaven, All's Right with the World' seemed to be diminishing.

It was at the time of concern over the Boer War that Creighton met Kaiser Wilhelm II of Germany and his wife while visiting Sandringham House. The royal couple were visiting Britain. Since Wilhelm's mother was Queen Victoria's eldest daughter, Wilhelm was on fairly good terms with his uncle Edward, Prince of Wales, in spite of the fact that Wilhelm possessed a deep dislike of his English mother. 'Who would have thought it ten years ago?', Mandell wrote to Ella Creighton, amazed that he was mingling with such people. 'It seems ridiculous that I should do such things ... I have been having a long talk with [the Emperor] about Germany and England, and the politics of Europe', he wrote. 'Such is life. [The Emperor] is a very nice and attractive man. The Empress also is quite bright and intelligent. We have been taking a long walk, Emperor and Empress, Prince and Princess of Wales, and all their children, and even a grandchild, Prince Edward of York.'[54] Creighton preached a sermon at the Sunday service that weekend entitled 'The Hope of the Future', which must have impressed the German Emperor for afterward he specifically asked to have a printed copy. Three-quarters of the sermon dealt with a commentary on Psalm 144, 'Yea happy is that people whose God is the Lord'. The final part, however—which Wilhelm liked best—was directed specifically to the royalty before him, and while the reference to the 'Teutonic race' dates his message, his warning to Kaiser and future King was almost prescient.

Patriotism is doubtless a great and necessary virtue; it must always regulate much that we do, but it should not therefore narrow our aspirations. A nation, like an individual, has much to learn, and must learn it, as the individual learns, mainly by sympathetic intercourse with like-minded nations. On this gradual education of nations, more than anything else, the hope of the world's future depends. Nations with like ideas of righteousness go forth on their separate ways, not that they may emphasise the differences which arise from differing experience, but that they may bring the results of their experience to a common stock. The Teutonic race has the same fundamental ideas. It has the same sense of duty, the same conception of conscience, the same aspiration after justice as the highest expression of national righteousness. We cannot shut our eyes to the responsibility which God's Providence has placed upon the nations of the Teutonic race ... It is not enough that each nation should recognise and glorify these ideas as it knows them. It must learn from the experience of other nations to understand them better and apply them more thoroughly. Is not this the task which lies before the great nations of the Teutonic stock? Shall we not combine in a spirit of comradeship to help one another to perform a work which we have in common? [55]

During those years of religious controversy and military conflict, the normal work of shepherding a large urban diocese continued to drain Creighton's strength. 'I have to think that I am useful, but I doubt it', he scribbled off to a niece, 'I rather pity my coachman who has a fine time of it, wandering about London. Last night I went to dine at Toynbee Hall, and then talked to an assembly of Trade Unionists and Socialists about education ... I never scarcely have time to read anything and seldom to write.' [56] Indeed, his literary life had come to a halt with no new books on history being conceived, let alone written.[57] The closest he came to any new work was a collection of edited sermons, published the year after be arrived in London, entitled *Lessons from the Cross*.[58]

In the course of those years, Creighton was able to squeeze a little time to write two short articles on history. When asked by Lord Acton, he agreed to write the 'Introductory Note' for the initial volume of the planned *The Cambridge Modern History*.[59] Likewise, he wrote a chapter on 'The Reformation' in the volume *The Church: Past and Present* that was published in 1900 and edited by Henry Gwatkin, the Dixie Professor of Ecclesiastical History.[60] Mainly, however, he whetted his scholarly appetite by giving occasional talks on history, which was barely satisfying: he spoke to the 'The Picturesque in History' at the Royal Institution of Great Britain in February 1897, and 'A Study of a Country' to a London University Extension gathering of students April 1897, and 'Heroes' to the Social and Political Education League in November 1898, and the 'Elizabethan London' at a meeting of the London Reform Union in November 1899.[61] Preparing for the latter, he told a niece that it 'rather amused' him sometimes 'to have a definite thing to read about. It is only this that drives me back again to consult old books.' [62]

Creighton carried the lion's share of work in preparing for a church congress in London in the autumn of 1899. The Albert Hall was filled to capacity at the opening session when he delivered the presidential address, his subject being the work of the English church in the modern state. He called upon his knowledge of history to show how the state had taken over much of the temporal work of the church; and with obvious reference to the ritual issue, he declared that the eyes of the church must be turned to the past for instruction, not imitation, stating that 'difficulties and differences arise because we have not a sufficiently lofty conception of the destiny of the English Church. If any disaster befalls it, the record that will be written hereafter will be that English Churchmen of this our day were not sufficiently large-hearted and high-minded to recognise the greatness of the heritage which was theirs.'[63] Creighton presided over every major session, and Louise on one occasion addressed a women's session.[64]

As the year 1900 began, the whole nation was struggling with deep anxiety over the South African War, and ritual peace within the church at home seemed as remote as ever. In the New Year's message to his diocese, Bishop Creighton said that his words 'must be words of warning, not encouragement. We cannot shut our ears to the voice of God, which is speaking to us as a nation.' A kind of pessimism seemed to be creeping into Creighton's public remarks and private letters, and in trying to explain his feelings to his young nephew Basil in simplest terms, he said:

> We [English] began our political and industrial life before other people; we went ahead very fast; we became quite content with ourselves: we have left off trying to improve things: we still think ourselves better than any other nation, whereas all the nations of Europe have come up to our level; many are working harder and more intelligently at many things; and we go on living in a fool's paradise. Take this war, for instance. What impresses me is that all the men who ought to have advised the government and were out there and knew the Boers, advised all wrong. They thought and said that 30,000 troops would finish the war in two months. Now the worst thing for any nation is not to judge aright. If Englishmen are growing so conceited that they cannot estimate properly, we are in a bad way. You ask if this can be helped. Yes, it can be helped by the young generation taking a more serious interest in what they do. You and such as you must set us right, by working harder, by thinking more wisely.[65]

The war and matters dealing with the Church of England took its toll on his normally upbeat, confident demeanour, but also there was probably an awakening of the growing problems disturbing the Victorian scene—the escalating urban plight and industrial blight, the rise of a disillusioned underclass along with the weakening of the middle and upper classes, and the withering of traditional mores that had kept the culture intact for much of the century, not to mention increasing challenges confronting Britain from Ireland, Empire and Europe. Whatever the case, Creighton was beginning to disclose a more sombre, sober tone in his sermons and his letters.

Helping to explain this in part was his diminishing health. During 1898 he began experiencing occasional bouts of stomach pain. After a busy Easter season that year, the pain became so acute that doctors advised him to take a few weeks off. He and Louise went to Switzerland, but the pain persisted. When he returned and threw himself back into his animated life, the symptoms appeared to diminish slightly. Towards the end of Lent in 1899, the Creightons went to Switzerland again, this time bringing Cuthbert and Walter along. After returning, he wrote: 'I do not find myself that taking a holiday makes it any nicer to come back to work.'[66]

That August the Creightons took their usual annual holiday, this time spending three weeks in Wales with the children, and with Polly and the nephews and nieces. After that, Louise and Mandell went off to the Swiss Alps and then down into northern Italy. A few weeks later, in the wake of the London church congress, Creighton began to suffer again from head-aches, dyspepsia and insomnia; and, shortly after having met the German Emperor at Sandringham in late November 1899, the pain in his stomach increased. In mid December he was invited to Windsor. Upon returning, his belly was on fire, what Louise called 'a sudden and most alarming attack of violent internal pain, the cause of which was never really discovered'.[67] He spent the next week in bed trying to prepare for the Christmas season while digesting the terrible news being reported from South Africa of one disaster after another. In early January 1900 he seemed to feel better and wrote to his niece Ella: 'I need cheering up, as I do not feel very vigorous yet, and my holidays are coming to an end, as I have to work hard again.'[68]

In the middle of February Creighton delivered his charge to the London clergy in St Paul's Cathedral, telling a niece on the following day that he 'found it less trying than I supposed to speak for an hour and a half in St Paul's. It will now afford material for everyone to attack me for a fortnight till they forget.'[69] In the charge, which seemed directed largely to the high church clergy, he spoke firmly about the need to bring about conformity of liturgy and doctrine, reminding them all that, because of the Reformation, the Church of England had embarked on its own distinct course and had formally withdrawn from the errors of the medieval church which tried 'to produce by external means the outward appearance of a Christian life without the inward conviction on which alone such a life can be based'.[70] It was one of Creighton's better and historically reasoned appeals to the ritualists.

On 7 April, he wrote to his niece Ella that he was 'pining for a holiday. I have never recovered since December, and it is time that I did improve a bit. I do not want to sink to a crock, just yet.'[71] Three days later Mandell and Louise went off to the Italian lakes in search of peace and quiet. 'He was not well', Louise remembered. 'This affected his spirits somewhat, though his energy and his interest in everything he saw was as great as ever.'[72] Returning to London at the end of the month, Creighton prepared for a diocesan meeting at which he proposed a round table conference for the autumn to discuss specific matters of dispute, particularly issues on holy communion. Administering a large and crisis-driven diocese had caused him anguish, and he sometimes told those closest to him that he often wished he were back in more peaceful Peterborough.[73] That summer his schedule remained full of the usual diocesan matters during the days and an array of social events in the evenings, though his health was obviously slipping. He gave a talk on Savonarola at St Paul's, on the church and national life at Sion College, and on religion at Alexandra Palace; he laid the foundation stone for a new building at London School of Economics, and he opened the Pan-African conference which was held in London for the purpose of discussing the future of the African peoples. August finally arrived and the Creightons took their usual holiday, this time renting a vacant boys' schoolhouse on Derwent Water near Keswick, Cumberland. Mandell predicted they would spend their time 'in a sort of boisterous picnic, which I enjoy greatly'.[74] After a few days of unseasonably cool, damp weather, he wrote to a friend that 'the weather began to amend', turning 'most beautiful. I have been going up hills with a vigour which is indecent in so old a man, but I never can reconcile myself to my age and infirmities.' He had just turned fifty-seven. Regrettably, in Louise's words, it was their 'last family summer holiday'.

> I don't think that I enjoyed this holiday very much. Max was not at all well. He took long walks with the children as usual, often further than I could go, but he often had a great deal of pain at night and did not sleep well ... I have few happy memories about this time. I believe that I should have insisted that Max should see Sir Thomas Barlow again before we went abroad, but he seemed as always so full of energy that I could not believe that there was anything seriously wrong.[75]

Mandell and Louise, along with Cuthbert, spent the next few weeks in northern Italy. On one occasion Mandell's pain was such that they called in the local doctor 'who did not seem to know much about what was wrong'. Louise said that she remembered 'a very black moment when I went alone to the neighbouring church where they were, I believe, preparing for a funeral. Finally we decided that we must go home at once.'[76] Back at Fulham the bishop was put to bed and the doctors called in, and then long weeks followed. A tumour in the stomach region was tentatively diagnosed, and the hope was that with proper rest and care, possibly an operation, Mandell would recover in a few months. 'I go on being an invalid, and am quite enjoying it in a way', he said to a niece. 'I am so tired of having been uncomfortable all this year, that I am really glad to have to set to work to mend things. I do not think, however, that it will be done in a hurry. So I take it calmly, and wait till a better time comes.'[77]

Creighton spent his mornings in bed, working with his chaplain, or his archdeacons or others as much as was needed. In the afternoons, when the weather was accommodating, he went for carriage rides accompanied by Louise or a friend. Louise claimed that he 'came to love Richmond Park with all its beautiful views'.[78] Evenings were given over to conversation or bridge games with friends, or quiet reading. To one of his nieces he spoke drearily of this 'humdrum style' of existence, saying that: 'I write letters. I read books, mostly novels; I take a drive; I have a game of bridge in the evening. It all goes on with strict monotony. People come to see me, sometimes in business, sometimes for friendship's sake; but I go nowhere, except to my dentist.'[79] Now the entire family, and close friends and associates, were beginning to take note of the seriousness of the bishop's illness, and Louise, especially, felt increasingly stressed about it. 'I could not speak, perhaps hardly think of my fears', she confessed.

I do not believe that at first they were very articulate. I went about my usual jobs, going to committees and speaking at meetings, though as little as possible. It was a fine autumn and there were always flowers to be found in the garden, and he enjoyed them. One of my most terrifying moments was when once walking with me out of the drawing-room window into the garden, he suddenly collapsed. I was able to help him up onto a chair and there were no further results, but it showed how weak he was. He began to talk as if he would have to resign and once asked me where I should like to live if he did, and we both agreed that we would like to live in the Lake District.[80]

Creighton had agreed earlier in the year to deliver a lecture on education to the Midland Institute at Birmingham in mid October, and after returning from Italy, continued to put the final touches on his paper which he called, 'A Plea for Knowledge'. Although too ill to give it, the paper was published in the *Contemporary Review* and ranks as one of his most interesting essays on education, and how he perceived its social implications on England in the late Victorian period.[81] He pointed out his belief that the English in the past were molded by 'three great powers', namely, the state, the church and the university; and while admitting certain alterations in modern society, he declared that 'it still remains an absolute truth that human life rests on three great primary requirements—order, conduct, knowledge'.[82] Thus, while the state and the church existed to provide people with a sense of order and right conduct, the educational system in England had failed to communicate the *value* of knowledge. He, of course, was not suggesting that England had ceased to produce eminent minds in various branches of learning or that society did not recognise them. What he meant was that the average English person of his day gave little thought to the *importance* of acquiring knowledge 'for the purpose of leading his own life efficiently'.[83]

'To put it briefly', Creighton had written, 'my opinion is that the great defect of England at present is an inadequate conception of the value of knowing in itself, and of its importance for the national life. I wish to see this remedied', he said, 'and it cannot be remedied till it is recognised.'[84] He stated, for example, that the 'point at which knowledge will cease to make a man a better wage-earner may be soon reached; but the point at which it will cease to make him a better and happier man will never be reached'.[85] Creighton made a distinction between education and training, and therefore claimed that the purpose of a society's educational system was to prepare its citizens to know how to live as well as to know how to make a living. Creighton thus believed in an educative state where cultural concerns transcended practical considerations. Sadly, he was naive in his optimism that succeeding generations would take full measure and pleasure in their educational opportunities, because as the twentieth century has demonstrated, modern states with all their wealth, leisure, and cultural advantages, still fail to place sufficient importance on elevating and ennobling the cerebral lives of its citizens. 'Men must learn to think for themselves, and so to form sound and deliberate opinions', he once said.[86] All this may have a familiar modern ring about it to the reader today, perhaps, but in Creighton's time such ideas were still very much limited. A week before he died, in one of his last recorded serious conversations, Creighton was asked what he considered the greatest danger of the coming century. Without hesitation he replied: 'I have no doubt what is the greatest danger—it is the absence of high aspirations.'[87]

Creighton's earlier proposal for a round table conference over issues revolving around holy communion began in October at Fulham Palace, with the bishop lying on a sofa in the drawing-room while a collection of selected clergy and suffragan bishops met in the adjoining hall. The conference, as most expected, brought no firm agreement between opposing sides over disputed rituals, but it did advance a better understanding among the participants which was pretty much what Creighton anticipated would happen, and that apparently satisfied him. Other church matters continued to vex him as autumn turned into winter and his health worsened. To a fellow bishop he wrote towards the end of November: 'I hope to make a new start in recovery on Saturday. I had a consultation yesterday with a surgeon. It is tolerably clear that there is some obstruction requiring an operation. Don't say anything about it as the operation suggests a cancerous tumour, which is not suspected. The surgeon hopes to restore me in a fortnight, if his diagnosis is right. He promises to make me good as new.'[88]

At last the doctors agreed on an operation which was then performed by one of London's top surgeons on the first day of December at Fulham. Mandell's condition seemed to improve. To her sister Sophie, Louise wrote on 7 December that he was 'quite cheery this morning and tho' of course he is not encouraged to talk, he is returning to an interest in life and the world around him ... I spend peaceful days now sitting in Max's room nearly all day and writing letters and taking little walks in the garden ... We shall keep the two nurses for at least a fortnight and and then one for a bit ... Next week I have one or too outside engagements which I must try and keep if possible, tho' I don't feel much in the mood for public appearances ...'[89] Friends of Creighton wrote letters wishing to call on him, but Louise restricted visitors to a minimum. She discouraged James Bryce from coming, saying that the doctors were 'quite satisfied with his progress ... I hope that when January comes he will be able to enjoy seeing his friends. I am glad to say that the doctors promise a complete recovery.'[90]

It was a bleak Christmas that year. All the children and other members of the extended family had gathered at Fulham as usual. Beatrice had just returned from a trip to America, Walter came home early from Germany, and Cuthbert, then in his first year as a master at Uppingham, arrived for the holidays. As the days passed, the doctors became dissatisfied with Creighton's progress and told Louise that there should be another operation. The second operation took place on Christmas Eve. Louise described the situation to her sister, Ida:

> Well we have had another terrible time. Last week I began to fear that things were not right; and when the surgeon came on Saturday his face and manner were enough to tell me that things were very wrong. On Sunday morning Dr Clarke told me that another operation would probably be necessary. I told Max that morning and his only wish was that he could be done with it all. However he was extraordinarily calm and quiet about it. He said he felt simply indifferent; and we went on reading a novel ... There was a consultation on Monday morning and they decided to operate that afternoon at two. It was a mercy that it was all settled so quick. I read aloud to him till a few minutes before the doctors were ready and then left him for another long period of waiting. Everything went very well and since the operation his progress has been marvellous.[91]

The optimism was short-lived, however. After a few days Louise was called one morning by a nurse and went into Mandell's room to find blood pouring from his mouth. Doctors were called and the haemorrhaging was stopped. After that, he seemed to make some progress throughout the early days of the new year, but on the afternoon of Monday 7 January, he took a turn for the worse. Early the next morning another severe haemorrhage occurred; and during the following week Mandell grew weaker, struggling between life and death, only sometimes fully conscious. On Sunday 13 January, he asked for Louise.

'I need to say I leave everything to you', he said. 'You are me and I am you. You will know what to do.'

'God's will be done', Louise uttered. 'They will pray for you in all the Churches.'

'Let them pray whether I live or die', he said. 'I want to think what message I shall send to the Queen.' He paused. 'Tell her that I love her and obey her, and will always obey her in all things.' He paused again. 'Now go. I don't want to keep you.'

Mindful that the end was near, Louise and the children spent restless hours in quiet wait; and they were all gathered at his bedside the next morning, Monday 14 January, when the end now appeared inevitable. Percival, the chaplain, stood nearby reading softly from the last chapter of St John's Gospel. 'Simon Peter saith unto them, I go a fishing. They say unto him. We also go with thee. They went forth, and entered into a ship immediately; and that night they caught nothing ...' Percival's voice trailed off as he paused. 'Go on,' Mandell urged him weakly. Percival returned to the Gospel. 'But when the morning was now come, Jesus stood on the shore: but the disciples knew not that it was Jesus ...' Then Mandell gave out a low cry. 'God', he said. And after a long exhale his laboured breathing ceased and he died. Louise began praying out loud. Walter broke down and sobbed uncontrollably, more so than the other children who wept silently. Then the nurses motioned to Percival to take everyone away.

'The next days are very vague to me', Louise said. 'The children were very dear. I believe Gemma came and slept with me the first night.' [92] And for the next two days Bishop Creighton's body lay in an open coffin in the chapel of Fulham Palace, his face peaceful for the first time in weeks, his body dressed in a purple silk cassock. The body was watched over around the clock by some of his clergy and several of the All Saints sisters from St James's Home. Upon hearing the news, hundreds of people began coming to the chapel, to file solemnly past the coffin. 'He looked very peaceful and beautiful', Louise said, and Wilfrid von Glehn, her artist-nephew, is said to have captured this in the sketch he drew of Mandell in the coffin, a drawing Louise framed and treasured thereafter.[93] On Wednesday evening the body was transferred to St Paul's Cathedral where great ornate candlesticks, not used since the funeral of the Duke of Wellington, were placed around the draped casket in the choir, watched all night by clergy.

The funeral was held on Thursday 17 January, an elaborate service of great solemnity worthy of a statesman or prince. The Queen, the Prince and Princess of Wales and other members of the royal family were represented, even the German Emperor; present, also, were great politicians and intellectuals, along with civic, religious and business leaders; and there were people from all classes and faiths. Creighton's two favourite hymns were sung during the service, 'Rock of Ages', and 'O God, Our Help in Ages Past'. The Archbishop of Canterbury committed his body to the grave, in front of the chapel of the Order of the British Empire in the eastern end of the crypt of St Paul's. Not for 280 years had a Bishop of London been buried in Wren's great masterpiece.[94]

Immediately following Creighton's death there was a great sense of public loss expressed, a 'universal sorrow' that swept the nation the next few days among people, it was said, 'of all classes and all shades of thought'.[95] And over the succeeding weeks and months, many spoke out or wrote at length about him with extraordinary unanimity and warmth. Here was a man out of the rural north country, not born to privilege or fortune, who pursued an academic-religious career not entirely fashionable in those times, who rose to the pinnacle of fame in late Victorian society by wielding his urbane wit and intelligence to become a leading scholar-statesman. When he died, Creighton was ranked as one of England's great historians and a noted ecclesiastical administrator who was surely destined for still higher preferment had his life not been tragically cut short at age fifty-seven. He was the last great scholar to fill the see of London.[96]

In one of his last lectures, entitled 'Heroes', he said: 'Few men, I imagine, who become great started on their career with the intention of becoming so. That intention generally accompanies the unsuccessful. The secret of real greatness seems to be a happy knack of doing things as they come in your way; and they rarely present themselves in the form which careful preparation would enable you to deal with.'[97] Creighton certainly demonstrated that 'happy knack of doing things' as they came his way. His social brilliance and intellectual capacity suggest that he could have achieved eminence in any vocation or situation. He brought a keen intellect to bear on any matter that confronted him throughout his life, and while sometimes expressing his opinions too enigmatically—or even too caustically—for some, he always seemed to size up every situation accurately and succinctly. A grandson speculated once that some people probably mistrusted him because of this, but that they were mistaken in thinking him an iconoclast or revolutionary; on the whole he was content to accept the general ideas and values of his time, but was scornful and critical of exponents of them who saw less clearly than he did.[98] Creighton's temperament drove him harder and faster than most, and he died as much of exasperation as of malignancy, suggested his nephew, 'of attacking suet puddings with a rapier. It answered his moral being.'[99]

Mandell Creighton's life, in retrospect, was much like an anthem—it began slow, spare and deliberate and ended up in a broad, colourful crescendo; and in the silence that followed his passing, many of his generation, even those who never really knew him, sensed that someone very interesting and relevant had been taken from them. As one obituary summed up: 'It is certainly rare to find so much intellectual force and so high a standard of conduct combined in one man.'[100] In a letter to a friend, about a month after Creighton's death, Beatrice Webb wrote: 'the more I think of Dr Creighton's death, the greater seems the loss. Every day brings a new revelation of one's affections for him as a human being.'[101] Mary Ward likened the loss of her friend and counsellor to a kind of catastrophe, 'as of some great tree fallen'.[102] Lord Rosebery spoke of Creighton as 'perhaps the most alert and universal intelligence that existed in this island at the time of his death'.[103] Even the critic Lytton Strachey, certainly no friend of the Victorians, wrote that it was 'difficult to believe that a man of Creighton's attainments will ever again be Bishop of London'.[104] Creighton's long-time high church friend, Canon Henry Scott Holland of St Paul's, said that Creighton 'was the most interesting personality alive in London', and pointed out that 'those who had known him long all agree that the Bishop was one who changed singularly little. The Merton undergraduate was in all essentials the same man as Bishop of London.'[105] Which, of course, was so true. Creighton the student, the don, the vicar, the professor, the canon, the bishop, remained essentially the same in attitude and outlook over the decades. And, finally, Beatrice Webb penned in her diary the day Creighton died:

> Mandell Creighton—Bishop of London—dead. One of our best friends. When we returned to London this autumn we found him invalided. He had broken down on his holiday, and was by the doctor's orders confined to the house. Three or four times I went down to Fulham to see him either with Sidney or alone. He was singularly gentle and sympathetic: eager to talk: the same delightful combination of banter and deep philosophy: the strange enigmatic view of all things, whether of God or man. The very last time, in fact, just before Christmas, I had a long talk with him whilst the other guests were at tea. I told him our plan for reforming the Church: our idea of religion as mental hygiene, and the way in which we thought the High Church doctrine more consistent with it, than the Evangelical. To all of which he listened, and half seriously and half playfully agreed.[106]

From Windsor Castle the ailing Queen sent Louise a note expressing her 'deep and heartfelt sympathy' at the 'great loss'.[107] On the evening following the funeral, Bishop Davidson, then Bishop of Winchester, paid a call on Louise at Fulham to comfort her, and while there a telegram arrived for

Davidson stating that the Queen was seriously ill and not likely to recover. The message suggested that Davidson, one of her favourite prelates, leave immediately for Osborne.[108] A few days later, on 22 January, Queen Victoria passed away at Osborne, and with that came the end of an era. So it was that Creighton's life virtually spanned the reign of Victoria. He was born six years after she ascended to the throne and died eight days before her death. Creighton was not only 'Victorian' by disposition but by chronology as well.

The last public meeting of Mandell Creighton and Queen Victoria occurred a few months before at an impromptu anti-Boer demonstration at Windsor, and it was captured by the author Shane Leslie who, as a boy at Eton, recalled the event vividly. 'In the evening the whole school marched up to Windsor with torches, to serenade the old Queen', Leslie recalled years later in the middle of the Great War of 1914–18: 'We entered and sang under the royal windows. The curtains were drawn aside by the Hindu attendants, and we beheld the Queen with the cadaverous Bishop of London (Creighton) standing in the background. The hand of death was over both of them, and indeed they died within a few days of each other in the following January. For a few moments the sad, stolid face of Victoria looked out upon the children and the grandchildren of the Victorians'.[109] Mandell, a few days after this demonstration, wrote the following letter to his young nephew:

Fulham Palace
May 30, 1900

Dearest Basil,

I was at Windsor on Saturday and saw rather a nice form of rejoicing in the evening. The Volunteers of the town and all the Eton boys marched up to the Castle and made a torchlight procession round the Great Court. Then they formed in line, saluted the Queen with their torches, and sang 'God save the Queen'. It was very pretty as a sight. The Queen was very well and very cheery. She forgot to ask about you, which was quite wrong of her ...

Your loving uncle,
M. Londin.[110]

Basil, then fifteen years of age, was a schoolboy at Uppingham, where Cuthbert was a master. The bishop had helped to get the boy into the public school, and though Basil's grades were somewhat inadequate in the bishop's eyes, he was heartened by the boy's growing interest in literature and poetry. Basil loved his uncle, and a short time after his death he penned the following lines:

Sadly on the muddy road
Drops a weary heavy load.
All its dimpling puddles swim
With a slowly widening brim.
Earth must with a patient eye
Reflect the humours of the sky.
All the colours are subdued
To the heavens' sorrow-mood.
Not a branch or twig may stir
In the weeping, weeping air.
Even the wind must hold its breath
Taking on the hush of death.
All the earth's being is subdued
To the heavens' sorrow-mood.[111]

Dear Mrs Creighton

'Dear Mrs Creighton—Your letters always have a steadying power of comfort, which helps me.'

Sir Edward Grey to Louise Creighton [1]

Now, at the age of fifty, Louise commenced her years of widowhood. The death of Mandell left a huge chasm to traverse, but though the loss robbed her of her life's companion, upon whom she was so dependent, she continued on with remarkable resiliency, albeit surreal in the beginning, to live another thirty-five years of active and productive life. Indeed, it was in her widowhood in fact that she ultimately defined Louise Creighton as a public person.

Within days after Mandell's death Louise fell seriously ill. She sensed something was wrong upon returning from a service a St Paul's on 27 January. 'I felt ill', she recalled, 'and sat by the fire unable to eat any lunch. I felt worse every minute and finally went to bed.' [2] It was fourteen weeks before she got out of bed again. Part of her ailment proved to be a complicated case of appendicitis requiring an operation, but the overall exhaustion and trauma of the lengthy illness and ultimate death of Mandell was obviously a factor. During her protracted recovery Charles Longman, Mandell's friend and publisher, called upon her to inquire if she would consider writing her husband's biography. Without much thought of the arduous task ahead, she consented. Then she began to realise the amount of preparation that would be needed to complete a biography. Fortunately for Louise, however, Mandell's estate provided her with sufficient income to cover her material needs for the remainder of her life. Friends and family helped in alleviating some of the costs of educating Gemma and several of the other children. For extras she would need to supplement her income by her writing. [3]

In the meantime, Louise had to decide where to live. She had no wish to live in central London, but still wanted to remain near the city. While considering what to do in the days immediately following her husband's funeral, an invitation came with a solution. Being the wife of a bishop, she was granted a modestly priced crown apartment at Hampton Court, the palace built originally by Cardinal Wolsey in the sixteenth century and later added to by Christopher Wren. The offer was given under the privilege known as 'grace and favour', where life tenancy apartments were extended by the crown to widows and families of state dignitaries (such as bishops, senior military officers, statesmen and other important civil servants) in recognition for services rendered to the nation. It was the last apartment granted by Queen Victoria before her death.[4]

After her recovery she moved into an apartment, No. 6, formerly Suite 23 and known as the Duke of York's apartment. It had been previously occupied by Lady Georgiana Grey, whom Louise had known years before at Howick, in Northumberland. A spacious four-bedroom apartment, it was located on the ground floor of Wren's New Palace on the south-east corner overlooking the beautiful gardens. On the south side, which now parallels the River Thames, was the orangery. The only drawback Louise found was that the apartment was directly under the public galleries on the first floor, thus the noise of people walking about overhead all day long came to be annoying. Also, since there were several windows and a small door opening out along the garden, Louise was sometimes startled to see inquisitive tourists peering inside. Besides the large bedrooms, there was a dining-room, a library and a drawing-room. 'We used to love staying there as children,' a granddaughter recalls, 'exploring the gardens and the corridors and the palace.'[5] Louise wrote later:

> I cannot remember how the rooms at Hampton Court struck me at first, but I remember walking out in the garden and going as far I think as the river and how we all felt as if we were in a dream and could not realise that this strange and wonderful place was to be our home. We could just manage to get in to the Apartment if all were at home. Gemma slept with me and Mary, and she shared the slip of a room which opened out of my room to dress in. Beatrice and Lucia had two rooms opening into one another through the drawing-room. Then there was a large pannelled [sic] bedroom with two beds and a little dark room opening into a little central yard, and here the three boys could put up when they were at home.
>
> The drawing-room and dining-room were beautiful large rooms with pannelled dados and large windows with splendid oak shutters opening onto the great terrace. From the dining-room opened my sitting-room, a corner room; and it and my bedroom, and the neighbouring large bedroom were all beautifully pan-nelled and would have made a splendid suite if they could all have been used as sitting-rooms, opening onto the dining-room and drawing-room and the wide corridor which connected them. In this corridor we placed our oak book cases standing out like a college library, and with these and more oak book cases in the study and dining-room I managed to find room for all my books. It was

perhaps foolish to keep them all, but their mere backs seem like friendly faces, part of my life.[6]

At Hampton Court, Louise kept a cook, a housemaid, a parlourmaid, and 'a girl for the morning to clean boots and knives'. She was able to live comfortably. In the beginning, the four girls lived with Louise. Gemma, the youngest, seemed the spirited one, especially kind and sensitive. Louise enrolled her at a nearby day school for girls, Surbiton High School, and later Gemma went off to Lady Margaret Hall at Oxford in 1906.[7] After completing her education she worked as a secretary to Professor Gilbert Murray, and through the Murrays met the classical scholar Cyril Bailey, a fellow of Balliol. Gemma and Cyril were married in 1912.[8]

Beatrice and Lucia worked at various jobs in the London area. Beatrice was the most attractive of the girls but possessed a cool icy streak, according to her cousin Basil. She had settled into the formidable job of rent collecting in London, but after a few years of that felt her calling was more in the direction of collecting souls, so she decided to become a deaconess in the Church of England; in 1908 she enrolled in the Deaconess Institute in Portsmouth, subsequently going out to India in 1913 where she spent most of her adult life. Lucia, the most awkward of the children, had several secretarial jobs and also did some teaching of domestic science (cooking, sewing and general household management) in elementary schools. During the First World War she did volunteer work in Serbia as a nurse's helper and a Red Cross organiser. According to her mother, she never really found an occupation that suited her.[9] Mary, the most artistic and charismatic of the children, finished up at the Slade Art School and set up a painting studio, first in one of the empty rooms at Hampton Court and then in Chelsea, London's fashionable artists' district.[10]

Cuthbert, the most academically inclined, was an assistant master and later chaplain at Uppingham from 1899 until the First World War. He had taken holy orders in 1902, and married Margaret Bruce in 1913. Walter, the most handsome of the sons, continued his singing lessons on the Continent and in Britain during the early Hampton Court years, hoping to fashion some sort of career as an actor and a singer. Louise felt some disappointment over his career, writing to her sister Ida in 1906 that she 'always wished that he could have chosen any other line of life but this'.[11] And Oswin, the youngest and the gentlest, went up to Oxford in the autumn of 1901. After completing his studies at Keble College, he went on to theological college, receiving holy orders and serving from 1912 to 1914 as a member of the Archbishop's Mission to Western Canada in the province of Alberta.[12]

Once Louise had recovered from her long illness, she began collecting available private correspondence and documents relating to Creighton's life for the projected biography. Having access to a number of his speeches, lectures, sermons and essays of course helped, and she set about editing eight volumes of them, all published by Longmans. They were *The Church and The Nation: Charges and Addresses* (1901), *Historical Essays and Reviews* (1902), *Thoughts on Education: Speeches and Sermons* (1902), *University and Other Sermons* (1903), *Historical Lectures and Addresses* (1904), *The Mind of St Peter and Other Sermons* (1904), *The Claims of the Common Life: Sermons Preached in Merton College Chapel, 1871–1874* (1905) and *Counsels for the Young: Extracts from the Letters of Mandell Creighton* (1905). One other book, a collection of religious essays, was edited by J. H. Burns and entitled *Counsels for Church People* (1901).[13] It came out a few months after Creighton died and was a part of a series of devotional books written by such persons as Archbishop Temple and Canon Henry Scott Holland.

In Louise's mind, virtually everything her husband had ever said or written had to be recovered and published if possible. It became almost an obsession, as if she needed to prove he really had been a serious scholar and a spiritually-minded person. Thus, she drove herself to write his biography, not out of deep devotion to the memory of her husband—though she was certainly consumed with that—but because she felt he might be misunderstood by his contemporaries. Men of large reputation and complicated demeanour can often be misunderstood. In Creighton's case, he seemed especially vulnerable to confusion because of his donnish manner. What was happening was that Creighton often seemed to stand too rigid and high-minded in some things—like a moral lightning rod attracting sparks of wonderment from all corners—and too frivolous, paradoxical and enigmatic in others.

'Strange', seemed to be a frequent word used to describe Creighton. Edmund Gosse, a friend of twenty-six years, thought his 'character and temperament' were more often than not 'the subject of discussion' among those who knew him; that while at Oxford, Creighton was 'more frequently and freely discussed than any other Oxonian of his years'. Creighton, he maintained, 'was too strong a man to be universally approved of: the dull thought him paradoxical, the solemn thought him flippant; already there was a whisper abroad that he was "not a spiritually-minded man".' Gosse considered his friend 'spiritually-souled', and admitted that Creighton was 'one of the strangest and the most original' men of his era.[14]

George Prothero, his fellow historian and close friend, claimed that Creighton's 'love of paradox, a shrewdness which some mistook for cynicism … and occasional lapses into flippancy as a protest against cant or a refuge from boredom, sometimes conveyed the wrong impression, concealing the natural kindness, the wide sympathy, the deep inner seriousness of a man who was more highly appreciated the more fully he was known'.[15]

The poet Robert Bridges, a former student of Creighton at Oxford, thought he had 'a very strange mind' and that he doubted 'if any one quite understood him for he was evidently not a man to be classed: and an offhand classification would have done him great injustice'. Creighton was 'extremely reserved', Bridges thought, and suspected that 'no one liked him on first acquaintance'. Yet, he admitted that Creighton could win 'everybody's heart very soon' because of what he called 'great gifts' of 'sympathy, kindness and sociability'.[16]

Beatrice Webb also used the word 'strange' in describing Creighton. 'Strange person—my friend the Bishop', she wrote in her diary, 'a cynic, an admirable man of business, a staunch believer in the Church—possibly also a believer in religion as a necessary element in society.' She even went so far as to suggest that others who knew him rather well wondered about the depth of his spirituality: 'Is Dr Creighton a convinced Christian? was the question perpetually canvassed by his friends.' She went on to write:

> I always felt it impertinence for an agnostic to raise the question. His tolerance, his desire to find a common basis with all his friends, made him deliberately stow away his Christian assumptions when he talked with heretics. 'Let us find something on which we can agree, and argue on that basis', was always his attitude of mind. He realised that the ultimate convictions of serious-minded persons could not be altered by a conversation: that they were rooted in their experience of life, or in the constitution of their minds. He never, therefore, tried to convert: all he did was to endeavour to sympathise and to justify. Probably this uncommon willingness to accept any person's fundamental assumptions, as a basis for argument, was the root of the feeling of many persons that he was intellectually insincere. Personally, I believe he had a firm belief in the validity of the Christian faith, and in its ultimate victory over other forms of thought.[17]

Yet more surprising perhaps was the opinion held by Randall Davidson, who had known Creighton from undergraduate days at Oxford. While appreciating his intellectual gifts, Davidson once privately penned a severe assessment of Creighton, stating that many who knew him 'found it difficult not to believe him to be a cynic, and there were those who doubted his real hold upon the dogmatic side of Christianity'. This last judgment he reckoned was probably due to Creighton's 'endeavour, mistaken and unsuccessful as I think it was, to appear as a finished man of the world with social experience and social gifts, who could meet other men of the world on equal terms'.[18]

When Louise's massive two-volume *The Life and Letters of Mandell*

Creighton appeared in 1904, readers were surprised at how thorough, honest and perceptive the work was. Despite Lytton Strachey's contention that the Victorian art of biography had 'fallen on evil times' because of those 'two fat volumes, with which it is our custom to commemorate the dead', Louise's biography was a momentous exception.[19] It was universally hailed as a masterpiece. Henry Scott Holland wrote that Louise had convinced 'a doubtful world' puzzled by Creighton's personality that 'the chief note in his character was to be found in a deep and steady consistency of purpose: that his dominant interest was serious and ethical: and that his ideal of life lay in simplicity of moral aim'.[20] The historian John Figgis, one who had watched Creighton since the Cambridge years, described the biography as one of the six best in the English language.[21] Even Bishop Davidson had to admit that he had not 'discovered or appreciated ... the deepest and best of [Creighton's] qualities' until he read the biography. 'I know of no instance in which the publication of a public man's biography has so greatly raised him in the estimation of good and thoughtful people', he said.[22] This judgment has withstood the test of time.[23]

Louise's biography, along with all his published speeches, sermons, lectures, essays and personal letters, convinced the sceptical that Mandell Creighton was a deeper man than they had thought. His spirituality, they learned, was at heart Christocentric, more practical and ethical than theoretical and theological. And in his correspondence, especially those letters written to his nephews and nieces, there was poignant evidence of his simple and abiding faith. Organisations and doctrines, he thought, were only useful 'as they keep open the way to Jesus'.[24] He sailed blithely past those screaming sirens of the age—such as the muscular Christianity movement, the *Lux Mundi* group, the evangelicals, the social-Darwinians, the positivists and the socialists—with never a glance, holding his steady course. And his knowledge of history and its many lessons in human behaviour seemed to be the map from which he charted his course. He favoured tolerance over persecution, freedom over control, moderation over extremism, which explains why he preferred the Renaissance over the Reformation. He was more comfortable with Erasmus than Luther, Aeneas Sylvius than Savonarola, Wolsey than Cranmer.[25] Because he was an historian, Creighton brought to his administrative affairs a wisdom of human character. Because he was a manager of men, he brought to his historical writings a sense of practicality and reality. What Louise did was to go far in explaining the man she knew, but which society openly wondered about.

There were other lasting monuments to Creighton, besides the biography and his edited works, erected in the wake of his death. A month after Creighton died, a Bishop Creighton Memorial Committee was formed at

Mansion House in London with a view to commemorating his public services.[26] A number of Creighton's friends joined the committee and they soon established a memorial fund. This committee, along with Louise's personal efforts, led to several memorials. William Hamo Thorneycroft, for example, was commissioned to sculpt the large statue that stands, today still, on the south choir aisle of the main level in St Paul's Cathedral. The famed artist Hubert Herkomer was assigned to paint a portrait which was given to Fulham Palace; copies of this portrait and one by Harris Brown were later given to Merton and Emmanuel colleges, and to the palace at Peterborough. Harris Brown also designed the memorial slab over Creighton's grave in the crypt of St Paul's. Louise wanted it to resemble a Siena pavement with the outline of the bishop's figure in robe and mitre along with an inscription. (Unfortunately, today the grave and colourful memorial slab is covered by a long carpet extending from the base of the altar to the entrance to the chapel.) Louise later had a replica made of the memorial slab which now can be seen in the choir aisle of Peterborough Cathedral. Among other tributes were the creation of a Creighton Memorial Lectureship for the School of Historical Research at the University of London, the establishment of the Bishop Creighton Settlement House at Fulham, and the naming in his honour of the new village centre building in Embleton.

Louise developed very few close friends at Hampton Court, finding that she had little in common with most of the men and women residents, many of whom had been connected with either the army or navy. In the beginning she tried to elevate the level of residential social life, but found that her efforts went mostly for naught. 'I used to meditate on how we could be drawn into some common life' at Hampton Court, she recalled later, 'and I thought that the right kind of chaplain might have done something in that direction, but our chaplain ... was a queer nervous man with no initiative, and a little unimpressive wife. He did not like it when I got up a meeting for the Bishop of London's fund for the Rescue work, and after a time I gave up trying to do anything of the sort at the Palace.'[27]

At one time she tried to instigate a weekly Bible study session, but found she 'had to discourse all the time. I could not get any of them to say much if anything'.[28] On another occasion she ran a class for the maids in the palace, but, as she said, 'could get nothing out of them, and never knew whether they cared about it'.[29] Failing to inject any serious intellectual or religious life into palace residents, Louise fell back on an outside social activity that had worked elsewhere. Apparently her only real contribution to the common life of the palace was the weekly dances she arranged that were held in a large common room, known as the Oak Room because of its oak paneling and floor, which she found especially suitable for dancing. Louise even gave up her Broadwood cottage piano to the cause. 'So as my work outside increased,' she admitted, 'I gave up my efforts in the Palace, and felt that I at any rate could do nothing to create any kind of community feeling.'[30]

Regarding her outside work, Louise continued her association with the Mothers' Union and the Girls' Friendly Society. She also developed renewed interest in the Church Missionary Society and the Society for the Propagation of the Gospel in Foreign Parts, eventually becoming a member of its standing committee and serving on several subcommittees, such as mission work, medical relief and India. Her interest in mission work was prompted greatly by the fact that two of her children were in church service abroad: Oswin in Alberta, Canada, working among the Indians and Beatrice in India with the Anglo-Indians. 'On the India Committee,' Louise said, 'I learned to know something about our work in India and gained a great and lasting interest in India.'

Louise remained connected with the London Council for the Promotion of Public Morality, the Women's Diocesan Association, the Girls' Diocesan Association, the Rescue and Prevention Association, and the Central Council for Women's Church Work, of which she was vice-chairman for more than twenty years. She served on two Royal Commissions: the London University Commission in 1909 and the Venereal Disease Commission of 1913; she also sat on the Joint Committee of Insurance Commissioners in 1912, being the only woman appointed.[31] She remained active with the National Union of Women Workers, which subsequently changed its name to the National Council of Women, where she served a third time as president.

It was at the 1906 conference of the NUWW at Tunbridge Wells that Louise publicly declared her support of women's suffrage, much to the disgust of certain friends like Mary Ward.[32] It was a heroic act brought on by years of reflecting on her earlier argument against women voting in national elections. She apparently changed her opinion because—whether in the Conservative Primrose League or in the Women's Liberal Party Association—women were dramatically expanding their role in party politics. 'I came to see that if they insisted on doing this they had better have the responsibility of the vote. The wild performances of the Suffragettes also influenced me. I thought that they needed to be steadied by responsibility.'[33] Louise also claimed that her sympathy with the industrial women in the north had led her to see the need of the vote to protect their interests as wage earners.[34] At first, Louise said she feared that people might think that it had been her husband's influence on her that made her anti-suffrage, and that it was his death that left me free to declare my own opinion. However, no one ever said this publicly, and of course there was no truth in it. I certainly should not after he was a bishop or indeed at any time have taken up a line opposed to him in any public political action. But he always left me absolutely free to form and express my own opinions. We never liked to differ and would generally go on discussing a question till we came to an agreement. I do not think he was at all strongly opposed to female suffrage at any time.[35]

Concerning two of her closest friends, Kathleen Lyttelton and Mary Ward, Louise said she was happy to be in agreement with Kathleen, who had come over to the cause of women's suffrage even before she had. Regarding Mary, Louise wrote regretfully:

[She] and I had never agreed on religious questions; she, as I discovered over the suffrage question, really loved controversy and her spirit rose at the thought of a fight, whilst I always wanted peace, and loved discussion tho' not argument or controversy. I do not think that our differences on the suffrage question interfered at all with our friendship; it was too deeply rooted, but it was trying to be working in opposite directions, and it in time became rather a closed subject between us. She would always have been ready to argue about it and to try to convince me, but I did not care to go over the old ground again and again and preferred to try to keep off it.[36]

Despite some differing views, Louise and Kathleen had been kindred spirits since Cambridge days, largely because their married lives were so similar as Kathleen's husband, Arthur Lyttelton, was an academic clergyman.[37] Kathleen's death in January 1907 left a void in Louise's life. 'She and I felt alike on so many points especially in religious matters', Louise said. Then Mary Ward died in March 1920. All her old friends were passing away.

The question of women's ministry, not only in the Church of England but even beyond, became an area of some concern for Louise in her later years. She began to argue more forcefully for greater participation by women, for example, in missionary life. She attended several world missionary conferences, actually chairing the women's meetings at the Pan-Anglican Congress of 1908, and she was an active participant of the Edinburgh World Missionary Conference in 1910, often regarded as the beginning of modern ecumenism.[38] During the First World War she became a vocal advocate for the National Mission of Repentance and Hope as well as the Life and Liberty Movement, the latter urging increased self-government in the Church of England. With the Assembly (Powers) Act passed by Parliament in 1919, the first national Anglican assembly was created, and Louise became a charter member, serving from 1920 to 1930.[39]

Louise was emerging more than ever as a national figure in her own right due to these social and religious works, and her published writing also contributed to her prominence. She wrote a number of articles, among them 'The Employment of Educated Women', in the *Nineteenth Century* (November 1901) and 'Women's Settlements', *Nineteenth Century* (April 1908).[40] During her widowhood, Louise wrote thirteen books. 'I think my mind, such as it was, was a student's mind', she once said. 'I liked hunting up information and following out obscure points. If I had had the training, and the time and opportunity, I believe I should have loved to do research work.'[41] Of those thirteen books, three were historical textbooks similar to the ones she had written earlier: *Heroes of European History* (1909), *Tales of Old France* (1924), and *Heroes of French History* (1925). Five were books on various social-political issues, such as *The Economics of the Household: Six Lectures Given at the London School of Economics* (1907), *The Art of Living and Other Addresses to Girls* (1909), *Missions: Their Rise and Development* (1912), *The Social Disease and How to Fight It: A Rejoinder* (1914), an essay on venereal disease, and *The International Crisis: The Theory of the State. Lectures Delivered in February and March 1916* (1916). The four remaining works, the best of the lot, were biographical studies: *Some Famous Women* (1909), a series of brief biographical sketches of twelve women ranging from St Hilda and Joan, the Maid of Kent, to Florence Nighingale, Mary Somerville and Queen Victoria; *Life and Letters of Thomas Hodgkin* (1917), Creighton's fellow historian and old friend from Embleton days; *G. A. Selwyn, D.D.: Bishop of New Zealand and Lichfield* (1923); *Dorothy Grey: A Memoir* (privately printed, 1907); and *Letters of Oswin Creighton, C.F., 1883–1918* (1920).

Three of these books warrant special discussion. Her book on venereal disease was Louise Creighton's boldest literary effort ever and established her as a recognised Christian moderate feminist in the British women's movement of the time.[42] The eighty-seven page book, written as a response to another book by the feminist Christabel Pankhurst, evolved in part from her long interest in the 'purity' issue, but principally from her work on the venereal disease commission over the previous two years. In her book Louise argued that in order to eradicate venereal disease, a serious social problem of the day, prostitution had to be checked, particularly in urban areas where the two were inexorably linked. Louise agreed with most feminists that the issue of venereal disease and prostitution should be an essential ingredient of the women's movement, what she termed the demand for a 'purer social life'. And she accepted the idea that the issue was tied to women's suffrage. Where Louise disagreed with the secular feminists was over their heavy emphasis on a political solution. 'The enfranchisement of women will, it is hoped, lead to greater attention being given to many matters affecting our social conditions', she said. 'Legislation can do something ... But we shall be wrong if we trust too much to legislation.'[43]

Louise differed from mainstream feminists by casting the issue more in a religious and moral context. 'Those who want to work for purity must be careful about the purity of their own souls', she warned, something many feminists probably did not accept. 'Women's influence on public opinion is even more needed than women's influence on legislation in these matters', Louise said.[44] Throughout the book her chief concern was to downplay a 'spirit of antagonism' against men whose 'weakness and wrongdoing', she thought, were the cause of 'the degradation of numberless women, and the suffering and disease which follows'. There was no doubt in her mind that such 'evils' would be remedied if the 'double standard which exacts purity for women and condones incontinence in men were abolished'. But she also admitted that 'chastity is more difficult for men than for women'.[45] Ultimately, she was sure that denominational religions had to do more in the battle against venereal disease and prostitution. 'It is a fight in which the Church has never really taken its full share', she lamented. Moreover, women must use their influence within the churches to fight for a purer society. 'If women are condemned to degradation because of the unchastity of men', she stated, then the same 'sin condemns men to degradation'. Women, she claimed, must 'struggle not only for the purity of women, but for the purity of men, and in this struggle they have not got to fight against men but win more men to fight with them'.[46]

Many within the women's movement by and large ignored Louise's argument, presumably because it centred more on religious morality rather than political rights. Undoubtedly many men would have disagreed with Louise's contention for gender reasons. Eric Gill, the noted Roman Catholic artist and controversial social philosopher, for instance, took particular offence at Louise's book, regarding it largely as an attack on males. A pity that he did not even bother to read it. In an unsolicited twenty-four-page letter to Louise, he wrote of seeing her little volume at a bookshop. 'I merely picked it up for five minutes', he stated, '. . . but that was sufficient for me to discover that it contained little I did not know and that it was badly conceived and not worth buying'.[47]

From there he launched into a long diatribe against Louise's contention that there was a 'double standard' when it came to judging the morals of men and women. Gill argued that women had to assume their share of responsibility; he offered some views on the problems of 'the degraded state' of existence under which many men and women were living in Britain, stating that 'poverty is not necessarily unhealthy. It is the utter degradation of modern life—particularly town life—and it is against this degradation that we have all of us, both men and women, to rebel'.[48] Summing up his lengthy letter, he told Louise that prostitution could not be considered apart from fornication, and that fornication was as much a habit of women as men; and therefore 'prostitution is not to be considered as a thing for which men are alone responsible [and] any attempt to eradicate or diminish prostitution must be preceded by a discovery of the cause which induce some women to ask money for an act which most are content to commit for nothing'. He then suggested four causes of women engaging in prostitution: sexual appetite, surplus of women over men, economic stress and the atrophy of religion. 'It is against these that your campaign must be directed', he declared. 'Any campaign against fornication or any other sin is *primarily* the affair of the church (in the confessional and in the school), and *secondly*, it is the affair of the parent. It is not at all the affair of the independent lay person except in the case of his or her own children. Finally, the natural and eternal and desirable antagonism between men and women must be taken into account and not glossed over.'[49]

Louise surely must have replied to Gill's epistle with a letter of her own, though there is no evidence of one. If she did, her letter would have pointed out to Gill, had he read her book entirely, that she had affirmed much of what he wrote.

The other two volumes dealt with painful tragedies. The memoir on Lady Dorothy Grey, formerly Dorothy Widdrington, was written after her tragic death in 1906. She was the wife of Sir Edward, and while Mandell had probably known her best in the Northumberland days, Louise came to renew the friendship with both Dorothy and Sir Edward after Mandell died. She found herself drawn close to Dorothy. The Greys had even extended to Louise a great kindness by lending, every year since 1902, their fishing cottage at Itchen Abbas in rural Hampshire about five miles above Winchester. Sir Edward was an avid fly-fisherman who found great solace in fishing the Itchen and other rivers in England and Scotland. Louise said that spending several weeks each autumn at the cottage 'never failed to refresh me, and to help me to find peace for myself'. Indeed it was at Itchen Abbas, on 3 September 1910, that Louise, sitting under the lime trees near the meadow with the murmur of the stream below and the air full of song birds, decided to write her autobiography.[50] Itchen Abbas had become a special place for Louise and it forged a powerful bond between her and the Greys.

In early February 1906, Dorothy was killed in a carriage accident. She had left the grounds of Fallodon Hall, the Grey's estate, and was driving by herself along a narrow Northumberland lane when the horse shied, throwing her out and onto her head. She never recovered consciousness and died a few days later. Louise learnt of the accident in London.

It was on February 2nd that I read in the newspaper that Dorothy Grey had been thrown out of her carriage about three miles from Fallodon and was lying in a cottage near by unconscious. Only a few days before she had driven me out in that high dogcart [51] with a swift poney [sic] which she seemed only just able to manage. I remember that it kicked up a lot of mud into her face and she could not find a handkerchief to wipe it off and borrowed mine. I hoped the account might be exaggerated, and I telegraphed at once for news and got the answer that she was still unconscious. I spent days of sickening anxiety. On Saturday came a telegram saying there was no hope, and another on Sunday saying that she was dead. [52]

In a long letter to her son Oswin in Canada, Louise explained her deep sorrow at losing her friend. [53]

I don't know whether you have any idea what a grief this is to me personally. She was quite different from other friends and filled a place that no one else can fill. She had been so extra-ordinarily kind and thoughtful to me during these last years. However, it was and is impossible for me to think of my own sorrow beside his [Sir Edward Grey]. I had a great fear at first that I might lose him too as a friend, for one can never tell how people will take a great sorrow, and he might have wished to shut himself off from old friends and old associations. So it was a great comfort to me to get a letter from him on Tuesday asking me to meet him at Darlington for the funeral on Wednesday and go back with him to Fallodon.

There would have been no time for me to get to Darlington on Wednesday morning and I telegraphed to the Peases that I would go to them that night. I had something that I ought to do in London that afternoon if possible, so I went first to my horrid meeting and then caught a 5.30 train at King's Cross and got to the Peases soon after eleven. The next morning Ella [Pease] and I went together to Darlington. We joined the special train that was bringing them from Fallodon at Newcastle and Edward sent for us to his saloon [car]. He was with Alice Graves and Constance Herbert. [54] There was also there Mr McGonigle, the clergyman at the little village where the accident took place. Dorothy had liked him very much.

Presently, Edward came and sat beside me and talked a great deal about her. He was absolutely natural and simple. It had been her own special wish to be cremated, expressed long ago, and he was glad to be carrying out her wish. I had never been at a cremation and felt rather a dread of it, but it was all very nice. The cemetery at Darlington is right out of the town amongst the fields, and it was a beautiful sunny day, with the snowdrops coming up in the grass. First we had a bit of the service in the little bare cemetery chapel; there were very few people there, a few servants and not more than six intimate friends besides ourselves and, of course, a few onlookers and loafers ... Then we followed the coffin on a bier a long way through the cemetery to the corner where the crematorium stands, and there we had the rest of the service, and the coffin was just slid away through some curtains, when the words committing it 'to be consumed' came; and then we all came away, and came back as we had come leaving Ella at Darlington and Constance Herbert at the Widdrington's station. Since then Alice, Edward and I have been living quietly here [at Fallodon].

It is a very wonderful time because he is so unlike anyone I have ever known in a great sorrow; there is no repining, no murmuring. He loved to talk about her and go over again all the memory of their past happiness. It has been a wonderful married happiness and I think that he is going to build on its memory a splendid life of service. He began his work again the day after the funeral, and on Sunday goes back to London to the Foreign Office. I stay here till then.[55]

Within a few days Louise had come up with the idea of writing a memoir of Dorothy. She spoke to Sir Edward about it and after some thought he agreed, writing to Louise: 'If a memoir is done at all I should like it to be done by you, but just now I am shrinking from the thought of having any of her letters published. I shall have to wait before I tell you.'[56] In time, he gave his permission to proceed on the basis that the memoir would be privately printed.[57] The *Memoir* as it turned out was a handsome, ivory-coloured volume on quality paper with an assortment of fine photographs of Dorothy and the special places that she held dear—the Hampshire cottage, Fallodon Hall, the rose garden and the new pond at Fallodon.[58] Louise's skill at writing honest biography, sensitive but not sentimental, was amply displayed as she wove a sparse narrative among excerpts of letters to and from Dorothy. Edward liked the *Memoir*, and said that he continued to find comfort in its pages, writing almost a decade later to Louise: 'Every time I look into the *Memoir* I am more and more grateful to you for having done it and am more and more impressed by the excellent way it is done. It is full of right things well said by you and the letters of Dorothy are so well selected. So are the quotations from the *Prelude* at the head of each chapter. So once more I want to say "Thank you".'[59]

During the succeeding years, Louise and Sir Edward carried on an active correspondence, she often visiting him at Fallodon in the summers or lunching with him in London. 'I think he liked to have me near to talk with as he went through deep waters, for he realised that I had gone through them too', she said.[60] Knowing how much Louise loved the his fishing cottage, Grey continued to offer it to her every year and she would usually spend a few weeks every August or September there communing with nature, either with some of her children or alone writing her own memoir. She wrote to one of her sisters relating that, 'Sir Edward Grey is always much on my mind and whenever I can I go to him and this has really made me see less of other people. It is a great thing to be able to be even of a little use to him, and it has helped me too. In a way their marriage was so like ours that I can speak more freely to him than anyone.' 61 Regarding their correspondence, the only letters that have survived, apparently, are Sir Edward's, and they exhibit a strong platonic friendship. He always began each with sentences like 'Dear Mrs Creighton—Your letters always have a steadying power of comfort, which helps me'; or 'Dear Mrs Creighton—There will be great difficulty about giving time to the Suffrage Bill this summer'; or, as on 9 August 1914 just after the Great War commenced: 'Dear Mrs Creighton—I found some weeks ago those hedges [at the cottage] had been cut down and grieved over it. But nothing matters now except this awful war.' 62 It is safe to say that he looked upon her as a kind aunt, and she felt herself to be a caring sister. As a member of the Creighton family put it: 'The bond that united them was the loss of their married partners and the memories which they shared.' 63

In 1916, during the middle of the Great War, Grey resigned from the government as Foreign Secretary, a post he had held since his wife's death. He was going blind, and shortly after he left tragedy struck. In May 1917 Fallodon Hall burnt to the ground. It was subsequently rebuilt, leaving off the upper floor. In 1922, much to the surprise of Louise, Grey married Pamela Glenconner, daughter of the Hon. Percy Wyndham, and widow of Edward Tennant, 1st Baron Glenconner. Then further tragedies: the Hampshire fishing cottage burnt down a year later, never to be rebuilt; then Pamela suddenly died in 1926, ending his brief second marriage. When Grey married Pamela, Louise's feelings for him may have cooled, though they continued to remain good friends. She admitted that the second marriage 'made a difference as there remained so little that he could need from me'. Louise wrote:

> To me Itchen Abbas was always full both of Dorothy and Edward and I loved it. My last visit there was just after the war broke out in August 1914. I meant to stay there but after a few days I felt the quiet and peace and being so out of the way of news were impossible and I never went there again. Later I never felt as if I could have gone there with Pamela, and I don't think he ever did; certainly he never stayed there with her. It seemed quite a right end when one night the cottage was burnt down without anyone seeing it. The woman who went down in the morning found nothing left. Some years later when I was visiting Laura Ridding, she drove me there and I went down the avenue and there was no sign of the Cottage but the chimney of the old stove standing up amongst some straggling remnants of the old flowers in the garden. I went down to the lasher and saw the last of the rushing Itchen, and that was the end of a place that had meant so much to me and done so much for me.64

Around 1932, shortly before he died, Grey wrote to Louise saying that he had intended to leave her a legacy, but thought he should give her the money then and there. He sent a cheque for £1000. 'He did not say why he gave it to me,' Louise said, 'but I suppose it was in some sense a recognition of the time spent on the memoir.' [65]

It was immediately after the First World War that Louise published the moving war letters of Oswin. All three of the Creighton sons served in the British army with distinction. Cuthbert became a chaplain, rising to the rank of captain. Walter served in the signal corps on the Western Front, was twice mentioned in dispatches, and received the Military Cross for valour. And Oswin returned from Canada and served as a chaplain, first at Gallipoli in 1915 and then in France after 1916. He wrote a small book, *With the Twenty-Ninth Division in Gallipoli* (1916). On 9 April 1918, roughly seven months before the armistice, Oswin's unit, the 3rd Artillery Division, was located just south of Arras. Reports arrived that a new German advance against the Allied lines in his sector was commencing. The 3rd Division was called to meet the assault, and Oswin volunteered to assist the dead and dying as the action began. There was general confusion, and a gunner reported seeing young Creighton 'dashing about in the same cheery manner as ever, as if nothing unusual were happening'. He had just gone up to a battery position, had greeted the men in his usual pleasant fashion, it was said, and as he was going into a hut, an enemy shell burst at the door, instantly killing Oswin and three of his companions.[66] Louise never got over this loss. Her volume, *Letters of Oswin Creighton, C.F., 1883–1918*, was published in 1920, and thereafter she seldom mentioned the tragedy. She never even referred to Oswin's death in her memoir and barely mentioned the war. After the war Louise seemed to find it difficult to maintain her connections with some of her German relatives, with the exception of her sisters Sophie and Ida and their families. While attending a conference of the World Alliance for Promoting Friendship between churches near Rotterdam shortly after the war, she wrote that the first time she heard German spoken outside her bedroom window at the hotel, it gave her 'a strange shock, almost a feeling of repulsion'.[67] Some of the von Glehns, as other families in Britain of German ancestry, altered their name as a result of the bitter experience of the war, dropping the 'von'. In the case of the Louise's relatives, the name was changed by two or three of her brothers to de Glehn, or later, simply Glehn. Wilfrid von Glehn, the son of Louise's brother Alick and a noted British portrait painter and close friend of John Singer Sargent, changed his name to de Glehn in May of 1917 while serving with the Artists' Rifles on the Italian front.[68]

In the years following the war, Louise came to be regarded as a strong but sensible voice for church reform in Britain. When compared with more radical church feminists of the day, such as Maude Royden the passionate preacher with whom she worked on occasion, Louise was a moderate on women's rights—a person who tried to apply reason over rhetoric to the critical issues.[69] When the controversy erupted over the question of priesthood for women in the Anglican Church, Louise worked to avoid the polarised positions that raged between liberal feminists and the more conservative. In an article for the *Guardian* in 1917 she contended that the move towards ordination of women should be approached with caution; that to accept it then 'would erect a hopeless barrier between the Church of England and the Roman Catholic and Orthodox Churches, and in such a matter it was essential that the whole Catholic Church should move together'.[70] She continued to have 'a sort of instinctive objection to women priests', she said a few years later, admitting, however, that it was probably just based on nothing more than natural 'prejudice'.[71] Yet the year before, during the 1916 National Mission when questions were being raised about women in the 'ministry of the word', that is, women preaching, Louise gave her support, and on two occasions, spoke her views in church—from the pulpit.[72]

When the Lambeth Conference of 1920 established certain restrictions against women's ministry Louise reacted with some disappointment.[73] She also supported an unsuccessful effort to remove the word 'obey' from the Anglican marriage service during discussion in the House of Laity on Prayer Book revision at the first Church Assembly.[74] Her general view on the role of women in the church centred on the fact that, if the bishops were expecting more and more from women, then women ought to be 'really given more responsibility'. In short, she felt the work being given to women in the church was 'not of a kind to attract the best brains amongst women'.[75]

A Sincere Fine Old Thing

'Widow Creighton ... I found her easy enough; a sincere fine old thing, her face emerging out of a mist of flesh, and looking infinitely seared and worn like an immensely old sun shining through the mist.'

Virginia Woolf about Louise Creighton [1]

Infirmity began to take its toll on Louise Creighton in the late 1920s, forcing her to abandon most of her public activities. In October 1927, she decided to give up her Hampton Court apartment and move to Oxford where she would be closer to her daughter Gemma and her family. She had lived at Hampton Court longer than she had ever lived anywhere else, but Oxford was the first home of her married life, a place where a young don first inquired about the young girl who had the courage to wear a yellow scarf. Gemma, her husband and their four children lived at a house called King's Mound in Mansfield Road. She stayed a short while with them until acquiring a comfortable, two-story brick house at 5 South Parks Road, about a hundred yards away. It was the former home of her friends from early Oxford days, Bertha and Arthur Johnson. Both had recently died and the house fell vacant at a convenient time. Louise brought along from Hampton Court her long-time cook, Louie, a countrywoman from Surrey, who became her close companion and nurse during her final years. Louise also hired a parlourmaid named Bertha to assist her in household duties.

Frail in body, her mind nevertheless remained sharp. Her final literary effort was her autobiography, a project begun one sunny September day at the Greys' Hampshire cottage back in 1910, and continued over the next fourteen years in on-again, off-again fashion. The autobiography ended up as a 433 page manuscript, written in a firm hand with an ink pen, virtually straight off with only few marginal notes and crossed out words here and there. Her last entry was penned in 1934.

Louise, while at Oxford, served on the governing board of Lady Margaret Hall, often inviting both dons and students to her house for meals. She enjoyed people, and especially looked forward to having students about her. Gemma's children recall escorting her on visits around the town and, as she grew lame and unable to walk long distances, they would push her in a Bath chair across the Parks so that she could participate in council meetings at Lady Margaret Hall, or to attend services at St Mary's. Louise became friends with the vicars of the university church and, according to her grandchildren, did not hesitate to criticise their sermons. In late 1931 she wrote: 'Now in my old age, the feeling that there is nothing for me to do and that I am no longer wanted is often hard to bear. I do not mean that my children make me feel that. I can never be thankful enough for their love and goodness to me.'[2]

Towards the end, Louise suffered two strokes and became bedridden; a resident nurse had to be employed to care for her. Gemma and other family members visited Louise often, checking to see how she was faring. Then, on Wednesday, 15 April 1936, Louise Creighton died peacefully at her home. In accordance with her wishes, her body was cremated, and, following a simple funeral service at St Paul's Cathedral on Saturday, 18 April, her ashes were buried in the same grave of her husband.[3]

In *The Times* a lengthy obituary opened with the words: 'Mrs Creighton, who died yesterday at her home in Oxford at the age of eighty-five, was a woman of strong personality and intellectual gifts. She was the widow and the biographer of Mandell Creighton, Bishop of London, and she herself wrote historical books; but her chief activities were concerned with Church work at home and overseas, in which she rendered long and valuable service.' It concluded:

> But a mere list of activities does not reveal a character or personality, and in Mrs Creighton's case these are not easy to describe. Her whole mind was set upon righteousness. Downright in manner and speech, with small regard for the graces and little diplomacies of life, she appeared at times uncompromising and even formidable. But to those who had eyes to see, behind all this lay unflinching sincerity and a deep fund of sympathy, not the least for young people. With characteristic honesty she was once heard to say to a friend of widely differing character from her own, 'As the years go on, I must grow gentler and you must grow sterner'.[4]

On the occasion of a portrait, painted by artist Glyn Philpot, being presented to her by her old friend Mary Ward at a gathering of friends in the Guard Room of Lambeth Palace, another friend recalled that, having 'got behind the stern look which some people found so formidable', she had the good fortune to see 'kindness behind the uncompromising manner' of Louise Creighton. 'Certainly she did not suffer fools gladly, but I remember complaining to her ... when she was presented with her portrait, that the artist had left out the twinkle.'[5] Even Virginia Woolf extended an oblique compliment, once meeting Louise at some event in the summer of 1918: 'I was pitched strangely enough into the arms of Widow Creighton who remembered me ... I found her easy enough; a sincere fine old thing, her face emerging out of a mist of flesh, and looking infinitely seared and worn like an immensely old sun shining through the mist.'[6]

Regarding the Creighton children, Cuthbert became headmaster of the King's School, Worcester, in 1919 and retired in 1936; he returned to King's for a time as chaplain and honorary headmaster during the early years of the Second World War. He and his wife, Margaret, had two sons, Thomas and Hugh. Margaret died after a stillborn birth, in 1923, and Cuthbert died in 1963.[7]

Walter continued his musical career after the First World War, eventually becoming a producer of pageants and films; he has been credited with the successful production of the Wembley Tattoo, among other events. He worked with or was on close terms with a number of notable British actors, artists and musicians, such as the composer Roger Quilter. Quilter dedicated seven of his compositions to Walter, one a choral piece *Non Nobis, Domine* that was introduced at the 1934 'Pageant of Parliament' which Walter produced.[8] During the Second World War, Walter served in several home front services, once as a personnel officer for a factory in Birmingham and later as a volunteer Red Cross organiser. He was a generous man, particularly kind to his friends and family; he never married and died in 1958.[9]

Beatrice, after becoming an Anglican deaconess, served in India from 1913 to 1947, only returning to England periodically for holidays. She founded St Faith's House in Madras, a residence for religious women who worked among the Anglo-Indians. A co-worker in India years later recalled that Beatrice 'had a strong will and personality', writing that the then Bishop of Madras, who was known for his strong personality too, used to profess himself in awe of the 'Deaconess Creighton'. She obviously possessed much of her mother's temperament. Beatrice retired to England during India's independence movement, and lived in Cambridge where she died in 1953.[10]

Lucia never married and spent her adult life in various jobs and social work. She died in 1947. Mary enjoyed a career as a painter; she married Arthur McDowall, writer and fellow of All Souls and a Thomas Hardy scholar. They had no children; he died in 1933 and she in 1951. Gemma and Cyril Bailey had four children, Mary, John, Rachel and Susan. Gemma died in 1959, a year after her husband.[11]

Polly Creighton, Mandell's sister, never married and spent her entire adult life in Carlisle engaged in civic and private philanthropy. She was especially interested in the education of children—no doubt because it had been one of the major omissions in her life—and in 1920 the Denton Holme School in the city was renamed 'Creighton School' in tribute to her. In 1927, she was awarded the freedom of the city, the first woman to be so honoured.[12] She died in 1944.

Of the Carlisle Creightons, Mandell's nieces and nephews, Robert, the eldest, never married and died in 1948; Ella married F. W. Halton, had five children and died in 1950; Winifred married P. J. Dormehl, had five children and died in 1967; Gilbert died of appendicitis in 1892; Harold married Flora Brown, had no children and died in 1923; Basil married Ursula Newton and had one child; he later married Frances Alderson, and he died in 1989 at the age of 104; Marjorie never married and became a Roman Catholic nun; she died in 1946.[13]

Basil Creighton, who stood in awe of his aunt, had long harboured some resentment toward Louise for what he thought were her feelings that Mandell Creighton was a changeling, that the Carlisle Creightons were to some degree backward and uncouth. In 1964, however, he happened by chance to read her unpublished memoir and wrote to one of the sons of his cousin Cuthbert Creighton: 'Louise's judgments were always sincere and never petty or malicious. She was truly a great woman.'[14]

Louise Creighton was indeed a great woman who achieved a successful public career in an era when women were necessarily confined to the private sphere.[15] Her non-historical writings and her recorded speeches, particularly those at church congresses and various conferences of the NUWW, argued consistently for women to be educated, professional and compensated—not only within the Church of England, but beyond. Louise chaired a session on 'The Training and Payment of Women Church Workers' at a 1899 church congress, for example, and openly chastised church leaders for taking advantage of women volunteers and for not supporting the women's cause. That same year she concluded her address to the International Congress of Women by pointing out that because a woman was fitted to make her own living did not make her unfit to be 'the very best wife and mother possible'. Two years later at an NUWW conference she stated flatly that improved education for women now prepared them to claim 'as much right as men to lead their own lives and to develop to the full their own capacities and to cease therefore to be mere appendages of men'.[16]

In some respects, one might argue, Louise's contributions equal those of Mandell because the things she wrote about and the things that she did have a wider relevancy today. As an author she wrote practical books to inform the uninformed, to educate a broad readership; as a religious worker, she advanced a strong concern for women in the church and in society at large; and she articulated the need to blend moral responsibilities with pragmatic social programmes. Indeed, she offered a balanced voice for women, but unlike other 'feminists' of her generation who also sought goals of equality, independence and individuality, she viewed the role of women within the context of both organised religion and the traditional family; and she framed these concepts within a world-view, a universal vision based on a realistic understanding of the human condition—a perspective that is still timely. In a way she appeared to became more progressive as she grew older, yet she could never quite let go of her Victorian outlook.

In a speech on 'Heroes' given in November 1898, Mandell Creighton said that one often learns more from the contemplation of a person's feelings than from the recognition of merits, adding that 'I do not think that we are acting ungenerously to great men of the past if we attempt to take into account not merely their definite achievements, but their influence on the conscience of their time.' [17] So it was with both Mandell and Louise Creighton. But beyond all this, the underlying purpose of this dual biography has been to explain two people, more interesting perhaps for who they were than for what they did.

Notes

Chapter 1: Who is That Girl?

1. Louise Creighton, *Life and Letters of Mandell Creighton*, 2 vols (1904), i, p. 77.
2. John Ruskin (1819–1900), the critic who dominated the middle and late Victorian world of artistic tastes, was the Slade Professor of Art at this time.
3. William Morris (1834–1896), artist, writer, printer and socialist, was one of the leaders of Victorian art and taste. Sir Edward Burne-Jones (1833–1898), painter and decorator, was a Pre-Raphaelite.
4. Louise Creighton, *Memoir of a Victorian Woman: Reflections of Louise Creighton, 1850–1936*, ed. James Thayne Covert (1994), p. 33.
5. Louise Creighton, *Memoir*, p. 36.
6. See John Sutherland, *Mrs Humphry Ward: Eminent Victorian, Pre-Eminent Edwardian* (1991), pp. 48–58.
7. Ibid.
8. Louise Creighton, *Memoir*, p. 34.
9. Ibid.
10. Walter H. Pater (1839–1894), the noted essayist and critic, was a fellow of Brasenose College.
11. Sutherland, *Mrs Humphry Ward*, p. 52.
12. Louise Creighton *Memoir*, p. 36.
13. Ibid.

Chapter 2: The Nicest Man I Have Met

1. Louise Creighton, *Memoir of a Victorian Woman: Reflections of Louise Creighton, 1850–1936*, ed. James Thayne Covert (1994), p. 37.
2. Sutherland, *Mrs Humphry Ward: Eminent Victorian, Pre-Eminent Edwardian* (1991), p. 52.
3. Louise Creighton, *Memoir*, p. 38.
4. Sutherland, *Mrs Humphry Ward*, p. 53.
5. Louise Creighton, *Memoir*, p. 37.
6. Sutherland, *Mrs Humphry Ward*, p. 53. Pater and his sister, Clara, were both often described as a bit odd.
7. Louise Creighton, *Memoir*, p. 38.
8. Robert Brodie later became headmaster of Whitgift School, Croydon. *Alumni Oxonienses*, iii, p. 528.

9. Ibid.

10. Henry Parry Liddon (1829–1890), Anglican theologian who was a strong Puseyite advocate of the Tractarians. At Oxford, he served as vice president of St Edmund Hall for a time and was professor of exegesis.

11. Benjamin Jowett (1817–1893), Regius Professor of Greek, was elected master of Balliol College in 1870 and served as vice chancellor of the university from 1882 to 1886.

12. Thomas Henry Huxley (1825–1895), biologist and ardent exponent of Darwinism.

13. Louise Creighton, *Memoir*, pp. 37–38. The full text of the letter can be found in the original memoir manuscript, Creighton Family Papers.

14. Louise Creighton, *Memoir*, pp. 38–39.

15. Louise writes guildhall, but Town Hall is more likely. Ibid., p. 39.

16. Ibid.

17. Ibid.

18. J. R. Green to Louise von Glehn (6 March 1871), Bodleian Library, MS eng. lett. e. 48. fos 70–83; also, J. R. Green, *Letters of John Richard Green, 1837–1883*, ed. Leslie Stephen (1901), p. 287.

19. Louise Creighton, *Memoir*, pp. 13, 16, 40.

20. Ibid., p. 39.

21. Besides the random physical descriptions of Creighton in Louise's biography and her memoir, see Rudolph de Cordova, 'Bishop of London', *Strand Magazine* (November 1899), pp. 526–35, and Edmond Gosse, 'Mandell Creighton, Bishop of London', *Atlantic Monthly* (May 1901), pp. 677–89.

22. Louise Creighton, *Memoir*, p. 39.

23. W. G. Fallows, *Mandell Creighton and the English Church* (1964), p. 1.

24. Louise Creighton, *Memoir*, p. 39.

25. Ibid., p. 41.

26. Louise Creighton, *Life and Letters of Mandell Creighton*, 2 vols (1904), i, p. 77–78.

27. Ibid.

28. Louise Creighton, *Memoir*, p. 41.

29. Ibid.

30. Sutherland, *Mrs Humphry Ward*, p. 55.

31. Louise Creighton, *Memoir*, pp. 40, 42.

32. All of the following excerpts come from Louise Creighton, *Life and Letters*, i, pp. 90–126.

33. Owen Chadwick, *Creighton on Luther: An Inaugural Lecture* (1959), p. 22.

34. Louise Creighton, *Memoir*, p. 42.

35. Creighton Family Papers, MS letter, Louise von Glehn to Agnes von Glehn, 13 July 1871.

36. Louise Creighton, *Memoir*, pp. 42–43, 80.

37. In the words of one nephew, 'Louise von Glehn, coming ... from her southern, suburban and semi-continental background, was shocked to find herself in the North country, where people did not speak exactly as she did, and so she took Mandell to be a changeling or a being of another clay', adding that to the

Carlisle Creightons, Mandell 'was the kind and indulgent uncle, all the more because we were very English, and in tune with his own inheritance. The von Glehn strain was alien.' MS letter, Basil Creighton to author, 10 September 1965.

38. Louise Creighton, *Memoir*, p. 44.

39. Ibid., p. 42.

40. Ibid., pp. 42–43.

41. Ibid.

42. Ibid., pp. 44.

43. Louise Creighton, *Life and Letters*, i, p. 83.

44. Ibid., pp. 83–84.

45. Ibid., p. 85.

46. Louise Creighton, *Memoir*, p. 40.

47. Ibid.

48. Ibid.

49. Ibid., p. 41.

50. Louise Creighton, *Life and Letters*, i, p. 86.

51. Ibid., p. 87.

52. Louise Creighton, *Memoir*, p. 44.

53. Those who know Oxford suggest that Louise's description of the house being on 'St Giles Road East' could not accurate. It was probably in the present-day Banbury Road. Louise Creighton, *Life and Letters*, i, p. 127.

54. Louise Creighton, *Life and Letters*, i, p. 88.

55. Louise Creighton, *Memoir*, p. 44. Louise refers to Woollams and Co., one of the most notable high-quality handprinted wallpaper manufacturers in England. William Woollams (1782–1840) established the London firm in 1807, and it was carried on by his sons, William and Henry. The company specialised in high quality handprinted wallpaper. Ibid., p. 158.

56. Ibid., pp. 44–45.

57. Louise Creighton, *Life and Letters*, i, p. 88.

Chapter 3: A Most Promising Scholar

1. Creighton Family Papers. Durham Grammar School 'Report of Progress and Conduct', 29 September 1862.

2. Kenneth Smith, *Carlisle* (1969), pp. 5–56. For a pictorial history of Carlisle since the early nineteenth-century, see Laurie Kemp and Jim Templeton, *175 Years of Carlisle* (1990).

3. See Creighton's own account of his city and county in Mandell Creighton, *Carlisle* (1889), and 'Cumberland' in Mandell Creighton, *The Story of Some English Shires* (1897), chapter 4, pp. 109–22.

4. Ibid., pp. 115, 122.

5. Hawthorne, the American author, was US consul at Liverpool. Nathaniel Hawthorne, *The English Note-Books*, ed. Randall Stewart (1962), p. 498.

6. See A. Hamilton Thompson, 'The Life and Work of Mandell Creighton: An

Address Delivered in Carlisle Cathedral on the Occasion of the Creighton Centenary, Sunday, 4th July 1943' (1943); Ernest Williams, 'Mandell Creighton: Modern Carlisle's Greatest Son', *Carlisle Journal* (1933).

7. Creighton Family Papers, MS letter, Mary Ellen Creighton to Cuthbert Creighton, 29 April 1939. Also, see Louise Creighton, *Life and Letters of Mandell Creighton*, 2 vols (1904), i, pp. 1–16, for Creighton's childhood years.

8. Creighton Family Papers. A family document mentions Robert Creighton's 'brothers' and 'sisters'. Mary Ellen Creighton to Cuthbert Creighton, 29 April 1939. No records of the birth dates of Robert and Jane exist. See Genealogical Chart, p. 131.

9. Creighton Family Papers, MS letter, Mary Ellen Creighton, 'Genealogy Fragment with Notes of Mandell Family', c. 1902.

10. Creighton Family Papers, MS letter, Mary Ellen Creighton to Cuthbert Creighton, 29 April 1939; H. Mandell to Mary Ellen Creighton, 1901, and J. Eubank to Mary Ellen Creighton, 11 May c. 1902.

11. The only personal recollections of Mandell's childhood during the Carlisle years come from his sister, Mary Ellen. She wrote two documents, around 1902, for Louise Creighton who was then preparing the materials for her husband's biography. Creighton Family Papers, MS letter, Mary Ellen Creighton to Louise Creighton, c. 1902.

12. Some family documents suggest Polly was born in 1850. Her baptismal date, however, was 2 May 1849 according to city archives. Confirming this are the dates 1849–1944 inscribed at the base of a lectern in Carlisle's Cathedral donated in Mary Ellen Creighton's memory shortly after her death. Baptismal Records, Carlisle City Archives.

13. Creighton Family Papers, Louise Creighton' s original memoir.

14. Louise Creighton, *Memoir of a Victorian Woman: Reflections of Louise Creighton, 1850–1936*, ed. James Thayne Covert (1994), p. 44.

15. Louise Creighton, *Life and Letters*, i, pp. 3, 10.

16. Creighton Family Papers, MS letter, Mary Ellen Creighton to Louise Creighton, c. 1902. Also *Louise Creighton, Life and Letters*, i, pp. 3, 10.

17. Creighton Family Papers, MS letter, Mary Ellen Creighton to Louise Creighton, c. 1902.

18. Ibid. Also, *Louise Creighton, Memoir*, p. 42: Louise Creighton, *Life and Letters*, i, p. 31.

19. Creighton Family Papers, MS letter, Mary Ellen Creighton to Louise Creighton, c. 1902.

20. Ibid.

21. *Louise Creighton, Life and Letters*, i, p. 4. Also Louise Creighton, *A Victorian Family as Seen Through the Letters of Louise Creighton to her Mother, 1872–1880*, ed. James Thayne Covert (1998), 15 April 1877, p. 166.

22. Louise Creighton, *Life and Letters*, i, p. 5.

23. Louise Creighton, *Memoir*, p. 158; *Carlisle Grammar School Memorial Register, 1264–1924*, comp. and ed. G. B. Routledge (1924), p. 123.

24. Chance, *Some Notable Cumbrians*, p. 101.

25. Louise Creighton, *Life and Letters*, i, p. 16.

26. Ibid., p. 6; *A Register of Durham School, January 1840-December 1907* (n.d.), pp. 78, 263, 292.

27. G. R. Elton, 'Introduction', reissue of Mandell Creighton, *Queen Elizabeth*, p. vii.

28. Creighton Family Papers, MS letter, Mandell Creighton to Ella Creighton, 8 November 1899.

29. See *A Register of Durham School*, p. 11.

30. Louise Creighton, *Life and Letters*, i, p. 6. Creighton Family Papers. Durham Grammar School, 'Report of Progress and Conduct'. Interestingly, his school-boy notebooks are still available and readily thumbed through by boys currently in the sixth form room.

31. Louise Creighton, *Life and Letters*, i, pp. 8–9; *Quarterly Review* (April 1901), p. 585.

32. Louise Creighton, *Life and Letters*, i, pp. 10–15. Also published in Mandell Creighton, *Counsel for the Young: Extracts from the Letters of Mandell Creighton*, ed. Louise Creighton (1905), pp. 1–7.

33. Henry Scott Holland, *Personal Studies* (1905), p. 210; at that time, Holland was dean of St Paul's.

34. David Newsome, *Godliness and Good Learning: Four Studies on a Victorian Ideal* (1961), p. 1, passim.

35. Ibid., pp. 32–33.

36. Louise Creighton, *Life and Letters*, i, p. 15.

37. Ibid., p. 9.

38. Fallows, *Mandell Creighton and the English Church* (1964), p. 3.

39. This is what Louise Creighton wrote, but realising that it is about 240 miles between Oxford and Durham, some have questioned that he actually walked the distance in three days. Creighton's eldest son has a note penned in the margin by his copy of Louise's biography of Mandell Creighton that reads simply: 'Not possible.' See Louise Creighton, *Life and Letters*, i, p. 15.

40. Ibid., p. 15.

41. Louise Creighton, *Letters to her Mother*, 6 June 1875, p. 91, October 1877, p. 182.

42. *Quarterly Review* (April 1901), p. 585.

43. Rudolph de Cordova, 'Bishop of London', *Strand Magazine* (November 1899), p. 527.

44. MS letter, Basil Creighton to author, 10 September 1965. Also see the Bishop of Durham's recollections of Creighton's interest in hiking as quoted in Newsome, *Godliness and Good Learning*, p. 70. Just a little over a year before he died he spoke about his life-long 'delight in walking' and how 'perfectly happy' he was if he could 'get two hours' tramping a day'. See 'Obituary of Mandell Creighton', *Quarterly Review*, 143, no. 386 (April 1901), p. 586; also de Cordova, 'Bishop of London', *Strand Magazine*, p. 527.

45. See Bibliography listing Creighton's books and articles on English towns and shires.

46. Louise Creighton, *Life and Letters*, i, pp. 9–10.
47. *Quarterly Review* (April 1901), 585; Louise in her biography claims that the headmaster's wife only prophesied that he would someday be a bishop. Louise Creighton, *Life and Letters* i, pp. 9–10.
48. De Cordova, 'Bishop of London', *Strand Magazine*, p. 526.

Chapter 4: Undoubtedly the Ablest Man

1. Louise Creighton, *Life and Letters of Mandell Creighton*, 2 vols (1904), i, p. 27.
2. Ibid., pp. 16, 297.
3. W. R. Ward, *Victorian Oxford* (1965), p. xv.
4. See Owen Chadwick, *The Spirit of the Oxford Movement: Tractarian Essays* (1990); Eugene R. Fairweather, ed., *The Oxford Movement* (1964).
5. Alfred W. Benn, *The History of English Rationalism in the Nineteenth Century* (1906), ii, p. 421. See Bibliography for general works on the history of Oxford University during this period.
6. See Owen Chadwick, *The Victorian Church* (1970), ii, chapter 1, pp. 90ff, and chapter 2, passim; Richard Helmstadter and Bernard Lightman, eds, *Victorian Faith in Crisis: Essays on Continuity and Change in Nineteenth-Century Religious Belief* (1990), passim.
7. Thomas Hill Green (1836–1882) was fellow of Balliol College and a prominent philosopher and interpreter of Hegel. He married Charlotte Symonds, sister of essayist and critic John Addington Symonds.
8. Newsome, *Godliness and Good Learning: Four Studies on a Victorian Ideal* (1961), p. 228.
9. For a history of Merton College, see Bernard W. Henderson, *Merton College* (1899).
10. Edmund A. Knox, *Reminiscences of an Octogenarian, 1847–1934* (1935), p. 83.
11. Charles E. Mallet, *A History of the University of Oxford*, 3 vols (1924–27), iii, p. 397. Some of these books are still chained to the shelves.
12. J. R. L. Highfield, *Merton College Chapel: A Lecture* (n.d.), p. 15. The chapel was officially the church of St John the Baptist.
13. Louise Creighton, *Life and Letters*, i, p. 24.
14. V. H. H. Green, *Oxford Common Room: A Study of Lincoln College and Mark Pattison* (1957), p. 120n.
15. Louise Creighton, *Life and Letters*, i, p. 17.
16. Knox, *Reminiscences*, p. 93.
17. Louise Creighton, *Life and Letters*, i, p. 31.
18. Ibid., p. 22.
19. Knox, *Reminiscences*, pp. 75–76.
20. See 'Biographical Memoir' by A. Blyth Webster in George Saintsbury, *A Saintsbury Miscellany: Selections from his Essays and Scrap Books* (1947), pp. 27–73.
21. Louise Creighton, *Life and Letters*, i, p. 18.
22. Ibid., p. 22. Reginald Copleston, not to be confused with Edward Copleston

of Oriel College, became fellow and tutor of St John's College, Oxford, before becoming Bishop of Colombo and then Calcutta. John Sutherland, *Mrs Humphry Ward: Eminent Victorian, Pre-Eminent Edwardian* (1991), p. 51.

23. Rudolph de Cordova, 'Bishop of London', *Strand Magazine*, p. 527. Henderson, *Merton College*, p. 274.

24. William Tuckwell as quoted in Newsome, *Godliness and Good Learning*, p. 206.

25. Louise Creighton, *Life and Letters*, i, p. 23.

26. Ibid., p. 35.

27. Ibid. Daniel Pool, *What Jane Austen Ate and Charles Dickens Knew* (1993), p. 391.

28. Louise Creighton, *Life and Letters*, i, pp. 29, 30, 80, 199, 214.

29. Mandell Creighton, *Counsel for the Young: Extracts from the Letters of Mandell Creighton*, ed. Louise Creighton (1905), p. 147; Louise Creighton, *Life and Letters*, i, p. 29.

30. Ibid., p. 40.

31. Ibid., pp. 24–25.

32. Ibid.

33. Ibid., p. 39.

34. As quoted in Sutherland, *Mrs Humphry Ward*, p. 48.

35. Cf. Louise Creighton, *Life and Letters*, i, p. 29 and Saintsbury, *Saintsbury Miscellany*, p. 30.

36. Louise Creighton, *Life and Letters*, i, p. 18.

37. Ibid.

38. Ibid., pp. 34–35.

39. Ibid., p. 36.

40. Creighton Family Papers. Copy of Mandell Creighton's poem.

41. Louise Creighton, *Life and Letters*, i, chapter 2, passim.

42. Ibid., p. 20.

43. Ibid., pp. 20, 25.

44. See Sutherland, *Mrs Humphry Ward*, p. 50.

45. Louise Creighton, *Life and Letters*, i, pp. 21, 27.

46. Newsome, *Godliness and Good Learning*, p. 2.

47. Louise Creighton, *Life and Letters*, i, pp. 33–34.

48. Ibid, p. 55.

49. De Cordova, 'Bishop of London', *Strand Magazine*, p. 530.

50. Louise Creighton, *Life and Letters*, i, p. 27.

51. Mandell Creighton, *Historical Lectures and Addresses*, ed. Louise Creighton (1903), p. 24.

52. Louise Creighton, *Life and Letters*, i, p. 36.

53. MS letter, Mandell Creighton to James Bryce, Bryce Papers, Bodleian Library, Oxford. No date appears on this letter, but Bodleian authorities list it as 1864.

54. Louise Creighton, *Life and Letters*, i, pp. 40–41.

55. De Cordova, 'Bishop of London', p. 526.

56. Louise Creighton, *Life and Letters*, i, p. 39.

57. Ibid.

58. Ibid., pp. 39–40.

59. Ibid., p. 41. This letter is missing from the Bryce Papers in the Bodleian Library.

60. Melvin Richter, *The Politics of Conscience: T. H. Green and his Age* (1964), p. 84.

61. Louise Creighton, *Life and Letters*, p. 42.

62. MS letter, Mandell Creighton to James Bryce, 7 January 1867. Bryce Papers, Bodleian Library, Oxford.

63. G. W. Prothero, 'Mandell Creighton', *Dictionary of National Biography*, xxii supplement, p. 507.

Chapter 5: A Glorious Game

1. Louise Creighton, *Life and Letters of Mandell Creighton*, 2 vols (1904), i, p. 54.

2. Cf. W. R. Ward, *Victorian Oxford* (1965), chapter 10 passim; Bernard Henderson, *Merton College* (1899), pp. 166–69. Also see Bibliography for other general works on Oxford University.

3. Charles E. Mallet, *A History of the University of Oxford* (1924–27), iii, p. 375.

4. Great Britain, House of Commons, *Sessional Papers*: 'Oxford University Act, 1854', 5, pp. 289ff; 'Oxford Royal Commission, 1852', 22, pp. 1ff. Cambridge followed with its parliamentary royal commission and subsequent reform Act. See Ibid., 'Cambridge Royal Commission, 1853', 44, pp. 1ff; and 'Cambridge University Act, 1856', 1, pp. 411ff.

5. Mark Pattison as quoted in Ronald A. Knox, *Let Dons Delight: Being Variations on a Theme in an Oxford Common-Room* (1939), p. 206; Mark Pattison, *Memoirs* (1885), p. 245.

6. For further general studies on English education in the nineteenth century with sections concerning university reforms, see John W. Adamson, *English Education, 1789–1902* (1930); Roger Armfelt, *The Structure of English Education* (1955); H. C. Barnard, *A History of English Education from 1760* (1964); S. J. Curtis, *History of Education in Great Britain* (1948).

7. John Richard Green, *Oxford Studies*, eds Mrs J. R. Green and Miss K. Norgate (1901), p. 264.

8. Besides the works previously cited, see A. J. Engel, *From Clergyman to Don: The Rise of the Academic Profession in Nineteenth-Century Oxford* (1983).

9. Ibid., pp. 116, 127.

10. As quoted in ibid., p. 116.

11. See V. H. H. Green, *Oxford Common Room: A Study of Lincoln College and Mark Pattison* (1957), especially chapters 8 to 12; Christopher Hobhouse, rev. Marcus Dick, *Oxford as it Was and as it Is Today* (1952); Charles Mallet, 'Modern Oxford,' *Handbook to the University of Oxford*, pp. 1–41; Cyril Bailey, 'The Tutorial System', ibid., pp. 261–68.

12. Besides works previously cited, see Marjorie Cruickshank, *Church and State in English Education* (1963); S. R. Dongerkery, *Universities in Britain* (1953); J. F. C. Harrison, *Learning and Living, 1790–1960: A Study in the History of the*

English Adult Education Movement (1961); Robert G. McPherson, *Theory of Higher Education in Nineteenth-Century England* (1959); Cyril Norwood and Arthur H. Hope, *Higher Education for Boys in England* (1909); and S. C. Roberts, *British Universities* (1947).

13. Between the founding of the University of Durham in 1832 and the granting of a university charter to Bristol University in 1908, over a dozen new universities appeared. These were the civic or 'redbrick' universities, so-called because they were constructed out of brick as opposed to the old stone buildings of Oxbridge and were established in urban centres with strong municipal relationships. By attracting the middle classes, these universities broke the monopoly of the two medieval residential institutions (Oxford and Cambridge), long characterised by their aristocratic and clerical remoteness.

14. G. M. Young, *Victorian England: Portrait of an Age* (1936, 1960), p. 158.

15. Green, *Oxford Studies*, p. 260.

16. Edmund Knox, *Reminiscences of an Octogenarian, 1847–1934* (1935), p. 90.

17. Melvin Richter, *The Politics of Conscience: T. H. Green and his Age* (1964), p. 15.

18. Attributed to Noel Annan, as quoted in David Newsome, *Godliness and Good Learning: Four Studies on a Victorian Ideal* (1961), p. 7.

19. When it came to practising religion, both men 'grew where they were planted, surveyed the world and were content', as one writer put it. 'Their faith was Christian and Catholic; their religion the Church of England; their view High— Creighton's more liberal than Saintsbury's.' A. Blyth Webster's biographical memoir in *A Saintsbury Miscellany: Selections from his Essays and Scrap Books* (1947), pp. 31–32.

20. A grandson believed that Creighton 'had a very real personal religion, though the exact nature of it was something of an enigma even to those closest to him'. MS letter, Hugh Creighton to author, 4 May 1965.

21. Louise Creighton, *Life and Letters*, i, p. 75.

22. Ibid., pp. 45–46, 93.

23. Ibid., p. 32.

24. Knox, *Reminiscences*, pp. 83–84, 100. Warden Marsham died in 1880 and was succeeded by George Brodrick, who in the late 1860s was a promising tutor at the same time as Creighton. For an interesting depiction of the life of a Merton don in the late 1860s and early 1870s, see chapter 5, pp. 82–101. Edmund A. Knox, of Corpus Christi, became a fellow of Merton in 1868 and tutor in 1875.

25. Louise Creighton, *Life and Letters*, i, p. 26.

26. Ibid., pp. 56–57.

27. Ibid.

28. Ibid., p. 52.

29. Ibid., p. 53.

30. Ibid., p. 58.

31. Knox, *Reminiscences*, pp. 82–83.

32. Louise Creighton, *Life and Letters*, i, p. 54.

33. Edmund Gosse, *Portraits and Sketches* (1913), p. 172.

34. Louise Creighton, *Life and Letters*, i, p. 55.

35. Ibid., p. 56.

36. Ibid.

37. Pattison, *Memoirs*, p. 331.

38. Louise Creighton, *Life and Letters*, i, p. 50.

39. Ibid., pp. 58–59. Dates and positions of Creighton's official record at Merton were: Junior Dean (1868, 1871–74), principal of postmasters (1869–75), and Knightley lecturer (1870). College Register, i, p. 5, courtesy of J. R. L. Highfield, librarian of Merton College. Principal of postmasters was a college officer in charge of the postmaster scholars. The Knightley lectureship was originally founded in 1589 and re-established in 1635. Also see Henderson, *Merton College*, p. 162.

40. Louise Creighton, *Life and Letters*, i, p. 50–51.

41. Engel, *From Clergyman to Don*, pp. 113, 124. Creighton's income was supplemented later by fees he received as examiner of the Modern History School and for lectures presented during vacations as a part of both the extension programme and the Ladies' Association lecture series. Louise Creighton makes no mention in her biography about her husband's financial income at Merton or in his later career. There are a few sparse references, however, about his income as bishop in her private memoir.

42. A third condition regarding terms for accepting a 'living' or holding property may have been imposed. Knox, *Reminiscences*, p. 82.

43. Creighton's colleagues at Merton included F. H. Bradley, George Brodrick (later warden), Edward Caird, William Esson, Noel Freeling, George Hammond, Edmund Knox, Andrew Lang, John Coleridge Patteson (later Bishop of Melanesia), John James Randolph, John Rhys, Henry Savile Roundell, William Sidgwick, William Wallace and Robert Wilson. Ibid., pp. 82–85.

44. Louise Creighton, *Life and Letters*, i, p. 59–60.

45. Engel, *From Clergyman to Don*, pp. 82–85.

46. Knox, *Reminiscences*, p. 90.

47. Engel, *From Clergyman to Don*, pp. 83–84; Louise Creighton, *Life and Letters*, i, pp. 59–60.

48. W. G. Addison, *J. R. Green* (1946), see section on the New Historical School, pp. 44–59.

49. William Stubbs (1825–1901) was for a time librarian at Lambeth Palace and editor of the Rolls Series before his appointment as Regius Professor of History at Oxford, 1864–84. His *Constitutional History of England* (1873–78), a landmark work, brought him deserved recognition. He was appointed Bishop of Chester in 1884, and then Bishop of Oxford in 1888.

50. Louise Creighton, *Life and Letters*, i, p. 61.

51. Mallet, *University of Oxford*, iii, p. 342.

52. Knox, *Reminiscences*, p. 88.

53. Mandell Creighton, 'The Endowment of Research', *Macmillan's Magazine*, 34 (1876).

54. Ibid., pp. 189–90.

55. Ibid., p. 190.
56. Ibid.
57. Ibid., p. 192.
58. Ibid., p. 191.
59. It is surprising that Louise Creighton never reprinted this article when she collected and published almost everything else her husband wrote.
60. For a description of the tutorial system at Oxford, see Mallett, *University of Oxford*, iii, pp. 56ff.
61. Louise Creighton, *Life and Letters*, i, p. 64.
62. James Bryce, comparing Creighton to William Stubbs as a teacher, wrote that Stubbs was 'full of wisdom, and sometimes full of wit' but 'not effective as a teacher' as was Creighton, 'who won his reputation at Merton College long before he became professor of ecclesiastical history at Cambridge'. James Bryce, *Studies in Contemporary Biography* (1911), p. 289.
63. Louise Creighton, *Life and Letters*, i, p. 63.
64. Ibid.
65. Ibid., p. 65.
66. Ibid.
67. Ibid., pp. 243, 138–39.
68. As quoted in Shane Leslie, *Men Were Different: Five Studies in Late Victorian Biography* (1937, 1967), p. 19.
69. Gosse, *Portraits and Sketches*, p. 170.
70. As quoted in Winston S. Churchill, *Lord Randolph Churchill* (1951), pp. 41–42.
71. Ibid., p. 202, and Louise Creighton, *Life and Letters*, i, p. 64.
72. Knox, *Reminiscences*, p. 182.
73. Mandell Creighton, *University and Other Sermons*, pp. 220–21.
74. Louise Creighton, *Life and Letters*, i, p. 67.
75. Ibid., p. 68.
76. Edmund Gosse, *Selected Essays* (1928), pp. 44–45. Cf. Owen Chadwick, *Creighton on Luther: An Inaugural Lecture* (1959), p. 11.
77. Louise Creighton, *Life and Letters*, i, p. 93–94.
78. Ibid.
79. A. C. Benson, *Walter Pater* (1908), pp. 195–96.
80. Creighton Family Papers, MS letter, Mandell Creighton to Winifred Creighton, 11 November 1898. Cf. Louise Creighton, *Life and Letters*, ii, p. 348.
81. Ibid., i, p. 184.
82. Norman F. Cantor, ed., *William Stubbs on the English Constitution* (1966), p. 4.
83. Louise Creighton, *Life and Letters*, i, p. 106.
84. Ibid., p. 93.
85. Mrs Humphry Ward, *A Writer's Recollections* (1918), i, pp. 146–47, 188–189.
86. Ibid., pp. 146–47.
87. Louise Creighton, *Life and Letters*, i, pp. 69–70.
88. Ibid., p. 71.
89. Ibid., pp. 71–72.

90. Ibid., pp. 72–73.
91. Ibid., pp. 75–76.
92. Mrs Humphry Ward, *A Writer's Recollections*, i, p. 189.

Chapter 6: The Peak

1. Published letter from Ernest de Glehn (formerly von Glehn) in the *Sydenham, Forest Hill and Penge Gazette* (12 May 1933) on the occasion of the demolition of Peak Hill Lodge. Some of the members of the von Glehn changed their name to de Glehn during the First World War.
2. Louise Creighton, *Memoir of a Victorian Woman: Reflections of Louise Creighton, 1850–1936*, ed. James Thayne Covert (1994), p. 1.
3. MS letter, John Coulter (Sydenham historian) to author, 12 July 1998.
4. LCM, 13. For archival photographs of Sydenham in the last half of the nineteeth century, see *Sydenham and Forest Hill*, compiled by John Coulter and John Seaman (1994), and John Coulter, *Sydenham and Forest Hill Past* (1999).
5. MS letter, John Coulter to author, 23 August 1998.
6. Louise Creighton, *Memoir*, p. 3.
7. Creighton Family Papers, 'Abstract of the Diary of Robert von Glehn', ed. Louise Creighton (1928), unpublished document, pp. 9–17; Louise Creighton, *Memoir*, p. 2.
8. Creighton Family Papers, 'Abstract Diary'; also Louise Creighton, *Memoir*, pp. 1–3, 154.
9. Creighton Family Papers, 'Abstract Diary', p. 9.
10. Ibid., p. 9; Louise Creighton, *Memoir*, p. 3.
11. Louise Creighton, *Memoir*, p. 9.
12. Ibid. Also see Genealogical Chart for more on the von Glehns, p. 71.
13. Ibid., pp. 9, 13.
14. Ibid., pp. 3–4.
15. Ibid.
16. Ibid., p. 4.
17. Ibid.
18. Ibid., pp. 3–4.
19. Ibid., p. 11.
20. Ibid.
21. Ibid., p. 5.
22. Ibid.
23. Ibid., p. 6.
24. Ibid.
25. Ibid., p. 7.
26. Ibid., pp. 32–33.
27. Ibid., p. 8.
28. Ibid., pp. 6–7.
29. Ibid., p. 9.

30. See MS letter, R. A. Greenhill to K. E. Richardson (27 February 1979), in Dr Kenneth Richardson file, 'Research Papers on von Glehn Family', A82/7 File. Library Division, Lewisham Local History Centre, London.

31. Louise Creighton, *Memoir*, p. 10.

32. Ibid., p. 31.

33. Owen Chadwick, *The Victorian Church* (1966), i, p. 43; Louise Creighton, *Memoir*, p. 10.

34. Louise Creighton, *Memoir*, 10. Frederick Denison Maurice (1805–1872) was a controversial writer who championed Christian Socialism. F. W. Robertson, along with Maurice and Charles Kingsley, was a strong advocate of the Christian Socialist movement within the Church of England.

35. Ibid.

36. For commentaries on Sydenham's cultural life in the middle decades of the century, see Charles L. Graves, *Life and Letters of Sir George Grove, C.B.* (1903), p. 41; R. C. Lehmann, *Memories of Half a Century* (1908); John Wolfson, *Sullivan and the Scott Russells* (1984), pp. 11–12; Percy M. Young, *George Grove, 1820–1900* (1980), chapter 4.

37. As quoted in letter by Ernest von Glehn in the local newspaper, *Sydenham, Forest Hill and Penge Gazette* (12 May 1933). Also, see Richardson's file, Lewisham Local Studies Centre, London.

38. See Young, *George Grove*, passim; Louise Creighton, *Memoir*, p. 7.

39. Ernest von Glehn's letter in *Sydenham, Forest Hill and Penge Gazette* (12 May 1933).

40. John Richard Green (1837–1883). Among many other writings, Green is best remembered for his popular *A Short History of the English People* (1874), which brought him fame and an enormous reading public.

41. Louise Creighton, *Memoir*, p. 18.

42. She claimed, however, not to have suffered any 'great miseries of shyness'. Ibid., p. 16.

43. Ibid., p. 14.

44. See Laura Wortley, *Wilfrid de Glehn: John Singer Sargent's Painting Companion* (1989, 1997).

45. Louise claimed that Oswald only painted these 'two good pictures, which were exhibited in the Academy and sold'. Louise Creighton, *Memoir*, p. 14–15. See Wortley, *Wilfrid de Glehn*, p. 52.

46. Louise Creighton, *Memoir*, p. 15.

47. Ibid., pp. 24–25.

48. Ibid., pp. 29–30.

49. Ibid., p. 8.

50. Ibid., pp. 21–22.

51. Ibid., p. 24.

52. Edward Gibbon (1737–1794), the famous English historian, rationalist and author of the monumental six-volume study, *The Decline and Fall of the Roman Empire* (1776–88). Regarded by many as England's greatest historian, his *Decline and Fall*, along with his *Autobiography* (1796) are important literary works.

What has bothered some of his readers, then and today, was his scepticism that spilled over into an overly-rationalistic criticism of early Christianity.

53. Pope Pius IX, Bishop of Rome (1846–78). This was just before the Italian nationalists forcefully occupied the Papal States, after which the pope became a virtual prisoner within the Vatican.

54. Guido Reni (1575–1642), Renaissance painter of the Bolognese school, achieved renewed fame in the mid nineteenth century, in part due to John Ruskin's interest in him and subsequent criticism of Reni's style.

55. Louise Creighton, *Memoir*, pp. 28–29.

56. Ibid., p. 29.

57. J. R. Green to Louise von Glehn, Bodleian Library, MS lett. e. 48, fos 70–83; also J. R. Green, *Letters of John Richard Green, 1837–1883*, ed. Leslie Stephen (1901), p. 240.

58. Louise Creighton, *Memoir*, p. 27.

59. Ibid.

60. Ibid.

61. Ibid., pp. 33–34.

Chapter 7: A Charm About Oxford

1. MS letter, J. R. Green to Louise von Glehn, Bodleian Library, MS Eng. e. 48, fos 70–83; also J. R. Green, *Letters of John Richard Green, 1837–1883*, ed. Leslie Stephen (1901), p. 241.

2. Louise Creighton, *Memoir of a Victorian Woman: Reflections of Louise Creighton, 1850–1936*, ed. James Thayne Covert (1994), p. 45.

3. Ibid., p. 46.

4. Louise Creighton, *A Victorian Family: Letters of Louise Creighton to her Mother*, ed. James Thayne Covert (1998), 12 January 1872, pp. 15–16.

5. Louise Creighton, *Life and Letters of Mandell Creighton*, 2 vols (1904), i, p. 127.

6. Louise Creighton, *Memoir*, p. 47.

7. Ibid., pp. 47–48.

8. Louise Creighton, *Letters to her Mother*, 17 January 1872, p. 18.

9. LCM, 48. She later added a nurse after the first child was born.

10. Louise Creighton, *Life and Letters*, i, p. 131.

11. Creighton Family Papers, MS letter, Louise Creighton to Mary Emilie von Glehn, 12 May 1872.

12. Louise Creighton, *Life and Letters*, i, p. 131.

13. Ibid.

14. 'Obituary of Louise Creighton', *Women in Council*, May 1936.

15. Louise Creighton, *Letters to her Mother*, 25 January 1872, p. 18.

16. Ibid., 18 April 1872, p. 22.

17. For a revealing description of Oxford life in the 1870s and the role of the wives of academics, see Georgina Battiscombe, *Reluctant Pioneer: A Life of Elizabeth Wordsworth* (1978), chapter 3 'Oxford Encounters', pp. 48–62.

18. Louise Creighton, *Memoir*, p. 48.

19. Louise Creighton, *Letters to her Mother*, 18 April 1872, p. 23.

20. Andrew Lang (1844–1912) was educated at Balliol College before becoming a fellow of Merton College. He married Leonora Alleyne in 1875.

21. George James Howard (1843–1911) later became the ninth Earl of Carlisle (1889). His wife was Rosalind Frances, daughter of Baron Stanley of Alderley.

22. Louise Creighton, *Memoir*, p. 48.

23. Bonamy Price (1807–1888) was Drummond Professor of Political Economy. Friedrich Maximilian Müller (1823–1900) was Taylorian Professor of Modern European Languages.

24. Louise Creighton, *Memoir*, p. 48. Cf. Janet Trevelyan, *The Life of Mrs Humphry Ward* (1923) and John Sutherland, *Mrs Humphry Ward: Eminent Victorian, Pre-Eminent Edwardian* (1991).

25. Louise Creighton, *Memoir*, p. 53.

26. Ibid., p. 55.

27. Ibid.

28. Louise Creighton, *Letters to her Mother*, 14 July 1872, p. 29.

29. Louise Creighton, *Memoir*, p. 53.

30. Both books were published in 1872. Louise Creighton, *Letters to her Mother*, 5 May 1874, p. 56.

31. Louise Creighton, *Memoir*, p. 55; Louise Creighton, *Life and Letters*, i, p. 128.

32. Louise Creighton, *Memoir*, p. 53.

33. Louise Creighton, *Life and Letters*, i, pp. 128–29.

34. Edmund A. Knox, *Reminiscences of an Octogenarian, 1847–1934* (1935), p. 90.

35. Edward A. Freeman (1823–1892), a former Trinity College man, was a noted historian of the age and was appointed regius professor of modern history at Oxford in 1884. Freeman influenced a generation of students, and is largely remembered today for his emphasis on the Anglo-Saxon impact on English institutions. His major work was the *History of the Norman Conquest* (1867–79).

36. Charles E. Mallet, *A History of the University of Oxford*, 3 vols (1924–27), iii, p. 348.

37. Mandell Creighton, *The Claims of the Common Life: Sermons Preached in Merton College Chapel, 1871–1874*, ed. Louise Creighton (1905).

38. Louise Creighton, *Life and Letters*, i, p. 89.

39. Creighton's income as don is discussed below. See A. J. Engel, *From Clergyman to Don: The Rise of the Academic Profession in Nineteenth-Century Oxford* (1983), p. 126.

40. Knox, *Reminiscences*, p. 89.

41. Louise Creighton, *Memoir*, pp. 56–57.

42. Ibid., p. 57.

43. Cf. Albert Mansbridge, The *Older Universities of England: Oxford and Cambridge* (1923), p. 176; Mrs Humphry Ward, *A Writer's Recollections* (1918), i, p. 203; Mallet, *University of Oxford*, pp. 431–32; Melvin Richter, *The Politics of Conscience: T. H. Green and his Age* (1964), p. 371; J. F. C. Harrison, *Learning and*

Living, 1790–1960: A Study in the History of the English Adult Education Movement (1961), pp. 238–39; and Jane Lewis, *Women and Social Action in Victorian and Edwardian England* (1991), p. 240.

44. H. C. Barnard, *A History of English Education* (1964), pp. 159–160.
45. Bertha Johnson, 'The First Beginnings, 1873–90', *Lady Margaret Hall: A Short History*, ed. Gemma Bailey (1923), p. 25.
46. Ibid., p. 26. Beatrice Creighton was born in 1872.
47. Louise Creighton, *Memoir*, p. 57.
48. Leopold von Ranke (1795–1886), the noted German historian who sought to apply scientific method to historical investigation.
49. All six volumes were eventually published by Clarendon Press in 1875. Louise Creighton, *Memoir*, p. 53.
50. William Stubbs, Regius Professor of History 1866 to 1884. Stubbs was one of Mandell Creighton's examiners for the Law and Modern History School in 1866, along with James Bryce, later Viscount Bryce (1838–1922), historian and Regius Professor of Civil Law.
51. Louise Creighton, *Memoir*, p. 53.
52. W. G. Fallows, *Mandell Creighton and the English Church* (1964), p. 10.
53. Louise Creighton, *Memoir*, p. 54.
54. Mandell Creighton, *Primer on Roman History* (1875); see Bibliography for a complete list of Creighton's published works.
55. Louise Creighton, *Life and Letters*, i, p. 146.
56. Louise Creighton, *England: A Continental Power, From the Conquest to Magna Carta, 1066–1216* (1876); see also Bibliography for a list of Louise's published works.
57. Louise Creighton, *Memoir*, p. 54.
58. Ibid., p. 57.
59. Louise Creighton, *Letters to her Mother*, 18 April 1872, pp. 21–23.
60. Ibid., 8 June 1872, p. 24; Louise Creighton, *Memoir*, p. 58.
61. Louise Creighton, *Letters to her Mother*, 27 July 1872, p. 30.
62. Ibid., 8 June 1872, p. 24.
63. Ibid., 7 October 1872, p. 37.
64. Ibid.
65. Louise Creighton, *Memoir*, p. 57.
66. Ibid., pp. 57–58.
67. Ibid.
68. Louise Creighton, *Life and Letters*, i, p. 133.
69. Louise Creighton, *Memoir*, p. 58.
70. Louise Creighton, *Life and Letters*, i, p. 136.
71. Louise Creighton, *Memoir*, p. 59.
72. Louise Creighton, *Letters to her Mother*, 25 September 1873, pp. 50–52.
73. Ibid.; Louise Creighton, *Memoir*, p. 59.
74. Louise Creighton, *Memoir*, p. 59; Christopher Brooke and Roger Highfield, *Oxford and Cambridge* (1988), p. 59.

75. Louise Creighton, *Memoir*, p. 60.

76. Originally the parish was a part of the barony of Simon de Montfort and later, after de Montfort's death, was confiscated by Henry III who gave it to his younger son Edmund, Earl of Lancaster. In 1274 Edmund gave the endowed parish over to Merton College, and the college has been its patron ever since. Income from the parish continues to remain a part of Merton's endowment and most vicars, until recent times, have been Merton men. Louise Creighton, *Life and Letters*, i, p. 148; see also Edward Bateson, *A History of Northumberland* (1895), ii, p. 19 passim.

77. Louise Creighton, *Life and Letters*, i, p. 137; besides his *Claims of the Common Life* sermons, also see Mandell Creighton, *University and Other Sermons*, ed. Louise Creighton (1903), passim.

78. Engel, *Clergyman to Don*, p. 126.

79. Ibid., p. 124.

80. Ibid.; E. T. Raymond, *Portraits of the Nineties* (1921), p. 158.

81. Louise Creighton, *Life and Letters*, i, p. 141.

82. Ibid., p. 140.

83. Ibid., p. 141.

84. Ibid.

85. Louise Creighton, *Memoir*, p. 60.

86. Louise Creighton, *Letters to her Mother*, 22 October 1874, p. 60.

87. Ibid., 5 November 1874, p. 61.

88. Louise Creighton, *Life and Letters*, i, p. 143.

89. Ibid.

90. Ibid.

Chapter 8: Exile

1. Louise Creighton, *Memoir of a Victorian Woman: Reflections of Louise Creighton, 1850–1936*, ed. James Thayne Covert (1994), p. 62.

2. Stead only lived in Embleton a few months after he was born in 1849. See Estelle W. Stead, *My Father: Personal and Spiritual Reminiscences* (1912).

3. Louise Creighton, *Life and Letters of Mandell Creighton*, 2 vols (1904), i, pp. 153–54.

4. Ibid., pp. 154–155.

5. Louise Creighton's 'Foreword' in R. B. Dawson, *A Short History of Embleton Church and the Fortified Vicarage* (1933).

6. So thought Andrew Lang, then a tutor of Merton, when visiting the Creightons. Ibid. For a vivid description of Northumberland, see Mandell Creighton, *The Story of Some English Shires* (1897), pp. 13–38.

7. R. B. Dawson, *A Short History*, p. 20.

8. Cf. Ibid., and Louise Creighton, *Life and Letters*, i, pp. 148–157.

9. Owen Craster, *A History of Embleton Parish Church* (privately printed pamphlet, c. 1978).

10. For details about the history of the vicarage see Lyall Wilkes, *Tyneside Portraits: Studies in Art and Life* (1971), pp. 123–32; also, Dawson, *A Short History*, p. 37. The author also used material from interviews and correspondence over the years 1987–99 with owner of Embleton Tower, Kay Seymour-Walker.

11. One guess is that the tower resembles more what is known as 'solar', fortified structures used in medieval country houses. Dawson, *A Short History*, p. 37. See Robert Hugill, *Borderland Castles and Peles* (n.d.), 'Embleton Tower', pp. 91–92.

12. Louise Creighton, *Life and Letters*, i, p. 151. There are rumours still of some subterranean passage that once ran from its 'donjon' to Dunstanburgh Castle. Embleton Tower was one of several fortified vicarages in the district. Also see H. L. Honeyman 'Embleton Vicarage', in *Archaeologia Aeliana: or Miscellaneous Tracts Relating to Antiquity*, ed. C. H. Hunter Blair (1928), pp. 87–101.

13. Dawson, *A Short History*, pp. 37–38.

14. Louise Creighton, *Life and Letters*, i, p. 144.

15. Ibid., p. 145.

16. P. F. Ryder, *Fallodon*, privately printed, 1987.

17. See G. M. Trevelyan, *Grey of Fallodon: The Life and Letters of Sir Edward Grey, Afterwards Viscount of Fallodon* (1937), passim.

18. Louise Creighton, *Life and Letters*, i, p. 145.

19. Louise Creighton, *Memoir*, p. 60.

20. Louise Creighton, *Life and Letters*, i, p. 254.

21. A. J. Engel, *From Clergyman to Don: The Rise of the Academic Profession in Nineteenth-Century Oxford* (1983), p. 124.

22. Acland became vice-president of the committee of council on education under Prime Minister Gladstone and is remembered for his educational reforms.

23. Louise Creighton *Memoir*, p. 61; Louise Creighton, *Life and Letters*, i, pp. 160 and 178. When Creighton left Embleton, Earl Grey gave Green the living at Howick. Green later became vicar of Chulmleigh in Devonshire.

24. Louise Creighton, *Memoir*, p. 62.

25. Louise Creighton, *Life and Letters*, i, p. 157.

26. Ibid., p. 159.

27. Ibid., pp. 177–78.

28. Ibid., pp. 163–64.

29. Attributed to Albert Grey by his biographer. Harold Begbie, *Albert, Fourth Earl Grey: A Last Word* (1918), p. 44.

30. Louise Creighton, *Life and Letters*, i, p. 166.

31. Ibid.

32. Louise Creighton, *Memoir*, pp. 63–64.

33. Ibid., p. 63.

34. Ibid.

35. Ibid.

36. Louise Creighton, *Life and Letters*, i, p. 196.

37. Ibid., p. 167. Also, MS letter, Rev. G. H. P. Karney (vicar of Embleton) to author, 16 September 1965.

38. Louise Creighton, *Memoir*, p. 63.

39. Ibid., p. 64.

40. Louise Creighton, *Life and Letters*, i, p. 169; Louise Creighton, *Memoir*, p. 64.

41. Louise Creighton, *Letters to her Mother*, 29 January 1877, pp. 148–49.

42. Louise Creighton, *Life and Letters*, i, p. 168.

43. In the 1960s the vicar of Embleton was saddened that the hall had 'fallen on evil days. Village people today', he said, 'have cars and television, so for their entertainment they either leave the village altogether or they sit at home glued to the TV ... The result is that Creighton Hall is not much patronized by village organisations or functions and consequently cannot pay its way.' MS letter, Rev. G. H. P. Karney to author, 9 August 1966.

44. Louise Creighton, *Life and Letters*, i, p. 168.

45. Louise Creighton, *Letters to her Mother*, 8 January 1877, p. 144.

46. The Band of Hope was particularly prominent at that time in nonconformist denominations such as Methodism. See Colin Ford and Brian Harrison, *A Hundred Years Ago: Britain in the 1880s in Words and Photographs* (1983), pp. 91, 101.

47. Louise Creighton, *Letters to her Mother*, 23 May 1875, p. 87.

48. Ibid., 27 January 1879, pp. 246–47.

49. Louise Creighton, *Memoir*, p. 65.

50. Louise Creighton, *Letters to her Mother*, 30 November 1880, p. 305.

51. Louise Creighton, *Memoir*, pp. 65–66.

52. Ibid., p. 64.

53. Great Britain, *Report of the Committee of Council on Education (England and Wales)*, 187, pp. 605–8.

54. Edward Bateson, *History of Northumberland* (1895), ii, p. 71.

55. The Embleton school was named the Vincent Edwards Church of England Primary School after a former vicar who actually built the school out of his own funds.

56. James T. Covert, 'Mandell Creighton and English Education' (unpublished University of Oregon doctoral dissertation, 1967).

57. Louise Creighton, *Life and Letters*, i, p. 168.

58. Ibid., ii, pp. 170–71.

59. Ibid., i, p. 168.

60. Mandell Creighton, *Thoughts on Education: Speeches and Sermons*, ed. Louise Creighton (1902), pp. 28–29, 39.

61. Louise Creighton, *Letters to her Mother*, 25 April 1875, pp. 78–79.

62. Mandell Creighton, 'Duties of Guardians with Regard to Education', *Reports of the Poor Law District Conferences* (1877), pp. 170–81; (1878), pp. 142–49. See Louise Creighton, *Life and Letters*, i, p. 187.

63. Mandell Creighton, 'Duties of Guardians', *Reports of the Poor Law*, (1881) pp. 80–81. See Louise Creighton, *Life and Letters*, i, pp. 204–5.

64. Frances Knight, *The Nineteenth-Century Church and English Society* (1995), p. 1.

65. Mandell Creighton, *University and Other Sermons*, ed. Louise Creighton (1903), pp. 71–89.

66. Ibid., pp. 90–123.
67. Louise Creighton, *Life and Letters*, i, pp. 186, 198.
68. Louise Creighton, *Letters to her Mother*, 9 April 1878, pp. 209–10.
69. Louise Creighton, *Life and Letters*, i, p. 206.
70. Ibid., p. 222.
71. Ibid., p. 208; Owen Chadwick, *The Victorian Church* (1970), ii, p. 346.
72. Louise Creighton, *Life and Letters*, i, pp. 212, 242–43. The Church of England inaugurated the first church congress in the 1860s as a means of broadening input from diocesan clergy and laity regarding national church policy. They were conducted periodically thereafter. See Owen Chadwick, *Victorian Church*, ii, pp. 359ff.
73. Louise Creighton, *Life and Letters*, i, p. 243.
74. See Mandell Creighton, 'Clerical Inaccuracies in Conducting Church Services', *Clergyman's Magazine*, 18 (1884), pp. 168–76.
75. Louise Creighton, *Life and Letters*, i, pp. 206–7.
76. See Chapter 16 below for discussion of the ritual controversy.
77. Louise Creighton, *Memoir*, p. 66.
78. Ibid.
79. See Trevelyan, *Grey of Fallodon*, passim.
80. Louise Creighton, *Memoir*, p. 67.
81. Louise Creighton, *Life and Letters*, i, p. 234.
82. Mandell Creighton, *Memoir of Sir George Grey, Bart, G.C.B.* (1884, 1901).
83. Louise Creighton *Memoir*, p. 67. Charles Lindley Wood, second Viscount Halifax.
84. Ibid., Albert eventually became the fourth Earl Grey.
85. Ibid., pp. 67–68.
86. Ibid., pp. 68–69.
87. Louise Creighton, *Letters to her Mother*, 17 November 1879, p. 269.
88. Louise Creighton *Memoir*, p. 69.
89. Louise Creighton, *Life and Letters*, i, p. 197.
90. Rudolph de Cordova, 'Lord Bishop of London', *Strand Magazine* (November 1899), p. 530.
91. Louise Creighton, *Life and Letters*, i, p. 224.

Chapter 9: The Happiest Years

1. Rudolph de Cordova, 'Bishop of London', *Strand Magazine* (November 1899), p. 528.
2. Ibid.
3. Louise Creighton, *Memoir of a Victorian Woman: Reflections of Louise Creighton, 1850–1936*, ed. James Thayne Covert (1994), pp. 62–63.
4. Louise Creighton, *Memoir*, p. 80.
5. Ibid., pp. 69–70.
6. Marion Lockhead, *The Victorian Household* (1964), 108. Also see John Sutherland, *Mrs Humphry Ward: Eminent Victorian, Pre-Eminent Edwardian* (1991), passim.

7. A photograph of this portrait is included in this book, plate 18.

8. See Mandell Creighton and Mrs J. R. Green correspondence in A. C. Green Papers, National Library of Ireland, Dublin. Mrs Green had a habit of not dating her letters, but from contents it is evident that this letter and several others were written during the last three years Creighton was at Embleton.

9. Ibid.

10. Sir George Otto Trevelyan's maternal uncle was Thomas Babington Macaulay, the great historian; one of his sons was George Macaulay Trevelyan, eminent historian and biographer in his own right.

11. The Bosanquets of Rock Hall came from an old Huguenot family and were associated with the Charity Organisation Society of London.

12. Louise Creighton, *Letters to her Mother*, 21 April 1879, p. 257.

13. Louise Creighton, *Memoir*, p. 70. Also see Louise Creighton, *Letters to her Mother*, passim.

14. Louise Creighton, *Memoir*, p. 70.

15. Louise Creighton, *Letters to her Mother*, 12 September 1875, p. 101.

16. Louise Creighton, *Memoir*, p. 71.

17. Ibid., pp. 71–72.

18. Ibid., p. 72.

19. Louise Creighton, *Life and Letters of Mandell Creighton*, 2 vols (1904), i, pp. 193–94.

20. Creighton Family Papers, MS letter, Mandell Creighton to Basil Creighton, 28 October 1899. Louise seemingly carried on this tradition with her grandchildren, engaging them in stories, more historical than fanciful no doubt, while taking them for long rambles. To one granddaughter, 'the walks she took us on and the stories she told us' remained vivid memories for her. MS letter, Mary Bailey to author, 21 February 1998.

21. Louise Creighton, *Life and Letters*, i, p. 258.

22. Ibid.

23. Ibid.

24. Ibid., p. 259.

25. Ibid.

26. Ibid., p. 258.

27. Louise Creighton, *Letters to her Mother*, 30 November 1880, p. 306.

28. Louise Creighton, *Memoir*, p. 72.

29. Louise Creighton, *Letters to her Mother*, 8 October 1876, p. 131.

30. Ibid., 12 February 1877, p. 152.

31. Ibid., 2 April 1878, pp. 207–8.

32. Ibid., 22 April 1878, p. 212.

33. Ibid., 13 May 1878, p. 217.

34. Ibid., 21 May 1878, pp. 219–20.

35. Ibid., 4 June 1878, p. 224.

36. Ibid., 10 June 1878, p. 231.

37. Ibid., 24 June 1878, p. 279.

38. Ibid., 1 March 1880, p. 280.
39. Ibid., 30 March 1880, p. 289.
40. Ibid., 12 July 1880, p. 289.
41. Louise Creighton, *Memoir*, p. 72.
42. Louise Creighton, *Letters to her Mother*, 15 April 1877, p. 166. This same punishment was applied to Creighton by a teacher at the Carlisle dame's school. See Louise Creighton, *Life and Letters*, i, p. 4.
43. Louise Creighton, *Letters to her Mother*, summer 1876, p. 129.
44. Ibid., p. 130.
45. Ibid., 9 July 1877, pp. 174; 5 November 1877, p. 188.
46. Ibid., 2 May 1875, p. 81.
47. Ibid., 23 January 1876, p. 106.
48. Ibid., 25 April 1875, p. 78.
49. Ibid., 8 October 1876, p. 131.
50. Ibid., 22 April 1878, pp. 211–12.
51. Ibid., 13 April 1880, p. 283.
52. Ibid., 12 November 1876, p. 136.
53. Ibid., 1 January 1877, pp. 142–43.
54. Ibid., 14 January 1877, p. 145.
55. Ibid., 18 February 1877, pp. 154–56.
56. Ibid., 17 May 1878, p. 222.
57. Keith Thomas, *Man and the Natural World: Changing Attitudes in England, 1500–1800* (1983), p. 239.
58. Louise Creighton, *Memoir*, pp. 70–71.
59. Louise Creighton, *Letters to her Mother*, 20 November 1877, p. 189.
60. Louise Creighton, *Memoir*, p. 75.
61. For a history of the Pease family, see Joseph Gurney Pease, *A Wealth of Happiness and Many Bitter Trials: The Journals of Sir Alfred Edward Pease, Restless Man* (1992).
62. Louise Creighton, *Memoir*, p. 75.
63. Louise Creighton, *Letters to her Mother*, 29 October 1877, p. 184.
64. Ibid., 2 January 1878, pp. 194–95.
65. Ibid., 6 January 1878, p. 197.
66. Following the custom of the day, for the following year the initial page of the Creightons' stationery was edged in black.
67. Louise Creighton, *Letters to her Mother*, 28 January 1878, p. 199.
68. Louise Creighton, *Memoir*, p. 76.
69. Ibid. One wonders if Walter was born by Caesarean section.
70. Ibid.
71. Ibid.
72. Ibid., pp. 78–79.
73. Ibid.
74. Ibid., p. 79.
75. Ibid., p. 77.

76. Ibid.

77. Louise Creighton, *Life and Letters*, i, p. 211.

78. Louise Creighton, *Memoir*, pp. 77–78.

79. Ibid., p. 78.

80. Ibid., p. 71.

81. Louise Creighton, *Letters to her Mother*, 24 June 1878, p. 230.

82. Louise Creighton, *Memoir*, p. 71.

83. Louise Creighton, *Life and Letters*, i, pp. 180, 193.

84. Louise Creighton, *Memoir*, p. 71 and Louise Creighton, *Letters to her Mother*, 12 July 1880, pp. 288–89.

85. Louise Creighton, *Memoir*, p. 71.

86. Louise Creighton, *Life and Letters*, i, p. 209.

87. G. M. Trevelyan, *Grey of Fallodon: The Life and Letters of Sir Edward Grey, Afterwards Viscount of Fallodon* (1937), p. 18.

88. Ibid.

89. Ibid., p. 36.

90. Joseph G. Pease, *The Journals of Sir Alfred Edward Pease*, pp. 10–11.

91. Ibid, p. xiii; Louise Creighton, *Life and Letters*, i, pp. 215–19, and passim.

92. Ibid., p. 219.

93. Ibid, p. 347.

94. Trevelyan, *Grey of Fallodon*, p. 23.

95. Louise Creighton, *Life and Letters*, i, p. 201.

96. Ibid.

97. Louise Creighton, *Letters to her Mother*, 13 April 1880, p. 282.

98. Trevelyan, *Grey of Fallodon*, pp. 22–23.

99. Louise Creighton, *Life and Letters*, i, pp. 202–3.

100. Trevelyan, *Grey of Fallodon*, p. 23.

101. Ibid., pp. 23–24; Louise Creighton, *Life and Letters*, i, p. 203.

Chapter 10: A Great Work

1. Louise Creighton, *Life and Letters of Mandell Creighton*, 2 vols (1904), i, p. 191.

2. See Bibliography for a complete list of Mandell and Louise Creightons' published books.

3. Louise Creighton, *Life and Letters*, i, pp. 182–83.

4. Ibid., p. 182.

5. Ibid.

6. See G. A. N. Lowndes, *The Silent Social Revolution: An Account of the Expansion of Public Education in England and Wales, 1895–1935* (1937).

7. Louise Creighton, *Memoir of a Victorian Woman: Reflections of Louise Creighton, 1850–1936*, ed. James Thayne Covert (1994), p. 54; Louise Creighton, *Life and Letters*, i, pp. 146–47.

8. Louise Creighton, *Memoir*, p. 54.

9. Louise Creighton, *Life of Edward the Black Prince* (1876), p. 63.

10. Louise Creighton, *Letters to her Mother*, 6 March 1876, p. 113. Also see Louise Creighton, *Life and Letters*, i, pp. 182–84.

11. Louise Creighton, *Letters to her Mother*, summer 1876, p. 28.

12. Ibid., 12 November 1876, p. 137.

13. Ibid., 5 November 1877, p. 188.

14. Ibid., 21 May 1878, p. 220.

15. Ibid., 27 January 1879, p. 247.

16. Ibid.

17. Ibid., 11 October 1880, pp. 300–1. Louise refers to Edward Freeman's six-volume study of the Norman Conquest.

18. Ibid., 30 November 1880, p. 306.

19. Louise Creighton, *Memoir*, p. 73.

20. *Spectator* (6 May 1882), pp. 598–99.

21. Louise also claimed to have written a short story of village life hoping that it might be suitable for the Society for Promoting Christian Knowledge, but this manuscript too was not accepted by a publisher and now no longer exists. Louise Creighton, *Memoir*, p. 73.

22. *Academy*, vol. 12, no. 152 (3 April 1875); also see vol. 12 to vol. 13, no. 321 (29 June 1878), and specifically, vol. 11, no. 255 (24 March 1877), pp. 242–43, and vol. 12, no. 271 (14 July 1877), pp. 30–31.

23. Mandell Creighton, 'Aeneas Sylvius Piccolomini, Pope', *Macmillan's Magazine*, 27 (1872), pp. 113–22, 294–309; and 'Dante', ibid., 29 (1873), pp. 554–63, 30 (1874), pp. 56–67. Reprinted in Mandell Creighton, *Historical Essays and Reviews*, ed. Louise Creighton (1902).

24. Mandell Creighton, 'A Schoolmaster of the Renaissance', *Macmillan's Magazine*, 32 (1875), pp. 509–19; 'A Learned Lady of the Renaissance', ibid., 42 (1880), pp. 136–44. Reprinted in Mandell Creighton, *Historical Essays and Reviews*.

25. See Chapter 5 above. Mandell Creighton, 'The Endowment of Research', *Macmillan's Magazine*, 34 (1876), pp. 186–92.

26. Mandell Creighton, 'The Northumberland Border', *Macmillan's Magazine*, 50 (1884), pp. 321–33; also published with appendices in *Archeological Journal*, 42 (1885), pp. 41–89. Reprinted in Mandell Creighton, *Historical Essays and Reviews*.

27. Louise Creighton, *Life and Letters*, i, pp. 237–238. See Frederic Seebohm, *The English Village Community* (1882).

28. Mandell Creighton, 'Alnwick Castle', *Magazine of Art*, 5 (1881–82), pp. 140–45, 195–200.

29. Louise Creighton, *Life and Letters*, i, p. 239; see also Edward Bateson, ed., *A History of Northumberland*, 15 vols (1895-).

30. Creighton Family Papers, MS letter, Mandell Creighton to J. Peile, 25 November 1892.

31. Mandell Creighton, 'Hoghton Tower', *Magazine of Art*, 10 (1887), pp. 19–24, 68–72.

32. Mandell Creighton, 'Alnwick Castle', ibid., p. 140.

33. Mandell Creighton, 'A Man of Culture', ibid. (*c.* 1882), pp. 270–77. Reprinted in Mandell Creighton, *Historical Essays and Reviews*.

34. Mandell Creighton, 'Influence of the Reformation on England, with Special Reference to the Writings of John Wiclif', *Church Congress Reports* (1884); see Mandell Creighton, *The Church and the Nation*, ed. Louise Creighton (1901), pp. 166–76 for reprint.

35. Mandell Creighton, 'John Wiclif at Oxford', *Church Quarterly*, 5 (October 1877), pp. 489–92.

36. Louise Creighton, *Life and Letters*, i, pp. 190, 189.

37. Louise Creighton, *Life and Letters*, i, pp. 190–91.

38. Ibid.

39. The first two volumes appeared in October 1882; but, when it became clear to him over the next decade and a half that he could not complete the series, the title was changed in the last edition when the final volume appeared in 1894 to *A History of the Papacy from the Great Schism to the Sack of Rome*, thus covering the years 1378 to 1529.

40. Louise Creighton, *Letters to her Mother*, 30 November 1880, p. 306.

41. Louise Creighton, *Life and Letters*, i, p. 196.

42. Pope Leo XIII's decision to open the Vatican archives to all scholars was in 1883. Ludwig von Pastor was the first to gain access to the Vatican archives which made his massive history of the papacy (sixteen volumes, 1886–1933; English translation, forty volumes 1891–1953) supersede the works of Creighton or Ranke. J. T. Covert, 'Ludwig von Pastor', *New Catholic Encyclopedia*.

43. The major work of an English Roman Catholic priest-historian, Horace K. Mann, was the *Lives of the Popes in the Middle Ages* in nineteen volumes, (1902–32).

44. G. P. Gooch, *History and Historians in the Nineteenth Century* (1913, 1959), p. 352.

45. Acton, Lord, *Selections from the Correspondence of the First Lord Acton*, vol. 1, eds John N. Figgis and Reginald V. Laurence (1917), p. 306.

46. Louise Creighton, *Life and Letters*, i, p. 219.

47. Ibid., p. 222.

48. Ibid., p. 231.

49. Mandell Creighton, *A History of the Papacy from the Great Schism to the Sack of Rome* (1882, 1901), i, pp. v, viii.

50. See Claude Jenkins, 'Bishop Creighton's View of History', *Church Quarterly Review*, 218 (January 1930), p. 202. Also, Andrew Fish, 'Acton, Creighton and Lea: A Study in History and Ethics', *Pacific Historical Review*, 16 (February 1947), pp. 59–69.

51. The original two volumes carried the papacy up through the councils of Basel and Ferrara-Florence (1438–39), to the final death of the conciliar theory and the restoration of the papal monarchy with the elections of Pope Nicholas V and Pope Pius II in the mid fifteenth century.

52. Mandell Creighton, *History of the Papacy*, i, pp. vi–vii.

53. Lord Acton, 'Review of *A History of the Papacy*', *Academy*, 22 (9 December 1882), p. 407; also see Louise Creighton, *Life and Letters*, i, p. 227.

54. Ibid., p. 226.

55. Lord Acton, 'Review of *A History of the Papacy*', *Academy*, p. 407. Also see Fish, 'Acton, Creighton and Lea', *Pacific Historical Review*, p. 61.

56. Louise Creighton, *Life and Letters*, i, p. 265.

57. Attributed to Henry Sidgwick. Gooch, *History and Historians*, p. 365.

58. Acton, 'Review of *A History of the Papacy*', pp. 407, 408.

59. Louise Creighton, *Life and Letters*, i, p. 265.

60. Ibid., pp. 228–29.

61. Ibid., pp. 229–30.

62. J. R. Green, *Letters of John Richard Green, 1837–1883*, ed. Leslie Stephen (1901), p. 483.

63. H. A. MacDougall, 'Acton, John Emerich Edward Dalberg', *New Catholic Encyclopedia*.

64. Mandell Creighton, *Historical Lectures and Addresses*, ed. Louise Creighton (1903), p. 261.

65. Louise Creighton, *Life and Letters*, i, p. 231.

66. Ibid., p. 265; see also Owen Chadwick, *Creighton on Luther: An Inaugural Lecture* (1959), p. 35; and Jenkins, 'Bishop Creighton's View of History', pp. 214–15; also Gooch, *History and Historians* for more on Ranke, Creighton, Acton et al.

67. Louise Creighton, *Life and Letters*, i, p. 243.

68. Ibid.

69. 'Accounts of Dixie Fund', ref. SCH. 1.16, Emmanuel College Archives; see also Shuckburgh, *Emmanuel College*, passim.

70. Louise Creighton, *Life and Letters*, i, p. 245.

71. Ibid., pp. 274–75. It has been suggested that, when she printed the letter to Creighton in her biography, Louise Creighton failed to ask Gwatkin's permission, and, according to G. G. Coulton, 'as Mrs Gwatkin always confessed, her husband would not have granted it', p. 105.

72. Creighton wrote a strong letter of recommendation to James Bryce, one of the electors. See early part of Chapter 13 below. MS letter, Mandell Creighton to James Bryce, 7 June 1891, James Bryce Papers, Bodleian Library, Oxford.

73. Edmund A. Knox, *Reminiscences of an Octogenarian, 1847–1934* (1935), p. 101.

74. Merton College Register, MCR 1.5a, 30 October 1884.

75. Louise Creighton, *Life and Letters*, i, p. 248.

76. Ibid., p. 247.

77. Ibid., p. 248.

78. MS letter, Mandell Creighton to Mrs J. R. Green, 31 July 1884, A. S. Green Papers, National Library, Dublin; also Louise Creighton, *Life and Letters*, i, pp. 248–49.

79. MS letter, Mandell Creighton to Mrs J. R. Green, 22 May 1884.

80. Louise Creighton, *Life and Letters*, i, p. 251.

81. Frances Knight, *The Nineteenth-Century Church and English Society* (1995), p. 201.
82. See ibid.; also K. S. Inglis, *Churches and the Working Classes in Victorian England* (1963), pp. 1, 7, 18, and passim.
83. Owen Chadwick, *The Victorian Church* (1970), ii, p. 472; see also Alan D. Gilbert, *Religion and Security in Industrial England: Church, Chapel and Social Change, 1740–1914* (1979), pp. 28–29.
84. David Newsome, *Godliness and Good Learning: Four Studies on a Victorian Ideal* (1961), p. 33.
85. M. Creighton, 'A Charge Delivered to the Clergy of the Diocese of London at St Paul's Cathedral Church on 21 February 1900', *The Church and the Nation: Charges and Addresses*, ed. Louise Creighton (1901), pp. 287–323.
86. Louise Creighton, *Life and Letters*, i, p. 251.
87. Louise Creighton, *Memoir*, p. 80.
88. For an edited version of Creighton's 'Farewell Sermon', see Louise Creighton, *Life and Letters*, i, pp. 252–54.
89. See A. R. Gray, 'Mandell Creighton, Pastor, Scholar and Man', *Sewanee Review*, 15 (1907), pp. 232–34.

Chapter 11: A Breath of Fresh Air

1. E. S. Shuckburgh, *Emmanuel College* (1904), p. 173.
2. Louise Creighton, *Life and Letters of Mandell Creighton*, 2 vols (1904), i, p. 274; in Louise Creighton, *Memoir of a Victorian Woman: Reflections of Louise Creighton, 1850–1936*, ed. James Thayne Covert (1994), p. 81, the size of the land is given as a quarter of an acre, but this is a misprint according to her original memoir document.
3. Louise Creighton, *Memoir*, p. 81.
4. Ibid., p. 83.
5. Ibid., pp. 81–82.
6. Ibid., p. 82.
7. Ibid.
8. Ibid.
9. Mary Kathleen Lyttelton, the daughter of George Clive of Perrystone Court, Herefordshire, married Arthur Lyttelton in 1880. They had three children. She died in January 1907.
10. A fourth woman friend was Nea Ryle, wife of Cambridge fellow Herbert Edward Ryle, later Hulsean Professor of Divinity and Bishop (of Exeter and of Winchester), and then Dean of Westminster. As it turned out her choice of the first three women 'was perfectly successful', she said. 'I did not make very real friends with Mrs Ryle at Cambridge, though I liked her and laid a good foundation for future friendship in later years.' Louise Creighton, *Memoir*, p. 82.
11. Beatrice Webb, *Our Partnership*, eds Barbara Drake and Margaret I. Cole (1948), p. 206. Elsewhere Beatrice suggests she met the Creightons 'in the autumn of

1888'. See Beatrice Webb, *My Apprenticeship* (1926), p. 338 n. 1. The former is probably correct.

12. Ibid.

13. B. Webb, *Our Partnership*, p. 206.

14. Louise Creighton, *Memoir*, p. 83. Louise, in the biography of her husband, refers to Beatrice and Sidney Webb as 'his friends'. Louise Creighton, *Life and Letters of Mandell Creighton*, ii, p. 444.

15. Louise Creighton, *Memoir*, p. 83.

16. F. J. H. Jenkinson, diary for 1890. Cambridge University Library, Add. MS 7413, 31 January and 14 June 1890.

17. Louise Creighton, *Memoir*, p. 83.

18. Louise Creighton, *Life and Letters*, i, p. 292–96.

19. MS appreciation, William Chawner, MAS. 2.1.2, Emmanuel College Archives, Cambridge; also Louise Creighton, *Life and Letters*, i, p. 297.

20. See Owen Chadwick, *The Victorian Church* (1970), ii, p. 176.

21. Louise Creighton, *Life and Letters*, i, p. 256.

22. Mandell Creighton, *Historical Lectures and Addresses*, ed. Louise Creighton (1903), p. 225.

23. Louise Creighton, *Life and Letters*, i, p. 297.

24. Ibid.

25. Ibid., p. 275.

26. See Bibliography; also H. A. MacDougall, 'Acton, John Emerich Edward Dalberg', *New Catholic Encyclopedia*, pp. 101–2.

27. Mrs Humphry Ward, *A Writer's Recollections* (1918), ii, p. 50.

28. Lord Acton, *Letters of Lord Acton to Mary, Daughter of the Right Hon. W. E. Gladstone*, ed. Herbert Paul (1904), p. 197.

29. James Bryce, *Studies in Contemporary Biography* (1911), p. 387.

30. Edmund Gosse, *Portrait and Sketches* (1913), p. 184.

31. See L. Wiese, *German Letters on English Education: Written during an Educational Tour in 1876*, trans. and ed. by Leonhard Schmitz (1877), p. 135; Noel Annan, *Leslie Stephen: His Thoughts and Character in Relation to his Time* (1952), p. 22; and W. E. Heitland, 'Cambridge in the "Seventies"', in H. Granville-Barker, ed. *The Eighteen-Seventies: Essays by Fellows of the Royal Society of Literature* (1929), p. 262.

32. A. J. Grant, ed., *English Historians* (1906), pp. 75–76.

33. G. P. Gooch, *History and Historians in the Nineteenth Century* (1913, 1959), pp. 344–45.

34. L. E. Elliott-Binns, *The Development of English Theology in the Later Nineteenth Century* (1952), pp. 45–46.

35. Owen Chadwick, *Creighton on Luther: An Inaugural Lecture* (1959), pp. 2–3; Louise Creighton, *Life and Letters*, i, pp. 277–79.

36. Ibid., pp. 276–277.

37. Another feature was the decision to give students greater option to explore either theoretical or practical history. Ibid., p. 277.

38. Ibid., pp. 282–83.
39. See MS letters, Mandell Creighton to F. J. H. Jenkinson, 25 December 1889, 13 February 1890, and 7 May [1891], Jenkinson Papers, University Library, Cambridge.
40. Louise Creighton, *Life and Letters*, i, p. 282.
41. Ibid., i, p. 278–82. Also see entire lecture reprinted in Mandell Creighton, *Historical Lectures and Addresses*, pp. 1–28.
42. Cf. Claude Jenkins, 'Bishop Creighton's View of History', *Church Quarterly Review*, 218 (January 1930), p. 226; Elliott-Binns, *Development of English Theology*, p. 59; and Chadwick, *Creighton on Luther*, p. 5.
43. Mandell Creighton, *Historical Lectures and Addresses*, pp. 5–6.
44. Ibid., pp. 7–8.
45. Ibid., p. 27.
46. Ibid., p. 18.
47. Ibid., p. 19.
48. Ibid.
49. Edmund Gosse *Portraits and Sketches*, p. 184.
50. Louise Creighton, *Life and Letters*, i, pp. 285–86.
51. Ibid., p. 284.
52. Ibid., pp. 284–85.
53. Ibid., p. 287.
54. Ibid., p. 286.
55. John N. Figgis, *Churches in the Modern State* (1914), pp. 233–34.
56. Ibid., pp. 231–32.
57. Edmund Gosse, *Portraits and Sketches*, p. 169.
58. Louise Creighton, *Life and Letters*, i, p. 290.
59. See Alice Gardner, *A Short History of Newnham College Cambridge* (1921).
60. Ibid., pp. 96–97; Louise Creighton, *Life and Letters*, i, pp. 288–89, 304, 341; also James W. Thompson, *A History of Historical Writing* (1942), i, pp. 394–95.
61. Ibid., pp. 298–99.
62. MS appreciation, William Chawner, MAS. 2.1.2., Emmanuel College Archives, Cambridge.
63. MS source as quoted in W. G. Fallows, *Mandell Creighton and the English Church* (1964), p. 14.
64. Creighton once publicly admitted just before his death: 'If I venture to talk about teaching, it is because I have spent a great part of my life in teaching.' Louise Creighton, *Life and Letters*, i, p. 78; and Mandell Creighton, *Thoughts on Education: Speeches and Sermons*, ed. Louise Creighton (1902), p. 70.
65. Louise Creighton, *Life and Letters*, i, p. 275.
66. Louise Creighton, *Memoir*, p. 84.
67. The Perse School for Girls was established in 1881 from part of the endowment of the more renowned boys' school of the same name which was founded centuries earlier. See M. A. Scott, *The Perse School for Girls: The First Hundred Years, 1881–1981* (1981).

68. Creighton Family Papers, MS letter, William Gladstone to Mandell Creighton, 9 June 1885.

69. Louise Creighton, *Life and Letters*, i, pp. 305–6.

70. Ibid., p. 310.

71. Louise Creighton, *Memoir*, p. 84.

72. Louise Creighton, *Life and Letters*, i, p. 312; Louise Creighton, *Memoir*, pp. 84–85.

73. Ibid., p. 84.

74. Ibid., p. 85.

75. Ibid., pp. 85–86.

76. Louise Creighton, *Life and Letters*, i, pp. 312–13.

77. Ibid., p. 313. Both Mandell and Louise edited a number of his sermons, such as *The Claims of the Common Life: Sermons Preached in Merton College Chapel, 1871–1874*, ed. Louise Creighton (1905); *The Heritage of the Spirit and Other Sermons* (1896); *Lessons from the Cross* (1898); *The Mind of St Peter and Other Sermons*, ed. Louise Creighton (1904); *University and Other Sermons*, ed. Louise Creighton (1903).

78. Louise Creighton, *Life and Letters*, i, p. 316.

79. Ibid., pp. 318–19.

80. Ibid., p. 317.

81. K. S. Inglis, *Churches and the Working Classes in Victorian England* (1963), p. 1, and passim.

82. Louise Creighton, *Life and Letters*, i, p. 314.

83. Ibid., p. 315.

84. Barbara Caine, *Victorian Feminists* (1992), p. 211.

85. Louise Creighton, *Life and Letters*, i, p. 392; Louise Creighton, *Letters to her Mother*, p. 317 n. 14; and Louise Creighton, *Memoir*, p. 172 n. 9. Also Jane Lewis, *Women and Social Action in Victorian and Edwardian England* (1991), pp. 10, 13ff. Creighton likely first learned of the COS through a Northumberland neighbour, Charles Bosanquet of Rock Hall, who was its first national secretary and half-brother of Bernard Bosanquet, Idealist philosopher and husband of social reformer and theorist Helen Dendy Bosanquet. Helen Dendy was a student at Newnham in those days and more than likely knew Mandell Creighton.

86. Louise Creighton, 'Women's Settlements', *Nineteenth Century* (1908), pp. 607–13. Also see Jane Lewis, *Women and Social Action in Victorian and Edwardian England*, p. 209.

87. Mandell Creighton, *University and Other Sermons*, p. 183.

88. B. Webb, *Our Partnership*, pp. 206–7.

89. Louise Creighton, *Memoir*, p. 86.

90. Ibid., p. 86.

Chapter 12: Inspiring Influences

1. Beatrice Webb, *My Apprenticeship* (1926), p. 338 n. 1.
2. Founder of the National Vigilance Association. See Chapter 11 above.
3. Louise Creighton, *Memoir of a Victorian Woman: Reflections of Louise Creighton, 1850–1936*, ed. James Thayne Covert (1994), pp. 89–90.
4. Beatrice Webb, *Our Partnership*, eds Barbara Drake and Margaret I. Cole (1948), p. 136. See also Jane Lewis, *Women and Social Action in Victorian and Edwardian England* (1991), p. 133.
5. Cf. Lewis, *Women and Social Action*, pp. 2–9, 87, 133, 249; Barbara Caine, *Victorian Feminists* (1992), pp. 216, 235; John Sutherland, *Mrs Humphry Ward: Eminent Victorian, Pre-Eminent Edwardian* (1991), p. 325.
6. Louise Creighton, *Memoir*, pp. 88–89.
7. Ibid., p. 145. While such reasoning may seem odd in more modern times where political solutions regarding social policy, at the national level, are widely accepted, in those more simplistic days of Victorian England, before big government, problems and solutions in society were conceived to be more locally oriented.
8. Ibid., p. 89.
9. Louise Creighton, 'The Appeal Against Female Suffrage: A Rejoinder', *Nineteenth Century* (August 1889), pp. 347–54.
10. According to John Sutherland, this 'Rejoinder' article was of Mary Ward's doing and that she used Louise 'as her front woman' to draft the response. Sutherland, *Mrs Humphry Ward*, pp. 198–99.
11. Janet Trevelyan, *The Life of Mrs Humphry Ward* (1923), pp. 228–29.
12. Louise Creighton, 'A Rejoinder', p. 347.
13. Ibid., p. 347. The Fawcett allusion was incorrect. It was actually six hundred in Alfred, Lord Tennyson's poem *The Charge of the Light Brigade*.
14. Ibid., p. 348.
15. Ibid., p. 349.
16. See Lewis, *Women and Social Action*, p. 247.
17. Louise Creighton, 'A Rejoinder', pp. 350–51.
18. The term 'feminist' has a twentieth-century origin. B. Caine, *Victorian Feminists*, p. 4.
19. Louise Creighton, 'A Rejoinder', p. 354.
20. See Chapter 17 below.
21. Sutherland, *Mrs Humphry Ward*, p. 198.
22. Louise Creighton, *Memoir*, p. 90.
23. Ibid.
24. Ibid., pp. 90–91.
25. John Harvard left half of his estate—a goodly sum—to the college in 1638 along with his four hundred volume collection of books on theology, the classics, and general literature.

26. Louise Creighton, *Life and Letters of Mandell Creighton*, 2 vols (1904), i, pp. 355–57.
27. Ibid., p. 358.
28. Louise Creighton, *Memoir*, p. 88.
29. Louise Creighton, *Life and Letters*, i, p. 359.
30. MS letter, Mandell Creighton to James Bryce, 27 October 1886, James Bryce Papers, Bodleian Library, Oxford.
31. Material on the celebration was taken from various files in the Harvard archives, e.g. Francis Ellingwood Abbot, 'Diary', 1886; Dan Louis Smith, scrapbook (Class of 1888); Albert Thorndike, scrapbook (Class of 1881), Harvard University Library Archives, Cambridge, Massachusetts.
32. Louise Creighton, *Life and Letters*, i, p. 361.
33. MS fragment, Notes of J. R. Lowell's Anniversary Address at Harvard, Emmanuel College Archives; also see Louise Creighton, *Life and Letters*, i, p. 363.
34. *Boston Herald*, Thursday, November 11, 1886, Harvard University Archives.
35. Louise Creighton, *Memoir*, p. 88.
36. Louise Creighton, *Life and Letters*, i, p. 366.
37. Louise Creighton, *Life and Letters*, ii, p. 192.
38. Louise Creighton, *Memoir*, p. 91.
39. Ibid., pp. 83–84.
40. Ibid., pp. 86–87.
41. Ibid., p. 87.
42. Louise wrote in her biography of Mandell Creighton that this trip occurred in September 1889, but it was more likely the year earlier. See Louise Creighton, *Life and Letters*, i, p. 384. Also Louise Creighton, *Memoir*, p. 91.
43. Louise Creighton, *Memoir*, p. 91; Louise Creighton, *Life and Letters*, i, pp. 385–86.
44. Louise Creighton, *Memoir*, p. 91.
45. Ibid., 91–92.
46. Ibid., p. 93.
47. Ibid., p. 92.
48. Ibid.
49. Ibid., pp. 92–93.
50. Ibid., p. 93.
51. Louise Creighton, *Life and Letters*, i, p. 333.
52. *English Historical Review*, vol. 1, no. 1 (January 1886).
53. Louise Creighton, *Life and Letters*, i, p. 339.
54. 'Notes on the Greville Memoirs', *English Historical Review*, vol. 1, pp. 105–37. Also, Creighton Family Papers, William Gladstone to Mandell Creighton, five letters, 1884–87.
55. *English Historical Review*, vol. 1, p. 340.
56. Mandell Creighton, *Cardinal Wolsey* (1888).
57. Ibid., p. 2.
58. Ibid., p. 295.
59. Mandell Creighton, *Carlisle* (1889).

60. Mandell Creighton, 'The Italian Bishops of Worcester', *Worcester Diocesan Architectural and Archeological Society's Publication* (1889). Reprinted in Mandell Creighton, *Historical Essays and Reviews*, ed. Louise Creighton (1902).

61. Mandell Creighton, 'The Teaching Work of the Church', *Church Congress Reports* (1885), pp. 338–43; see reprint of his 'Church in History', in Mandell Creighton, *The Church and the Nation: Charges and Addresses*, ed. Louise Creighton (1901), pp. 156–65.

62. Mandell Creighton, 'Harvard College', *Emmanuel College Magazine*, vol. 1, no. 1 (May 1889), pp. 2–9; and Mandell Creighton, 'The Harvard Commemoration', *The Times* (22–23 November 1886). Reprinted in Mandell Creighton, *Historical Essays and Reviews*.

63. Mandell Creighton, 'The Hope of Our Founder', *Emmanuel College Magazine*, vol. 2, no. 2 (1891), pp. 49–59. Reprinted in Mandell Creighton, *University and Other Sermons*.

64. MS letter, Mrs J. R. Green to Mandell Creighton, no date; also see G. W. Prothero, 'Mandell Creighton', *Dictionary of National Biography*, xxii supplement, p. 513.

65. See 'John Richard Green', *Dictionary of National Biography*, 8, pp. 489–92; and 'Philip II' *Encyclopedia Britannica*, xviii, 9th edition. Creighton also wrote a 'History of the Waldenses'.

66. Lytton Strachey, *Portraits in Miniature and Other Essays* (1931, 1962), pp. 205, 207.

67. Louise Creighton, *Life and Letters*, i, p. 368.

68. Ibid.

69. Ibid.

70. As quoted in ibid.

71. Ibid. Also see Jenkins, 'Bishop Creighton's View of History', *Church Quarterly Review*, p. 213.

72. Louise Creighton, *Life and Letters*, i, pp. 369–70.

73. Lord Acton, *Essays on Freedom and Power*, selected with introduction by Gertrude Himmelfarb (1955), pp. 329–39; also see Louise Creighton, *Life and Letters*, i, pp. 371–72.

74. Lord Acton, *Essays in the Liberal Interpretation of History* (1967), xiv–xv.

75. As quoted in Louise Creighton, *Life and Letters*, i, p. 372 and Acton, *Essays on Freedom and Power*, pp. 335–36.

76. Louise Creighton, *Life and Letters*, i, p. 372.

77. Ibid., p. 373; also Acton, *Essays on Freedom and Power*, p. 342.

78. Mandell Creighton, 'The English National Character', *Historical Lectures and Addresses*, ed. Louise Creighton (1903), p. 214.

79. Louise Creighton, *Life and Letters*, i, pp. 374–75; also Acton, *Essays on Freedom and Power*, p. 344.

80. Louise Creighton, *Life and Letters*, i, p. 375; also Acton, *Essays on Freedom and Power*, p. 345.

81. Lord Acton, *Selections from the Correspondence of the First Lord Acton*, John Figgis and Reginald Laurence, eds (1917), i, pp. 309–10.

82. See *English Historical Review*, vol. 1, pp. 571–81.

83. Louise Creighton, *Life and Letters*, i, p. 369.

84. Acton, *Essays on Freedom and Power*, p. 51. Also see Henry Steele Commager, 'Should the Historian Make Moral Judgements?', *American Heritage*, 17 (February 1966), p. 90.

85. Louise Creighton, *Life and Letters*, i, p. 266.

86. Ibid., p. 265.

87. Ibid., pp. 377–78.

88. Mandell Creighton, *Persecution and Tolerance* (1895). This will be discussed in Chapter 13 below.

89. Mandell Creighton, *The Church and the Nation*, p. 205.

90. Mandell Creighton, 'Historical Ethics', *Quarterly Review*, (1905), pp. 32–46; also see reprint in *Living Age*, vol. 28, series 7, no. 3190 (26 August 1905), pp. 515–24.

91. Mandell Creighton, *Quarterly Review*, pp. 39–40, 44; *Living Age*, pp. 519–20, 522.

92. Mandell Creighton, *Quarterly Review*, p. 46, and *Living Age*, p. 524.

93. To counter these moral-minded historians, however, Henry Steele Commager— one of the most respected American historians of the twentieth century—wrote an intriguing article in the 1960s in which he warned historians not to confuse moral judgments with 'professional judgments'. He believed that the historian, in the same way as a judge, or priest, or teacher, or physician, is a creature of his nationality, his culture, and at best can only offer professional assessments that flow from professional training. Commager based his argument on the notion that 'all the relevant evidence is never available, and there are no universal standards' when it comes to history. Henry Steele Commager, 'Should the Historian Make Moral Judgments?' *American Heritage* (1966), pp. 91–93.

Chapter 13: The Blow has Fallen

1. Louise Creighton, *Life and Letters of Mandell Creighton*, 2 vols (1904), i, p. 399.

2. Ibid., p. 224.

3. Ibid., p. 396; also Creighton Family Papers, MS letter, Lord Salisbury to Mandell Creighton, 1 December 1890.

4. Ibid.

5. Louise Creighton, *Life and Letters*, i, p. 397. One advantage—besides the extra income—was the fact that Windsor was near Oxford. MS letter, Mandell Creighton to Miss Owen, 7 December 1890, Bodleian Library, MS Eng. lett. e. 27, fol. 161, pp. 161–62.

6. MS letter, Mrs J. R. Green to Mandell Creighton, 9 December 1890, A. S. Green Papers, National Library of Ireland, Dublin.

7. Louise Creighton, *Memoir of a Victorian Woman: Reflections of Louise Creighton, 1850–1936*, ed. James Thayne Covert (1994), p. 94.

8. Ibid.

9. Louise Creighton, *Life and Letters*, i, pp. 398–99; Louise Creighton, *Memoir*, p. 94.

10. Louise Creighton, *Life and Letters*, i, p. 398.

11. Robert Blake and Hugh Cecil, eds, *Salisbury: The Man and his Policies* (1987), pp. 38, 56, 73, 195.

12. Dudley W. Bahlman, 'The Queen, Mr Gladstone, and Church Patronage', *Victorian Studies*, 3 (June 1960), pp. 252–53

13. Queen Victoria, *The Letters of Queen Victoria: A Selection from Her Majesty's Correspondence and Journals between the Years 1886–1901* (1931), ed. George E. Buckle, 3rd series, iii, p. 9.

14. Ibid.

15. Ibid.

16. In the play the Queen decides to elevate a 'Canon Clayton' to a bishopric in order to remove the canon's wife from court. Louise, of course, must have known of the play, though she never alluded to it, even in her private memoir. More likely Housman, who probably wrote the play in the 1920s, was responding to Louise's public persona at that time. Laurence Housman, 'Promotion Cometh', *Victoria Regina: A Dramatic Biography* (1934), pp. 413–36.

17. Louise Creighton, *Life and Letters*, i, p. 399.

18. Ibid., pp. 399, 401.

19. Ibid., pp. 401–2.

20. Ibid., p. 400.

21. E. Gosse, *Portraits and Sketches* (1913), p. 188.

22. *Cambridge Review: A Journal of University Life and Thought*, 12 (20 February 1891), p. 209.

23. Louise Creighton, *Life and Letters*, i, p. 405.

24. For several of his reviews, see Mandell Creighton, *Historical Essays and Reviews*, ed. Louise Creighton (1902).

25. MS letter, Mandell Creighton to James Bryce, 7 June 1891, James Bryce Papers, Bodleian Library, Oxford. George Coulton, *Fourscore Years: An Autobiography* (1943), p. 105.

26. Ibid.

27. MS letter, Mandell Creighton to James Bryce, 21 February 1891, James Bryce Papers, Bodleian Library, Oxford.

28. Louise Creighton, *Memoir*, p. 100.

29. MS letter, Rachel von Glehn to Fanny von Glehn, 31 October 188?, de Bruyne Family Papers (private collection). Rachel was the daughter of Louise's brother, Alick. Letter in possession of Rachel von Glehn's granddaughter, Anne-Cecile de Bruyne.

30. Interview between Basil Creighton and author, June 1969.

31. Louise Creighton, *Memoir*, pp. 97–98.

32. John Sutherland, *Mrs Humphry Ward: Eminent Victorian, Pre-Eminent Edwardian* (1991), p. 92.

33. Edmund Gosse, *Silhouette* (1925), p. 206.

34. Janet Trevelyan, *The Life of Mrs Humphry Ward* (1923), p. 45.

35. Ibid., p. 65. See also Sutherland, *Mrs Humphry Ward*, p. 108, and Mrs Humphry Ward, *A Writer's Recollections* (1918), passim.

36. Sutherland, *Mrs Humphry Ward*, p. 260.

37. Mrs Humphry Ward, *A Writer's Recollections*, ii, p. 6.

38. Ibid., ii, p. 7.

39. As quoted in Louise Creighton, *Memoir*, p. 98.

40. Ibid.

41. Louise Creighton, *Life and Letters*, ii, pp. 6–8. As one London ticket agent warned the author in 1969: 'There is nothing there but the cathedral!'

42. Mandell Creighton, *The Story of Some English Shires* (1897), p. 300.

43. Louise Creighton, *Life and Letters*, ii, pp. 10.

44. Ibid., p. 25.

45. Ibid., p. 13.

46. Ibid., p. 11.

47. Ibid., pp. 18, 31, 32.

48. Ibid., p. 7.

49. 'Mandell Creighton', *Quarterly Review*, vol. 193, no. 386 (April 1901), p. 605.

50. Louise Creighton, *Life and Letters*, ii, p. 13.

51. Herbert Paul, 'The Late Bishop of London: A Personal Impression', *Nineteenth Century and After*, vol. 50 (July 1901), p. 112.

52. See Louise Creighton, *Life and Letters*, ii, pp. 38–41, 44.

53. Ibid., p. 53.

54. Ibid., pp. 63, 112, 280, 282–83, 349, 375.

55. Ibid., p. 384.

56. G. W. Prothero, 'Mandell Creighton', *Dictionary of National Biography*, xxii, supplement, p. 509.

57. Louise Creighton, *Life and Letters*, ii, p. 114.

58. Ibid., pp. 131, 114–16.

59. Ibid., p. 116.

60. Ibid., p. 115.

61. Hugh McLeod, *Religion and the Working Class in Nineteenth-Century Britain* (1984), pp. x, 60.

62. E. R. Norman, *Church and Society in England, 1770–1970* (1976), p. 157.

63. Louise Creighton, *Life and Letters*, ii, p. 120.

64. Ibid.

65. Ibid., pp. 121–22.

66. Ibid., pp. 124–26.

67. Ibid., p. 130.

68. Ibid.

69. Reprinted in Mandell Creighton, *The Church and the Nation: Charges and Addresses*, ed. Louise Creighton (1901); also see Louise Creighton, *Life and Letters*, ii, pp. 95–96.

70. Mandell Creighton, *The Church and the Nation*, pp. 56–58.

71. Louise Creighton, *Life and Letters*, ii, pp. 95–96.

72. Mandell Creighton, *The Heritage of the Spirit* (1896).

73. See reprint in Mandell Creighton, *The Church and the Nation*, pp. 1–7, 177–86, 207–15; also Louise Creighton, *Life and Letters*, ii, pp. 79, 174–75.

74. Mandell Creighton, 'Laud's Position in the History of the Church of England', *Historical Lectures and Addresses*, ed. Louise Creighton (1903), p. 164.

75. Ibid., p. 176.

76. Ibid., p. 179.

77. Ibid., p. 183.

78. Ibid., p. 185.

79. Most of these are reprinted in Mandell Creighton, *Historical Lectures and Addresses*, or in his *The Church and the Nation*.

80. Louise Creighton, *Life and Letters*, ii, pp. 97–98.

81. Reprinted in Mandell Creighton, *The Church and the Nation*, pp. 187–206.

82. Louise Creighton, *Life and Letters*, ii, p. 97. These include D.C.L., Oxford and Durham; LL.D. Glasgow and Harvard; Litt.D. Dublin.

83. Mandell Creighton, *History of the Papacy from the Great Schism to the Sack of Rome, 1378–1527*, second edition, 6 vols (1897).

84. James B. Mullinger, 'Review of Mandell Creighton's *History of the Papacy*', *English Historical Review* (October 1894), pp. 777, 782.

85. Louise Creighton, *Life and Letters*, ii, p. 87.

86. See Owen Chadwick, *Creighton on Luther: An Inaugural Lecture* (1959), p. 6, passim; also Louise Creighton, *Life and Letters*, ii, p. 86.

87. As quoted in Louise Creighton, *Life and Letters*, ii, p. 91.

88. Mandell Creighton, *Persecution and Tolerance* (1895).

89. Louise Creighton, *Life and Letters*, ii, p. 90.

90. See Chapter 12 above regarding Acton's criticisms of volume 3 and 4 of Creighton's *History of the Papacy*.

91. Mandell Creighton, *Persecution and Toleration* (1895), pp. v, 1.

92. Ibid., pp. 2–3.

93. Louise Creighton, *Life and Letters*, ii, p. 92.

94. Ibid.

95. W. G. Fallows, *Mandell Creighton and the English Church* (1964), p. 16.

96. Mandell Creighton, *Persecution and Toleration*, pp. 123, 137.

97. Louise Creighton, *Life and Letters*, ii, p. 89.

98. Mandell Creighton, *Queen Elizabeth* (1896).

99. See G. R. Elton 'Introduction' to the reprint of *Queen Elizabeth* (1966); also A. L. Rowse, 'Queen Elizabeth and the Historians', *History Today*, vol. 3, no. 9 (September 1953), p. 640.

100. Elton's 'Introduction', Mandell Creighton, *Queen Elizabeth*, pp. x–xi.

101. Mandell Creighton, *The Story of Some English Shires* (1897).

102. Ibid., p. 5.

103. Ibid., p. 6.

Chapter 14: I Went to Visit the Queen

1. Creighton Family Papers, MS letter, Mandell Creighton to Winifred Creighton, 7 December 1894; also see Louise Creighton, *Life and Letters of Mandell Creighton*, 2 vols (1904), ii, p. 100.
2. Louise Creighton, *Memoir of a Victorian Woman: Reflections of Louise Creighton, 1850–1936*, ed. James Thayne Covert (1994), pp. 98–99.
3. Ibid., 99.
4. Louise Creighton, *Memoir*, p. 118.
5. Ibid.
6. Ibid., p. 119.
7. Ibid., p. 116; Louise Creighton, *A First History of France* (1893).
8. Louise Creighton, *Memoir*, p. 98.
9. Ibid., p. 100.
10. Ibid.
11. Ibid., pp. 100–1.
12. Ibid.
13. Ibid., p. 112.
14. Ibid.
15. Ibid.
16. Ibid.
17. Ibid., p. 114.
18. Ibid.
19. Cf. Owen Chadwick, *The Victorian Church* (1970), ii, pp. 269–99, and Jane Lewis, *Women and Social Action in Victorian and Edwardian England* (1991), pp. 9–16ff.
20. Louise Creighton, *Memoir*, p. 114.
21. In the wake of the Oxford Movement, there occurred a revival of Anglican monasteries and nunneries. One of the earliest was the Wantage Sisters, founded by W. J. Butler, vicar of Wantage, in 1848. See Owen Chadwick, *The Victorian Church*, i, pp. 505–11.
22. Louise Creighton, *Memoir*, p. 115. Later in her life, as will be discussed in Chapter 17 below. Louise wrote a short work, published in 1914, on the subject entitled *The Social Disease and How to Fight It.*
23. Louise Creighton, *Memoir*, p. 115. See Chapter 17 below for more of her thoughts on this issue.
24. Ibid.
25. Ibid.
26. Ibid., p. 116.
27. Ibid.
28. Cf. Great Britain, *Lords' Journal*, 128 (1896), p. 7; Great Britain, 4 *Hansard's Parliamentary Debates*, 37 (1896), pp. xxii and 7.
29. Louise Creighton, *Life and Letters*, ii, p. 143.
30. Ibid.

31. Ibid., p. 7.
32. Louise Creighton, *Memoir*, p. 102.
33. Louise Creighton, *Life and Letters*, ii, p. 73.
34. Louise Creighton, *Memoir*, pp. 102–3.
35. Ibid., p. 102.
36. Ibid., p. 117.
37. Ibid., p. 101.
38. Ibid., p. 99.
39. Ibid.
40. Ibid., p. 110.
41. Creighton Family Papers, MS letter, Mandell Creighton to Ella Creighton, 15 September 1896.
42. Louise Creighton, *Memoir*, p. 102.
43. Ibid.
44. Ibid.
45. Creighton Family Papers. See Genealogical Chart.
46. Louise Creighton, *Memoir*, pp. 117–18.
47. 'M. Petriburg.' Latinising the term was the traditional way bishops signed their letters. Creighton Family Papers, MS letter, Mandell Creighton to Winifred Creighton, 4 December 1894. Also see edited letter in Louise Creighton, *Life and Letters*, ii, pp. 100–1.
48. Ibid., p. 135.
49. Virginia Cowles, *Gay Monarch: The Life and Pleasure of Edward VII* (1956), p. 217.
50. Comment by his friend Henry Scott Holland; see Henry Scott Holland, *Personal Studies* (1905), p. 211.
51. Louise Creighton, *Life and Letters*, i, p. 220.
52. Louise Creighton, *Memoir*, pp. 101, 118.
53. MS letter, Basil Creighton to author, 10 September 1965.
54. Louise Creighton, *Memoir*, p. 110.
55. Louise Creighton, *Life and Letters*, ii, p. 18.
56. Ibid., p. 77.
57. Ibid., p. 79; Louise Creighton, *Memoir*, p. 110.
58. Louise Creighton, *Life and Letters*, ii, p. 83.
59. MS letter, Mandell Creighton to Samuel Butler, 11 July 1893, British Library, Add. MS 44034.
60. Clara G. Stillman, *Samuel Butler: A Mid-Victorian Modern* (1932), pp. 248–49.
61. Louise Creighton, *Memoir*, p. 111. Louise probably refers to Henry Festing Jones's biography of Butler (1919) or C. E. M. Joad's biography (1924). Samuel Butler (1835–1902), a man who in many ways came to express the antithesis of Louise's Victorian beliefs, wrote, among other works, *The Way of All Flesh* (1903), an autobiographical novel that shocked the religious sensibilities of many Victorians, most especially those of Louise.
62. Louise Creighton, *Life and Letters*, ii, p. 93; Louise Creighton, *Memoir*, p. 111.

63. Joseph Gurney Pease, *A Wealth of Happiness and Many Bitter Trials: The Journals of Sir Alfred Edward Pease, Restless Man* (1992), p. 106.

64. Louise Creighton, *Memoir*, p. 111.

65. Ibid.

66. Louise Creighton, *Life and Letters*, ii, pp. 146–47.

67. 'Obituary of Mandell Creighton', *Annual Register* (January 1901), p. 104.

68. Louise Creighton, *Memoir*, p. 112.

69. Louise Creighton, *Life and Letters*, ii, p. 148.

70. Ibid., pp. 152–53.

71. Ibid., pp. 153–54.

72. Ibid., pp. 156–57.

73. G. W. Prothero, 'Mandell Creighton', *Dictionary of National Biography*, xxii, supplement, p. 509.

74. Louise Creighton, *Life and Letters*, ii, pp. 158–59.

75. Ibid., pp. 158–60.

76. See reprint, Mandell Creighton, 'The Imperial Coronation at Moscow', in *Historical Essays and Reviews*, ed. Louise Creighton (1902), pp. 297–329.

77. Creighton Family Papers, MS letter, Queen Victoria to Mandell Creighton, 8 September 1896; also Louise Creighton, *Life and Letters*, ii, p. 164.

78. Lytton Strachey, *Portraits in Miniature and Other Essays* (1931, 1962), p. 214.

79. Louise Creighton, *Life and Letters*, ii, p. 161.

80. Creighton Family Papers, MS letter, M. Pobiedonostzeff to Mandell Creighton, 16 September 1897.

81. Louise Creighton, *Life and Letters*, ii, 163–64.

82. Ibid., p. 150.

83. Ibid., pp. 150–51.

84. Ibid., p. 176.

85. Ibid.

86. Ibid., p. 177.

87. Ibid., pp. 177–78.

88. John Jay Hughes, *Absolutely Null and Utterly Void: The Papal Condemnation of Anglican Orders, 1896* (1968), p. 81.

89. Louise Creighton, *Life and Letters*, ii, pp. 178–79.

90. See George H. Tavard, *A Review of Anglican Orders: The Problem and the Solution* (1990), p. 10. See also Hughes, *Absolutely Null and Utterly Void*, pp. 162–63.

91. Tavard, *A Review of Anglican Orders*, p. 134; Hughes, *Absolutely Null and Utterly Void*, p. 287.

92. Louise Creighton, *Life and Letters*, ii, p. 179.

93. Tavard, *A Review of Anglican Orders*, pp. 114–17.

94. Louise Creighton, *Life and Letters*, ii, p. 180–82.

95. Creighton Faamily Papers, MS letter, Lord Salisbury to Mandell Creighton, 28 October 1896; also Louise Creighton, *Life and Letters*, ii, p. 197.

96. Queen Victoria, *The Letters of Queen Victoria: A Selection from Her Majesty's*

Correspondence and Journal between the Years 1886–1901 (1931), ed. George Earle Buckle, 3rd series, iii, p. 106.

97. Ibid., pp. 94–97.

98. Ibid., pp. 100–3; also see G. K. A. Bell, *Randall Davidson, Archbishop of Canterbury* (1935), i, pp. 284–86.

99. Marie Mallet, *Life with Queen Victoria: Marie Mallet's Letters from Court, 1887–1901*, ed. Victor Mallet (1968), p. 94.

100. Louise Creighton, *Memoir*, p. 119.

101. Fallows, *Mandell Creighton and the English Church*, p. 14.

102. Elton, 'Introduction', to Mandell Creighton, *Queen Elizabeth*, p. vii.

103. Louise Creighton, *Memoir*, p. 119.

104. 'Memorials of the Bishops of Peterborough', Diocese Books, Palace Library, Peterborough, England.

105. Stephen Paget, ed., *Henry Scott Holland: Memoir and Letters* (1921), p. 209; also Louise Creighton, *Life and Letters*, ii, p. 198.

Chapter 15: Fulham is a Nice Place

1. Louise Creighton, *Life and Letters of Mandell Creighton*, 2 vols (1904), ii, p. 201.

2. Ibid., p. 202.

3. Creighton Family Papers, MS letter, Louise Creighton to James Bryce, 8 November 1896.

4. Louise Creighton, *Life and Letters*, ii, p. 201.

5. Ibid., pp. 222, 224–25.

6. Bridget Cherry and Nikolaus Pevsner, *London*, iii, *North West* (1991), pp. 235, 238. Fulham Palace ceased to be the official residence of the Bishops of London in the 1970s.

7. Louise Creighton, *Memoir of a Victorian Woman: Reflections of Louise Creighton, 1850–1936*, ed. James Thayne Covert (1994), p. 120. A 'victoria' was a four-wheeler with a collapsible roof, a seat for two passengers and an elevated seat for the driver.

8. Fulham Palace Papers, 132. Thought by some to have been destroyed in the Blitz in the Second World War, London House, with the symbol of the Bishop of London's coat-of-arms visible on the twin drain pipes near the roof line, still stands; it is no longer the city residence of the Bishop of London.

9. Louise Creighton, *Memoir*, p. 120.

10. Ibid., pp. 120–21.

11. Ibid., p. 121.

12. Ibid.

13. MS letter, Louise Creighton to Mary Ward, 9 April 1897, author's collection.

14. Louise mentions the figure of £10,000 in her memoir. She also states that they received a legacy from Creighton's father, and may have received something from the estate of his brother James. Louise Creighton, *Memoir*, p. 135; also A. J. Engel, *From Clergyman to Don: The Rise of the Academic Profession in*

Nineteenth-Century Oxford (1983), p. 124. Incomes for bishops in the Church of England had been established in the reign of William IV earlier in the century, and were not changed until 1902; see G. F. A. Best, *Temporal Pillars: Queen Anne's Bounty, the Ecclesiastical Commissioners and the Church of England* (1964), p. 321.

15. Louise Creighton, *Memoir*, p. 110.

16. Creighton Family Papers, MS letter, Arthur Balfour to Mandell Creighton, 4 March 1898.

17. Louise Creighton, *Life and Letters*, ii, pp. 220–21.

18. Creighton Family Papers, MS letters, M. Creighton to Basil Creighton (nephew), 28 October 1899; Mandell Creighton to Ella Creighton (niece), 1 April 1897, 9 October 1897; Mandell Creighton to Basil Creighton, 7 February 1900; Mandell Creighton to Winifrid Creighton (niece), 22 October 1898.

19. Louise Creighton, *Life and Letters*, ii, pp. 230–32; also F. Temple, *Memoirs of Archbishop Temple by Seven Friends*, ed. E. G. Sandford (1906), ii, pp. 172, 174.

20. Schools under sponsorship of the nondenominational British and Foreign School Society.

21. Schools under sponsorship of the National Society for Promoting the Education of the Poor in the Principles of the Church of England.

22. Sidney Webb, *London Education* (1904), p. 206.

23. Louise Creighton, *Life and Letters*, ii, p. 504.

24. See Mandell Creighton, *Thoughts on Education: Speeches and Sermons*, ed. Louise Creighton (1902), passim; also, Mandell Creighton, *The Church and the Nation*, ed. Louise Creighton (1901), passim.

25. Mandell Creighton, *Church and the Nation*, p. 70.

26. Louise Creighton, *Life and Letters*, ii, p. 189.

27. Great Britain, *Hansard's Parliamentary Debates*, 48 (1897), pp. 67–72. Cf. Louise Creighton, *Life and Letters*, ii, pp. 232–33.

28. Refers to the W. Cowper-Temple clause to the Forster Bill, to be known as the Education Act of 1870. See Bibliography for works devoted to English education at this time.

29. Great Britain, *Hansard's Parliamentary Debates*, 48, p. 67, passim; Cf. Louise Creighton, *Life and Letters*, ii, p. 233.

30. Great Britain, *Hansard's Parliamentary Debates*, 48, p. 72. Louise's concluding sentence is slightly different but with the same meaning. She may have used the actual draft of Creighton's speech whereas the *Hansard Debates* were paraphrased, rather than recorded verbatim. Cf. Louise Creighton, *Life and Letters*, ii, p. 233.

31. Ibid., p. 233.

32. Creighton Family Papers, MS letter, Mandell Creighton to Ella Creighton, 1 April 1897; Cf. Louise Creighton, *Life and Letters*, ii, p. 233.

33. Mandell Creighton, *The Church and the Nation*, pp. 218–19.

34. Louise Creighton, *Life and Letters*, ii, pp. 511–512. Cf. James T. Covert, 'The

Church-State Conflict in Late Nineteenth-Century English Education: One Victorian's View', *University of Portland Review*, 27 (Spring 1975), pp. 33–52. A fuller discussion can be found in the doctoral dissertation by the author, 'Mandell Creighton and English Education' (University of Oregon, 1967).

35. Louise Creighton, *Life and Letters of Thomas Hodgkin* (1917), p. 263.

36. Louise Creighton, *Life and Letters of Mandell Creighton,* ii, p. 225.

37. Ibid., pp. 217–18.

38. Creighton Family Papers, MS letter, Mandell Creighton to Winifred Creighton, 13 February 1898.

39. Louise Creighton, *Life and Letters*, ii, p. 249.

40. Ibid., p. 223.

41. As quoted in ibid., p. 320.

42. Louise Creighton, *Memoir*, p. 123.

43. Lytton Strachey, *Portraits in Miniature and Other Essays* (1931, 1962), pp. 208–9.

44. Margot Asquith, *The Autobiography of Margot Asquith* (1920).

45. One of the many books on this period is Karl Beckson, *London in the 1890s: A Cultural History* (1992). See also Bibliography.

46. *Vanity Fair* (22 April 1897), opposite p. 273.

47. See the collection of photographs and sketches at the National Portrait Gallery.

48. Louise Creighton, *Memoir*, p. 123.

49. Creighton Family Papers, MS letter, Mandell Creighton to Basil Creighton, 14 February 1899.

50. Louise Creighton, *Memoir*, p. 123.

51. Ibid.

52. Ibid., pp. 121–22.

53. Ibid., p. 124.

54. Ibid.

55. R. C. K. Ensor, *England, 1870–1914* (1936, 1963), p. 239.

56. Louise Creighton, *Life and Letters*, ii, p. 238. See reprint of 'National Aspirations' in Mandell Creighton, *The Mind of St Peter and Other Sermons*, ed. Louise Creighton (1904), pp. 55–66.

57. Creighton Family Papers, MS letter, Queen's secretary to Mandell Creighton, 26 June 1897.

58. Louise Creighton, *Life and Letters*, ii, p. 239. No Jubilee description exists in the Creighton Papers.

59. Creighton Family Papers, MS letter, Sir Francis Knollys to Mandell Creighton, 22 June 1897.

60. Louise Creighton, *Life and Letters*, ii, p. 241.

61. Creighton Family Papers, MS letter, Mandell Creighton to Basil Creighton, 23 March 1899.

62. Louise Creighton, *Life and Letters*, ii, p. 241.

63. Louise Creighton, *Memoir*, pp. 126–27.

64. Ibid., p. 125.

65. Ibid., p. 126.

66. Louise Creighton, *Life and Letters*, ii, p. 331.
67. Various student records, Emmanuel College archives.
68. Creighton Family Papers, MS letter, Mandell Creighton to Winifred Creighton, 14 April 1898.
69. Student records, Emmanuel College archives.
70. Louise Creighton, *Memoir*, p. 126.
71. Louise Creighton, *Life and Letters*, ii, p. 328–29.
72. See Louise Creighton, *Memoir*, pp. 135, 160, 167.
73. MS letter, Basil Creighton to author, 10 September 1965.
74. Louise Creighton, *Life and Letters*, ii, p. 331.
75. Creighton Family Papers, MS letter, Walter Creighton to Cuthbert Creighton, no date.
76. Louise Creighton, *Life and Letters*, ii, pp. 128–29.
77. Louise Creighton, *Memoir*, p. 124.
78. Ibid., p. 123.
79. Ibid., p. 122.
80. Ibid.
81. Beatrice Webb, *Our Partnership*, eds Barbara Drake and Margaret I. Cole (1948), pp. 102, 195–96; 198.
82. Richard B. Haldane, *An Autobiography* (1929), p. 138. Also James T. Covert, 'Reorganisation of the University of London, 1884–1900: An Example of Government Intervention in Higher Education', *Duquesne Review*, 14 (Spring 1969), pp. 16–40.
83. See W. H. Allchin, *An Account of the Reconstruction of the University of London*, 3 vols (1905–1912); also Covert, 'Reorganisation of the University of London, 1884–1900', pp. 16–40.
84. Sir Philip Magnus, *Educational Aims and Efforts* (1910), p. 52.
85. Louise Creighton, *Life and Letters*, ii, p. 339.
86. Ibid., pp. 339–340.
87. Great Britain, House of Commons, *Sessional Papers*, 'Report of Statues and Regulations made by the Commissioners appointed under the University of London Act' (1900), p. 57.
88. See Sir Sydney Caine, *The History of the Foundation of the London School of Economics and Political Science* (1963), pp. 78, 80–81; Janet Beveridge, *An Epic of Clare Market: Birth and Early Days of the London School of Economics* (1960), pp. 16–17, 46–48.
89. Louise Creighton, *Life and Letters*, ii, pp. 321, 509.
90. Creighton Family Papers, MS letter, Mandell Creighton to Winifred Creighton, 23 June 1898; also Louise Creighton, *Life and Letters*, ii, p. 322.
91. Ibid., p. 325.
92. 'The Creighton Memorial', *Carlisle Journal*, 7 October 1898.
93. Ibid.

Chapter 16: Tell Her That I Love Her

1. Louise Creighton, *Memoir of a Victorian Woman: Reflections of Louise Creighton, 1850–1936*, ed. James Thayne Covert (1994), p. 131.
2. John Sutherland, *Mrs Humphry Ward: Eminent Victorian, Pre-Eminent Edwardian* (1991), p. 186.
3. Louise Creighton, *Life and Letters of Mandell Creighton*, 2 vols (1904), ii, p. 402.
4. Creighton Family Papers, MS letter, Mandell Creighton to Winifred Creighton, 3 November 1899. Louise Creighton, *Life and Letters*, ii, p. 403.
5. See ibid., pp. 284–315.
6. Ibid., p. 215; 'Mandell Creighton', *Quarterly Review*, vol. 193, no. 86 (April 1901), p. 609.
7. Owen Chadwick, *The Victorian Church* (1970), ii, p. 101, passim.
8. John R. H. Moorman, *The Anglican Spiritual Tradition* (1893), pp. 186, 193.
9. Owen Chadwick, *The Victorian Church*, ii, pp. 355–56.
10. G. I. T. Machin, *Politics and the Churches in Great Britain, 1869–1921* (1987), p. 235.
11. Louise Creighton, *Life and Letters*, ii, p. 284.
12. Ibid., p. 285.
13. Ibid.
14. Mandell Creighton, *The Church and the Nation*, ed. Louise Creighton (1901), p. 316.
15. Ibid., pp. 290–91.
16. Louise Creighton, *Life and Letters*, ii, pp. 295–96.
17. Ibid., p. 286.
18. Ibid., p. 298.
19. Ibid., p. 287.
20. Ibid., p. 299.
21. W. G. Fallows, *Mandell Creighton and the English Church* (1964), pp. 87–88.
22. Ibid., p. 90.
23. Louise Creighton, *Life and Letters*, ii, pp. 360–61.
24. Fallows, *Mandell Creighton and the English Church*, pp. 90, 102; Louise Creighton, *Life and Letters*, ii, p. 287; Owen Chadwick, *The Victorian Church*, ii, pp. 355–57; Machin, *Politics and the Churches in Great Britain, 1869–1921*, p. 237.
25. Queen Victoria, *The Letters of Queen Victoria, 1886–1901* (1931), ed. George Earle Buckle, 3rd series, iii, p. 342.
26. Louise Creighton, *Life and Letters*, ii, pp. 286, 293, 291.
27. Ibid., p. 302.
28. Creighton Family Papers, MS letter, Mandell Creighton to [no name], 24 October 1898.
29. Louise Creighton, *Life and Letters*, ii, p. 292.
30. Ibid., p. 298.
31. Creighton Family Papers, Mandell Creighton, 'Untitled and Unpublished Notes

Concerning Ritual Controversy in 1890s', *c.* 1899, which reveals his genuine effort to understand.

32. *Louise Creighton, Life and Letters*, ii, p. 300.

33. Ibid., p. 307.

34. Ibid., p. 288.

35. Ibid., pp. 291–92.

36. Ibid., pp. 313–14.

37. Ibid.

38. Creighton Family Papers, MS letter, Mandell Creighton to Ella Creighton, 8 November 1898; Louise Creighton, *Life and Letters*, ii, p. 341.

39. Mandell Creighton, *The Mind of St Peter and Other Sermons*, ed. Louise Creighton (1904), p. 98.

40. Louise Creighton, *Life and Letters*, ii, p. 336; Mandell Creighton, *The Mind of St Peter*, pp. 98–99. See remarks about Creighton's lecture on Laud in Chapter 13 above.

41. Louise Creighton, *Life and Letters*, ii, p. 351.

42. Ibid., pp. 368–69; also Mandell Creighton, *The Church and the Nation*, pp. 231–47.

43. Louise Creighton, *Life and Letters*, ii, p. 382.

44. MS letter, Reginald L. Poole to Mrs Giles, 24 May 1922, MAS. 3.4.1., Emmanuel College archives.

45. Louise Creighton, *Life and Letters*, ii, pp. 382–83.

46. John Figgis, *Churches in the Modern State* (1914), pp. 238–39.

47. G. K. A. Bell, *Randall Davidson, Archbishop of Canterbury* (1935), i, p. 258. Randall Davidson was Bishop of Rochester, 1891–95, of Winchester, 1895–1903, and Archbishop of Canterbury, 1903–28.

48. Ibid., pp. 221–22.

49. Creighton Family Papers, MS letter, Mandell Creighton to Winifred Creighton, 24 May 1899 and 4 October 1896.

50. Alfred Havighurst, *Twentieth-Century Britain* (1966), p. 32; L. C. B. Seaman, *Victorian England: Aspects of English and Imperial History* (1973), pp. 19–24, 419–20.

51. Fallows, *Mandell Creighton and the English Church*, pp. 103–4.

52. Creighton Family Papers, MS letter, Mandell Creighton to Ella Creighton, 28 October 1899.

53. Ibid., MS letter, Mandell Creighton to Winifred Creighton, 16 December 1899; also Louise Creighton, *Life and Letters*, ii, p. 405.

54. Ibid., MS letter, Mandell Creighton to Ella Creighton, 26 November 1899; also Louise Creighton, *Life and Letters*, ii, p. 404. Louise made a mistake on the date, writing that it was 29 November, and also mistakenly transcribed the sentence to read, 'The Empress also is quiet and intelligent', instead of what is written: 'The Empress also is quite bright and intelligent.'

55. Louise Creighton, *Life and Letters*, ii, p. 404; see reprint in Mandell Creighton, *The Mind of St Peter*, pp. 161–71.

56. Creighton Family Papers, MS letter, Mandell Creighton to Winifred Creighton, 9 April 1897.

57. It is true that a new six-volume edition of Creighton's original five volume history of the papacy appeared in 1897 under the revised title *History of the Papacy from the Great Schism to the Sack of Rome, 1378–1529*, and that his previously written collection of essays on English shires was released in 1897 as *The Story of Some English Shires* (1897), but he wrote nothing new.

58. Mandell Creighton, *Lessons from the Cross* (1898).

59. Mandell Creighton, 'Introductory Note', *The Renaissance*, vol. 1 of *The Cambridge Modern History*, eds A. W. Ward, G. W. Prothero and Stanley Leathes, (1907), pp. 1–6.

60. Mandell Creighton 'The Reformation', *The Church: Past and Present. A Review of its History by the Bishop of London, Bishop Barry and Other Writers*, ed. H. M. Gwatkin (1900), pp. 125–34.

61. See reprints in Mandell Creighton, *Historical Lectures and Addresses*, ed. Louise Creighton (1903).

62. Creighton Family Papers, MS letter, Mandell Creighton to Winifred Creighton, 26 October 1899.

63. Louise Creighton, *Life and Letters*, ii, p. 396; cf. Mandell Creighton, *The Church and the Nation*, p. 285.

64. Louise Creighton, *Memoir*, p. 127.

65. Creighton Family Papers, MS letter, Mandell Creighton to Basil Creighton, 8 November 1900.

66. Louise Creighton, *Life and Letters*, ii, p. 389.

67. Ibid., p. 405.

68. Creighton Family Papers, MS letter, Mandell Creighton to Ella Creighton, 11 January 1900; also Louise Creighton, *Life and Letters*, ii, p. 406.

69. Creighton Family Papers, MS letter, Mandell Creighton to Winifred, 22 February 1900.

70. Mandell Creighton, *The Church and the Nation*, p. 296; also see Louise Creighton, *Life and Letters*, ii, p. 425.

71. Creighton Family Papers, MS letter, Mandell Creighton to Ella Creighton, 7 April 1900; also see Louise Creighton, *Life and Letters*, ii, p. 440.

72. Ibid., p. 440.

73. Creighton Family Papers, MS letter, Mandell Creighton to Basil Creighton, 30 May 1900.

74. Louise Creighton, *Life and Letters*, ii, p. 444.

75. Louise Creighton, *Memoir*, p. 129.

76. Ibid., p. 130.

77. Creighton Family Papers, MS letter, Mandell Creighton to Winifred Creighton, 24 September 1900; Louise Creighton, *Life and Letters*, ii, p. 445.

78. Louise Creighton, *Memoir*, p. 130.

79. Creighton Family Papers, MS letter, Mandell Creighton to Winifred Creighton, 18 November 1900.

80. Louise Creighton, *Memoir*, p. 130. This edited memoir omitted the words 'where I should *like to* live', which can be found in the original unedited memoir, ii, p. 182.

81. See reprint in Mandell Creighton, *Thoughts on Education: Speeches and Sermons*, ed. Louise Creighton (1902), pp. 196–215.

82. Ibid., pp. 189–99.

83. Ibid., p. 206.

84. Ibid.

85. Ibid., p. 212.

86. Louise Creighton, *Life and Letters*, ii, p. 382.

87. Ibid., p. 463.

88. Ibid., pp. 462–63. More likely, from what limited evidence there is now, Creighton may have been suffering not from a tumor but from a bleeding duodenal ulcer, presumably brought on by stress and over work. He had never learned to pace himself.

89. Creighton Family Papers, MS letter, Louise Creighton to Sophie Hasse, 7 December 1900.

90. Ibid., MS letter, Louise Creighton to James Bryce, 14 December 1900.

91. Ibid., MS letter, Louise Creighton to Ida Koch, 26 December 1900.

92. Louise Creighton, *Memoir*, p. 131; Louise Creighton, *Life and Letters*, ii, p. 464.

93. Louise Creighton, *Memoir*, p. 132; Wilfrid, son of Alick and Fanny, became a noted British artist. See Chapter 17 below.

94. Louise Creighton, *Life and Letters*, ii, pp. 464–65.

95. Richard Garnett, 'Obituary of Mandell Creighton', *English Historical Review*, 16, no. 1 (April 1901), pp. 21, 213; 'Obituary of Mandell Creighton', *Quarterly Review* (April 1901), p. 584.

96. Besides the above obituaries, see 'Obituary of Mandell Creighton', *American Historical Review*, 6, no. 3 (April 1901), p. 615; also Sir Charles Petrie, *The Victorians* (1960), p. 29.

97. Mandell Creighton, *Historical Lectures and Addresses*, p. 319.

98. MS letter, Hugh Creighton to author, 4 May 1965.

99. MS letter, Basil Creighton to author, 10 September 1965.

100. 'Obituary', *Quarterly Review*, p. 622.

101. Creighton Family Papers, MS letter, Beatrice Webb to Mrs G. W. Prothero, 18 February 1901.

102. Sutherland, *Mrs Humphry Ward*, p. 237; Janet Trevelyan, *The Life of Mrs Humphry Ward* (1923), p. 176.

103. Louise Creighton, *Life and Letters*, ii, p. 465.

104. Lytton Strachey, *Portraits in Miniature and Other Essays* (1931, 1962), p. 204.

105. Henry Scott Holland, *Personal Studies* (1905), p. 207; Louise Creighton, *Life and Letters*, ii, p. 75.

106. Webb, *Our Partnership*, pp. 205–6.

107. *Annual Register* (1901), p. 6.

108. The telegram came from Sir Arthur Bigge, the Queen's private secretary. Louise

wrote in her *Memoir* that Davidson was instructed to go to 'Windsor', though she must have been mistaken in her recollection because the Queen was then at Osborne. Bell, *Randall Davidson*, i, p. 351; Louise Creighton, *Memoir*, p. 132.

109. Shane Leslie, *The End of a Chapter* (1916), p. 157.
110. Creighton Family Papers, MS letter, Mandell Creighton to Basil Creighton, 30 Many 1900.
111. Basil Creighton, *Poems* (privately printed by Alethea Creighton and Christian Creighton, 1991), p. 1.

Chapter 17: Dear Mrs Creighton

1. MS letter, Sir Edward Grey to Louise Creighton, 4 February 1911, MSS Eng. lett. e. 73/1, 2, Bodleian Library, Oxford.
2. Louise Creighton, *Memoir of a Victorian Woman: Reflections of Louise Creighton, 1850–1936*, ed. James Thayne Covert (1994), p. 132.
3. Ibid., p. 135; Creighton Family Papers, MS letter, Louise Creighton to Ida Koch, 28 September 1907.
4. According to Hampton Court records, see List of Occupants of Private Apartments, 1891–1989.
5. MS letter, Mary Bailey to author, 27 November 1992.
6. Louise Creighton, *Memoir*, p. 134.
7. As revealed in her letters and diaries. See Gemma Bailey, 'Diaries and Letters', unpublished typescript edited by Mary Bailey (1990), pp. 19, 70.
8. Ibid.
9. Creighton Family Papers, Louise Creighton's original memoir, iii, p. 59.
10. Ibid.
11. Creighton Family Papers, MS letter, Louise Creighton to Ida Koch, 22 July 1906.
12. Creighton Family Papers. Also Keble College register.
13. See Bibliography.
14. Edmond Gosse, 'Mandell Creighton, Bishop of London', *Atlantic Monthly* (May 1901), pp. 680, 687–88.
15. G. W. Prothero, 'Mandell Creighton', *Dictionary of National Biography*, xxii, supplement, p. 511.
16. Donald E. Stanford, ed. *The Selected Letters of Robert Bridges* (1983), i, p. 376.
17. Beatrice Webb, *Our Partnership*, eds Barbara Drake and Margaret I. Cole (1948), pp. 142, 207.
18. G. K. A. Bell, *Randall Davidson, Archbishop of Canterbury* (1935), i, p. 358. Also see W. G. Fallows, *Creighton and the English Church* (1964), pp. 106–7.
19. Lytton Strachey, *Eminent Victorians* (1918), p. viii.
20. Henry Scott Holland, *Personal Studies* (1905), p. 207.
21. John N. Figgis, *Churches in the Modern State* (1914), p. 231.
22. Bell, *Randall Davidson*, i, p. 359.
23. Owen Chadwick, Dixie Professor of Ecclesiastical History at Cambridge from

1958 to 1968, and Regius Professor of History thereafter, stated that 'the biography of her husband is confessed by all critics to be a masterly performance—a portrait of a man, faults and all ... Though she selected well, at times selected brilliantly, she could not quite bring herself to wield the knife without a tremor of pity; and in consequence the two volumes are somewhat too long. Yet if they are too long, they are intellectually so, not sentimentally'. In all, Chadwick reckoned that Creighton was 'in every sense blessed in his wife, one of the remarkable women of her age'. See Owen Chadwick, *Creighton on Luther: An Inaugural Lecture* (1959), pp. 16–17; also Montgomery Belgion, 'Why You Should Read It: *Life and Letters of Mandell Creighton*', *Theology*, 52, no. 352 (October 1949), pp. 377–83.

24. Louise Creighton, *Life and Letters*, ii, p. 507.

25. Owen Chadwick, *Creighton on Luther*, p. 9; Fallows, *Creighton and the English Church*, p. 34. See also G. W. Prothero, 'Mandell Creighton', *Dictionary of National Biography*, xxii supplement, p. 512.

26. Ibid.; also *The Times*, 25 and 26 February 1901, pp. 10 and 12.

27. Louise Creighton, *Memoir*, pp. 137–38.

28. Ibid., p. 138.

29. Ibid.

30. Ibid.

31. See Sir Frederick Maurice, *Haldane, 1856–1915: The Life of Viscount Haldane of Cloan* (1937), 241. Cf. *Whitaker's Almanack* (1914), pp. 796, 816; *Annual Register* (1916), pp. 27–31; Jane Lewis, *Women and Social Action in Victorian and Edwardian England* (1991), p. 69.

32. It was thought from her *Memoir* that she spoke out for women's suffrage at the 1912 conference, but her *Women in Council* obituary claims it to have been in 1906.

33. Louise Creighton, *Memoir*, p. 146.

34. 'Louise Creighton Obituary', *Women in Council Newsletter*, May 1936.

35. Louise Creighton, *Memoir*, p. 89.

36. Ibid. See also John Sutherland, *Mrs Humphry Ward: Eminent Victorian, Pre-Eminent Edwardian* (1991), p. 325.

37. Arthur Temple Lyttelton was a former tutor at Keble College and later suffragan Bishop of Southampton.

38. See Adrian Hastings, *A History of English Christianity, 1920–1990* (1991), p. 87; Brian Heeney *The Women's Movement in the Church of England, 1850–1930* (1988), p. 17.

39. Heeney, *Women's Movement*, pp. 92–93, 110–11.

40. See Bibliography; Louise had co-authored, prior to these, an article with H. Bosanquet and Beatrice Webb, 'Law and the Laundry', *Nineteenth Century* (January-June 1897), pp. 224–35.

41. Louise Creighton, *Memoir*, p. 99.

42. Louise Creighton, *The Social Disease and How to Fight It* (1914).

43. Ibid., pp. 80–81.

44. Ibid., pp. 82–83.

45. Ibid., pp. 12–13.

46. Ibid., pp. 34–35, 86.

47. Creighton Family Papers, MS letter, Eric Gill to Louise Creighton, 22 August 1914.

48. Ibid.

49. Ibid.

50. Louise Creighton, *Memoir*, p. xvii.

51. A dogcart was a small, two-wheeled open carriage with two seats back to back, the rear seat being such that it could be closed to form a box for holding sportsmen's dogs.

52. For details on Dorothy Grey's death, see G. M. Trevelyan, *Grey of Fallodon: The Life and Letters of Sir Edward Grey, Afterwards Viscount of Fallodon* (1937), pp. 103–4ff; also Louise Creighton, *Dorothy Grey* (1907).

53. Sir Edward, two months before, had joined the new Liberal government of Sir Henry Campbell-Bannerman as Foreign Secretary—a post he would hold in succeeding Liberal cabinets until the middle of the First World War.

54. Alice Emma Graves was the sister of Sir Edward who had married Charles Graves. Miss Constance Herbert was a friend of Dorothy's and lived near Fallodon. See Trevelyan, *Grey of Fallodon*, genealogical table and pp. 19, 37, 338, 350.

55. Louise Creighton, *Memoir*, 140–41.

56. Trevelyan, *Grey of Fallodon*, p. 147; MS letter, Sir Edward Grey to Louise Creighton, 17 February 1906, Bodleian Library, MSS Eng. lett. e. 73/1, 2.

57. G. M. Trevelyan, in his biography, wrote that Sir Edward conceived the idea of the memoir and requested her to write it, but one must accept Louise's word that she thought of it and asked Sir Edward's permission. See Trevelyan, *Grey of Fallodon*, pp. 36n., 147.

58. When Sir Edward died, his ashes were buried at the edge of this 'new fishing pond'.

59. Louise Creighton, *Memoir*, p. 142. MS letter, Sir Edward Grey to Louise Creighton, 6 August 1915, Bodleian Library, MSS Eng. lett. e. 73/1, 2.

60. Louise Creighton, *Memoir*, p. 141.

61. Creighton Family Papers, MS letter, Louise Creighton to Ida Koch, 22 July 1906.

62. MS letter, Sir Edward Grey to Mrs Louise Creighton, 10 June 1910, 4 February 1911 and 9 August 1914. There are 156 letters of Sir Edward to Louise in the Bodleian Library (see Bibliography). None of Louise's letters apparently exist. Also see G. M. Trevelyan, *Grey of Fallodon*, passim.

63. MS letter, Mary Bailey to author, 25 March 1999.

64. Louise Creighton, *Memoir*, p. 143.

65. Ibid., p. 142.

66. Sources include Keble College archives and Louise Creighton, *Letters of Oswin Creighton, C.F., 1883–1918* (1920), pp. 222–23.

67. Creighton Family Papers, Louise Creighton's original memoir, iii, p. 67.
68. Laura Wortley, *Wilfrid de Glehn, R.A., John Singer Sargent's Painting Companion: A Painter's Journey* (1998), p. 9.
69. Brian Heeney, *Women's Movement*, p. 93; Louise Creighton, *Memoir*, p. 146.
70. *Guardian* (22 February 1917), as quoted in Brian Heeney, *Women's Movement*, p. 135.
71. Louise Creighton, *Memoir*, p. 146.
72. Brian Heeney, *Women's Movement*, pp. 108, 124; Louise Creighton, *Memoir*, pp. 146–47.
73. Ibid., p. 146.
74. Ibid., p. 147.
75. Ibid.

Chapter 18: A Sincere Fine Old Thing

1. As quoted in Brian Heeney, *Women's Movement*, p. 93, from *The Diary of Virginia Woolf, 1915–1918*, entry for 1 July 1918, p. 162.
2. Louise Creighton, *Memoir of a Victorian Woman: Reflections of Louise Creighton, 1850–1936*, ed. James Thayne Covert (1994), p. 139.
3. Details from ibid., p. 151, and personal recollections by members of Creighton family.
4. 'Obituary of Louise Creighton', *Times*, 16 April 1936.
5. 'Obituary of Louise Creighton', *Women in Council Newsletter* (May 1936).
6. As quoted in Brian Heeney, *Women's Movement*, p. 93.
7. Sources include Emmanuel College archive material, Alec Macdonald, *A History of the King's School, Worcester* (1936), and Creighton Family Papers.
8. Private source: Valerie Langfield, Cheshire, England, author of 'Roger Quilter' in the new *Dictionary of National Biography*.
9. Sources include Emmanuel College archives and Creighton Family Papers.
10. MS letters, Dorothy de la Hay to author, 31 March 1969, and Mary Tattersall to author, 28 November 1968, 10 December 1968, 24 January 1969.
11. Details from Creighton Family Papers, Gemma Bailey, 'Diaries and Letters'.
12. 'City of Carlisle Education Committee Creighton and Margaret Sewell Selective Central School Official Opening', programme document (17 April 1940), p. 2; Chance, *Some Notable Cumbrians*, p. 101.
13. See Genealogical Charts, pp. 71, 131 above.
14. Creighton Family Papers, MS letter, Basil Creighton to Hugh Creighton, summer 1964.
15. Jeanne Peterson, *Family, Love and Work in the Lives of Victorian Gentlewomen* (1989), pp. 188–89.
16. As quoted in Heeney, *Women's Movement*, pp. 85, 99.
17. Mandell Creighton, 'Heroes', *Historical Lectures and Addresses*, ed. Louise Creighton (1903), p. 322.

Bibliography

PRIMARY SOURCES

Creighton Family Papers

Barbara Adcock Papers, West Sussex.
Mary and Susan Bailey Papers, Wiltshire.
Basil Creighton Papers, London.
Hugh Creighton Papers, Oxfordshire.
Thomas Creighton Papers, Somerset.
Joan Duncan Papers, Ipswich.
Penelope Fowler Papers, Kent.
Rachel Moss Papers, West Midlands (also Lambeth Palace Library as 'Louise Creighton Letters').

Diaries, Notebooks, Papers

Abbot, Francis Ellingwood, 'Diary', 1886, Harvard University Library, Cambridge, Massachusetts.
Baptismal Records, Carlisle City Archives.
Bailey, Gemma, 'Diaries and Letters', unpublished typescript, ed. Mary Bailey, Wiltshire.
Chawner, William, 'First Thing I Remember about Creighton' (unpublished MS appreciation), Emmanuel College Library, Cambridge, MAS. 2.1.2.
Creighton, Louise, 'Abstract of the Diary of Robert von Glehn', 1928, Hugh Creighton Family, Oxfordshire.
Creighton, Louise, 'Memoir of Louise Creighton', Original Memoir Manuscripts, 1910–34, Creighton Family Papers, Thomas Creighton Family, Somerset.
Creighton, Mandell, 'Friendship' (an unpublished poem in the album of Mrs Caroline Potter at Stanley Mount, Oxton, Birkenhead, August 1865), Hugh Creighton Family, Oxfordshire.
Creighton, Mandell, MS document 'Inaugural Address as Dixie Professor', 1884 (with MS donation letter from Louise Creighton dated 1905), Emmanuel College Library, Cambridge.
Creighton, Mandell, 'Untitled and Unpublished Notes Concerning Ritual Controversy in 1890s', c. 1899, Hugh Creighton Family, Oxfordshire.

Creighton, Mary Ellen, 'MS Genealogy Fragment with Notes on the Mandell Family', n.d., Hugh Creighton Family, Oxfordshire.

Diocese Books, Bishop's Palace, Peterborough.

'Durham Grammar School Progress Report on Mandell Creighton', 1862, Hugh Creighton Family, Oxfordshire.

Fulham Palace Papers, 1897–1900, nos 59–65, no. 460 (photo album), no. 132 (London House), Lambeth Palace Archives, London.

Jenkinson. F. J. H., Diary, 42 vols for 1886, 1880, 1886–1923. Add. MSS 7406–447, Cambridge University Library.

Richardson, Kenneth, Research Papers on von Glehn Family, A82/7 File, Library Division, Lewisham Local History Centre, London.

Smith, Dan Louis, Scrapbook (Class of 1888), Harvard University Library Archives, Cambridge, Massachusetts.

Testimonial to E. Moore, 20 January 1886, MS Eng. misc. e 84, fol. 140, Bodleian Library, Oxford.

Thorndike, Albert, Scrapbook (Class of 1881), Harvard University Library Archives, Cambridge, Massachusetts.

Letters

British Library, London (Samuel Butler Papers)

Butler, Samuel to Mandell Creighton, two letters, 8 July 1893, 7 January 1896, Add. MSS 44034 and 44036.

Creighton, Mandell to Samuel Butler, four letters, 1 July 1893, 26 September 1894, 14 October 1896, 6 January 1900, Add MSS 44034, 44036, and 44040.

Bodleian Library, Oxford

Creighton, Louise to James Bryce, four letters 30 June c. 1889, 8 November c. 1896, 14 December 1900, 16 December 1906 (James Bryce Papers).

Creighton, Louise to Sir Sidney Lee, 5 May 1902, MS Eng. misc. d. 176, fol. 187.

Creighton, Mandell to James Bryce, eighteen letters 1864–99 (James Bryce Papers).

Creighton, Mandell to Charles E. Doble, 19 Janary 1881, MS Autogr. d. 12, fol. 48.

Creighton, Mandell to Augustus Jessopp, 8 March 1888, MS Eng. lett. c. 144, fol. 56.

Creighton, Mandell to Sir Sidney Lee, two letters, 30 May 1891 and 4 June 1892, MS Eng. misc. d. 176, fos 191–94.

Grey, Lady Dorothy to Mandell Creighton, four letters, c. 1886–99. MSS Eng. lett. e. 73/2, fos 167–81.

Grey, Lady Dorothy to Louise Creighton, eight letters, 1901–5, MSS Eng. lett. e. 73/2, fos 182–97.

Grey, Sir Edward to Louise Creighton, 156 letters, 1901–31, MSS Eng. lett. e. 73/1, 2.

Creighton, Mandell to Sir E. Ommanney, 17 October 1900, MS Don. c. 72, fol. 151.

Creighton, Mandell to Miss Owen, 7 December 1890, MS Eng. lett. e. 27, fol. 161, pp. 161–62.

Creighton, Mandell to R. W. Rees, 22 March 1900, MS Don. e. 20, fos 34.

Creighton, Mandell to W. Sanday, three letters, 2 August 28, August, 4 October 1900, MSS Eng. misc. d. 122 (2), fol. 479, pp. 480–86.

Creighton, Mandell to Sir Leslie Stephen, 31 May 1889, MS Eng. misc. d. 176, fos 189–90.

Creighton, Mandell to H. G. Woods, four letters, 21 April 1879, 7 January 1880, 7 November 1882, 21 February 1891, MSS Eng. lett. d. 183, fol. 1.

Creighton, Mandell to Canon Yeatman, 20 February 1891, MS Autogr. b. 8, no. 1583.

Green, J. R. to Louise Creighton, four letters, 1871–77, MSS Eng. lett. e. 48, fos 70–83.

Cambridge University Library (Jenkinson Papers)

Creighton, Mandell to F. J. H. Jenkinson, four letters, 6 January 1888, 24 December 1889, 13 February 1890, 7 May 1891, Jenkinson Papers.

Creighton, Mandell to J. Peile, 25 November 1892, Add. 2596/xx/11.

Creighton (Mary Bailey), Family Papers, Wiltshire

Creighton, Mandell to Mary Ellen Creighton, four letters, 10 March 1896, 29 August 1897, 30 August 1898, 26 August 1899.

Creighton (Basil) Family Papers, London

Creighton, Mandell to Basil Creighton, thirty-seven letters, 8 February 1897 to 13 November 1900.

Creighton (Hugh and Christian) Family Papers, Oxfordshire

Balfour, Arthur to Mandell Creighton, 4 March 1898.

Bridges, Robert to Mandell Creighton, 13 October 1889.

Creighton, Basil to Hugh Creighton, Summer 1964.

Creighton, Mandell to Edward Freeman, eleven letters, 22 August 1884 to 11 December 1890.

Creighton, Louise to Lady Mildred Buxton, 4 July 1915.

Creighton, Mandell to Louise Creighton, thirteen letters, 21 June 1887 to 17 July 1887.

Creighton, Mandell to Walter Creighton, nine letters, 24 February 1893 to 14 February 1899.

Creighton, Mary Ellen to Cuthbert Creighton, 29 April 1939.

Creighton, Mary Ellen to Louise Creighton, two letters c. 1902.

Creighton, Walter to Louise Creighton, notes, c. 1902.

Edward, Prince of Wales to Mandell Creighton, three letters, 26 February, 27 February, 22 June 1897.

Eubank, J. to Mary Ellen Creighton, 11 May 1902.

Eulenburg, Count August to Mandell Creighton, 14 December 1899.

Gill, Eric to Louise Creighton, 22 May 1914.

Gladstone, William to Mandell Creighton, five letters, 1884–87.

Glehn von (relative) to Louise Creighton, one fragment letter in German concerns von Glehn genealogy, c. 1910.

Grey, Sir Edward to Mandell Creighton, 29 November 1885.

Mandell, Mrs H. to Mary Ellen Creighton, 1901.
Pobiedonostzeff, M. to Mandell Creighton, 16 September 1897.
Verrall, Dr to Louise Creighton, c. 1902.
Victoria, H.M. Queen (or secretary) to Mandell Creighton, five letters, September 1896 to October 1897 (three letters in Queen's hand).
Webb, Beatrice to Mrs G. W. Prothero, 18 February 1901.

Creighton (Barbara Adcock-Penelope Fowler) Family Papers, West Sussex and Kent

Creighton, Mandell to Winifred Creighton, eighty-one letters, 23 October 1893 to 18 November 1900.

Creighton (Joan Duncan) Family Papers, Ipswich

Creighton, Mandell to Ella Creighton, fifty-six letters, 1894–1900.

Creighton (Rachel Moss) Family Papers, West Midlands and Lambeth Palace Library

Creighton, Louise to Agnes von Glehn, 159 letters plus fragments, 10 January 1872 to 22 November 1880.
Creighton, Louise to Mimi von Glehn, nine letters, 12 May 1872 to 20 July 1884.

National Library of Ireland, Dublin (A. S. Green Papers)

Creighton, Mandell to Mrs J. R. Green, eleven letters, 1883–95.
Green, Mrs J. R. to Mandell Creighton, nine letters, c. 1882 to c. 1896.

Documents

Carlisle Grammar School Memorial Register, 1264–1924, compiled and edited by G. B. Routledge (Carlisle: Charles Thurnam and Sons, 1924).
City of Carlisle Education Committee Creighton and Margaret Sewell Selective Central School Official Opening, programme document (17 April 1940), p. 2.
Great Britain, *Lord's Journal*, 128 (1896).
Official Programs of Harvard Commemoration (1886), HUA 886.71, Harvard Library Archives.
Record of the Commemoration, November Fifth to Eighth, 1886, of the Two Hundred and Fiftieth Anniversary of the Founding of Harvard College (Cambridge: John Wilson and Son, 1887).
Register of Durham School, from January 1840 to December 1907 (Durham: privately printed, n.d.).

Books by Louise Creighton

The Art of Living and Other Addresses to Girls (London: Longmans, Green and Co., 1909).
The Bloom off the Peach (London: Rivingtons, 1882).
Dorothy Grey, A Memoir (privately printed, 1907).

The Economics of the Household: Six Lectures Given at the London School of Economics (London: Longmans, Green and Co. 1907).

England: A Continental Power, From the Conquest to Magna Carta, 1066–1216 (London: Longmans, Green and Co., 1876).

A First History of England (London: Longmans, Green and Co., 1881).

A First History of France (London: Longmans, Green and Co., 1893).

G. A. Selwyn, D.D.: Bishop of New Zealand and Lichfield (London: Longmans, Green and Co., 1923).

The Government of England (London: Rivingtons, 1883).

Heroes of European History (London: Longmans, Green and Co., 1909).

Heroes of French History (London: Longmans, Green and Co., 1925).

The International Crisis: The Theory of the State: Lectures Delivered in February and March 1916 (Oxford: Oxford University Press, 1916).

Letters of Oswin Creighton, C.F., 1883–1918 (London: Longmans, Green and Co., 1920).

Life of Edward the Black Prince (London: Rivingtons, 1876).

Life of John Churchill, Duke of Marlborough (London: Rivingtons, 1879).

Life and Letters of Mandell Creighton, 2 vols (London: Longmans, Green and Co., 1904).

Life and Letters of Thomas Hodgkin (London: Longmans, Green and Co., 1917).

Life of Sir Walter Raleigh (London: Rivingtons, 1877).

Missions: Their Rise and Development (London: Williams and Norgate, 1912).

Memoir of a Victorian Woman: Reflections of Louise Creighton, 1850–1936, edited by James Thayne Covert (Bloomington: Indiana University Press, 1994).

The Social Disease and How to Fight It: A Rejoinder (London: Longmans, Green and Co., 1914).

Social History of England (London: Rivingtons, 1887).

Some Famous Women (London: Longmans, Green and Co., 1909).

Stories from English History (London: Rivingtons, 1883).

Tales of Old France (London: Longmans, Green and Co., 1924).

A Victorian Family as Seen Through the Letters of Louise Creighton to Her Mother, 1872–1880, edited by James Thayne Covert (Lewiston, New York: Edwin Mellen Press, 1998).

Major Articles by Louise Creighton

'The Appeal Against Female Suffrage: A Rejoinder', *Nineteenth Century* (August 1889), pp. 347–54.

'The Employment of Educated Women', *Nineteenth Century* (November 1901), pp. 806–11.

[With H. Bosanquet and Beatrice Webb] 'Law and the Laundry', *Nineteenth Century* (January-June 1897), pp. 224–35.

'Women's Settlements', *Nineteenth Century* (April 1908), pp. 607–13.

Books by Mandell Creighton

The Age of Elizabeth (London: Longmans, Green and Co., 1876).

Cardinal Wolsey (London: Macmillan, 1888).

Carlisle (London: Longmans, Green and Co., 1889).

The Church and the Nation: Charges and Addresses, edited by Louise Creighton (London: Longmans, Green and Co., 1901).

The Claims of the Common Life: Sermons Preached in Merton College Chapel, 1871– 1874, edited by Louise Creighton (London: Longmans, Green and Co., 1905).

Counsels for Church People, edited by J. H. Burn (London: Elliot Stock, 1901).

Counsels for the Young: Extracts from the Letters of Mandell Creighton, edited by Louise Creighton (London: Longmans, Green and Co., 1905).

The Heritage of the Spirit and Other Sermons (London: Sampson Low, Marston and Co., 1896).

Historical Essays and Reviews, edited by Louise Creighton (London: Longmans, Green and Co., 1902).

Historical Lectures and Addresses, edited by Louise Creighton (London: Longmans, Green and Co., 1903).

History of the Papacy from the Great Schism to the Sack of Rome, 1378–1527, second edition, 6 volumes (London: Longmans, Green and Co., 1897. The first edition was five volumes under the title of *History of the Papacy during the Period of the Reformation* (1894).

Lessons from the Cross (London: James Nisbet and Co., 1898).

Life of Simon De Montfort, Earl of Leicester (London: Rivingtons, 1877).

Memoir of Sir George Grey, Bart, G.C.B. (London: Longmans, Green, and Co., 1901), reprint from a privately printed edition in 1884.

The Mind of St Peter and Other Sermons, edited by Louise Creighton (London: Longmans, Green and Co., 1904).

Persecution and Tolerance: Being the Hulsean Lectures Preached before the University of Cambridge in 1893–94 (London: Longmans, Green and Co., 1895).

Primer on Roman History (London: Macmillan, 1875).

Queen Elizabeth (London: Boussod, Valadon and Co., 1896).

The Shilling History of England (London: Longmans, Green, and Co., 1879).

The Story of Some English Shires (London: Religious Tract Society, 1897).

Thoughts on Education: Speeches and Sermons, edited by Louise Creighton (London: Longmans, Green and Co., 1902).

The Tudors and the Reformation (London: Longmans, Green, and Co., 1876).

University and Other Sermons, edited by Louise Creighton (London: Longmans, Green and Co., 1903).

Major Articles by Mandell Creighton

'The Abolition of the Roman Jurisdiction', *Church Historical Society* (1896).

'Aeneas Sylvius Piccolomini, Pope', *Macmillan's Magazine*, 27 (1872), pp. 113–22, 294–309.

'A Learned Lady of the Sixteenth Century (Olympia Fulvia Morata)', *Macmillan's Magazine*, 42 (1880), pp. 136–44.

'Alnwick Castle', *Magazine of Art*, 5 (1881–82), pp. 140–45 and 195–200.

'A Man of Culture (Gismondo Malatesta of Rimini)', *Magazine of Art* (1882), pp. 270–77.

'A Schoolmaster of the Renaissance (Vittorino da Feltre)', *Macmillan's Magazine*, 32 (1875), pp. 509–19.

'The Church and History', *Church Congress Reports* (1887).

'Church and State', *Oxford House Papers*, 3 (London: Longmans, Green, and Co. 1907), pp. 31–43.

'Clerical Inaccuracies in Conducting Church Services', *Clergyman's Magazine*, 18 (1884), pp. 168–76.

'Christian Ethics', *Church Congress Reports* (1892).

'Dante', *Macmillan's Magazine*, 29 (1873), pp. 554–63; 30 (1874), pp. 56–67.

'Duties of Guardians with Regard to Education', *Reports of the Poor Law District Conferences* (1877), pp. 170–81; (1878), pp. 142–49.

'The Endowment of Research', *Macmillan's Magazine*, 34 (1876), pp. 186–92.

'The Fenland', *Archeological Journal*, 49 (1892), pp. 263–73.

'Harvard College', *Emmanuel College Magazine*, vol. 1, no. 1 (May 1889), pp. 2–9.

'The Harvard Commemoration', *The Times* (November 22–23, 1886).

'Historical Ethics', *Quarterly Review* (1905), pp. 32–46; reprinted in *Living Age*, 28, series 7, no. 3190 (26 August 1905), pp. 515–24.

'Hoghton Tower', *Magazine of Art*, 10 (1887), pp. 19–24, 68–72.

'The Hope of Our Founder', *Emmanuel College Magazine*, vol. 2, no. 2 (1891), pp. 49–59.

'The Idea of a National Church', *Church Congress Reports* (1896) and *Church Historical Society* (1898).

'The Imperial Coronation at Moscow', *Cornhill Magazine* (September 1896), pp. 305–25.

'Influence of the Reformation on England, with Special Reference to the Writings of John Wiclif', *Church Congress Reports* (1884).

'Introductory Note', *The Renaissance*, vol. 1 of *The Cambridge Modern History*, edited by A. W. Ward, G. W. Prothero and Stanley Leathes (New York: Macmillan Co., 1907), pp. 1–6.

'The Italian Bishops of Worcester', *Worcester Diocesan Architectural and Archeological Society's Publication* (1889).

'John Richard Green', *Dictionary of National Biography*, pp. 489–92.

'John Wiclif at Oxford', *Church Quarterly*, 5 (October 1877), pp. 119–41.

'Laud's Position in the History of the English Church', *Archbishop Laud Commemoration*, ed. by W. E. Collins, (1895), pp. 3–29.

'Life and Work', *The Girls' Quarterly*, 1, no. 4 (September 1895), pp. 73–75.

'The National Church and the Middle Ages: Its Continuity in Order, Doctrine, and Autonomy', *Church Congress Reports* (1895), pp. 371–75.

'The Northumberland Border', *Macmillan's Magazine*, 50 (1884), pp. 321–33; also published with appendices in *Archeological Journal*, 42 (1885), pp. 41–89.

'Philip II', *Encyclopedia Britannica*, 9th edition, vol. 18, pp. 743–46.

'The Reformation', *The Church: Past and Present: A Review of its History by the Bishop of London, Bishop Barry and Other Writers*, edited by H. M. Gwatkin (London: James Nisbet and Co., 1900), pp. 125–34.

'Remarks Following a Paper on Workhouse Management', *Reports of the Poor Law District Conferences* (1881), pp. 80–81.

'The Rise of European Universities', *The Daily Crimson* (now *Harvard Crimson*), 10, no. 38 (November 11, 1886).

'St Edward the Confessor', *Cornhill Magazine* (1896).

'Science and Faith', *Church Congress Reports* (1893), pp. 350–52.

'Sermon Preached at the Close of the Birmingham Church Congress in Worcester Cathedral', *Church Congress Reports* (1893), pp. 554–61.

'Some Literary Correspondence of Humphrey, Duke of Gloucester', *English Historical Review*, 10 (1895), pp. 99–104.

'The Teaching Work of the Church', *Church Congress Reports* (1885), pp. 338–43.

'What the Church Does for the Nation', *Nye's Popular Illustrated Church Annual* (1893), pp. 7–11.

Books

Acton, Lord, *Essays on Freedom and Power*, edited by Gertrude Himmelfarb (New York: Meridian Books, 1948, 1955).

——, *Historical Essays and Studies*, edited by John N. Figgis and Reginald V. Laurence (London: Macmillan and Co., 1908).

——, *Letters of Lord Acton to Mary, Daughter of the Right Hon. W. E. Gladstone*, edited by Herbert Paul (London: George Allen, 1904).

——, *Selections from the Correspondence of the First Lord Acton*, vol. 1, edited by John N. Figgis and Reginald V. Laurence (London: Longmans, Green and Co., 1917).

Arnold, Matthew, *Thoughts on Education, Chosen from the Writings of Matthew Arnold*, edited by Leonard Huxley (New York: Macmillan Co., 1912).

Asquith, Margot, *The Autobiography of Margot Asquith* (London: Thornton Butterworth, 1920).

Bailey, Gemma, ed., *Lady Margaret Hall: A Short History* (London: Oxford University Press, 1923).

Bateson, Edward, ed., *A History of Northumberland*, vol. 2 of 15 vols published by Northumberland County History Committee (London: Simpkin, Marshall, Hamilton, Kent and Co., 1895).

Begbie, Harold, *Albert, Fourth Earl Grey: A Last Word* (London: Hodder and Stoughton, 1918).

Benson, A. C., *Walter Pater* (London: Macmillan and Co., 1906).

Bridges, Robert, *The Selected Letters of Robert Bridges*, ed. Donald E. Stanford., 2 vols (London: Associated University Presses, 1983–84).

Bryce, James, *Studies in Contemporary Biography* (New York: Macmillan Co., 1911).

Collier, Price, *England and the English: From an American Point of View* (New York: Charles Scribners' Sons, 1909, 1910).

Emerson, Ralph Waldo, *English Traits* (New York: T. Y. Crowell and Co., 1899).

Fawsley, Lady, *The Journals of Lady Knightley of Fawsley*, edited by Julia Cartwright (London: John Murray, 1915).

Figgis, John Neville, *Churches in the Modern State* (London: Longmans, Green and Co., 1914).

Foster, Joseph, *Alumni Oxonienses: The Members of the University of Oxford, 1715-1886*, vol. 1 (Oxford: James Parker and Co., 1891).

Freeman, Edward A, *General Sketch of History* (American edn, New York: Henry Holt and Co., 1876).

Gardner, Alice, *A Short History of Newnham College Cambridge* (Cambridge: Bowes and Bowes, 1921).

Gosse, Edmund, *Books on the Table* (New York: Charles Scribner's Sons, 1921).

——, *Portraits and Sketches* (London: William Heinemann, 1913).

——, *Selected Essays* (First Series) (London: William Heinemann, 1928).

——, *Silhouettes* (New York: Charles Scribner's Sons, 1925).

——, *Some Diversions of a Man of Letters* (London: William Heinemann, 1919).

Granville-Barker, Harley, ed., *The Eighteen-Seventies: Essays by Fellows of the Royal Society of Literature* (Cambridge: Cambridge University Press, 1929).

Grey, Viscount Edward, *Fallodon Papers* (Boston: Houghton Mifflin Co., 1926).

——, *Twenty-Five Years, 1892–1916*, 2 vols (New York: Frederick A. Stokes Co., 1925.

Green, John Richard, *Letters of John Richard Green, 1837–1883*, edited by Leslie Stephen (New York: Macmillan Co., 1901).

Green, John Richard, *Oxford Studies*, edited by Mrs J. R. Green and Miss K. Norgate (London: Macmillan and Co., 1901).

Gwatkin, H. M., ed., *The Church: Past and Present; A Review of its History by the Bishop of London, Bishop Barry and Other Writers* (London: James Nisbet and Co., 1900).

Haldane, Elizabeth S, *From One Century to Another: The Reminiscences of Elizabeth S. Haldane* (London: Alexander MacLehose and Co., 1937).

Haldane, Viscount Richard Burton, *An Autobiography* (New York: Doubleday, Doran and Co., 1929).

Hawthorne, Nathaniel, *The English Note-Books by Nathaniel Hawthorne*, edited by Randall Stewart (New York: Boston: Russell and Russell, Inc., 1962).

Henderson, Bernard W., *Merton College*, 'University of Oxford College Histories' series (London: F. E. Robinson, 1899).

Henson, Herbert H., *Bishopric Papers* (London: Oxford University Press, 1946).

Holland, Henry Scott, *A Bundle of Memories* (London: Wells Gardner, Darton and Co., 1915).

——, *Personal Studies* (London: Wells Gardner, Darton and Co., 1905).

Huxley, Thomas H., *Autobiography and Selected Essays*, edited by Ada L. F. Snell (Boston: Houghton Mifflin and Co., 1909).

Knox, Edmund A., *Reminiscences of an Octogenarian, 1847–1934* (London: Hutchinson and Co., 1935).

Knox, Ronald, A., *Let Dons Delight: Being Variations on a Theme in an Oxford Common-Room* (London: Sheed and Ward, 1939).

Lecky, William E. H., *Democracy and Liberty*, 2 vols (New York: Longmans, Green and Co., 1899).

Lehmann, R. C., *Memories of Half a Century* (London: Smith, Elder and Co., 1908).

Leslie, Shane, *The End of a Chapter* (London: Constable and Co., 1916).

——, *Men Were Different* (Freeport, New York: Books for Libraries Press, 1937, 1967).

Maas, Henry. *The Letters of A. E. Housman* (Cambridge: Harvard University Press, 1971).

Mallet, Charles E., *A History of the University of Oxford*, 3 vols (London: Methuen and Co., 1924–27).

Mallet, Marie, *Life with Queen Victoria: Marie Mallet's Letters from Court, 1887–1901*, edited by Victor Mallet (Boston: Houghton Mifflin Company, 1968).

Masterman, C. F. G., *The Condition of England* (London: Methuen and Co., 1910).

McCarthy, Justin, *Portraits of the Sixties* (New York: Harper and Brothers, 1903).

Morley, John, *The Struggle for National Education* (London: Chapman and Hall, 1873).

Oman, Sir Charles, *Memories of Victorian Oxford and of Some Early Years* (3rd edn, London: Methuen and Co., 1942).

Paget, Stephen, ed., *Henry Scott Holland: Memoir and Letters* (New York: E. P. Dutton and Co., 1921).

Pattison, Mark, *Memoirs* (London: Macmillan and Co., 1885).

Paul, H. W., *Stray Leaves* (London: John Lane and Co., 1906).

Pease, Joseph G., *A Wealth of Happiness and Many Bitter Trials: The Journals of Sir Alfred Edward Pease, A Restless Man* (York: William Sessions, Ltd, 1992).

Saintsbury, George, *Saintsbury Miscellany: Selections from his Essays and Scrap Books* (New York: Oxford University Press, 1947).

Shuckburgh, E. S., *Emmanuel College* (London: F. E. Robinson and Co., 1904).

Tate, George, *The History of the Borough, Castle and Barony of Alnwick*, 2 vols (Alnwick: Henry Hunter Blair, 1866).

Temple, F., *Memoirs of Archbishop Temple by Seven Friends*, edited by E. G. Sandford, 2 vols (London: Macmillan and Co., 1906).

Tuckwell, Rev. W., *Reminiscences of Oxford* (London: Smith, Elder and Co., 1907).

Victoria, Queen, *The Letters of Queen Victoria: A Selection from Her Majesty's Correspondence and Journal between the Years 1886–1901*, edited by George Earle Buckle, vols 2 and 3, 3rd series (London: John Murray, 1931).

Ward, Mrs Humphry, *A Writer's Recollections*, 2 vols (New York: Harper and Brothers, 1918).

Webb, Beatrice, *My Apprenticeship* (New York: Longmans, Green and Co., 1926).

——, *Our Partnership*, edited by Barbara Drake and Margaret I. Cole. (London: Longmans, Green and Co., 1948).

Webb, Sidney, *London Education* (London: Longmans, Green and Co., 1904).

Wiese, Dr. L., *German Letters on English Education: Written during an Educational Tour in 1876*, translated and edited by Leonhard Schmitz (London: William Collins, Sons and Co., 1877).

Articles

Acton, Lord, 'Review of Mandell Creighton's *History of the Papacy*', vols 1 and 2, *Academy*, 22 (9 December 1882), pp. 407–9.

——, 'Review of Mandell Creighton's *History of the Papacy*', vols 3 and 4, *English Historical Review* (July 1887), pp. 571–81.

Boston Herald (November 11, 1886).

Cambridge Review: A Journal of University Life and Thought, vols 9–12 (1889–91).

Cambridge University Calendar (Cambridge: Deighton Bell and Co., 1888–92).

Carlisle Journal (7 October 1898), p. 1.

'College News', *Emmanuel College Magazine*, vol. 2, no. 3 (1891), 136–37; vol. 3, no. 1 (1891), p. 41.

'Combating Venereal Disease', *Whitaker's Almanack* (1917), pp. 816–17.

'Creighton, Louise H.', *A Supplement to Allibone's Critical Dictionary of English Literature and British and American Authors*, ed. John Foster Kirk (Philadelphia: Lippincott, 1902), i, p. 412.

'Creighton, Mandell', *Encyclopedia Britannica* (11th edn), vii, pp. 401–42.

'Creighton, Rev. Mandell', *A Supplement to Allibone's Critical Dictionary of English Literature and British and American Authors*, ed. John Foster Kirk (Philadelphia: Lippincott, 1902), i, p. 412.

'Creighton and Stubbs', *Church Quarterly Review* (October 1905), pp. 134–63.

De Cordova, Rudolph, 'The Lord Bishop of London [Mandell Creighton]', *Strand Magazine*, 18 (November 1899), pp. 526–35.

Gosse, Edmund, 'Mandell Creighton, Bishop of London', *Atlantic Monthly*, 87 (May 1901), pp. 677–89.

Gray, A. R., 'Mandell Creighton, Pastor, Scholar and Man', *Sewanee Review*, 15 (1907), pp. 227–43.

Hopkinson, Sir Alfred, 'The New Universities', *Fifty Years: Memories and Contrasts. A Composite Picture of the Period 1882–1932 by Twenty-Seven Contributors to The Times* (London: Thornton Butterworth, 1932, 1936), pp. 99–107.

Mullinger, James Bass, 'Review of Mandell Creighton's *History of the Papacy*', *English Historical Review* (October 1894), pp. 771–82.

'Obituary of Louise Creighton', *The Times*, 16 April 1936.

'Obituary of Louise Creighton', *Women in Council Newsletter*, May 1936.

'Obituary of Mandell Creighton', *American Historical Review*, 6, no. 3 (April 1901), p. 615.

'Obituary of Mandell Creighton', *Annual Register*, 1901, pp. 104–5.

'Obituary of Mandell Creighton, Bishop of London', by Richard Garnett, *English Historical Review*, 16, no. 1 (April 1901), pp. 211–18.

'Obituary of Mandell Creighton', *Quarterly Review*, vol. 193, no. 386 (April 1901), pp. 584–622.

Paul, Herbert, 'The Late Bishop of London: A Personal Impression', *Nineteenth Century*, 50 (July 1901), pp. 103–13.

Prothero, G. W. 'Mandell Creighton', *Dictionary of National Biography*, xxii, supplement, pp. 507–13.

'Report of Royal Commission on Venereal Disease', *Annual Register*, 1916, pp. 28- 31.

'Review of *The Bloom Off the Peach*, by Lois Hume [Louise Creighton]', *Spectator*, 55 (6 May 1882), pp. 598–99.

SECONDARY SOURCES

Books

Abbott, Mary, *Family Ties: English Families, 1540–1920* (New York: Routledge, 1993).

Abbott, Wilbur C., *Adventures in Reputation* (Cambridge: Harvard University Press, 1935).

Adamson, John W., *English Education, 1789–1902* (Cambridge: Cambridge University Press, 1930).

Addison, W. G., *J. R. Green* (London: Society for Promoting Christian Knowledge, 1946).

Allchin, Sir William Henry, *An Account of the Reconstruction of the University of London*, i (London: H. K. Lewis, 1905); ii (London: H.M. Stationery Office, n.d.); iii (London: H.M. Stationery Office, 1912).

Altick, Richard D., *The English Common Reader: A Social History of the Mass Reading Public, 1800–1900* (Chicago: University of Chicago Press, 1957).

Annan, Noel et al., *Ideas and Beliefs of the Victorians: An Historic Revaluation of the Victorian Age* (London: Sylvan Press, 1949).

——, *Leslie Stephen: His Thoughts and Character in Relation to his Time* (Cambridge: Harvard University Press, 1952).

Armfelt, Roger, *The Structure of English Education* (London: Cohen and West, 1955).

Ausubel, Herman, *In Hard Times: Reformers Among the Late Victorians* (New York: Columbia University Press, 1960).

——, *The Late Victorians: A Short History* (New York: D. Van Nostrand Co., 1955).

Balfour, Graham, *The Educational Systems of Great Britain and Ireland* (2nd edn, Oxford: Clarendon Press, 1903).

Banks, J. A., *Victorian Values: Secularism and the Size of Families* (London: Routledge and Kegan Paul, 1981).

Barnard, H. C., *A History of English Education from 1760* (London: University of London Press, 1947, 1964).

Battiscombe, Georgina, *Reluctant Pioneer: A Life of Elizabeth Wordsworth* (London: Constable and Co., 1978).

Beaver, Patrick, *The Crystal Palace, 1851–1936: A Portrait of Victorian Enterprise.* (London: Hugh Evelyn, 1970).

Beckson, Karl, *London in the 1890s: A Cultural History* (New York: W. W. Norton and Co., 1992).

Begbie, Harold, *Painted Windows: Studies in Religious Personality* (New York: G. P. Putman's Sons, 1922).

Bell, G. K. A., *Randall Davidson: Archbishop of Canterbury*, 2 vols (New York: Oxford University Press, 1935).

Benn, Alfred William, *The History of English Rationalism in the Nineteenth Century*, 2 vols (London: Longmans, Green and Co., 1906).

Benson, A. C., ed., *Cambridge Essays on Education*, introduction by Viscount Bryce (Cambridge: Cambridge University Press, 1918).

Bentley, James, *Ritualism and Politics in Victorian Britain* (Oxford: Oxford University Press, 1977).

Best, G. F. A., *Temporal Pillars: Queen Anne's Bounty, the Ecclesiastical Commssioners and the Church of England* (Cambridge, England: Cambridge University Press, 1964).

Beveridge, Janet, *An Epic of Clare Market: Birth and Early Days of the London School of Economics* (London: G. Bell and Sons, 1960).

Blake, Robert and Hugh Cecil, eds, *Salisbury: The Man and his Policies* (New York: St Martin's Press, 1987).

Bowen, Desmond, *The Idea of the Victorian Church: A Study of the Church of England, 1833–1889* (Montreal: McGill University Press, 1968).

Bradley, A. G., A. C. Champneys, and J. W. Baines, *A History of Marlborough College during Fifty Years from its Foundation to the Present Time* (London: John Murray, 1893).

Briggs, Asa, *Victorian People: A Reassessment of Persons and Themes, 1851–1867* (New York: Harper and Row, 1963).

——, *Victorian Things* (Chicago: University of Chicago Press, 1988).

Brooke, Christopher and Roger Highfield, *Oxford and Cambridge* (Cambridge: Cambridge University Press, 1988).

Brown, Alan Willard, *The Metaphysical Society: Victorian Minds in Crisis, 1869–1880* (New York: Columbia University Press, 1947).

Brown, C. K. Francis, *The Church's Part in Education, 1833–1941: With Special Reference to the Work of the National Society* (London: National Society and Society for Promoting Christian Knowledge, 1942).

Burgess, H. J. and P. A. Welsby, *A Short History of the National Society* (London: National Society, 1961).

Caine, Barbara, *Destined to Be Wives: The Sisters of Beatrice Webb* (Oxford: Clarendon Press, 1986).

——, *Victorian Feminists* (Oxford: Oxford University Press, 1992).

Caine, Sir Sidney, *The History of the Foundation of the London School of Economics and Political Science* (London: G. Bell and Sons, 1963).

Chadwick, Owen, *The Spirit of the Oxford Movement: Tractarian Essays* (Cambridge: Cambridge University Press, 1990).

——, *The Victorian Church*, 2 vols (New York: Oxford University Press, 1966, 1970).

Chance, Sir Frederick, *Some Notable Cumbrians* (Carlisle, England: Charles Thurman and Sons, 1931).

Cherry, Bridget and Pevsner, Nikolaus, *London, iii, North West* (London: Penguin Books, 1991).

Churchill, Winston S., *Lord Randolph Churchill* (London: Odhams Press, 1951).

Clark, G. Kitson, *The Making of Victorian England* (Cambridge: Harvard University Press, 1962).

Cole, G. D. H. and Raymond Postgate, *The British Common People, 1746–1946* (London: Methuen and Co., 1961).

Colloms, Brenda, *Victorian Country Parsons* (Lincoln and London: University of Nebraska Press, 1977).

Cotton, Edward H., *The Life of Charles W. Eliot* (Boston: Small, Maynard and Co., 1926).

Coulter, John, *Sydenham and Forest Hill Past* (London: Historical Publications, 1999).

Coulter, John and John Seaman, compilers, *Sydenham and Forest Hill* (Stroud, Gloucestershire: Chalford Publishing Co., 1994).

Coulton, Geo. G., *Fourscore Years: An Autobiography* (Cambridge: Cambridge University Press, 1943).

Cowles, Virginia, *Gay Monarch: The Life and Pleasure of Edward VII* (New York: Harper and Row, 1956).

Cox, Jeffrey, *The English Churches in a Secular Society: Lambeth, 1870–1930* (Oxford: Oxford University Press, 1982).

Craster, Owen, *A History of Embleton Parish Church* (Embleton: privately printed, 1978).

Cruickshank, Marjorie, *Church and State in English Education, 1870 to the Present Day* (New York: St Martin's Press, 1963).

Curtis, S. J., *History of Education in Great Britain* (London: University Tutorial Press, 1948).

Daunton, M. J., *House and Home in the Victorian City: Working-Class Housing, 1850–1914* (London: E. Arnold, 1983).

Dawson, Robert B., *A Short History of Embleton Church and the Fortified Vicarage* (London: The Crypt House Press, 1933).

Dodds, Madeleine Hope, *A History of Northumberland*, xv (Northumberland County History Committee, 1940).

Dongerkery, S. R., *Universities in Britain* (London: Oxford University Press, 1953).

Edwards, David L., *Christian England: From the Eighteenth Century to the First World War*, iii (Grand Rapids, Michigan: Eerdmans Publishing Co., 1984).

——, *Leaders of the Church of England, 1828–1944* (London: Oxford University Press, 1971).

Elliott-Binns, L. E., *The Development of English Theology in the Later Nineteenth Century* (London: Longmans, Green and Co., 1952).

Ellmann, Richard, ed., *Edwardians and Late Victorians: English Institute Essays* (New York: Columbia University Press, 1960).

Engel, A. J., *From Clergyman to Don: The Rise of the Academic Profession in Nineteenth-Century Oxford* (Oxford: Oxford University Press, 1983).

Ensor, R. C. K., *England, 1870–1914* (Oxford: Clarendon Press, 1936).

Fairweather, Eugene, ed., *The Oxford Movement* (New York: Oxford Universtiy Press, 1964).

Fallows, W. G., *Mandell Creighton and the English Church* (London: Oxford University Press, 1964).

Fletcher, Sheila, *Victorian Girls: Lord Lyttelton's Daughters* (London: The Hambledon Press, 1999).

Ford, Colin and Brian Harrison, *A Hundred Years Ago: Britain in the 1880s in Words and Photographs* (New York: Allen Lane-Penguin Books, 1983).

Gardiner, A. G., *The Life of Sir William Harcourt*, 2 vols (New York: George H. Doran Co., n.d.).

Garvin, J. L., *The Life of Joseph Chamberlain*, 3 vols (London: Macmillan and Co., 1934).

Gilbert, Alan D., *Religion and Security in Industrial England: Church, Chapel and Social Change, 1740–1914* (London: Longmans, 1979).

Gooch, G. P., *History and Historians in the Nineteenth Century* (Boston: Beacon Press, 1959; originally published 1913).

Gourvish, T. R. and Alan O'Day, eds, *Later Victorian Britain, 1867–1900* (New York: St Martin's Press, 1988).

Grant, A. J., ed., *English Historians* (London: Blackie and Son, 1906).

Graves, Charles L., *Life and Letters of Sir George Grove, CB* (London: Macmillan, 1903).

Green, V. H. H., *Oxford Common Room: A Study of Lincoln College and Mark Pattison* (London: Edward Arnold, 1957).

Haig, Alan, *The Victorian Clergy* (London: Croom Helm, 1984).

Halévy, Elie, *Victorian Years, 1841–1895* (New York: Barnes and Noble, 1961).

Harrison, J. F. C., *Learning and Living, 1790–1960: A Study in the History of the English Adult Education Movement* (London: Routledge and Kegan Paul, 1961).

Hastings, Adrian, *A History of English Christianity, 1920–1990* (London: SCM Press, 1991).

Havighurst, Alfred F., *Twentieth Century Britain* (New York: Harper and Row, 1966).

Heeney, Brian, *The Women's Movement in the Church of England, 1850–1930* (Oxford: Clarendon Press, 1988).

Heyck, T. W., *The Transformation of Intellectual Life in Victorian England* (New York: St Martin's Press, 1982).

Himmelfarb, Gertrude, *Lord Action: A Study in Conscience and Politics* (Chicago: University of Chicago Press, 1962).

——, *Marriage and Morals Among the Victorians and Other Essays* (London: I. B. Tauris and Co., 1989).

Hobhouse, Christopher, *Oxford as it Was and as it Is Today*, revised by Marcus Dick (London: B. T. Batsford, 1952).

Hobsbawn, E. J., *Labouring Men: Studies in the History of Labour* (New York: Basic Books Inc., 1964).

Holcombe, Lee, *Wives and Property: Reform of the Married Women's Property Law in Nineteenth-Century England* (Toronto: University of Toronto Press, 1983).

Hollis, Patricia, *Women in Public, 1850–1900: Documents of the Victorian Women's Movement* (London: George Allen and Unwin, 1979).

Honeyman, H. L., 'Embleton Tower', in Blair, C. H. Hunter, *Archaeologia Aeliana:*

or Miscellaneous Tracts Relating to Antiquity (Newcastle: Northumberland Press Ltd), chapter 8, pp. 87–101.

Horn, Pamela, *Victorian Countrywomen* (Oxford: Basil Blackwell Ltd, 1991).

Houghton, Walter E., *The Victorian Frame of Mind, 1830–1870* (New Haven: Yale University Press, 1957).

Housman, Laurence, *Victoria Regina: A Dramatic Biography* (London: Jonathan Cape, Ltd, 1934).

Hughes, John Jay, *Absolutely Null and Utterly Void: The Papal Condemnation of Anglican Orders, 1869* (Washington, D.C.: Corpus Books, 1968).

Hughes, Kathryn, *The Victorian Governess* (London: The Hambledon Press, 1993).

Hugill, Robert, *Borderland Castles and Peles* (London: ed. J. Burrows and Co., n.d.)

Humberstone, Thomas L., *University Reform in London* (London: George Allen and Unwin, 1926).

Hutchinson, Horace Gordon, *Portraits of the Eighties* (New York: Books for Libraries Press, 1970).

Inglis, K. S., *Churches and the Working Classes in Victorian England* (London: Routledge and Kegan Paul, 1963).

Jalland, Pat, *Women, Marriage and Politics, 1860–1914* (Oxford: Clarendon Press, 1986).

James, Henry, *Charles W. Eliot, President of Harvard University, 1867–1909*, 2 vols (Boston: Houghton Mifflin Co., 1930).

Johnson, Dale A., *Women in English Religion, 1700–1925* (New York: Edwin Mellen Press, 1983).

Jones, Henry Festing, *Samuel Butler, A Memoir*, 2 vols (London: no publisher named, 1919).

Kent, John, *William Temple: Church, State and Society in Britain, 1880–1950* (Cambridge: Cambridge University Press, 1992).

Kemp, Laurie, and Jim Templeton, *175 Years of Carlisle* (Cheshire: Archive Publications, 1990).

Kingsmill, Hugh, *After Puritanism, 1850–1900* (London: Duckworth, 1929).

Kirby, M. W., *Men of Business and Politics: The Rise and Fall of the Quaker Peace Dynasty of North-East England, 1700–1943* (London: George Allen and Unwin, 1984).

Knight, Frances, *The Nineteenth-Century Church and English Society* (Cambridge: Cambridge University Press, 1995).

Levine, Philippa, *Feminist Lives in Victorian England: Private Roles and Public Commitment* (London: Basil Blackwell, 1990).

Lewis, Jane *The Politics of Motherhood: Child and Maternal Welfare in England, 1900–1939* (London: Croom Helm, 1980).

——, *Women in England, 1870–1950: Sexual Divisions and Social Change* (Bloomington: Indiana University Press, 1984).

Lewis, Jane, *Women and Social Action in Victorian and Edwardian England* (Stanford: Stanford University Press, 1991).

Liddington, Jill and Jill Norris, *One Hand Tied Behind Us: The Rise of the Women's Suffrage Movement* (London: Virago Press, 1978).

Lochhead, Marion, *The Victorian Household* (London: John Murray, 1964).

MacDonald, Alec, *A History of the King's School, Worcester* (London: Ernest Benn, 1936).

Machin, G. I. T., *Politics and the Churches in Great Britain, 1869 to 1921* (Oxford: Clarendon Press, 1987).

Mack, Edward C., *Public Schools and British Opinion since 1860, The Relationship between Contemporary Ideas and The Evolution of an English Institution* (New York: Columbia University Press, 1941).

Malmgreen, Gail, ed., *Religion in the Lives of English Women, 1760–1930* (Bloomington: Indiana University Press, 1986).

Mansbridge, Albert, *The Older Universities of England: Oxford and Cambridge* (Boston: Houghton Mifflin Co., 1923).

Marsden, Gordon, ed., *Victorian Values: Personalities and Perspectives in Nineteenth-Century Society* (London: Longmans, 1990).

Marsh, P. T., *The Victorian Church in Decline: Archbishop Tait and the Church of England, 1868–1882* (Pittsburg: University of Pittsburg Press, 1969).

Mathew, David, *Lord Acton and His Times* (London: Eyre and Spottiswoode, 1968).

Maurice, Sir Frederick, *Haldane, 1856–1915: The Life of Viscount Haldane of Cloan* (London: Faber and Faber, 1937).

McDowell, R. B., *Alice Stopford Green: A Passionate Historian* (Dublin: Allen Figgis, 1967).

McLeod, Hugh, *Class and Religion in the Late Victorian City* (London: Croom Helm, 1974).

——, *Religion and the Working Class in Nineteenth-Century Britain* (London: Macmillan, 1984).

McPherson, Robert G., *Theory of Higher Education in Nineteenth-Century England* (Athens: University of Georgia Press, 1959).

Mintz, Steven, *A Prison of Expectations: The Family in Victorian Culture* (New York: New York University Press, 1985).

Mitchell, Sally, ed., *Victorian Britain: An Encyclopedia* (New York: Garland Publishing Inc., 1988).

Morley, John, *The Life of William Ewart Gladstone* (New York: Macmillan Co., 1932).

Morris, Jan, ed., *The Oxford Book of Oxford* (Oxford: Oxford University Press, 1978).

Morse, David, *High Victorian Culture* (New York: New York University Press, 1993).

Newsome, David, *Godliness and Good Learning: Four Studies on a Victorian Ideal* (London: John Murray, 1961).

Nord, Deborah Epstein, *The Apprenticeship of Beatrice Webb* (Ithaca, New York: Cornell University Press, 1985).

Norman, E. R., *Church and Society in England, 1770–1970* (Oxford: Clarendon Press, 1976).

Norwood, Cyril, and Arthur H. Hope, *Higher Education of Boys in England* (London: John Murray, 1909).

Nowell-Smith, Simon, ed., *Edwardian England, 1901–1914* (London: Oxford University Press, 1964).

Olsen, Donald J., *The Growth of Victorian London* (New York: Holmes and Meier, 1976.

Peardon, Thomas Preston, *The Transition in English Historical Writing, 1760–1830* (New York: Columbia University Press, 1933).

Peterson, M. Jeanne, *Family, Love and Work in the Lives of Victorian Gentlewomen* (Bloomington: Indiana University Press, 1989).

Petrie, Sir Charles, *The Victorians* (London: Eyre and Spottiswoode, 1960).

Pool, Daniel, *What Jane Austen Ate and Charles Dickens Knew: From Fox Hunting to Whist—The Facts of Daily Life in Nineteenth-Century England* (New York: Simon and Schuster, 1993).

Powicke, F. M., *Modern Historians and the Study of History* (London: Odhams Press, 1955).

Raymond, E. T., *Portraits of the Nineties* (London: T. Fisher Unwin, 1921).

Richter, Melvin, *The Politics of Conscience: T. H. Green and his Age* (Cambridge: Harvard University Press, 1964).

Roberts, S. C., *British Universities* (London: Collins, 1947).

Rothblatt, Sheldon, *The Revolution of the Dons: Cambridge and Society in Victorian England* (New York: Basic Book, Inc., 1968).

Rowse, A. L., *Oxford in the History of England* (New York: G. P. Putnam's Sons, 1975).

Russell, George W. E., *Afterthoughts* (London: Grant Richards, 1912).

Ryan, Barbara, *Feminism and the Women's Movement: Dynamics of Change in Social Movement, Ideology and Activism* (New York: Routledge, 1992).

Schuettinger, Robert L., *Lord Acton: Historian of Liberty* (La Salle, Illinois: Open Court Publishing Co., 1976).

Seymour-Jones, Carole, *Beatrice Webb: A Life* (Chicago: Ivan R. Dee, 1992).

Shaw, William A., *A Bibliography of Historical Works by Dr Creighton, Dr Stubbs and Dr S. R. Gardiner and Lord Acton* (London: Office of Royal Historical Society, 1903).

Sheils, W. J. and Diana Wood, eds, *Women in the Church* (London: Basil Blackwell, 1990).

Shiman, Lilian Lewis. *Women and Leadership in Nineteenth-Century England* (New York: St Martin's Press, 1992).

Sigsworth, Eric M., ed., *In Search of Victorian Values: Aspects of Nineteenth-Century Thought and Society* (Manchester: Manchester University Press, 1988).

Simon, Brian, *Education and the Labour Movement, 1870–1920* (London: Lawrence and Wishart, 1965).

——, *Studies in the History of Education, 1780–1870* (London: Lawrence and Wishart, 1960).

Smith, Kenneth, *Carlisle* (Carlisle: Carlisle Corporation, 1969).

Smith, Warren Sylvester, *The London Heretics, 1870–1914* (New York: Dodd, Mead and Co., 1968).

Stillman, Clara G., *Samuel Butler: A Mid-Victorian Modern* (London: Martin Secker, 1932).

Strachey, Lytton, *Eminent Victorians* (London: Chatto and Windus, 1918, 1921).

——, *Portraits in Miniature and Other Essays* (New York: W. W. Norton and Co., 1931, 1962).

Sutherland, John, *Mrs Humphrey Ward: Eminent Victorian, Pre-Eminent Edwardian* (Oxford: Oxford University Press, 1991).

Tavard, George H., *A Review of Anglican Orders: The Problem and the Solution* (Collegeville, Minnesota: The Liturgical Press, 1990).

Thomas, Keith, *Man and the Natural World: Changing Attitudes in England, 1500-1800* (Oxford: Oxford University Press, 1983).

Thompson, James Westfall, *A History of Historical Writing*, ii (New York: Macmillan Co., 1942).

Thomson, Sir J. J., *Recollections and Reflections* (New York: The Macmillan Co., 1937).

Trevelyan, George M., *British History in the Nineteenth Century and After, 1782-1919* (New York: Harper and Row, 1966).

——, *English Social History* (Toronto: University of Toronto Press, 1944).

——, *Grey of Fallodon: The Life and Letters of Sir Edward Grey, Afterwards Viscount Grey of Fallodon* (London: Longmans, Green and Co., 1937, 1948).

Trevelyan, Janet Penrose, *The Life of Mrs Humphry Ward* (New York: Dodd, Mead and Co., 1923).

Vicinus, Martha, *Suffer and Be Still: Women in the Victorian Age* (Bloomington: Indiana University Press, 1972).

Ward, W. R., *Victorian Oxford* (London: Frank Cass and Co., 1965).

Warner, Rex, *English Public Schools* (London: Collins, 1946).

Webb, Clement, C. J., *A Study of Religious Thought in England from 1850* (Oxford: Clarendon Press, 1933).

Whitehall, David, *Monstrous Regiment: The Story of the Women of the First World War* (London: The Macmillan Co., 1965).

Wiener, Martin J., *English Culture and the Decline of the Industrial Spirit, 1850–1980* (Cambridge: Cambridge University Press, 1982).

Wilkes, Lyall, *Tyneside Portraits: Studies in Art and Life* (Newcastle: French Graham, 1971).

Williams, C. H., *The Modern Historian* (London: Thomas Nelson and Sons, 1938).

Wingfield-Stratford, Esmé, *Those Earnest Victorians* (New York: Williams Morrow and Co., 1930).

——, *The Victorian Sunset* (New York: William Morrow and Co., 1932).

Winstanley, D. A., *Later Victorian Cambridge* (Cambridge: Cambridge University Press, 1947).

Wohl, Anthony S., *Endangered Lives: Public Health in Victorian Britain* (Cambridge: Harvard University Press, 1983).

Wolfson, John, *Sullivan and the Scott Russells* (Chichester: Packard Publishers, 1984).

Wortham, H. E., *Victorian Eton and Cambridge: Being the Life and Times of Oscar Browning* (London: Arthur Barker, 1927).

Wortley, Laura, *Wilfrid de Glehn, RA, John Singer Sargent's Painting Companion: A Painter's Journey* (London: The Studio of Fine Arts, 1989, US revised edition by Spanierman Gallery, 1997).

Wright, Thomas, *The Life of Walter Pater*, 2 vols (New York: Haskell House Publishers, 1907, 1969).

Young, G. M., *Daylight and Champagne* (London: Rupert Hart-Davis, 1937, 1948).

——, *Victorian England: Portrait of an Age* (London: Oxford University Press, 1936, 1960).

Young, Percy M., *George Grove, 1820–1900* (London: Macmillan, 1980).

Articles and Pamphlets

Backstrom, Jr, Philip N., 'The Practical Side of Christian Socialism in Victorian England', *Victorian Studies*, 6 (June 1963), pp. 305–24.

Bahlman, Dudley W. R., 'The Queen, Mr Gladstone and Church Patronage', *Victorian Studies*, 3 (June 1960), pp. 349–80.

Belgion, Montgomery, 'Why You Should Read It: *Life and Letters of Mandell Creighton*', *Theology*, 52 (October 1949), pp. 377–83.

Brose, Olive, 'F. D. Maurice and the Victorian Crisis of Belief', *Victorian Studies*, 3 (March 1960), pp. 227–48.

Chadwick, Owen, *Creighton on Luther: An Inaugural Lecture* (Cambridge: Cambridge University Press, 1959).

Clive, John, 'British History, 1870–1914, Reconsidered: Recent Trends in the Historiography of the Period', *American Historical Review*, 68 (July 1963), pp. 987–1009.

——, 'More or Less Eminent Victorians: Some Trends in Recent Victorian Biography', *Victorian Studies*, 2 (September 1958), pp. 5–28.

Commager, Henry Steele, 'Should the Historian Make Moral Judgements?' *American Heritage*, 17 (February 1966), pp. 26–27, 87–93.

[Covert, James T.] 'Mandell Creighton', *New Catholic Encyclopedia*, 4 (1967), p. 438.

Covert, James T., 'The Church-State Conflict in Late Nineteenth-Century English Education: One Victorian View', *University of Portland Review*, 27 (Spring 1975), pp. 33–52.

——, 'Reorganization of the University of London, 1884–1900: An Example of Government Intervention in Higher Education', *Duquesne Review*, 14 (Spring 1969), pp. 16–40.

Craster, Sir Edmund, 'Co-Operation between College Libraries', *Oxford Bibliographical Society's Publications*, new series, 4 (1950), pp. 44–52.

'Creighton, Mrs Louise', *Who Was Who, 1929–1940* (London: Adam and Charles Black, 1941), p. 307.

'Creighton, Louise (Hume)', *Who Was Who Among English and European Authors, 1931–1949* (Detroit: Gale Research, 1978), i, p. 362.

De Janosi, F. E., 'Correspondence between Lord Action and Bishop Creighton', *Cambridge Historical Journal*, 6 (1940), pp. 307–21.

De Laura, David J., 'Pater and Newman: The Road to the Nineties', *Victorian Studies*, 10 (September 1966), pp. 39–69.

Fish, Andrew, 'Action, Creighton and Lea: A Study in History and Ethics', *Pacific Historical Review*, 16 (February 1947), pp. 59–69.

Fletcher, Ian, 'The 1890s: A Last Decade', *Victorian Studies*, 4 (June 1961), pp. 345–54.

Harrison, John F. C., 'Recent Writing on the History of Victorian England', *Victorian Studies*, 8 (March 1965), pp. 263–70.

Hickman, R. G. K., *The Relationship between Churches and Schools* (London: National Society, 1961).

Highfield, J. R. L., *Merton College Chapel: A Lecture* (Oxford: Merton College Pamphlet, n.d.).

Honeyman, H. L., 'Embleton Vicarage', *Archaeologica Aeliana*, 4th series (1928), v, pp. 87–101.

Jenkins, Claude, 'Bishop Creighton's View of History', *Church Quarterly Review*, 218 (January 1930), pp. 193–238.

Madden, William A., 'The Victorian Sensibility', *Victorian Studies*, 7 (September 1963), pp. 67–97.

Matteisen, Paul F., 'Gosse's Candid Snapshots', *Victorian Studies*, 8 (June 1965), pp. 329–54.

Merton College (Oxford: University Press, n.d.).

Musgrove, F., 'Middle-Class Education and Employment in the Nineteenth Century', *Economic History Review*, 2nd series, 12 (August 1959), pp. 99–111.

Reckitt, Maurice B., 'When Did "Victorian" End?', *Victorian Studies*, 1 (March 1958), pp. 268–71.

Roach, J. P. C., 'Victorian Universities and the National Intelligensia', *Victorian Studies*, 3 (December 1959), pp. 131–50.

Rowse, A. L., 'Queen Elizabeth and the Historians', *History Today*, 3 (September 1953), pp. 630–41.

Ryder, P. F., *Fallodon* (Fallodon, Northumberland: privately published, 1987).

Smith, Kenneth, *Carlisle* (Carlisle: Carlisle Corporation, 1969).

Thompson, A. Hamilton, *The Life and Work of Mandell Creighton: An Address Delivered in Carlisle Cathedral on the Occasion of the Creighton Centenary, Sunday, 4th July, 1943* (Carlisle: Charles Thurnam and Sons, 1943).

Williams, Ernest, 'Mandell Creighton: Modern Carlisle's Greatest Son', *Carlisle Journal* (Carlisle, 1933).

Index

For a complete list of published articles and books by
Mandell and Louise Creighton, see Bibliography

Academy, The 128, 157, 160, 166, 167
Acland, Arthur 110, 111, 140
Acland, Mrs 122
Acton, John, Lord 163, 165–168, 179, 184, 204–10, 227–28, 283
Ad Anglos (Pope Leo XIII) 249
Aesthetic movement 2, 23, 61–62
Age of Elizabeth, The (Mandell Creighton) 155
Agricola 23
Albert Hall (London) 117, 283
Alberta, Canada 297, 302
Alderson, Frances (Basil Creighton's second wife) 316
Alexander III, Tsar of Russia 243–44
Alexander VI, Pope 206–7, 209
Alexandra Palace 286
Algeria 243
Alice in Wonderland by 'Lewis Carroll' (Charles Dodgson) 136
All Saints sisters 290
All Souls College, Oxford 90, 128, 315
Alleyne, Leonora Blanche 128, 130
Allnut, Miss 255, 267
Alnwick Castle 124, 160, 161, 212
Alps and Sanctuaries of the Piedmont and the Canton Ticino (Samuel Butler) 242
American Antiquarian Society 257
American Drolleries by 'Mark Twain' (Samuel Clemens) 129
American Episcopal Church 77

Anglican, *see* Church of England
Anglo-Catholic movement, see Church of England
Anti-Suffrage League 196
Apostolicae curae (Pope Leo XIII) 249
'Appeal Against Female Suffrage: A Rejoinder' (Louise Creighton) 195
Appleton, Charles Edward 128
Archaeological Institute 230
Archbishop's Mission to Western Canada 297
Architectural Association 260
Arnold, Mary, *see* Ward, Mrs Humphry Ward
Arnold, Matthew 2, 41, 86
Arnold, Thomas of Rugby 2, 34, 41, 44, 76, 172
Arnold, Thomas (son of Thomas Arnold of Rugby) 41
Artists' Benevolent Society 260
Asquith, Lady 267
Asquith, Margot 261
Assembly Powers Act, see Church of England
Association for the Education of Women 90
Association of Tutors (Oxford) 56
Athenaeum 261
Austen, Jane 159

Bacon, Roger 38
Bailey, Cyril (Gemma Creighton's husband) 297, 315

Bailey, John (Gemma Creighton's son) 315

Bailey, Mary (Gemma Creighton's daughter) 315

Bailey, Susan (Gemma Creighton's daughter) 315

Balfour, Arthur 256, 260

Balliol College, Oxford 29, 38, 45, 47, 52, 55, 150, 297

Baltic Exchange 68

Balzac, Honoré de 41, 63

Balzani, Count 253, 264

Bamburgh Castle 106

Band of Hope 116

Barlow, Sir Thomas 286

Barring, Bishop C. T. 108

Basel, Council of 165

Bateson, Mary 184–85

Beam Hall (Oxford) 98, 99

Beardsley, Aubrey 261

Beatrice, Princess 240

Becket, Thomas à 188

Beerbohm, Max 261

Beeton, Isabella 88

Bell, Hugh 128

Bell, William 27

Belvoir Castle 232

Benson, Archbishop E. W. 243–44, 246, 249–50

Berrington, Trevor 149–50, 152

Bethnal Green (London) 278

Bevan, Paul 149

Bigg, Charles 185

Bishop Creighton Memorial Committee 300–1

Bishop Creighton Settlement House (Fulham) 267, 301

Blackheath Proprietary School 77

Bloom off the Peach, The (Louise Creighton) 159–60

Board of Trade 223–24

Board schools, see Education

Bodleian Library (Oxford) 92, 163

Boer War (South African War) 271, 282

Book of Common Prayer, see Church of England

Boot and Shoe industry strike 223–24, 268, 277

Booth, William 234

Borgia, Cesare 209

Borough Farm (Ward's rented summer house) 216

Bosanquet, Charles 129

Boston Herald 199

Bowdler, Thomas 67

Boyd, C. T. 43, 44, 128

Brace, Charles Loring 197–98

Bradford, William 257

Bradley, Daisy (Mrs C. H. Woods) 128

Brasenose College (Oxford) 1, 2, 3, 5, 6, 8, 13, 38, 43, 63, 128

Bridges, Robert 89, 128, 299

Briennios, the Patriarch of Constantinople 244

Bright, J. F. 89, 128, 171

British Museum 11, 163, 256

Brodie, Sir and Lady Benjamin 1, 5–7

Brooke, Stopford 80–81, 149–50

Brown, Flora (Harold Creighton's wife) 316

Brown, Harris 301

Browning, Oscar 155, 162, 169–70

Browning, Robert 41, 129

Bruce, Margaret (Cuthbert Creighton's wife) 297

Bryn Mawr College (USA) 198

Buckingham Palace 261, 263

Burckhardt, Jacob 164

Burne-Jones, Edward 1, 62

Bury, J. B. 205

Butler, Samuel 242–43

Byron, Lord 70

Caird, Edward 37, 45, 55, 89

Calvin, John 165

Cambridge Modern History, The 179, 283

Cambridge Review 214

Cambridge, University of, *see* specific colleges

Cardinal Wolsey (Mandell Creighton) 205, 229

Carlisle (Mandell Creighton) 206

Carlisle Grammar School 27–29

Carlyle, Thomas 41

Carmichael, Sir Thomas 150

Catholic Church, *see* Roman Catholic Church

Catholic Way movement 272

Central Council for Women's Church Work 302

Chamberlain, Joseph 262, 271

Charity Organisation Society 190

Charles, Bonnie Prince 23

Charteris, Hugo, Lord Elcho 150

Chawner, William 178, 185

Children's Aid Society (USA) 198

Choate, Joseph H. 198–99

Christ Church (Oxford) 222

Christ's College (Cambridge) 25, 28, 227

Christian Social Union 234

Christon Bank (Northumberland) 105, 108, 111

Church, R. W. 204

Church and the Nation, The: Charges and Addresses (Mandell Creighton) 298

Church Army 234–35

Church Association 272

Church Benefices Bill 275

Church Congress Reports 162

Church Discipline Bill 275

Church Gospel Army 234

Church Historical Society 226

Church Militant Mission 234

Church Mission Army 234

Church of England:
  Anglo-Catholic movement 123, 247–48, 272–75
  Assembly Powers Act (1919) 303, 311

Book of Common Prayer 273–74, 277, 279

broad church 76, 213, 273, 276

communion service 27, 33, 41, 273, 274, 276, 286, 288

diocesan conferences 121, 237, 274, 276, 279

disestablishment 154, 224

evangelical wing 51, 172, 219, 272–75, 280, 292, 300

high church 29, 35, 41, 44, 51, 213, 225–26, 272–80, 285, 292

House of Laity, Church Assembly 311

loss of attendance 189, 259, 281

low church 272–73, 275–78

nonconformists 222, 258–59, 272, 281

priesthood for women issue 311

ritual issue 37, 52, 122, 213, 221, 226, 247, 271–85, 288

Church Quarterly 162

Church Salvation Army 234

Churchill, John, Duke of Marlborough 156–57

Civilisation of the Renaissance in Italy, The (Jacob Burckhardt) 164

Clifton College 149

Club, The (London) 261

Communion service, *see* Church of England

Connaught, Duke of 240

Conservative Party 152, 250, 256, 302

Conservative Primrose League 302

Constance, Council of 146, 163, 165–66

Contemporary Review 287

Co-operative Society (Peterborough diocese) 222

Coulton, George 215

Cranmer, Thomas 300

Creighton, Basil (Mandell's nephew) 241, 262, 266, 284, 293, 297, 316

Creighton, Beatrice (Mandell and Louise's daughter) 95–96, 98, 123,

125, 132–37, 144, 158, 186, 200–1,
219, 237–38, 242–43, 266, 268, 289,
296–97, 302, 315
Creighton, Caroline 'Carrie' *née* Hope
(Mandell's sister-in-law) 16, 17, 239
Creighton, Cuthbert (Mandell and
Louise's son) 130, 135–38, 144, 186,
202–4, 237, 243, 265, 285–86, 289,
293, 297, 310, 315–16
Creighton, Ella (Mandell's niece) 241,
259, 281–82, 285, 316
Creighton, Gemma (Mandell and
Louise's daughter) 201, 238, 255,
266–67, 290, 295–97, 313–15
Creighton, Gilbert (Mandell's nephew)
239, 316
Creighton, Harold (Mandell's nephew)
316
Creighton, Hugh (Cuthbert
Creighton's son) 315
Creighton, James (Mandell's brother)
16–17, 25, 27–28, 129, 239, 269–70
Creighton, Jane (Mandell's maiden
aunt) 16, 24–25, 146
Creighton, Louise:
   birth and family 68–72
   childhood activites 67–68, 71–76
   atmosphere in von Glehn home 9,
      71, 75–77
   Sydenham cultural life 68, 76
   early education 1, 72, 77–78
   intellectual and literary development
      78, 80–81
   interest in painting and music 78,
      80, 114
   father's business and financial status
      68–69, 70
   first trip to Continent 1, 78–80
   physical appearance 2
   character traits 75, 77, 85, 177,
      315–16
   early religious views 76
   appreciation of John Ruskin 1, 21,
      80

   early friendship with J. R. Green 8,
      76, 80
   early friendship with Humphry
      Ward 1–3, 80–81
   meeting Mandell Creighton 2–3
   engagement and courtship 5–22
   feelings about Mandell's family 11,
      15–17
   marriage and honeymoon 83–84
   first home ('Middlemarch') 20–21, 84
   married life adjustments 84–86
   household management in early
      marriage 84, 88
   letter-writing 85
   Oxford society 86–87
   Oxford friends 86–87, 89
   daily routine at Oxford 87–88
   interest in women's education
      90–91, 313–14
   begins social work 91
   first interest in writing history 91
   writes first book 93
   birth of Beatrice 91, 93–95
   first trip to Italy with Mandell 96–98
   move to Beam Hall 98–99
   birth of Lucia 99
   reluctance to leave Oxford 99–103
   feeling of 'exile' at Embleton 105,
      111, 127
   views on Northumberland life and
      people 105–109, 111, 114–15
   description of Embleton vicarage
      107–108, 110
   duties as vicar's wife 111–18
   social work at Embleton 115–18
   social life and visitors to Embleton
      122–25, 127–30
   birth of Cuthbert, Mary, Walter and
      Oswin 130
   thoughts about her children 130, 132
   education and discipline of children
      at Embleton 132–38
   household management at
      Embleton 139–43

interest in gardening, sketching and painting 143–44, 148

trips to Continent during Embleton years 144–48

illness on trip to Italy 145–46

death of mother 146–47

relationship with mother 147

views on Mandell's resident pupils 149–52

early friendship with Sir Edward Grey 150–51

marital relationship 152

literary achievements at Embleton 155–60

move to Cambridge 175

Cambridge society 175–76

Cambridge friends 176–77

friendship with Beatrice Webb 176–77

children's education in Cambridge years 186, 203–4

begins life at Worcester 187

death of father and sister, Mimi, 187

social and religious work at Cambridge 191–97

role with National Union of Women's Workers 193–97

early views on women's suffrage 194–97

trip to America 197–99

impressions of America 199–200

literary work at Cambridge 200

children's illnesses 200–201

birth of Gemma 201

misses Golden Jubilee 201

trips to Continent during Cambridge years 201–3

reluctance of Mandell becoming canon of Windsor 212

feelings about moving to Peterborough 216–18, 231

duties as bishop's wife 231–33

literary work at Peterborough 232

social work at Peterborough 233–36

views on 'purity question' 235–36, 304–6

social and family life at Peterborough 237–41

children's education and activities at Peterborough 237–38

feelings about Mandell's nephews and nieces 239

trips to Continent during Peterborough years 241–51

trip to Ireland 242

move to London 254–65

social life in London 262–63

holidays and trips to Continent 264, 269, 285

children's education and activities in London years 265–67

church and social work at London 267–68

addresses session of London Church Congress (1899) 284

last family holiday and trip to Continent 286

Mandell's final illness 286–90

Mandell's death and funeral 290–91

illness following Mandell's death 295

decision to write Mandell's biography 295

move to Hampton Court apartment 295–96

children after Mandell's death 296–97, 302, 313, 314–15

editing Mandell's writings and speeches 297–98

writing biography of Mandell 298–300

memorials to Mandell 300–1

life at Hampton Court 301–2

social and religious work after Mandell's death 302–3, 304–6, 310–11, 313–15

supports women's suffrage 302–3

close friends 303

published writings in later years
304–8, 310
efforts to combat venereal disease
304–6
differs from mainline feminists 305,
310–11
death of Lady Dorothy Grey 306–8
writes autobiography 306, 313
writes *Memoir* of Lady Dorothy
Grey 308
relationship with Sir Edward Grey
308–10
death of Oswin 310
views on church issues 310–11
move to Oxford 313
illness and death 314
obituaries and reflections 314–15,
316–17
lives of Mandell's sister, nieces and
nephews 315–16
Creighton, Lucia (Mandell and Louise's
daughter) 99, 135–38, 144, 186, 201,
238, 242, 262, 266, 296–97, 315
Creighton, Mandell:
birth and family 24–28
childhood 26–36
religious development 26–27,
35–36, 41, 51–52
early intellectual interest 27, 29–30
at Carlisle Grammar school 27–28
at Durham Grammar school 28–36
early interest in some sports 35, 40,
87
physical appearance 10
letter on monitors' duties 30, 32–34
at Merton College 37, 39–47
social life and friends at Merton
39–41, 42–44
early political views 42
first interest in history 45–47
interest in poetry and literature 41,
63–64
enjoys long walks 34–35, 40, 64, 97,
148, 160, 201, 220, 238

poem to a friend 43
favourite teachers 45–47
academic interest and degrees 45–47
takes holy orders 51, 65
character and personality
misunderstood 42–44, 51–52, 54,
65, 177, 298–301
decision to teach 47
elected fellow of Merton 47, 51–52
teaching at Merton 49–65, 83–103
views on teaching 52–53, 55, 57–59,
61
interest in intercollegiate lectures
56–59
avoids university politics 54–55
financial income as fellow 55
views on 'common life' of college
53–54, 89
tutoring the Duke of Albany and
Lord Randolph Churchill 59–61
interest in aestheticism 61–63
early trips to Continent 64–65
discovers Italy 64
early lectures for women 17–18, 90,
94
meets Louise von Glehn 2–3
engagement, courtship and
courtship letters 5–22
thoughts about letter-writing 13–15,
55, 240–41
issue over married fellowships 12,
19–20, 22
marriage and honeymoon 83–84
married life adjustments 84–85
nicknamed 'Max' 12
interest in rowing 87
life as a tutor 87–90
sermons at Merton 89–90, 99
appointed examiner to new school
of history 90
writes first book 92–93, 155
early thoughts on parenthood 91,
96
first trip to Italy with Louise 96–98

begins history of popes 98
offer of Embleton living 99
annual income at Merton and Embleton 100, 110
decision to leave Oxford 99–103
move to Embleton 105–10
work as a vicar 110–25
preaching style 112
work with schools and board of guardians 118–20
as examining chaplain and rural dean 119–22
as history examiner 119–21
works on history of popes 126
love of children 132–34
trips to Continent during Embleton years 144–48
death of father 145
death of aunt 146
resident pupils at Embleton 149–152
questions concerning his spirituality 152
political views on Gladstone's policies 152–54, 186
controversy over 1884 election 153–54
historical writings at Embleton 155 58, 160–68
completed first two volumes of history of popes 162–65
Lord Acton's reviews 165–68
views on Reformation 165
comparison with Ranke 168
applies for Regius Professorship at Oxford 168–69
elected Cambridge professor 169–71
annual incomes as vicar and professor 169
reads first paper at church congress 171
thoughts on Reformation in England 171–72
farewell sermon at Embleton 172–73
begins professorship 175

friendship with Beatrice Webb 176–77
views on Creighton at Cambridge 177–79
relationship with Lord Acton 179–79
issue over historical tripos 179–81
inaugural lecture 181–83
views on church history 181–83
lecturing style 183–84
work as fellow of Emmanuel 184–85
preaching at Emmanuel 185
teaching at Newnham and Girton 184–85
appoinment as canon of Worcester 186
canon's life 187–91
views on day schools 188–89
views on cathedral life 189
growing social concern 189–91
trip to America 197–99
represents Emmanuel at Harvard anniversary 198–99
impressions of America 199–200
trips to Continent during Cambridge years 201–3
first editor of English Historical Review 204–5
historical writing at Cambridge 205–6
completed second two volumes of history of popes 206
views on Renaissance popes 206–10
disagreements with Lord Acton 207–10
chance to become canon of Windsor 211
appointed Bishop of Peterborough 212–14
brief illnesses 216–17
friendship with Mrs Humphry Ward 216–17
working with clergy 219–21
views on nonconformists and Roman Catholics 221

relationship with working and middle classes 221–23

role in industry strike 223–24

primary charge to clergy (1894) 224–25

sermons and church congress speeches 225

thoughts about Archbishop Laud 225–26

lectures and writings at Peterborough 226–30

completed final volume of history of popes 226–27

reviews of final volume 227

views on 'toleration' 227

enters House of Lords 236–37

death of sister-in-law and brother 239

relationship with nephews and nieces 239–41

visits with royal family 239–40, 285

trips to Continent during Peterborough years 241–51

trip to Ireland 242

trip to Algeria 243

trip to Russia for coronation of Tsar 243–47

discussion with Archbishop of St Petersburg 246–47

geopolitical assessment of Europe 246

issue over Anglican orders 247–49

mentioned as possible Archbishop of Canterbury 250, 251

appointed Bishop of London 250–51

feelings about becoming Bishop of London 253–54

annual income as bishop 256

Privy Council and other committees 256

interest in log of the *Mayflower* 256–57

defends voluntary schools 257–59

argues for Voluntary School Bill in House of Lords 258–59

growth of administrative work 260

some sermons and speeches in London years 260, 283, 286, 287–88

London life 261–62

involvement in Diamond Jubilee (1897) 263

Pan-Anglican Conference (1897) 264

holidays and trips to Continent during London years 264, 269, 285

views about his children 265–67

work on London University commission 268

first president of London School of Economics 269

funeral of W. E. Gladstone 269

last trip to Carlisle 269–70

views on Boer War 271, 284, 285

ritual controversy 272–82

meets Kaiser Wilhelm II 282–83

historical writing during London years 283

London Church Congress (1899) 283–84

charge to London clergy (1900) 285

Pan-African Conference in London (1900) 286

last holiday and trip to Continent 286

final illness 285, 286–90

final thoughts on society 287–88

Round Table Conference at Fulham 288

death and funeral 290–91

obituaries and reflections 291–94, 298–301, 317

memorials 300–1

Creighton, Marjorie (Mandell's niece) 316

Creighton, Mary (Mandell and Louise's daughter) 130, 238, 266, 296–97, 315

Creighton, Mary Ellen 'Polly' (Mandell's sister) 16–17, 25–28, 83,

99, 123, 129, 144–46, 239, 243, 264, 270, 285, 315

Creighton, Oswin (Mandell and Louise's son) 130, 186, 204, 238, 266, 297, 302, 304, 307, 310

Creighton, Robert (Mandell's father) 11, 16, 24–26, 28, 145

Creighton, Robert (Mandell's nephew) 316

Creighton, Sarah Mandell (Mandell's mother) 24–25

Creighton, Thomas (Cuthbert Creighton's son) 315

Creighton, Walter (Mandell and Louise's son) 130, 137, 146, 186, 200, 202, 204, 237, 243, 265–66, 285, 289–90, 297, 310, 315

Creighton, Winifred (Mandell's niece) 231, 239, 241, 260, 269, 271, 281, 316

Creighton Memorial Lectureship (London University) 301

Creighton School (Carlisle, formerly Denton Holme School) 316

Crimean War 68

Crompton, Henry 89

Cruttwell, C. T. 128

Crystal Palace 6, 68, 74–76, 78

Daily Telegraph, The 281

Dalmatian coast 201–3

Dante, Alighieri 15, 17, 65, 90, 95, 99, 115, 130, 160, 201

Darwin, Charles 38, 52, 63, 176, 300

Darwin, Horace 176

Darwin, Ida 176

Davey, Lord 268

Davidson, Bishop Randall 212–13, 216, 244, 250, 280–81, 292–93, 299–300

Deaconess Institute (Portsmouth) 297

Denton Holme School, *see* Creighton School

Diamond Jubilee (Queen Victoria) 263

Dictionary of National Biography 206

Dilke, Mrs Ashton 194–95

Diocesan Penitentiary Association, Worcester 189

Disestablishment of the Anglican Church, see Church of England

Dixie, Sir Thomas 169

Dobson, John 107

Dormehl, P. J. (husband of Winifrid, Mandell's niece) 316

Dorothy Grey, A Memoir (Louise Creighton) 304, 306

Drummond, Henry 124

Drummond, Louisa, see Duchess of Northumberland

Duns Scotus 38

Dunstanburgh Castle 106

Durham Cathedral 29, 35–36, 38, 273

Durham Grammar School 23, 28–30, 32, 34–36, 46, 132, 189, 217

Durham, University of 29, 51, 149

Ecce Homo 180

Ecclesiastical and Political History of the Popes (Leopold von Ranke) 168

Economics of the Household, The (Louise Creighton) 304

Edinburgh World Missionary Conference (1910) 303

Edinburgh, University of 39, 176

Education:
　board schools 156, 257–58
　college reforms (*see* specific colleges)
　Compulsory Attendance Act (1876) 118, 120
　Education Act (1870) 257
　Embleton parish schools 118
　establishment of London School of Economics 269, 286
　inspectors ('Payment by Results' policy) 118–19
　London University commissions (1900, 1909) 268–69, 302
　monitorial system 30, 32–35
　Oxford University Act (1854) 49
　Oxford University reforms 49–51

school of law and modern history at Oxford (divided in the 1871) 45, 90
university extension movement 50, 90
Voluntary School Bill (1897) 257–59
voluntary schools 118, 257–59
women's higher education 1, 17, 51, 78, 90–91, 184, 313, 316; see also specific women's colleges
Edward, Prince of Wales (later King Edward VII) 244, 250, 260–61, 263, 282
Edward, Prince of Wales (later King Edward VIII) 240, 282
Edward, the Black Prince 156–57
Edward IV, King 107
Edward VI, King 273
Elizabeth I, Queen 155, 218, 229–30, 273, 276
Eliot, Charles W. 198–99
Embleton (Northumberland):
parish schools 118
parish and region, description of 105–6
vicarage, description of 107–8, 110
village life and people, description of 105–15
Emmanuel College Magazine 206
Emmanuel College (Cambridge) 169, 171, 175, 177–78, 181, 184–85, 197, 199, 201, 206, 265, 301
England: A Continental Power. From the Conquest to Magna Carta, 1066–1216 (Louise Creighton) 93, 155, 157
Englische Geschichte (Leopold von Ranke) 91–92
English Church Union 247, 272
English Churchman 272
English Historical Review 204–5, 207–8, 211, 215, 227
'Epochs of Church History' series 205
'Epochs of English History' series 155–56, 158

'Epochs of European History' series 155
Essays and Reviews 38
Esson, William 56
Estonia 69
Eton, public school 59, 293
Eucharist, see Church of England, communion service
Eugenius V, Pope 46
Evangelical, see Church of England

Fabian Society 191, 261, 268
Fallodon Hall 105, 109, 118, 122, 123, 150, 154, 306–9
Farrer, Sir Thomas (later Lord Farrer) 176
Fawcett, Millicent Garrett 194–95
Feltre, Vittorino da 160
Figgis, John N. 184, 300
First History of England, A (Louise Creighton) 158, 200
First History of France, A (Louise Creighton) 200, 232
First World War 199, 297, 303, 310, 315
Fortnightly Review 128
Foster, William H. 43–44
Fox, Helen and Mary (of Falmouth) 125
Franciscans (Order of Friars Minor) 248
Franco-Prussian War 64
Free Library movement 235
Freeling, N. 128
Freeman, Edward A. 89, 158, 169, 204, 206
Fulham Palace 171, 251, 253–55, 257, 260–64, 267, 272, 286, 288–89, 290, 292–93, 301

G. A. Selwyn, D.D.: Bishop of New Zealand and Lichfield (Louise Creighton) 304
Gairdner, James 205
Gardiner, S. R. 205, 227

Gardner, Alice 184

Garnet, Richard 229

General Election (1880) 153

General Election (1884) 154

Gennadius, Patriarch, Archbishop of St Petersburg 246

Gibbon, Edward 79, 103

Gilbert and Sullivan 76, *see also* Sullivan, Arthur

Gill, Eric 305–6

Gilman, Daniel C. 198–99

Girls' Friendly Society 117, 191, 234, 267, 302

Girton College (Cambridge) 91, 184

Gladstone, Mary 179

Gladstone, William E. 42, 50, 154, 179, 186, 205, 212, 269

Glehn, Agnes von (Louise's mother) 2, 5–6, 9–10, 16, 19, 21, 69–72, 75, 77–79, 81, 83–86, 88, 93–95, 97, 102, 116–17, 120, 124, 129, 135, 139, 141–47, 149–50, 153, 157–58, 200

Glehn, Alexander 'Alick' von (Louise's brother) 68, 70, 77, 310

Glehn, Alfred von (Louise's brother) 70, 72, 77

Glehn, Ernest von (Louise's brother) 1, 6, 67, 68, 70, 72, 73, 77

Glehn, Harry von (Louise's brother) 70, 72, 77, 198

Glehn, Ida von (Louise's sister) 21, 70, 72, 289, 297, 310

Glehn, Mary Emilie 'Mimi' von (Louise's sister) 9, 11, 12, 19, 21, 70, 76, 78, 80, 85, 187

Glehn, Olga von (Louise's sister) 9, 11–13, 21, 70, 80

Glehn, Oswald von (Louise's brother) 70, 72, 77, 265

Glehn, Rachel von (Louise's niece) 215

Glehn, Robert von (Louise's father) 8–9, 11, 67–72, 74–79, 81, 84, 146–47, 187, 194

Glehn, Sophie von (Louise's sister) 70, 72, 78, 243, 289, 310

Glehn, Wilfrid von, later de' Glehn (Louise's nephew, son of Alick) 77, 290, 310

Glehn, Willie von (Louise's brother) 19, 68, 70, 77

Glenconner, Pamela 309

Goethe, Johann Wolfgang von 15, 41

Golden Jubilee (Queen Victoria) 201, 263

Gore, Charles 272

Gosse, Edmund 54, 128, 179, 184, 214, 298

Government of England, The (Louise Creighton) 158

Graves, Alice 307

Great Exhibition 68

Great Schism 103, 165

Green, Alice Stopford (J. R. Green's wife) 128, 166, 168, 171, 194, 206, 209, 212, 229

Green, C. E. 111–12, 119

Green, Charlotte (T. H. Green's wife) 84, 87, 89–91, 128, 130, 194

Green, John Richard 8, 50–52, 65, 76, 80–81, 83, 89, 92, 128, 158, 168, 204, 206

Green, Thomas Hill 38, 45–47, 52, 84, 87, 89, 128, 130

Gretna Green (Scotland) 25

Greville, Charles 205

Grey, Albert Henry George, fourth Earl Grey 123

Grey, Charles, second Earl Grey (of Reform Bill fame) 109

Grey, Constance (Sir Edward Grey's sister) 123

Grey, Lady Dorothy, *née* Widdrington 151, 254, 264, 304, 306–9

Grey, George, Lieutenant Colonel (Sir George Grey of Fallodon's son) 123

Grey, Harriet Jane Pearson (Lieutenant Colonel George Grey's wife) 123

Grey, Lady Anna Sophia (Sir George Grey of Fallodon's wife) 122
Grey, Sir Edward, Viscount Fallodon (Lieutenant Colonel George Grey's son) 123, 150–54, 186, 201, 254, 271, 295, 306–9
Grey, Lady Frederick 117
Grey, Sir George (son of Earl Grey of Reform Bill fame) 107
Grey, Sir George of Fallodon (nephew of Earl Grey of Reform Bill fame) 122–23, 150
Grey, Lady Georgiana 296
Grey, Henry George, Viscount Howick, and third Earl Grey 107
Grillions Club (London) 261
Grove House School 151
Grove, Sir George 6, 76, 128, 160
Guardians, board of 119–20, 124
Gunson, William 25, 28, 102
Gwatkin, Henry M. 169–70, 180, 215, 283

Haldane, Richard, later Lord 268
Halifax, Charles Lindley Wood, second Viscount Halifax 123, 247–49, 272
Halton, F. W. (husband of Ella, Mandell's niece) 316
Hamlyn, Vincent 144
Hampton Court Palace 265, 296–97, 301, 313
Harcourt, Sir William 275
Hardy, Thomas 315
Harrison, Frederic 89
Harvard University (USA) 77, 197–99, 206, 242
Harvard, John 197, 199
Haverford College (USA) 198
Hawthorne, Nathaniel 24, 138
Hebdomadal Council (Oxford University) 49, 54
Henry III, King 38
Henry VIII, King 218, 248

Henry, Prince of Battenberg 240
Herbert, Constance 136, 307–8
Heritage of the Spirit and Other Sermons, The (Mandell Creighton) 225
Herkomer, Hubert 301
Heroes of European History (Louise Creighton) 304
Heroes of French History (Louise Creighton) 304
High church, see Church of England
'Highways of History' series 158–59, 200
'Historic Towns' series 206
'Historical Biographies' series 156
Historical Essays and Reviews (Mandell Creighton) 298
Historical Lectures and Addresses (Mandell Creighton) 298
Historische Zeitschrift 204
History of the Norman Conquest (Edward Freeman) 158
History of the Papacy from the Great Schism to the Sack of Rome, 1378–1527 (Mandell Creighton) 126, 151, 160–66, 197, 205, 213–15, 226–27, 229, 246
Hodgkin, Barnett, Pease, Spence and Co., bank of Newcastle 125
Hodgkin, Thomas 125–26, 160, 163–64, 167, 178, 209, 259, 304
Hoghton Tower 161
Holden, Dr Henry 23, 29–30, 32–33, 35, 38, 46, 217
Holiday House (Catherine Sinclair) 73
Holland, Henry Scott 34, 49, 52, 54, 251, 272, 292, 298, 300
Holmes, Oliver Wendell 198–99
Homer 27, 59
Hood, Mr and Mrs H. J. 8, 12–13, 43, 127–28, 130
Hope, Caroline, see Creighton, Caroline
Hopkins, Ellice 190, 193
Hort, F. J. A. 178–79

House of Laity (first Church Assembly) 311

Housman, Laurence 213

Howard, George James, ninth Earl of Carlisle 86, 128, 130, 153

Howick Hall 109, 117–18, 123–24, 296

Hughes, Thomas 77, 198

Hume, Elisa 68, 159

Hume, Joseph MP 68

Hume, Lois (Louise Creighton) 159

Hus, John 146, 166

Huxley, Thomas H. 7, 38, 194

Indian Civil Service examinations 149

Intercollegiate lectures (Oxford University) 56–57

International Congress of Women (1899) 316

International Crisis, The: The Theory of the State (Louise Creighton) 304

Irish Home Rule 152, 186

Italy and Her Invaders (Thomas Hodgkin) 126

Itchen Abbas cottage (Hampshire) 306, 309

James I, King 218

Jane Eyre (Charlotte Brontë) 41

Jenkinson, Francis J. H. 177

Jesus College (Oxford) 54

Jewry, Mary, *Warne's Every-Day Cookery* 88

Joan, the Maid of Kent 304

Johns Hopkins University (USA) 198–99

John of Gaunt 106

Johnson, Arthur 90, 128, 313

Johnson, Bertha (Arthur Johnson's wife) 87, 89, 91, 128, 313

Joint Committee of Insurance Commissioners (1912) 302

Jowett, Benjamin 6, 37, 45–47, 86, 150

Julius II, Pope 206

Katherine of Aragon, Queen 218

Keble College (Oxford) 90, 111, 128, 176, 297

Kensit, John 272–73, 275, 277–78

Khartoum 186

King's College (Cambridge) 176

King's College (London) 77

King's School (Worcester) 188, 315

Kingsley, Charles 180

Knox, Edmund A. 39, 53–54, 57, 59, 89, 170

La vie de Jésus (Ernest Renan) 63

Ladies Association (Oxford) 17, 90

Lady Margaret Hall (Oxford) 90, 297, 313–14

Laing, Robert 56

Lake District 15, 35, 264, 287

Lambeth Palace 245, 251, 279, 314

Lambeth Palace Conference (1897) 264

Lambeth Palace Conference (1920) 311

Lambeth Palace Hearing (1899) 279–80

Lang, Andrew 86, 89, 127–28, 130

Langdale Lodge 175

Laud, Archbishop William 225–26, 278–79

Le Havre, France 77

Lea, Henry Charles 198, 209, 227

Leisure Hour 230

Leo X, Pope 179

Leo XIII, Pope 249, 272

Leopold, Prince, Duke of Albany 59, 169

Leslie, Shane 293

Lessons from the Cross (Mandell Creighton) 283

Letters of Oswin Creighton, C.F., 1883–1918 (Louise Creighton) 304, 310

Lewes, G. H. 63

Liberal Party 26, 70, 124, 152–54, 186, 191, 261, 268–69, 275, 302

Liddon, Henry P. 6

Life and Letters of Mandell Creighton (Louise Creighton) 299

Life and Letters of Thomas Hodgkin (Louise Creighton) 304
Life and Liberty movement 303
Life of Edward the Black Prince (Louise Creighton) 156–57
Life of John Churchill, Duke of Marlborough (Louise Creighton) 156–57
Life of Simon De Montfort, Earl of Leicester (Mandell Creighton) 156, 160
Life of Sir Walter Raleigh (Louise Creighton) 156–57
Lightfoot, Bishop Joseph 121, 180
Lightfoot scholarship (Cambridge) 120
Lincoln College (Oxford) 37, 64
Literae humaniores 45, 47, 56
Literary and Philosophical Institute (Peterborough diocese) 222
Literary Philosophical Institute (Newcastle) 119
London Brighton and South Coast Railway 67
London Church Congress (1899) 285
London Church Reading Union 260
London Council for the Promotion of Public Morality 267, 302
London Illustrated News 261
London Reform Union 283
London School of Economics 260, 269, 286
London University Commission (1900) 268–69
London University Commission (1909) 302
London University Reorganisation Bill 268–69
London, University of 1, 78, 268–69, 283, 301–2
Longman, Charles J. 156, 162, 204, 295
Longmans (publishers) 155–56, 158, 162–63, 200, 204–5, 232, 295, 298
Lord Mayor of London 262
Lords, House of 153, 236–37, 258, 263

Louise, Princess 240
Low church, *see* Church of England
Lowell, James Russell 199
Luther, Martin 165, 167–68, 226–27, 300
Lux Mundi 272, 300
Lymington, Lord, later Earl of Portsmouth 149–50
Lyttelton, Arthur 176, 303
Lyttelton, Kathleen 176, 193–94, 216–18, 233, 236, 303

Macaulay, Thomas Babington, Lord 167
Macbeth (William Shakespeare) 115
Maclagan, Archbishop W. D. 250
Macmillan's Magazine 57, 128, 160
Magazine of Art 160–61
Magee, Bishop William 212, 221
Maitland, Frederic 184
Malatesta, Gismondo, of Rimini 161–62
Manchester Guardian, The 93, 128, 311
Mandeville, Walter de 25
Mansion House 262, 301
Marlborough House 261
Marlborough School 15, 186, 203–4, 237, 258, 266
Marlborough, Duchess of 60–61
Marshall, Alfred 176
Marsham, Robert Bullock 52
Mary Tudor, Queen 183
Mary, Queen of Scots 23–24
Maud, Princess of Wales 240
Maurice, F. D. 76
Mayflower, The, log of 256–57
McDonald, Eleanor 114
McDowall, Arthur (Mary Creighton's husband) 315
Medici family 167
Memoir of Sir George Grey, Bart, GCB (Mandell Creighton) 123
'Memorials of the Bishops of Peterborough' (scrapbook) 251

Merton College (Oxford), reforms of 52–53

Merton College (Oxford) 3, 5, 8, 12–13, 19–20, 22, 38–40, 42–45, 47, 51–57, 59, 61, 63, 83–84, 86–89, 98, 100, 103, 107, 126, 128, 130, 170, 184–85, 188, 273, 292, 298, 301

Merton College (Oxford), issue over married fellows 12, 19–20, 22

Merton, Walter de 38, 130

'Middlemarch' (Louise and Mandell's first home) 84, 91

Midland Institute (Birmingham) 287

Mildmay, Sir Walter 206

Mill on the Floss, The, by George Eliot (Mary Ann Evans) 41

Mill, John Stuart 38, 52

Mind of St Peter and Other Sermons, The (Mandell Creighton) 298

Miss Bretherton (Mrs Humphry Ward) 216–17

Missions: Their Rise and Development (Louise Creighton) 304

Modern Painters (John Ruskin) 164

Monitorial system, see Education

Montfort, Simon de 156, 160

Morata, Olympia Fulvia 160

Morley, John 128

Morris, William 1, 18, 21, 62–63, 110

Moss, Rachel (Gemma Creighton's daughter) 315

Mothers' Union 116–17, 191, 233–34, 267, 302

Mrs Beeton's Every-Day Cookery and Housekeeping Book (Isabella Beeton) 88

Müller, Georgiana (Mrs Max Müller) 86, 90, 194

Müller, Max 86

Mullinger, James Bass 227

Muratori, Ludovico Antonio 163

Murray, Gilbert 297

'Mystic Circle' (also 'The Saints') 44

National Mission of Repentance and Hope 303, 311

National Portrait Gallery (London) 256

National Protestant Church Union 272

National Union of Women Workers 193–94, 196–97, 235–236, 267, 302–3, 316

National Vigilance Association 190

Natural History Museum 256

New College (Oxford) 77

'New Machiavellian' (Webbs' house) 261

New Poor Law (1834) 119

New Rugby (Thomas Hughes's settlement in America) 77

Newnham College (Cambridge) 91, 184–85, 238, 262, 266

Newton, Ursula (Basil Creighton's first wife) 316

Niagara Falls (USA) 198

Nicholas II, Tsar of Russia 243–45

Nicholas V, Pope 46

Nightingale, Florence 304

Nineteenth Century, The 194–95, 304

Nobody's Friends club (London) 261

Non Nobis, Domine (Roger Quilter) 315

North Eastern Railway 105–106

Northampton Educational Society 258

Northampton Trades Council 224

Northumberland, Algernon George, sixth Duke of Northumberland 124

Northumberland, Duchess of (Louisa Drummond) 109, 124

Norton, Charles Eliot 198

Order of the British Empire Chapel (crypt in St. Paul's) 291

Oriel College (Oxford) 45, 55–56, 128

Orthodox Church, see Russian Orthodox Church

Osborn, Montagu Francis Finch 170

Osborne Palace 293

Oswy, King of Bernicia 130

Owens College (Manchester) 204

Oxford Movement 37–38, 52, 247, 272
Oxford Union 42, 153
Oxford University Act (1854), see Education
Oxford University reforms, see Education
Oxford, University of, see specific colleges

'Pageant of Parliament' (Walter Creighton, producer) 315
Pan-African conference (1900) 286
Pan-Anglican Conference (1897) 264
Pan-Anglican Congress (1908) 303
Pankhurst, Christabel 304
Papillon, T. L. 55
Parkman, Francis 198
Pater, Clara 5, 19, 89, 91, 128
Pater, Walter 2, 38, 61–62, 84, 87, 89, 164
Pattison, Mark 37, 39, 45, 49, 54
Pavia-Siena, Council of 165
Paxton, Sir Joseph 68
Peak Hill Lodge (Sydenham) 8–9, 13, 16–17, 67–69, 72–77, 80, 83, 144, 147, 187
Pease, Alfred 150–52, 243
Pease, Ella 241, 307–8
Pease, Emma (Effie) 144
Pease, John William (of Newcastle and Alnmouth) 125
Pease, Joseph 'Jack', later Lord Gainford of Headlam 144
Pease, Sir Joseph Whitwell (of Hutton Hall in Yorkshire) 144
Peile, Dr John 227–28
Percival, Bishop John 260
Percival, Dr (of Clifton College) 149
Percival, Lancelot 260, 287, 290
Perse School for Boys (Cambridge) 186
Perse School for Girls (Cambridge) 186
Persecution and Tolerance (Mandell Creighton) 209, 228

Peterborough Cathedral 217–18, 224, 231
Phear, Dr Samuel G. 197–99
Philip II, King of Spain 206
Philpot, Glyn 314
Philpott, Bishop Henry 211, 213
'Plea for Knowledge, A' (Mandell Creighton) 287
Pisa, Council of 165
Pius II, Pope (Aeneas Sylvius) 147, 160, 300
Pius IX, Pope 79
Pobiedonostzeff, M. 244–46
Pole, Cardinal 183
Poole, R. L. 204–5
Porchester, Lord 150
Portal, Abbé E. F. 247–48
Potter, Beatrice, see Webb, Beatrice
Potter, C. A. 43
Potter, Mrs Caroline 43
Powell, Frederick York 204
Pre-Raphaelites 1, 62
Price, Bonamy 86
Primer on Roman History (Mandell Creighton) 92–93, 155
Prince of Wales' Hospital Fund 260
Privy Council 20, 256, 260
Promotion Cometh (Laurence Housman) 213
Protestant Alliance 272
Protestant Reformation Society 272
Protestant Truth Society 272, 278
Prothero, George W. 160, 176, 180–81, 298
Prothero, Mary Frances (George W. Prothero's wife) 176
'Purity question' 235, 304–5

'Quadrilateral, The' 44
Quarterly Review 209
Queen Elizabeth (Mandell Creighton) 229–30
Queen's College (Cambridge) 25
Queen's Hall (London) 117

Quilter, Roger 315

Ragosine Oil Company 68
Raikes, R. T. 43–44, 128, 130
Raleigh, Sir Walter 156–57
Ranke, Leopold von 91–92, 164, 167–68
Reform Act (1832) 107, 109, 122–23
Reform Act (1867) 158
Regius Professorship of Modern
    History (Oxford and Cambridge) 45,
    56, 168–69
Reierson, Mr and Mrs (Louise's
    grandparents) 69–70
Renaissance in Italy, The (John
    Symonds) 164
Renan, Ernest 63
Reni, Guido 80
Reports of the Poor Law District
    Conferences 120
Rescue and Prevention Association 302
Rescue movement 234–35, 267, 301–2
Rescue Work Association 267
Response of the Archbishops of England
    to the Apostolic Letter of Pope Leo
    XIII 249
Review of Reviews 261
Revue historique 163, 204
Richmond Park 287
Ritual controversy, see Church of
    England
Rivingtons (publishers) 156, 158–59,
    200
Robert Elsmere (Mrs Humphry Ward)
    217
Robertson, Fred 76
Robertson, George 124–25
Robertson, Mrs George 124–25
Roman Catholic Church 79, 146–47,
    163–64, 166, 168, 179, 206–7, 209,
    221, 225, 247, 249, 254, 257, 272–74,
    276, 279, 305, 311, 316
Roman Wall 15, 23, 126
Rookes, Charles and Mrs 109–10
Rosebery, Lord, fifth Earl of 237, 292

Rossetti, Dante Gabriel 41
Round Table Conference at Fulham
    Palace (1900) 285–86, 88
Royal Academy (London) 77
Royal Institution of Great Britain 283
Royden, Maude 311
Rugby public school 2, 34, 41, 55, 76
Ruskin, John 1–2, 7, 21, 62, 65, 80,
    164, 202
Russell, Scott 67–68
Russian Holy Synod 244
Russian Orthodox Church 244, 246,
    311
Rutland, Duke of 232

St Anselm 46
St Augustine's Confessions 44
St Bartholomew's church (Sydenham)
    76, 83
St Bees boarding school (Cumberland)
    27–28
St Catharine's College (Cambridge) 184
St Cuthbert 23
St Faith's House (Madras, India) 315
St Francis of Assisi 96
St Hilda's College (Oxford) 1, 91, 304
St Hugh's College (Oxford) 90
St James's Home (London) 290
St John's College (Cambridge) 25, 227
St John's College (Oxford) 54
St Mary-le-Bow church (London) 272
St Oswin 130
St Paul's Cathedral 202, 204, 226, 251,
    254–55, 263, 285–86, 290–92, 295,
    301, 314
St Peter's church (Leicester) 258
St Petersburg (Russia) 69, 246
Saintsbury, George 39–40, 42–43, 51,
    89, 128
Salisbury, Lord, third of Marquess of
    211–13, 243–44, 250–51, 257, 261
Salvation Army 234
Sand, George (Lucile-Aurore Dupin)
    15, 41, 63

Sandringham Palace 240, 263, 282, 285
Sanitary Congress (Worcester) 190
Sargent, John Singer 77, 310
Saturday Examiner 157
Savile Club (London) 261
Savonarola, Girolamo 166, 286, 300
Sayce, Archibald Henry 128
Schleswig-Holstein, Prince and
  Princess of 240
School of Historical Research (London
  University) 301
Schwabe, Mary 95, 128
Scott, C. P. 89, 93, 128
Scott, Sir Walter 23, 29, 135
Secret History of the Oxford Movement,
  The (Walter Walsh), 272
Seebohm, Frederic 160
Seeley, John 180–81, 204
Selwyn College (Cambridge) 176
Servants:
  Allnutt, Mrs (nurse-governess) 155,
    167
  Bertha (parlourmaid) 313
  Eliza (nurse-governess) 96, 137,
    140, 142
  Hardman, Mrs (cook-housekeeper)
    255, 262
  Holmes, Mr (groom) 141–42
  Holmes, Mrs (cook) 141–43
  Janie Thompson (nurse-governess)
    175
  Louie (nurse) 313
  Marie (nursemaid) 140
  Turner (gardener) 255
  Wilkin (butler) 237, 255
Settlement house movement 190, 234,
  267, 301, 304
Shadwell, C. L. 56
Shakespeare, William 67, 115
Shilling History of England, The
  (Mandell Creighton) 158
Shirley, Walter 45–46, 164
Short History of the English People (J. R
  Green) 128, 158

Sidgwick, William 45, 55, 64
Siegfried (Richard Wagner) 2243
Sinclair, Catherine 73
Sion College 286
Sitwell, Sir George 149–50
Sixtus IV, Pope 206
Slade School of Art (London) 77, 266,
  297
Smith, Mrs Pearsal 193
Smith, Robertson 179
Smith, Samuel 275
Social and Political Education League
  283
Social Disease and How to Fight It
  (Louise Creighton) 304
Social History of England (Louise
  Creighton) 200
Society for Promoting Christian
  Knowledge 267
Society for the Propagation of the
  Gospel in Foreign Parts 267, 302
Society of Friends (Quakers) 125, 152,
  259
Some Famous Women (Louise
  Creighton) 304
Somerville College (Oxford) 90
Somerville, Mary 304
South African War, *see* Boer War
Spectator, The 159
Spencer, Herbert 38, 52, 138
Stamford, Earl of 220
Stanley, Arthur Penrhyn 76
Stead, William T. 105
Stocks (Wards' country house in
  Hertfordshire) 271
Stories from English History (Louise
  Creighton) 258
Story of Some English Shires, The
  (Mandell Creighton) 230
Strachey, Lytton 206, 261, 292, 300
Strand Magazine 261
Streatfeild, C. W. 124
Stubbs, Bishop William 45, 47, 56–57,
  63, 92, 164, 168, 180, 204, 215

Studies in the History of the Renaissance (Walter Pater) 164
Sullivan, Sir Arthur 76
Sumner, Mary 233
Surbiton High School 297
Swinburne, Algernon 41
Sydenham, culture and society 67–68, 74–76, 78
Symonds, John Addington 164

Tait, Archbishop Archibald 23
Talbot, Edward 56, 90, 128
Talbot, Lavinia (Mrs Edward Talbot) 90
Tales of Old France (Louise Creighton) 304
Temperance Society 116
Temple, Archbishop Frederick 249–51, 255, 257, 262, 274, 279, 298
Temple, Mrs Frederick 267
Tennant, Edward, first Baron Glenconner 309
Tennyson, Alfred Lord 41
Thirty Years War 69
Thorneycroft, William Hamo 301
Thoughts on Education: Speeches and Sermons (Mandell Creighton) 298
Thring, Edward 29
Thursfield, J. R. 54, 88–89, 128
Times of London, The 128, 206, 216, 275, 314
Titanic, the 105
Tower Bridge 261
Toynbee Hall (London) 260, 283
Toynbee, Mrs Arnold 194
Tractarians, *see* Oxford Movement
Trade unions 277, 283
Trent, Council of 146, 162, 167, 226–27
Trevelyan, George Otto 129
Trevelyan, Janet (Ward) 195
Trinity College (Cambridge) 151
Trinity College (Dublin) 242
Trinity College (Oxford) 272
Tripos (Cambridge) 28, 179–83, 214, 265–66

Tudors and the Reformation, The (Mandell Creighton) 155
Twain, Mark (Samuel Clemens) 129

Ullswater 264
Ultramontanism 273
Unionist-Conservatives 152
University and Other Sermons (Mandell Creighton) 298
University College (Oxford) 43, 128
University of Cambridge, *see* Cambridge
University of Durham, *see* Durham
University of Edinburgh, *see* Edinburgh
University of London, *see* London
University of Oxford, *see* Oxford
Uppingham, public school 29, 241, 289, 293, 297
Urban VI, Pope 165

Vanity Fair 27, 261
Vatican, the 163
Vaughan, Cardinal Herbert, Roman Catholic Archbishop of Westminster 249
Venereal Disease Commission (1913) 302
Victor Emmanuel II, King of Italy 145
Victoria, Princess 240
Victoria, Queen 59, 201, 211–13, 231, 239, 240, 245, 250, 263, 271, 275, 282, 290, 292–93, 296, 304
Victorian attitudes and interests 15, 26, 34, 40–41, 44–45, 51, 70, 74–76, 93, 129–30, 132, 138, 143, 172, 234, 240, 259, 263, 284, 287, 292–93, 300, 317
Voluntary School Bill (1897) 257–59
Voluntary schools, *see* Education

Wagner, Richard 61, 64, 243
Wallace Collection (Hertford House, London) 262–63
Wallace, Lady 263
Walsh, Walter 272

Wantage Sisters 235
Ward, Adolphus 204
Ward, Agnes 80–81
Ward, Dorothy 243
Ward, Humphry 1–2, 5–6, 13, 19,
    80–81, 87, 128, 168, 216, 243, 271
Ward, Mrs Humphry (Mary Arnold) 2,
    5, 13, 19, 41, 63, 65, 87, 90–91, 128,
    170, 176, 179, 193–95, 216–17, 255,
    292, 302–3, 314
Warne's Every-Day Cookery (Mary
    Jewry) 88
Webb, Beatrice, née Potter 176–77,
    190–91, 193–94, 261, 268–69, 292,
    299
Webb, Sidney 176–77, 268, 292
Wellington, Duke of 290
'Wembley Tattoo' (Walter Creighton,
    producer) 315
West Point Military Academy (USA)
    198
Westminster Abbey 76, 216, 218, 226,
    237, 244, 269
Westminster Gazette 261
Wetton, Bunnie 128
whist 26, 40–41, 124, 127, 129
Widdrington, Dorothy, see Grey,
    Dorothy
Wilberforce, Bishop E. R. 121, 211
Wilberforce, Bishop Samuel 38
Wilde, Oscar 261
Wilhelm II, Kaiser of Germany 282,
    285, 291

William of Ockham 38
Wilson, Robert 55, 83, 89, 128
Winchester, public school 123, 150
With the Twenty-Ninth Division in
    Gallipoli (Oswin Creighton) 310
Wolsey, Cardinal 205–206, 225, 229,
    296, 300
Women's Diocesan Association 267,
    302
Women's education, see Education
Women's Friendly Society 236
Women's Liberal Party Association 302
Women's suffrage 194–96, 263,
    302–305, 309
Wood, H. G. 89, 128
Woolf, Virginia 313–15
Worcester Cathedral 187–89, 201
Worcester Diocesan Penitentiary
    Association 189–90
World Alliance for Promoting
    Friendship (between churches) 310
World, The 261–62
Wren, Christopher 255, 291, 296
Wyclif, John 162, 188
Wyndham, Hon. Percy 309

Yellow Book 261
York, Duchess of 240
York, Duke of 296
Young Men's Improvement
    Association (Alnwick) 119

Zwingli, Ulrich 165